BRITAIN'S MERCHANT NAVY

Edited by
SIR ARCHIBALD HURD

*With more than forty explanatory drawings
specially prepared by L. Ashwell Wood*

ODHAMS PRESS LIMITED, LONG ACRE, LONDON, W.C.2

MINESWEEPER'S GUN CREW AT ACTION STATIONS

The work of Britain's minesweepers in keeping the sea lanes clear and the convoy lines open is of the utmost importance to ships of the Merchant Navy. It is carried out unceasingly, day and night, by mine-sweeping patrols, well armed against attack. Many of the crews on these vessels were fishermen in peace time. All round the coasts of Britain these ships keep their perilous watch, seeking out and destroying mines, ensuring the safety of our shipping

CONTENTS

SHIPPING IN THE ROYAL ALBERT DOCK

On the north side of the Thames the Royal Albert Dock and the adjoining King George V Dock comprise the largest enclosed dock water space in the world. The five large docks of the Port of London have nearly fifty miles of quays for loading and unloading goods

CHAPTER 1

Britain's Life-line

Britain's vital need for ships. One year's cargoes—67,000,000 tons. Britain's ships in every port. The enemy's main target. Food and essential supplies. New tasks, new dangers, new weapons. Achievements of science. Heroism of Britain's seamen. New standards of safety. Lifeboats, life jackets and rafts. Orange smoke signals to guide rescuers. Grand work of the convoys. Keeping the sea lanes clear.

WHEN war broke out in the autumn of 1939 Britain possessed nearly 18,000,000 tons of merchant shipping—more ships than any other country in the world. These British ships numbered 9,000, but many of the vessels were quite small—under 500 tons gross—and more than 1,200 of the remainder ranged from 500 tons gross to 2,000 tons. There were only 4,000 of upwards of 2,000 tons gross, for use in ocean trading.

Because Britain is a small island nation with a large population—about 48,000,000 men, women and children—Britain's Merchant Navy was her very life blood.

SHIPS ON EVERY ROUTE

The ships, varying from the 80,000-ton luxury liner *Queen Mary* to the modest but vastly important tramp, were the foundation upon which the whole economic and industrial prosperity of the nation had been built up. From the ends of the earth they came, day by day in a constant stream, ploughing their way through foul weather and fine, braving all the forces of Nature—storms, fog, high seas, hidden currents—and they were handled with superb courage and fine seamanship by British Merchant Service officers. In the year before the second World War, British ships brought to our ports cargoes weighing more than 67,000,000

tons. Think what that meant! Twenty-two million tons were food and drink; 28,500,000 were raw materials for Britain's industries; 9,500,000 were oil fuel, so important in this modern mechanical age.

BRITAIN'S SEA-BORNE TRADE

The remainder consisted of manufactured goods; all sorts of things, which, although not perhaps absolutely necessary, made life much more pleasant for us all.

But if Britain relied upon her ships to bring her all these things, she relied upon them just as much to carry her wares abroad. She needed her ships if she were to sell her goods in the markets of the world, to increase her financial prosperity and to be able to pay for the goods she needed from those who had them to sell.

Thus, there is hardly an industry in the country that does not rely upon the Merchant Navy, and hardly a person whose prosperity and general well-being is not bound up in this vast and complicated organization. It is a vital life-line without which this island kingdom could not maintain her position in the forefront of World Powers—without which, indeed, the people of the island could not live. In times of peace, Britain's ships sailed the oceans of the world upon their "lawful occasions." There was scarcely a port of any size in the world where you could not see the "Old Red Duster" fluttering proudly in the breeze, not a trade route along whose length a British ship could not be found engaged upon these lawful occasions of her trading, loaded down to her marks with her precious cargo.

THE MEN OF THE SEA

The men who sailed these ships —and there were nearly 157,000 of them at the beginning of the second World War—were a hardy race with the mark of the sea in their faces and the salt of the sea in their blood. Their lives were bound up with the sea and ships. They were happiest when they had left the land far behind them and were out upon the ocean highways, resourcefully pitting their strength against the forces of Nature or sailing serenely upon a placid sea. They were a simple, peaceloving race untrained in the arts of war, who asked for no more than that they should be permitted to get on with their job undisturbed.

Then came the war. Overnight these men and the ships they sailed assumed an even greater importance. The Merchant Navy took its place by the side of the three fighting Services as one of the main bulwarks of Britain's safety.

To the hazards they encountered from storm, fog, or treacherous currents were added the dangers of attack from bomb, torpedo and hidden mine. The Merchant Navy became at once the main target of an unscrupulous enemy who realized that, if Britain were to be beaten, her ships must be sunk or driven from the seas. Foodstuffs and vital war materials, the enemy realized, must be prevented from reaching Britain's shores at all costs.

If the Merchant Navy was important in time of peace, it was doubly important in time of war. Food still had to be brought to feed the population—about half of all the food and practically all the raw materials for factory and workshop—

but other calls were made upon the ships and the men who manned them. The Navy lacked sufficient auxiliary vessels; the Merchant Navy had to find them. Luxury passenger ships were transformed into armed merchant cruisers; trawlers became minesweepers.

Ships had to be found for the transport of troops and materials of war to all the fronts on which Britain was engaged— the Merchant Navy had to supply them. Not an aeroplane could operate unless it had ocean-borne oil fuel. But the merchant ships had still to carry out their primary function of stocking the nation's larder.

Britain's seamen knew only too well the dangers that they would have to face. In the first World War, Britain's Merchant Navy had lost nearly 8,000,000 tons of valuable ships by enemy action and the lives of 13,000 seamen had been sacrificed, and in those days aircraft were a comparatively new weapon—so new, in fact, as to be hardly worth considering.

GERMANY'S FIRST BLOW

Our seamen knew that in the second World War more deadly weapons would be used and that the sea war of 1914 was only a shadow of things to come in 1939 and after. But they never wavered. With a good ship under them, and by the grace of God and the help of the British Navy, they were willing, and even eager, to face whatever dangers lay ahead. They would show the enemy that his hopes of winning the war by cutting Britain's life-lines were vain.

The enemy was not long in beginning his sea war. Within a few hours he claimed his first victim. With no warning, he torpedoed the liner *Athenia*, outward bound to Montreal with over 1,000 persons aboard, many of whom were women and children. Fortunately all but 112 were picked up by ships that hurried to her assistance. This was only the beginning,

SHIPWRECKED SEAMEN RESCUED FROM RAFTS

Exhausted survivors from a torpedoed merchant vessel are being helped aboard a rescuing ship. They lashed together two rafts and drifted for fifteen days, with no food and very little water, until they managed to attract the notice of their rescuers by flashing tin lids in the sun

WITH CARGOES OF FOOD SUPPLIES AND WAR MATERIAL CONVOYS

Making the Merchant Navy his chief target, the enemy strove desperately to stop supplies from reaching our shores. His efforts were in vain. In face of relentless attacks by torpedoes from U-boats, by bombs from aircraft, great convoys of Britain's ships sailed continually,

but it was a pointer to the future. It showed that the Germany of 1939 had lost none of the barbarity she had exhibited in the first World War—that she was still a foe who disregarded not only the laws drawn up and agreed to by the nations of the world, but, worse, far worse, the laws of humanity and God as well.

As the months passed, the number of sinkings increased, but the spirit of Britain's seamen did not waver. Added to the dangers from submarines, surface raiders and moored mines, there were new and terrible weapons, the chief of which was the aeroplane. The enemy used aircraft in large numbers to attack merchant ships. Diving out of the sun or cloud, they dropped their bombs almost at mast height, whilst the ships' officers and crews shot at them with any weapon they could lay hands on—rifles, revolvers and even shot guns were used. Later these ships were armed with powerful guns as well as multiple machine guns for defence against air attack. These accounted for many U-boats and numerous raiding aircraft.

Two other weapons were added to the already long list of perils faced by mariners. The first was the magnetic mine, which was detonated by the magnetic field set up by the steel hull of the ship, and the second was the acoustic mine, exploded by sound waves from the ship's propellers. At first, the seamen could make no reply to these weapons. They were sinister robots that struck without warning. But Britain's scientists soon came to the aid of their comrades at sea, and

SAILED NIGHT AND DAY TO KEEP BRITAIN'S LIFE-LINES CLEAR
daring every menace and every weapon the enemy could bring against them. The Merchant Navy was one of the main bulwarks of Britain's safety. The records of the convoys are full of stories of the dauntless heroism of the men who manned the ships

evolved ways and means of reducing—if not entirely eliminating—these perils.

As tales of heroism and suffering reached the Ministry of War Transport, it was realized that everything humanly possible had to be done to succour the seamen in their distress. The Ministry became in no long time a scientific hothouse. Devices which were considered the last word in 1939 were progressively improved and a host of new ones produced. These measures were the means not only of saving thousands of lives, but also of avoiding much hardship and suffering. A new standard of safety was established.

As Lord Leathers pointed out in an article in *The Shipping World* of September 23, 1942, the most pressing need was to provide rafts which could be easily launched, and life jackets (described as waistcoats to distinguish them from pre-war types), which could be worn continuously while men were in dangerous waters. Improvements came later, until rafts were at last produced which afforded so high a degree of protection that, in one case, nine men survived the perils of a shark-infested sea until rescued in good condition, after thirty-four days, during which the raft had successfully ridden out heavy seas.

As a result of these measures the hardships of survivors in boats and on rafts were mitigated by the best equipment which science could devise, including weatherproof suits, manual pumps and massage oil, and by more varied and nutritious rations, with greatly increased

Grim skies and the grey seas of war threaten
this oil tanker as she thrashes home with
her precious cargo, her well-deck awash. On
the horizon a watchful destroyer keeps guard

allowances of water. The means of calling help or attracting aid were multiplied and bettered. Rafts were automatically lighted up when they floated free of the ship. Life jackets and waistcoats were fitted with small electric lamps—the seamen's safety lamp—to guide the rescue boats to survivors. Special equipment was issued to protect the crews of tankers.

NEW SMOKE SIGNALS

When a passenger ship was torpedoed in the third year of the second World War, the crew and passengers, numbering 335 persons, took to the boats and rafts. The next day an aircraft was sighted and hopes ran high, but the plane disappeared without seeing them. Some hours later another aircraft was sighted and this time they succeeded in attracting the attention of the pilot, who dropped a message saying that he was sending help immediately. Surely enough, first a merchant vessel and then a warship appeared, and every one of those survivors was saved. The signal which proved so effective in attracting aid was the new orange-coloured smoke signal first introduced a year before, which became a compulsory part of the equipment of every lifeboat and raft.

As an indication of what these requirements meant, in terms of manufacture and supply, it may be mentioned that down to the end of 1942, the Government had issued to ships over 50,000 smoke signals, more than 150,000 weatherproof suits and thousands of portable wireless transmitting sets. Over 1,000 tons of new foods had also been supplied in airtight containers of 2 lb. for lifeboats and 1 lb. for rafts. Among the new measures which were made compulsory were several intended to help seamen to make a quick get-away from sinking vessels.

All who have co-operated with the Ministry in this work—owners and men, manufacturers of ship equipment and

scientific and other experts—noted with pride that the recommendations made by the Joint Maritime Commission of the International Labour Office at their meeting in London in the summer of 1942 followed very closely the measures adopted in this country. When the war is over, we must not return to the old peacetime standards. Both sides of the industry are agreed, in principle, that wartime improvements must be preserved. It is sure that both sides will recognize equally the need for continuing efforts to mitigate the hardships and diminish the risks of the seaman's calling. In war or in peace, the aim must be to provide the maximum degree of safety. Nothing less will do.

The full story of the war at sea can never be properly told. If it could, it would fill many volumes and form a library of heroism the like of which has seldom been equalled. It would tell of British seamen—sleepless and haggard—striving to bring their sinking ships into port, of men in oil tankers, with thousands of tons of highly inflammable liquid under their feet, sailing calmly through a hail of bombs and shells. It would tell how sometimes these missiles found their mark and how the crew overcame the flames and brought their cargoes safely home.

RECORDS OF GALLANTRY

The records of the convoys to Malta and to Russia are full of stories of the heroism of British seamen who set sail time and time again—in the one case to take food and supplies to a besieged outpost of the Empire and in the other to carry war material to a gallant and hardpressed ally. On every voyage they knew the perils before them, knew they would be lucky to get through unscathed.

Again, there is the story of the gallant men in the minesweepers—the fishermen of England who hunted far more dangerous prey. How, in their tiny trawlers, they swept the sea lanes along which our

GUN PRACTICE ON A MERCHANT SHIP

To meet enemy attack became an essential addition to good seamanship, and the men of the Merchant Navy learnt to lay, load and fire the guns with which their vessels were fitted

supplies had to come. How they battled constantly with enemy aircraft and with fast, heavily armed E-boats, which sought to interfere with their work.

The bravery and endurance of the men of the Merchant Navy are beyond praise; our debt to them is beyond repayment. Their ships may be sunk under their feet; they may suffer desperate privation and misery in open boats before they reach land or are rescued; but no hardship deters them from setting forth in another ship as soon as opportunity occurs. Their steadfast courage stands star high.

After Napoleon had surrendered on board H.M.S. *Bellerophon* he said: "In all my plans I have been thwarted by the British fleet." There may well be a time when Hitler will say the same—and add "and by the British Merchant Navy."

UNDER FULL SAIL—THE "FLYING CLOUD"

The clippers were a royal race of sailing ships, "never excelled for beauty, grace, and speed."
One of the most famous was the "Flying Cloud." The first clippers were built in America,
but British shipbuilders produced rival ships, which made sailing history by their fast passages

CHAPTER 2

The Freedom of the Seas

Policy of the closed seas. Merchantmen in wartime. Protection of British shipping. Navigation laws and their repeal. Coming of the clipper ships. Sail versus steam. Iron ships. Increase of British and world shipping. First World War. Restrictions by foreign governments. Position of British shipping at start of second World War. Bravery of our seamen.

THE era of ocean trading—not only for Great Britain but for the world—opened when Queen Elizabeth threw down the gauntlet to the great sea powers of the period, Spain and Portugal. They claimed exclusive rights of navigation on the seas which their pioneer navigators had discovered. "The use of the sea and the air," Elizabeth declared to the Spanish Ambassador in London, who had protested against Drake's latest voyage into the prohibited waters, "is common to all, and no title to the ocean can belong to any nation since neither Nature nor regard for the public use permits any possession of the ocean." It was a proud statement.

THE CLOSED SEAS

It was one of the most courageous declarations in history. England—for Scotland was then a separate kingdom, and Ireland was in rebellion—had a population of only about five or six millions, and all the vessels engaged in ordinary commerce were estimated at little more than 50,000 tons burthen. Antwerp and Bruges, and not London, were the marts of the world, to which English merchants sent wool and drapery and other things that they had to sell. They used such little ships as they could secure, mostly under foreign flags, since there was little need for larger ships as long as the outer seas were closed to the traders of this country. Seamen of Spain had discovered the

American continent and the Portuguese had made voyages round the Cape of Good Hope to India, for it was not until 1869 that the shorter route by the Suez Canal was opened to traffic. The success of these pioneers encouraged the rulers of their two countries to demand that no other seamen but Spaniards and Portuguese should enter the hitherto unknown oceans. The Pope, after studying the map of the New World, decided to give them his support. In effect, he divided the New World between these two countries.

For centuries past certain countries had claimed rights in specific seas, and restricted the movements of shipping and traders of other nations. The republics of Venice and Genoa had controlled all navigation in the Adriatic Sea and the Ligurian Sea respectively. Sweden and Denmark had claimed "absolute" command of the Baltic. Great Britain exercised a limited sovereignty over "the Narrow Seas," the North Sea, and the Atlantic from North Cape as far as Cape Finisterre.

MARITIME SOVEREIGNTY EXTENDED

When the great navigators broke into seas of which little or nothing had been known, this policy of "the closed seas" was extended and was generally recognized. Portugal claimed sovereignty over the whole of the Indian Ocean and of the Atlantic south of Morocco, and Spain over the Pacific and the Gulf of Mexico.

This policy was effective for many years. In 1478 Frederick III, Emperor of Germany, had to ask the permission of Venice for a cargo of corn to be carried for Apulia through the Adriatic Sea. As late as the seventeenth century England compelled foreigners to take out licences for fishing in the North Sea; when in 1636 the Dutch began fishing without such licence they were attacked and compelled to pay £30,000 as the price for the indulgence. Again, in 1554, when Philip II of Spain was on his way to marry Queen Mary, the English admiral who met him in the "British Seas" fired on his ship for flying the Spanish flag. The King of Denmark, returning from a visit to James I in 1606, was forced by a British captain, who met him off the mouth of the Thames, to strike the Danish flag.

HONOURING THE FLAG

Maritime sovereignty found expression, however, mainly in ceremonials, vessels being required to honour the flag of the foreign state concerned. Even as late as 1805, the year of Trafalgar, the Regulations of the British Admiralty contained an order that "when any of His Majesty's ships shall meet with the ships of any foreign Power within His Majesty's seas (which extend to Cape Finisterre), it is expected that the said foreign ships do strike their topsail and take in their flag, in acknowledgment of His Majesty's sovereignty in those seas; and, if any do resist, all flag officers and commanders are to use their utmost endeavours to compel them thereto, and not to suffer any dishonour to be done to His Majesty."

With her protest against the policy of Spain and Portugal in the New World, Queen Elizabeth opened up a new and brilliant chapter in the history of ocean navigation. She based her defiance on the ground that England had never pressed her claim so far as to attempt the prohibition of free navigation on the so-called British Seas, whereas Spain and Portugal had attempted to keep foreign ships altogether out of the seas over which they claimed sovereignty.

It was no little matter for the queen of a small and sparsely populated island with few ships of war or commerce, and with no colonies from which to draw wealth as Spain and Portugal drew wealth, to proclaim the new doctrine of the freedom of the seas.

Her declaration may be regarded as the charter of ocean-going shipping. Thenceforward English seamen, at no little risk to themselves, sailed wherever they liked—Drake, Raleigh, Cavendish, Howard, Frobisher. The strength of the country at this time lay in its merchant ships and not in the Royal Navy, which was of little account. Queen Elizabeth had only twenty-six men-of-war with which to oppose the Spanish Armada, and the remainder of the 191 vessels were merchantmen from London, Bristol and other ports. When war broke out it was the custom for the sovereign to requisition whatever merchant ships were needed. Professor Sir Geoffrey Callender*, Honorary Secretary of the Society of Naval Research, has told us what happened on the outbreak of war when ships were required in emergency to co-operate with the Royal Navy.

NAVY ON HIRE

In the absence of roads in most districts, small vessels carried cargoes from port to port, other craft fished for herring and haddock round the coasts, bigger vessels went as far afield as Iceland after whale, and others ventured into the Mediterranean.

When war was imminent, all these ships were inspected. If suitable they were hired by the Sovereign and fitted for the carriage of soldiers; for it was as transports that they were usually needed. At either end of the ship, carpenters erected a tower

---

*The Naval Side of British History

1852
A BLACKWALL
FRIGATE
Length 200 Ft.

1860
THE FAMOUS
CLIPPERS
Length 212 Ft.

1890
THE ACME OF SAILING SHIPS
STEEL BARQUE
Length 300 Ft.

1802
THE FIRST STEAMSHIP
"CHARLOTTE DUNDAS"

1829
SAIL & STEAM
FIRST P & O SHIP
Length 207 Ft.

1843 FIRST SCREW SHIP TO CROSS ATLANTIC
S.S. GREAT BRITAIN *Length 315 Ft.*

1860 "GREAT EASTERN"
LARGEST SHIP OF ITS TIME
Length 692 Ft.

1884 "ETRURIA"
SAIL & STEAM *Length 519 Ft.*

1939 "MAURETANIA"
Length 772 Ft.

FROM SAIL TO STEAM

The fascinating progress of merchant ships, over a period of a hundred and forty years, is vividly shown above. The first practical steamship, "Charlotte Dundas," serving as a tug on the Forth-Clyde canal, developed into the "Mauretania," the largest ship built in England

EAST INDIAMAN "HEREFORDSHIRE"

Fig. 1. *The East India Company (1600) built a fleet of armed merchantmen—a complete cargo-carrying navy. These fine ships had a monopoly of our trade with India and China. In 1803 the Company lent ships to the Government to guard against a French invasion (Crown copyright. By courtesy of the Director of the Science Museum, South Kensington)*

or turret—a structure something like the scaffolding which is used in building a house. Fir poles were set up and lashed together with ropes. Cross-bars gave additional support to the ship's stout deck, and stouter bulwarks gave a strong foundation. On the top of this cagework there was a floor of 3-inch plank, round which a crenellated breastwork for the protection of the fighting men was made. In time, the scaffolding was given an outer wall of pine planks or painted hides. These fighting stations were known as "castles," though they had none of the strength or permanence which the name implies.

In the forecastle of the converted merchantman, the soldiers were assembled. The man in the crow's nest would warn the captain if the enemy were sighted and the ship would be prepared for action with such weapons as were on board—bows

and arrows, javelins, spears, quicklime and stones and even harpoons if the transport had been a whaler. Grappling irons were also carried; picked men gathered in the vessel's waist in readiness to carry the enemy by boarding as soon as she had been grappled and held.

After Queen Elizabeth made her proclamation of the freedom of the seas, the differences between ships of the Royal Navy and ships of commerce increased. As trade overseas grew it became necessary to build larger and more seaworthy ships which could load bigger cargoes. The invention of heavy cannons meant that room had to be found for ammunition which took up a lot of space at the expense of cargo. So the strength of the Royal Navy was increased, and the merchant ships' armament, for protection against enemies or pirates, lessened.

When the seas were thrown open to free navigation Drake sailed from Plymouth on November 15, 1577, for the circumnavigation of the world.

Five ships set out. The largest was the *Pelican* (afterwards rechristened the *Golden Hind*) which was of only 120 tons; the *Elizabeth* was of eighty tons. The sloops *Swan* and *Marigold* were of fifty and thirty tons respectively, and there was also a pinnace of twelve tons. What courage was exhibited by Drake and his companions in setting forth for seas into which neither they nor any of their fellow-countrymen had ventured before ! The seas were as strong and fogs as dense as they are today when the Cunarder *Queen Elizabeth* of 85,000 tons is the pride of Britain's Merchant Navy.

As trade developed, many larger ships were needed. Our forefathers decided, in accordance with the economic theories then in fashion, that if shipping was to prosper, some form of protection should be given to the English merchantmen against competition, and Navigation Acts were passed. They were developed in later years until they confined British trade, in the main, to British ships. By the seventeenth century this legislation was regarded by British shipowners as their sheet anchor.

(1) Nothing could be imported into or exported from any English possession in Asia, Africa or America except in English ships.

(2) English ships only could carry to this country any goods of native production or manufacture from Asia, Africa or America.

(3) Only English ships could engage in the coasting trade round Britain.

THE "CRUSADER"—A THOROUGHBRED OF THE OCEAN

Fig. 2. *The clipper ships were the dying effort of sail in its losing battle with steam. Built for speed, with tall masts and a magnificent spread of canvas, they were the most beautiful sailing ships ever known. Their captains, superb seamen, took all risks to make their record passages*

ROYAL MAIL MOTOR SHIP "CAPETOWN

In their time the royal beauty of the clipper sailing ships delighted every beholder, and pictures of them still give a thrill to us all. We get no less a thrill to see a great ship of today, such as the "Capetown Castle." Her beauty of line and grace of form are undeniable and the

The protection of the English shipping industry, which had been the object of legislation since the time of Richard II, was thus made complete: practically all competition was ruled out.

As a result of the new epoch in trading which began with the declaration of the freedom of the seas, English merchants, who frequently owned their own trading ships, sought charters for privileges in various parts of the world. One of these companies was known as the Merchant Venturers, another was the Muscovy Company, yet another the Turkey Com-

pany, and, in 1600, Queen Elizabeth granted a charter to the greatest and longest lived of these associations, the East India Company, which built, manned and armed its own fleet of ships—a complete cargo-carrying navy (Fig. 1).

The influence of these great companies on shipping may be judged from the wording of the grant to the Muscovy Company. "For the better maintenance of the Navy and mariners of this realm, be it provided and enacted that it shall not be lawful for the said fellowship and company to carry and transport or cause

CASTLE" LARGEST UNION CASTLE LINER

picture conveys a striking impression of disciplined power and speed. Compare her with pictures of the early steamships on a previous page. A twin-screw motor vessel, she is the largest Union Castle liner, 27,000 tons. Built at Belfast in 1938, she carries 800 passengers

to be carried and transported any commodity of this realm to their new trade, but only in English ships and to be sailed for the most part with English mariners." The prosperity of the enterprising merchants was linked with the prosperity of British shipping. In later years the most successful competitors of this country on the high seas were the Dutch, and it was against them that the Navigation Laws in their final form were directed. Though the great economist, Adam Smith, was an out-and-out Free Trader, he commended such legislation on the ground that "de-

fence was more important than opulence"; and he declared that this system was "perhaps the wisest of all the commercial regulations of England."

For long years, British shipping gained in strength and importance. But there came a time when the absence of competition sapped efficiency, and traders protested that the Navigation Laws were a serious handicap to them in developing overseas trade. At last the Government decided to investigate. In 1843 enquiries were sent to British consuls all over the world. Their reports showed that many

GREAT RACE BETWEEN "TAEPING" AND

Fig. 3. *Two of the most famous clippers were the "Taeping" and the "Ariel." The "Ariel" was the finest "ghoster" ever built—she could glide through the water with scarcely a breath of wind. These two ships ran a wonderful race from China. Starting at the same time, they*

ships were ill-found, that a number of officers and men were careless in their duties, and that drunkenness was responsible for the loss of many vessels. Exposure of the abuses which the restrictive policy had encouraged led to an agitation for the repeal of the Navigation Laws. Step by step the various prohibitions which applied to foreign ships were swept away, and in 1854 even the coasting trade was thrown open to foreign ships.

Queen Elizabeth had made the seas of the world free to all nations. By the repeal of the Navigation Laws and the cancellation of the charters to the trading companies, the carrying trade of the whole British Empire was thrown open to all comers. Shippers of goods could employ ships under any flag. It was natural that shipowners should fight against this

change in policy, protesting that it would ruin them, but British shipping took a fresh lease of life. Whether this was due to the spur of foreign competition, to the industrial progress of this country, which was becoming "the workshop of the world," or to the skill of British shipbuilders in producing finer ships of iron instead of wood than were to be found under foreign flags is a matter of controversy. But it is certain that the tonnage under the British flag steadily increased in the following half-century. Also, under the influence of competition, the status of the industry was gradually raised.

By the beginning of the nineteenth century the number of British merchantmen exceeded 20,000, making more than 2,000,000 tons in all. In due course, bigger and more seaworthy ships were designed,

"ARIEL"—CHAMPIONS AMONG THE CLIPPER SHIPS

docked in London within a few hours of each other, after ninety-nine days at sea! The race was made a dead heat. Once the "Ariel" made a record London-Hong Kong passage, 79 days, 21 hrs. (By courtesy of the Controller of H.M. Stationery Office. "Sailing Ships," Part I)

to carry larger cargoes at cheaper rates.

An impetus to the development of British shipping was given by the keen competition of American shipbuilders. They turned out clippers which were for a time so superior in speed, as well as in sea qualities, to contemporary vessels built in this country that many owners ordered new ships from American yards or chartered American vessels for their trade. The clipper ship was an American development, and the rivalry between the American and British ships of this type makes one of the most exciting chapters in the commercial history of the two countries.

The clipper ship (Fig. 2) was the dying effort of the sailing ship to compete with the steam ship. The clipper ship had bows that cut the waves so as to set up less skin friction than the vessels which had

hitherto been built, gaining much in speed. Marine architects in America defied convention by modifying the design of the stern in such a way that, instead of squatting and holding the dead water, the ship slid through it cleanly with a minimum of resistance. The one object of the American designer was to build a ship that should outsail every other craft and so obtain the maximum of cargo carrying. Besides the improvement in bow and stern, the Americans lengthened the ship until she became five or six times longer than her breadth, against four times the beam in the case of the East India Company's ships.

This enabled them to add a fourth mast to the ship and to carry more sails. The sails themselves were improved in cut. In contradistinction to the East Indiamen, these American ships did not reef down in anticipation of the gale that was to follow hours afterwards, but took in sail with the greatest reluctance.

The part played by the American clippers between the close of the Napoleonic Wars and the beginning of the American Civil War is one of vast importance in the development of the sailing ship. Even when steamers began to cross the Atlantic in 1840, these wonderful racing clippers were able to sail across the ocean in about a fortnight.

TWO FAMOUS CLIPPERS

British shipowners were not slow to learn their lesson in ship design from the Americans, and a keen sporting competition occurred between the clippers of the two countries. It was especially marked in the China tea trade, and also during the Gold Rush to Australia from 1851 onwards.

The great race home of the *Ariel* and the *Taeping* (Fig. 3) marks an unforgettable epic of clipper-ship rivalry. These two ships left Foochow in China on the same day, London bound. The date was May 30, 1866. There was bad weather, with squalls and driving mist, but the captains clapped on sail.

Twenty-one days out, the *Ariel* and the *Taeping* passed Anjer Point, and both ships made this landmark on the same day. Off the Cape of Good Hope the *Taeping* and the *Ariel* were close together. On August 12, when the ships had been over seventy days at sea, the *Ariel* made the Cape Verde Islands. She led the race for the first time—but the *Taeping* was only a day behind.

Ninety-eight days out, on September 5, the *Ariel* sighted the Bishop Rock Light in the Scilly Isles. The *Taeping* showed swiftly with the same day's dawn, and the two great ships swept together up the Channel. In the end, the *Ariel* and the *Taeping* docked in London within an hour or so of each other. The race was declared a dead heat and the captains shared the prize of £100 and the premium of ten shillings a ton for the first cargo home.

The speed which a crack clipper ship attained under favourable wind conditions put her far in advance of the economic rate of an ordinary cargo carrier of today.

The passage from Hong Kong to London was made in 1850 by the American clipper *Oriental* in ninety-seven days. The British ship *Lightning* reached Liverpool from Melbourne in sixty-three days. On one voyage the latter ship exceeded for a period of a week a speed of 15½ knots, whereas the tramp ship of today makes only 10 to 11 knots. But whereas the sailer might be becalmed for many days on end, the steamer was to a great extent independent of weather conditions.

The sailing ship made a gallant fight, but its fate was sealed as the marine steam engine was improved and became more reliable for long distance voyages. But as late as 1892 there was built on the Clyde the *Marie Rickmere* with a sail area of no less than 56,500 square feet, over four miles of steel wire for shrouds, stays, and so on, and not far short of six miles of running cordage. She was a ship of wonder! But though such ships were still being launched in this and other countries, the issue of the battle between sail and steam was never in doubt.

STEAM CONQUERS SAIL

As time went on, the steamship drove the sailing ship off the sea. Now the sailing ship does not count for anything in international trade—a gain in efficient transport, but an æsthetic loss, for the sailing vessel was a thing of great beauty.

The Americans had shown that they could build the finest and swiftest clipper ships. In 1814 they launched their first steamship on the great waters of the Mississippi, and immediately proceeded to develop their internal maritime communications. Such was the spirit of enterprise of the Americans that by the early sixties the British lead amounted to little more than a quarter of a million tons. Then came the Civil War. The North possessed only a small fighting fleet, and, in the emergency, the authorities turned to the mercantile marine in order that economic pressure, by means of a blockade of the numerous ports of the Confederacy, might be applied without delay. Warships were improvised, but at a terrible cost to the Merchant Marine.

As time went by, the decline not only of American, but of other foreign fleets, reflected the skill and enterprise of British shipowners who realized that the ball was at their feet and took full advantage of it.

In an official report published in 1875, the Secretary of the Board of Trade, writing from his office in London, stated that whilst the British tonnage in the trade of the United Kingdom had increased from sixty-five per cent of that trade in 1850, to sixty-eight per cent in 1870,

TRANSATLANTIC PIONEER

Fig. 4. *The first large Transatlantic iron steamer was the "Great Britain," the first ship fitted with a screw propeller to cross the Atlantic. Her departure from Bristol, where she was built in 1843, had to be postponed for a year as she was too wide to pass through the dock gates. She convinced even the doubters of the strength and practicability of iron ships (Crown copyright. By courtesy of the Director of the Science Museum, South Kensington)*

A number of ships under foreign flags took the place of the American vessels on some of the principal trade routes.

The recovery of American shipping was retarded by the discovery that ships could be built of iron, which many people had disputed, instead of wood. British shipyards, with plenty of iron ore near at hand, began building ships of iron propelled by the marine steam engine (Fig.4).

United States tonnage, which had sixty per cent of the trade to the United States in 1850, had only thirty-eight per cent of it in 1870. French tonnage, which had forty-one per cent of the trade of France in 1850, had only thirty-one per cent in 1870. Dutch tonnage, with forty-two per cent of the trade of Holland in 1850, had only twenty-eight per cent in 1870. Prussian tonnage, which had forty-nine per cent of the trade of Prussia in 1850, had forty-six per cent in 1870. Swedish tonnage fell from forty-three per cent in 1850 to thirty-two per cent in 1870. Although the marine trade of Norway had rapidly grown, her tonnage, which had seventy-three per cent of her trade in 1850, decreased to seventy per cent in 1870.

In these years, British merchant shipping underwent a revolution, partly owing to the increased interest which Parliament took in its welfare by insisting on better seaworthiness and partly owing to the action of leading shipowners in setting their own house in order.

BRITAIN'S SHIPS LEAD WORLD

Lloyd's Register made rules for design and construction in advance of those prescribed from Whitehall; underwriters helped this movement to improve the character of merchant ships of all classes by issuing a certificate only to those vessels which conformed to the rules of the Register. Plimsoll's agitation in the seventies, which ensured a mark being placed on every vessel to check overloading was another most valuable contribution towards the greater safety at sea of passengers, crews and goods.

Under these conditions, British owners took a great pride in their ships, and officers and men at sea acquired high qualifications. The industry forged ahead, and the shipbuilding industry shared its prosperity.

A few figures will show the progress made in the years preceding the war of 1914-18. As late as 1884 eight out of every ten merchant ships under all flags, as well as many foreign men-of-war, were of British construction; even in 1914 the percentage of merchant ships of the world built in this country was as high as 61·9.

"There are few important industries," a Departmental Committee reported in 1918 "where the predominance of British manufacturers has been more marked than in shipbuilding and marine engineering." The report stated that compared with twenty years previously, the output from British shipyards and marine engine works

ONE HUNDRED YEARS OF PROGRESS

The tiny "Britannia," a pioneer of the Atlantic crossing, and the mighty " Queen Mary" are here compared. In 1840, the "Britannia," driven by paddle-wheel engines, took fourteen days to cross. In 1936, the " Queen Mary," five times as long as the "Britannia," made the 3,000-mile passage from Southampton to New York in four days, five hours,

had shown a decline in the proportion which it bore to the world's output; but it added that "the normal production of British shipyards was, before the war, still greater than that of all foreign shipyards put together." As to shipping, in 1890 the gross tonnage owned by Great Britain and Ireland amounted to 10,439,000 tons; this gradually increased until in 1914 it had reached a total of 19,256,000 tons, representing an increase of eighty-five per cent. But during the same period, the tonnage of the rest of the world rose from 11,410,000 tons to 30,098,000 tons, representing an increase of 164 per cent.

Then (1914-18) came the U-boat campaign of the Germans. Seven million tons of British shipping were sunk and the lives of 13,000 seamen were sacrificed. Could the industry recover from such blows? Many observers in foreign countries were satisfied that here was the opportunity to undermine the maritime industries of the British Isles. New shipyards were laid out and subsidies were paid to enable the newly built vessels to compete successfully with British shipping on the great trade routes of the world. At the same time foreign governments continued to reserve all coastal shipping to vessels under their national flags, while British ports remained open on terms of equality to ships of all nations in accordance with the principles of Free Trade which were then officially held.

CAUSES OF DECLINE

What happened? Without State aid British shipowners could not fight successfully against foreign shipyards and foreign shipowners, spoon-fed by their national treasuries. The course of events can best be indicated by a few figures. In 1919, the tonnage owned in Great Britain and Ireland amounted to 16,555,000 tons and after increasing to 20,438,000 tons in 1930, it had fallen to 17,984,000 tons in 1938. During the same period, the tonnage of the rest of the world had grown from 34,331,000 tons in 1919, to 50,063,000 tons in 1932, and then, after a fall,

IN TRANSATLANTIC TRAVEL
forty-six minutes, although she was delayed by fog. She made a run of 766 miles in a single day, at an average speed of thirty knots. The "Britannia," built of wood, was 1,150 tons, 740 horse power—speed only nine knots. The "Queen Mary" is 60,744 tons, 200,000 horse power. (Crown copyright. By courtesy of the Director of the Science Museum, S. Kensington)

SURVIVORS RESCUED AS SHIP GOES DOWN

A collier sinks after striking a mine. The keel of the sinking vessel can be seen in the background. Victims are swimming in the ocean, and survivors are being helped aboard one of the ship's lifeboats, which is rowing towards the rescue ship. Three of the crew were lost. The collier was in convoy and the photograph was taken from one of the convoy's escort ships

had risen to 51,455,000 tons in 1939.

When the war began in September, 1939, there was not sufficient tonnage under the British flag. If it had not been for the ships of Norway, France, Greece, Denmark, Belgium and Holland which eluded the Germans and sheltered in our ports—amounting to about 8,000,000 tons—the country would have been hard pressed to survive; and that is to put the matter in its most moderate terms. Those ships bridged the interval between the opening of the struggle and the launching of great numbers of vessels from the shipyards of the British Isles, the United States, Canada and Australia. It was not long before our position was considerably improved through the unremitting efforts of Empire and United States shipbuilders, who did everything possible.

SERIOUS HANDICAPS

The British people, dependent for most of their raw materials as well as half their food on overseas supplies, entered the war which was forced upon them in the autumn of 1939, under a serious handicap.

As compared with 1914, there was a shortage of 2,000,000 tons of sea-going ships, and the number of seamen had also declined. The enemy had U-boats with a greater radius of action than in the former struggle, and much improved mines. A menacing new danger was the bomber.

BRITAIN'S PERIL

The courage, skill and resourcefulness of British seamen saved a situation which was full of peril for the 48,000,000 men, women and children of the British Isles. The Germans, with the support of the Italians, had the odds heavily in their favour, and these were further increased when they overran the Low Countries and Northern France and thus obtained convenient bases for their piratical operations, which extended far out on the Atlantic Ocean as well as to the Mediterranean. The position worsened when Japan in the autumn of 1941, with a perfidy even exceeding that of her Axis partners, entered the war, for she possessed not only a large navy but a merchant fleet nearly twice as large as that which had existed in 1914.

Future generations will acclaim as without parallel in history the valiant spirit in which British merchant seamen, in their frail ships, fought for the freedom of the seas against the twentieth-century pirates armed with the gun, the torpedo, the bomb and the mine. They carried on in face of Nature's handicaps, storms and fog, and the carefully planned attack of three powerful enemies. Many thousands of them paid the forfeit of their lives in order that the world's seas might remain open for the freedom-loving nations. Thousands of others, after surviving the hardships inevitable in open boats, reached shore only to demand that they should be allowed to go to sea again— such was their courage. In the records of the sea, there is nothing comparable to the manner in which these seamen, as well, let it be added, as those of Norway, Holland, Belgium, Greece and the other Allies, opposed their weakness, as civilians untrained in the acts of war, to the long-planned campaign of the Axis Powers. Our enemies had all the advantages in their favour except one. This was the spirit of the brotherhood of the sea which, in past centuries, led to the suppression of piracy and slave trading, and to the charting of the oceans so that men of all races might go down to the sea in ships and do their business in the great waters.

EPIC BRAVERY

Historians have praised the daring, courage and resourcefulness of the Elizabethan sailors after the Virgin Queen had declared the seas of the world open to the seamen of all the maritime nations. But nothing has happened in the past 1,000 years which compares with the dauntless courage, endurance and skill of our merchant seamen, who stood up, without flinching or complaining, to the onslaught of the pirates of the twentieth century.

ANOTHER ATLANTIC VICTIM

Slowly sinking after being torpedoed by a U-boat, this ship is about to make her death plunge into the Atlantic. The picture was taken from a plane which signalled the position of lifeboats containing survivors. Patrol planes have saved many lives in the Battle of the Seas

PASSENGER AND MAIL LINER "ALCANTARA"

Passenger liners with large cargo accommodation have always been highly important ships in the Merchant Navy. The "Alcantara," of over 17,000 tons gross, was built for trade to the River Plate from Southampton, and is a most efficient unit of Merchant Navy power

CHAPTER 3

Ships of the Merchant Navy

Britain's lead in merchant tonnage. Tonnage terms. The passenger liner. Cross-Channel ships. Cargo liners. Advantages of oil fuel Empire food ships. Fruit and meat carriers. Tramps. Flush-deckers and three-island tramps. Ore carriers. Oil tankers. Whale-oil factories. Coasters and colliers. Paddlers. Trawlers and drifters. Tugs. Dredgers and hoppers. Salvage ships. Cable-layers. Ferries and train carriers.

PICTURES of convoys of merchant ships with their precious cargoes of food, raw materials and munitions, will in after years be among the most important documentary evidence of the vital part played by Britain's Merchant Navy in the second World War, and of the purposes for which different kinds of ships were employed. A big war convoy may include practically every type of ship; cheek by jowl with a large oil-carrying vessel will be a small ship designed for trading to the Baltic; alongside a ship well known in the South American trade. That is one of the reasons why a study of ship types is so important, and fascinating.

WARTIME DISGUISES

If there were convoys in peace time, it would still be hard for the lover of ships to identify the different types which the convoy had gathered together.

In wartime, the snowy white decks, the glistening upper works, gaily coloured funnels, slim hulls outlined in mauve or white or black—all the usual aids to recognition—have utterly vanished. Everything presents a drab and sinister sameness; yet all the types of peace time are there, but disguised.

The British Mercantile Marine has more ships than any other country. At the outbreak of war in the autumn of 1939 they totalled nearly 19,000,000 gross tons, and there were not far short of 9,000 individual ships, or bottoms, as they are often called. In addition there were over 3,000,000 tons of shipping owned in the British Dominions and Colonies. These amounted to well over 2,000 ships.

So the British Empire started the war in 1939 with more than 11,000 individual ships, having a total tonnage of over 21,000,000 gross—most of them in peril from enemy action. The problem of the shipbuilder was to maintain that number, in spite of losses due to gun, torpedo, bomb and mine and marine casualties from weather or other causes. It was a problem somewhat akin to trying to keep full of water a bucket with a hole in its bottom. The size of the hole depends upon the success of the enemy's attack and upon the effect of the offensive and defensive measures taken by the naval authorities to counteract them.

ALL THE WORLD'S SHIPPING

Grim though the picture has been from time to time as the war went on, we may thank the sturdy sea spirit of our seamen, and the individualism of the owners, for having kept the Mercantile Marine so strong and e ficient in time of peace, beset as they were for many years by economic di ficulties and international storms.

Great Britain, in association with her Allies, and later the United States, was probably in a better position to face total sea war than any other nation. This is clear from a brief survey of the leading mercantile marines of the world (Fig. 1).

At the beginning of the war the United States held second place as a commercial sea power, even if the large number of ships which traded on the Great Lakes were excluded. Her sea-going tonnage amounted to more than 9,000,000 gross tons. The Lakes contributed nearly 2,500,000 tons.

Japan came third, with over 4,000,000 gross tons, followed by Norway, much of whose 4,000,000 tons worked for the Allied cause from the time when she was overrun by the Germans.

POSITION OF GERMANY

Germany was fifth on the list with less than 4,000,000 gross tons and then came Italy, with 3,050,000 gross tons. A fine group of fast ships had been built by Italy in the years preceding the war.

France—with nearly 3,000,000 gross tons—owned excellent merchant ships and was seventh, while friendly Holland stood eighth in order of precedence. Greece, one of the biggest tramp ship owning countries in the world, possessed nearly 2,000,000 gross tons. At the tail of the list came Sweden, with just over 1,500,000 gross tons, Russia, Spain and Denmark.

Russia's contribution to the merchant sea power of the world was nearly 1,200,000 tons.

Lloyd's Register gives its figures in tons gross. What is the meaning of the various tonnage terms which are in use? Tonnage measurement is an old art, complicated in conception and, like many old things, somewhat unfitted to modern conditions. It goes back to the days when tons were tuns—i.e., tuns (or casks) of wine.

Gross tonnage is a measure of the ship's internal capacity, expressed in tons of 100 cubic feet. Gross tonnage is usually employed when referring to ships like passenger liners, or cross-Channel ships, to paddle vessels, cable-layers, or ships which are not specifically designed for the carrying of cargo in quantity or bulk. On the other hand, ships which carry masses of cargo—what is called bulk cargo—such as tramps, tankers, coasters, ore carriers and so on, are usually referred to in tons of 2,240 lb., the deadweight capacity of a ship being the amount of tons of material which she can carry. Some of the biggest oil tankers are capable of carrying up to 15,000 tons, whilst an ordinary tramp may carry between 9,000 and 10,000 tons. Conversely, and perversely, it is sometimes possible to think of these capacities in terms of cubic feet—not to be confused with the cubic feet (100 per ton) by which gross tonnage is measured.

Then there are other kinds of tonnage, such as net tonnage, upon which light dues are based; displacement tonnage, which is the actual weight of a ship in the water. To avoid confusion, however, it is well for our present purpose to use the terms gross tons and tons of deadweight capacity, for by so doing the discussion of various ship types will be much easier to understand.

GROWING NUMBER OF TYPES

There is another dimension to be considered; that is draught—the amount of water a ship draws or the amount under her keel. A cargo ship is designed with a certain maximum or greatest draught: she floats at this only when fully loaded. When half loaded or with little or no cargo she is at light draught. It is interesting to note that the difference may be as much as twenty feet in a big ship.

The number of merchant ship types has grown appreciably in recent years; indeed trading fleets have been growing in complexity for the last fifty years or so. In Napoleon's day, the relatively few types

PRINCIPAL MARITIME POWERS AT OUTBREAK OF WAR

Fig. 1. *This diagram-survey clearly shows the British Empire's position in commercial sea power—with 20,000,000 tons of merchant shipping—at the beginning of the second World War*

BOILER
UPTAKES

AIR SUPPLY TRUNK
TO BOILER ROOM

SPORTS DECK

SUN DECK

PROMENADE DECK

MAIN DECK

"A" DECK

"B" DECK

"C" DECK

FANS

OIL FUEL
TANKS

BOILERS

DOUBLE
BOTTOM
TANKS

CROSS SECTION OF LINER SHOWING DECKS

WIRELESS AERIALS

ENGINE ROOM HATCH

VERANDAH CAFE

CARGO HATCHES

DOCKING BRIDGE

STARBOARD
PROPELLER SHAFT

TANKS

STARBOARD PROPELLER

RUDDER

ASHWELL
WOOD

THE 'NEW' "MAURETANIA"
A FAST INTERMEDIATE PASSENGER LINER

WIRELESS AERIALS

FORECASTLE

CARGO HATCHES

STREAMLINED FUNNELS

NAVIGATING BRIDGE

THIRD CLASS SPORTS DECK

No I BOILER ROOM

TURBO GENERATING ROOM

No 2 BOILER ROOM

WATERTIGHT BULKHEADS

ENGINE ROOM

OIL FUEL TANKS

KEY TO NUMBERS

1. CREW'S QUARTERS
2. STEWARDS' QUARTERS
3. THIRD CLASS CABINS
4. REFRIGERATED SPACE
5. CARGO
6. FRESH WATER TANKS
7. LIFT
8. CABIN CLASS CABINS
9. CABIN CLASS DINING SALOON
10. THIRD CLASS DINING SALOON
11. KITCHEN STORES
12. KITCHENS
13. SERVICE ROOMS
14. LIFT
15. TOURIST CLASS DINING-ROOM
16. TOURIST CLASS CABINS
17. SWIMMING POOL
18. LIFT
19. CAR STOWAGE
20. CARGO SPACE
21. TOURIST CLASS CABINS

THE "QUEEN MARY"

Fig. 2. *This aerial picture of the famous Cunard liner gives a vivid impression of her giant size and power. Built on the Clyde at a cost of £5,000,000, she is a triumph of the shipbuilding industry. She was built to carry 2,000 passengers and has over 1,000 crew. Her four propellers are probably the largest ever constructed, each weighing thirty-five tons. She was launched by H.M. Queen Mary in 1934, and made a record day's run on her first trip to New York*

existing could easily be transformed from freighter into warship. Speed and manœuvrability usually governed the selection, whenever it became necessary, and many merchantmen, being armed, were well able to look after themselves.

Something similar happened when war broke out in 1939, though merchant ships had not been designed fundamentally to be armed.

First and foremost among the ship types, by reason of size, prestige, luxury of equipment and speed, is the passenger liner, ranging from the *Queen Mary* and *Queen Elizabeth* (Figs. 2 and 3)—floating palaces—down to relatively small vessels like, say, the *Rangitiki* (Fig. 4), which in

peace time ran to New Zealand via the Panama Canal; a ship of nearly 17,000 gross tons with a large passenger capacity and, incidentally, a fairly big cargo space insulated for the carriage of frozen meat. Ships of this class have sometimes been dubbed Empire food ships, but the *Rangitiki* is a passenger vessel as much as a cargo vessel. Between the 85,000 gross tons of the *Queen Elizabeth* and the 17,000 tons of the *Rangitiki*, there is an enormous gap, bridged by many fine ships. The *Georgic* of nearly 27,000 gross tons (Fig. 5) is a case in point. This fine ship carries in normal times, 504 cabin class and 551 tourist class, as well as 466 third-class passengers, across the Atlantic, and, in addition, manages to find space for over 500,000 cubic feet of cargo. That is rather like imagining a big double row of shops in a busy town's main street, provisioned with all kinds of freight, being transported across the Atlantic inside one ship. Another good example is the *Dominion Monarch*, built to link Great Britain with South Africa, Australia and New Zealand (Fig. 6).

The internal characteristics of passenger liners vary much according to the route on which they run. In peace time, for example, a 23,000 tonner, trading to the Far East via the Mediterranean, differs from a ship operating on the North Atlantic, if only because the hotter-weather route calls for wide open decks.

The best way to think of a passenger vessel is to imagine the largest luxury hotel which has ever been built, in a street of shops, with an electric power station, capable of operating the lighting for the whole of the town. In the days before the second World War, this floating hotel travelling at twenty-five to thirty knots, offered the most wonderful food to be found anywhere ; and the wine cellars of the big transatlantic mammoth ships had a magnificent tradition. A liner of over 48,000 tons carries enough fuel oil to drive 55,000 motor cars a distance of 625 miles. Her electrical equipment could provide light for a city of more than 200,000 inhabitants.

What influences the great aeroplane of today will have on the big passenger ship of about 800 feet in length and with between 130,000 to 140,000 h.p. in her engine-room is a matter of conjecture. Will passengers, who are willing to pay highly to travel as fast as a ship can be driven through the sea, be prepared to pay a still higher fare to be transported at

BRITAIN'S QUEEN OF THE SEA

Fig. 3. *Robbed by war of her rightful place in transatlantic travel alongside the "Queen Mary," the "Queen Elizabeth" was "Queen Mary's" sister ship. Her design was affected by that of the "Normandie," whose shadow is cast upon her side as the ships lie in harbour in New York*

PASSENGERS, MAIL AND CARGO

Fig. 4. *One of the finest passenger and mail liners engaged in the United Kingdom—New Zealand service, the "Rangitiki" introduced oil-engine drive to this trade, which demanded big, fast, luxurious ships. Nearly 17,000 tons gross, the "Rangitiki" has a large passenger capacity and has also considerable cargo space, insulated for the carriage of frozen meat*

an even greater speed—the shortening of the passage offering them compensation for reduced space and the absence of many of the amenities of the ship of the sea? Will another *Queen Elizabeth* be built?

It is likely that we shall see a compromise between the supporters of the liner and the aircraft, though the future of the mammoth liner may well be in jeopardy. Many of the beautiful ships operating to the Cape, to South America, to the Far East and elsewhere will probably continue to be built, but their internal structure and the luxury of the accommodation may be varied. Since many wealthy passengers and people in a hurry will travel by air the ships will be provided for travellers

of more modest means, as well as for special freight—too heavy or too bulky to be carried in the aeroplane. Full details of a luxury passenger ship will be found in the illustrations on pages 34 and 35.

The next type of ship, the cross-Channel vessel (Fig. 7), like the big passenger vessel, is likely to be affected considerably by air travel. Every night before the second World War there radiated from ports of the British Isles and from the coasts of the Continent, numbers of fast, streamlined, beautifully equipped little vessels of this class. By day, too, these luxury services ran regularly as clockwork over the Channel, and these efficient ships were the indispensable links of pleasure and business between Britain and the Continent.

The cross-Channel ship can be regarded as a passenger liner in miniature. She has almost everything a passenger liner has. There are *suites de luxe*, comfortable dining saloons, special cabins on the upper decks, less comfortable cabins on the lower decks, smoking rooms, a recreation room and, last but not least, ample space for carrying special perishable cargo.

The cross-Channel ship, too, adopted many of the big passenger liner's characteristics as regards appearance—high, piled-up decks, big streamlined superstructure, surmounted by squat funnels, fine hull lines, and—what is more—a speed closely resembling that of her big sisters. A census of cross-Channel ships, in September, 1939, revealed—in proportion to the total number—almost as many vessels

capable of a speed of over twenty knots as in the bigger ocean-going class.

Let us take a typical night-service vessel of this class. It is true that her gross tonnage is under 4,000, but with a speed of twenty-one knots, she can carry 700 first-class and 800 second-class passengers. Some of the day-service vessels, of slightly less tonnage and greater speed, were very popular. They found space for over 1,200 passengers, and at the same time carried two or three "shops full" of cargo.

CARGO LINERS

Next in the list of ship types, in order of size, though not necessarily in importance, is the cargo liner. When Kipling wrote about the liner "being a lady" and the cargo ship very much the reverse, there were no cargo liners. There was then a very sharp line of demarcation between the passenger vessel and the tramp.

THE MOTOR-PROPELLED "GEORGIC"

Fig. 5. *Smaller than the "Queen Elizabeth" and the "Queen Mary," the "Georgic," 27,000 gross tons, is nevertheless a magnificent Transatlantic ship. In addition to accommodating over 1,500 passengers, in normal times she can carry over half a million cubic feet of cargo*

THE "DOMINION MONARCH"

Fig. 6. *Another fine example of Empire ships is the "Dominion Monarch." Possessing no less than four screws for propulsion, this motor-ship is unique among the passenger and mail liners of Great Britain. She formed a valuable link in the Empire chain, maintaining a service to New Zealand and Australia. Her oil engines are remarkable for their economy of operation*

But the cargo liner does exactly the same things with special cargo as the passenger liner does with passengers and mail; she runs to a rigid schedule, usually between two ports only, at the highest possible speed. Because of her speed and the completeness of her equipment, she is able, however, to offer facilities for upwards of a dozen passengers. The law requires that if a ship carries more than a dozen passengers, it is *ipso facto* a passenger liner, and all the Board of Trade regulations regarding safety of life at sea which apply to a passenger liner must be strictly observed. Many shipowners provide the extra equipment in their cargo liners, and endeavour to bridge the gap between the cargo liner proper and the passenger liner by providing space for upwards of a hundred passengers.

ADVANTAGES OF OIL FUEL

The cargo liner is a product of the last two and a half decades. Nor in any subdivision of cargo liners must we omit the Empire food ship (Fig. 8), of which many particularly fine examples have come from the famous Belfast shipyards of Messrs. Harland & Wolff.

In their many big holds and 'tween decks (as the various deck levels are called), upwards of 500,000 cubic feet are available for refrigerated cargo. It is difficult to visualize 500,000 cubic feet, and more helpful to look at it in terms of mutton, beef, pigs and so on. One ship of this type can carry 137,000 individual carcasses of mutton, and in another part of her hold space she is able to stow 13,000 bales of wool. Such a ship is over 400 feet long, has a deadweight tonnage of 10,390 tons, and steams or motors some seventeen land miles an hour. It would require several thousand lorries to transport such a load on land. Such a ship is illustrated on pages 42 and 43.

When we talk of a ship motoring, we mean that she is a motor-ship propelled by enormous engines of similar type to those which drive London buses. Many modern ships are motor-ships which must always use oil. Steamers can use oil or coal because they have boilers, but numbers of modern steamers, such as passenger liners in which cleanliness is essential, burn oil only. It is not only clean, but much more handy than coal to take aboard and store space for storage of fuel on ocean trade routes is a vital matter.

Looking again to the future, many people consider that the cargo liner, or Empire food carrier type, is one of the most important and one that should be still far more developed. They suggest that she will steam at even more than seventeen land miles, but with the same amount of carcases of mutton, or an equivalent number of bunches of bananas or cases of apples, pears, plums, or grape-fruit, or even perhaps other perishable foodstuffs. In time to come, the type will no doubt be built in increasing quantities. It is urged that the streamlined fast vessel of this kind could do much of the work formerly done by the passenger liner.

In normal times cargo liners may be found on the main routes radiating from British ports, South Africa, New Zealand via Panama, Australia via the Cape, the Pacific north-west coasts via Panama, and other important lines of communication which are dealt with fully in Chapter 6.

SPECIALIST FOOD CARRIERS

There are two main classes, the meat and dairy produce carrier, and the fruit ship. This again is specialized so as to provide for the carriage of bananas only or other kinds of fruit. Generally, the fruit ship is smaller than the meat ship. Both are specialist cargo liners.

The cargo liner, it may be claimed, is beginning to encroach on the duties

CROSS-CHANNEL SHIPS

Fig. 7. *Cross-Channel ships can be described as liners in miniature, resembling their big sisters in their smart streamlined appearance. Fast and comfortable, in happier times they were links of pleasure and business between Great Britain and the Continent, carrying passengers, motor cars and mail by day and night services across the narrow seas*

INTERIOR OF
INSULATED HOLD,
SHOWING ARRANGEME
OF BRINE PIPES

NAVIGATING BRIDGE

3 TON
DERRICKS

Nº 2
HATCH

5 TON
DERRICKS

Nº 1 HATCH

ELECTRIC WINDLASS

GENERA
CARGO

STORES

FROZEN PORK 15°F

CHILLED SPACES
(CHEESE & FRUIT) 40°F

LASHWELL
WOOD

42

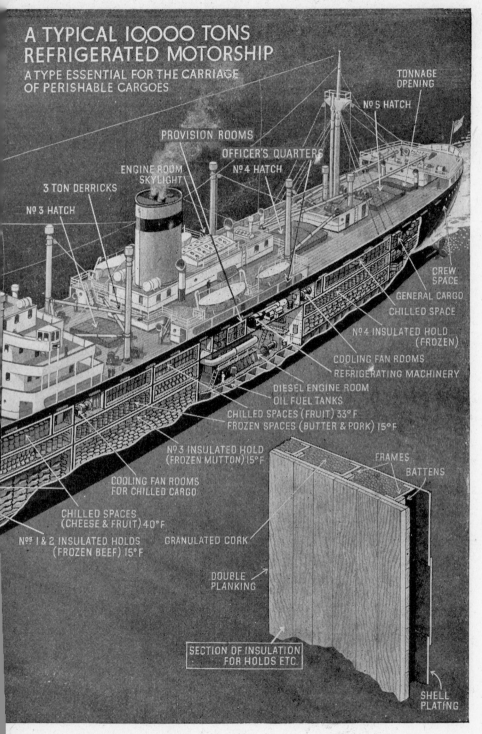

A TYPICAL 10,000 TONS REFRIGERATED MOTORSHIP

A TYPE ESSENTIAL FOR THE CARRIAGE OF PERISHABLE CARGOES

TONNAGE OPENING

Nº 5 HATCH

PROVISION ROOMS

OFFICER'S QUARTERS

ENGINE ROOM SKYLIGHT

Nº 4 HATCH

3 TON DERRICKS

Nº 3 HATCH

CREW SPACE

GENERAL CARGO

CHILLED SPACE

Nº 4 INSULATED HOLD (FROZEN)

COOLING FAN ROOMS

REFRIGERATING MACHINERY

DIESEL ENGINE ROOM

OIL FUEL TANKS

CHILLED SPACES (FRUIT) 33°F

FROZEN SPACES (BUTTER & PORK) 15°F

Nº 3 INSULATED HOLD (FROZEN MUTTON) 15°F

FRAMES

BATTENS

COOLING FAN ROOMS FOR CHILLED CARGO

CHILLED SPACES (CHEESE & FRUIT) 40°F

GRANULATED CORK

Nºs 1 & 2 INSULATED HOLDS (FROZEN BEEF) 15°F

DOUBLE PLANKING

SECTION OF INSULATION FOR HOLDS ETC.

SHELL PLATING

(*Above*) *Empire food ship. with cargo capacity of half a million cubic feet for meat cargo ;* (*Left*) *Fast ship plying between Australia and U.S. with cargoes of lumber and copra*

(*Right*) *Another Empire food ship trading with New Zealand, carrying refrigerated meat cargo and dairy produce;* (*Below*) *General cargo carrier equipped with special derricks*

Fig. 8. SPECIALIST CARGO CARRIERS—EMPIRE FOOD SHIPS

formerly carried out exclusively by the passenger liner. This is probably true. It is certainly correct that the tramp is doing much of the work which was formerly carried on, especially in the early days after the first World War, by the cargo liner.

THE UNIVERSAL TRAMP

The tramp (Fig. 9) is a maid of all work. Many people say that in the future the tramp will continue to hold the same

to design. Her owner does not know what cargo his ship may get or where she will have to go; what kind of fuel she will have to burn; what waters his ship will go into. All this is fixed in an international chartering market, usually the Baltic Exchange in London, the centre of the world for these matters.

Tramps carry a tremendous variety of cargoes. Tramp ships may be chartered for work for a few months in the Pacific,

TRAMPS IN CONVOY

Fig. 9. *In peace time a general servant of the sea, the tramp is taking her full share in the battle of the Atlantic. An escorting destroyer, from which this picture was taken, keeps watch on a convoy entering U-boat areas, through which the convoy passed without loss*

important position as hitherto, but others declare that its day is over because specialization will be the new order. It is probable, however, that tramps will continue as the general servants of industry for many years. They are handy ships, most of them capable of carrying about 9,000 tons of cargo, the equivalent of about four huge coal dumps which may be seen alongside a quay at a South American port. Despised though the tramp may be by some of the liner companies, she is, nevertheless, a tricky ship

may then have to carry lumber or scrap iron between North America and Japan, which may easily be followed by a cargo of case oil—i.e., oil in tins—between California and Australia. On occasion, she may have to load a cargo of ore of various kinds, and bring it home to smelting plants. The holds, therefore, must be strong; the cargo-handling gear equally strong and reliable; hatches must be as large as possible. Accommodation for the crew must be comfortable, but cannot be luxurious. The tramp ship is a cheap

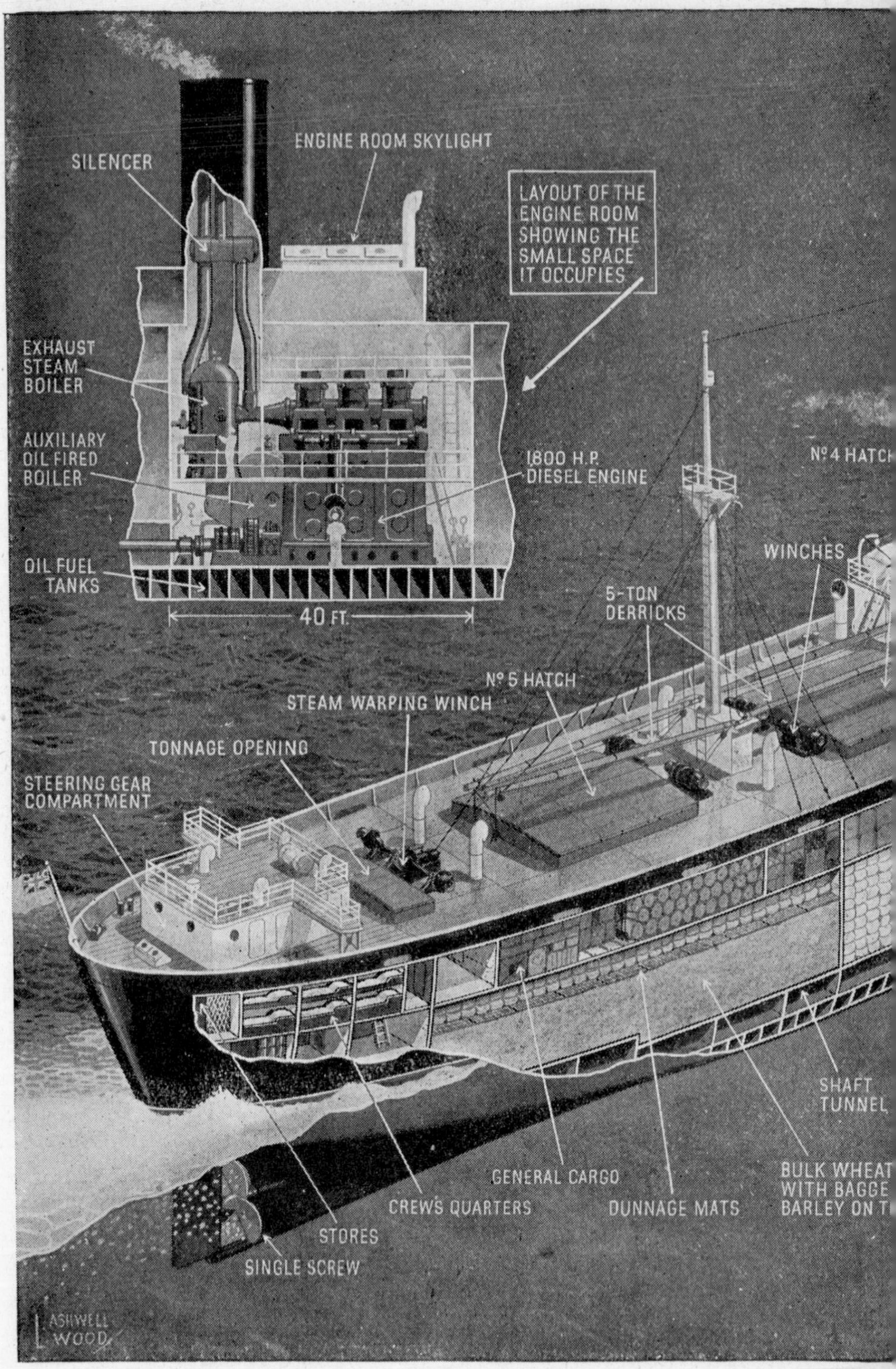

SILENCER

ENGINE ROOM SKYLIGHT

LAYOUT OF THE
ENGINE ROOM
SHOWING THE
SMALL SPACE
IT OCCUPIES

EXHAUST
STEAM
BOILER

AUXILIARY
OIL FIRED
BOILER

1800 H.P.
DIESEL ENGINE

N° 4 HATCH

OIL FUEL
TANKS

WINCHES

40 FT.

5-TON
DERRICKS

N° 5 HATCH

STEAM WARPING WINCH

TONNAGE OPENING

STEERING GEAR
COMPARTMENT

SHAFT
TUNNEL

GENERAL CARGO

BULK WHEAT
WITH BAGGE
BARLEY ON T

CREWS QUARTERS

DUNNAGE MATS

STORES

SINGLE SCREW

ASHWELL
WOOD

46

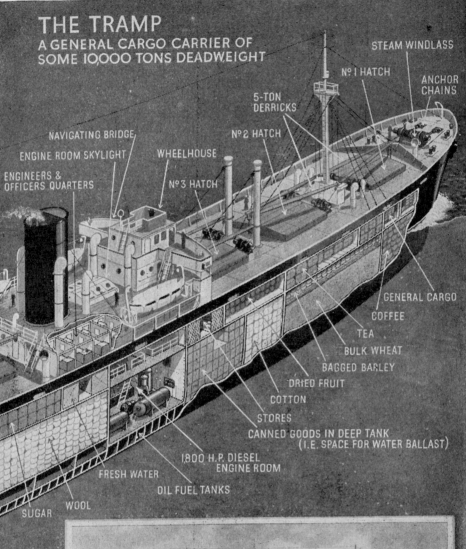

THE TRAMP
A GENERAL CARGO CARRIER OF SOME 10000 TONS DEADWEIGHT

STEAM WINDLASS

Nº 1 HATCH

ANCHOR CHAINS

5-TON DERRICKS

NAVIGATING BRIDGE

Nº 2 HATCH

ENGINE ROOM SKYLIGHT

WHEELHOUSE

ENGINEERS & OFFICERS QUARTERS

Nº 3 HATCH

GENERAL CARGO

COFFEE

TEA

BULK WHEAT

BAGGED BARLEY

DRIED FRUIT

COTTON

STORES

CANNED GOODS IN DEEP TANK
(I.E. SPACE FOR WATER BALLAST)

1,800 H.P. DIESEL ENGINE ROOM

FRESH WATER

OIL FUEL TANKS

SUGAR

WOOL

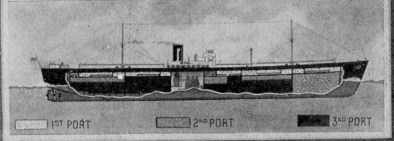

1ST PORT   2ND PORT   3RD PORT

CARGO PLAN SHOWING DISPOSITION OF CARGO
IN RELATION TO PORTS OF CALL

vessel in first cost, and must be equally cheap to her owners in running cost.

As shipbuilding technique improved in the fifteen years preceding the second World War, tramps became more efficient. They increased in size until they resembled some of the big ships which have been mentioned, and they increased in speed. Before the first World War about six knots was considered to be ample for a vessel to wallow out, loaded with coal, to the Plate. Now at least twelve knots is considered necessary.

So there is the tramp—a maid of all work. If she occasionally appears dirty, islands when the ship was loaded, and running in stormy weather, with waves crashing on board all the time. A tramp carrying 9,000 tons of cargo has four hold spaces and two decks. Each hold space has a large hatch. Goods can be lowered into or raised from these holds by derricks on the masts. The propelling machinery is placed amidships.

We have mentioned ore carriers, but reference should be made to some vessels which can carry nearly 15,000 tons of ore in specially arranged holds, on a fixed route. On the other hand, it would be just as possible to use them—provided they

A TYPICAL OIL TANKER

Fig. 10. *The M.T. "Orville Harden," one of the largest tankers, carries a liquid cargo of 15,000 tons. Strong steel bulkheads run fore and aft, and are divided to make transverse bulkheads, forming huge tanks to hold the oil. The engine-room and funnel are aft to minimize risk of fire ; the bridge and crew's quarters are amidships. Pumps are installed for unloading*

then it's the fault of the cargo she carries, and the fact that she may never be in the same port twice for many years. Full details of a typical tramp are given in the illustrations on pages 46 and 47.

Most tramps today are what is known as flush-deckers, that is to say, the topmost or weather deck is level fore and aft, but some of the older ones were known as three-island ships, having a building forward known as a fo'c'sle, one amidships known as a bridge or centre castle, and one aft, known as a poop. The term three-island was formerly due to the fact that these excrescences were literally were not too big for the ports—on other routes. The ore carrier can often run as an ordinary tramp when business in the ore trade is bad. A tramp, too, carries ore cargoes when the demand is brisk. But the specialized ore carrier usually has her machinery aft, and in convoy might well be mistaken for an oil tanker.

OIL TANKERS

Oil tankers are among the most numerous and certainly the most important class of ships in the world today, and it is upon their safe running that war operations by sea, on land and in the air largely depend.

OIL TANKER UNLOADS CARGO

*Safe in port after a perilous passage, a tanker discharges its vital cargo by means of pumps.
This tanker was one of the many ships in a convoy which safely reached home ports after
successfully withstanding repeated attacks by day and night from torpedoes and from the air*

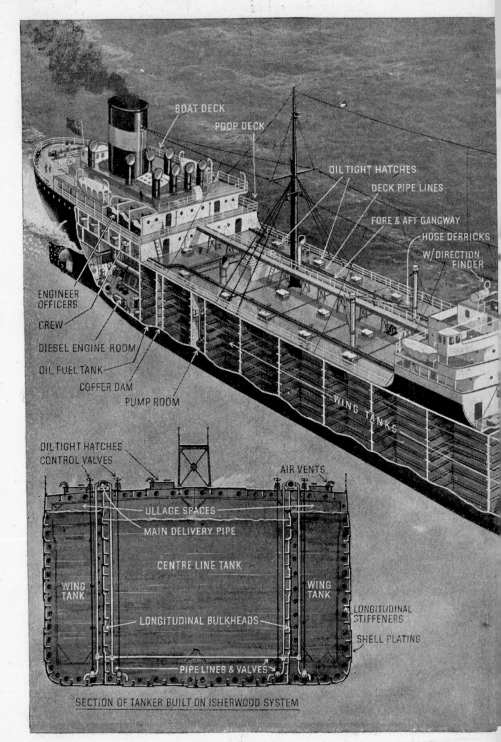

BOAT DECK

POOP DECK

OIL TIGHT HATCHES

DECK PIPE LINES

FORE & AFT GANGWAY

HOSE DERRICKS

W/DIRECTION FINDER

ENGINEER OFFICERS

CREW

DIESEL ENGINE ROOM

OIL FUEL TANK

COFFER DAM

PUMP ROOM

WING TANKS

OILTIGHT HATCHES
CONTROL VALVES

AIR VENTS

ULLAGE SPACES

MAIN DELIVERY PIPE

CENTRE LINE TANK

WING
TANK

WING
TANK

LONGITUDINAL
STIFFENERS

SHELL PLATING

LONGITUDINAL BULKHEADS

PIPE LINES & VALVES

SECTION OF TANKER BUILT ON ISHERWOOD SYSTEM

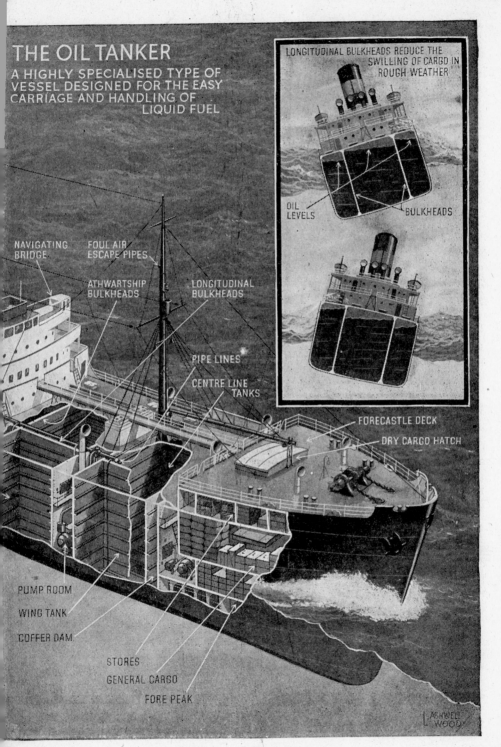

THE OIL TANKER

A HIGHLY SPECIALISED TYPE OF VESSEL DESIGNED FOR THE EASY CARRIAGE AND HANDLING OF LIQUID FUEL

LONGITUDINAL BULKHEADS REDUCE THE SWILLING OF CARGO IN ROUGH WEATHER

OIL LEVELS

BULKHEADS

NAVIGATING BRIDGE

FOUL AIR ESCAPE PIPES

ATHWARTSHIP BULKHEADS

LONGITUDINAL BULKHEADS

PIPE LINES

CENTRE LINE TANKS

FORECASTLE DECK

DRY CARGO HATCH

PUMP ROOM

WING TANK

COFFER DAM

STORES

GENERAL CARGO

FORE PEAK

L. ASHWELL WOOD

IN THE COASTWISE TRADE

Fig. 11. A typical example of the little vessels which carry freight coastwise and to near ports across the Channel, is the coaster "Jersey Queen" shown here. In normal times express services of coasters run between London and Liverpool, Newcastle and London, and other ports. They can off-load from big ships and take cargoes up narrow waterways to smaller ports

At the beginning of the first World War there were under 1,500,000 gross tons of oil tankers. When war again broke out in 1939 the total had grown to nearly 11,000,000 tons. The biggest of these ships can carry 16,000 tons of liquid cargo.

BRITAIN'S LEAD

There are two classes of tankers. The clean tankers carry the clean oils, i.e., petrol, paraffin, etc. The dirty tankers transport the heavy fuel oils, lubricating oils, etc. Heating is necessary because, if the cargo were not warmed in cold weather the oil cargo might go solid. In one case, it had to be dug out of the tanks in winter weather in Liverpool. In September, 1939, Great Britain had the greatest number of tankers, followed by the United States, Norway, Holland, Panama, Japan, Italy, France, Germany, Sweden.

No survey of our merchant ships would be complete which did not include the enormous whale-oil factories which go to the Antarctic with attendant trawler-like catchers to capture and boil up the whales. Some whale factories are equipped to carry as much as 20,000 tons.

An oil tanker can be easily recognized because her machinery as well as her funnel is aft, and her bridge just forward of amidships (Fig. 10). The whole of the hold space, possibly 400 feet in length in a big ship, is divided by two steel structures running from the bow to the stern or vice versa, and parallel with the centre line of the ship. These are known as fore and aft bulkheads, and the three long trough-like spaces so formed are further subdivided by cross divisions, or transverse bulkheads. There may be as many as ten or twelve of these, making nearly thirty individual tanks, into which and out of which oil must be moved by pumps with the greatest possible dispatch. These pumps control the oil flow in each of the three lines of compartments, and some of them are able to pump 2,800 gallons of fuel a minute. Other pumps keep the air pure to guard against explosions.

COASTERS AND COLLIERS

Most coasters, also, have their engines aft. The coaster (Fig. 11) as her name tells, carries freight coastwise. In normal times companies handling coasters ran express services between Newcastle and London, between London and Liverpool, and other ports. Much of the Newcastle-London traffic, consisting of coal, is handled by colliers. The collier is a stocky little ship, sometimes with engines aft, and sometimes with the machinery amidships (Fig. 12). Some colliers trade to the near

Continent ports, returning with a cargo of pit props for the mines. Those colliers which come up the Thames as far as Fulham or Battersea, are known as flat-irons, because, with their hinging funnels aft—lowered to pass under bridges—and their low superstructure, they resemble this household article. Ships of this kind are a type exclusive to Great Britain.

Before the war, many Dutchmen were engaged in the coasting trade, and the shipyards of Northern Holland were turning out standard vessels, well equipped, fast, and capable of carrying upwards of 800 tons of cargo. Holland was extremely competitive, both with her own shipyards and shipowners. These little ships can off-load from big ships in main harbours, and take portions or parcels of cargo up narrow tortuous waterways, to semi-inland ports. This is a most useful ship type characterized by its good looks and efficiency.

THE BUSY COLLIER

Fig. 12. *Colliers are hard-working ships very familiar in East Coast ports and on the Thames. The ship above, built at Burntisland, is typical of many turned out in British ship-yards for this important trade. 972 tons gross cubic capacity, 68,650 feet., her speed is 10½ knots*

The smaller motor coaster, carrying no more than 500 tons, has been a growing rival to the larger steam-driven short sea trader, such as the Baltic timber carrier, a three-island ship which carries some of her cargo on deck. Faster and smaller than the steamer, she can trade to a wide range of ports.

As a frequenter of the Narrow Seas and shoal water, the coaster is frequently a

A complete contrast to the paddler is the hard-working fishing vessel. In size and appearance she resembles the coaster.

Two types operate from our ports, and the Royal Navy has considerable work for both in wartime. They are trawlers and drifters. The biggest is the trawler. She is a ship of over 100 feet in length, if she goes long-distance fishing in the White Sea. The smaller craft—intended

HOLIDAY SHIPS

Fig. 13. *Paddle-steamers once travelled the oceans. Modern paddle-steamers were used for holiday traffic and for happy excursions on the Clyde and around the south coast, as well as to connect ports inaccessible—in estuaries—to rail and coach services. They maintain a high standard of comfort for passengers. Here is the Southern Railway steamer "Whippingham"*

neighbour of the paddler. This is a type of excursion ship very popular on the Clyde, where it maintains regular passenger services, and on the south-east coast in summer time.

Many magnificent ships of this kind have been built in recent years, and the standards of speed, luxury and comfort for passengers have all increased. A typical excursion paddler is shown in Fig. 13.

mainly for work in the North Sea and round the coast—are considerably smaller.

Such vessels are characterized by their stocky appearance and by their ability to stand any pounding which the sea and wind may give them. In contrast to the ordinary cargo vessel, they run out light, i.e., with no fish cargo, but a full cargo of bunkers or fuel. They return with their fish holds full and bunkers almost empty.

ALL-WEATHER SHIPS OF THE FISHING FLEET

Figs. 14 and 15. *The trawler steams forward when at work—drifters (below) drift. Trawlers go far out to sea to find the deep water fish, dragging the net along the sea bottom to gather up the catch, and life on a trawler means hard and unremitting work for the crew. A strong ship of about 150 feet in length, in wartime the trawler is tremendously useful for mine sweeping and other duties. The stoutly-built little drifter, smaller in size than the trawler, is shown below, plunging in a heavy sea. Employed in the North Sea herring fishery, drifters use drift nets to catch the surface-swimming fish, mainly herring. Although steam vessels, drifters carry a steadying sail on the mizen mast to keep the ship's head to wind*

A TUG ON THE JOB

Fig. 16. *Tugs are invaluable little vessels, strength and seaworthiness their stock in trade. With their strong hawsers and towing gear they do wonderful work in salvaging damaged ships. This crippled ship has been taken in hand by tugs, and one of them is about to start pulling her into harbour for repair. Thames tugs are used exclusively for handling barges*

The trawler actually trawls (or tows) when fishing, her tow consisting of a large conical-shaped net, the mouth of which is kept open by two flat boards known as otter boards. Some of the largest trawlers are really ocean-going ships. They have plant for dealing with cod and other fish l'vers; they catch some of the choicest fish. In some cases, refrigerating machinery, such as we find in a fruit ship or meat ship, is fitted.

The trawler is a handsome little vessel, with raking stem, streamlined hull, tall funnel, tall bridgehouse and two masts. As will be seen from Fig. 14 she is unmistakable at sea, though she may sometimes be confused with a pilot cutter, the ship which cruises near a port entrance

or harbour mouth to put pilots in incoming ships and pick them up from departing vessels.

The drifter (Fig. 15) is often a wooden ship. As her name indicates, she literally drifts when fishing, putting out a vertical wall of net in front of her, the net being as far as possible athwart the stream of herring. When the net is hauled in by the capstan, the gills of the fish are entwined in the net from which they are shaken free on the deck. They are then put down in the hold for the run home.

Never was the term harvest of the sea more correctly applied than to the herring industry, and to the ships which run it. You could stand on the quay at Great Yarmouth during the herring season in

September, and watch thousands of shining fish being poured into baskets, which were then hoisted from ship to quayside.

In size, there is some similarity between the fishing vessel and the large ocean-going tug. When running out into the middle of the Atlantic to pick up a ship to be salvaged, the tug may have a speed of as much as seventeen knots. Her powerful pumps enable her to clear the water from a ship's hold. Her hawsers and towing gear are so strong that she can bring a 12,000-ton tanker across the Atlantic to the shipyard which will repair her. Such big tugs are not so numerous as the small and efficient little vessels which surround a big ship when she is docking. These are ship-handling tugs, and do not normally go far outside the harbour limit. There are even smaller tugs on the River Thames, exclusively for the handling of barges, an important feature in the work of the river. A typical tug is shown in Fig. 16.

Lastly, we come to a big, miscellaneous group of vessels. Some of them may be classed under the heading of "Subsidiary Transport," important in the sense that without their work no other transport could go on for long.

Take, for example, the dredger. Unless the entrance to big harbours are kept clear of sand or rock or mud, the draught of ships using the port would be limited, and hence the trade of the port would diminish. The bucket dredger (Fig. 17)—one of the most important—has an endless chain of buckets, worked by gear wheels from an engine in the hull. This digs the lip of each bucket into the sand or material to be dredged, brings it up to the top of the structure, and discharges it from each side of the structure either into the hull of the dredger itself or into little ships called hoppers on either side.

But where there are large quantities of sand, it is more profitable to use the type of dredger which is, in actual fact, a sand sucker. Such craft, very numerous in ports like Liverpool, Rotterdam, Hamburg in peace time, and in other ports

BUCKET DREDGER IN DOCK

Fig. 17. *The dredger's job is to keep the entrances to harbours clear of sand and mud. There are many types. The bucket dredger accomplishes its task by means of an endless chain of buckets which dig out the sand and discharge it into the dredger itself or overside into hoppers*

where there is considerable silting up, have powerful centrifugal pumps which are driven by enormous engines, capable of moving thousands of cubic feet of sand per hour.

Then there is another class of dredger which you find round the entrances to docks and locks. This is a grab dredger, which lifts coal out of trucks, and mud away from dock entrances.

Salvage ships are sometimes tugs, but tugs are not always salvage ships. Such vessels are fast, with powerful portable pumps and wrecking gear. This equip-

cable when it runs out. Fresh water is stored within the tanks proper. Sometimes cable ships work out in mid-ocean; on other occasions they are stationed near sturdy bluff red lightships marking a special channel or dangerous sandbank.

Finally, a word about ferries. They range from the rowing boat on the upper Thames to the large sleeping-car-train-carrier which in normal times runs between Dover and Dunkirk. The types have many features in common.

It will be obvious that if vehicles as well as passengers are carried, or vehicles only,

TYPICAL CABLE-LAYER

Fig. 18. *The cable ship has beautiful yacht-like lines because of the nature of her work—a broken cable can be easily picked up over the curving raked bow. Her hundreds of miles of cable are wound round conical tanks, which hold fresh water. She raises and repairs cables, in addition to laying them. Being at sea for long periods, she must have large fuel capacity*

ment enables them to stand by a ship which has run, say, on the rocks.

Cable-layers are among the most beautiful of ships afloat, because of the nature of their work. To pick up a broken cable over the bow and lay the mended cable over the stern, or indeed merely to lay a new cable over the stern, calls for a curving raked bow and a graceful yacht-like stern (Fig. 18).

Her hundreds of miles of cable are kept in holds, which form conical tanks, so that the cable is wound round and round the tank, every care being exercised to ensure that there are no kinks in the

they must have a flat deck considerably strengthened on the under side, a depth of hold not too great, a big beam or width in proportion to their deck, and plenty of engine power.

So shipping, it is apparent, is rapidly dividing itself into many distinct groups. Each has its particular work to do. Without a well-balanced Mercantile Marine, the people of the British Isles could not live in comfort in time of peace, enjoying to the full the fruits of the whole world, nor could they fight an enemy when war occurs. In the final issue of war, everything must depend on shipping.

THE SIZE AND CAPACITY OF MERCHANT SHIPS

An average ship type as below has a:	Length of	When loaded floats in	Speed Loaded of	Tonnage of	Loading capacity of
PASSENGER LINER	657·6 ft.	34 ft. 1½ in.	19 knots	17,350 gross	658,960 cub. ft. 517 pass.
CARGO LINER ...	516·3 ft.	29 ft. 7 in.	17 knots	12,320 gross	750,839 cub. ft. 12 pass.
OIL TANKER ...	462·8 ft.	27 ft. 0 in.	11 knots	8,012 gross	12,000 tons o l
TRAMP	414 ft.	25 ft. 3½ in.	11 knots	4,719 gross	585,420 cub. ft.
ORE CARRIER ...	387·1 ft.	24 ft. 4 in.	10 knots	5,787 gross	161,380 cub. ft.
CROSS-CHANNEL SHIP	353 ft	15 ft 1 in.	17½ knots	4,320 gross	725,755 cub. ft. 1,000 pass.
TUG (SALVAGE)...	198·3 ft.	17 ft. 11 in.	17 knots (without tow)	793 gross	No loading capacity: carries tire and salvage pumps
COASTER... ...	197 ft.	8 ft. 6 in.	9 knots	200 gross	62,480 cub. ft.
TRAWLER ...	134·6 ft.	11ft. 9in.	11 knots	130 gross	400,000 lb. fish

GUN DRILL ON A MERCHANT SHIP

Men of the Merchant Service have become gunners as well as seamen, for the ships which daily deliver vital supplies have constantly to meet enemy attack. Picture shows seamen gunners at drill under the Red Ensign. This is the distinctive flag of merchant ships. It has a Union Jack in the corner, and is affectionately known as the Old Red Duster

CHAPTER 4

Men of the Merchant Navy

Uniform. Shipping Act of 1854. Rank. The articles. The master. First mate. Boatswain and carpenter. Quartermasters. Seamen and boys. Engineers. Greasers, firemen and trimmers. The purser. Stewards. Merchant ships in the Royal Navy. Monotony of patrol duties. Fishing vessels and their crews. Mine sweeping. Allied merchant seamen

I T is surprising how little is known by the general public of a nation of islanders about the men of their Merchant Navy. This may be because in peace time officers are rarely seen ashore, and the men of the deck, engine-room and stewards' department do not wear uniform. Unless you lived at a seaport, and close to the docks, you would never see them in their work-a-day clothes. Indeed, in my early days at sea it was an unwritten law that the master of the ship should don his top hat and frock coat before going ashore to hand in his report at the shipping office at the end of a voyage.

FIRST TRAINING SHIP

To understand fully the position of the British Mercantile Marine, it is necessary to learn a little about our naval history for from time immemorial the two great sea Services of Supply and Defence have been interwoven in the strand of our national life. In medieval times there was no such thing as a fighting navy. There were certainly Royal Ships, but these were usually merchant ships engaged in trading to help fill the royal coffers, and were entirely a business transaction on the part of the monarch. When war did break out, the monarch called on as many merchant ships as were lying in harbours to come to his aid and fight for king and country.

It was not until the early part of the eighteenth century that the two sea services separated into the Merchant Navy and the Royal Navy. It was only then that the Royal Navy as a fighting force was established. Then it was that Parliament ordered all merchant ships to wear a distinctive flag. This flag was to be a Red Ensign, in the canton of which (that is to say, the top corner next to the flagstaff) was placed a small Union Jack. Today this is the flag which men of the Merchant Navy affectionately call the Old Red Duster. It is known the world over.

Soon after this, the Marine Society was formed, which meant much to our sailors, for it was the first organized attempt to train men for the profession. The Society provided uniform and kit for lads entering either the Royal or the Merchant Service. A ship named the *Beatty* was purchased for the training of these lads; she was the first training ship in the world. Anchored in the Thames between Deptford and Woolwich she did excellent work.

MERCHANT NAVY RECOGNIZED

Up to this time there was no uniform either in the Royal Navy or in the Merchant Service. George II, however, decided on blue and white as the distinctive colours for uniform for officers in the former service. It is said that one of his lady loves wore a pretty dress of these colours, which impressed the monarch. It was many years afterwards that the men of the lower deck were placed in uniform;

though certainly some wealthy captains used to rig their boat's crew in a livery of their own design, which they provided at their own cost.

But when the Shipping Act of 1854 was passed, embodying all previous legislation, merchant seamen were at once placed on a better footing. Furthermore, the Act regulated the method of engagement and discharge. Shipping offices were set up in the principal ports, and articles of agreement were drawn up between the owners and the crew.

The official log book was born, and the health of our seamen was given primary importance for the first time.

CONDITIONS IMPROVED

As the years passed, new shipping companies, which became leaders in the industry and were more interested in passengers than cargoes, came into the field, and soon the conditions for all on board such ships improved, to some extent, as the result of competition. These owners insisted on officers wearing distinguishing uniforms. In most cases the uniforms were fashioned on those in use in the Royal Navy, with alterations in badges and decorations.

It was the wealthy East India Company that introduced uniform for its officers. So good were conditions in this company's ships that many men preferred to serve in them, rather than in the King's Navy. This is how we got the term Merchant Service and King's Service. There is no standard uniform for officers in the Merchant Service today. They wear the uniform chosen by the company with which they serve, together with distinctions of rank which are recommended by the Board of Trade. The master usually wears four gold stripes which vary in design. Some masters like to wear plain circles round the sleeve of the coat, others have distinctive stripes on the coat shoulder. The first mate sports three, the

second two, and other officers one stripe (Fig. 1). Caps carry a crown and anchor.

At one time there was a great deal of rivalry amongst the big shipping companies as to whose officers should be the most smartly dressed, and one line, which shall be nameless, tried to put their officers in uniform as nearly as possible like those worn in the Royal Navy. The story goes that the chairman of the company wrote to Whitehall requesting permission for their officers to wear epaulettes. A well-known admiral dictated the reply to the effect that permission would be granted—if the officers concerned would wear three! No suggestion was made in the letter as to where the third epaulette was to be worn.

Different departments are frequently distinguished by coloured cloth between the gold, as in the Navy. The deck department has no colour, just the blue of the cloth sleeve. Engineer officers show a purple band, pursers a white one, and doctors red. On the quartermaster's sleeve a steering-wheel is represented.

R.N.R. AND R.N.V.R.

The badge of the Royal Naval Reserve officer is two thin gold bands plaited (Fig. 2). One thin band undulating round the coat sleeve signifies that the wearer is in the Royal Naval Volunteer Reserve (Fig. 3), known as the " Wavy Navy." The number of rings designates the rank. A captain has four, a commander three, a lieutenant-commander two and a half, a lieutenant two, while a sub-lieutenant sports only one. Warrant rank does not carry a gold band, but only buttons on the sleeve. This also is the distinguishing uniform of a midshipman. The three buttons on the sleeve have given rise to the name by which the midshipman is usually known—snotty.

In the dark winter nights, the bridge of a ship is not too comfortable, and a bitter east wind would cause the nose of a lad to

CAPS AND SLEEVE MARKINGS OF THE MERCHANT NAVY

Fig. 1. *The above markings are recommended for general use by the Board of Trade.* 1, Master; 2, Chief Officer; 3, Second Officer; 4, Third Officer; 5, Uncertified Junior Officer; 6, Second Master; 7, First Officer; 8, Junior Second Officer; 9, Chief Engineer; 10, Second Engineer; 11, Third Engineer; 12, Fourth Engineer; 13, Uncertified Junior Engineer; 14, Second Chief Engineer; 15, Junior Second Engineer; 16, Junior Third Engineer; 17, Junior Fourth Engineer; 18, Surgeon; 19, Assistant Surgeon; 20, Senior Purser; 21, Purser; 22, Assistant Purser; 23, First Wireless Operator; 24, Second Wireless Operator; 25, Third Wireless Operator; 26, Cadet; 27, Chief Steward; 28, Assistant Chief Steward; 29, Steward; 30, Assistant Steward; 31, Steward (cargo ships); 32, Boatswain; 33, Boatswain's Mate; 34, Quartermaster; 35, Quartermaster's Mate; 36, Cook; A, Master's Cap; B, Officer's Cap; C, Petty Officer's Cap

CAPTAIN, R.N.R.   COMMANDER, R.N.R.   LIEUT. COMMANDER, R.N.R.

LIEUTENANT, R.N.R.   SUB LIEUTENANT, R.N.R.   SKIPPER, R.N.R.
(CHIEFLY FISHING TRAWLERS)

RANKS OF ROYAL NAVAL RESERVE

Fig. 2. *Many Merchant Navy officers volunteer in peace time for training in the R.N.R., which is the first line of reserve for the Royal Navy. The highest rank they can obtain in the Royal Navy is Commodore. The badge of R.N.R. officers is two gold bands plaited*

run somewhat freely. Apparently it was the custom in days of old for these young gentlemen to remove offending drips from the ends of their noses with the sleeves of their coats. To prevent this, three large buttons were placed on the sleeve, just above the wrist band, which it was hoped would render such a deplorable habit more difficult of accomplishment.

HOW THE CREWS SIGN ON

Nowadays, in peace time, the crew of a merchant ship is signed on articles before a shipping master at the port from which the ship is sailing. The crew attend the shipping office, as do the heads of the departments. The mate will see to men of the deck department, the second engineer will look after the men in the engine-room and stokehold; and the purser or chief steward is responsible for the stewards, cooks, and so on, necessary for running the victualling side of the ship.

The articles, or, as this document is officially known, T 124, are read out to all men intending to sign on. The tacit consent of the men is taken to mean that they agree to the clauses which are as binding on both parties—the men and the owners—as any legal document. Then every member of the crew signs his name to the agreement. Against his name are his rate of pay and occupation. The articles are opened by the master.

It may come as a surprise to some to learn that there is no such rank as captain in the Merchant Navy. The man who is often called captain is actually the master of the ship. In the early days of trade, the owner of the ship, who was usually a merchant, was known as the captain, and he employed a navigator whose duty it was to navigate the ship from and to the various ports as instructed by him. This navigator was called the master of the ship.

Neither are there any officers in the merchant service. The men who assist the master in the navigation of the ship are called mates. Thus the chief officer, next to the captain, would be the first mate on articles, the next the second mate, and so on. The officer titles given them today are entirely honorary.

The duties of the deck department are considerably less today than they were in the days of sail. Since mechanical propulsion has taken the place of the winds of heaven in driving ships across the waters, the engine-room staff has increased pro-portionately and the deck department has considerably decreased.

The master of the ship is responsible for the safety of all on board and although he may not take an active part in the navigation, nevertheless, it is his job to see that this is correctly done. Even when he has a skilled pilot on his bridge, his responsibility still remains; should the pilot run the ship ashore it is the master who must take the blame, as it is argued that he should be a better judge of pilots!

RESPONSIBILITIES OF THE MASTER

Think for a moment of what the master of a big liner has under his care. Apart from the lives of passengers and crew there is probably a valuable cargo and, added to this, the hull and fittings of his ship. In many cases the monetary value

DISTINCTIONS OF RANK IN R.N.V.R.

Fig. 3. *The undulating gold band is the mark of the R.N.V.R., the "Wavy Navy." Four rings mark a captain, three a commander, while a lieutenant-commander has two broad rings, with a thin ring between them. Two rings mark a lieutenant, and one a sub-lieutenant*

MASTER AND MATE

On the bridge of an oil tanker, master and mate admirably typify the merchant seamen engaged in the battle of the seas. The master (left) returned from retirement when the war started, after thirty years in ships. His second mate (right) has had fifty years at sea

is exceedingly high, yet the pay of these men is small compared with salaries ashore for posts of far less responsibility.

The first mate is usually known as the chief officer in passenger ships. In a way, he corresponds to the first lieutenant in a man-of-war. He is the executive officer, and it is up to him to see that cargo is properly stowed and discharged at the correct port. He has also to see to the general cleanliness of the ship. He does not often keep a watch; this is done by the other mates who, of course, help in the running and navigation of the ship.

The boatswain and carpenter come next in the deck staff. They have a crew of their own in large ships and come into line with men of warrant rank in the Royal Navy. The term boatswain is common to both services and is a very old word. Actually, it means the man in charge of the largest boat in the ship. In olden days it was customary for the captain-owner to travel in his ship.

OLD SHIP CUSTOMS

He was not a sailor, and when the ship reached port he would have to go ashore to conduct his business. Gangways were non-existent or very primitive, and it was difficult for a landsman to negotiate them, so the owner was lowered down to the waiting boat in a chair slung on a block and tackle. The crew would stand by on the end of the tackle and the boatswain would keep an eye on the descending chair, and signal to the crew to hold fast when the chair was close enough to the boat to allow the occupant to step out of it. On his return, the reverse action would take place to get the captain-owner inboard. The boatswain gave the signal with a whistle, which he wore suspended round his neck by a small silver chain. This whistle is the boatswain's pipe and this is the origin of the custom, when an important person joins or leaves a ship, of piping him over the side.

Quartermasters are next on the list. They are men who have had a good deal of sea-going experience and are able to take a turn at the wheel. Then come the able-bodied seamen, ordinary seamen, and boys. This is the deck part of a ship's complement today in liners and cargo liners. The principle is the same for other ships, but is naturally adjusted to suit tonnage and trade conditions.

WORK BELOW DECKS

The chief engineer is the head of the engine-room staff. On him falls the whole responsibility for the main and subsidiary machinery. Here again conditions call for slightly different personnel, but in the main he has a staff of juniors according to the size of the ship and her cargo. If she is carrying perishable goods, such as meat, fruit, dairy produce, etc., she will have refrigerator holds, and a special engineer is told off for this duty. Electrical engineers are carried in all big ships. In an ocean greyhound engaged on the Western Ocean trade, there will be as many as fifty engineer officers.

There are no stokers in the merchant service. The greasers are experienced firemen who assist the engineers in the smooth running of the machinery and keep an eye on the firemen and trimmers. Today many ships are oil fuelled and then there is no need for so many hands in the engine-room.

If coal is used, the firemen have the job of working in the stokehold to keep the fires burning underneath the boilers. In coal-fuelled ships, this is not an easy task and in the tropics these men suffer considerable inconvenience from the heat. Alongside each fireman is a heap of coal and it is no easy matter to throw a shovelful of coal into a furnace when the ship is rolling. It is the job of the trimmers to carry the coal from the bunkers to the stokehold. Also when the ship is coaling, trimmers have to be in the bunkers to see that the incoming coal is evenly distributed, by no means an easy task.

In large passenger ships the purser's department is of the greatest importance. He will have as his assistant the chief steward and a personnel of anything between three or four hundred stewards. He is responsible for the entire victualling of the ship, and has many other duties.

PROBLEMS OF THE PURSER

Consider a large passenger ship starting on a voyage in peace time. She would have a crew of approximately 1,100, as well as 2,500 passengers of all classes, totalling something like 3,700 people—more than the population of many villages in Britain. It would be a big job to supply all these people with food daily even on shore with shops at hand, so think what it means to do this at sea.

Vast quantities of stores have to be carried in the holds and refrigerators and the amounts must be worked out almost to the fraction of a pound. Yet this work is efficiently carried out by the stewards' department in the ship. The chief steward may have as many as 150 cooks, butchers and bakers and a small army of stewards under him; the galleys have electrical devices to peel potatoes, cut beans, shell peas, stone raisins and wash dishes, etc.

Besides this, the purser has to act as host to the passengers, a position requiring a great deal of tact. People who are not used to shipboard life ask the most curious and inane questions—and a polite and satisfying answer must always be found.
"*And then there is the purser,*
Most polite and suave converser,
With a repertoire of anecdotes o'erflowing.
His one lifelong desire is
Just to answer such inquiries
As 'Please, purser, will you tell me where
I'm going?'"
In smaller ships such as cargo liners, a purser is not needed, and a chief steward combines the two jobs.

One of the duties of a purser is to make up the Portage Bill, which is a detailed account of the financial transactions of every member of the crew and the amounts due to each man when the ship pays off. When the crew is a large one, this necessitates a considerable amount of close clerical work, and the purser has in his office one or two assistant pursers. But when the crew is small, this job falls to the chief steward.

The crew of a tramp steamer is smaller than in passenger ships. Her deck department is much the same, as is the engine-room. She carries very few stewards, just a cook or two and a few stewards to act as personal servants to some of the officers.

The tanker, a special type of ship, is usually well found, with comfortable quarters and good food. On account of the inflammable nature of her cargo, there are certain restrictions on board which may become irksome, and by way of compensation extra food and comfort are provided. For this reason the tanker is popular among merchant seamen.

LINERS CHANGED TO WARSHIPS

At the outbreak of war in 1939, many of our merchant ships of all types were requisitioned for the Royal Navy. The fast ocean-going liners were rushed into dock. All the trappings of passenger days were ruthlessly torn down and all inflammable material removed. Decks were stiffened to carry gun mountings and soon these ships, flying the White Ensign, were able to take their place as fighting auxiliaries of the Royal Navy.

A regular naval captain was appointed to the command of each of them, with naval gunnery officers. It was necessary also to appoint a signal officer and certain naval ratings. The original captain, if he were not already in the Naval Reserve, was given a temporary commission as commander and retained to advise the

SEARCHING FOR MINES

From the bridge of a minesweeper at work off the East Coast, keen eyes search the sea for enemy mines. Many trawlers are constantly employed in this dangerous job, sometimes retaining their old crews, and their skippers are given warrant rank in the Royal Naval Reserve

IN THE ENGINE-ROOM

The importance of the chief engineer's job cannot be over emphasized, especially in wartime. In emergency the safety of the ship may depend on his quickness and resource. He bears the whole responsibility for the main and subsidiary machinery of the ship, and is supreme in his kingdom below decks. This chief engineer (right), who has had forty years service on the sea, is shown in charge of the engine-room of an oil tanker. Tankers are popular with seamen, as extra comforts compensate for necessary restrictions due to the dangerous cargo

naval man. Nearly all the engineers were retained, as the extra strain on the engines demands the skill and knowledge of men used to working them. These officers were also given temporary commissions commensurate with their standing in peace time. In many cases, the men in the ship were in the Royal Fleet Reserve or Royal Naval Reserve, so they were accustomed

lower deck were several petty officers and ratings from the Royal Navy, and the remainder were made up of the merchant seamen already serving in the ship. When it came to the matter of signals, few merchant seamen were experts, and men from the R.N.V.R. took over these duties.

The great weakness in converting passenger ships into warships is the question

STEWARDS AT LIFEBOAT DRILL

The purser is responsible for the entire victualling of a large passenger ship. The chief steward and more than three hundred stewards assist him in seeing to the comfort of the passengers. A big liner will have 2,500 passengers to look after. Stewards are seen at lifeboat drill

to naval routine and speedily adapted themselves. Naturally the men from the Merchant Service found the work different, but all of them were proud of their uniform and a chance to serve their king and country in the Royal Navy.

In the ship in which I served in the first World War, we carried a naval captain, a commander R.N.R., a lieutenant-commander R.N., and seven or eight lieutenants R.N.R. who were in the ship when she was taken over. Two doctors were signed on and an extra paymaster. On the

of protective armour plating. A certain amount is placed round the guns for the protection of the gun's crew, but the hull of these ships is very vulnerable—a fraction of an inch thick. This was demonstrated in the second World War. The gallant *Rawalpindi* had no chance whatever against the formidable *Deutschland*, nor had the *Jervis Bay* against overwhelming odds. Both these ships had been converted into merchant cruisers (Fig. 4). The stories of their heroic encounters with the enemy thrilled the world.

Some of these converted ships are employed on patrol work. This is one of the most monotonous jobs, and its very monotony may become a danger. Daily alterations must be made on the routes taken, because, if the work fell into a matter of mere routine, the enemy would soon become informed of that fact. He the great net which is trawled astern. Another feature of these trawlers is the otter boards. These consist of two right-angle planes of wood which are attached to the trawl wires when trawling is in progress, in order to keep the mouth of the huge net open. Many trawlers are now minesweepers, and do grand work.

PULL ALL TOGETHER, BOYS!

In off-duty spells, while not actually engaged on a sweep, minesweeper crews welcome the opportunity to do a little fishing for the ship's company, and a good catch often rewards their efforts. This picture, taken with a mine sweeping flotilla in the North Sea, shows the nets being hauled in after a successful trawl. In the background the cook waits expectantly

would then only have to watch for a favourable opportunity to break through.

There are no finer ships sailing the seas than the trawlers which harvest our fish. They can be seen at work round our coasts, and are easily recognizable by two queer contraptions aft. These are called gallows and are on each side of the hull. It is through these that the wires pass to

The master of such a vessel signs on T 124 and is generally known as skipper. He has a mate and six or seven deck hands in his department. The engines are in the charge of the first and second enginemen and there are two or three firemen, according to the size of the ship. The average size of a trawler is about 120 feet long, but she is pretty broad in

ARMAMENT OF TYPICAL CARGO SHIP
3 IN. A·A GUN
6 IN. Q.F. GUN
STRENGTHENING STANCHIONS
STERN

PORT SEARCHLIGHT
RANGE FINDER
STARBOARD SEARCHLIGHT
A·A GUN
ARMOURED WHEELHOUSE
CARLEY FLOATS
A·A GUN
FORWARD 6 IN. GUNS
AMMUNITION TRUNK TO HOLD

MERCHANT CRUISER ARMAMENT
FORWARD TWO 6 IN. GUNS
TWO A·A GUNS
TWO 6 IN. GUNS
TWO A·A GUNS
STERN 6 IN. GUN

LINER CHANGED TO CRUISER

Fig. 4. *Many famous liners have been converted into armed merchant cruisers. Drawing shows a typical example, with details of her armament. Top, the armament of a cargo ship*

LOWERING AND MANNING THE LIFEBOAT

On H.M.S. "Gordon," one of the Navy's dry land "ships" which trains men for the Merchant Navy, men are taught everything about seamanship. They pass from instructor to instructor learning how to steer a ship and read a compass, how to stow cargo, how to knot and splice, how to shoot, and how to take soundings. Here they are learning to lower and man a lifeboat

the beam to enable her to withstand the fierce buffeting of the North Sea in winter. I served in such ships as these during the first World War and was really astonished at their seaworthiness.

Some of the larger trawlers are at sea for as long as a week on end, and are frequently to be seen engaged in trawling as far away as the stretch of water between Iceland and Norway. A smaller type of fishing craft is the drifter. She is usually seen near our shores and, as her name implies, she handles a drift net which is much lighter than a trawl. She is a wonderful boat for all weathers.

A large number of trawlers were requisitioned at the outbreak of hostilities in the autumn of 1939 because they can be so admirably adapted for war work; the larger vessels for patrol duties, and the smaller ones in the dangerous and hazardous work of mine sweeping. The gallows that used to handle the huge trawl took the sweep wires, and the otter boards kept this wire at the necessary depth to catch the mooring of hidden mines. The crew remained the same as in the peaceful days of fishing, with the addition of a naval petty officer for signal duties. The skipper was given warrant rank in the Royal Naval

Reserve and wore the peak cap and reefer jacket of this rank. Some of the fishermen were naval reservists and had had a certain amount of training in the Lewis gun and the twelve-pounder. Little knowledge have these fishermen of mines and submarines, but they set out with a quiet deliberation and as simple a demeanour as if they were off to shoot the trawl for the earning of their daily bread.

IN THE FRONT LINE

Some day the full story of the courage and endurance and skill of British merchant seamen and fishermen in the war will be written, and the nation will realize that these men were in the front line of the most important of all the battles which were fought in various parts of the world. For if they were to fail, nothing could save the cause of the United Nations. The Battle of the Seas is decisive, for the sea controls the land; every international war has been won by sea and the army of the victors has then done "the mopping up." In that task aircraft, which are of such value to both the Navy of Defence and of Supply, take their part.

And when tribute is paid to British merchant seamen, it would be ungenerous if praise were not also given to the seamen of Norway, Holland, Denmark, Fighting France, Poland and Greece, as well as to the seamen of the Dominions. Their ready co-operation with the British seamen in fighting the Battle of the Seas— and their unflinching bravery—is one of the great surprises for the Axis Powers.

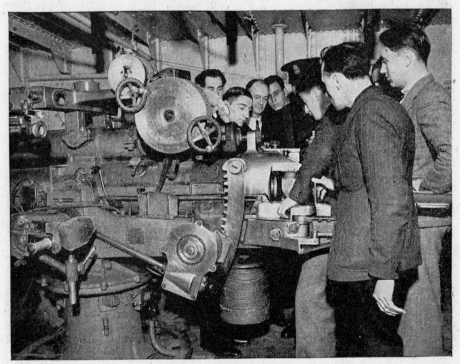

LEARNING THEIR NEW TRADE

Men of the Merchant Navy are given special courses by Royal Navy instructors in gunnery, plane recognition, the use of depth charges, etc. Here young seamen are learning the mechanism of a 4-inch gun. Navigation and all branches of seamanship are taught at special schools

MINESWEEPERS AT WORK

Fig. 1. *The approaches to all harbours are regularly swept by a great fleet of minesweepers of all types. The work of the minesweepers never stops. It goes on night and day, and has saved numbers of ships from being blown up or seriously damaged. Here the sweeping apparatus is being lowered into the sea by a crane. Many trawlers have been adapted for use as minesweepers*

CHAPTER 5

The Merchant Navy in Wartime

A ship puts to sea in peace time. Many changes with the coming of war. Sailing under orders. Routine of entering harbour. Outer and inner defences. The boarding officer. Ministry of War Transport. Director of Merchant Ship Repairs. Seamen's pool. Arming of merchant ships. Dangers encountered by ships. Magnetic mines. Degaussing. Compass adjustments. The acoustic mine. Catapulting of fighter aircraft. Preparations for the next voyage. Convoy conference. Back to sea again

CAPTAIN JOHN SMITH walks down the steps to the street, and stops to draw a deep breath of relief.

He is always rather relieved to escape from shipping offices. They give him a feeling of oppression; for Captain John Smith, of London, or Newcastle, or Leith, or Aberdeen, or Glasgow, or Liverpool, or Cardiff, or Bristol, or Plymouth, or wherever else in the British Isles he hails from, is a bluff, hard-headed, forthright fellow, and, for the life of him, he can't see what all these people—men and women, boys and girls—in the shipping offices do with themselves all day long.

OUT OF HIS ELEMENT

People rushing this way and that, doors banging, telephones shrilling and squawking, pencils scribbling, pens scraping, typewriters clicking—yet always plenty of time to ease down and have a comfortable yarn with Captain John Smith, over a cigar and the business that brings him there. Office life puzzles Captain Smith.

He likes the cigar and the yarn; but just the same he is glad to get out into the open again, with all his papers crammed into the battered old brief case under his arm, or the still more battered attaché case that looks so incongruous dangling from one great paw. It swings as he walks.

He has squared up everything now—customs clearance, manifests, ship's articles—everything. His crew is complete, cargo stowed and hatches battened down under the efficient and watchful eye of the mate, he is complete with bunkers for the voyage, and drinking water, and boiler water, and stores—everything.

GOING ABOARD

For weeks or months he will be independent of the shore; his ship will become a little, compact microcosm moving on the great waters; and he, John Smith, will be master—" under God," as they say in the insurance policies—of that small self-contained world.

In his tweed coat and soft felt hat, looking as little like a seafarer as he can contrive, for he would never dream of wearing his uniform ashore, he sets off for the docks; walking deliberately, setting each foot down in front of him with emphasis, firmly, as he has learned to do in thirty or forty years of making his way along the steel deck or the wooden bridge of a vessel seldom steady under his feet. And you could not possibly mistake him for anything but what he is.

The dock policemen salute him, recognizing him on sight. He goes on board his ship, battered tramp or sombre looking, black hulled cargo liner, her name in small metal letters on the bows, *British Freighter*, and painted on her counter, with her port of registry underneath. He goes straight to his cabin, and is busy there for a short time, before the mate appears, to report.

The pilot is on board, the dock master has been warned, the ship is at immediate notice for steam, and the chief engineer is standing by. Everything is set.

FULL AHEAD !

Captain John Smith takes the bridge. The mate goes forward to the forecastle head, the second mate to the poop, the third mate (if there is a third mate) joins the master on the bridge. The engine-room telegraph drags, its bell trills, and is answered from down below; a whistle blows, a winch hisses and clanks and warps are eased. The screw thumps lazily, greenish water suddenly swirls along the hull, disturbing the scum that floats on the surface of the still, unruffled dock, the ship trembles a little, and begins to glide away from the quay wall.

She swings, deliberately. The pilot, the master, and the third mate peer down over the side, judging distances, watching, waiting. Mate and second are alert, ready to spring into action when the signals come from the bridge. The ship edges out, swings slowly round, slips out through

the narrow dock entrance, and enters the wider yet still confined waters of the river.

Half ahead now, with a sharp lookout; and she slides smoothly down river, making her way quietly, without commotion, through the busy traffic—fussing tugboats, impatient, hurrying ferry boats, red-sailed deeply laden barges, stolid, slow-moving lighters and puffers, swift sleek river steamers — all the multifarious thronging traffic of a great artery of trade.

The river widens, the land recedes, open sea lies ahead. The pilot is dropped. The master's hand goes to the telegraph: Full ahead!

The *British Freighter* is at sea. For days, for weeks, she will thrust her steadfast,

stolid way over the limitless grey desert of sea, towards a horizon that steadily recedes as she steadily advances; and now Captain John Smith, master—" under God "—of the steamship *British Freighter*, is indeed master. He is back at his job.

His word is law. The ship is his. He is beyond interference, beyond any questioning of his authority. Even if his owners choose to alter his orders, he still remains master, and final arbiter of the ship's fate. He will obey the new orders only if he considers that the safety of his ship and her cargo is not jeopardized thereby.

The courses he steers, the speed he calls for, even, in emergency, the port he makes for—these are matters for his decision alone; for his is the sole responsibility, and he has been trained, through years of sea service, to accept that responsibility, which he willingly shoulders, to make his decisions for himself, and to command.

SEALED ORDERS

September 3, 1939—a curt wireless message in code—and Captain John Smith knows that it has come at last. Britain is at war with Germany. He is not taken by surprise. Already, in the past year, he has been amply warned; preparations have been made. His officers have been ashore to attend short, intensive courses in gunnery and in other matters essential to the safety of their ship at sea in wartime. At his last port of call, he received certain instructions—a packet of sealed orders to meet this eventuality.

So now, quietly, he goes to his office and opens these orders. He is to proceed to the nearest of a list of British ports,

SHIPS IN CONVOY

An impressive view of ships sailing in convoy. The convoy system has been perfected by experience to give our merchant ships, themselves well armed, the greatest protection against enemy torpedoes and bombs. Convoys are escorted by destroyers or corvettes upon part of their journey

ANOTHER CONVOY FORMATION
LINE ABREAST

STARBOARD WING CORVETTE

VICE-COMMODORE

FIGHTER PLANE PROTECTION
FROM CATAPULT

CRUISER ESCORT AHEAD

ARMED TRAWLER MINESWEEPER

DESTROYERS
WEAVING AHEAD OVER
1500 YARD RANGE

LONG RANGE
RECONNAISSANCE FLYING BOAT
(COASTAL COMMAND)

CRUISERS, PLANES, CORVETTES, MINESWEEPERS,

*This drawing shows the measures taken for a convoy's protection. Cruiser escort is ahead
and minesweepers patrol. Ahead and astern, destroyers search for submarines. Port and*

RELIEF RECONNAISSANCE AIRCRAFT
(COASTAL COMMAND)

BEST U-BOAT ATTACK ANGLE
"COFFIN CORNER"

TRAVELLING
BALLOON BARRAGE

ASTERN DESTROYER SCREEN

VITAL CARGO SHIPS TRAVEL IN CENTRE OF CONVOY

800 YDS

PORT WING CORVETTE

CONVOY COMMODORE

4 INCH GUN

TRAWLER BOW

A·A GUN

DEPTH CHARGE
THROWER

DEPTH CHARGES

THE CORVETTE
DESIGNED SPECIALLY FOR CONVOY
ESCORT WORK & U-BOAT HUNTING

GUARD ONE OF BRITAIN'S VITAL CONVOYS

starboard, corvettes on the alert, and coastal command aircraft keep watch. Vital cargo ships
travel in centre of convoy. Inset (left) another convoy formation ; (right) details of a corvette

MERCHANT SHIPS OF BRITAIN STEAM OUT TO SEA ON THEIR LAWFUL
There is a sense of excitement and pride in this vigorous picture of a convoy in progress.
The convoys sail almost daily, their crews unconcerned about the hazards they must face
on every voyage from bomb, torpedo, and mine. The disposition of merchant ships in convoy
is carefully planned to give the smallest target for lurking submarines. For further protection

report himself to the naval authorities, and there await further orders. He is to adopt at once certain measures of defence and certain evasive procedure; he is to mount forthwith a special anti-submarine and anti-aircraft lookout, day and night; and he is to use his best speed to reach safety. There are other instructions.

PART OF THE WAR MACHINE

He obeys without hesitation. He issues orders, he studies charts, he makes calculations; and he realizes he is still master of the steamship *British Freighter*, his word is still absolute law; but he is no longer his own master. His owners, even, have become a secondary consideration. His ship is no longer a peaceful argosy of trade, earning dividends for a group of shareholders and incidentally a livelihood for himself and his crew and for scores of people ashore—shipowners, agents and their staffs, ship chandlers, shipyards, custom officials, insurance brokers, and the rest. Instead, she is an integral part of a vast and complex war machine; and as such she is under orders al. the time.

Henceforth Captain John Smith is under orders. He can no longer sail when he pleases, lay his own courses as he likes, steam at whatever speed he thinks fit, bunker where he pleases, and use his own discretion to earn dividends for the shareholders. He is under orders. His comings and goings will henceforth be controlled; he may even be taken out of his ship and put into another without being consulted; his officers and crew may be changed; and every moment of his waking life, afloat or ashore, he will be conscious of this immense change.

It may be that at first he will find it irksome. But very soon he understands just how important his ship and himself are in the struggle into which they have been plunged; and he becomes acquainted gradually with the enormous organization that has sprung into being with one sole object—to get his ship to sea as quickly as possible, to get her across the seas as safely as possible, and to get her back home laden to the Plimsoll line with the thousand and one commodities that have become overnight the sinews of war—the raw materials,

OCCASIONS: ANOTHER CONVOY SAILS WITH ESSENTIAL SUPPLIES
*against torpedo attack, the whole convoy frequently makes abrupt changes in course,
zigzagging on patterns previously arranged. Destroyers and corvettes flank the convoy
on both sides, and destroyers steam ahead. At night, when submarines can attack on the
surface, and in narrow waters, the disposition of the convoy is completely changed*

the oil, the aeroplanes and tanks and guns and shells, and above all, foremost of all, the food for Britain's millions which he carried in such vast quantities in peace time, and which Britain's millions, in peace time, seemed to take so completely for granted.

We are going to watch Captain John Smith and the *British Freighter* in war; and we cannot do better than follow him home to a British port, keep him company there while he discharges his cargo and loads again, and accompany him back out across the Western Ocean.

Of course the organization was not built up and perfected in a night. Of course it must be flexible, it must grow, day by day and week by week; and the weeks pass into months, and the months into years while the process goes on, until now it is complete, fully equipped, fully manned, and running smoothly. But it remains flexible, and can adapt itself swiftly to changing conditions—for, of course, conditions change, almost week by week, and measures that were sufficient to secure his safety a short time ago have been made obsolete

by some new device, some new technique of the enemy's relentless and unceasing attack. Counter measures must be taken.

So we shall see Captain John Smith bringing his ship in to port after crossing the Western Ocean, and we shall stand beside him while he interviews this officer and that; and we shall begin to understand just how much he owes to those men who can be seen in every seaport in the British Isles, and in every British seaport abroad —naval officers, many of them elderly, Most of them will be retired or temporary officers of the Royal Naval Reserve, or the Royal Naval Volunteer Reserve.

ALTERING COURSE

Also how much we owe to Captain John Smith, that bluff, hard-headed, stout-hearted fellow who gets on with his job— just as the officers ashore get on with theirs —quietly, efficiently, and as a matter of course.

The *British Freighter* has made her landfall. The long, hazardous voyage across the Western Ocean is over, she is within sight now of safety. Captain John

Smith studies the instructions given him for the approach to his destination—the courses to be steered, the identification flags to be hoisted, the regulations to be obeyed.

He reaches the first given position, and there alters course. He is entering the swept channel—a wide channel searched diligently by the minesweepers, little sturdy vessels, which patrol the seas in all weathers, to ensure that ships may enter port in safety (Fig. 1).

THROUGH THE MINEFIELDS

Their work, perhaps one of the most monotonous jobs of the Royal Navy in wartime, is endless. Week after week, month after month, the same channels must be swept—and week after week may pass without sight of an enemy mine.

A moment's carelessness, a moment's lack of vigilance, and disaster may come in a second to the sweeper and her crew.

Captain John Smith keeps punctiliously to the courses laid down for him. In this way, in daylight or in darkness, in clear weather or in fog, he will avoid the out-going traffic of the port, and other dangers as well. The outer approaches are mined, so that should any enemy craft attempt to force a passage into the harbour it would only be by a series of the most amazing flukes that it could avoid being blown sky-high. Captain John Smith has a wholesome respect for these minefields, whether of moored mines or of controlled mines operated from the shore.

As the end of his voyage draws near, Captain John Smith has his first encounter with the naval authorities, who now govern his every movement. A little vessel heaves in sight. Only the fact that her gun is mounted forward instead of aft, and that instead of the familiar Old Red Duster she proudly wears the White

VITAL CONVOY FOR RUSSIA BEATS
On the bitter and perilous route to Northern Russia, convoys of the United Nations have successfully withstood many fierce assaults from the air. Torpedo-carrying Heinkels swooped upon this convoy from the low-hanging clouds—they can be seen zooming and climbing

Ensign indicates that she carries the authority of the Royal Navy with her. She may be a small trawler, a converted steam or motor yacht, or even a large herring drifter or a tug ; what matters is that she is the outer examination vessel, and her job is to identify all ships approaching the estuary.

Captain John Smith hoists the flags that will prove his identity ; there is a slight pause, and then he is allowed to proceed. The outer examination vessel is satisfied that he is friend, not foe.

The *British Freighter* steams on ; and in due course she is stopped by another patrol vessel—generally a smaller type of ship—and is ordered into the examination anchorage, where, under the guns of the batteries ashore, she is to be boarded and inspected. A brief formality, perhaps, since she can so readily establish her bona fides, but the young officer—R.N.R. or R.N.V.R.—who commands the inner

examination vessel has keen eyes, and experience has taught him what to look for. Although the vast bulk of the shipping entering the port is British, there is also a considerable tonnage of Allied vessels, and of neutrals ; and although magnificent work is being done by the merchant seamen of many nations— Dutch, Norwegian, Polish, Belgian, Fighting French, Jugoslav, Greek, as well as Swedish and Danish—the possibility of fifth column activity can never be overlooked for a single day.

PORT DEFENCES

The outer and inner examination vessels are under the command of the Chief Examination Officer, who organizes the patrols, passes on information, and, in general, is responsible for this first link in the defences of the port. He, in turn, comes under the Extended Defence Officer, organizing and commanding the

OFF DESPERATE ENEMY ATTACK

to evade the shell bursts from the guns of the ships, whose heavy fire broke the attack and made the enemy's torpedoes ineffective. Two enemy planes were brought down, and ten others were hit. One of the ships of the convoy was sunk, but the others got safely to port

TORPEDO STRIKES A DOOMED SHIP

A German surface raider attacked this merchant ship and sank her by torpedo, after taking off the captain and crew. The track of the torpedo can be seen as it strikes home and explodes. From the deck of the raider the captain saw his ship go down. Captain and crew were saved

controlled minefields, the shore batteries, signal stations, and so on, of the estuary.

Having been released from the examination anchorage—probably without being required to anchor—the *British Freighter* proceeds up river, and picks up her pilot.

ANTI-SUBMARINE NETS

Now she approaches the inner defences —the boom, a line of anti-submarine nets stretching from shore to shore across the estuary. Boom defence vessels stand guard by "the gate," a gap which can be opened to allow ships to proceed through.

As our ship approaches, the gate is opened for her, and as she slips through the narrow gap she is identified again, both by the boom defence vessel and by the signal station ashore. Journey's end.

Now she has reached safety. Perhaps she is to proceed direct up river to dock, for the discharge of her cargo ; or is to be brought to an anchor for discharge overside, or to await a vacant berth, or to proceed to some other discharging port along the coast. The pilot has brought the orders out with him, and knows what to do ; he has also brought with him a sheaf of instructions, and a formidable questionnaire which the captain must fill up. These come from the Admiralty Berthing Officer, or the King's Harbour Master in a naval port—usually a captain, R.N. or R.N.R. on the retired list.

The Admiralty Berthing Officer's job is to control the harbour. His jurisdiction begins inside the boom, and he allocates anchor berths for all incoming ships, organizes boat services and ferries, and works along in close co-operation with the civil harbour or port authorities.

He must know everything about the ship, not only for his own information but for that of the various officials and naval officers concerned with dealing with her and her cargo. The essential thing is to get that cargo discharged, and shipped off by rail or road or coaster to its final destination, as quickly as possible.

The instructions that Captain John Smith has to study deal with harbour and anchorage regulations, motor launch and ferry boat services, facilities and amenities, orders about anchor watch, signalling, permits for members of the crew to land, air raid precautions and fire-fighting regulations and organization, and so on.

The pilot carries the completed questionnaire ashore with him, for he leaves the ship as soon as the anchor is down; and so the necessary information is in process of speedy distribution to all departments concerned.

Captain John Smith, who has been on the bridge almost continuously for several days past, has no sooner got rid of the pilot than he receives another visitor.

THE BOARDING OFFICER

He would like nothing better than to get his head down for a good twelve hours of sound sleep. But there's a war on.

This visitor is a naval officer, the boarding officer of the Naval Control Service, whose specific function is the control of all merchant shipping, coastwise and overseas. The Naval Control Service Officer requires certain information about the ship and her cargo, so

EXPLODING A MINE

The billowing cloud of smoke rises to mark the funeral of a German mine. Swept up in the North Sea, the mine has been exploded by gunfire from a trawler. The Germans have laid a great number of mines both from minelayers and from the air. Their ever-present menace to our ships is checked by the work of our minesweepers, which continually clear the seas

another form has to be filled up. He wants to know her speed, light and loaded, her consumption of fuel at various speeds (from which the amount of bunkers necessary for her next voyage can be calculated), her defensive armament and equipment, and so on—details which decide whether she will sail alone next time, or escorted, or in convoy, and, in that case, in which convoy she is to sail. These details must be known well in advance of her sailing, so that as soon as she is ready for sea there will be the minimum delay in getting her away once more.

REPAIRS AND ADJUSTMENTS

The Boarding Officer may obtain further information required by other authorities—what bunkers, stores, water, etc., are needed, whether the ship needs any repairs, or her degaussing equipment inspected, or her compasses adjusted, or any other work done on board. She may require replacements of crew; she may have suffered storm damage; she may have lost lifeboats. Word of her needs must be got ashore as speedily as possible.

Thereafter, Captain John Smith is instructed to report ashore to the Naval Control Service; because, while all the other naval organizations have their hand in the pie, it is essentially the Naval Control Service under whose orders he acts.

Examination Service, Extended Defence, Admiralty Berthing Officer, degaussing, and all the allied branches of naval organization in a port are under the authority of the local Flag Officer-in-Charge (a vice- or rear-admiral) or the Naval Officer-in-Charge (usually a captain, R.N.). The

GUARDING A CONVOY

One of the destroyers escorting a convoy sweeps round the ships in its charge—the picture gives a vivid impression of alertness, efficiency and speed. With the protection of destroyers, the untiring watchdogs attending the merchant ships, the vital supplies of the United Nations are safeguarded, and our convoys confidently carry out their perilous journeys over the seas

WRENS IN THE OPERATIONS ROOM

Wren ratings and officers do valuable work in many branches of the Navy. In this Naval Operations Room, a signal has been received ordering a destroyer to the scene of action, and the Wren on right is moving a counter representing a destroyer to its new position

Naval Control Service, however, is in an entirely different category. There is a Naval Control Service Officer in every port of consequence, and generally a sub-office in all the smaller ports, throughout not only the British Isles but the Dominions and every sphere of British occupation or control; and each of these is directly responsible to the Admiralty Trade Division. It has its headquarters in Whitehall and its branches everywhere, each branch being self-contained and under the immediate authority of the Trade Division.

This arrangement gives the Naval Control Service Officer a free hand—subject of course to the approval of the Trade Division—in dealing with Merchant Navy vessels, without reference to the local naval authority, thus reducing naval interference with the Merchant Navy to a minimum. The arrangement also pre-vents any tendency to allow the interests of merchant shipping to become secondary to the interests of naval vessels.

N.C.S. PERSONNEL

While the Naval Control Service Officers are in the main retired captains, R.N., the great bulk of the personnel is provided by the Royal Naval Reserve, which is drawn, of course, from the Merchant Navy; there is, in addition, a limited number of R.N.V.R. officers, mostly with special qualifications (experience in shipping offices, or intimate knowledge of the Merchant Navy). All these officers are either medically unfit for sea service or are considered to be more usefully employed ashore than they could be at sea.

The prime function of the Naval Control Service is to get the ships across the seas as speedily and as safely as can be managed. Their main work, therefore, is in routeing ships to their destinations, and in making up and dispatching convoys.

Let us accompany Captain John Smith as he makes his report.

His first call is at the Duty Office of Naval Control. Here he makes his report, and here the record of his ship's movements is kept up to date by card index.

FULL REPORT OF VOYAGE

The real reason for this call is the packet of instructions received at his last port, which he must now surrender intact, for destruction. That off his chest, Captain John Smith can relax and enjoy a brief chat. What sort of voyage did he have? Any incidents to report? Was he attacked at all? Has he suffered any damage? How long does he reckon it will be before he will be ready to sail? Are there any changes in the details about his ship—armament, equipment, sea speed maintainable, fuel consumption, and so on? Is there anything he wants to know? In a word, can the Naval Control Service do anything for him while he is here?

Captain Smith thinks not. But—well, where can he find the Ministry of War Transport? And—oh, yes, the Confidential Book Officer? He would like to leave his confidential books to be brought up to date, and he has a coding table to hand in. Anything else? Well, he had better see about his degaussing, and then, of course, the compasses will have to be adjusted, and there's the question of a kite balloon.

He learns where he will contact everybody he wants to see, and so goes on to the Confidential Book Officer, usually a paymaster lieutenant, R.N.V.R., or more recently, a Wren officer. There are Wren ratings employed as confidential book correctors, and their familiarity with every modification and alteration makes it an easy matter for them to bring his books up to date, a job which would take him many hours, even days, of close work.

Then, unless the Naval Control Service Officer wishes to see him personally, to raise any point concerning his route, or his ship, he goes on to the Ministry.

The Ministry of War Transport—formerly the Ministry of Shipping—is the authority concerned with all the business of ship management, cargo discharge, and so on.

Its members are all men of long experience in shipping or rail and road transport. Some are not paid by the Ministry, receiving their salaries from the shipping companies and agencies who have lent their services; others are in the category of temporary civil servants.

The Ministry has had ample warning of the expected arrival of the *British Freighter*. The local representative has made all arrangements for quick discharge of her cargo. Warehouses, rolling stock, the whole complicated structure of commercial transport—these have been arranged for well in advance, so that the cargo, whatever it may be, will reach its ultimate destinations—the factories and workshops, the warehouses, the shipyards, the wholesalers, and the shops—with the least delay.

TRANSPORT PROBLEMS

That is normal peace time work, speeded up to meet wartime requirements. But it is vastly complicated in wartime by the enormous calls on transport necessitated by the movement of large bodies of troops, or huge loads of military and naval stores and equipment.

But how seldom does this normal work proceed normally! Storms, concentrated U-boat attacks, or fog may force a convoy to disperse. Engine breakdowns, storm damage, all manner of things may cause a ship to fall behind, to straggle, or even, in certain cases, to push on ahead of her convoy with the result that she arrives not at the time anticipated but even several days ahead of it.

Ships bound for one port may be compelled to put into another. Cargoes urgently required elsewhere may be brought into port through stress of weather or other circumstances over which the master has no control. And then the fun begins.

What is her cargo? Is it consigned to the Ministry of Supply or the Ministry of immediate notice to tranship cargo? What subsidiary ports could receive it?

The ship needs repairs. Very well. Another department immediately takes a hand—the Director of Merchant Ship Repairs. Surveyors are rushed out, they inspect the damage or breakdown, and a preliminary report is rushed ashore. Repairs will take forty-eight hours, or a week,

HUNTING THE U-BOATS

Exploding depth charges have just been dropped by the destroyer over the spot indicated by the submarine-detecting apparatus, and members of the crew are eagerly awaiting evidence to register the end of another U-boat. Destroyers and corvettes employed on escort duty to convoys are responsible for many U-boat sinkings in the Battle of the Atlantic

Food? Is the ship damaged? Will she require repairs here—and, if so, how long will they take? Telephones tinkle, urgent priority calls go through, questions are asked, orders are given, the lines hum.

Can the ship be docked in the river? Can the port accept her cargo? Can the railways handle it? What warehousing facilities are available? Exactly how urgent is it? What coastal craft are free at or a fortnight. The chief engineer of the ship has already got the repairs in hand; or if he is unable to do anything, the ship must be docked. If she has to be docked, and repairs are likely to take a week or so, then her cargo must be discharged while the repairs are being done. The way in which the job is to be tackled must be arranged so that it will not interfere with the discharge of cargo—and the discharge

SEAMEN AT GUNNERY SCHOOL

The ships of Britain's Merchant Navy are now armed to meet all emergencies, and the men who man the ships must learn how to man the guns. They are willing pupils. Instructors from the Royal Navy train the seamen in gunnery, and themselves learn the handling of new weapons at a gunnery school. Here an instructor is teaching the use of Marlin A.A. guns.

of cargo must not hinder the repairs.

Nowadays it is no longer a question of a shipowner losing a little money by the slow turn-round of a ship. It is a matter of life and death to a whole nation. The leisurely ways of peace are forgotten; the ship is no longer merely a source of profit and dividends; she has become one highly important unit in a vast and vital organization which is an Empire's lifeline.

MINISTRY OF WAR TRANSPORT

So the Ministry gets to work—and, like the Navy, the Ministry works twenty-four hours a day. Its offices are manned continuously. "It'll do in the morning," has dropped out of its phrase book; and gone are the early days of the war when ships might lie at anchor for days before beginning to discharge their cargoes.

Captain John Smith, then, interviews the Ministry of War Transport.

He answers more questions, hears what arrangements have been made, and then comes the question of his next voyage. His orders have already come through. On completion of discharge, he is to sail for Halifax, or New York, or the Mexican Gulf, or Spain, or West Africa, or South Africa, or India, or Australia, or anywhere else in the Seven Seas. He may load cargo outward, or sail in ballast. More often than not, he sails in ballast unless there is a cargo absolutely ready, for a country at war has little time to spare for the export trade of peace.

But even before he starts discharging, Captain John Smith knows where he is going next—and gets to work preparing for the outward voyage. First of all, bunkers: how much does he need? Very well, arrangements will be made accordingly. There are colliers and oilers available. Water? It will be delivered. Stores? That matter, too, is thoroughly organized. And now comes the crucial question—his crew. Is he signing off? Is he short? Is he dissatisfied with any of his men? This is where the Seamen's Pool comes in. It operates simply and effectively.

This is a new organization which became urgently necessary when it was made clear that the old casual system of signing on and paying off crews after each voyage would not do in wartime. Between voyages, the seafarer had been nobody's business. A steady man would always be fairly sure of being re-engaged when his ship was ready to sail again; but there was no security about it, and no guarantee that

the spell on the beach would be short enough for his money to last out. It was all far too haphazard, and the merchant seaman had every right to feel himself badly treated in comparison with the skilled men in other trades of importance.

HOW CREWS ARE FOUND

The pool was intended to do away with the disadvantages of the old system from both points of view—that of the seaman himself, and that of the owner. Finding his crew had always been one of the jobs a captain had to attend to himself. But with the enormous increase in his responsibilities and his work brought about by war conditions, it became a sheer impossibility for captains to round up crews themselves. Somebody had to do that job for them. The old ways would not work.

FIGHTING THE MINE MENACE

After first making use of the moored mine, the enemy employed the magnetic mine as a new underwater threat to our ships. Members of a minesweeper's crew throw out one of the units of the magnetic sweeper, showing the sinker and the floats, which are known as blobs

Not only that, but it was very much more difficult to find crews. The war was weeding out the poorer material, the men who were only concerned with putting up with the hardships of the round trip for the sake of the cash at the end of it, and a spree. And there was another vital difficulty. Under the old system, there was no kind of priority, no guarantee that the ship the captain's behalf, and, if the men he needs are not available in that port, there will be others in other ports who can be sent for, and who will be put into the first train and sent to join, irrespective of the distance they have to travel. All that matters is that the ship gets her full complement of men, and that they are all on board in good time before she sails.

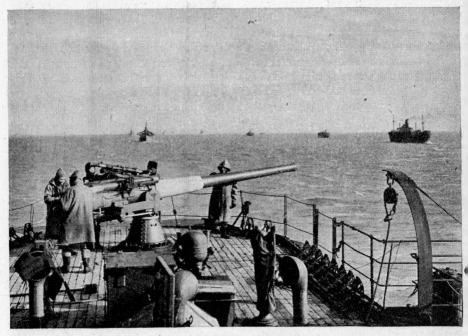

JOURNEY'S END

Fig. 2. *Thousands of guns of many types have been fitted to our merchant ships, and these guns have enabled them to repel countless enemy attacks by surface raiders, by U-boats, and by aircraft. Ranging from light machine guns to big naval guns, they are manned by merchant seamen gunners. Picture shows the gun crew of an oil tanker cleaning a 4·7-inch gun as their convoy reaches safe waters near the home port. Outgoing convoy on right*

which had to get away within a few hours would get preference over the ship that was not to sail for several days.

The pool obviates these delays. All seamen, on being discharged, revert to the pool—and receive their wages while ashore. At any time, they may be required to report on board a certain ship, sign on, and sail forthwith. So the Ministry of War Transport gets in touch with the pool on

That question disposed of, Captain John Smith collects permits for his crew to come ashore—without these, in ports where the piers or wharves are defended areas, they would not be allowed to land —and goes on to report to the Director of Merchant Ship Repairs. If he has nothing to report, he is received with affable thankfulness; if he has a defect list to hand over, the D.M.S.R. officials get to work on it at once. It may be that a winch has broken down, or the engine-room telegraph is faulty, or there has been some trouble with the main engines, or the pumps, or the steam steering gear. Jobs like that can be carried out while the ship is discharging cargo.

And, at last, Captain John Smith is free to go and see the man who in peace time would have been the only person he had to bother about—his agent, who represents his owners in the port and who, in peace time, would have done all his business, leaving him a spell of freedom ashore.

STORES AND GUNS

So he reports to his agent, and gets all the details from him that he has not been given already, and arranges about stores, and goes over the ship's papers, and gets back for a little while into the old familiar atmosphere: although even here there is a great change. Girls and young lads have taken the places of the older shipping clerks, some of whom have gone into the Services, others into the Ministry of War Transport or other Ministries where their special training and ability are important.

But Captain John Smith has still a great deal yet to do before he can take a rest. He wants to see the officers of the department of Defensively Equipped Merchant Ships, known generally as D.E.M.S. When the war broke out, there were over two thousand British merchant ships on the high seas. Since then, there has never been less than that number, often very many more, and to date more than thirteen thousand guns of all kinds have been fitted to these ships (Fig. 2). That total represents a vast amount of urgent work, and also a vast amount of experiment, trial and error, experience, forethought, and expert knowledge.

Innumerable attacks on individual ships and on convoys have been beaten off by these guns—attacks by surface raiders, by U-boats, and by aircraft. The men who man them have done, and are doing, a great job of work with a coolness and precision worthy of the highest traditions of British seamanship.

The guns range from light machine guns of the shoulder type to big 6-inch naval guns, and the job of fitting them has presented many problems; for British ships were built for peaceful trade. not for war.

You cannot simply mount a heavy gun —or even a machine gun—on the deck of a ship. Considerable strengthening of the structure is necessary first, and many other things have to be taken into consideration. The gun must be mounted where it will do most good, where its crew can reach it quickly and get it into action on the shortest notice, where it will not be rendered useless in heavy weather and where it will not interfere with the normal working of the ship.

So it was necessary for scores of experts to carry out inspections and to make structural alterations before the guns could be fitted. And when they were fitted they had to be manned.

GUN CREWS

They had to be manned, too, by men who could give their whole time to the job. The purely volunteer crew from among the ship's company is not sufficient, since ships' companies in the Merchant Navy are always the minimum needed for working the ships: there are no spare hands. So, in addition to the large number of regular seafarers, deck hands, seamen, firemen, cooks, stewards, as well as engine-room and deck officers, who underwent gunnery training, there was created a corps of merchant seamen gunners, mostly young fellows who were keen to do their bit at sea, and signed on with the crews for the specific job of manning the guns in the danger zones.

Meantime, while the ship is in port, an officer from D.E.M.S. will pay her a visit,

ON EVERY VOYAGE OUR CONVOYS ARE

Fig. 3. *The enemy employs many weapons and many methods. Convoys have to meet torpedo attack from U-boats, E-boats, and from Heinkel bombers adapted to carry torpedoes (inset, top). They can be shelled by surface raiders, and are harassed by incendiaries and high*

HOW THE HEINKEL He III K. BOMBER
IS ADAPTED FOR TORPEDO ATTACK

TORPEDOES RELEASED AT
100 Ft & 1000 Yds. RANGE

TWO 18 In. TORPEDOES SLUNG ON
EXTERNAL RACKS

U-BOAT TORPEDO ATTACK

HEINKEL He. III K.
AIRBORNE TORPEDO ATTACK

MOORED MINEFIELD

BRITISH CONVOY

SHORE
BASE

ACOUSTIC MINES

MAGNETIC MINES

HOW LONG RANGE
GERMAN AIRCRAFT
WIRELESS POSITION
OF A CONVOY VIA
BASE TO U-BOATS

U-BOAT PACK

THREATENED FROM SEA, UNDERSEA AND SKY

*explosives from aircraft. Beneath their keels, contact, magnetic, and acoustic mines are
constant perils, but the convoys get through with their cargoes. Long-range German
aircraft wireless convoy's position (inset, bottom) to the waiting U-boat pack*

and inspect her armament. His job is to see that all the defensive equipment is in perfect order before the ship sails again.

But guns—machine guns, 12-pounders, 3-inch, 4-inch or 6-inch naval guns—are only a part of a merchant ship's defensive equipment. There are many other things, inventions of several kinds that have been produced to meet the constant threat of submarine and bombing attack. There are the reinforced bridge shelters to protect the men on the bridge from machine gun and cannon attack by aircraft, from bomb splinters, and from shells. There are gadgets designed to ward off bombing and machine-gunning attacks, or to interfere with the bomber's aim. There are kites and captive balloons to be flown above the ship.

Captain John Smith may send word that he requires replacement of this and that, or that he wants to make sure of being given a balloon before he sails again. He cannot afford to delay his ship—and he cannot afford, either, to sail unless all his defensive equipment is in first-class order.

Very little imagination is needed to visualize the many dangers threatening Captain John Smith's ship, as she makes her way over the hostile seas (Fig. 3).

Whenever Captain Smith's ship approaches shallow water, the mine is a great danger. There are several types.

CONTACT MINES

Mines have been used, in one form or another, for centuries. But the present war has seen a tremendous intensification of mine warfare, and a great deal of ingenuity has been shown in devising new mines and means of dealing with them.

The standard type of mine is the moored mine, which is laid in comparatively shallow water in the approaches to harbours. It is a contact mine, exploding on impact, and in principle it is simple. The main charge is electrically fired, and for this purpose a complete electric circuit is incorporated. But the batteries are dry, there is no acid in them and so they are not live. The acid is contained in glass phials protected by metal covers, which are the horns of the mine. If one of these horns is crushed by impact against a ship's hull, the glass is broken, the acid pours down into the batteries, the circuit becomes live—and the mine is detonated.

THE MAGNETIC MINE

But a much more subtle type of mine was soon in use—the magnetic mine. This is detonated not by impact, but by the movement of a compass needle which is affected by the magnetic field of the ship passing near or over it. It is laid, therefore, on the sea bed, usually in shallow water, because the magnetic field of a ship does not extend very far; and its effect is infinitely greater than that of the moored mine (Fig. 4).

There is a very simple reason for this. The force of an explosion takes the line of least resistance. Water offers great resistance, which increases with depth. A mine striking a ship's side is near the surface, and the force of the explosion is dissipated. It will spread out in all directions, and only part of it will burst through the ship's side. But when a mine explodes underneath a ship the circumstances are very different. The thin shell of a ship's bottom offers far less resistance to the explosion than the solid weight of water all around it; so the explosion goes directly upwards through the ship, and thereby achieves an infinite deal of damage.

The magnetic mine took a heavy toll before British scientists, working at feverish speed, evolved means not only of sweeping it, but of protecting ships. The method evolved is known as degaussing. Briefly, the ship's magnetism is neutralized, and thus it does not actuate the compass needle that controls the trigger of the mine (Fig. 5).

But degaussing requires frequent overhaul and testing; so the Degaussing and Ranging Officer in the port examines the master's report and decides whether a test is required. If so, arrangements are made for the ship to go over the range, where the efficiency of her degaussing is be altered, the ship's compasses will be affected, and so will require adjustment. That is done first of all by swinging the ship and taking bearings on known objects or fixed landmarks ashore, and so finding out the errors of the compass, then making the necessary adjustments to com-

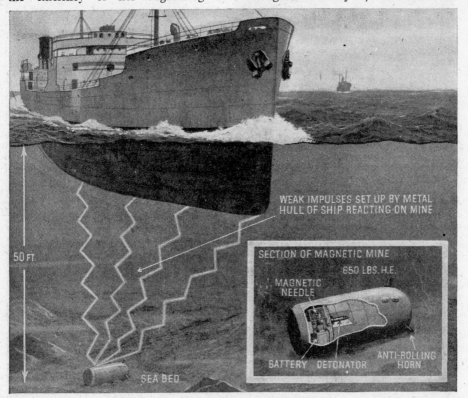

WEAK IMPULSES SET UP BY METAL
HULL OF SHIP REACTING ON MINE

50 FT.

SECTION OF MAGNETIC MINE
650 LBS. H.E.

MAGNETIC
NEEDLE

BATTERY   DETONATOR

ANTI-ROLLING
HORN

SEA BED

HOW THE MAGNETIC MINE WORKS

Fig. 4. *The magnetic mine operates successfully only in shallow water. It comes to rest on the sea bed in such a position that the magnetic needle is always uppermost. When a ship passes over it, weak magnetic impulses from the metal hull react on the needle, which moves upwards, and fires the charge of 650 lb. of high explosive by means of an electric circuit and relays. It is far more devastating than the moored mine. Inset, details of mine*

measured. If it is all right, she is free to proceed immediately. If not, the ship is held until necessary adjustments are made.

Working in with the Degaussing and Ranging Officer are the compass adjusters, civilian experts who work on a pool system, so that one is always available. It follows that, if the degaussing has had to pensate for them. Needless to say, the work of the compass adjusters has been enormously increased by the introduction of this magnetic warfare.

The approaches to all harbours are regularly and methodically swept by a great fleet of minesweepers of all types, from converted drifters and trawlers to

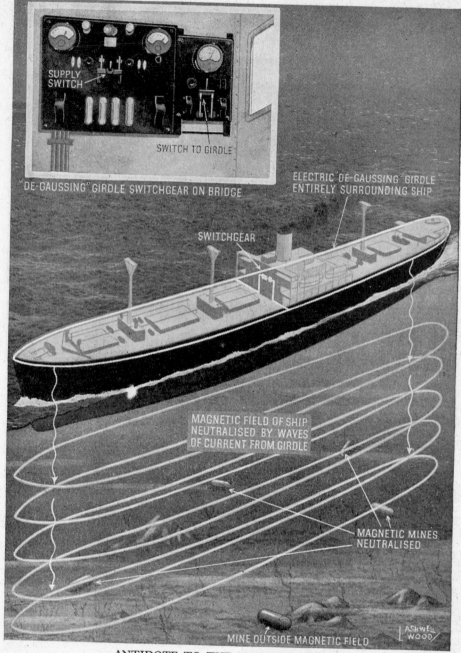

SUPPLY SWITCH

SWITCH TO GIRDLE

"DE-GAUSSING" GIRDLE SWITCHGEAR ON BRIDGE

ELECTRIC "DE-GAUSSING" GIRDLE ENTIRELY SURROUNDING SHIP

SWITCHGEAR

MAGNETIC FIELD OF SHIP NEUTRALISED BY WAVES OF CURRENT FROM GIRDLE

MAGNETIC MINES NEUTRALISED

MINE OUTSIDE MAGNETIC FIELD

ASHWELL WOOD

ANTIDOTE TO THE MAGNETIC MINE

Fig. 5. *The menace of the magnetic mine was, to a large extent, overcome by the ingenious degaussing girdle which was fitted to British ships. Current supplied to the girdle by a generator causes electric waves to pass down to the sea bed and render the mines inoperative*

large, specially constructed fleet mine-sweepers; and this untiring and hazardous labour has accounted for very large numbers of enemy mines, and has undoubtedly saved a great many ships from being blown up or seriously damaged.

or sunk by rifle fire. Then the magnetic mine was introduced, and took its toll before counter measures were designed. Later still came the acoustic mine, in which the pistol is actuated by sound—not by the ship's magnetism, but by the

SOUND WAVES FROM SHIPS' PROPELLERS

AREA OF GREATEST FREQUENCY

TREMBLER CIRCUIT

HYDROPHONE

EXPLOSIVE

AREA OF GREATEST FREQUENCY OVER MINE WHICH THEN EXPLODES

ACOUSTIC MINE

Fig. 6. *Following the magnetic mine, the next development was the acoustic mine. In some respects similar to the magnetic, it is operated by sound instead of magnetism. To fire the charge, a trembler circuit is touched off by the sound vibrations produced by a ship's propellers, the mine being exploded when these vibrations reach the area of greatest frequency*

At the beginning of the war the enemy made use chiefly of the ordinary moored mine, which could be dealt with by sweepers towing gear that cuts the mooring wire and so allows the mine to bob up to the surface, where it can be destroyed

sound vibrations produced by her engines and propeller (Fig. 6). This in turn necessitated the designing of a new type of sweeper to counter it successfully.

The Merchant Navy has had to face one ever present and very real danger

FROM THE COCKPIT
A FOCKE-WULF KURIER OUTMANOEUVRED BY CATAPULTED FIGHTER

RETARDING CABLES & PULLEYS

GLYCERINE CHAMBER AND CUSHION CYLINDER

PISTON

PULLEYS ATTACHED TO SLIDING CROSSHEAD

COMPRESSED AIR CYLINDERS AND PIPES

HOW FIGHTER AIRCRAFT ARE CATAPULTED FROM

Fig. 7. *Some merchant ships have catapult gear, which launches fighter aircraft into the air to attack long-range Focke-Wulf Kuriers. Main picture gives in detail the method of cata*

FIGHTER JUST RELEASED FROM TROLLEY

RELEASE HOOKS

SHOCK ABSORBERS

TROLLEY

CATAPULT EXTENSION

ACCELERATING CABLE & PULLEYS

COMPRESSED AIR CYLINDER AND CONTROL VALVES

FIGHTER AIRCRAFT "DITCHED" WHEN TOO FAR FROM LAND & PILOT BEING PICKED UP

SHIPS TO REPEL LONG RANGE ENEMY BOMBERS

pulting. Inset (top left) shows from the cockpit of a British fighter a Focke-Wulf set on fire by a direct hit. Inset (right) shows a ditched pilot being rescued by another ship in the convoy

unknown, or almost unknown, in the last war. This was the bomber aircraft.

This threat was not serious at first; but with the fall of France, with enemy aerodromes and seaplane bases established not only along the English Channel but on the Atlantic seaboard as well—some of them within fifteen minutes flying time of vital British harbours and sea lanes, others within easy bomber reach of our convoy routes in the Atlantic—the danger became acute.

It was met by concentrated anti-aircraft fire power, not only in escort vessels, but on the merchant ships themselves; but it also led to the employment of fighter aircraft catapulted from ships (Fig. 7).

CATAPULT FIGHTERS

The fighter aircraft is launched by means of a catapult, which hurls it forward violently. At the same time, the engine is opened full out, the machine picks up speed, dipping only very slightly as it leaves the catapult, and then climbs rapidly to engage the enemy.

It is a breath-taking business. The fighter rests on the catapult, ready to be launched. The pilot climbs into the cockpit, starts up his engine—which is kept constantly warmed up, ready for instant action—and opens the throttle. The officer in charge awaits the pilot's signal. When he receives it, he launches the aircraft. Simultaneously, the pilot opens to full throttle.

It is a job for steady nerves, for firm hands and a clear head and swift reactions, for it is no easy matter to be sitting at ease in the cockpit of a stationary aircraft one moment, and to be airborne and hurtling forward at more than a hundred miles an hour the next. To be able to stand the sudden shock, and to take instant control of the plane, and switch your whole attention a second later to the business of bringing down your enemy—that calls for a very special kind of nerve.

Add to this that the chances of making a comfortable landing on an aerodrome are very remote, and you realize the kind of men these pilots are—youngsters, all of them, specially selected for the work. At sea, they are on duty continuously, ready to take off at a moment's notice. On the approach of enemy aircraft, they go into action. In a space of time that seems incredibly short, they are airborne, and as the enemy aircraft, usually a Focke-Wulf, unsuspecting, closes in on its prey, the columns of lumbering merchant ships, the fighter swoops down for the kill. And so the hunter becomes the hunted, and is shot down into the sea, or at best sent racing for home with the fighter on his tail.

And the fighter pilot? If he is lucky, he may find that there is an aerodrome within reach. But he is seldom lucky in that respect. His range is short, and even a short scrap will burn up petrol at an alarming rate. Then two courses are open to him: he can bring his aircraft down into the sea, or bale out and come down by parachute, near one of the ships of the convoy, which will stand by to pick him up. Either course is not pleasant; and it demands a high degree of expert cooperation on the part of the ship. This is particularly the case when a high sea is running and visibility is bad.

PILOT'S RISKS

So the pilot regains contact with the convoy, and makes his decision. If he thinks he can safely bring the aeroplane down on the water, he flies low over the ship, in the direction in which she is proceeding, and pancakes down a short distance ahead. But if he has to bale out, he must rely upon the ship's captain to gauge accurately the drift of his parachute, so as to be on the spot as nearly as possible at the moment when he strikes the water. In either case, the pilot is in for a very cold bath—and a very risky one. But the catapult aircraft fliers take it all as part of their job, and many Focke-Wulf aircraft have fallen to these daring young pilots.

Captain John Smith is lucky if he has any time to himself at all in port. The quick turn round saves shipping space, makes up for shortage of tonnage. There are no leisurely refits, no casual delays, in wartime.

And while he is interviewing all these people, whose business it is to help him get back to sea, the cargo is being taken out of his ship, by gangs of stevedores, either in the dock, or into lighters if he is out in the stream.

Before he has really had time to feel that he has been in port, he is thinking of his next voyage, and soon he has fixed a date when he will be ready to begin it.

READY TO SAIL

Then he makes his pilgrimage to the Duty Officer at the Naval Control Service. "I'll be ready—barring accidents—on Saturday." He states his destination—it may be Halifax, or Boston, or New York, or Aruba, or Curacao, or Galveston, or Houston, or Lagos, or Calcutta, or any remote spot where the Old Red Duster can be seen flying. Probably he finds that his sailing date has been anticipated—his agent may have given a hint—and he is already entered for a suitable convoy. It has to be a convoy whose speed will be less than the speed he can be certain of maintaining. He must always have half a knot or so in hand—for accidents. He knows, just as well as the naval officers know, the fate that awaits the straggler. He gauges his speed conservatively, to be on the safe side. You never know these days, especially with inexperienced firemen.

Captain John Smith is entered for the first available convoy, and then he departs to interview the Ministry of War Transport and deal with any remaining business —and the Naval Control Service gets on with its job. First of all, his ship has to be allotted a definite place in the convoy.

He has to be provided with sailing orders and convoy instructions; his routes have to be worked out to his destination and he has also to be given alternative routes, and approaches to various harbours —again in case of accidents.

His convoy equipment must be in order —signalling lamp and flags, navigation and special convoy lights, blackout, fog buoys, and the rest. He has a certificate signed by a Convoy Equipment Officer stating that everything is in order. Is it up to date? If not, the equipment must be inspected again and defects made good.

There is also a Convoy Signal Officer whose business is to deal with all matters affecting his wireless equipment. This officer works in with the Post Office inspectors who test his transmitters and receivers, and who also test all the privately owned receiving sets on board.

Practically all receiving sets reradiate —that is, they act as small transmitters. It is this that enables the Post Office officials to detect wireless licence dodgers by locating their sets. It is this that might betray a ship to the lurking U-boat; and so every set must be tested meticulously; and in many cases sets have to be sealed up and condemned as unfit for use at sea.

CONVOY CONFERENCE

There seems, in fact, to be no end to the innumerable details that must be thought of before a ship can go to sea.

But at last the day of sailing arrives, and Captain John Smith goes to attend the convoy conference (Fig. 8).

A launch is sent to collect him and the other masters—just a part of the service, and seemingly an insignificant one, but somebody has to sweat over it, for it is no simple matter to keep a fleet of launches in service, day in, day out, in all weathers, and with scores of people clamouring at all hours for boats.

ORDERS FOR THE VOYAGE

Fig. 8. *The convoy is soon to sail. Now the masters of the ships attend the conference at the offices of the Naval Control Service, to receive full instructions regarding the course to be taken, the position their ships must keep in the convoy, action in emergencies, speed, and special signals. The R.N.R. officer in front row, commodore of the convoy, will command the fleet. Every possible mischance on the voyage is considered and guarded against*

The conference is held generally at the Naval Control Service offices, in a special room. The Naval Control Service Officer presides, and when the masters have assembled, and have reported to the Duty Officer, he plunges directly into what he has to say. He is as brief as possible. He runs through the convoy instructions, making certain that every one understands every detail—and taking particular care that Dutch, Norwegian, Greek, Belgian, French, Panamanian, Swedish, and other Allied and neutral captains have grasped every word, every phrase. Then questions may be asked, points may be raised and discussed, and the commodore of the convoy—a commodore, R.N.R., who is usually a retired rear admiral, R.N., serving in this rank—addresses the conference.

Every minute detail, every conceivable eventuality, is considered. Nothing that could possibly happen to create confusion, or difficulty, or crisis is overlooked. Fog, storm, bombing attack, U-boat attack, surface raider attack, engine breakdown, damage due to stress of weather, collision, the closing of a harbour through enemy action—there are precise instructions covering everything.

And so the conference breaks up, and the masters are pounced on by the Ministry of War Transport. "Is your crew complete? Got all your stores, bunkers, water?"

"No defects? No last-minute hitch likely to delay you? All right, captain. Good-bye—and good luck!" The masters leave, in little groups. They are satisfied.

There is nothing more to be done—except to be ready to sail at the given hour.

Under weigh! Anchors have been hove short as zero hour approaches. The Boarding Officer is going his rounds, in his launch, hailing each ship.

"All correct, captain? Fine—good-bye. Take care of yourself. Good luck!"

LAST MOMENTS BEFORE SAILING

The commodore signals. He is getting under weigh, moving down to the gate, to pass out through the boom and lead the way down channel. Many convoys sail at night, for a variety of reasons. But daylight or dark, it makes no difference. One after another the ships slip out, at regular intervals, through the gate.

Ashore, men are watching. The signal station has the list of ships, telephones

through as each ship is identified passing out. The Naval Control Service officers are waiting for the last ship to go through, which means that the convoy has sailed, and word can be passed on to all the departments concerned. The Ministry of War Transport's officials are on the pier, waiting—ready for any last-minute emergency.

One ship has not weighed anchor yet. What is wrong? Why is she delaying? The Boarding Officer flashes a signal ashore. Two men short. Should have arrived by train three hours ago—no sign of them. The Ministry gets to work. It telephones for two more men—two local men who can be routed out—it may be one o'clock in the morning, but no matter! —and hustled out to the ship. Telephone to the N.C.S.O., and find out how long

READY TO GO

Now the convoy assembles off the pier. The ships are ready to slip out, one by one, through the boom, and sail down channel on the first stage of another hazardous voyage. Each ship knows its place in convoy, allotted according to tonnage and destination. All emergencies are provided for, and no measure which contributes to the convoy's safety has been overlooked

grace the ship can have. If she has several knots in hand beyond the convoy speed, she may still be able to sail, and overtake it, some hours later.

Then find out if the two missing men have by any chance arrived. They may actually be on their way out to the ship. Have they been seen? Has a launch been sent off with them? Hustle around the pier and ask questions. No sign of them? Missed their connexion, probably. All right—what about those local men from the Pool? More telephoning—two men have been found, are being rushed down to the pier. Get a launch ready for them, then. Get the Boarding Officer—let the master know.

Good! That's his winch starting up— he's heaving short. Hullo, here are the two men. Bad luck, lads—but there's a war on! All right, off you go. Telephone

Naval Control—tell 'em the ship will be passing the boom exactly an hour and a half late. Tell the Extended Defence Officer, so he'll know to keep the gate open. . . .

Phew! There she goes. All right. Through the gate in less than half an hour now. She is through the gate. The convoy has sailed. The Duty Officer of the Naval Control Service puts through his call to the Admiralty, and sends off a signal addressed to all the authorities concerned.

Another convoy has got away. The whole complex organization can relax— for a few hours. It is working at full pressure again very soon; for the convoys sail almost daily, in spite of enemy propaganda and the U-boat blockade.

So Captain John Smith is at sea again. But he cannot relax—not even for a few hours. For every moment that he is at sea

MALTA CONVOY GETS THROUGH

Fighters and torpedo bombers ranged on the flight deck of an aircraft carrier in the harbour of Malta. In the background are ships of the convoy she helped to escort. They reached the fortress with much-needed supplies and reinforcements, in spite of most determined attacks

NEAR MISS ON MERCHANT SHIP IN CONVOY

Dramatic picture of a near miss on a merchant ship, which afterwards reached Malta safely. In the face of massed air, sea and submarine attacks, the object of the convoy—to get stores through to Malta—was attained. The First Lord of the Admiralty sent personal letters to all masters of the merchant ships before they set out on their hazardous voyage

is fraught with danger, and never a day passes without some emergency signal from the commodore, as information comes through of U-boats located in this position or that, U-boats on the prowl.

STAFF WORK

And ashore, there are others who never relax, who are thinking of Captain John Smith and his fellow shipmasters day and night: Fighter Command headquarters, so long as the convoy is within range of fighter protection; Coastal Command, while it can still be reached by long-range patrol aircraft; the staffs at the bases from which the escorts work, operational staffs

at the Admiralty, plotting its position, piecing together information about U-boat activity, or about the occasional surface raider, so that the commodore may be warned in good time.

And naval and civilian staffs on the other side, consular officers, shipping agents in neutral ports, are waiting for news, and working so that they will be all ready to receive the ships.

So the vast complex machine of organization works; and Captain John Smith, that simple, good-natured, stolid fellow, is the core round which the whole structure is built. All of us owe him our gratitude and thanks.

UNLOADING CARGO IN THE PORT OF LONDON

From all the seas of the world, in normal times, our merchant ships come with goods of all kinds to the port of London, one of the largest and busiest ports in the world. In prosperous years before the war, the average annual value of London's imports was 470 million pounds. London and Liverpool together handled over half the foreign trade

CHAPTER 6

Sailing the Seven Seas

Great sea roads. World's busiest ocean. Passenger lanes. Billions of bananas. Treasures from Pacific coast. South American trade. Key ports of South Africa. Empire food ships. Short-sea trades. Panama and Suez Canals. Manchester, Kiel, Gota. Sault Sainte Marie. New canals planned. World's aircraft routes. Sky-shipping.

THE Battle of the Atlantic began with the sinking of the liner *Athenia* on September 3, 1939. It spread and became the Battle of the Oceans—a struggle for the maintenance or disruption of the trade routes along which move our foodstuffs and our raw materials; our troops and our war stores.

WORLD'S TRADE ROUTES

In the peaceful summer of 1939 the United Kingdom was the hub of a mighty wheel, from which trade routes radiated over the seas to every part of the world. For routes read cargoes, bearing in mind the many types of ships described in Chapter 3. Certain kinds are built for certain routes, and for this reason, the establishment of a new route often brings on the seas a new type of ship.

Figs 1 and 2 show the world's principal trade routes in the Atlantic and Pacific oceans. It is on these routes that ships of sixty-seven million gross tons which the world owned in 1939 went about their peaceful business; the Grand Banks trawlers in the North; the whale factories of the Southern seas; the cargo liners of the Atlantic and Pacific; the meat carriers of the South Atlantic; the banana merchantmen of the Caribbean. So let us see how they run, the cargoes they carry, and the ports where they load and discharge. These routes are Britain's lifelines. The world's water spaces, for

our investigation, can be divided into two. One takes in the North and South Atlantic Oceans, and the Indian Ocean. The other is the Pacific Ocean.

In both diagrams (Figs. 1 and 2) the intensity of the traffic is depicted by the broadness of the route lines, and it is clear that the North Atlantic route is the busiest in the world. The main routes are from the United Kingdom to North America; from the United Kingdom to Central America and the Caribbean; from the United Kingdom southward to South America, and to the Cape. The North Atlantic services are not only the busiest, but the most subject to severe weather conditions. As a consequence the route taken by ships varies according to whether it is winter or summer.

PASSENGER TRAFFIC

The main trade, say, from Southampton to New York, or New York to Liverpool, concerns passengers and high-class freight, as well as manufactured goods of every kind, from motor cars to typewriters, from machine tools to silk stockings. Much of this merchandise is carried in the holds of large passenger liners. Other goods come in fast cargo liners.

Noteworthy in this important North Atlantic trade, also, are bulk cargoes. These include west-bound quantities of iron ore from the Swedish ore mines, at the top of the Gulf of Bothnia, to the big

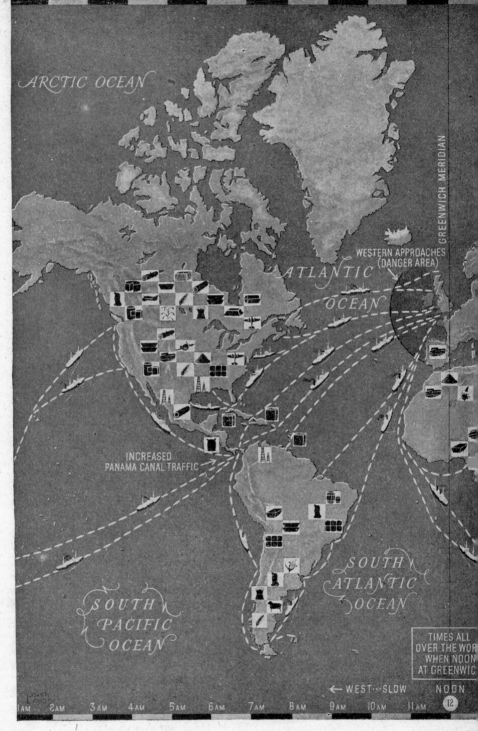

ARCTIC OCEAN

GREENWICH MERIDIAN

WESTERN APPROACHES
(DANGER AREA)

ATLANTIC
OCEAN

INCREASED
PANAMA CANAL TRAFFIC

SOUTH
PACIFIC
OCEAN

SOUTH
ATLANTIC
OCEAN

TIMES ALL
OVER THE WOR
WHEN NOON
AT GREENWIC

← WEST···SLOW   NOON

1 AM 2 AM 3 AM 4 AM 5 AM 6 AM 7 AM 8 AM 9 AM 10 AM 11 AM 12

BRITAIN'S VITAL LIFE LINES ON THE SEVEN SEAS

Pictorial map showing the imports necessary to the well-being of Britain in time of war and the ships required to maintain the vital sea routes. Each ship represents a convoy of 50 vessels at sea

KEY TO SYMBOLS OF IMPORTS

PETROLEUM	OILS & FATS	TIMBER	NICKEL
MEAT	SUGAR	CHEESE	ALUMINIUM
TIN	COFFEE	BACON	MANGANESE
COPPER	PAPER	BUTTER	JUTE
COTTON	ZINC	FERTILIZERS	ESPARTO
WHEAT	COCOA	HEMP	OIL NUTS
WOOL	RUBBER	OATS	TINNED FOODS
BARLEY	TEA	RICE	ARMAMENTS
MAIZE	IRON	LEAD	AIRCRAFT

SUEZ CANAL CLOSED TO ORDINARY SHIPPING

NORTH PACIFIC OCEAN

INTERNATIONAL DATE LINE

INDIAN OCEAN

WAR-TIME LONG ROUTE ROUND THE CAPE

ANTARCTIC OCEAN

EAST ·· FAST →

2PM   3PM   4PM   5PM   6PM   7PM   8PM   9PM   10PM   11PM   12PM   1AM

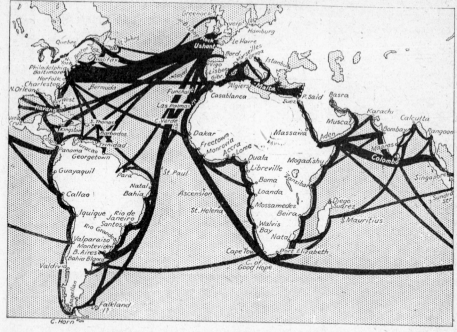

NORTH AND SOUTH ATLANTIC ROUTES

Fig. I. *The intensity of the traffic along the main trade routes from Great Britain is depicted by the thickness of the black lines, and the map shows clearly that the North Atlantic route is the busiest in the world. Its main trade in peace time comprises passengers, high-class freight, and goods of all kinds. Other important routes are to South America and to the Cape*

Pennsylvania steel works, and east-bound large quantities of grain from the St. Lawrence estuary. The grain comes from the vast growing spaces of the American Middle West, and from the Canadian prairies. During the eight months that the St. Lawrence is open for navigation, that is to say, when it is not blocked by ice, tremendous stores of grain are carried to Europe in ships of the tramp type— British, Norwegian, Greek and other nationalities. The grain is first brought to inland ports like Buffalo, on Lake Erie, one of the enormous sheets of fresh water totalling some ninety-five thousand square miles in area which are a feature of the North American continent. Special types of ships known as lake freighters are employed (Fig. 3) for this vast traffic. In a good year nearly twelve million tons of grain can be brought down the Great Lakes. During the season, Buffalo, to take one example only, receives every week enough golden grain from the western prairies to make almost half a million loaves of bread. This traffic from only one wheat port emphasizes the vital importance of this cargo. Two methods of unloading are shown in Figs. 4 and 5.

Over this broad stream, depicted by the white line on the diagram, the waters of the North Atlantic route, over which millions of tons of valuable merchandise flow annually, are among the most stormy in the world, though there are many trade routes in which distances are greater.

From the Bishop Rock light, a convenient landfall and departure point for ships crossing the Atlantic, to New York is about 2,850 nautical miles. To Boston it is 2,650 miles, whilst the run to the St. Lawrence is slightly shorter—a point made much of in travel propaganda before the war for the benefit of passengers fearing sea-sickness.

The North Atlantic is often known as the Western Ocean. The Bishop Rock Lighthouse is a kind of starting-off point to the wastes of the Western Ocean. There some of the routes diverge. Almost equally important trade routes run further south to ports in the Gulf of Mexico, and to the Caribbean Sea. Countries bordering on the Caribbean Sea supply many thousand tons of oil.

The routes to the Caribbean proper are of two kinds: those which terminate in the Caribbean and those which proceed further, via Panama. Here they may divide —first, northward to the Pacific north-west coast ports with their great cargoes of grain, oil, lumber, canned goods and fresh fruit. Other ships turn south to the coastal regions served by ports all the way down as far as Valparaiso. Thirdly, ships sail straight on, across the Pacific to the Antipodes (Fig. 2), Some ships do not call at any of the intermediate islands, but others call at Honolulu, Tahiti, Suva for copra, pineapples, and other products.

OIL FROM COLOMBIA

Trade to the Caribbean proper is concerned to a great extent with oil, from the Columbia oilfields. In the Gulf of Maracaibo the oil wells themselves are drilled by machines actually on the water of the lake, the oil being taken in small ships at high-water across the Bar leading to the lake, to the refineries on the islands fringing the coast. Curacao is one of the principal islands engaged in this work. In peace time there is an almost continuous stream of tankers, carrying upwards of

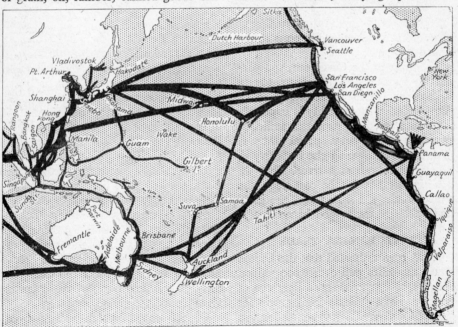

SEA ROADS OF THE PACIFIC

Fig. 2. *All main Pacific routes are given in this map, which emphasizes the trade significance of the Panama Canal, connecting the Pacific north-west coast ports with their cargoes of grain, oil, lumber and canned goods. It also links the great group of ports in South America*

MONSTER SHIP IN SERVICE ON THE GREAT LAKES—

Fig. 3. *The "Lemoyne," one of the largest grain ships afloat, is in service on the Great North American lakes, the vast sheets of fresh water which have a total area of 95,000 square miles. In a good year nearly 12,000,000 tons of grain can be brought down the Great Lakes. In one week Buffalo, the inland port on Lake Erie, receives enough golden grain from the*

10,000 tons of cargo at a time, trading to Thameshaven and other big ports in the United Kingdom.

The fruits of the Caribbean, and particularly bananas, are so important as to make an export trade in themselves. Note that whenever a commodity is imported, or manufactured for export in sufficient quantities to demand a special group of ships which do nothing else but carry it, it becomes known as a trade. Thus we talk of the oil trade, the coal trade, the lumber trade, the fruit trade, the grain trade, the ore trade—and banana trade.

HUGE BANANA TRADE

It has been estimated that the United States consumes well over 6,000 million bananas in a year; even so long ago as 1914 an average of sixty-five bananas per head of the United States population was imported annually. And the European market was very large and expanding rapidly, to satisfy demands from many centres, up to the outbreak of war.

Bananas come from the Central American Republics, from the island of Jamaica, and are exported to the United Kingdom, as well as to the American ports of New Orleans and Boston. Trade in the Caribbean Sea, and in the Gulf of Mexico, was becoming the subject of intense international competition prior to the second World War. It is unfortunate to record that British ships were by no means the most successful traders, the Dutch and German both ranking above them in the type of ships employed.

As for distances: from Bishop Rock to Curacao is 3,800 miles. To Kingston, Jamaica, it is 3,850 miles, to the island of Barbados 3,400 miles, and to New Orleans direct 4,350 miles. To Colon, at the Atlantic entrance to the Panama Canal, it is 4,350 miles.

Of the routes which radiate from Panama, it is convenient, first of all, to consider those running to the Pacific North-West Coast, for although this part of the world strictly comes within the

THE GRAIN-CARRYING VESSEL "LEMOYNE"

western prairies to make half a million loaves of bread. The navigation season lasts eight months only—for four months of the year the St. Lawrence is blocked by ice. British, Greek, and Norwegian ships of the tramp type carry the grain to Europe. The "Lemoyne" can carry 571,000 bushels of wheat. She is 630 feet long, and has a gross tonnage of 10,480

Pacific Ocean, it is naturally linked to the Atlantic for a great deal of its trading.

The opening of the Panama Canal (Fig. 6) automatically opened up a vast volume of trade in the States of California, Washington, and in British Columbia. It also revitalized trade to the Caribbean. The export activity of the Pacific Coast, embracing the Southern California, Northern California, Columbia River, Puget Sound, and British Columbia, is notable for its increase and consistent development. In a single year, ships laden with 11,500,000 tons of raw material and manufactures have sailed from the Pacific Coast to other shores carrying canned, dried and frozen foods, machinery, petroleum and petroleum products, grain, fertilizers, scrap material, textiles, and timber.

The world-famed San Francisco harbour, with its land-locked sea waters, embracing a shore line of 100 miles, has an area of 450 square miles. There are forty-three piers and terminals, giving

17 miles of berthing space, and 186 acres of cargo area, with a capacity of over 2,000,000 tons. San Francisco is just over 8,000 miles away from London, more than 7,000 miles from Liverpool, and 5,262 miles distant from New York, via the Panama Canal. Before the opening of this international waterway, it was necessary to steam all the way down to Cape Horn, through the Straits of Magellan, and up the eastern seaboard.

PORTS LINKED BY PANAMA CANAL

The short cut more than halves distance and steaming time. Incidentally, the canal presents all ports on the Pacific Coast seaboard, both Canadian and the United States, with a two-way approach to the ports of South America, and makes it possible for ships starting from, say, Los Angeles to circle the South American continent. It is a shorter distance to Buenos Aires from Los Angeles via the Straits of Magellan than it is via the Panama Canal, the latter distance being

8,406 miles compared with 7,243 miles. Many services actually make the round trip, circling the continent in doing so.

The Panama Canal connects another great group of ports—those in the South American Continent. The ports of Peru, with its ore trade, and Chile, ports like Mollendo, Iquique, Arica and Antofagasta, with open roadsteads in which ships

and along the rocky shore countless sea lions bask and tumble, and queer diving birds swoop and flash above the surf. It is from these ports that heavily laden ships start out on their long haul back to London or Liverpool via the Panama Canal. On occasions they may go south-about via Cape Horn, touching at some of the chief ports on the River Plate.

UNLOADING GRAIN BY ELEVATOR

Fig. 4. Great quantities of grain come from the wide spaces of the American Middle West and from the Canadian prairies. Modern granaries and machines called elevators in Canada and the United States, not only provide safe storage for the grain, but deal with the unloading of it. Grain cannot be handled without creating dust, and as air and dust in certain proportions combine to make a mixture highly liable to explode, precautions are taken against this risk

anchor, receiving and discharging their cargo with the aid of lighters. Mollendo is on high cliffs above the Pacific Ocean, and high above these again are the awe-inspiring Andes.

The Tape-line Republic, as Chile is known because of its shape, has a length of about 3,000 miles and a maximum breadth of only about 130. Antofagasta is strung along the coast at the foot of brown uplands; in the slow Pacific rollers

Reference to the map (Fig. 2) shows that the width of the trade lanes from these South American eastern states is rather greater than that of the routes to South Africa, and second only to the broad North Atlantic lanes.

Buenos Aires, and the many inland ports on the River Plate and its associated waterways, are the big granaries and butchers' shops for ever-hungry Europe. It is 5,900 miles from Buenos

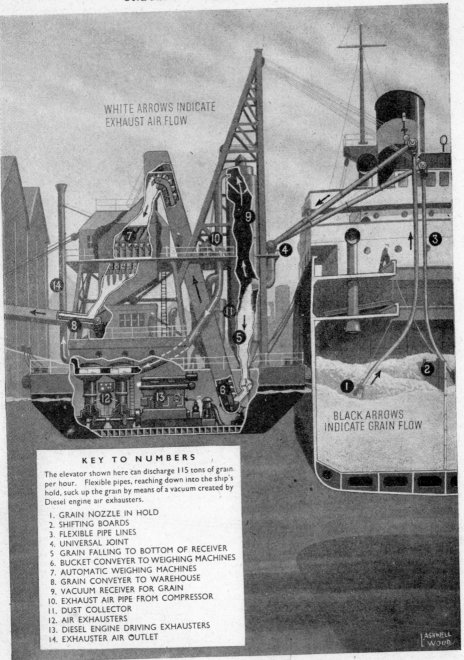

WHITE ARROWS INDICATE
EXHAUST AIR FLOW

BLACK ARROWS
INDICATE GRAIN FLOW

KEY TO NUMBERS

The elevator shown here can discharge 115 tons of grain per hour. Flexible pipes, reaching down into the ship's hold, suck up the grain by means of a vacuum created by Diesel engine air exhausters.

1. GRAIN NOZZLE IN HOLD
2. SHIFTING BOARDS
3. FLEXIBLE PIPE LINES
4. UNIVERSAL JOINT
5. GRAIN FALLING TO BOTTOM OF RECEIVER
6. BUCKET CONVEYER TO WEIGHING MACHINES
7. AUTOMATIC WEIGHING MACHINES
8. GRAIN CONVEYER TO WAREHOUSE
9. VACUUM RECEIVER FOR GRAIN
10. EXHAUST AIR PIPE FROM COMPRESSOR
11. DUST COLLECTOR
12. AIR EXHAUSTERS
13. DIESEL ENGINE DRIVING EXHAUSTERS
14. EXHAUSTER AIR OUTLET

HOW THE WHEAT IS UNLOADED

Fig. 5. *Vast quantities of wheat come from Canada and America. Much of this grain, transported by lake freighters, is efficiently handled at the European end by floating grain elevators, which are sometimes moored between ship and warehouse, or barge, and work by suction*

LINKING THE ATLANTIC AND THE PACIFIC

Fig. 6. *With the completion of the Panama Canal in 1914, a vast volume of trade was opened up. Forty-three miles long, the Canal is a vital waterway in the world's commerce*

Aires to Ushant, which is the landfall light for ships coming in from the southward, loaded with grain or meat, or rubber, or coffee from Brazil.

The grain trade from the River Plate is of international importance; it yearly absorbs thousands of tons of ships of the tramp type. They are mostly chartered for one, two, or more voyages at the Baltic Exchange in London.

These ships may proceed to an anchorage at the mouth of the River Plate in ballast, or they may, perhaps, bring a cargo of coal or of general nature.

SHIPS FOR SOUTH AMERICA

Some of the main outward shipments to Brazil and the Argentine are large manufactured goods, such as electric power plant, railway coaches and locomotives. Another important export from Europe to South America, which generally comes under its own power, is the completed ship. The rivers Parana and Paraguay, which discharge into the triangular muddy delta known as the River Plate, carry an enormous amount of traffic, and some of the ships transporting freight and passengers go so far inland that at their terminal they are nearer to the Pacific than to the Atlantic Ocean. The River Plate junction of the Rivers Parana and Uruguay is a shallow estuary draining a basin nearly 4,000,000 square kilometres in area. The Plate itself is about 150 miles long.

Most of these ships are built in Europe, many of them in Great Britain. Their design, whilst specialized, is based upon the design of seagoing ships, and they make the journey out from their builders' ports under their own power. One company alone owns 360 passenger and cargo motor ships, steamers, barges, tugs and cattle carriers.

But it is not only with Europe that South America does so much trading. The routes between South and North America have developed enormously in importance in recent years, and prior to the outbreak of war between Japan and America a regular service was maintained with ships of high speed and quality.

It is 3,610 miles from Montevideo to Cape Town, or about sixteen days steaming at the old-fashioned tramp ship speed of ten knots—a time which can be cut to just over nine days in a modern 18-knot ship.

Cape Town is the leading port of South Africa, and one of the most important ports in the Empire. The citizens of Cape Town realized its possibilities, and had on the eve of the second World War plans which would have made Cape Town not only the most up-to-date bunkering station in the world. but also the best equipped to deal with a variety of freight, both through cargoes and transit cargoes. In 1937 Cape Town handled nearly £22,000,000 worth of imports such as textiles, apparel, yarns and fibres, iron and steel goods, and foodstuffs. Exports were valued at over £92,000,000, and these included gold, diamonds, fruit, maize and fish.

IMPORTANCE OF CAPE TOWN

Cape Town is the terminal of a most important trade route from Great Britain. Cape Town reached its highest prosperity when the coal-firing of ships was at its peak and the emigrant trade to Australia was a matter of great importance.

The increasing use of oil as a marine fuel meant that the rich deposits of coal to be found in Natal were no longer necessary for bunker purposes for long-distance passenger liners, and so the importance of the Cape lessened. Unsettled conditions, and the fact that the modern oil-using ship could go much farther than her predecessor without bunkering, made it just as convenient for shipowners to use the southern route in preference to Suez.

To secure speed in bunkering modern oil-using ships, the oil companies put up installations which were equal to anything in the world. Cape Town followed by constructing dry docks and increasing its harbour area, and adopted a plan for a new port with no less than three miles of quays and a water area of over 360 acres.

KEY PORTS OF SOUTH AFRICA

Like the harbours of the Pacific North-West Coast, Cape Town is a port which, whatever the future may bring, cannot fail to grow, and the same is true of other key ports of the Union : Port Elizabeth, East London, and Durban. One of the principal connexions is with the United Kingdom, the distance from London to Cape Town being 6,181 miles, or 5,978 miles from Southampton, which is the usual terminal port for the mail ships. Generally, these big 23,000-ton vessels make an intermediate call at Madeira, 1,306 miles from Southampton.

Madeira and the Canary Islands are interesting and important calls on the routes both south to the Cape, south-west to South America, and to the west coast of Africa. They carry on a large trade, principally in fruit and vegetables, and several lines of ships are employed, especially in the trade between these islands and the United Kingdom. Norway had a large stake in this business before the outbreak of the second World War.

Rich and valuable cargoes are carried home from the African western seaboard. Not the least important among them are vegetable oils and ground nuts, which form the basis of such a valuable foodstuff as margarine.

Just as the name Union Castle—one of whose fine ships is illustrated in Chapter 3—will always be associated with the South African trade, so the name of the Elder Dempster Line is bound up with West African shipping. The Union Castle ships girdle the African continent, for some of their vessels run out to Gibraltar, then proceed on through the Mediterranean, down the Red Sea, and down the African eastern seaboard. At all ports, from Zanzibar downwards they make contact with ships which cross the Indian Ocean.

Before Japan joined in the second World War, the link between South Africa and the Far East was becoming stronger. The Dutch had a great deal to do with this, and the vessels they constructed were in no small way responsible for the success of these developments. Some of the most luxurious passenger ships in the world, with ample cargo accommodation, were built to connect Cape Town with Hong Kong by numerous island ports and via Colombo, Singapore, Saigon, and other important trading centres; they could hardly be equalled on any route for luxury and good service.

DOMINION TRADE

The more one examines the map of the Atlantic Ocean, the more one is convinced of the strategic position of Cape Town. And so, using it as a jumping-off point, we move on to Australia, which sends us wheat and meat, and fruit and dairy produce, as does also the sister Dominion, New Zealand. Ships have, for a long time, been accustomed to go to Australia either by the Cape, with the long haul to Fremantle, and then round the Australian coast, or via the Suez Canal and then straight down to Fremantle, or on occasion via the South Atlantic Ocean and Cape Horn. The more general way out and home for British ships trading to New Zealand—the Empire food ships—is via the Panama Canal and the Pacific Ocean.

Distances are long, so speed is of paramount importance. From Panama to Wellington, New Zealand, is 6,500 miles. Six thousand miles at the old-fashioned 10-knot speed takes twenty-five days. Imagine, therefore, the advantages of a

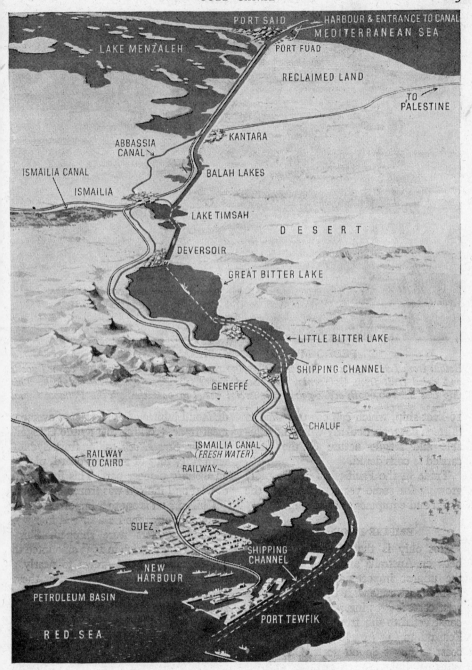

BRITAIN'S GATEWAY TO THE EAST

Fig. 7. *The Suez Canal consists of four lakes linked together by channels dredged out of the sand. Ships carry 26,578,000 tons of cargo through the canal in a typical year*

PEDRO MIGUEL LOCK, PANAMA CANAL

Bound from Los Angeles to London with 7,850 tons of general cargo, mostly canned goods and dried fruit from California, the "Steel Exporter" enters Pedro Miguel lock. This ship was the 100,000th ocean-going commercial vessel to pass through the Panama Canal

19-knot ship, which can cut this time to thirteen days, particularly when the valuable and fragile nature of the cargo carried is considered.

Trade in the Pacific has been rapidly growing for some years, an! so has the speed and equipment of the ships.

EMPIRE FOOD SHIPS

Not only is the Inter-Empire trade between Australia and New Zealand of the utmost importance, but the sister Dominions' trade with the Pacific north-west coast is growing. Special ships are constructed to run from Sydney via New Zealand, to Los Angeles, and then up the coast to Puget Sound ports. One of the principal links, and a growing one for meat, fruit, dairy produce, and lumber is that between Panama and New Zealand. In 1938 the British Empire celebrated the diamond jubilee of the immense overseas meat trade, recalling that a little Glasgow steamer, *Strathleven*, sailing from Sydney with forty tons of meat on board, played an historic pioneer part. This forty tons of beef and mutton was frozen on board.

Chilled beef is another important cargo in the Empire food ships, and in 1937, 350,000 quarters were shipped. Shipments of pigs, which in 1933 amounted to 70,500 carcases, had grown to nearly a quarter of a million in 1937. For these increasing quantities of foodstuffs the ships built and building before the second World War, and the routes on which they operated were of great importance.

This concludes the survey of the principal long-distance trade routes, especially as they affect Great Britain.

Mention must now be made of the busy trades which are maintained in peace time between the United Kingdom and ports in the Western Mediterranean and in the Levant. Whilst increasing quantities of our fresh fruit came from New Zealand ports, much was provided from the Levant and Spanish ports, particularly oranges and lemons.

The shorter haul has many advantages, because there is no need for refrigeration; surface ventilation is sufficient.

SHORT-SEA TRADES

Nearer the British Isles there are the short-sea trades, the coastal routes which surround the British Isles, carrying much trans-shipment freight from the ships running on the long Empire hauls, as well as cargo in competition with the railways and the roads. The North Sea and English Channel are crossed and criss-crossed with routes in peace time. For pit props from the Baltic countries form an exchange cargo for coal and coke;

Denmark sends fish and dairy produce; Holland sells us eggs and fresh vegetables. We send coal to Holland.

The routes to the Baltic are among the most important in Northern Europe. There are two ways of reaching the Baltic: one is north-about, via the Skagerrak and Kattegat, down to the Sound, round the south of Sweden and up into the Gulf of Bothnia. The other is along the flat Frisian coast to Brunsbuttel at the North Sea entrance to the Kiel Canal, and thence to Holtenau, at the other entrance.

The Kiel Canal, which is one of the most important strategic waterways in the world, is in peace time one of its most important trade lanes, since there is a great saving in distance for ships bound for the English Channel, if they pass through the Kiel Canal instead of going down the Kattegat and through the Sound.

Ship canals have a very considerable influence upon the trade routes of the

MERCHANTMAN AND WARSHIP, SUEZ CANAL

The "British Courage" steams past one of H.M. ships in the Suez Canal, which was opened for navigation in 1869. The Suez Canal has no locks, and the average time for merchant ships to pass through is 15 hours, 20 minutes. Its terminal ports are Port Said and Suez

PANAMA AND SUEZ CANALS

Opened for navigation	... Panama Canal, 1914 (August 15)	Suez Canal, 1869
Connects	... Atlantic and Pacific	... Mediterranean and Red Sea
Ports at each end...	... Colon (Cristobal) Panama (Balboa)	Port Said, Suez (Port Tewfik)
Length	... 43.84 nautical miles	... 85 nautical miles
Number of locks ...	... Three	... None.
Depth of Channel	... 57 feet for all sections	... 30 feet (maximum draught of ship)
Width of Channel	... 300 feet minimum	... 240 feet minimum
Approximate average time of transit for ordinary merchant ships...	... 8 hours	... ... 15 hours, 20 minutes.

world. Most important of the world's ship canals are Panama and Suez. Running them very close in importance, and exceeding in an eight months operated year the volume of traffic both carry, is the Sault Sainte Marie Canal on the Great Lakes of North America, which connects Lakes Superior and Huron, and overcomes the 21-foot difference in levels between them. It is popularly known as the Soo Canal (see Table).

In addition to the Kiel Canal, there are the North Sea Canal, connecting the important port of Amsterdam with open water at Yjmuiden, the Manchester Ship Canal, which performs a similar function for the port of Manchester as far as the

River Mersey is concerned, and a much smaller canal, the Gota Canal, which is serviceable to ships of coaster type; it links Stockholm with Gothenberg, and runs across the Swedish peninsula.

But to return to the Panama Canal ; it is one of the engineering wonders of the world.

It connects the Atlantic and Pacific Oceans by means of two bays, an artificial lake 164 square miles in extent, and a natural lake. There are three systems of locks. Contrary to the general impression, its direction is from north-west to southeast, i.e., almost at right angles to the strip of land it crosses. Passage from the Atlantic to the Gatun, a great artificial lake, is

CANAL TRAFFIC COMPARISONS IN A TYPICAL YEAR

	PANAMA	SUEZ	SAULT SAINTE MARIE (SOO)
Number of transits ..	4,673	5,337	21,975
Net tonnage... ...	22,855,151	26,761,735	68,546,412
Tons of cargo ...	23,958,826	26,578,000	91,379,658
Total: Panama and Suez	50,536,826		
Total dues paid ...	$119,203,342	Fr. 193,515,145	Nil. Free canal
Period of operation...	12 months	12 months	8 months

made in the three steps of the Gatun locks; the descent from Gatun Lake to the Pacific is made by one step on the Pedro Miguel Lock, the Miraflores Lake, and two steps in the Miraflores Lock. All the locks are double, so that there can be a two-directional flow of ships.

It is instructive to compare the Panama and Suez Canals physically. Other inter-

of locks. The building of the other involved the linking up of a system of lakes. Both canals have the same function: to save mileage on seaways. Each handles a great volume of traffic. The Suez Canal has no locks throughout its eighty-five nautical miles of length. It comprises a string of lakes which are linked together by channels dredged out of the sand.

LAKE FREIGHTERS ON SOO CANAL

Special types of ships, lake freighters, bring grain and ore over the Great Lakes of North America to inland ports. The Sault Sainte Marie Canal (the Soo), operating only eight months of the year, carries a greater volume of traffic than the Suez and Panama together

esting comparisons—length and transit time—are made in the tables opposite.

Suez is dead flat throughout its length. Panama requires a lift of 85 feet and a drop of 31 feet, followed by a second drop to sea level. The construction of Panama involved literally digging through a large mass of land, and the creation of a system

The canal channel is banked up throughout most of its length, so as to form a secure waterway for ships of up to 32-foot draft. Differing vitally though each does from the other from a physical point of view, each cuts in half the land masses of its respective hemispheres. Suez revitalized a large inland sea—the

Mediterranean—and made of it, in railway parlance, a through station; formerly it had been a terminus. Panama did the same for the Caribbean. Events have caught up with Suez, and thanks to the low fuel consumption of the modern ship, it was, prior to September, 1939, no longer necessary for vessels to pass through this canal and down the Red Sea on the way to the Antipodes, and even to the Far East. The importance of Cape Town is again emphasized.

Political events have left Panama more or less untouched. Modern machinery permits ships to go via Magellan rather than via Panama if necessary, but Panama is still the short cut to the Antipodes from the United Kingdom, and effects a great saving in sea miles from chief ports of Europe to important Pacific ports. The two principal ship canals in the world are in a category by themselves.

Dividing continents, Panama and Suez link oceans; Kiel cuts an isthmus and joins vital seas. Located at the narrowest land portion of the continents, the construction of Panama and Suez was carried out in the teeth of unbelievable difficulties—Suez because civil engineering was a young science in those days, and Panama because of the contour of the land. It took ten years to construct.

NEW CANALS PROJECTED

There has been some talk of a rival to the Panama Canal via Lake Nicaragua. Before the Panama Canal was built, the Nicaraguan route was strongly advocated. Also Siam has considered the building of a canal across the Kra Isthmus, joining the South China Sea and the Bay of Bengal. The Kra Isthmus, which is a narrow neck of land ten miles wide, links the Malay Peninsula to Tenasserim.

MANCHESTER SHIP CANAL

Built at a cost of £15,000,000, the Manchester Ship Canal transformed Manchester from an inland city into one of the leading ports of Great Britain, with an immense annual revenue. Great difficulties had to be overcome during its construction. Picture shows the "Pacific Enterprise," with tugs, passing through the canal, which is thirty-five miles long

RIVERS AND LAKES SERVE THE GOTA CANAL

Linking the Baltic with the Kattegat, the Gota Canal is 240 miles long, but only about fifty-six miles consist of artificial canals, the remainder being rivers and lakes. The differences in level along the route are regulated by seventy locks. Above, a ship leaving Trollhättan Lock

It is extremely doubtful, however, if the canal would be feasible, owing to the mountainous terrain, though modern engineering is not necessarily baffled by such difficulites.

From a traffic point of view, more impressive than either the Panama Canal or the Suez Canal is the Soo Canal. It links two large freshwater seas and is a vital point in the through flow of grain and iron ore from west to east. Through this narrow bottle-neck pass in an average navigation year of eight months, nearly 22,000 ships, with over 91,000,000 tons of freight.

Two other canals are the Manchester Ship Canal, 35½ miles in length, and the North Sea Canal, 15 miles in length. The North Sea Canal is as clean as the Manchester Ship Canal is dirty, and it is joined at certain points by tributary canals, which are all part of the Dutch

Inland Waterways system. Indeed, the whole of Holland, and of Northern Europe is one vast canal system, upon which large quantities of freight are annually moved. These canals are convenient substitutes for road and railway, and are not part of the world's main trade routes.

The Gota Canal is a 240 mile river and lake route, partly canalized, connecting Gothenberg with Stockholm. It is not a ship canal in the accepted sense, as it does not handle ocean- or sea-going tonnage, and actually only fifty-six miles are canalized, the remainder being a channel through lakes. Part of this canal—the Trollhättan portion—handles sea-going traffic. In 1938 over 2,500,000 tons of freight passed through. The largest cargo was 2,000 tons of iron ore, another example of the growing importance of inland water transport.

In ships specially designed for the work the canal transports considerable quantities of merchandise, and in the summer months has a large tourist traffic.

There are differences of level of 300 feet on the canal route, and these are overcome by means of no less than seventy locks at various points.

Thus we realise why there is a tendency these days to produce small, fast, highly efficient ships. These are ideally suited to canal traffic. Indeed, the production of ships capable of carrying merchandise at high speed on rivers, canals and seas is certain to be one of the developments of the future.

It may be asked: What is going to be the effect of aircraft on the ships and routes of the future? It is instructive to examine a map specially prepared to show the number and direction of aircraft routes which were in regular use in September, 1939 (Fig. 8).

These show clearly the similarity between air and sea routes, at any rate, as far as the terminal ports are concerned. The map indicates, too, that pre-war air routes were successfully operating

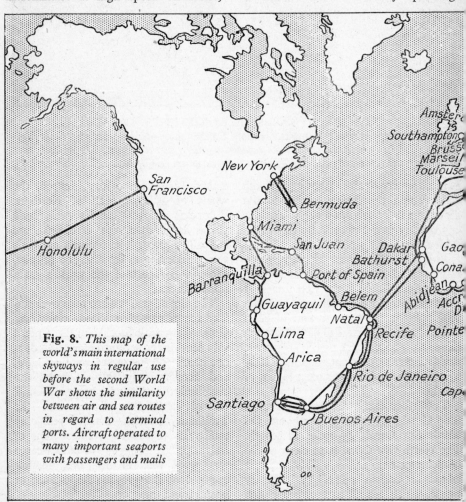

Fig. 8. *This map of the world's main international skyways in regular use before the second World War shows the similarity between air and sea routes in regard to terminal ports. Aircraft operated to many important seaports with passengers and mails*

to the most important of the world's seaports with passengers and mails.

The use of aircraft—call it sky-shipping—will increase. The question is: how much will the routes be sea routes, i.e., with flying-boats, and how much will they be land routes, spanning the seas and oceans merely as part of their regular flight? One thing is certain. Development will depend very largely upon ready supplies of oil. That is why the most enduring trade is that which carries liquid fuel on the trade routes. Because of this Cape Town has come into its own again

as a world port. Here, again, we stand at the threshold of big developments.

That aircraft, the heaviest liquid fuel user, will completely eliminate the ship is unthinkable; that aircraft will affect the design and operation of ships is likely. That aircraft will alter the direction of trade lanes does not seem possible, because these are established with regard to the optimum distance between ports with regard to weather conditions. What is at least certain is that ships will be faster and that the time taken between ports will be very considerably reduced.

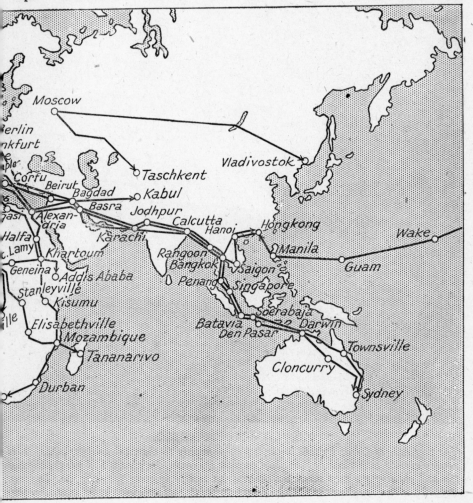

NON-STOP SHIPBUILDING

The shipyards of Great Britain responded magnificently to the vital need for ships. This newly launched tanker can be seen about to enter the water. Before she had left the slipway the keel plate of the next vessel for construction was being slung into position. The men stopped work only to cheer the launching, and started immediately upon building another ship

CHAPTER 7

Shipbuilding and Repairing

Strain on Britain's shipping. Serious losses and a gain: past lessons neglected. Seven standard types of ships. Pre-fabrication. New ships in record time. The glory of a new ship. "Surgeons" for sick ships. Ships torn in half. Liner into cruiser. Triumphs of the salvage service.

ONLY after about two and a half years of war—intermittent on land and in the air, but continuous at sea—did the fact of Britain's sea dependence fully impress itself on the country. Britain had then lost nearly a third of the merchant fleet that flew the Red Ensign on September 3, 1939.

And the tasks of the merchant ships had been multiplied. They had to bring food, raw materials and munitions over greater distances, and Britain's munition workers had trebled their consumption of raw materials. Ships had to support and supply larger armies in the Far East and the Middle East, with the Mediterranean highway practically cut off. Ships were required to carry great quanties of weapons and materials through the Arctic to Russia. No wonder there was the cry for "Ships, Ships, and yet more Ships!" Fortunately, there had been some profit from the experience of 1914-18, and the shipyards had not been idle.

BRITAIN'S FOURFOLD PROBLEM

Britain's sea problem—her chief war problem—was fourfold. Firstly, though the Royal Navy had been greatly reduced in strength in the preceding twenty years or so, the merchant ships had to be protected, which meant the maintenance of naval supremacy, the organization of convoys, and the fitting of defensive armament and other equipment to meet new developments of enemy attack.

Secondly, the enemy's weapons had to be destroyed or blunted as far as possible, by the use of the most effective strategy and counter-weapons at sea, and by bombing bases, ports, shipyards and factories supplying the enemy's shipyards.

Thirdly, each ship had to be put to the fullest and most effective use by the careful organization of imports, supply routes, of particular ships in relation to routes and imports, and by efficiently overhauling all port arrangements.

TASKS OF THE SHIPYARDS

Finally, lost ships had to be replaced, and damaged ships must be brought back to port and returned to service with the least delay. It is with this part of the vast and intricate sea problem that this chapter is mainly concerned. The other factors provide the perspective. The task of the shipyards would have been great enough even if losses had been small, for Britain entered the second World War with too few sea-going ships—2,000 less than on the eve of the first World War. But the losses were by no means negligible, and the most determined efforts of the shipyards, in shipbuilding and ship repairing, were vital to victory.

The measures adopted by the naval authorities soon had their influence on the sinkings. For some time after September, 1939, the losses of neutral ships—most of them then sailing singly —exceeded British losses. This was evidence, not only of Nazi lawlessness, but of the success of the convoy system.

In the spring of 1940 the shipping situation took a violent turn for the worse. By occupying Norway, Denmark, Holland, Belgium, and all the Channel and Atlantic coastal areas of France, Germany gained ideal 'bases for U-boats, motor torpedo-boats, and long-range bombers. At the same time, when she could least afford it, Britain lost the considerable assistance of the French Navy, suffered serious naval casualties in evacuating British troops from the Continent, and had to meet the challenge of the Italian Fleet in the Mediterranean, requiring a diversion of strong forces from the Atlantic. She also lost the near sources of supply for dairy produce, iron ore, and other important commodities, which was the equivalent of losing ships, since more ships were required to carry these essential things—and over greater distances. The Atlantic route to America became the nearest and principal supply route. A further heavy strain on shipping came later, with Russia's entry into the war. Quantities of war materials had to be sent to the Persian Gulf, to Murmansk, and to Archangel past German air bases in Norway.

SHIPS FROM OUR ALLIES

Against these formidable setbacks there was one solid gain. By his military conquests on the Continent, Hitler sent into friendly British ports more than 7,000,000 tons of merchant ships, including 3,800,000 tons of the markedly efficient Norwegian fleet, and 2,620,000 from the Netherlands.

Later, the total of Allied ships was increased to more than 8,000,000 tons when Greece was occupied. With the ships came their officers and crews, eager to carry on the struggle for the liberation of their countries. It is true that some of these ships were already chartered to the British Government, but they were only

a portion of the whole, and henceforward their continued service was guaranteed.

This great addition to Allied shipping strength may have saved an otherwise disastrous situation, but it did not alter the new strategic advantages for attack which the Germans had gained ; rather it increased the number of their targets.

DEFENCE MEASURES IMPROVE

The graph of shipping losses slanted sharply upwards. In March, 1940, less than 100,000 tons gross of British, Allied and neutral ships had been sunk. In June the figure had risen to more than 500,000 tons. During the next nine months the losses averaged nearly 400,000 tons a month compared with a previous average of 182,000 tons.

In the following spring of 1941 the Germans intensified their campaign. For three months the shipping losses averaged 534,000 tons. Germany was trying hard to defeat Britain by strangling her jugular vein. But the blitzkreig failed, although battleships and cruisers and armed raiders were sent out on the trade routes. Merchant shipping losses fell to about 180,000 tons a month ; they were lower, in fact, than at any time since the over-running of Europe. The improvement was not due to any slackening of effort by Germany. It was brought about by stronger naval and air escorts, by great prowess and courage on the part of British merchant seamen and naval personnel, and by the help of the American Navy, which patrolled the Atlantic as far west as Iceland, and escorted convoys.

Then a major upheaval in the course of the war, the most far-reaching of all, turned the tide once more against Britain and the Allies. When Japan launched her treacherous and powerful blow at the American Fleet in Pearl Harbour, a new phase of the sea war began. It was a desperate phase, yet one full of hope and encouragement, for the

RIVET HEATERS AT WORK

Intent on their job of preparing rivets for the plates of a new ship, these workers make a vivid shipyard picture. When the platers have finished their task of putting the plates of the ship into position, the riveters follow on. For speedy construction, plates are now welded together by heat in some shipyards, and many ships have been built in an astonishingly short time

BUILDING A MERCHANT SHIP

Platers are tightening the bolts of the bottom plates of a new ship. Ships were built in record time, both in British and American shipyards. The output per man of the British shipyard worker was the highest in the world, but for a considerable time the yards were handicapped by a shortage of labour

Shipping losses in the early part of 1942 were again heavy, too heavy for the rapid assembly and concentration of striking power which the military situation demanded.

To build up their strength at sea was the first task of Britain and America, and everything else hung on that task being successful. In spite of all the democracies' might, mobilized and potential, the dictators could, even at this stage, still have won the war by winning at sea—not in a pitched naval battle but by the slow pressure of attrition, by the sinking of merchant ships on a scale which exceeded replacement capacity over a long period, or prevented effective use of existing tonnage. Britain's sea power, composed of warships and merchant ships, is Britain's strength, but it is also her weakness in time of war. For merchant ships, the base of her economic and fighting strength, are especially vulnerable to torpedo and bomb.

Against this background can be seen the vast importance of the work in the shipyards. On the ability of the shipyards to replace losses, naval and mercantile, and to do more—to increase the strength of both these arms—depended the issue of the war and its duration.

One of the lessons of the first World War was that to neglect the building of merchant ships was to court disaster. This is clear from production figures. In 1913 British shipyards launched about

great American nation, with her untold resources, her power in men, was now a partner in arms with Britain, Russia, and the free peoples of Europe.

Because of President Roosevelt's leadership the Americans had shown greater awareness of the tremendous significance of ships in the war picture. But they were not prepared for a blow such as Pearl Harbour. For the time being it tilted the balance of sea power in Japan's favour, made possible Japan's rapid military victories in the East, and seriously affected the sea war in the West.

2,000,000 tons gross of merchant ships; in 1915 the total fell to 660,000 tons, and in the following year to 630,000 tons. The Government had concentrated on the building of naval vessels and had ignored merchant shipbuilding as a national problem. In addition, the claims of the Army on men and materials had been allowed to impair the efficiency of shipbuilding.

With a sudden rise in shipping losses in the spring of 1917 the menace of a broken supply line of merchant ships was at last recognized and panic expedients were at once adopted to meet a desperate situation.

What happened on the outbreak of the second World War? The Government had been blind to the menace of Britain's weakness at sea. For a long time it had been officially declared that Britain's merchant fleet was adequate for peace and war, and that even if it were not, the country could rely on neutrals. And so the warnings from all sides were ignored, and the shipbuilding industry languished for want of new orders.

There was more widespread unemployment than in any other industry. Thousands of men left the yards for better-paid and more regular work. Official complacency continued until the gathering war clouds were almost overhead. Then, in the spring of 1939, the British Shipping (Assistance) Bill

was presented to Parliament. Its immediate purpose was to fill some of the empty shipbuilding berths, and that part of the Bill was put into operation in advance of Parliamentary sanction. The misery in the shipbuilding districts made quick action necessary.

But before the Bill had reached the Statute Book the clouds of war had burst, and this belated legislation was dropped.

Following years of semi-starvation the shipbuilding industry was suddenly faced with a prodigious task, and attacked the emergency with ability and courage. The

HAMMERING THE RIVETS

To hammer the rivets connecting a ship's plates, once driven in by hand by squads of workers, pneumatic hammers are now employed, as the picture shows. When the riveter has finished his work, all plate junctions are firmly secured by caulking. With welded plates, one third of the labour can be saved

NEW SHIPS TAKE SHAPE

To build up her strength at sea was the first and most important of all the prodigious tasks before Britain. Upon the ability of the shipyards to build new vessels as speedily as possible, and to replace losses, the duration of the war largely depended. This shipyard scene shows ships under construction. In the foreground, protected from flying sparks, a welder at work

response to the national call reflects great credit on everyone associated with the shipbuilding industry.

The theme of those first months of war was "Get on with the Job!" The discussion and regulation of details were postponed if they threatened to hold up work for a day. And the shipyards did get on with the job.

One lesson of 1914-18 was heeded. Control of the shipbuilding effort was vested in practical men of proved organizing ability and drive, men who knew their job from A to Z. It is not customary for bouquets to pass between controllers and controlled, but in shipbuilding, efficient direction was generally acknowledged. The gain on this score was very

considerable. At first merchant ship construction came within the province of the Ministry of Shipping, but, in the interests of co-ordination, was later transferred to the Admiralty, the department responsible for warship building. The types and design of the merchant ships were, however, decided in co-operation with the Ministry of Shipping, later Ministry of War Transport.

The shipyards first concentrated on those types of ships with which they were most familiar. That was the general policy, subject to adjustment according to strategical needs and to steady progress in the direction of standardization. It was helped by the fact that in the previous decade there had developed a decided tendency among many individual ship-builders to produce semi-standardized ships.

Several yards, for example, specialized in their own design of "economy" cargo vessels; others had been accustomed to build tankers of very similar types ordered by one or two of the big oil companies; while some builders had achieved a reputation for the construction of special types of meat-carrying cargo liners. On these general types the wartime programme was based. This was another important improvement on the programme of 1917. Then standardization had been carried too far and too quickly; it made insufficient allowance for changes between one shipyard and another and between districts. The policy of gradual

standardization avoided disorganization, and kept all the many departments of a shipyard familiar with what they were doing. There is little doubt that the policy paid in terms of tons built.

Eventually, seven main types of war-time merchant ships evolved. Chief of these was a tramp ship, or cargo vessel, with a carrying capacity of about 10,000 to 10,500 tons deadweight, usually propelled by steam reciprocating, or triple expansion engines, and simple Scotch boilers. Variations of this type were confined to details or the substitution of Diesel engines for steam.

The standard tramp lacked many of the frills of a peace time vessel, and modern refinements in the engine-room were lacking. But she was an efficient vessel by

WOMEN WORKERS IN THE SHIPYARDS

Women played a valuable part in the wartime programme which demanded as many ships as possible in the shortest time, and in a year the number of women employed in the industry trebled. Here they are heating rivets, which are made of tested steel, ready for the riveters

THE PRE-FABRICATED SHIP
A NEW METHOD OF CONSTRUCTION IN SEPARATE UNITS

COMPLETE
MAST UNITS

PRE-FABRICATED
BULKHEADS

MAIN DECK PLATING
& HATCH OPENINGS

MAIN FRAMES AND
OUTER SHELL PLATING

BREAKWATER

WINCH

KEEL PLATES

BETWEEN DECK PLATING

COMPLETE BOW UNIT

PRE-FABRICATED
DOUBLE BOTTOM
AND TANK TOPS

ASHWELL
WOOD

COMPLETE BRIDGE
& DECK HOUSE UNIT

COMPLETE AFTER DECK HOUSE
& GUN PLATFORM

WARPING WINCH

PRE-FABRICATED
STERN SECTION

PROPELLER
& RUDDER

SHAFT TUNNEL

RECIPROCATING
STEAM ENGINE UNIT

BOILER UNITS

ENGINE ROOM

THE COMPLETED 10,000 TON DEADWEIGHT
CARGO SHIP WITH FITTINGS

comparison with the tramp of 1917, with a higher speed, and excellent crew's accommodation, and was well equipped for war service. In normal times such a ship—her defensive equipment replaced by the features of efficiency considered unessential in wartime—might take anything from nine to twelve months to build from the laying of the keel.

SHIPS BUILT IN SECTIONS

At the huge mass-production shipyard established at Hog Island, in America, during 1914-18 the record construction time for a far simpler vessel was ten months. British shipyards, short of labour, cut this time to six months, four months on the stocks and two fitting out. The speed-up was achieved by hard and efficient work and by the adoption of special wartime construction methods. Six months was a good average building rate. But these times are now considerably bettered. A notable instance was a tramp ship laid down in a Scottish yard on December 17, 1941. That was the worst time of the year because daylight hours were short, and very little work could be done after dark because of the blackout. Weather always interferes with shipbuilding, but that winter was particularly severe. Blizzards stopped all work on this vessel for twelve days. Yet she was launched at the beginning of April and sailed south on May 13, less than five months from the laying of her keel. That was not a record, but it was a very fine achievement in view of the difficulties of winter work.

This vessel, like others, was built on the system of pre-fabrication—one of the chief special construction methods that aimed at rapid production. Normally, a ship is assembled, bit by bit, as it lies on the stocks. With pre-fabrication, sections of different sizes are constructed on the ground, or sometimes even outside the shipyard at constructional engineering or similar works, and then lifted by cranes into place and joined up to the main structure. (*See* pp. 140-141.)

In the emergency, shipyards sprang up in the United States of America where pre-fabrication was used on a very large scale, because the older yards could be speedily extended and new yards laid out with that end in view. Ships were pieced together in huge sections weighing up to thirty or forty tons. Practically all joints and plates were welded together instead of riveted. With welding the two pieces of metal are fused by the application of intense heat, generated by an electric spark, and the deposit of additional molten metal from a rod or electrode. This also helped speedy construction because it was quicker to train welders than riveters, and the majority of American shipyard workers were new to their jobs.

These methods were not alone responsible for the sensational speeds at which ships were built in the United States.

SHIP BUILT IN TEN DAYS

Tramps were delivered by American yards in less than fifty days from keel-laying. In September, 1942, ten days after its keel was laid, a 10,500-ton Liberty cargo ship was launched at Mr. Henry Kaiser's Pacific Coast shipyard. Such records were possible because work was carried on for twenty-four hours a day, seven days a week. That meant employing at least three separate shifts of workers, nearly three times the labour force required for single shift working. This is mentioned because it touches the roots of the limited output of British shipbuilding. There were not enough workers.

The shipyard labour force was increased by many expedients. Men who had left the industry in the years of depression were recalled. New labour was trained. Women were employed on a considerable scale for a variety of jobs, from rivet heating, welding, and painting to general labouring, carpentry and machine-shop work, but always there was room for more labour.

In the pre-war years of depression many shipyards had been closed down by a voluntary movement in the industry. The purpose was to cut out the facilities which, created to meet the war demands of 1917, were surplus to any possible needs of peace. In this way work was concentrated in the more efficient yards, huge overheads were saved amounting to enormous sums in a year, and the industry as a whole was put on a sound basis.

The move aroused considerable political controversy, mainly because it tended to aggravate the effects of the depression in some districts. It was often overlooked, however, that it also relieved conditions to a corresponding extent in other districts. Rationalizing the shipyards did not reduce the amount of work available, nor did it reduce the numbers employed in shipbuilding. The reduction was due to the world economic situation and to Britain's policy of disarmament.

SHORTAGE OF LABOUR

Many of the closed yards were reopened when war requirements once more superseded those of peace. Twenty-three were again in commission by the middle of 1942. The experience of one of these well illustrates the situation that dominated British shipbuilding from September, 1939. In the spring of 1941 this yard was put into working order, and a keel laid down. Over a year passed, however, before the first ship was launched and all the building berths were occupied. And the explanation was simply that the yard could not be properly manned, although there was no hesitation in taking on as many women as possible. At any time it could have absorbed at least twice the number employed.

The output of merchant ships was not spectacular by comparison with the peak years of peace time construction. But that was because so much was demanded by warship construction and by repairs of naval and mercantile vessels. The naval programme—the long-neglected effort to strengthen the Royal Navy—made very considerable inroads on the production from berths that would otherwise have been filled with merchant ships.

GREAT EFFORTS OF THE WORKERS

Repairing and conversion of ships were also carried out on a tremendous scale, and such work could not be classified as shipbuilding. For this reason the shipyard effort could not be measured by the normal standard of mercantile tonnage *launched*. But, relating that tonnage to the proportion of men and facilities devoted to building merchant ships, the effort was astonishing. The output per man of the British shipyard worker was the highest in the world. No effort was more important in the whole field of war production than that of the shipyards, and none more creditable.

A new merchant ship calls vividly to the imagination. It is a vast creation, with a character of its own, a brain in the bridge and a rhythmic heart in the engine-room—and the Seven Seas and a thousand ports within its reach.

Created by mind and muscle from sheets of steel, thick girders, bends and angles, planks of wood, brass and delicate instruments, a ship is as shapely and self-contained as the human body. A new ship symbolizes adventure—from the human dramas that may be lived on the bridge, in the saloon, or far down in the heat and noise under deck and under sea-level, to the cargoes that may lie in the holds. A large mass of grain may seem unexciting, but the dullest imagination can find adventure in the thought that it comes to our tables from a field 8,000 miles away.

SAVING CRIPPLED SHIPS

Salvage work is as important as the building of new vessels, for every damaged ship must be returned to service in the minimum of time. Tugs try to bring a shipping casualty to a quayside, but often they have to beach her in the harbour mouth, where the Admiralty Salvage Officer takes her in charge. This tug is drawing alongside a crippled ship, which is still smoking

A new ship is impressive. In war its colour is a sombre, purposeful grey instead of the bright freshness of a peace ship, but the hull, decks, and deckhouses are clean. The grey is in keeping with the grim duties ahead, and also with that gun in the stern, the tough little gun above and other guns farther forward.

ROMANCE OF A NEW SHIP

Later there will be signs of rust and dirt, perhaps a buckled top plate, scars from bullet and shrapnel; but, just completed, the ship is a clean hull with clean derricks and masts, new ropes and efficient winches. You glance back; and there is the open piece of ground, bordered by untidy scaffolding, and at one end a muddy river from which this huge, intricate, purposeful animal has sprung. It is now partly filled by an untidy, gaunt skeleton of rusty-looking steel, bare, metallic, lifeless. The achievement is wonderful. And seeing it in this way brings meaning to the knowledge that a ship has been completed in fifty days and less.

A new ship stirs the imagination of us all, although the British public may not be as sea-conscious as it should be in view of the history, economy, and geography of Britain.

Ship repairing is less romantic, but no less important. The repaired ship, old, perhaps, and ugly judged by modern standards, lacks the imaginative appeal she had when she slid down the ways with a rumble of chains, a cloud of dust and smoke, and waves of water washing her on either beam; she is less impressive than when she pulled away from the fitting-out berth for her trials. She gets no mention in the papers. But if it were not for the work of the men who repair ships—the labourers' skill, the technicians' knowledge, the managers' experience and organizing ability—the British Merchant Navy would have been immobilized before the second World War was twelve months old. In the first three years 23,000 warship repairs and refits were carried out : 35,000 merchant ships and 140,000,000 tons gross were put back into service. In a single week 1,000,000 tons were sent to sea. Such achievements bear out the proud claim of the ship repairer,

who is often also a shipbuilder, that his repairing job is a far more ticklish one than that of building. A firm may build a very good tramp ship of 10,000 tons deadweight, or smaller, but a high-class refrigerated liner would be most probably outside its range and an oil company might have to go elsewhere to discuss the building of a new tanker.

SPECIALIST TASKS

A ship repairer, on the other hand, must be able to apply the knowledge and skill of shipbuilders who specialize in several different classes of tonnage, from the barge to the passenger liner. He must be a skilled engineer and boilermaker, capable of handling many different types and makes of marine engines, and able to

SALVAGE WORK ON TIMBER SHIP

This damaged ship is floating on her cargo of timber, and salvage men are working on her. They have flooded the crew space forward to improve her trim. Amidships they are keeping pumps working at top pressure to get rid of water which poured into her when she was holed

solve technical and structural problems of his own. To borrow an analogy, the ship repairer is the marine surgeon and physician who must be ready always to tackle every marine ill and accident with all the surgeon's skill.

The British ship-repairing industry is the largest in the world. It is scattered around the coasts, an important strategical advantage. There are large ship-repairing centres, such as those on the north-east coast, and on the Mersey, but considerable facilities are found in Northern Ireland, South Wales, Falmouth, Southampton, and in Scotland on the Clyde and at Leith, with smaller yards at many other ports. The efficient maintenance of these dispersed yards should be a key part of Britain's maritime policy.

Ships are repaired in dry dock if the damage is below the waterline, or if the under-water part of the hull needs to be scraped, painted, or inspected. The function of the dry dock is to place the ship back on the building berth, and, like the building berth, it is served by cranes and derricks. It is the operating table.

MARINE HOSPITALS

But when the work is completed there is no complicated launching procedure. The water, which has been pumped out of the dock, is let in again until the ship is afloat once more, the dock gates are opened, and the repaired vessel towed out to open water. Dry docks are usually owned by ship-repairing firms who, as has been stated, may also be shipbuilders. But sometimes they belong to the port authority, or railway company, constructed as an investment and an addition to the port facilities; this applies to some of the docks in London, on the Mersey, at Southampton, Belfast, and elsewhere. The public dock, or railway dock, is hired to the specialist ship repairer for the purpose of carrying out the work.

There are about 125 large dry docks capable of taking ocean-going ships spread over thirty different ports, and more than half are privately owned. In addition there are the Royal dockyards maintained by the Admiralty, and a large number of smaller dry docks, pontoons, or floating docks, and slipways. To every larger repair necessitating dry-docking, there may be four or five ships requiring attention to deck, superstructure, or machinery which have suffered varying damage.

HEAVY DEMANDS OF WAR

These are attended to alongside a wharf, or wet dock. They are the out-patients of the marine hospitals.

All these extensive facilities, apart from the Royal dockyards, were provided to meet the peace time requirements of the mercantile marine, and not by any means *all* the mercantile marine, for a large number of British ships, trading between distant countries, seldom entered home waters. Their overhaul and repairs were done abroad.

What are these requirements in peacetime ? Occasional damage from the effects of heavy weather, collision or stranding, but more often the normal maintenance needed to ensure safety, seaworthiness and economical efficiency. Scraping of scale and marine growth from the ship's bottom, repainting, periodical overhauls required by law and carried out at the instance of the classification societies, the examination of corroded plates, and so on—all more or less routine work to keep the ship in a healthy condition.

How vastly different are the demands of war! What claims on ingenuity, initiative and even improvisation! Dramatically the whole scene changes overnight.

It is no longer a question of the frills of life, but life itself. Every ship must be returned to service in the absolute minimum time; every battered hull, however aged, that is capable of repair, must be

SHATTERED SHIPS MADE WHOLE AGAIN

Fig. 1. *Top pictures show how ships broken in two have been successfully salved and made fit for sea again. Lower picture, methods by which sunken ships are lifted from the sea-bed by means of "camels." Filled with compressed air, they rise to the surface with the wreck*

repaired, though in normal times it might be abandoned or merely sold for scrap.

Normal maintenance work may be slightly reduced to ease the demand. No more fancy paint, for instance. But it cannot be left undone. And on top of that come bomb, torpedo, shell and mine damage; attendance to gaping wounds in the side, broken pipes, cables and machinery parts; reconstruction of deck-houses and cargo spaces gutted by fire.

TRICKS PLAYED BY MINES

The freakish behaviour of bomb and blast was observed by everyone who experienced air raids. At sea miraculous escapes and unexpected destruction, particularly the latter, followed the explosions not only of bombs but of mines and torpedoes.

Shell damage was more "according to the book," but the powerful German magnetic and acoustic mines sometimes played extraordinary tricks on ships that managed to survive. The whole of a ship's engine might be shattered into a thousand pieces without the hull being pierced. In cases of lesser damage it was up to the ship repairer to piece the bits together like a jig-saw puzzle, whether it was a smashed bilge pump or a main Diesel engine, possibly an engine of foreign design and manufacture, just one of many different sorts of jobs that had never been met before.

It was, perhaps, the chief feature of ship-repairing in the war that began in 1939 that there was no precedent to the demands, neither the general demand on facilities nor the particular technical demand of the work to be done. They could not have been met by an inefficient industry, nor one without a tradition of initiative.

They could not have been met if the workmen themselves had not been inspired by that same tradition, backed by their individual skill and willing labour.

Bombs damaged more ships than they sank, and it needs little imagination to picture the volume of coastal and overseas ships that came under this heading. For aerial attacks were almost continuous around the British coasts, far out into the Atlantic, and on the northern route to Russia past Norwegian bases. Bombs, incidentally, were not unknown in the building and repair yards themselves! Added to the damage from war weapons were higher marine casualties—so they were termed—due to sailing in convoy, navigation without lights, voyages on routes that would be unheard of in peace time, and other consequences of war.

Collisions, strandings and weather damage were all increased. Besides these extra demands, repairs to the huge fleet of Allied shipping had to be done mainly in British yards, where formerly all the facilities of Europe were open. After a time the United States and the Dominions gave increasingly valuable help, which must be fully acknowledged. But this by no means cancelled the extra tonnage dependent on Britain's ship-repairing industry, apart altogether from the unusual attention these ships required.

MENDING BROKEN SHIPS

The ship repairer had to be more than a marine surgeon; he must act as physician, diagnostician, osteopath, and "plastic" surgeon. The plastician's art was demonstrated in the wonderful reconstruction of ships that had broken in half, one portion lost and the other salved (Figs. 1 and 2).

The *Imperial Transport*, a tanker of 12,460 tons dead weight, was struck by a torpedo in the Atlantic early in 1940. Within five minutes she broke her back. The crew took to the boats, but when they found the after part still afloat they boarded it, and set to work to save their caricature of a ship, square to the sea, with twisted, broken shell plates and slanting deck. They corrected the trim by

THE SHIP THAT BROKE HER BACK

Fig. 2. *Struck by a torpedo, the motor tanker "Imperial Transport" broke in half in five minutes. The crew found the after part still afloat and boarded her. For two days their half-ship drifted in high seas, and was then towed home. The smashed stern half, salved, is in dry dock, showing great damage to deck and bulkhead. Side plates are marked off for cutting*

transferring water from one tank to another, and started the engines. The half-ship's behaviour under power was far from satisfactory, and in view of the high seas it was decided to let her drift. Two days went by. Wind and sea having dropped, engines were put ahead, and what was left of the *Imperial Transport* steamed for forty-eight hours at about 3½ to 4 knots. Eventually an escort came to the rescue, and a tug, the *Buccaneer*, took the half-ship in tow.

A new fore part was built to the ship's original plans and was launched bow first, with deckhouse, mast, derricks and auxiliary equipment complete (Fig. 3). Meantime the damaged half had been docked, the battered bulkhead cut away and side plates cut back to avoid a straight vertical join. The deck plates were also staggered. The docking of the new half had to be done in such a way that the already docked portion did not float off the blocks on which it rested.

AS GOOD AS NEW

Then the two parts were aligned and the new bow, supported by a specially built cradle, was "launched" by block and tackle into the correct position for riveting, an operation that meant working to exact measurement. The joining of plates and frames was fairly straight-forward, but pipes, cables, and the pump system had all to be connected up.

This was an impressive demonstration of ship repairing success. In such an adventure are concentrated the dangers and violence of the battlefield of the sea; the brave resourcefulness of the men who fight upon it; the salvor's part and his skill; the different skill of builder and repairer, working on slipway and in dry dock—and the defiance of maritime Britain.

Another tanker, of about the same size as the *Imperial Transport*, was mined and broke in two. I saw her lying at an angle in a muddy north-east coast river, with her plates still jutting and bent. She looked forlorn, lifeless, "beyond repair." But a little farther down on the opposite bank, from where the crescendo of rivet-ing din blazed forth the opposite theme, another half was beginning to take shape, though it strained the imagination to associate one with the other, or either with a complete immaculate ship.

The new fore part was about 200 feet long, and it was built at the top of the berth. With a good clear run to give it momentum sufficient to clear the ways, this half was launched bulkhead, or square end, first (Fig. 4). Both halves were docked, and within a few weeks the tanker was at sea again, soon to return with 12,500 tons of a cargo on which every fighting service is absolutely dependent —oil fuel. As efficient and valuable as before, she now had a special claim to attention, for she was an international ship. Two countries helped to build her.

The original vessel was built in Sweden before the second World War. Compared with an entirely new vessel she represented a saving of considerable time and labour, about 1,500 tons of steel, a great deal of complicated equipment, and a 6-cylinder Diesel engine. At a casual glance the new vessel presented an entirely normal outboard appearance, as would be expected. But a close inspection would reveal her unmistakable birthmark, her war medal, perhaps. The sides, or shell plates, of the Swedish stern portion presented the smooth surface that is one of the attributes of welding. The plates of the British bow were lapped and riveted, though they covered some welded joints.

THE INFLEXIBLE RULE

Examples of other major repairs, such as patching up holes the size of a house-side, were legion. They required just as much skill, sometimes more, just as much ingenuity. In all cases the work was governed by a rigid rule, one that was unknown in peace time: everything to make the ship seaworthy and sea-going must be done but no more, for the pressing need was the ship at sea.

Like shipbuilding, ship repairing in the second World War gained much by efficient direction and control. The allotment of work between different yards according to available facilities, the position of the ship and the amount of work already in hand could so easily have been

JOINING THE TWO HALVES TO MAKE A NEW SHIP

Fig. 3. *From the shattered half of the "Imperial Transport" a new ship was created. This job was a good example of the excellent and intricate repair work continually being carried out in the shipbuilding yards of Britain. After the damaged stern half was repaired, a new fore portion was built to the original plans of the ship. This was docked on a specially built cradle so that it could be manœuvred into exact position for riveting to the after part. The new half-ship was docked to within 9 feet 8 inches of the repaired half in such a way that the latter would not float off the blocks. Then hydraulic jacks started the new half-ship moving until both halves were correctly aligned. This operation completed, the rest was straightforward repair work. The two halves are shown in position in dry dock, ready for the final assembly*

LAUNCHING A NEW HALF-SHIP

Fig. 4. *Complete with deckhouse, mast, derricks and auxiliary equipment, a new half-ship is launched. In care of tugs, it is now on its way to dry dock, where it will be joined up to the repaired half. In some cases ships broken in half have been repaired and made seaworthy in a few weeks, providing impressive demonstrations of ship-repairing skill and success*

muddled. It was not. And that meant more ships at sea, for the speed of repairs was a major factor in the war with the U-boat.

The function of control was also to see that existing facilities were employed to the greatest advantage, that the methods were the best and most efficient, and that facilities and plant were expanded and modernized. It demanded energy, ability, and a thorough technical and general knowledge of the industry. Fortunately, these qualities were not lacking. A spirit of enthusiastic drive was infused into the ship-repairing effort. It did not slacken.

EFFICIENCY OF CONTROL

There is an instance that illustrates the way things were done. A thousand miles from a British repair port, a ship put in to a small harbour severely damaged. She could be brought home with comparative safety, but a fair amount of repair work would have to be done. A description of the damage was wired to repair head-

quarters. When that ship arrived at her destination not long after, plates, girders, and new equipment were waiting on the dock, cut, shaped, and ready for assembly. The time for that job was halved.

But repairs, so numerous and complicated though they were, by no means limited the demands on the industry. The rival and fluctuating calls of building war and merchant ships, of repairs and of conversions have already been mentioned. Conversions were no less important than the other tasks of the shipyards—some were at the top of the priority list. The volume of work they represented was considerable, perhaps as much as the equivalent, in a single year of war, of the entire output of merchant ships in a slack peace year.

Under the heading of conversion may be put everything ranging from the installation of a gun—converting a defenceless merchant ship into a vessel that could sink a U-boat—to the metamorphosis or liners into auxiliary cruisers. The work of conversion was divided between the building and repair yards, but the bulk of it fell on the repairers. At the outbreak of the second World War there were about 3,800 British steamers and motor ships of 500 tons and over, and 1,760 of these were engaged in overseas voyages. Nearly all these ships, coasters as well as ocean-going vessels, had to be fitted, at some time, with guns, degaussing apparatus for countering magnetic mines, emergency rafts, and a great quantity of other safety equipment, some of which had to be specially installed and not just taken on board.

Fitting a gun was not just a matter of a few bolts through the deck. A special platform had to be built and more often than not it was necessary for extra stiffening to be introduced to enable the hull to stand the strain of the gun's recoil.

Bridge-houses had to be protected from aerial machine gun fire. This was done in some cases by fitting concrete slabs, and armour-plating and an ingenious bulletresisting plastic were also used. Other parts of the ship had also to be altered.

CONSTANT CHANGES

Adding considerably to the total amount of work, was the fact that it could not all be done at one time. Requirements changed with changes in the enemy's weapons and tactics, and as defensive answers were found. Early in the second World War, while many ships were having their defensive guns installed, scientists were still grappling with the reply to the magnetic mine ; those ships had to return to the repair yard for the installation of a degaussing cable, which was the successful countermeasure to the new weapon.

BACK TO SEA AGAIN
The new "Imperial Transport" leaves her dock, to return to her job of conveying cargoes of oil fuel, upon which all the fighting services depend. The importance of speedily returning the "Imperial Transport" to service needs no emphasizing, for she can carry 12,500 tons of oil

Similarly, merchant ships were originally equipped with a single gun aft in the vain hope that the Germans would abide by International Law, which provided that a defensively armed ship must be warned before attack and the safety of the crew and ship's papers must be assured. When air attacks developed, however, additional anti-aircraft guns of different types were fitted in different parts of the ship. Again, this necessitated more visits to the repair or "conversion" yards.

MANNING THE GUNS

What this involved in the way of extra work is shown by these few facts about the arming of merchant ships. In the first six months of the second World War 1,900 ships were defensively armed, and by the end of the first year nearly 3,000 had been equipped. Yet in a later year, 1941, all but 13,000 anti-aircraft guns were fitted in merchant ships; some of this work was done abroad, but most of it in the ports of the United Kingdom. On top of that, 4,843 ships of different sizes and nationalities were fitted with anti-aircraft devices other than guns. There was practically an unending flow of this sort of work.

D.E.M.S. PERSONNEL

With all this gun-power on board, defensive though it was, merchant ships somewhat changed their character. The guns had to be manned and that meant trained gunlayers. Thus the maritime regiments of " Defensively Equipped Merchant Ships " gunlayers gradually evolved. The additional personnel had to be accommodated: easy enough in a new ship to rob a bit more cargo or deck space for larger crews' quarters; by no means easy in a vessel built twenty years ago, with quarters already cramped! Here was one more conversion demand of considerable size. It had to be met.

Most of the war-servicing of merchant ships, though it weighed heavily on sorely taxed facilities and labour, represented minor conversion work considered as individual jobs. But it all had to be dovetailed into the shipyard programme so that congestion was avoided as far as possible, so that sufficient ships were kept at sea, and so that the seamen were, with least delay, given every available means of hitting back at the enemy.

Major conversions were of a different nature. A passenger liner with spacious rooms and expensive furnishings will not make an efficient auxiliary cruiser without a great deal of work and a lot of new equipment. The accommodation must be practically stripped, public rooms redesigned, hull strengthened, guns—offensive guns—installed fore and aft, extra buoyance provided, armour-plating fitted, and a hundred other things that make up the difference between a floating hotel and a fighting ship. Many large liners were transformed in this way.

CONVERSION OF MERCHANT SHIPS

Little less extensive was the work of converting passenger ships to troop transports and hospital ships. They might be small cross-channel vessels, or huge liners, the *Queen Mary* and *Queen Elizabeth* among them. It was not unknown for a troopship to be converted into a cargo carrier and reconverted as a trooper between one voyage and the next so great was the pressure on shipping space.

There were many other sorts of conversion jobs involving the largest and the smallest of vessels. Trawlers and excursion steamers into minesweepers and minelayers were among the many jobs. The functions of many hundreds of ships changed with war, and usually the ship had to be changed accordingly.

Routes changed also. Ships built for no more arduous a winter route than the South Atlantic carried tanks and aeroplanes to Russia's arctic ports, through ice and blizzard and temperatures of 52 degrees of frost. They could not do that without alteration to equipment and accommodation—additional heating, lining of cabins, improved ventilation, and strengthening the hull against ice pressure.

Conversions, as well as repairs were, in fact, out of all proportion to the work carried out in 1914-18. That must be remembered when output is compared with output. The war was begun in 1939 with barely a third of the shipyard workers employed in 1918. Though it was man-

than at any time in the last war, when there were more yards, more men and no blitz and blackout. And at that time nearly half the shipbuilding labour of the country was employed on repair work! Though new labour was by then coming along very slowly, production continued to advance, and the shipyards received a measure of priority that had been lacking. No class of war production could better the record of the British shipyards, if it is fully examined.

ARMING BRITAIN'S MERCHANT SHIPS

D.E.M.S., the department of Defensively Equipped Merchant Ships, was responsible for fitting vessels with guns and equipment to withstand U-boats and other enemy attacks. For installing guns, the structure of the ship had to be strengthened, and this work was divided between building and repair yards. Picture shows a gun being lowered to deck of a merchant ship

power that placed the limit on production, yet in the first two and a half years of war British shipyards built a greater tonnage of naval and merchant ships than in the first three years of the first World War, apart from the tremendous volume of repair and conversion work, far exceeding that turned out in all 1914-18.

The Deputy Prime Minister declared in the spring of 1942 that the actual current production of ships was then greater

If it is true that no two ship repair jobs are alike, that is equally true of salvage. No disabled ship presents exactly the same problem to the salvor as another. Yet every vessel capable of being saved must, in wartime, be brought into port, despite the constant dangers while limping home without convoy protection.

As in the case of repairs, the demand for salvage services from the outbreak of war far exceeded the needs of peace. The authorities were able to fall back on the great experience gained in 1914-18, but, unfortunately, the fine equipment and salvage fleet built up in those years, no longer existed when the call came in 1939. Owing to lack of support and to the keen competition of continental firms, particularly Dutch and German, British salvage facilities had been allowed to decline seriously. Extensive Admiralty equipment had been dispersed.

The Admiralty Salvage Service in 1914-18 had been built up largely on the vessels and personnel of the Liverpool Salvage Association. This Association was formed in 1857 by shipowners, merchants, and underwriters of marine insurance to act in their common interests. Between the two wars, it was amalgamated with the Glasgow Salvage Association, another old established concern operating on similar lines.

Again in 1939 the Liverpool and Glasgow Salvage Association, with its specially designed plant and trained personnel, formed the nucleus of the country's salvage resources. In a single year (1941) the Association successfully salved a number of merchant ships representing 385,400 tons gross, much of it loaded with valuable cargoes, which were also saved. Besides the association, which is a non-profit making concern, there were three or four important private salvage and towage firms as well as a number of smaller companies normally engaged chiefly in towage.

A MILLION TONS SAVED

Between the spring of 1940 and March 1941 the number of salvage vessels available had doubled. In less than eighteen months more than 1,000,000 tons had been rescued, as well as much cargo and equipment from vessels that had had to be abandoned. The jobs, all vitally important, varied from such complicated tasks as the raising of the submarine *Thetis* in Liverpool Bay (she sank before the outbreak of

war) to a simple towage in calm weather.

Not all towage operations, however, are simple. The rescue of the cargo steamer *Macbeth* was typical of the sort of work the salvage tugs might expect at any time. The ship broke down in mid-Atlantic during the notorious winter storms of 1941-42. A tug stationed at a Canadian base was sent to tow her back to Canada.

The gale was in the wrong direction and got steadily worse; after towing the steamer about 400 miles the tug was compelled to return to her base to refuel, leaving the *Macbeth* wallowing helplessly, a sitting target for any prowling U-boat.

A NOTABLE RESCUE

While the tug was refuelling for another rescue attempt, it was decided to send a tug from the British side of the Atlantic to tow the *Macbeth* to a United Kingdom port, and the *Zwarte Zee*, a famous Dutch salvage tug, with her Dutch crew, was detailed for the job. The *Zwarte Zee* was the largest and most powerful salvage vessel in the world, but she got a hammering from the weather on her way out. Her lifeboat and jollyboat were washed overboard, the raft was smashed, all the hatch covers were torn off. At times this powerfully engined vessel, capable of over seventeen knots, could not exceed five knots. Nevertheless, she found the *Macbeth*, rolling heavily in a beam sea. Soon afterwards the other tug arrived from the Canadian side. She was eventually sent back to her base.

The *Zwarte Zee* got her heavy 6-inch towing wire ready; no easy matter with heavy seas constantly crashing over the deck and throwing the gear all over the place. Oil was pumped overboard to calm the sea, and a heavy line was somehow got across to the *Macbeth*. As the *Macbeth* could not raise steam on her winches or anchor windlass, her entire crew were mustered to haul in, first a 3-inch rope and, finally, the heavy 6-inch towing wire.

After tremendous efforts the wire was got on board and made fast to the anchor cable, and the *Zwarte Zee* started her long tow through hail and snowstorms. At last the weather moderated. In six days the *Macbeth* was towed a distance of 900 miles and brought safely into port.

Many wonderful feats of salvage were performed by ships' crews without the aid of special salvage craft. Another vessel, with her back partly broken, beached and given up for lost, was brought to port under her own power, with improvised steering gear, a distance of 2,000 miles through many air attacks. In the Atlantic a ship was hove to in a tremendous storm when her engines stopped. This exposed her to the full brunt of the storm. Then came a crash which shook the vessel as if she had struck a mine; in the engine-room pieces of metal were sent flying and clouds of steam followed. The exhausted crew waited for the end, expecting the vessel to sink. Eventually, it was discovered that the crash had come, not from mine or torpedo, but from a tremendous wave which had smashed in the hull plates and seriously fractured a steam pipe.

SAVING A WHALER

Ten days later that vessel reached port with a full cargo of oil. Another tanker, the *Tachee*, partly steaming under her own power and partly in tow by a corvette, was brought 592 miles in 5½ days after having been torpedoed and set on fire. The master and chief engineer of the *Tachee* were awarded the O.B.E.

A valuable ship which was saved under great difficulties was the whaling factory ship *Svend Foyn*, a British vessel of 14,800 tons manned by Norwegians. She was homeward bound with 20,000 tons of oil in her tanks when she ran into bad weather. Two of her lifeboats were washed away, and two of her rafts were pounded to pieces on her decks. Then she was attacked by a U-boat and torpedoed.

The *Svend Foyn* opened fire on the U-boat and drove her off, but a hole had been blown in her side, and the sea came washing in. The ship had to be trimmed, and some of the fuel oil pumped from her tanks, but the valves lay 10 feet deep below swirling black oil and water.

SIX BOILERS ADRIFT

In the meantime the storm had increased. Down in the 'tween decks some of the 60-ton boilers, in which whale blubber is rendered down, had broken adrift and were crashing about with the movement of the ship. Six of these huge boilers smashed their way through the gap in the ship's side and fell into the sea, enlarging the hole to 70 feet wide by 40 feet deep.

But the valves had to be freed. Under the direction of the chief engineer four young pump men in their 'teens put on diving equipment and went down into the swirling oil, seawater, and crashing machinery. It was useless to attempt to use an underwater torch—the most powerful torch made would not penetrate 6 inches through the black, viscous oil. Everything had to be done by touch. It was a dangerous as well as difficult task. At last they succeeded in freeing the valves, the pump got to work, and the ship was restored to an even keel.

The *Svend Foyn*'s troubles were not over. In the words of the captain: "For two and a half days we experienced really terrible weather, heavy storms and a gale from the south-west. I was afraid the ship would break amidships, as the seas were so heavy, and the vessel vibrated a great deal." But this vessel, built on the Tees, was worthy of the seamanship of men trained in the hard school of the Antarctic. The *Svend Foyn* was brought safely into port, with the bulk of her precious cargo intact—now a job for the repairer.

Such were the men and methods that kept the Red Ensign flying.

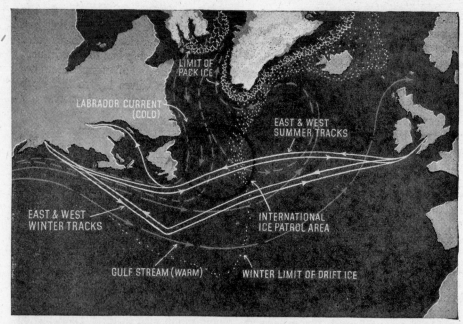

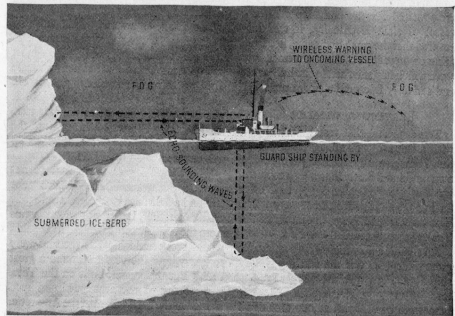

INTERNATIONAL ICE PATROL

Fig. 1. *After the sinking of the "Titanic" in 1912, the International Ice Patrol was established. Top shows the wide area of the North Atlantic over which the Patrol operates to guard against the recurrence of such disasters, and also the limits of the ice drifts. Lower picture indicates fog areas. The guard ship stands by to warn vessels of the presence of an iceberg*

CHAPTER 8

How Ships Find Their Way

Fixing position by the stars. The first chronometer. Winds, tides and currents. Soundings for depth of water. The magnetic compass. How the gyro-compass works. Improvements in the sextant. The Patent Log. Hurricane perils. Pilots, lighthouses, lightships. Rules of the road at sea. Navigating by wireless, lights and buoys.

"CAN you tell me where I am?" or "Can you tell me how to get to Marbury?"—or some other town or village. How frequently pedestrians or motorists have put such a question to passers-by, though they were in their own country and had well-made roads, with distinctly marked signposts, at their service—at least, in times of peace. Consider the difference when a ship puts out from port, and her captain must find his way over the great waste of waters.

You can better appreciate the vast extent of the sea, and, consequently, how difficult the problems of navigation are, if you keep a few simple facts in mind. The superficial area of the earth is 196,836,000 square miles; only about one-third is land, and the rest is sea.

We speak of the seven seas, but you could say that they are all one, for there are no boundaries as on the land. So how does a ship find its way when it passes out of sight of land? It is very rarely that the captain loses his way, though he has no signposts or roads. He navigates his ship towards its destination with complete confidence that he will get there, and, in these days of steam or motor power, we can make sure of getting there on a certain day, if not at a specified hour.

The sea has its deeps and shallows. Islands standing out of the ocean, level for all to see in clear weather, may be shrouded from sight in fog or mist. Rocks awash at half tide may be covered at full tide, and the navigator must know the exact position of these perils. Coral reefs, marked on the chart (P.D.) to indicate that their position is doubtful, provide yet another snare for the mariner. Icefields of varying size, which move from the North Polar regions southwards annually have to be taken into account. Icebergs which float northward towards Cape Horn from the South Polar regions —some are 20 miles in length—are a very real danger to shipping in the North Atlantic at certain times of the year (Fig. 1), especially in the fog areas.

BRITAIN'S LEAD IN RESEARCH

The disaster to the *Titanic*, which sank in 1912 after colliding with an iceberg, led to the establishment of the International Ice Patrol in the North Atlantic.

There are also islands which appear and disappear, such as the questionable Elizabeth Island of Drake, some hundreds of miles west of Cape Horn, which was probably of volcanic origin.

The British nation has expended much money, has devoted much time and research to the scientific improvement of navigation, and this work has been of great benefit to the whole world.

Flamsteed, the English Astronomer Royal and a friend of Isaac Newton,

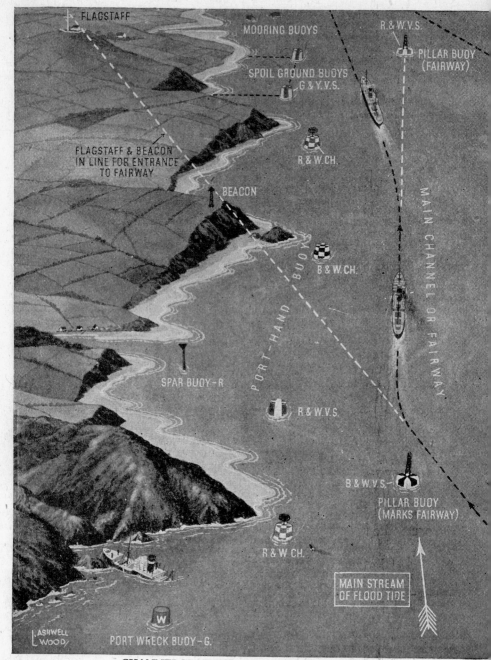

FLAGSTAFF

MOORING BUOYS

R. & W. V.S.

PILLAR BUOY
(FAIRWAY)

SPOIL GROUND BUOYS
G. & Y. V.S.

R. & W. CH.

FLAGSTAFF & BEACON
IN LINE FOR ENTRANCE
TO FAIRWAY

BEACON

B. & W. CH.

PORT-HAND BUOYS

MAIN CHANNEL OR FAIRWAY

SPAR BUOY—R

R. & W. V.S.

B. & W. V.S.

PILLAR BUOY
(MARKS FAIRWAY)

R. & W. CH.

MAIN STREAM
OF FLOOD TIDE

ASHWELL
WOOD

PORT WRECK BUOY—G.

CHANNELS, SANDBANKS, WRECKS, MOORING GROUNDS,

*This composite drawing shows how the different types of buoys are placed to help mariners
and their ships. As in Admiralty Charts, they are indicated by letters (inset, right). Starboard-
hand buoys are always conical in shape, and painted one colour. Port-hand buoys, in two*

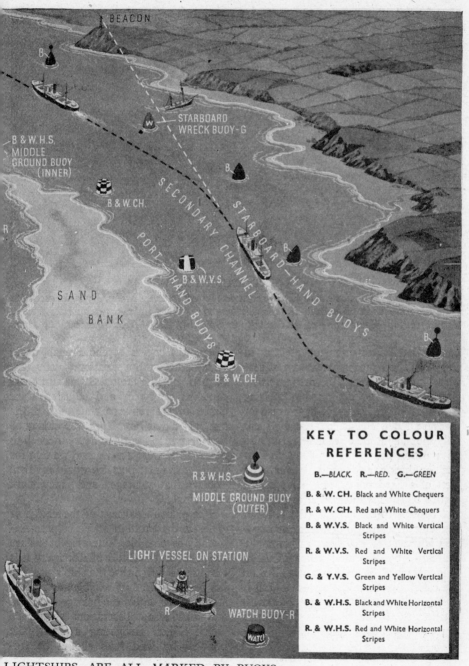

BEACON

B

STARBOARD
WRECK BUOY-G

B & W.H.S.
MIDDLE
GROUND BUOY
(INNER)

B & W. CH.

B

R

SAND

BANK

B & W.V.S.

B & W. CH.

B

R & W. H.S.
MIDDLE GROUND BUOY
(OUTER)

LIGHT VESSEL ON STATION

R

WATCH BUOY-R

KEY TO COLOUR REFERENCES

B.—BLACK.   R.—RED.   G.—GREEN

B. & W. CH.	Black and White Chequers
R. & W. CH.	Red and White Chequers
B. & W.V.S.	Black and White Vertical Stripes
R. & W.V.S.	Red and White Vertical Stripes
G. & Y.V.S.	Green and Yellow Vertical Stripes
B. & W.H.S.	Black and White Horizontal Stripes
R. & W.H.S.	Red and White Horizontal Stripes

LIGHTSHIPS, ARE ALL MARKED BY BUOYS

colours, are always can shaped. Middle-ground buoys wear horizontal stripes and are spherical. Spar buoys mark special positions, such as wrecks. Pillar buoys indicate the fairway, and watch buoys tell the position of lightships. Details of all types of buoys are given on page 180

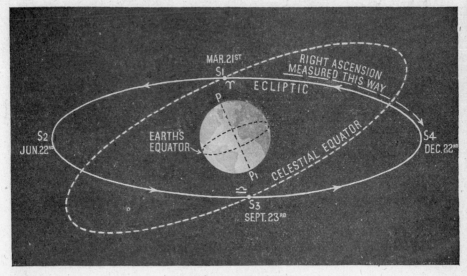

RIGHT ASCENSION

Fig. 2.   *A ship's position can be fixed by observations of heavenly bodies. By right ascension of a heavenly body is meant its celestial longitude. The right ascension runs from 0 degrees to 360 degrees, or—as it is usually expressed in time—from 0 hours to 24 hours*

compiled the first catalogue of stars in the English language for the use of seamen. It was, probably, the first extensive compendium of astronomical data. Using the meridian of Greenwich as the zero for measurements, Flamsteed provided not only the magnitude of each star, but also its position from the equator and its position during the day and night east and west of a fixed point. The plane of the earth's equator is inclined at an angle of $23\frac{1}{2}$ degrees to the ecliptic (the plane of the sun's apparent path). The right ascension is measured eastwards in hours and minutes from the first point of Aries (Fig. 2), which is used as a meridian on the celestial sphere just as Greenwich is used on the earth. Owing to the earth's rotation, the whole celestial sphere seems to rotate about the celestial axis.

FIXING SHIP'S POSITION

Flamsteed's list of stars became the *Nautical Almanac*, a title it still retains. He gave to seamen the Prime Meridian,

which was copied by the French, using Paris, and by the Russians, using St. Petersburg. The United States and other countries followed, and adjusted their clocks to the required time. When the sun is rising at New York, the citizen of San Francisco has three hours of sleep to come. If he were a navigator, waiting for daylight to enter port, he would regulate orders for pilotage and movement accordingly.

The primary concern of the navigator is to fix the position of his ship as frequently as possible. When log books are called for in the Court of Admiralty it is essential to prove that the ship's position has been obtained by reliable observation at noon each day of the passage. At dawn and dusk also, observations should be taken. When navigating a coast, the position by land fixes should be frequently taken to avoid dangers.

At sea, when out of sight of land, both latitude and longitude must be found in order to obtain the position of the ship by

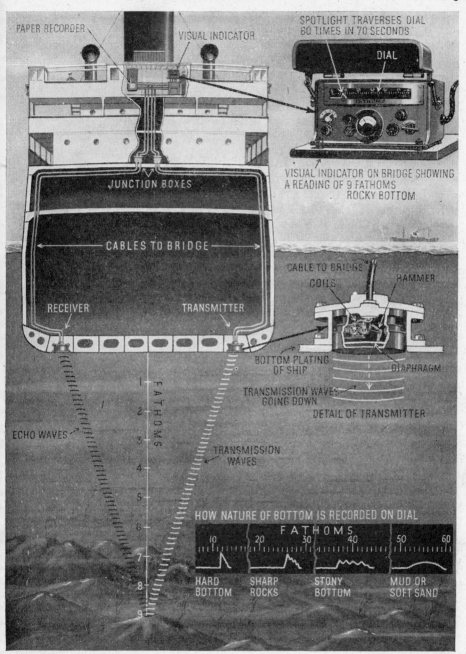

PAPER RECORDER

VISUAL INDICATOR

SPOTLIGHT TRAVERSES DIAL
60 TIMES IN 70 SECONDS

DIAL

VISUAL INDICATOR ON BRIDGE SHOWING
A READING OF 9 FATHOMS
ROCKY BOTTOM

JUNCTION BOXES

CABLES TO BRIDGE

RECEIVER

TRANSMITTER

CABLE TO BRIDGE
COILS   HAMMER

BOTTOM PLATING
OF SHIP

DIAPHRAGM

TRANSMISSION WAVES
GOING DOWN

DETAIL OF TRANSMITTER

FATHOMS

ECHO WAVES

TRANSMISSION
WAVES

HOW NATURE OF BOTTOM IS RECORDED ON DIAL

FATHOMS

10   20   30   40   50   60

HARD
BOTTOM

SHARP
ROCKS

STONY
BOTTOM

MUD OR
SOFT SAND

AUTOMATIC RECORDS OF DEPTH OF WATER AND NATURE OF SEA BED

Fig. 3. *This apparatus electrically records depth of water under a ship, and shows the nature of the sea bed. An electrically controlled hammer strikes a diaphragm in the transmitter. The impulses pass to the sea bed, return to the receiver, and are recorded on the bridge*

the intersection of their two lines. These "lines of position" are obtained by observing the altitude and position of two or more stars. In coastal navigation a "fix" is obtained by cross-bearings, two, or more, points of land being used to do this. It is obvious that both these operations amount to the same in effect, and are fundamentals in navigation.

SAILING BY THE POLE STAR

The Vikings, who before A.D. 1000 were covering voyages exceeding 2000 miles, did not trouble about longitude: they used the land to give them their "eastery" and "westery" landfalls. Probably they observed the Pole star for latitude on their many voyages from Bergen to the Shetlands, Faröe Islands, and Greenland, because this star has the distinction, not available for the help of the mariner in any other star of such magnitude, of giving the latitude in degrees approximately according to its elevation. That is to say, if you are in the latitude of 40 degrees north, about the latitude of New York, the Pole star will be riding the heavens 40 degrees above the horizon level. This ready check was known to the Alexandrians and, later, to the Moors, who were navigating long before the Vikings.

Magellan and his successors found the need for determining longitude. Our Elizabethan seamen, Drake, Davis and others, developed the practice of taking simultaneous observations of two stars.

There was great need for some form of watch to gauge the correct intervals of time, and mark the difference of longitude. In 1766 the British Government offered a reward for a clock capable of maintaining a very high standard of correctness for navigation. The result was a chronometer designed with a compensation balance to meet changes of climate. It was invented by John Harrison, of Yorkshire, who received £20,000 for his ingenuity. At this time Captain Cook was preparing for one of his many long voyages of discovery.

The British began seriously to survey the Seven Seas in 1795, in which year the Hydrographic Department of the Admiralty was formed. Since that date it has grown to be the largest organization of its kind in the world, producing charts, sailing directions, and the most complete information possible of winds, tides, and currents in every part of the globe.

England, always in the forefront of maritime discovery, ultimately laid down the method by which the time of tide (high water), and height of tide (level), could be predicted, and issued tide tables for the use of mariners. Later, Professor William Thomson, who became Lord Kelvin, invented and patented a machine for the easy prediction of these elements without figuring out details by mathematics. This revolutionary achievement enabled tide tables to be prepared for all parts of the world.

Lord Kelvin again came to the help of sailors with a method of ascertaining the depth of water. Measurement in deep water was not only a laborious operation, but sometimes required that the ship should be stopped, and caused delay.

LORD KELVIN'S DISCOVERIES

Lord Kelvin coloured sounding tubes with chemical solution, and the pressure of water, as the sounding-lead descended, caused the tube to become changed in colour and so to represent the increase in depth. His sounding machine enabled vessels, proceeding at speed, to take deep water soundings without stopping. For thousands of years, in his dugout, raft, or sea-going vessel, man had been using a line with a weight attached, but all this was changed by the practical application of the new method. In the years that followed deep-sea sounding became the subject of much intensive research.

During the voyage of H.M.S. *Beagle* (1831-36), oceanography—the science which deals in detail with the depths of the ocean—was made the subject of special study by Charles Darwin, who reported many profound matters with a most valuable simplicity.

About the year 1909 some American engineers, by using a Fessenden oscillator, found it possible to gauge the depth under a ship by sending a note downwards and listening for the echo, much as one can do in the atmosphere where there exists a wall or means for creating the reverberation to reflect the sound. What was wanted was an accurate method of measuring the depth or distance. Acoustic sounding had been born. In the research that followed the first World War, the British Admiralty produced the echo sounder, by which a hammer sent out a note receivable on a measuring dial actuated by an electric current (Fig. 3). Variation of depth could be known by the rise and fall in the hammer notes with variation of speed. An ordinary loudspeaker trumpet was used in these early stages, and even in shallow water the depth could be measured within three feet. In 1924 the Port of London Authority fitted one such machine, made by Henry Hughes & Son, in their survey ship *St. Katharine.*

From the acoustic to the non-acoustic has been a short step. It was quickly found by trial and error that it was not necessary to hear the note at all, as a high-frequency electrical impulse, noiseless yet more accurate in its behaviour, would register without noise. Moreover, it could be connected to a make-and-break light, as is done with another type, and be made to indicate the depth visually on a scale. A roll of photographic paper, set moving during soundings, gives a permanent record.

The Magnetic Compass deserves a place of honour to itself, for it is as indispensable as the seaman's anchor, which holds a ship fast when the engines are stopped, or the sails are furled. When the ship is under way the compass indicates;

POINTS OF THE COMPASS

Fig. 4. *There are thirty-two points of the compass—four cardinal points: N, S, E, W; four half cardinal points: NE, NW, SE, SW; eight three-letter points: NNE, ENE, etc.; sixteen "by" points: N by E, NE by N, etc. In the compass there are 360 degrees, which are divided into quarters of 90 degrees each. One point = 11¼ degrees*

(*a*) the direction in which the ship is going, (*b*) the positions of headlands, buoys, lights, sun, moon and stars. All these are measured on a horizontal circle with reference to the North-South line.

The compass is constructed on the principle of suspending magnets in such a manner that, remaining horizontal, they are free to take up the direction in which the magnetism of the earth draws them. This direction is termed the magnetic meridian. A circular compass card is fixed to the compass needles, or magnets, and divided into four quarters of a circle—North, South, East, West. Each quarter is divided into eight equal parts called points, making thirty-two points of the compass (Fig. 4). The edge of the card is graduated into 360 degrees. Dry card compasses are used for ships where shock is not severe, but where heavy guns are discharged the compass card is confined in a bowl containing spirit, thus reducing vibration. The compass itself is mounted on gimbals, so that in bad weather, however much the ship may roll or pitch, the compass continues to remain, as it were, on an even keel.

PRINCIPLES OF GYRO-COMPASS

The gyro-compass is a later development. This instrument has the same utility as the magnetic compass from the seaman's standpoint, but, whereas the magnetic compass does not require energy to make it useful, the gyroscope is of no use without that energy. Like a top, it must be started spinning, and like a hoop speeding along the surface of a road it remains on its course, travelling in a straight line, as long as it has momentum. If a force is impressed at the top of the right-hand side, the hoop then travels to the left and falls over to that side; to correct it again a force must be impressed at the top left-hand side. This movement in the hoop is reproduced in the gyro-compass, and is known as *precession*. The gyro comes under the laws of rotating bodies, which state that "Any rotating mass, such as a spinning wheel, tends to swing round so as to bring its axis of rotation parallel to that of any externally applied force, and in such relation that its direction of rotation is the same as that of the applied force" (Fig. 5).

With the gyro-compass the applied force is that of the earth revolving about its axis. At the equator, where the earth's directive force is at maximum, the gyro-compass points true North, but, as a ship with a gyro-compass changes latitude, the directive force lessens until it becomes nil at the Pole. The adjustments of the gyro-compass may be found in the handbooks dealing with this instrument.

CHARTS AND THEIR USES

Gyroscopic control, to keep a ship, or an aeroplane, on its course, belongs to the same field of research that developed fire control and torpedo directors in the navy. An advantage the gyro-compass control has over the magnetic is that the former is not affected by electrical or magnetic disturbances of the earth.

For very many years the compass existed without the chart, but today, in first-class navigation, consideration of the chart is indispensable for a proper answer to the question : "How do ships find their way ?"

The chart is a representation of part of the earth's surface—it also has the depths of the sea marked on it. It shows capes, islands, headlands, and topography. As the earth is an oblate spheroid —i.e. it is round but flattened at the poles —the flat surface of a chart cannot show the curvature or rotundity. So for many years navigators had difficulty until Mercator, the Flemish geographer, invented his system of projection which showed the meridians of longitude parallel and not converging. In the new method the convergence was compensated for by adjusting the lines of latitude according to the curvature correction.

Mercator's chart was invented as long ago as the sixteenth century, but it still holds favour with navigators.

The sextant is now an essential part of a navigator's equipment, and is the principal instrument used in finding positions at sea. The position of ships may be fixed by means of direction-finding wireless bearings transmitted from suitable stations on land, but these are not infallible, an accuracy greater than a 6-inch theodolite. Since the radius of the sextant is greater, the subdivisions can be bisected to ten seconds of arc—which is hardly possible on a small theodolite.

During the past thirty years improvements in sextants include: (1) greater

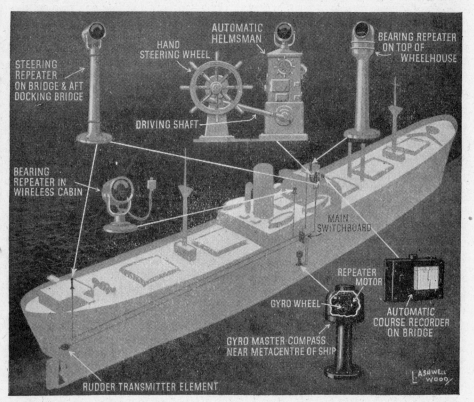

THE GYRO-COMPASS AND MECHANICAL PILOT

Fig. 5. *The gyro-compass is operated by the rotation of the earth and points to the north. A gyro-wheel spinning at high speed has a strong tendency to maintain its axis in a fixed direction—this is made to coincide with true north. The automatic helmsman keeps the ship on a straight course. From the master compass repeaters constantly indicate the direction of the ship's head*

and the ship's receiver may become damaged, whereas the sextant, a more durable instrument, can be subject to much hard wear and tear without injury.

The sextant is used to measure angles of sun, moon, or stars on the vertical or horizontal planes—or even at oblique angles. For horizontal angles it possesses telescopic range for star operations; (2) the micrometer method of reading the Vernier subdivisions; (3) wider field of observation. In the matter of accuracy let this fact be considered. The writer has, in co-operation with other officers (their observations being averaged), fixed by sextant the ship's position within 300 to 400 yards of the precise measurement by taut wire during cable-laying operations in the Atlantic.

To use the sextant, one has only to remember that the angle at which a celestial object strikes down at the mirror of the sextant (angle of incidence) is equal to the angle measured to the horizon (angle of reflection). Hence, the observer must look steadily at the horizon, moving the index, or mirror, arm until he finds that he has the vertical dimension. He then clamps the arm to the arc and, turning the sextant face upwards, reads the degrees on the arc and the minutes and seconds on the Vernier (Fig. 6).

The ship's chronometer (Fig. 7) is used for determining longitude. This it does with great accuracy owing to Harrison's invention (1766) of a compensation, or expansion, balance to meet changes of temperature. It is a specialized clock which carries Greenwich Mean Time to any part of the world, and also fixes longitude at sea.

The difference between a ship's time in mid-Atlantic and the chronometer time is longitude because time in hours, minutes and seconds is convertible into degrees, minutes and seconds of arc by the equation that one hour of sun travel is equal to 15 degrees of longitude. Therefore, when it is noon at Greenwich, it is only 11 hours a.m. at 15 degrees west longitude. There is the rhyming rule:—

Longitude East Greenwich time least
Longitude West Greenwich time best

WHY SHIP'S TIME CHANGES

The navigator, like the tailor, chops off or cuts up as much as he requires for his navigation. When travelling westward, he is moving towards the setting sun. He is going to places where noon is always later than at Greenwich. When travelling eastward, moving towards the rising sun, he finds that his clock, adjusted for longitude, is showing noon to be earlier than Greenwich.

In order that we shall not turn day into night we have to put our ship's clock right at least every twenty-four hours, if not more frequently, while keeping the chronometer at Greenwich Mean Time. Thus, we are stealing a march on the sun —owing to the earth's rotation from left to right—and in travelling or flying around the world eastwards we gain twenty-four hours on the clock as compared with the time when we left Greenwich. This gain of clock time was used by Jules Verne in his famous story-book, "Around the World in Eighty Days." The traveller, on reaching Westminster, thought he had nearly lost his wager, only to find that, owing to this gain in time, he had done the journey in seventy-nine days, thus winning the wager with a day to spare.

HOW THE LOG WORKS

Ships are able to measure their passage through the water by means of a rotating propeller-like metal contrivance attached to a specially woven line. This line does not twist, but imparts to a clock on the stern of the ship a number of revolutions according to speed. This is called the Patent Log. The propeller, or rotator, is streamed so as to keep fairly in the water at distances varying with the type of ship. The clock is read regularly, usually every two hours, and the distance noted in the log-book.

Patent Logs also operate from tubes in the bottom or sides of a ship, in which case the pressure due to speed is the registering factor (Fig. 8). A handicap with this type, however, is its tendency to become weed-grown and choked. Before the invention of the Patent Log, sailing ships used a sand-glass, which measured the seconds taken for a line to run out, the line having knots to mark the speed at which the ship was moving. Hence the term "knot," which is used to denote the number of nautical miles covered by a ship in one hour. When we say a ship is

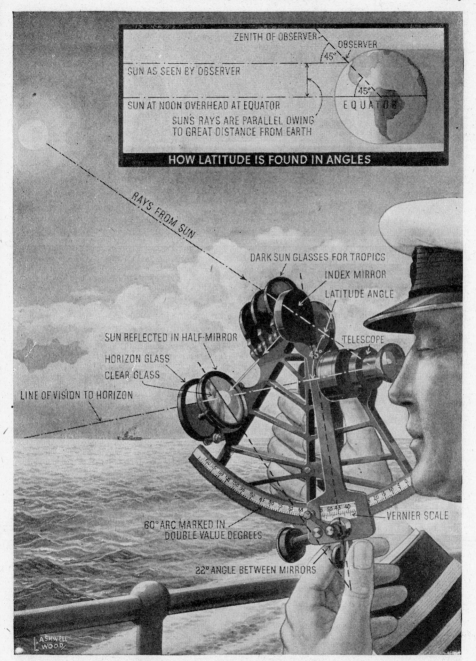

ZENITH OF OBSERVER
OBSERVER
45°
SUN AS SEEN BY OBSERVER
SUN AT NOON OVERHEAD AT EQUATOR
EQUATOR
45°
SUN'S RAYS ARE PARALLEL OWING
TO GREAT DISTANCE FROM EARTH

HOW LATITUDE IS FOUND IN ANGLES

RAYS FROM SUN

DARK SUN GLASSES FOR TROPICS
INDEX MIRROR
LATITUDE ANGLE

SUN REFLECTED IN HALF-MIRROR
HORIZON GLASS
CLEAR GLASS
TELESCOPE
45°
LINE OF VISION TO HORIZON

60° ARC MARKED IN
DOUBLE VALUE DEGREES
VERNIER SCALE

22° ANGLE BETWEEN MIRRORS

FINDING LATITUDE FROM THE SEXTANT

Fig. 6. *The sextant, so called because its arc is one-sixth of a circle, is used to measure the altitude of the sun. Obtaining the angle as shown above, the mariner finds his latitude. Inset is shown latitude of 45 degrees when the sun is overhead at noon at the equator*

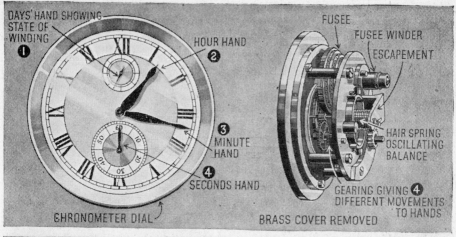

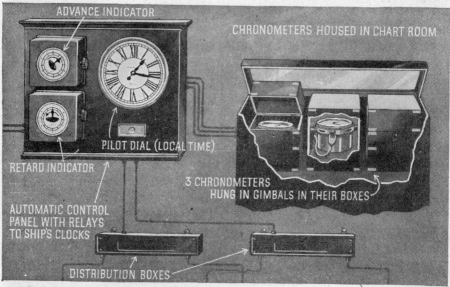

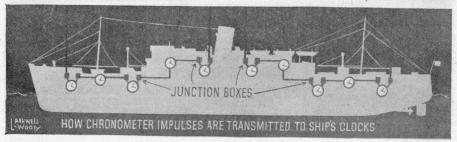

DETAILS OF SHIP'S CHRONOMETERS

Fig. 7. *British chronometers are wonderfully accurate—an error of ten seconds a month being the only rectification needed. Used with the sextant, the chronometer gives exact longitude*

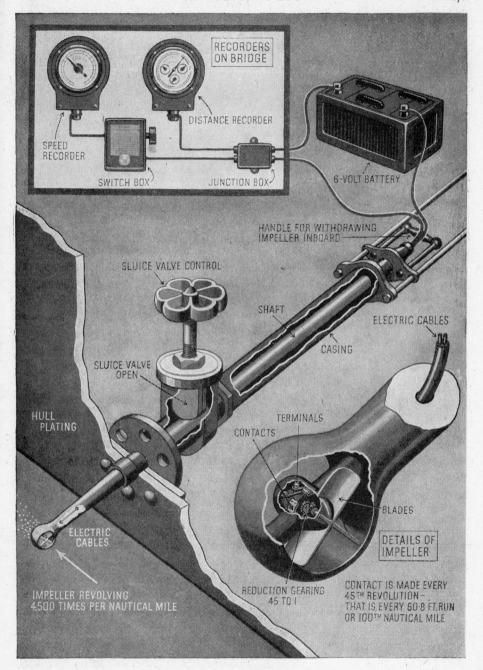

RECORDERS ON BRIDGE

DISTANCE RECORDER

SPEED RECORDER

SWITCH BOX

JUNCTION BOX

6-VOLT BATTERY

HANDLE FOR WITHDRAWING IMPELLER INBOARD

SLUICE VALVE CONTROL

SHAFT

ELECTRIC CABLES

CASING

SLUICE VALVE OPEN

HULL PLATING

TERMINALS

CONTACTS

BLADES

DETAILS OF IMPELLER

ELECTRIC CABLES

REDUCTION GEARING 45 TO 1

IMPELLER REVOLVING 4,500 TIMES PER NAUTICAL MILE

CONTACT IS MADE EVERY 45TH REVOLUTION — THAT IS, EVERY 60.8 FT. RUN OR 100TH NAUTICAL MILE

SPEED AND DISTANCE MEASURED BY PATENT LOG

Fig. 8. *This new electric ship's log gives a continuous record of speed and total distance run by measuring in units of rotation the distance run at any speed from zero to 40 knots*

steaming twenty-one knots we mean that she is covering twenty-one sea miles in one hour. To say "knots per hour" is wrong.

With the instruments and appliances which have been described, let us now set out on a voyage from a West Indian port. Our ship is bound for London.

Pilotage is usually compulsory in foreign ports, and the master, or his agent, orders the pilot on board when the ship is ready for sea. The orders of the pilot rank as the orders of the master. In deep water outside the harbour the pilot is dropped, and we are well started across the Pacific on our four thousand miles journey from Jamaica to London.

HURRICANES AND CYCLONES

Notwithstanding the robust build of ships, weather must always be considered, especially in the hurricane seasons. Hurricanes may be encountered in the vicinity of Rodriguez and Mauritius, or in the West Indies. Cyclones are encountered in the Bay of Bengal, and typhoons in the China Seas. The writer was at Bermuda when H.M.S. *Aeolus* was caught in a hurricane in the West Indies. It was eight bells (noon) and the crew were about to start dinner. There was no dinner on board H.M.S. *Aeolus* that day, for the hurricane threw the ship on her beam ends in a welter of livid foam. She was saved, with great difficulty, by the superb seamanship of Captain Northan, her commander. In the year 1937 a liner navigating the Caribbean Sea became involved in a hurricane which uprooted the funnel, carrying it overboard, together with all deck fittings. The heroic efforts of an apprentice, who crawled from place to place about the stricken vessel in order to stop the inwash of water, contributed to the saving of the ship.

So the mariner finding his way must have good knowledge of the path and velocity of hurricanes. Hurricanes are rotary storms. In northern latitudes they rotate left-handed (or anti-clockwise) and in southern latitudes in the reverse direction. The velocity of the wind in its rotary motion may reach 150 miles per hour, but about 100 miles per hour is more general. Meanwhile, it is progressing on a track which has geographical limitations at the rate of 200 miles per day, but a thousand miles per day has been proved as a possible onward movement. As you can imagine, in the centre of this storm—the vortex—the sea is like a boiling cauldron, rising and falling in pyramidal confusion, magnificent but terrible. Very few ships can survive it.

To avoid the dread danger of the vortex, laws of storms must be known and contact maintained with meteorological centres locally. These storms originate between latitudes 10 and 20 degrees north and south, and on reaching latitudes 20 to 30 degrees recurve and peter out as they travel northwards and southwards. Trinidad escapes the North Atlantic hurricanes which reach Jamaica in the heart of the Caribbean. As they pass over the islands they devastate the vegetation, tear up dwellings as if they were cardboard, and cause incredible damage. The season for these hurricanes in the North Atlantic is between July and October.

DANGEROUS CURRENTS

Ships sailing coastwise have special points in navigation to consider. It is near the land that currents are most unreliable. For instance, in the Bay of Fundy, Canada, the range of tide may exceed forty feet, which causes a great indraught on the flood tide. Therefore, a look-out must be kept for the coastal lights, and the ship's position checked when the lights are observed. The lights vary considerably in power, according to the position of the lighthouse. If the position commands the approach of shipping the candlepower of a lighthouse, such as that at the Lizard in Cornwall, for example,

DIFFERENCE OF SPEED BETWEEN WIRELESS SIGNAL AND SOUND SIGNAL
DETERMINES DISTANCE
WIRELESS 186,000 MILES A SECOND
SOUND SIGNAL 1,100 FEET A SECOND

RADIO DIRECTION FINDER
ON SHIP

WIRELESS WAVES GIVING
CODE SIGN OF LIGHTHOUSE

TWIN FILAMENT LAMPS

PRISM LENSES GIVING
158,000 CANDLE POWER

SOUND WAVES
FROM SIREN

TRANSMITTING
AERIAL

SIREN

KEEPER
ON DUTY

AIR COMPRESSOR
HOUSE

SERVICE ROOMS

OCCULTING CLOCK

COMPRESSED
AIR STORAGE
CYLINDERS

RADIO AND SOUND WARNINGS TO SHIPS

Fig. 9. *Lighthouses warn ships in fog by an automatic recorder which broadcasts the code sign of the lighthouse every 70 seconds. Three blasts are sent out on the fog siren, and the difference of speed between radio and sound warnings enables navigators to fix distances*

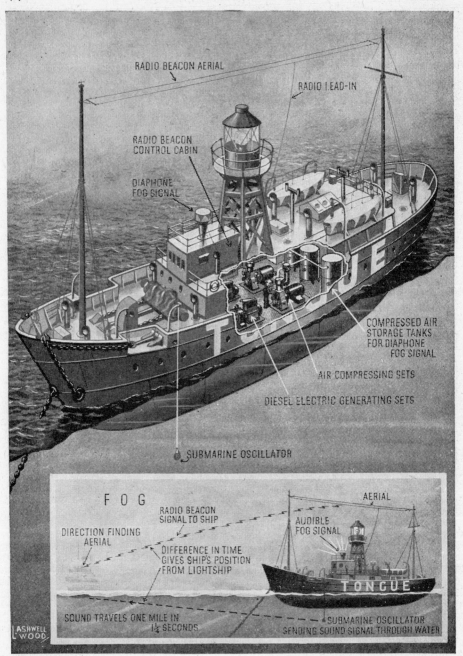

RADIO BEACON AERIAL

RADIO LEAD-IN

RADIO BEACON
CONTROL CABIN

DIAPHONE
FOG SIGNAL

COMPRESSED AIR
STORAGE TANKS
FOR DIAPHONE
FOG SIGNAL

AIR COMPRESSING SETS

DIESEL ELECTRIC GENERATING SETS

SUBMARINE OSCILLATOR

FOG

RADIO BEACON
SIGNAL TO SHIP

AERIAL

AUDIBLE
FOG SIGNAL

DIRECTION FINDING
AERIAL

DIFFERENCE IN TIME
GIVES SHIPS POSITION
FROM LIGHTSHIP

TONGUE

SOUND TRAVELS ONE MILE IN
1¼ SECONDS

SUBMARINE OSCILLATOR
SENDING SOUND SIGNAL THROUGH WATER

ASHWELL WOOD

LATEST TYPE LIGHTSHIP WITH SUBMARINE OSCILLATOR

Direction and distance in times of fog can be obtained from some lightships. The ship receives a warning radio signal in code, and morse dashes every 1¼ seconds are counted. Upon receipt of submarine oscillator signals the distance is known, as every dash represents a mile

may b: of several millions, and .he distance at which it is visible about 25 sea miles on a clear night. In less important positions, lights of lesser power are used (Fig. 9). By means of the Sun Valve, the lamp, when clear daylight comes, can be automatically extinguished. Conversely,

They are employed, however, in special positions which demand a number of lights, when distinguishing characteristics for beacons or buoys are essential. Group-flashing lights, in which two or more flashes are separated by varying intervals of darkness, are used. One of the

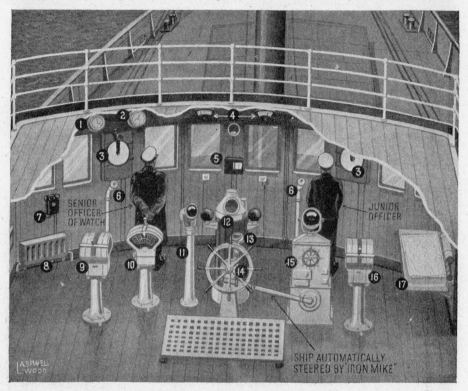

EQUIPMENT ON BRIDGE OF A MODERN MERCHANT SHIP

1, Local time; 2, Greenwich time; 3, clear view screens; 4, revolution indicators; 5, course recorder; 6, voice pipes; 7, telephone; 8, heating radiator; 9, port engine-room telegraph; 10, docking telegraph; 11, gyro steering repeater; 12, magnetic compass; 13, rudder indicator; 14, hand steering; 15, automatic helmsman; 16, starboard engine-room telegraph; 17, chart table

it can be arranged that the lamp becomes illuminated when darkness falls. The ship's position off the coast can be fixed by means of bearings of lights, used as cross bearings, just as in daytime headlands are used for the same purpose.

Coloured lights in lighthouses are used as little as possible, for the simple reason that they lack the intensity of white lights.

most famous of Britain's lighthouses is the Eddystone. The Eddystone rocks lie about fourteen miles off Plymouth, and four lighthouse towers have been built on the reef. Probably the most exposed lighthouse in the world is the Bishop Rock, westernmost rock of the Scilly Isles.

Before the 1914-1918 war it was found possible to use wireless telegraphy for the

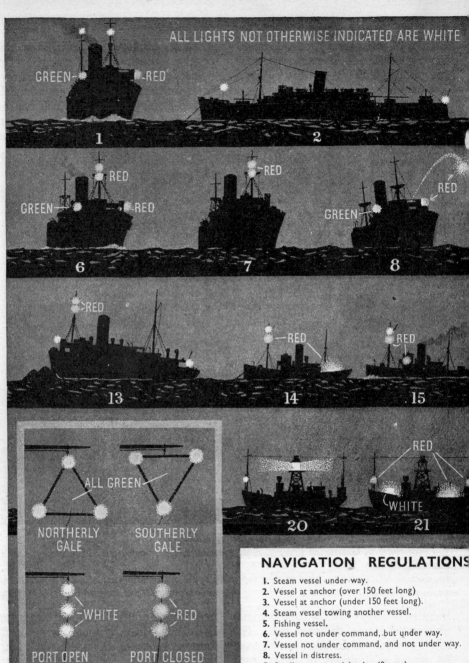

ALL LIGHTS NOT OTHERWISE INDICATED ARE WHITE

GREEN — RED

1

2

RED
GREEN — RED

6

RED

7

RED
GREEN

8

RED

13

RED

14

RED

15

ALL GREEN

NORTHERLY GALE

SOUTHERLY GALE

WHITE

PORT OPEN

RED

PORT CLOSED

HARBOUR SIGNALS

20

RED

WHITE

21

NAVIGATION REGULATIONS

1. Steam vessel under way.
2. Vessel at anchor (over 150 feet long)
3. Vessel at anchor (under 150 feet long).
4. Steam vessel towing another vessel.
5. Fishing vessel.
6. Vessel not under command, but under way.
7. Vessel not under command, and not under way.
8. Vessel in distress.
9. Small steam vessel (under 40 tons).
10. Steam trawler under way.
11. Cable ship not under way.
12. Cable ship under way.

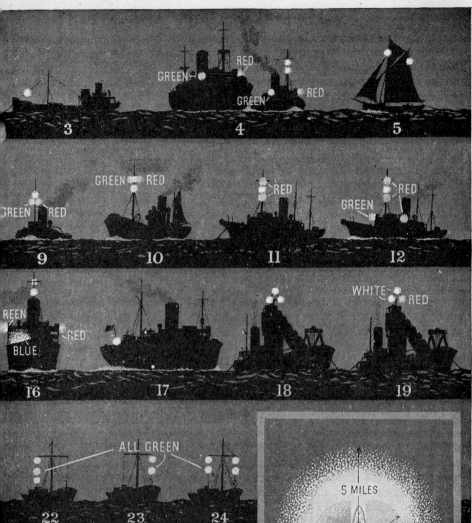

FOR SHIPS' LIGHTS & FLARES

13. Vessel aground.
14. Steam pilot vessel at anchor.
15. Steam pilot vessel under way.
16. Pilot required.
17. Overtaking stern light.
18. Dredger at work (pass either side).
19. Dredger at work (pass on white side only)
20. Lightship on station.
21. Lightship off station.
22. }
23. } Wreck Lights { Pass on starboard hand.
24. } { Pass on port hand.
{ Pass on either side.

RANGE AND POSITION OF
SHIP'S NAVIGATION LIGHTS

correction of chronometers in ships at sea and time signals were transmitted from various high-powered wireless transmission stations for this purpose. It was soon discovered that the direction of the station from the ship could be found by rotating a receiver until the full force of the station was registered, and that by noting the direction of the signal a line could be drawn on the chart to prove that the ship was somewhere on that line of bearing. Fog signals were introduced on this principle, and wireless direction finding of position at sea was thus born.

FIXING POSITION BY WIRELESS

By shutting out other arcs of reception a directional beam was developed, and it was thus possible, by using two stations suitably situated, to obtain cross bearings and thereby fix the position of the ship.

There are two ways in which mariners can obtain a fix by wireless means. Either they can pick up signals from two shore stations, as already described, or they can themselves send out a signal to be picked up by two shore stations which are immediately able to work out the position of the ship and wireless it back. Navigators, however, generally prefer to receive the bearings rather than send them to the chosen stations, as the land stations have more facilities for gauging the accuracy of the signals, which vary in precision by day or by night. They are clearer by night (Fig. 10).

NORTH POLE WIRELESS

As the signals are received over long distances, the shape of the globe must be considered in plotting. This allowance is named convergency, because the meridians converge to the Pole.

If a wireless message were sent from the North Pole, the direction would be south as there is no east and west there. A North Pole wireless station would be situated in an unenviable part of the world from the operator's point of view, but the direction-finding value of the station would be as useful in navigation as the Pole star, and its future installation is probable.

While at sea, ships arrange the hour of arrival in port for the purpose of docking. Large seaports, like London and Liverpool, have dock systems capable of holding many ships, and great quays, with cranes, warehouses, and all facilities for receiving and dispatching cargo.

Docking at low tide means a loss of water in the dock, as the lock must be run down to tide level. Ports, therefore, prefer that ships should enter dock at high tide. To estimate the rise and fall of tide at any place, standard tidal ports are enumerated in tide tables published by the Admiralty in Britain and the U.S. Hydrographic Bureau in the United States. To these standard ports' corrections for various places are supplied.

IMPORTANCE OF TIDES

These are called tidal constants. If the seaman has no tables for tides, he finds by the chart the time of high water at full moon and new moon. To this he adds about forty-five minutes for every twenty-four hours elapsed since these times, which will give him the approximate time of high tide on any day. In the Mediterranean, there is hardly any rise and fall. In the Bristol Channel the rise and fall may exceed 40 feet. At Liverpool it may exceed 30 feet, at London it may exceed 20 feet. Southampton has double tides, i.e., four high levels in each 24 hours. This is due to the flood and ebb of the Channel tide visiting the estuary. Portsmouth, which has a narrow entrance to its harbour (close to Southampton), shuts out the second high water.

Soundings shown in depths on charts are reduced to the common denominator of Low Water Spring Tides. Thus the least favourable conditions for

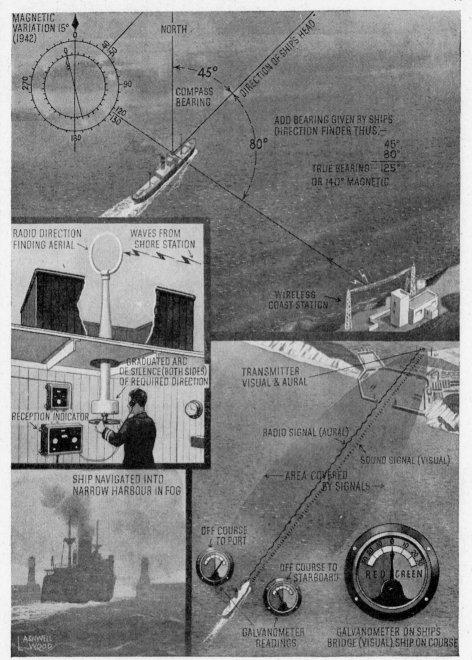

MAGNETIC VARIATION 15° (1942)

NORTH

45°

COMPASS BEARING

DIRECTION OF SHIPS HEAD

80°

ADD BEARING GIVEN BY SHIPS DIRECTION FINDER THUS:—
45°.
80°.
TRUE BEARING 125°
OR 140° MAGNETIC

RADIO DIRECTION FINDING AERIAL

WAVES FROM SHORE STATION

WIRELESS COAST STATION

GRADUATED ARC OF SILENCE (BOTH SIDES) OF REQUIRED DIRECTION

TRANSMITTER VISUAL & AURAL

RECEPTION INDICATOR

RADIO SIGNAL (AURAL)

SOUND SIGNAL (VISUAL)

AREA COVERED BY SIGNALS

SHIP NAVIGATED INTO NARROW HARBOUR IN FOG

OFF COURSE TO PORT

OFF COURSE TO STARBOARD

RED GREEN

GALVANOMETER READINGS

GALVANOMETER ON SHIPS BRIDGE (VISUAL) SHIP ON COURSE

ASHWELL WOOD

RADIO DIRECTION FINDING AND HARBOUR BEACON SIGNALLING

Fig. 10. *By radio direction finding, ships determine exact position by transmissions from known shore stations (top and centre). Harbour beacon signalling permits ships to safely negotiate even the narrowest harbour entrances in fog by aural and visual course indicators (bottom)*

ALL TYPES OF BUOYS WHICH GUIDE THE MARINER

Buoys are used to mark channels, sandbanks, wrecks, shoals and all danger spots. Their positions are marked on charts. Most buoys round our coasts are in charge of Trinity House. International agreement determines buoyage and fixes a standard system to mark wrecks

SHIP C
1-KEEPS CLEAR OF-D
2-ALTERS COURSE TO STARBOARD
                    FOR-A
3-KEEPS ON COURSE FOR-B

SHIP D
1-KEEPS CLEAR OF-A
2- ..   ..   ..-B
3-KEEPS ON COURSE FOR-C

SHIP B
1-KEEPS CLEAR OF-C
2-KEEPS ON COURSE FOR D & A

SHIP A
1- KEEPS CLEAR OF B.
2-ALTERS COURSE TO STARBOARD FOR-C
3-KEEPS ON COURSE FOR-D

ASHWELL WOOD.

RULES OF THE ROAD FOR SHIPS BY DAY

The following principal regulations are illustrated in this composite picture: (1) Two vessels meeting end on, each alters course to starboard; (2) crossing—vessel with the other on her starboard bow keeps clear; (3) power-driven vessels keep clear of sailing craft; (4) vessels overtaking keep clear of the vessel overtaken; (5) vessels keep to the right of the fairway

entering, or lying in harbour, is made clear for the navigator on the chart. Buoys are noted when entering from seaward.

Long before the days of the motor car, which necessitated rules of conduct on the highway, seamen and legislators combined to draw up regulations for preventing collisions at sea, containing safeguards as to manœuvre, and also laying down the colour ranges and design of ships' navigation lights. The starboard side of a ship carries a green light and the port side a red light. On a steamer, or motor-propelled vessel, a masthead, or steaming, light is also carried. On a dark night with a clear atmosphere side lights have a range of about two miles. Masthead lights are visible for five miles.

The rule for navigation of the narrow seas is to keep to the right, that is to the starboard side of a channel. When two ships cross, the vessel having the other on the right, or starboard hand, must give way to the other by easing, stopping, or altering course. When overtaking another vessel the onus lies on the vessel overtaking to keep clear of the overtaken one. Steamers keep clear of sailing vessels, fishing vessels, and any vessels not mechanically propelled. In fog and thick weather, sound signals are used by ships to indicate their course and speed.

There is no international system of lighthouse operation, or any arrangement respecting lightships.

In 1936, international agreement was reached on questions of buoyage and on a standard system of marking wrecks by buoys. Great Britain signed this agreement conditionally on other countries bordering the North Sea and English Channel doing the same. Systems which are preferred in other maritime countries were admitted—thus the Cardinal system may be used where the authorities notify their wish to adopt it. In this system the points of the compass govern the laying of the buoyage. Great Britain uses the lateral system (pages 160-161).

The lie of the banks and other dangers is marked parallel to the routes or channels used. Both systems agree that when entering from seaward the colour of a buoy on the starboard side of the channel must be red, and black on the port side. Shapes by day and frequency

ROUND ISLAND
1 red flash every 20 seconds

BISHOP ROCK
2 flashes every
15 seconds

ST. MARY'S
1 flash every
20 seconds

SEVEN STONES
LIGHT VESSEL
3 flashes every
minute

WOLF ROCK
alternate white
and red every
15 seconds

LONGSHIPS
occulting white
and red every
minute

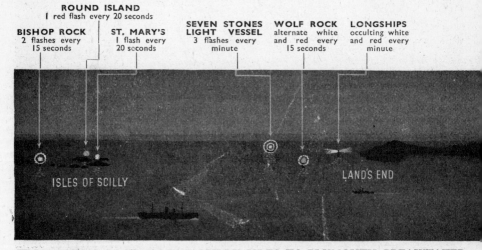

ISLES OF SCILLY

LAND'S END

FROM BISHOP ROCK ON THE SCILLY ISLES TO PLYMOUTH BREAKWATER,
Coming up Channel from the Scilly Isles to Plymouth, these lights would be noted by ships.
Flashing means showing an instantaneous light between periods of darkness. Continuous lights

of lights at night help to eliminate confusion. Pilots have to pass rigorous examinations in the positions, courses, and distances of all buoyage.

Before reaching harbour a ship may be in communication with the harbour authority for a long time. The range of wireless telegraphy has made this possible.

It is interesting to list briefly the various aids to navigation:—

(1) Direction, or position, finding by ship or shore station: wireless telegraphy.

(2) Fog signals (sound and radio): wireless telegraphy and telephony.

(3) Navigation warnings (ice prevalence, derelicts, etc.): wireless telegraphy.

(4) Time signals: wireless telegraphy.

(5) Meteorological signals: weather reports, gale warnings, synoptic data, etc.

(6) Lighthouse and lightship: communication, ships passing homeward and outward bound, and Lloyd's signal stations.

(7) Submarine sound signals emitted from lightships or shore stations.

Limited for space, charts can give only essential details, but the most extensive information is available for navigators in the sailing directions published by the British Admiralty, which detail all essential items of marine information.

For instance, there is the *North Sea Pilot*, Part III, comprising the east coast of England from Berwick to North Foreland, including the Rivers Thames and Medway. This volume contains the coastal meteorology: tidal streams and their probable velocity—period of slack water at the turn of the tide; life-saving stations; lighthouses; lightships, buoyage fixing fleets and where one may expect to encounter them during navigation; frequency of gales and fogs; temperature data; wireless stations for the use of navigation, where pilots may be found and tugs engaged; situation of Lloyd's signal stations and the coast guards; port facilities; storm signals.

The movements of ships covered by insurance, and the risks and premiums for sea risks vary with the venture and also depend on where the ship is going, what she is carrying, and the state of hull, wind and weather. England leads the world in this open market of insurance with Lloyd's of London.

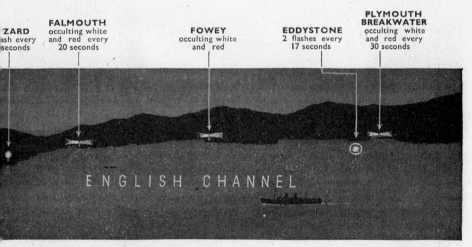

| ZARD
ash every
seconds | FALMOUTH
occulting white
and red every
20 seconds | FOWEY
occulting white
and red | EDDYSTONE
2 flashes every
17 seconds | PLYMOUTH
BREAKWATER
occulting white
and red every
30 seconds |

ENGLISH CHANNEL

CHANNEL LIGHTS IN WHITE AND RED FLASH WARNINGS TO MARINERS
with a sudden eclipse are called occulting lights. In alternating lights, different colours alternate at fixed intervals. Lighthouses, lightships and wireless are the chief aids to navigation

A CHANGE IN THE MENU

This picture of two happy fishermen was taken on a mine-sweeping trawler. They are taking a good haul of freshly caught fish to the cook's galley. When duties permit, members of a mine-sweeper's crew put their nets over to provide a welcome change from the usual menu

CHAPTER 9

Life on Board a Tramp

*Destination of cargo. Work in port. Getting in stores. Ready for sea.
Full ahead! The day's work. Keeping the watches. Jobs for the bo'sun.
Improvements in the forecastle. Care of the cargo. Responsibilities of
the master. The human element. Short sea routes. Homeward bound!*

A SHIP becomes a "tramp" when operated under an agreement called a charter party. The owner places the ship at the disposal of a charterer, who undertakes to provide a full and complete cargo ; the ship contracts to carry it from a port, or ports, in a given area, to a destination either agreed at once or to be determined later within the terms of the charter party. The reason for this is that the cargo on shipment need not necessarily be sold to an importer. It may be, and often is, offered for sale whilst on passage in the ship.

For example, a homeward-bound cargo of grain may be marketed whilst on passage and be bought by an importer, say, in Belfast, who may resell it to an importer in Rotterdam, who may later dispose of it to someone in London, Leith, Cardiff, or, in fact, any port which the ship can enter safely within the limits of the charter party.

But the final destination must be settled by the time the ship reaches the point where it is agreed final orders shall be given. This is usually one of the Atlantic islands, Gibraltar, or, in special circumstances, Falmouth, or when the ship reaches a given position, by wireless. This question of destiny of the cargo is the fundamental difference between the liner and the tramp. In the case of the liner, the voyage is predetermined precisely. With the tramp the scope of each stage of the voyage is more broadly defined.

Not until the sea pilot climbs down the rope ladder to his launch or cutter does the tramp ship enjoy that sense of independence which characterizes all her journeys and is a feature of her life.

The period spent in the home port, though having its compensations with a few days leave, is on the whole irksome in comparison with regular routine at sea.

OFFICIAL VISITORS

There are "intruders" : the Customs officials, the stevedores, the health authorities, the Factory Act inspector, the Board of Trade inspectors and, of course, the company's marine superintendent. All have questions to ask, investigations to make, visits here, there and everywhere, all over the ship. Although their object is to do everything possible to secure safety at sea and to ensure efficiency in all departments, their visits are bothersome.

The owner's visit, on the other hand, is welcome. It is satisfying to point to the work done last voyage, to be able personally to explain difficulties and suggest improvements, and also it is heartening to hear his words of appreciation and encouragement. But apart from official visitors there are others whose presence is a great joy. Those officers and engineers who cannot go on leave are joined by their wives on board, and though work constantly intervenes it is the next best thing to going home. Good-hearted women, these sailors' wives who, in order to spend a few days with their menfolk, put up with the noise and confusion of a ship working cargo.

Although some vessels load general cargo, a tramp ship's outward cargo from the United Kingdom is usually coal. Formerly we sold to foreign customers upwards of 70,000,000 tons a year.

The crew from the last voyage have been paid off and the ship is being worked with the help of "riggers," or "lumpers," old sea-dogs, mainly, who now work ashore in a sort of semi-retirement from the sea. The signing-off of the officers and engineers is in effect a formality, because they immediately sign on again, unless they are leaving the ship. The signing of the remainder of the crew is usually deferred until a day or so before sailing.

The chief officer watches the loading. Hatches and beams have been removed and derricks hoisted. The ship is moored alongside the coal-tips, and so the operation of tipping coal over coal-hoists into the ship's holds begins, accompanied by the rumble of coal and clouds of coal dust. Usually at the moment when the ship is at its very dirtiest, the stores arrive.

CHOOSING THE CREW

Barrels of oil, ropes, wires, paints, and a hundred and one things for the deck and engine departments ; cases of meat, tins of ship's biscuits, flour, tea, sugar, jams, in fact a complete grocer's shop, for the steward's reception. Later come the fresh meat and fish, together with ice for the ice box, unless a refrigerator is installed. Stores are stowed away, and in spite of the coal dust and the impediments of staging for trimming the cargo, everything finds its way to its appointed place. A hail from the shore announces that the waterman is ready to connect up, and the hosepipe is run aboard and the freshwater tanks are filled to their capacity. And now, with the loading of cargo nearing completion, the master announces the day and time for signing on the remainder of the crew. The chief officer selects his men and the second engineer selects his, and, following the usual procedure at the shipping office, the whole ship's company, including the wireless officer, has signed on articles. The master has selected the charts he requires for the voyage, and these have been delivered to the second officer, whose charge they become.

LAST DAYS BEFORE SAILING

By now the ship is almost down to her Plimsoll marks, and the chief officer is carefully watching trim and regulating the shipment of the last wagons of coal accordingly. Satisfied that enough is aboard, the cry goes out : "Up Chute," and coal teeming is over. The trimmers work on till all the coal is below deck and safely stowed. Staging is taken ashore, and preparations for sea follow. Beams and hatches and tarpaulins are put on, derricks stowed and secured.

But what of the engineers ? Has the period in port been in the nature of a holiday for them ? Not exactly a holiday, except that there is no watch keeping. Engine overhauls of a minor nature have been effected, and steam for working winches has been maintained on the donkey boiler. The main boilers have been opened up and scaled by shore labour, afterwards boxed up and filled with fresh water. Simultaneously with the completion of loading, steam is raised on the main boilers, and the engines are warmed through. In motor ships, whilst there is, of course, no steam to raise, the engineers have plenty of alternative work, such as adjustments, internal cleaning, and many other essential jobs.

By now the master has signed bills of lading for the cargo. He has cleared at the Consulate of his destination and at the dock office. The agent has ordered the dock pilot, tugs, and boatmen, and the ship

LEADING THE CONVOY

Ahead of a convoy, forging her way through heavy seas off the coast, a minesweeper carries on with her work of clearing the channel of mines for the safe passage of the merchant ships

heads for the lock gates. Here the channel, or sea pilot, boards her, and slowly the ship makes her way down the buoyed channel into deep water, where the pilot cutter is waiting to receive on board outward channel pilots and to place other pilots on board inward-bound ships.

And so, with expressions of good wishes for a pleasant voyage, the pilot says goodbye. The ship heaves gently to the ground swell, the steam safety valves call the ship's impatience to be on her way to her allotted destination.

Half ahead ! Full ahead ! The safety-valves close and there is a marked quiet. Only the gentle beat of the engines can be heard, the cries of the seagulls, and maybe the swishing of the hosepipes as the crew wash down on deck. At sea again ! Here, then, is the call of the sea at its strongest—the open expanse of ocean, the forthcoming battle with the elements, the spirit of adventure, and the crew's realization of dependence on the ship and on themselves. The helmsman repeats aloud the course set by the master, deftly he spins the wheel, bringing the ship's head on to her appointed course. The log is streamed, and the second officer is busy in the chart room, laying out the requisite charts, sailing instructions, and so forth, which are necessary for the voyage.

But whither bound ? Let us suppose that the coal cargo is destined for St. Vincent, Cape Verde Islands, which would be about a fortnight's voyage. But after St. Vincent, what then ?

Perhaps it may be the Gulf of Mexico, for sulphur, grain or cotton ; Cuba for sugar ; the River Plate for grain, or South

LARGEST CONVOY IN HISTORY CARRIES BRITISH AND

In this remarkable picture, taken from one of the aircraft of R.A.F. Coastal Command, ships of the Navy and the Merchant Navy seem to cover the sea as far as the horizon. They formed only one part of the mighty armada—some 500 transports, with 350 escorting naval vessels—bound

AMERICAN FORCES TO LAND ON THE NORTH AFRICAN COAST

for the coast of French North Africa. They made successful landings of British and U.S. troops at many places on the Mediterranean and Atlantic shores. Aircraft of R.A.F. and U.S. Army Air Forces maintained a great protecting air "umbrella" over the vast convoy

FISHING FLEET IN HARBOUR

In harbour at Yarmouth, this crowded assembly of little ships of the Scotch fishing fleet gives a forest-like effect of masts and funnels. The drifters follow the shoals of herring down the North Sea. Scottish girls clean and pack the fish as soon as it is unloaded

Africa for maize. And then? Home, maybe, but always with the possibility ol a destination farther afield. But wherever it is, the ship must remain self-sufficient, and a separate and complete entity.

So the ship's company settles down to sea routine: watch keeping for some, maintenance work for others; the firemen in the stokehold, the steward and his cook and boys attending to the commissariat. On the bridge, the chief officer takes the watch, both a.m. and p.m., from four to eight: the second officer takes the middle watch, which is twelve to four, and the third officer the eight to twelve watch, usually under the master's supervision.

The sailors take their turn at the wheel and the look-out. Below deck the firemen form into watches of four hours on and eight hours off. In the engine room the second engineer keeps the four to eight watch, the third engineer the middle watch, and the fourth engineer the eight to twelve watch, the chief engineer keeping him under his supervision.

From now on, until the arrival at the first port of call, the watches function with a smoothness born of habit. But, apart from watch keeping, there is much to do.

The bo'sun takes charge of the spare men of the watch and the deck boys, and sets about the work of maintenance. Derrick wires, topping lifts, and running gear are taken down, cleaned, greased and stowed away. Mooring ropes on the forecastle and poop are stowed below, and mooring wires either wound on their wheels or stowed in a dry and safe place.

In the storerooms and lockers, care is taken that everything is so stowed and lashed that it will not be deranged by the movements of the ship. The bo'sun finds time to look over the lamp locker and assembles the paints and sailing gear in readiness for use as soon as the work of putting everything shipshape is complete. In a steel ship, rust is the perpetual enemy, defeated only by constant scaling and painting.

Meantime, the ship's carpenter (familiarly known as Chippy), has oiled and greased the steering gear and sounded round—it is his daily practice—all tanks and bilges, recording his readings on a board at the top of the engine room, so that the engineer can see if any particular part of the ship requires pumping. He also sounds the freshwater tanks and keeps a record of how much water is being used.

He greases the winches to prevent working parts becoming seized up, and then turns his attention to such work as repairing hatches, lockers and doors, overhauling blocks and tackles, and the hundred and one other jobs which come within the scope of his trade.

The chief officer is responsible, under the master, for the maintenance and up-keep of the ship, and the bo'sun and Chippy are his right-hand men. To achieve success, apart from being hard working and skilful in their trade, they must be opportunists. For example, when the ship's holds are full of cargo, maintenance work is concentrated on deck, but when the ship is sailing in ballast attention is directed to maintenance of the holds and 'tween decks. In addition, the chief officer must keep his weather eye open and choose

JOURNEY'S END—SHIPWRECKED SEAMEN COME ASHORE

Stepping ashore at a Scottish port, these men remember a hard and eventful voyage. Their ship was torpedoed in the Atlantic and they endured fifteen grim days in lifeboats before being rescued. Survivors of sunk ships met the hardships they suffered with great courage

his day and place for putting the sailors to scaling and painting, so that their efforts may not be spoilt by rain and sea water.

In the engine room department there is plenty to do, in addition to the usual duties concerned with watch keeping. The relationship of the donkeyman to the fireman is equivalent to that of the bo'sun to the sailor. In sailing-ship days, when a boiler was sometimes carried to supply steam to operate the winches for loading and discharging cargo, this boiler came to be known as the donkey boiler, presumably because it did the donkey work. The man in charge was called the donkeyman, and this name is still applied to one who is, in fact, the leading fireman.

Most tramp ships and some motor ships carry a donkey boiler, and at sea it is the donkeyman's duty to clean and scale this boiler in readiness for use when the winches are next being worked. In addition, the donkeyman assists the second engineer on his watch, and is generally looked upon as the handyman of the engine room. Although uncertificated, the donkeyman becomes a skilled worker by long experience, and is of immense value on the engine room staff. In addition to watch keeping, the engineers themselves take the opportunity, when the ship is at sea, to overhaul winches and other auxiliaries which are used in port.

FIXING THE SHIP'S POSITION

At about eight o'clock in the morning and again just before noon, the master, together with his deck officers, stand by with chronometer and sextants to take sights and establish the ship's position. Eight a.m. is the time to find the latitude, and noon the longitude.

It is customary for all the officers to take their own sights, not only as a cross check on the master's observations but as experience for all. The modern ship, however, is still further assisted in the problems of navigation by electrical depth-sounding machines and wireless direction finders. The tendency of the future will doubtless be for radiolocation and other recent discoveries to be used for sea navigation.

But men must eat, and in the galley, as the kitchen is called, the cook, unperturbed by the heaving of the ship, is to be found preparing substantial and wholesome meals for an ever-hungry ship's company. Hard work and sea air ensure hearty appetites. It is not unusual for the master, chief engineer, and other first officers to dine together, as this arrangement gives them an opportunity of discussing the working of the ship and is conducive to full co-operation between the various departments. The other officers and engineers have their own messroom, and the sailors and firemen have separate messrooms adjacent to their quarters.

FORECASTLE ARRANGEMENTS

For years past it has been the custom to accommodate the deck officers in bridge housing, and the engineers in rooms built above and in way of the engine room. In these circumstances the crew's quarters were placed in the poop between decks, which are still called forecastles, although for crews to be housed in the forward end of the ship is an arrangement long discontinued in many ocean-going vessels.

That the crew's accommodation in the after poop is still called the forecastle is, of course, a habit which has come down through the years and dates from sailing-ship days, when the crew always lived forward and the master commanded from the after end. It would, perhaps, be too much to say that it is yet customary for all the ship's company to be housed amidships in a modern tramp vessel, but this arrangement was, in fact, introduced in several tramp ships during recent years. With the introduction of running hot and cold fresh water, central heating and other improvements, the advantage of concentrating accommodation amidships is emphasized.

KEEPING THE SHIP SMART

Constant scaling, chipping, and painting are necessary on a steel ship. The proper main-
tenance and upkeep of the ship demand unfailing attention, and rust is the perpetual enemy.
These two members of the crew are busily engaged in cleaning the vessel's smoke-stack

Certain it is that the days when the men's quarters were always placed below deck are passed, and ships of the future will, without doubt, accommodate their crews in rooms erected above the weather deck. Moreover, the example which has been set in a few modern tramp ships of

having a recreation room for the sailors and firemen, with wireless sets and a ship's library, will be followed in future ships.

As the course from Great Britain to St. Vincent, Cape Verdes, includes some westing, the ship's clock is adjusted daily accordingly. Leaving the Bay of Biscay behind, the ship runs into warmer climes, and with the approach to the first port of discharge, the chief officer turns his attention to the preparation of winches and cargo gear for discharging.

Once within shelter of the land and in smooth water, the derricks are hoisted, tarpaulins removed, and by the time the ship is moored in the harbour and the Customs and business formalities are over, everything is in readiness for the work of discharging to commence.

Coal and similar cargoes are discharged by various means, according to the facilities available in the port. These vary, and may embrace an elaborate system of travelling grabs, or a series of shore cranes operating grabs or tubs. The facilities may be limited to one or two cranes, working in co-operation with the ship's own gear, or there may be no shore facilities at all, in which case the cargo is discharged entirely by the ship's derricks and winches. Whatever may be the system, however, the work is done by labour from the shore, and is not the concern of the ship's crew.

There are, however, some members of the ship's company who have responsibilities, as, for instance, the donkeyman, who has to supply the necessary power for the winches. The ship's officers have to see that the shore appliances used to discharge the cargo do not in any way damage the ship. It is not customary to tally a

RECREATION IN THE FORECASTLE

Draughts and dominoes enliven the off-duty hours of these seamen, and they play with intent care, happily absorbed in the fortunes of the game. Spare moments are few, and too valuable to waste. Modern tramps have a recreation room for the crew, with wireless and a ship's library

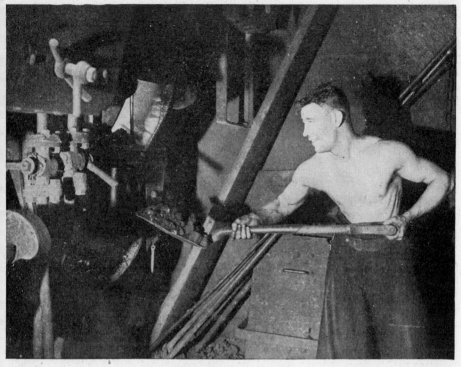

KEEPING UP STEAM

Hard at work in the boiler-room of a trawler. Many of the fishermen of Britain still man their stout little craft, hunting now for enemy mines instead of fish, clearing the channels of danger to ensure the safe conveyance of supplies. Many trawlers were equipped as minesweepers

homogeneous cargo, such as coal, but in the case of a general mixed or bagged cargo, where the ship has given a receipt in the form of a Bill of Lading for a certain number of packages, the ship's officers are concerned not only with the intake but with the correct out-turn. To assist in this check shore tallymen are usually employed.

The period spent in port discharging has given the members of the crew opportunities for excursions ashore, but, notwithstanding such attractions, it is true to say that the sailor is usually glad to be away on his voyage again.

The completion of discharge at the final stage of the outward voyage is always accompanied by a definite sense of achievement, and there certainly seems to be a different atmosphere in an outward bound ship from a homeward bound one. It is not a matter of homesickness, because one of the first things to be noticed about a sailor recently arrived home is his anxiety to be at sea again. Outward bound, all on board seem to be concerned with *beginning* jobs of work, whereas homeward bound, everything is being organized and timed for completion and to have everything in shipshape order for the arrival home.

In a tramp ship's life, until a cargo is aboard destined for home, the itinerary of the round voyage is always in doubt. A tramp ship which leaves home with an initial cargo without further engagements must, of course, receive instructions, either by wireless during the first outward passage or during the time of discharge at the first port of call, as to its next destination. The discharge having been completed and the instructions having been received, the vessel then proceeds, and unless the cargo fixed to be shipped happens to be actually at the port of discharge, the ship goes on her way in a state referred to as in ballast.

Here, again, is a legacy of sailing-ship terminology, dating back to the time when a sailing ship, undertaking a long voyage without cargo, had to take on board solid ballast for stability purposes. The modern tramp ship, however, does not take on board solid ballast, but instead fills the ballast water tanks, formed by the construction of the vessel's double underwater skin. The responsibility for running up ballast tanks and pumping out these tanks rests with the engineers, and the controlling valves and pumping machinery are situated in the engine room.

A voyage in ballast is a voyage with the holds empty, and it will therefore provide the opportunity for scaling and painting the ironwork in the holds and for effecting repairs to tank top ceilings, spar ceilings, and shifting board and limbers. Before receiving a cargo such as sugar in bags, bales of cotton, grain in bulk or in bags, the ship's hold must be scrupulously cleaned, and when the cargo is loaded no bag, package, or parcel which is stainable must be allowed to come into contact with anything which will stain or damage it.

CARE OF HOLDS AND CARGO

It can be seen, therefore, that the work of preparation to receive a fresh cargo is formidable, particularly when it is remembered that the preceding cargo may have been a dirty one, like coal, nitrate, or ore.

The holds, having been washed and brushed down, and thoroughly dried, are often dunnaged. This is done by the use of burlap, or fibre mats. But in stowing a perishable cargo there is the added consideration of ventilation. For certain cargoes the normal ventilation provided in the ship's construction is inadequate, and extra ventilation is effected by leaving gaps or shafts between the cargo.

Precautions, too, must be taken against damage to the cargo by condensation, or sweating, for a ship during a single voyage may experience many changes in climate, so that condensation is inevitable. It is customary for the ship's crew to carry out the cleaning of the holds, the work of dunnaging and provision of extra ventilation being performed by the shore stevedores as and when the cargo is loaded.

During the voyage the chief officer will regulate the ship's ventilators as may be necessary, in order to keep the cargo in good and sound condition.

The landsman, when he takes a voyage on the sea, is inclined to complain that sea life is monotonous. Not for the sailor.

IN CHARGE OF THE SHIP

Quite apart from the variety of work to be carried out on board in connection with the maintenance of the ship, the preparation for various types of cargo and its safe carriage through the hazards and perils of the sea, his life is one continual change and full of incident. So successful have been the efforts to reduce sea perils to the minimum that major disasters in peacetime are few, and this happy state of affairs is due to the naval architects and shipbuilders, and perhaps even more to the skill of the sea-going personnel.

The sight of a tramp ship lying in dock may suggest that such a vessel is a lumbering lifeless thing, but to see her in a seaway, heavily laden and skilfully handled, is to realize that a ship is a scientific instrument, seaworthy, adequately buoyant and alive ; she must be capable of withstanding heavy stresses and strains, and under the able control of a British master must be able to weather the storms and ward off the heavy and malicious blows of the green seas in a manner which might almost be termed graceful.

But even the most well-designed ship would not come through the ordeal of Atlantic gales and tropical storms without the skilful handling of the master, or, as he is usually referred to on board, the old man. It is at such times that the old man comes to be revered by the rest of the ship's complement.

Most of them have learnt enough of the sea to be able to appreciate that he knows what he is about. He seems to know just when to ease down, alter course a point or two, bring the wind and sea to a less dangerous angle, heave to, if things become worse, but always with a cool and settled confidence which is an inspiration.

It is difficult to find an experienced sailor who is afraid of heavy seas—but a sailor hates fog. In a storm he is master of his own destiny, but in a fog there is the ever-present danger of the unguessed movement of an unknown ship under another shipmaster's control.

The outward and any intermediate voyages having been accomplished, the ship arrives at the homeward loading port. The idea of being homeward bound has its own sentimental attractions, but apart from this all departments on board have in their minds the culmination of their efforts during the whole trip since leaving home, and the picture of their ship steaming into the home port looking her best inside and out, everything spick and span.

MAKE WAY FOR THE COOK
The cook brings back the dinner-tins from the mess deck.
They are very light to carry, for seamen's appetites are hearty

The ocean-going tramp ship may enter almost any trade and even circle the world in a round voyage. In practice, however, ships under their respective owners' management are usually to be found specializing in certain trades, primarily because of the knowledge the owners have accumulated of these trades by long experience, and also because, with the intention of concentration on certain trades, special features peculiarly suitable to conditions prevailing in those trades have

REGARDLESS OF NEAR MISSES SHIPS STEAM ON WHILE ESCORTING
Bombs fall among the ships of a convoy which steams resolutely on its way, and an escorting destroyer lays a smoke-screen to make a heavy black protective cloud. The thick pall of smoke will not disperse for a long time. Smoke-floats are sometimes dropped overboard to make this

WARSHIPS LAY SMOKE-SCREENS TO PROTECT THE CONVOY
concealing fog. Dense white smoke can be produced by the use of chlor-sulphonic acid, released from drums at a ship's stern.   With modern oil-fired boilers a smoke-screen is easily produced by arranging for the oil to enter the furnaces through a specially adjusted nozzle

been introduced into the ship's design. So, generally speaking, when ships leave outwards from the United Kingdom the owner has in mind a definite round voyage, even if the arrangements for such a voyage have not been completed. Market conditions must, obviously, influence him, and also the law of supply and demand.

Given reasonably normal conditions a ship outward bound for an Eastern Mediterranean destination would follow with a cargo from the Black Sea to the United Kingdom, or U.S.A., or would pass through the Suez Canal to lift a cargo from India or Burma. Alternatively, the ship may be sent to load in Australia.

An outward-bound vessel with anthracite from South Wales to Canada is obviously intended to load a homeward cargo in the River St. Lawrence. To many destinations for homeward loading there is no suitable outward cargo from the United Kingdom, as, for instance, the Pacific Coast of U.S.A. and Vancouver. The ships proceed outwards in ballast.

THE HUMAN ELEMENT

From Vancouver they may load homewards or for Australia, New Zealand, or the Western Pacific. The owner's business is to employ his ship profitably, and with this end in view he aspires to an itinerary which finds the vessel so positioned that the market with the greatest demand for ships is within easy and timely reach.

The ship's company, in their respective spheres, supply the essential requirements in human effort and ability to operate the instrument of sea carriage—the ship. Navigation—withstanding and overcoming the hazards of the sea—maintaining the ship in a condition of seaworthiness which will enable the safe carriage of the cargo and its delivery at destination in good order—in all these matters the crew work as a team. The master has extra responsibilities concerned with the business side of the adventure, and he must

also be medical adviser and doctor to the crew when at sea. Repeated experience in a particular sea " trade " gives the master expert knowledge and a preference for that trade. The same with seamen—if a man likes the East he will endeavour to remain with a company specializing in that trade.

There are ships which stay abroad for long periods trading on the coast of Australia, or between Australia and the Western Pacific or on the Indian coast.

SHORT SEA ROUTES

Then there are what are known as the short sea traders. These are ships of the smaller type ranging from 2,000 tons to 4,000 tons dead weight, which trade regularly from the United Kingdom to North Africa, Spain and France, carrying out coal and bringing home ore, pit props, and sometimes general cargo. Again, there is the home coasting trade—small ships which work between home ports with an occasional trip to Northern France, Holland, or Germany. It is unusual to find seamen changing constantly from ocean-going to coasting ships. They usually settle down in one type or the other. Coasters are known as weekly ships. This means that the crew sign on under a running agreement. It would obviously be inconvenient to sign on and off at the end of each short coastal trip. Another condition peculiar to weekly ships is that the men customarily buy their own food.

Homeward bound! If from the Far East : through the heat and humidity of the Indian Ocean—avoiding, if possible, the monsoons, if it is the monsoon season. A call at Colombo and Port Said for bunker coal or oil, and then through the blue waters of the Mediterranean.

Passing Gibraltar, the ship will fall in with the north-bound traffic from the South Atlantic, and will encounter the Portuguese trade winds, prior to crossing the Bay, with its usual heavy ground

COTTON FROM U.S.A. REACHES A BRITISH PORT

Every ship that successfully braved the perils of the crossing from America and unloaded her cargo in a port of Britain is a unit of victory in the unceasing Battle of the Atlantic

swell. If from the Pacific, then through the Suez Canal and afterwards following the Gulf Stream towards Halifax and the North Atlantic circle (as in the case of homeward-bound ships from the Atlantic States seaboard and Canada), the ship will have the prospect of strong following winds and heavy seas.

All work of maintenance on board is now nearing completion, and except for the effects of wind and water on the hull, the ship is looking spick and span. Approaching the home port, the ensign and house flag are run up. As the pilot cutter on station is sighted the master rings the engine-room telegraph to stand by. Slowly the ship eases down and a rope ladder is lowered to assist the pilot aboard. In her deep sea wanderings the tramp has done another good job.

It will not be long now before the dock is entered and the ship made fast ready to discharge. Now comes the full sense of achievement—the successful completion of a purpose, of a most vital purpose, without which our country could not live.

BOOM DEFENCES TO GUARD HARBOURS

All harbours containing shipping have boom defences miles long, consisting mainly of anti-submarine and anti-torpedo nets, making a strong steel mesh curtain from the surface to the sea-bed. Constant attention is necessary to keep the boom in good order, and men of the boom defence repair ships are constantly at work in all weathers. Spherical floats keep the nets on the surface. Here a man of the boom defence is preparing to haul in some of the floats for repair

CHAPTER 10

How Britain's Merchant Navy Was Built Up

Pioneers of the shipping industry. Earliest steamships. From beach boy to shipowner. How the P. & O. started. First Atlantic fleet of mail steamships. Samuel Cunard's dreams. The Atlantic mail contract. Donald Currie and the Union Castle Line. Royal Mail Steam Packet Company. The load line. Great Scots shipowners. Safety at sea.

Oh, where are you going to, all you big steamers
With England's own coal, up and down the salt
    seas?
We are going to fetch you your bread and your
    butter,
Your beef, pork, and mutton, eggs, apples and
    cheese.
For the bread that you eat and the biscuits you
    nibble,
The sweets that you suck and the joints that you
    carve—
They are brought to you daily by all us big
    steamers,
And if anyone hinders our coming you starve.
                        RUDYARD KIPLING.

OF all the industries of Britain, shipping is the most adventurous, hazardous and romantic. "Yes," you may answer, "the officers and men must have a sense of adventure or they would never go to sea. They must face the perils of storm and fog. Their ships may possibly be cast ashore or posted at Lloyd's as 'missing.' But what is there romantic about those who manage the ships from their offices ashore?"

Let me tell you that there is a great deal of romance about the shipowners, the business men behind the ships. The ships they look after are really the property of hundreds, or even thousands, of investors; the Cunard Company, for instance, has as many as 9,000 shareholders on its books.

A shipowner, or manager, in the ordinary course of his business, has to be something of a financier, lawyer, accountant, linguist, engineer, ship designer, ship repairer, store dealer, and coal and iron expert. He must study the map of the world, particularly if he is a tramp owner, and know all about the produce of all countries. When war is on and his property is requisitioned by the Government, the shipowner must also be a bit of a politician, diplomat, underwriter, and philosopher—and business man as well.

British shipping has always been individualistic, resisting attempts of the Government to go beyond its obvious duty of ensuring that the ships are thoroughly seaworthy, and that officers and men are fit for their tasks. The shipping industry has great family traditions, represented by the Booths, the Holts, the Allens, the Bibbys, the Ropners, the Harrisons, the Hogarths, the Reardon-Smiths, the Runcimans, and many others, while some pioneers have hidden their identity, as with the P. & O., Royal Mail, Orient, Clan, Union Castle, and White Star. But whatever the designation which was chosen by the founders of a particular shipping business, its success depended on the initiative of a few men.

In many cases it depended on one man of progressive ideas, courage and business ability. Usually, the pioneer had very limited financial resources, and had to scratch up the money for acquiring his first ship as best he could, in many cases aided by friends who had faith in his star.

' LOSSES IN EARLY DAYS

In the days of the sailing ship the shipping industry was very precarious. Vessels loaded with costly cargoes would put out from their home ports amid the cheers of well-wishers, and after they had passed over the horizon the owners would know little or nothing of them for many months, since the mail services were slow and irregular, no cabling facilities existed, and wireless telegraphy was unthought of. It is understandable that in those days many fine ships were posted at Lloyd's as missing—nothing having been heard of them since they put to sea.

Nowadays, ships are rarely lost without trace, for owners are able to keep in constant wireless touch with them as they proceed on their voyages. The voyages, too, are more regular, as they depend for propulsion on the steam-engine instead of the wind. Sailing ships, even the crack clipper ships, would often get into "the doldrums." In those days seamen had to study the wind, for owners' profits, and often their own share of them, depended on the ships carrying as much canvas as they could safely spread, and their own lives depended on not spreading too much.

Who today knows the definitions which were familiar then? A 7-mile wind was a gentle air, 14 miles a light breeze, 21 miles a good steady breeze, 40 miles a gale, 60 miles a heavy storm, and 80 to 150 miles a hurricane which carried everything before it. The aim of an experienced sailor in the Atlantic and Pacific oceans was to pick up a steady "trade wind" which would send him bowling along with little thought or chance of disaster. What navigators then feared most, as likely to delay them, were the regions of calm, where the north and south trade winds in the two great oceans meet. When hindered in this way the sailors described themselves as being "in the doldrums," and abandoned hope of making a fast passage with the tea, or wood, or other cargo, so as to reach port before the market was flooded with goods brought in by ships which had been luckier, or had been better sailed. Nor were the "doldrums" the only trouble, for fogs were as frequent then as now, and the coasts were not as well lighted as they are today.

Life in the sailing days was full of danger and uncertainty, and the risks appealed to the seamen, as well as to the investors, of Britain. In following the sea, the seamen staked their lives, and their financial backers staked their money on a voyage as lightheartedly as a man will now stake a few pounds on a horse, or a few pence in a football pool. There were always plenty of volunteers for the merchant ships, where discipline was dictated only by the perils of the sea, and wind, and fog—and there were " no frills."

WHEN THE PRESS GANG RULED

Less desire was shown to join the Royal Navy. Men-of-war, in addition to the hazards which confronted merchant seamen, were exposed to the fury of the enemy, and often to brutal punishments for slight infringements of the King's regulations. In such circumstances the Press Gang had very often to be invoked in order to provide British men-of-war with crews in time of war.

Queen Elizabeth declared the seas to be free to all sailors, but the traffic upon them was on a small scale until the marine steam-engine was invented. As early as 1802 some enterprising Scotsmen were impressed by the possibilities which were opened up when the first practical steamship, the *Charlotte Dundas*, was built for

HELPING CRIPPLED SHIPS HOME

Every damaged ship saved and made seaworthy for service again is a victory over the enemy, and the crews of rescue tugs work under great difficulties to beach a crippled ship safely in a harbour mouth if they are unable to bring her to a quayside. Then the Admiralty Salvage Officer takes over. Here a strong line from a rescue tug is being taken aboard a torpedoed ship

use on the Forth and Clyde Canal. Her success was followed by the *Clermont*, which made the journey from New York to Albany, a distance of 130 miles, in thirty-two hours. But the ship was regarded only as an interesting experiment.

EARLY ATLANTIC STEAMSHIPS

A contemporary newspaper, the *Evening Sun* of New York, described how the *Clermont* "moved out into the stream, the steam connexion hissing at the joints, her crude machinery thumping and groaning, the wheels (paddle-wheels) splashing, and the smoke-stack belching like a volcano." She was described as "a monster moving on the water, defying the waves and the tide, and breathing flames and smoke." That was in 1807.

Ten years were to pass before the wooden-sailing ship *Savannah*, with a steam-engine for use when the wind failed her, crossed from the United States to Liverpool; and nearly twenty more years elapsed before the age of steam navigation on the Atlantic opened with the sailing of the *Sirius* and *Great Western* from England to the United States in just over a fortnight, a wonderful exploit at that time.

But even then there was a good deal of scepticism as to the possibility of the steamer, dependent on costly coal, competing successfully against the sailing ship, which got its power from the wind for nothing. The Sea Lords at the Admiralty were fiercely opposed to the steam-engine, and many business men were not easily convinced that the sailing ship was about to be driven off the seas. To some extent the sceptics were right, for it was many years before the tonnage of steam-propelled ships exceeded that of the sailing ships. In the eighteen-fifties, however, the Government decided that the mails going overseas from British ports could be carried more quickly and regularly by steamers. That decision marked a notable turning-point in the history of shipping.

The industry then increased in national importance owing to the increased demand for raw materials for the factories, and for food for the workers in them, for the British farmer could not supply them with all the corn and other things they required at the prices they were prepared to pay.

Thus, the shipowner, as we know him today, came on the stage. Shipowners do not have an easy life. They are not the masters of their own fortunes or misfortunes. Nature plays games with them at sea, with the result that their ships are lost. Again, the countries whose trade they have fostered by providing efficient and cheap transport may suffer financial or industrial reverses, as, for instance, the revolutions which occurred so frequently at one period in South America, disorganizing all trade at home and overseas.

They may make big profits during a "boom." But then will come a period, usually a long one, when it will be difficult to make ends meet owing to the falling off in the number of passengers who wish to travel, or the decline in the volume of cargoes to be carried from port to port. Consequently, wise shipowners are rather like squirrels—they store up in the summer the resources they will need in the winter. In times of prosperity they put by money to enable them, first, to withstand the losses in the years of depression; and secondly, to build more efficient and economic ships in place of their older vessels which are wearing out. Conservative finance has been the secret of the success of British shipping.

START OF THE "P. & O."

My claim that the shipowner is a romantic figure in industry can be supported by relating the story of Arthur Anderson, who, in association with his less daring partner, Brodie Willcox, founded the Peninsular and Oriental Steam Navigation Company, which opened up trade to the East, and especially to India.

In order to appreciate his achievements it may be added that today, what is now known as the "P. & O. Group" is one of the most important shipping combinations under any national flag. It embraces the British India Steam Navigation Company, Ltd., the Eastern and Australian Steamship Company, Ltd., the Federal Steam Navigation Company, Ltd., the Hain Steamship Company, Ltd., the New Zealand Shipping Company, Ltd., James Nourse, Ltd., the Orient Steam Navigation Company, Ltd., and the Strick Line (1923), Ltd., as well as, of course, the P. & O. Steam Navigation Company. Other companies are also included in the group as, for instance, the Union Steamship Company of New Zealand.

FROM BEACH BOY TO PARTNER

To trace the beginning of this group, in which each company still preserves its own identity, we must go back one hundred and fifty years, to the bleak Shetland Islands, which were mainly occupied by poverty-stricken men enjoying few of the necessities and none of the conveniences of life. A visitor at that time to Bressey, which adjoins Lerwick, might have seen a beach boy named Anderson, in his early teens, scrubbing and washing the fish which had been landed that morning. This lad also had to run messages for his employer, Mr. Thomas Bolt, a general merchant and fish-curer, and on occasions row him across the sound to Lerwick, the business centre of the Shetlands. It was not a promising opening to the career of a man who was to become one of the outstanding figures in the history of British shipping.

Anderson was ambitious. Though there was no school at Bressey for such as he, the boy had had some education from a local parson. In his spare time he read any books on which he could lay his hands. His employer, pleased with the way he did his dull work, at length took him into his office, and there he gained a knowledge of business methods. But the lad wanted adventure. Before he was sixteen years of age he secured a passage to Portsmouth, where, by the influence of Thomas Bolt, he entered the Royal Navy, became captain's clerk and sailed for the Baltic.

When this cruise came to an end, Anderson returned to Portsmouth. He was discharged from the Royal Navy, only to find that no one in the town had any job by which he could earn his living. So he walked to London, penniless and friendless. For a time he found that London had no more use for him than Portsmouth.

Eventually, however, through the influence of an uncle, he entered the office of Brodie Willcox, a London shipbroker in a moderate way of business. Anderson revealed himself as a genius in shipping affairs, and within seven years Willcox made him his partner. Though still young, he soon became the leader in the firm. Keen and ambitious, he was ready for any adventure that promised a profit.

The first investment of the firm was an American schooner, which had stranded at Dover. A revolution was running its course in Portugal, with which country the firm had business links. With Anderson on board, the schooner, after having been refitted, set sail with a cargo of ammunition for Lisbon. Anderson took a gallant part in winning the throne for the young Queen, Dona Maria. Thus he gained, in a literal sense, "a friend at court." He returned to London with dreams which would have seemed utterly impossible of attainment to a less courageous man.

CONTRACT FOR MAILS

His first act was to form, in 1837, the Peninsular Steam Company. His second was to secure the contract for carrying the mail every week from Falmouth to Gibraltar, with calls at Vigo, Oporto, Lisbon and Cadiz, the Government agreeing to pay a subvention of £29,600 a year.

Later, the name of the company was changed to The Peninsular & Oriental Steamship Company. "To Arthur Anderson and the Melbourne Ministry of 1835-41 must be given the credit for a complete break with tradition, which had an effect which neither of them can have contemplated. It is hardly too much to say that the contract drawn up between them in August, 1837, laid, quite unconsciously, the foundations of the modern British mercantile marine, which most of us have been brought up to regard with some national pride." (From *British Shipping*).

STORY OF THE CUNARD LINE

It is unnecessary to trace in detail the subsequent history of this line. The directors had to fight against the conservatism of Government departments as well as the monopoly of the East India Company, then on its last legs. But Anderson and the colleagues he had gathered round him were undaunted by obstacles, and in later years, with the former beach boy as chairman, the P. & O. Company extended its services. He lived to see P. & O. ships navigating not only the Mediterranean, but also the Red Sea and the Indian Ocean, with a service to China. And the P. & O. possessed its own repairing depots at Malta, Suez, Alexandria, Aden, Bombay, Calcutta, Hong Kong, Shanghai, and Point de Galle.

The names of Anderson and his partner, Brodie Willcox, are forgotten; their identity was merged in the title of the shipping company which they founded. It was otherwise with Samuel Cunard. Of all names associated with the shipping industry none, perhaps, is so familiar, for the company he founded won, held for many years, and still held on the outbreak of war in 1939, the Blue Ribbon of the Atlantic, unquestionably the premier trade route of the Seven Seas.

Consider the romance of Samuel Cunard, the shipowner who dreamed great dreams, and of the company he founded. There was nothing in its early history to suggest that the time would come when it would represent the prestige of this country on the sea route over which more passengers pass, and in a greater measure of comfort and even luxury, than on any other. The passenger liners *Queen Mary* and *Queen Elizabeth*, of 81,233 tons and 85,000 tons respectively, may be regarded as monuments to the progressive spirit of Samuel Cunard, who was responsible for the building of the first Atlantic fleet of mail steamships, the *Britannia*, *Arcadia*, *Caledonia* and *Columbia*. Each of these was little over 1,000 tons, with a speed of about $8\frac{1}{2}$ knots as compared with $28\frac{1}{2}$ and 30 knots of the great ships which, under conditions of peace, can cross the Atlantic in a shuttle service in about four days.

Samuel Cunard had already celebrated his fiftieth birthday when he determined to create a bridge of ships across the North Atlantic. He was living in Halifax, Nova Scotia, earning what was apparently a sufficient income by running sailing ships from Boston and Newfoundland to Bermuda. There was no reason why he should put his whole future to the hazard by founding a shipping company in England, the success of which would depend on his optimistic belief in the development of traffic between the two branches of the English-speaking world.

SAMUEL CUNARD'S SUCCESS

But he had faith in the marine steam-engine, and when he read an advertisement for tenders for the conveyance of the mails between England and the United States he decided that his day had dawned.

He appears to have had only one influential friend in England when he crossed the Atlantic to submit his tender —the Secretary of the East India Company. The success of his mission represented a triumph over difficulties which would have defeated a man of less vision and courage, for it was generally assumed that the mail contract would be secured by the owners of the famous *Great Western*, of 1,340 tons, the largest steamship which had been built up to then. Cunard was undoubtedly fortunate from the day he landed. He secured an introduction to the

Cunard had all his plans "cut and dried," he submitted his tender to the Government for the new mail service. It was accepted, to the great chagrin of the owners of the *Great Western*, and it was agreed to pay him £50,000 a year. The next step was to raise what, in those days, was regarded as a large sum of money

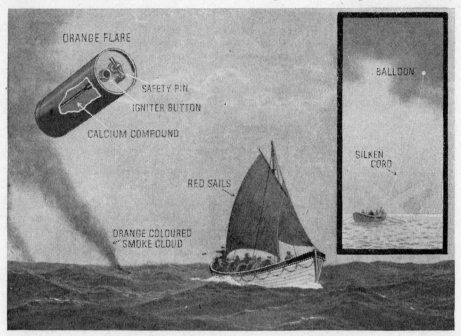

ORANGE FLARE

SAFETY PIN

IGNITER BUTTON

CALCIUM COMPOUND

BALLOON

SILKEN CORD

RED SAILS

ORANGE COLOURED SMOKE CLOUD

EMERGENCY EQUIPMENT FOR LIFEBOATS

Lifeboats must now carry red sails and special equipment, including buoyant smoke signals. Thrown on the water, these give off orange-coloured smoke which can be seen several miles away. Lifeboats also carry small balloons (inset) which rise on a silken cord to a great height

pioneer marine engineer of the day, Robert Napier, who was impressed with his ambitious scheme. At that time George Burns and Donald McIver who, for some time, had been the owners of rival lines of coasting steamers plying between Glasgow and Liverpool, had just amalgamated their business, and were ready for some fresh adventure. Napier suggested that Cunard should talk the matter over with them. Experienced shipowners, they caught his enthusiasm and promised their ungrudging support. When Samuel

to pay for the ships which were needed. Burns, McIver and Cunard got together, and it was agreed that the two former should buy a half-share in the contract for £25,000 and form a separate company to raise that sum. But the arrangement was clumsy and not likely to work well. So a new scheme was evolved, a co-partnership, with a capital of £270,000; Cunard was one of the partners and consented to surrender the contract in return for shares. The canny Glasgow business men made it a condition of the co-partnery, as it was

ALPHABETICAL FLAGS

FLAGS USED IN THE NEW INTERNATIONAL CODE

The new International Code of Signals has been translated into English, French, German, Italian, Japanese, Spanish, and Norwegian. Nautical and technical phrases are adjusted so

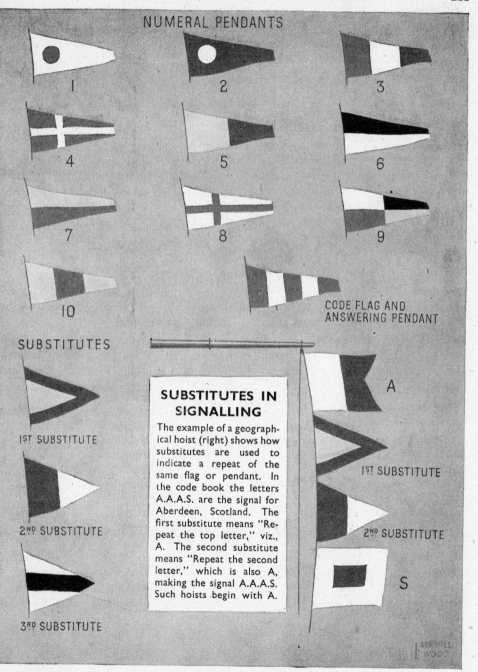

NUMERAL PENDANTS

1

2

3

4

5

6

7

8

9

10

CODE FLAG AND
ANSWERING PENDANT

SUBSTITUTES

1ST SUBSTITUTE

2ND SUBSTITUTE

3RD SUBSTITUTE

SUBSTITUTES IN SIGNALLING

The example of a geographical hoist (right) shows how substitutes are used to indicate a repeat of the same flag or pendant. In the code book the letters A.A.A.S. are the signal for Aberdeen, Scotland. The first substitute means "Repeat the top letter," viz., A. The second substitute means "Repeat the second letter," which is also A, making the signal A.A.A.S. Such hoists begin with A.

A

1ST SUBSTITUTE

2ND SUBSTITUTE

S

SPEAK IN SEVEN DIFFERENT LANGUAGES

that correct information can be exchanged between people not speaking the same language. Substitutes (inset, above) indicate a repeat of the same flag or pendant in a hoist

called, that if they did not get 15 per cent on their investment, Cunard was to make good the deficiency out of the £50,000 which had been credited to him as the value of the mail contract.

In these circumstances, with the backing of the Government, the British and North American Steam Packet Company came into existence. The name was afterwards changed to the Cunard Steamship Company. The prospects were not too promising, but events proved that the foundations had been well and truly laid, for, if Cunard was a business-like dreamer, his partners brought to the adventure all their hardly won knowledge and years of experience as shipowners. The Company became famous for the speed of its ships, for the comfort provided for passengers, and for their safety. It is the proud boast of the Company that no life has ever been lost in any of its ships under peace conditions.

The Company has never been afraid of new departures in design and building. Early in its career the screw was adopted in place of the paddle; compound engines were fitted soon afterwards, and the Company was a pioneer in the fitting of the turbine, which many shipowners regarded as suited only to men-of-war.

Samuel Cunard lived until 1865, and had the good fortune to see the dreams which he had nurtured in far-off Nova Scotia more than realized. His company is now the pivot of what is known as the "Cunard group," which includes the Port Line and Thos. & Jno. Brocklebank.

UNION CASTLE LINE

The story of Samuel Cunard's achievement in founding the Cunard Company would not be complete unless something was said of the establishment, by Donald Currie, of the Castle Line, which, owing to its amalgamation with the Union Steamship Company, is now known as the Union Castle Line. Donald Currie was

a native of Greenock, where he was born in 1825. He came from a poor home, and there was nothing to suggest that he would found a fleet, enter Parliament, and become a national figure. When still a youth he entered a local shipping office, but it offered little scope for his ambitions. So, when only eighteen years of age, he left his native town for Liverpool, then entering upon a period of great prosperity. What idea prompted young Donald Currie to abandon his sure employment at Greenock for the uncertainties of keen competitive life in the great shipping city south of the border, we do not know.

TRADE WITH SOUTH AFRICA

But his intuition was not at fault. He obtained employment in the office of the Cunard Company. Currie was only twenty-five years of age when he was appointed its agent at Havre, to challenge the monopoly hitherto enjoyed by the Americans. Currie won his spurs by securing a large share of the freight traffic between France and America.

His success encouraged his employers to entrust him with pioneer work of a somewhat similar character at Bremen and Hamburg. Then they came to the conclusion that Currie, with his experience on the Continent, could be better employed in the head office at Liverpool. So about 1856 Currie moved back to Merseyside, and for the next six years was immersed in the affairs of the Cunard Company, still nursing the ambition to become a shipowner himself. He decided, however, that if ever he achieved his ambition he would not enter into competition with the Cunard Company, which had given him the first chance to study shipowning.

The mail service to South Africa was then operated by the Union Steamship Company, which had been formed in 1853 as the Union Steam Collier Company, a humble origin for a concern which was to link this country with South

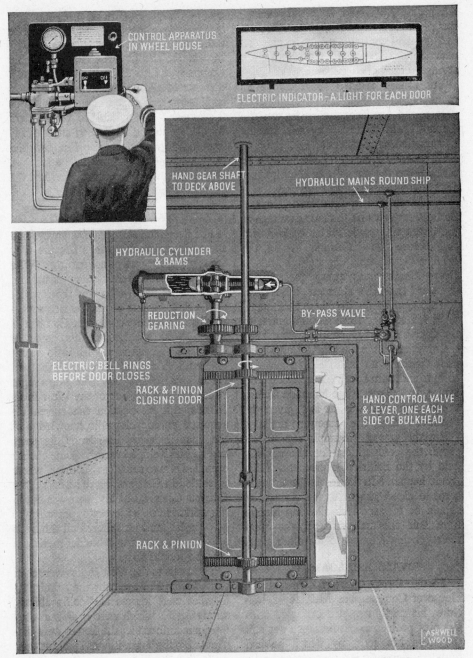

CONTROL APPARATUS IN WHEEL HOUSE

ELECTRIC INDICATOR - A LIGHT FOR EACH DOOR

HAND GEAR SHAFT TO DECK ABOVE

HYDRAULIC MAINS ROUND SHIP

HYDRAULIC CYLINDER & RAMS

REDUCTION GEARING

BY-PASS VALVE

ELECTRIC BELL RINGS BEFORE DOOR CLOSES

RACK & PINION CLOSING DOOR

HAND CONTROL VALVE & LEVER, ONE EACH SIDE OF BULKHEAD

RACK & PINION

ASHWELL WOOD

WATERTIGHT DOORS CONTROLLED FROM THE BRIDGE

Ships are divided into a number of watertight compartments so that the whole ship will not be flooded in the event of a collision. These compartments are fitted with watertight doors which can be opened or closed hydraulically from the bridge. In foggy weather they are kept closed

Africa and assist in its industrial development. The Union Steamship Company had the mail contract and its agencies all over South Africa. It was in a very strongly entrenched position.

But Currie decided to challenge its monopoly, as he had challenged the monopoly of the Americans when he was the Cunard agent at Havre. By this time he had made many friends, not only in Liverpool and London, but abroad. So he threw down the gauntlet to the directors of the Union Steamship Company.

He determined to build four steamers. So impatient was he to take advantage of the developing trade with South Africa that before the *Edinburgh Castle*, the *Windsor Castle*, the *Walmer Castle* and the *Dover Castle* were ready for sea he chartered two other steamers, the *Iceland* and the *Gothland*, with which he inaugurated his sailings from Southampton to the Cape of Good Hope in January, 1872 —four years before the Union Company's mail contract, no mean aid in running ships to and from South Africa, was due to expire. In the meantime he made friends at the Cape, and was, at last, given the contract to carry the homeward mail.

But the greatest triumph was still to come: the competition for the subsidy paid by the British Government. What would happen ? In the result the Government decided that Currie's enterprise should be rewarded by allowing him to have half the mail subsidy, the other moiety being allotted to his older rival.

RIVALS AMALGAMATE

Though Currie afterwards entered the House of Commons as M.P. for Perthshire, his mind was still occupied with shipping problems. His first love was still the steamship company which he had founded. It continued to prosper under his leadership, and, at last, in 1900 he and Sir Francis Evans, of the Union Steamship Company, agreed to call a truce to rivalry on the South African route, which had cost both concerns no mean sum. So the two fleets were amalgamated under the title of the Union Castle Steamship Company, Sir Francis becoming a director of the amalgamated companies and his former competitor chairman. Thus it happened that when the young clerk from Greenock died he had successfully founded a great steamship line and had swallowed the rival company, entrenched in a safe monopoly, which he had had the amazing courage to challenge.

ROYAL MAIL COMPANY

For Scotsmen shipping has always had an attraction; perhaps it is because they are romantic as well as adventurous. Who today remembers that other Scotsman, James MacQueen, who was the founder of the P. & O. line of the western seas— the Royal Mail Steam Packet Company ? At an early age he left his home in Crawford, Lanarkshire, with little except his brain as capital, and before he had reached his majority was managing a sugar estate at Grenada, one of the West India Islands. But his passion was travel. He acquired an encyclopædic knowledge of the Spanish Main, its islands, its ports and its undeveloped wealth. Some chance event led him to return to Scotland, where he settled in Glasgow. Here he edited the *Glasgow Courier*, but his heart was not in the work. He seized every opportunity to go overseas, and he suffered all the trials of voyages in ships whose chief merit was that they could float.

The mails to the West Indies were then carried from Falmouth by the Admiralty, in what were known as "coffin ships," sailing vessels which were as slow as they were uncomfortable; the letters were distributed to the larger islands by old 10-gun brigs into which steam-engines of 100 horse-power had been fitted. The cramped saloons in these brigs, which were placed over the boile᷄ ᷄ were lighted, of course, by oil lamps which swung to and fro as the ship pitched or rolled, giving off the familiar smell of this means of lighting, and they were without ventilation. The boilers used up vast quantities of coal, and when the capacious bunkers were being filled, the passengers had either to remain amid the coal-dust on deck, gradually taking on the appearance of negroes, or retreat to the airless saloon, however high the temperature.

MacQueen was a dreamer as well as a geographer and journalist, but where business men merely grumbled, he acted. In the year 1837 he submitted plans to the Government for a steam packet service —incidentally describing the Admiralty's ships as "a disgrace to the country."

His first overtures were not well received, but, nevertheless, he persevered with his ideas. Eventually he drew up a generous scheme for a mail communication between Great Britain and the eastern and western parts of the world, as well as Canton and Sydney, providing, incidentally, for the canal through the Central American isthmus, constructed many years later—after surmounting great difficulties—the Panama Canal.

POST OFFICE SUPPORT

He was not content to have his plan pigeon-holed and forgotten, but took the nation into his confidence, and soon gained the support of business men. He told them that "mails can never be carried either regularly or with certainty in vessels, the chief object and dependence of which is to carry merchandise," thus foreshadowing the luxury liners of later years. "Steamboats carrying mails," he went on to plead, "should be the mail coaches of the ocean, limited, as mail coaches on land are, as to cargoes." He summed up the matter in these words. "The object being a national one, it ought to be carried into effect by the nation," and he urged that "no narrow or parsimonious view

should be tolerated"—this appears to have been an obvious hit at the Treasury.

At the Post Office there was a man, Rowland Hill, who held much the same progressive views. Under the influence of these men of vision and in face of much opposition, the Government at last capitulated, the penny post was introduced in the British Isles, and tenders were sought for carrying the mails more or less in accordance with MacQueen's ideas, to the West Indies, North America, and the Far East. MacQueen's dreams were justified.

SUBSIDY FROM THE ADMIRALTY

But before this surrender to the all-conquering steamship, MacQueen had laid the foundations of the Royal Mail Company in 1839. He had gained the ears of the members of the West India Committee, which had existed in London since 1760, for large fortunes were made out of these dependencies in the eighteenth century. The Committee consisted of planters and merchants who had long been dissatisfied with existing shipping services, and were determined to improve them.

They were, at last, convinced that MacQueen's dream might become a reality; but they evidently had no high opinion of the dreamer's business ability; he was not made a director of the Company, but was grandly described as "General Superintendent of Affairs."

His first task was to obtain a Royal Charter. The Royal coat of arms was adopted as the company's seal, which was to be seen henceforth on all its ships, the noblest and the most humble, as well as on its tariff of charges. MacQueen's next act was to secure a subsidy from the Admiralty for a service of steam packets to Barbados, Grenada, Santa Cruz, St. Thomas, Nicola Mole, Santiago de Cuba, Port Royal, Savannah le Mar and Havana, with branch services to all the smaller islands as well as to New York and Halifax. Thus the Royal Mail Steam

Packet Company started on its long career.

The coming of steam gave a fillip to the British tramp ship—the ship which tramps the seas to pick up a profitable bulk cargo wherever one is on offer.

The tramp ship was the product of the industrial progress of this country. Many raw materials were demanded from overseas which had not been needed before, and the population, owing to the prosperity of the country, increased so rapidly that the soil of the British Isles could not produce all the food that was required; so, much of it had to be bought overseas, and, of course, in the cheapest overseas markets. The number of men, women and children in Great Britain in 1811 was only just over 10,000,000, but by the end of the century the figure had increased to upwards of 30,000,000, and in 1942 it had risen to not far short of 50,000,000.

As grain and other things were obtainable by the industrial workers at a small outlay, employers could keep their wages down, and the products of their industry could compete successfully with those of other countries—so successfully that year by year the national trading account showed a favourable balance. This was invested in the Dominions and in foreign countries in development schemes. Investors thus obtained higher rates of interest than British concerns would pay for their capital. It became a matter of exchange of British manufactures and coal for raw materials and food.

ERA OF NATIONAL PROSPERITY

The foundation of this economic structure was freedom of trading. No taxes were levied in order to keep imports out of British ports, and no restrictions were placed on foreign ships which carried immense quantities of commodities to and from the British Isles.

To the satisfactory trading position of the country early in the nineteenth century, the tramp ship made a great contri-

bution. It was built cheaply and operated cheaply. It was the expression of individual enterprise. Napoleon once declared that "in war it is not so much the men as the man that counts." That dictum also applies to tramp shipping, perhaps, more than to passenger liners, for the founder of practically every fleet of tramp ships was a seaman, or a clerk in a shipping office, with no capital but his brains, his shrewdness and his determination to improve his own position in the world.

TRAMP SHIP OWNERS

Lord Runciman, Sir Edward Nicholl, Sir William Reardon-Smith, Sir Edward Hain—all of them now dead—may be quoted as among the shipowners who began life as lads before the mast. There is talk these days of equality of opportunity. Each of these seamen, with no silver spoon in his mouth, made his own opportunity, and achieved success.

The tramp shipowner evolved an ingenious system by which he might become the owner of a ship—the sixty-four system, each ship being represented by sixty-four shares. Some shipbuilders built ships and set up managers to own them, retaining a mortgage on the ship until the instalments were paid. Throughout the country districts men were told of the profits which could be made in good times on sixty-fourth ships and freely invested their surplus profits in shares.

Down to about 1885 there were probably fewer than a dozen limited liability companies owning tramp steamers. When bad times came the "Sixty-fourthers," as they were commonly known, instead of receiving handsome dividends, found themselves liable for large calls. In consequence a new era opened when a shipowner conceived the idea of turning the ownership of a single vessel into a limited liability company. This development was popular, and the practice is still frequently adopted.

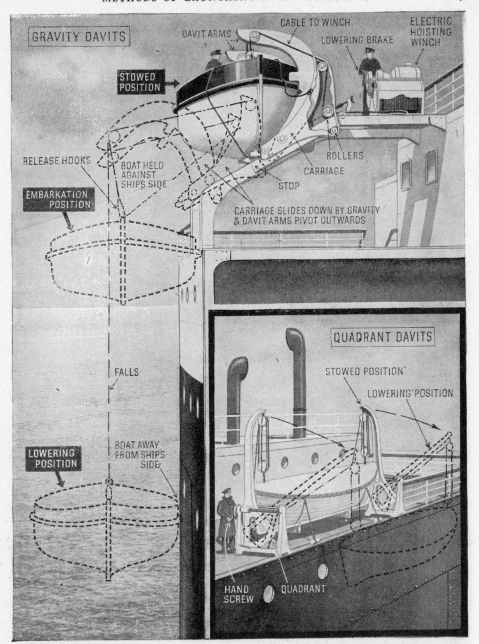

GRAVITY DAVITS

DAVIT ARMS

CABLE TO WINCH

LOWERING BRAKE

ELECTRIC HOISTING WINCH

STOWED POSITION

RELEASE HOOKS

BOAT HELD AGAINST SHIP'S SIDE

ROLLERS

CARRIAGE

STOP

EMBARKATION POSITION

CARRIAGE SLIDES DOWN BY GRAVITY & DAVIT ARMS PIVOT OUTWARDS

FALLS

QUADRANT DAVITS

STOWED POSITION

LOWERING POSITION

LOWERING POSITION

BOAT AWAY FROM SHIP'S SIDE

HAND SCREW

QUADRANT

LIFEBOATS LOWERED BY GRAVITY AND QUADRANT DAVITS

When the lowering brake is released, gravity davits slide down an inclined way. They then come to a stop and the davit arms swing outwards to hold the lifeboat in the correct embarkation position, ready for lowering. Quadrant davits (inset) bring the lifeboat to lowering position by the use of a hand screw. Hand davits of the old gooseneck type are now becoming obsolete

CONVOY WINS THROUGH TO MALTA DESPITE CONTINUOUS

*A salvo of bombs falls harmlessly between two of the ships of a big convoy for Malta. In the
foreground are anti-aircraft guns of one of the escorting warships which forced a way for*

ATTACKS BY E-BOATS, BY SUBMARINES, AND FROM THE AIR
the vessels in their charge. Enemy attack was relentless for several days. Two E-boats were sunk, and 66 Axis aircraft certainly destroyed. We also sank two enemy submarines

The secret of the success of the tramp was individualism—the thrift and enterprise of one man. When a young sailor, who had taken his master's certificate, decided to become a shipowner, he issued no prospectus inviting investors to come forward with their money. He would save all he could while serving at sea and then buy a second-hand ship, usually when there was a depression in freights, and the prices of tonnage were low. He might get a few friends to join him in the venture or he might mortgage the vessel to a bank.

ADVENTUROUS SHIPOWNERS

Most of the early tramp shipping companies were formed by "chapel" people, and especially by those who belonged to the Methodist chapels on the North-East coast, in Cornwall, and in Wales. They were thrifty men and women, and when one of the congregation who had made the sea his calling had gained their confidence, they would entrust him with their savings for investment in his first ship.

If he was fortunate in his trading, he would either use his savings to buy another vessel or would pay back the money which had been lent to him for the purchase of his first vessel, and then await the time when, out of his own pocket, he could pay for another. In this way many a tramp fleet was established.

By hook or by crook the aspiring owner would provide the necessary funds to purchase a ship. He would take command himself and thus make bigger profits than a vessel which was not operated by its owner. And he would continue to educate himself while afloat, and continue to save all he could during every voyage, until he was able to buy another vessel.

Thus he would slowly build up a fleet of tramp ships, always providing out of his earnings reserves against "a rainy day" and other reserves known as "depreciation," so that as each ship wore out he would be in a position to purchase another

one second-hand or place an order with a builder for a new one. It was a proud day for the ambitious owner when his wife, or daughter, broke a bottle of wine over the stern of the first ship constructed to his order and not bought in the sale market.

Sometimes if the owner and builder were friends there would be no written contract; the two men would meet, discuss the design of the new vessel, her speed, and so on, and haggle over the price in a friendly spirit. Having reached a figure which the owner considered reasonable they would shake hands on the bargain, and there was often no record of it on paper. By such methods the tramp section of the shipping industry was fostered in a fine spirit of adventure.

The captains and crews of a tramp ship in the Victorian era never lacked adventure, and in spite of the hardships, often including poor food, uncomfortable quarters and small wages, they enjoyed the life. Son would follow father and grandfather to sea. It was the calling they loved.

Most of us are familiar with the sea stories of Marryat, Stevenson, Conrad, Clark Russell and others, but many tramp owners of the last hundred years could tell tales of the sea which, for daring and adventure, and business risk, were far more exciting than those of the novelists.

SAFETY AT SEA

The story of how the British Merchant Navy was built up would not be complete without some account of the "Safety At Sea" movement, which eventually won for British ships the reputation of being the most seaworthy, well designed, well built, well managed, and well manned.

A few years ago Sir Westcott Abell wrote a book on this subject to which he had the courage, derived from a study of statistics of ship losses in the past, to give the title *The Safe Sea*. It is a record of achievement of which the nation may be proud, for Parliament had first to insist on reform, in face of considerable opposition; not all shipowners were conscious of their responsibility for the safety of the lives of the officers and men who sailed in their ships.

As the industrial movement in the British Isles made progress after the close of the Napoleonic wars and this country became increasingly dependent on shipping for its imports and exports, popular

Foreign Office, made inquiries of British Consuls throughout the world as to the condition of British shipping, especially in regard to the efficiency of the officers and men, which led to revelations of laxity in the performance of the ordinary duties on board ship. Further legislation was passed in 1846 to ensure greater safety at sea; in 1849 the last remnants of

WOMEN HELP WITH THE LIFEBOAT

When a lifeboat of the Royal National Institution was called out to a merchant ship in distress, thirty women of Newbiggin, Northumberland, helped to drag the lifeboat up a cliff and through the sand dunes, fighting all the way against a bitter gale and fierce sleet

interest in the conditions in the important shipping industry very naturally increased. In 1823 Parliament entered on the task of repealing the Navigation Laws; in 1836 a committee was appointed to inquire into the causes of wrecks, which were so numerous as to occasion public anxiety; in 1843 Mr. James Murray, of the

the Navigation Acts were swept away by Parliament; and in 1850 the Marine Department of the Board of Trade was established for the purpose of tightening up the application of the existing laws. In these circumstances the battle for the load line opened; the public demanded action in that direction, and the Govern-

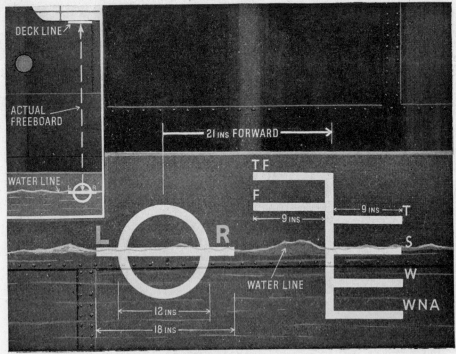

PLIMSOLL LOAD LINE

These lines are cut or painted on both sides of a ship to indicate the depths to which she can safely be loaded in any part of the globe. Initials indicate Tropical Fresh Water, Summer, Winter, Winter North Atlantic. Inset, the actual freeboard of a vessel from the waterline

ment of the day sat on the fence. In the 'sixties, James Hall, a shipowner of Tynemouth, called attention to the large number of ships which were lost at sea, and urged the Government to take action. He prepared the way for Samuel Plimsoll, who, from 1870 onwards, carried on an agitation in favour of a safety load line. He secured a seat in Parliament in 1868—not for a seaport, but for Derby. Having exposed the scandal of overloading and tried, unsuccessfully, to get Parliament to pass a bill which he had drafted for improving conditions at sea, Samuel Plimsoll prevailed, at length, on the Government of the day to agree to an inquiry into the scandal of what he described as "coffin ships."

This Royal Commission exposed the malpractices which were going on and the sufferings of the seamen serving bad owners. A reform bill was introduced into the House of Commons in 1875, but was subsequently dropped, to the chagrin of Plimsoll, who was bitterly disappointed.

But the case against these inhumane shipowners had impressed the country, and a bill to restrain them was passed in the following year. A load line, such as Plimsoll had advocated, was legalized.

In 1884, at the instigation of Mr. Joseph Chamberlain—then President of the Board of Trade—an amending act was placed on the Statute Book which strengthened the law.

In explaining this measure to the House of Commons, Mr. Chamberlain made it quite clear that he excluded from condemnation the majority of shipowners. In later years the movement to increase safety at sea owed its progress mainly to the action of what are called the classification societies, such as Lloyd's Register of Shipping, an offshoot of Lloyd's, the greatest marine insurance body in the world, and the British Corporation Register for the survey and registry of shipping. These bodies, on which shipowners, shipbuilders and underwriters are represented, supervise the building of all ships, and thus, apart from the law as administered by the Board of Trade, make doubly sure that a ship's design and equipment spell safety, and periodical surveys keep her seaworthy.

The classification societies, in the interest, not only of the officers and men, but in the interests of insurers and owners, now reinforce the law, and in some cases go far beyond it. The shipowner who acquires a good character owing to the care he takes of his ships can secure better insurance terms than one who is less scrupulous. In this way honesty in obeying the law, and even going beyond its provisions, has become the best policy.

By the action of Parliament and of the classification societies, the sea has been made increasingly safe. Under the

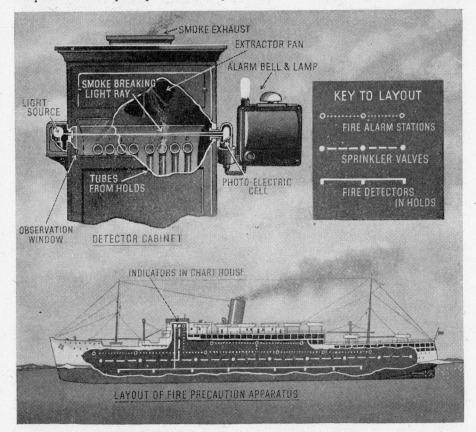

METHODS OF FIRE CONTROL ON SHIPS

The fire detector cabinet is on the bridge (top, left). A fan exhausts air from all the holds and closed spaces through small numbered pipes, and in the event of fire smoke is instantly drawn up and seen through the observation window. A photo-electric cell gives immediate warning of any smoke by breaking a ray which causes an alarm bell to ring and a lamp to light

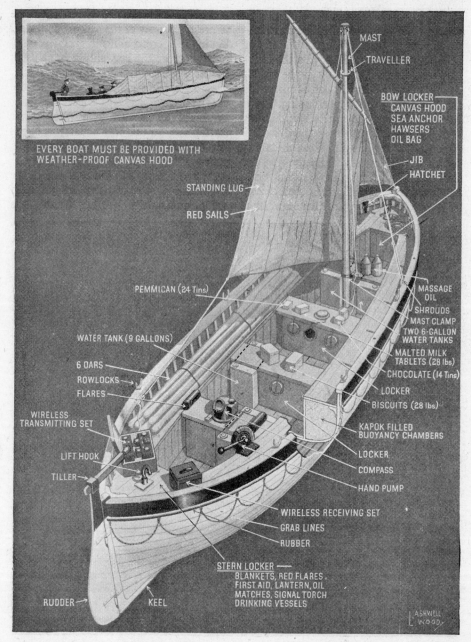

EVERY BOAT MUST BE PROVIDED WITH
WEATHER-PROOF CANVAS HOOD

MAST

TRAVELLER

BOW LOCKER
CANVAS HOOD
SEA ANCHOR
HAWSERS
OIL BAG

JIB

HATCHET

STANDING LUG

RED SAILS

PEMMICAN (24 Tins)

WATER TANK (9 GALLONS)

6 OARS

ROWLOCKS

FLARES

WIRELESS
TRANSMITTING SET

LIFT HOOK

TILLER

RUDDER

KEEL

MASSAGE
OIL

SHROUDS

MAST CLAMP

TWO 6-GALLON
WATER TANKS

MALTED MILK
TABLETS (28 lbs)

CHOCOLATE (14 Tins)

LOCKER

BISCUITS (28 lbs)

KAPOK FILLED
BUOYANCY CHAMBERS

LOCKER

COMPASS

HAND PUMP

WIRELESS RECEIVING SET

GRAB LINES

RUBBER

STERN LOCKER
BLANKETS, RED FLARES.
FIRST AID, LANTERN, OIL
MATCHES, SIGNAL TORCH
DRINKING VESSELS

L.ASHWELL
WOOD.

NEW LIFEBOAT AND COMPLETE SAFETY EQUIPMENT

Many improvements and life-saving devices help the men of the Merchant Navy. Picture
shows full details of equipment for ships' lifeboats, in accordance with new Ministry of
War Transport regulations. Water tanks contain enough water for a fortnight at sea.
Emergency rations of biscuits, chocolate, milk tablets, and meat extract must also be carried

Merchant Shipping Acts, passed between 1894 and 1906, it is compulsory for all British ships, with a few exceptions—such as sailing ships under eighty tons register engaged in the coasting trade, fishing vessels, certain coasting steamers and pleasure yachts—to be marked with a load line in accordance with freeboard tables. The Committee of Lloyd's Register is empowered to administer these regulations.

LIFEBOAT REGULATIONS

The extent to which a ship can be loaded is not always the same. The maximum load line varies: (a) if the ship is in fresh water; (b) if the ship is sailing during the Indian Summer between Suez and Singapore; or in other seas in winter and summer, there being special winter marking for the North Atlantic. The maximum load lines are by initial letters:

F.	...	Fresh water.
I.S.	...	Indian Summer.
S.	...	Summer.
W.	...	Winter.
W.N.A.	...	Winter, North Atlantic.

The principal rules applying to lifeboats provide that a ship shall carry on each side sufficient lifeboats not less than twenty-four feet in length, to accommodate every member of the crew, and, in addition, lifeboats of an aggregate capacity to take the total number of passengers the ship is permitted to carry. All lifeboat and launching gear must be kept ready to enable the lifeboats to be lowered without delay.

The launching gear must be of sufficient power to ensure that the boat can be turned out against the maximum list at which the lowering of the boats is possible. To comply with the rules of the Ministry the equipment of every lifeboat is remarkably complete against emergencies, and all items of equipment not kept in the lifeboat lockers, with the exception of the boathook, kept free for fending-off purposes, must be lashed within the boat. Rations on a specified scale include chocolate, milk tablets, pemmican (or other meat extract), and biscuits. Flare lights, smoke signals, rockets, charts are also compulsory.

Methods of fire prevention and control have been considerably improved.

On the outbreak of war in 1939 the work of the Marine Department of the Board of Trade was taken over by the Ministry of Shipping; later, that Ministry and the Ministry of Transport were combined in the Ministry of War Transport, dealing with all transport by land and sea.

In the course of years the casualties at sea, in peace time, have been greatly reduced, and there has been a consequent saving of life—of seamen as well as passengers. Between 1890 and 1913—that is, on the eve of the first World War—the rate of loss from all causes fell by nearly one half. Though later statistics have not been examined, it is known that the improvement has since continued, partly as a result of the more general adoption of wireless telegraphy in all but the smallest ships, and the fitting of direction-finders and depth-sounding apparatus, and partly owing to the provision of more lightships and buoys on the coasts, and of more lifeboats and seaworthy rafts for ships.

MAXIMUM SAFETY THE AIM

There will be no turning back in respect of the provision of wireless equipment, better lifeboats and more efficient life-saving appliances in the endeavour to secure the highest safety for our seamen.

It may be claimed that it is now safer under peace conditions to make a voyage on any of the Seven Seas in a British ship than to cross a crowded street in a great city, with its buses and motor cars. In 1937 the lives lost through wrecks at sea were only 134; 131 seamen and 3 passengers. In the same year no fewer than 6,633 persons were killed on the roads of Great Britain; in London alone the number who lost their lives was nearly 1,000.

AIR-SEA RESCUE SERVICE

In his rubber dinghy, hanging on to a Walrus amphibian aircraft, a pilot is waiting to be picked up. Launches and aircraft work together in the rescue of airmen forced down on the sea

CHAPTER 11

Battles Against Great Odds

Germany's savage war on merchant ships. "Sink at sight." Gallant fight of the "Rawalpindi." Tricks of enemy raiders. Heroines under fire. Great work of Merchant Navy gunners. How the "Jervis Bay" saved a convoy. Duels with submarines. H.M.S. "Cossack" sets British captives free. "City of Benares." Rescues by aircraft. Adrift for seventy days.

LESS than twelve hours after war was declared in 1939, Germany broke the agreement not "to sink or render incapable of navigation a merchant vessel without having first placed passengers, crew and ship's papers in a place of safety." Her first victim, the passenger liner *Athenia*, sailing from the United Kingdom to Canada, was torpedoed without warning when 200 miles from land. Americans were among the passengers.

The submarine came to the surface, fired a shell and left passengers and crew to their fate. More than a hundred were killed or drowned.

The Germans declared to the world that Mr. Churchill, then First Lord of the Admiralty, had had the liner torpedoed in order to create tension between the United States and Germany. The British Government answered this impudent propaganda by assuring the United States Government that the *Athenia* carried no guns, either as cargo or as armament, and that she had not been sunk by British mine, submarine, or destroyer.

It was soon evident that German submarines were operating on stations so far from home waters that they must have been sent out some time before war was declared. British merchant ships, on their peaceful errands, were scattered far and wide on the Seven Seas at the outbreak of war, and twenty-one vessels were lost in a couple of weeks. Neutral countries also suffered; a Belgian ship was sunk near Weymouth—it was believed, by a mine. The ship was cut clean in two. No British mines had been laid in this spot. If the cause of sinking was a mine, Germany had again violated International Law by not notifying the laying of a minefield.

In the weeks that followed German mines caused grievous loss to neutrals. By November five Dutch ships had been sunk, including the *Simon Bolivar*; and the British Admiralty suggested that the mine which sank the ship had been laid deliberately in the fairway used by neutral shipping. Among the survivors were several children and babies. A father saved his three-year-old daughter by putting her in an open box, which had been part of a deck game. As he swam behind her, the child asked: "Are we going to Trinidad in this, daddy?"

British minesweepers set to work, and drifters were called on to help in this dangerous job, with 2,000 volunteers, who were mostly fishermen, to man them. Then three months after war began, there came news in one weekend of sinkings by mines of Swedish, Norwegian, Danish, Italian, Lithuanian and Yugoslav ships. Protests from these neutrals did nothing to minimize their danger.

British merchant shipping also, of course, suffered. Day by day stories were published of British steamers sunk.

Sometimes just the bare statement: "The British steamer *Kennebec*, of 5,548 tons, has been sunk by submarine. Her crew was picked up"; or, more fully: "The captain and crew of twenty of the British steamer *Goodwood*, which was attacked in the North Sea, have been landed by a fishing boat which picked them up out of the water. The captain is in hospital with both legs broken."

There were personal stories like the narrative of a seaman from the Atlantic:

"In the last war, I was in the Merchant Navy and I knew what being attacked was; I was in a ship that was mined, in one shelled, and in one torpedoed. I hope to

be in another ship in less than a month. We first sighted the submarine not less than a hundred yards away. It fired twice with its gun, so the captain ordered us to abandon ship. We got our officers and crew away in the ship's boats.

"The submarine commander got impatient and fired again. The submarine came closer to us, and the commander spoke in perfect English to the captain. He said: "I am going to sink your ship, captain. Goodbye !""

"Sink at sight" with no warning, was Germany's policy and practice from the start. The second month of the war saw the sinking of the British liners *Yorkshire* and *City of Mandalay*. Some 300 were rescued by the American vessel *Independence Hall*, which, *en route* to help the

BATTLE OF THE ATLANTIC—PORTRAIT OF A SURVIVOR

This man is a survivor. He lies helpless and unmoving on his raft, unconscious through exposure to the bitter winter cold of the North Atlantic. He is one of the crew of a large merchant vessel sunk by submarine attack 160 miles off the coast. Ninety of his comrades lost their lives

FLYING BOAT SAVED TWENTY SEAMEN

This ship's lifeboat, crowded with twenty survivors, was 150 miles from land when an R.A.F. Sunderland flying-boat spotted it. The captain of the Sunderland signalled assurance of help and eventually succeeded in calling up a French vessel to rescue the men in the lifeboat

Yorkshire, received an SOS from the *City of Mandalay*. One of the passengers on the rescuing ship describes the scene:

"We were at dinner when the steward informed us that we were approaching the *City of Mandalay*. A terrible spectacle confronted us. From the deck we saw the doomed steamer sink into the sea.

"There were four small boats packed to sinking point. Men were swimming in the sea, and we heard the cries of children. The officers of the British ship were sublime. Only two of them escaped; all the rest went down with their ship.

"One officer, who was saved, was the last to jump from the *Yorkshire*. He was caught in the suction of the sinking ship and was then shot out of the water. He was the last person to be rescued." In these early days a few submarine commanders followed the traditions of the sea. The captain and officers of the

British ship *Truro* were taken aboard a U-boat and given the alternative of indefinite captivity or signing an undertaking to keep off the sea for the duration. They chose the latter course and were turned adrift after being provided with cigarettes and twenty-four bottles of beer!

Another German submarine which sank a British ship in the Atlantic had a considerate commander. Bread was handed out to the sunken ship's crew. They were given bandages for the injured, and an SOS was sent giving the position.

The Lifeboat Service was busy. In September, 1939, the Royal National Lifeboat Institution launched its boats fifty-two times, saving nearly 200 lives. During thirty-five months of war the Institution's lifeboats were launched to the rescue 2,531 times, saving 4,772 lives. For continued and valuable work in aiding the rescue of airmen compelled to force-land in the sea, the Institution received the thanks of the Air Council. But the chief help of the Lifeboat Service was given to the merchant ships, and the Service helped to save from destruction over two hundred boats and vessels.

By January, 1940, over half of Britain's merchant fleet had been equipped with anti-submarine and anti-aircraft guns, and men of the Merchant Navy were being trained to man the guns. This measure brought angry and hypocritical protests from the German press, which claimed that this armament justified merchant ships being treated as auxiliary cruisers. International Law, declared the Germans, does not recognize an armed merchant ship. Germany's preposterous contention was that she had kept strictly to the generally accepted principles of commercial warfare: Great Britain had repeatedly disregarded them!

In fact, British merchant ships were, at this time, armed purely for defence, their guns being placed aft so that they could not fire from an attacking position. A merchantman converted into an armed merchant cruiser was a different matter.

Such was the *Rawalpindi*, which, cruising one afternoon to the south-east of Iceland, sighted an enemy ship.

"RAWALPINDI'S" GALLANT FIGHT

The crew were ordered to action stations. The enemy was indentified as the 10,000-ton pocket battleship *Deutschland*. She was known to have a speed of twenty-six knots, while the *Rawalpindi's* maximum was eighteen. Course was altered to bring the enemy on the starboard quarter, and smoke-floats were lit to help screen the *Rawalpindi*. A second enemy ship was seen, also to starboard.

The *Deutschland* signalled to the *Rawalpindi* to stop, and, when she continued her course, fired across her bows. As the *Rawalpindi* ignored the warning the *Deutschland* fired her first salvo from her 11-inch guns. The *Rawalpindi* replied with her four starboard 6-inch guns. The third and fourth enemy salvoes put out all the lights, broke the electric winches of the ammunition supply, and shot away the bridge and the wireless-room. Meanwhile, the second enemy ship had manœuvred round to the *Rawalpindi's* port side and was firing from there. The gallant *Rawalpindi* continued to fight until every gun was out of action, and the ship ablaze.

ENEMY DISGUISES

After about half an hour of this hopelessly unequal duel, the enemy ceased fire, and three boats were lowered from the *Rawalpindi*. Eventually, the British ship foundered, with most of her crew.

The *Deutschland* was of the same class as the *Admiral Scheer* and *Admiral Graf Spee*, and had been operating in the Atlantic for some weeks. She had sunk the *Stonegate* and had seized the American steamer *City of Flint*, placing on board a German prize crew, an incident which set diplomats by the ears. The *Stonegate's* crew were taken on board the *Deutschland*, were given tobacco and cigarettes, and then transferred to the *City of Flint*.

Enemy raiders adopted many tricks of disguise. Some flew a neutral flag. For instance, the German liner *Windhuk*, which acted for a time as supply ship to the *Admiral Graf Spee*, had been refitted to carry the full armament of a raider, her speed being increased, and was disguised to resemble a British ship. The Hamburg-American liner *Cap Norte*, which was captured by the British Navy, had been repainted and renamed, the Swedish flag being painted on her side. The *Leander*, which was also captured, had been masquerading as a Russian vessel; and an American sea captain watched a fight between a British destroyer and a submarine in the Bristol Channel. The enemy submarine was disguised with rigging to resemble a fishing craft. Another raider

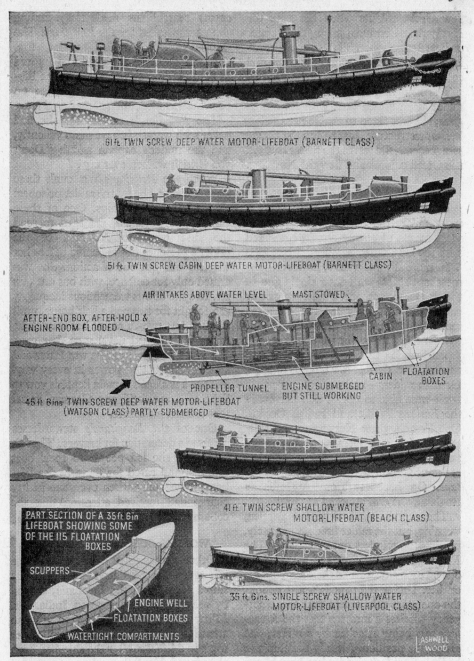

61 ft. TWIN SCREW DEEP WATER MOTOR-LIFEBOAT (BARNETT CLASS)

51 ft. TWIN SCREW CABIN DEEP WATER MOTOR-LIFEBOAT (BARNETT CLASS)

AIR INTAKES ABOVE WATER LEVEL   MAST STOWED

AFTER-END BOX, AFTER-HOLD &
ENGINE ROOM FLOODED

CABIN   FLOATATION
BOXES

PROPELLER TUNNEL   ENGINE SUBMERGED
BUT STILL WORKING

45 ft. 6 ins. TWIN SCREW DEEP WATER MOTOR-LIFEBOAT
(WATSON CLASS) PARTLY SUBMERGED

41 ft. TWIN SCREW SHALLOW WATER
MOTOR-LIFEBOAT (BEACH CLASS)

PART SECTION OF A 35 ft. 6 in.
LIFEBOAT SHOWING SOME
OF THE 115 FLOATATION
BOXES

SCUPPERS

ENGINE WELL

FLOATATION BOXES

WATERTIGHT COMPARTMENTS

35 ft. 6 ins. SINGLE SCREW SHALLOW WATER
MOTOR-LIFEBOAT (LIVERPOOL CLASS)

ASHWELL
WOOD

UNSINKABLE MOTOR-LIFEBOATS
*The many types of modern motor-lifeboats are of two main classes—deep water and shallow
water boats. They are launched down slipways, or down a beach on rollers, or from transporting carriages. During three years of the war R.N.L.I. lifeboats rescued 4,772 lives*

flew Greek colours when she sank the *Haxby* near Bermuda, taking the skipper on board as prisoner. She also used Brazilian and Dutch colours, and the name and colours of a Swedish vessel, the *Narvik*.

The captain of the *Haxby* reported this raider as an armed liner with six 6-inch guns; she was fitted to enable her to alter her superstructure. Just before the *Haxby* sank beneath the waves the raider covered the Greek colours and flew the Nazi flag.

PACIFIC SINKINGS

U-boats, which could operate 4,000 or more miles from their bases, were the main means of enemy attack, combined with the long-range bombers.

In more distant waters, however, lone merchant ships, with their single gun in the stern and, perhaps, a machine gun or two, were easy prey for the disguised merchant raiders that managed to slip past British patrols—or were fitted out in Japan while that country was still neutral. In the last few months of 1940, German raiders—perhaps not more than two—were able to reap a rich harvest in the Eastern Pacific and Indian Oceans. One French, three Norwegian and thirteen British and Dominion ships were sunk, some after gallant but hopeless resistance. Among these was the *Rangitane*. On her way from Australia to England, she was attacked at dawn.

The captain tried to give a wireless warning, but the raider fired immediately, putting the wireless out of action. The *Rangitane* opened fire, and two raiders, one on each side, turned their searchlights on her. Under the captain's instructions the operators calmly sent over the emergency wireless a message that the *Rangitane* was being attacked by a raider, and giving the position. Already the ship was badly battered, the bridge had been blown away, and there was a fire below. After heavy shelling the captain ordered the engines to be stopped. The glare of the enemy searchlights made range-finding almost impossible for the *Rangitane*. The ship's surgeon worked under fire. Stewards gathered the dead and injured in blankets and carried them to the lifeboats. Six of the forty-six women on board were killed, and another died later.

The *Rangitane*'s captain said he had never seen women behave more valiantly, and the raider's captain asked: "Don't you British women ever cry?"

When the *Rangitane* was sunk there were already on board the raider prisoners from several other ships. One of these vessels, the *Turakina*, managed to send the first news to Australia of the raider's presence in the Pacific before her wireless was put out of action. She was armed only for defence, with but one gun aft. In spite of this tremendous inequality she fought for two and a half hours, until she had lost two-thirds of her crew. The raider had trained naval men, her guns had greater range, and she was faster and superior in fighting power in every way. But the *Turakina*'s captain kept his vow to fight to a standstill any German vessel that crossed his course.

One of the *Rangitane*'s stewardesses received a decoration for bravery. Though wounded, she led people to their boat stations, and cared for them in the lifeboat; it was only when everyone in her charge had received attention that she collapsed, fainting from loss of blood.

WOMAN SURGEON'S HEROISM

Other women filled heroic rôles in the war at sea. Dr. Adaline Nancy Millar was ship's surgeon on the *Britannia*, shelled by a raider on a voyage to India. Dr. Millar went on deck during the firing to attend to the wounded, and continued her work in a lifeboat after the ship had been abandoned. Her father, who was on board an armed merchant cruiser, heard of the sinking of the *Britannia* over the wireless. After three days of anxiety the cruiser stopped a Spanish vessel and by an amazing twist of good fortune he found his daughter on board. Dr. Millar was awarded the M.B.E. A woman engineer was also decorated. When her ship was attacked by dive bombers she remained alone in the engine-room, coaxing more and more speed out of the engines, till the ship successfully eluded the enemy.

Navy won fame in these battles, no less than the men of the Fighter Command and the other services. The seamen faced their ordeal with wonderful spirit and determination—and accurate shooting.

Many gunners in merchant ships had old scores to wipe out, and were eager for an opportunity. Second Officer Peter Filcek, of the *Highwear*, had been in a ship

"KENSINGTON COURT" SUNK—ALL ON BOARD SAVED

An SOS from the torpedoed "Kensington Court," sinking in the Atlantic, was so promptly answered by flying-boats of the R.A.F. that not one of the thirty-four men on board was lost

Dive bombing and other forms of attack from the air were a terrible menace both to ocean-going and coastal shipping. Even defenceless lightships were bombed and machine gunned. But during the year March, 1941-42, when 82 per cent of the Luftwaffe's air attacks were made in daylight, the percentage of losses steadily decreased. For this the credit was due, largely, to the Royal Air Force, whose co-operation with naval escort ships protected coastal convoys. The men of the Merchant

sunk by the *Admiral Graf Spee*. He had been for weeks a prisoner in the *Altmark*, and had swum for his life from another torpedoed ship. His ship was sailing in convoy when a Dornier approached. Second Officer Filcek held his fire until the plane was only about 100 feet above the water and at 300 yards range he fired his Lewis gun. The Dornier hit the water, its bombs exploded, and when the spray had cleared there was nothing to be seen. In and out of convoy the stories of

"EMPRESS OF BRITAIN" IN FLAMES AFTER

One hundred and fifty miles off the Irish coast, the "Empress of Britain," 42,000 tons, the chief liner of the Canadian Pacific Company, was attacked by dive bombers, which made direct hits with both high-explosive and incendiary bombs, and left her blazing furiously. Later the great ship was torpedoed, and had to be abandoned. Salvage operations were speedily attempted, and tugs tried to bring her to port. These efforts were unsuccessful, and eventually the liner blew up and sank. There were 643 people on board, including military families and a small number of military personnel. Fortunately, there was little loss of life, 598 survivors being rescued and brought to port by British warships. Captain C. H. Sapsworth, C.V.O.,

ATTACK BY GERMAN DIVE BOMBERS

the commander of the "Empress of Britain," remained with his ship until she sank, and was then rescued. One of the survivors reported that the fire spread so rapidly that boats had to be got away with only a few men in them, in order that they could be safely floated and afterwards pick up the passengers and crew. The "Empress of Britain," one of the most important units of Britain's Merchant Navy, brought their Majesties the King and Queen back from Canada in 1939. Captain C. H. Sapsworth, who stayed on the bridge till it was burning under him, commanded the ship at that time also, and His Majesty invested him with the insignia of the C.V.O. as the liner steamed up the Channel on her homeward journey

courage and cool behaviour were legion. As ships left port and the protection of Fighter Command, they passed into the care of the long-range aircraft of Coastal Command. At sea, men would watch a distant speck. "Is it a Lockheed or is it a Sunderland?" and to quote the words of a merchant seaman, Frank Laskier: ". . . suddenly an idea flashes across the back of your mind. 'My God! It's a Jerry!' And you make one flying dash towards the Hotchkiss and you scream out 'Aircraft attack!'"

About three days out from Australia a ship's crew heard just such an approaching plane. It was flying low, and British markings could be seen. But hanging from it was a wire and plummet. This tore away the ship's aerial. A message dropped on deck ordered the ship to stop and not to use the wireless.

The captain rigged an emergency aerial. The plane returned and began dive bombing and machine gunning. Soon a raider, acting with the plane, appeared and gave chase. There was small chance of escape, as the raider had twenty knots to her victim's twelve. She began firing at close range, and the order to abandon ship was given. The raider took the crew on board.

NARROW ESCAPES

Afterwards they learned that the attack had been made in daylight and by very elaborate methods in an attempt to capture the ship undamaged for use as a store ship. The rigging of the emergency aerial frustrated this plan.

When it is remembered that mighty battleships like H.M.S. *Prince of Wales* and *Repulse* were sunk by bombs, the perils to small merchant ships from air attack are plain. The success of the British Merchant Navy gunners was all the more commendable. The seamanship of the Merchant Navy, too, upheld the highest traditions under the stress of modern warfare. Shooting

planes down was not the only way of destroying them. By clever handling, the *Jamaica Producer* contrived to foul a Heinkel with her fore topmast and to send it crashing into the sea. There were no casualties on board, but, when the ship was examined in daylight, it was found that a bomb had passed through the screen of the bridge and through the funnel.

NEW BASES FOR ENEMY

The small steamer *Highlander* had a similar adventure in the North Sea, and destroyed two German planes. Attacked at night by bombs and with machine gun fire, she hit a German plane with her defensive gun, and saw it crash. Two minutes later bombs from another aircraft just missed the *Highlander*, and the ship's gunner secured another hit which caused the plane to lose height. One wing hit a lifeboat, and the impact swung the plane round, smashing it against the poop of the little steamer. The *Highlander* steamed into harbour the next morning with the wreckage still there as evidence. Only two of her crew were wounded.

The collapse of France gave Germany new aerodromes and submarine bases from which to attack Allied shipping. In October, 1940, a big passenger liner was hit by bombs and set on fire. The Canadian Pacific liner *Empress of Britain*, of 42,000 tons gross, was some 150 miles off the Irish coast, homeward bound, when she was attacked and machine gunned. Then a high-explosive bomb got a direct hit; incendiaries started a fire, which drove the ship's company into the boats.

Women and children carried on with great bravery, obeying orders calmly. An eleven-months-old baby was saved by a sailor, who carried the child, tied in a blanket, on his back as he slid down a 60-foot rope into a lifeboat. The sight of a British flying-boat put heart into everyone. It signalled help on its way, and soon warships were taking survivors on board.

MERCHANT SERVICE FIGHTER UNIT

A Hurricane of the Merchant Service Fighter Unit goes aboard its parent ship. M.S.F.U.
planes travel on merchant ships in convoy, and are catapulted into action against enemy aircraft

ACTION STATIONS ON ESCORT VESSEL

Keeping their multiple guns at the ready, this gun crew of an escort vessel, clad in oilskins,
faces heavy weather and turbulent seas in its work of protecting the convoy against air attack

Captain Sapsworth stayed on the bridge until it was burning under his feet. Efforts were made to save the ship, and she was taken in tow, but some hours later she was torpedoed by a submarine. Revenge was taken on the U-boat, but the *Empress of Britain*, one of the finest liners, sank.

So much courage was shown at sea during these months, and such spirit in adversity was shown on many occasions, that it is difficult to claim that one man's act was more heroic than another's.

The story of the last fight of the *Jervis Bay* will take a proud place in the history of sea warfare. Thirty-eight ships were steaming across the Atlantic in convoy on a November afternoon in the care of a single armed merchant cruiser, the *Jervis Bay*, of 14,164 tons. The weather was fine, with blue sky and some cloud; visibility was excellent. The raider was sighted nearly ten miles away. The commodore aboard one of the merchantmen, the *Cornish City*, signalled to all the ships to alter course away from the raider. Almost simultaneously the enemy fired her first salvo right into the middle of the convoy.

SAVING THE CONVOY

Before she had time to fire again, the escort drew away from the convoy, towards the enemy, and opened fire. A number of other merchant ships within range also fired, and one master claimed two direct hits. The commodore ordered his ships to scatter and put on all speed. One master declared that his vessel, normally capable of nine knots, managed to knock up twelve.

Meanwhile, the *Jervis Bay*, heavily knocked about at the start, partly out of control, and blazing furiously, continued to keep the raider occupied, diverting the fire from the escaping convoy. No one could have known better than Captain E. S. F. Fegan, R.N., posthumously awarded the V.C., and his officers and crew, that they had not the ghost of a

chance in view of the superior armament, speed and gun range of the enemy. But the ship's quick action and ready sacrifice kept the raider at bay for nearly three hours. After sinking the *Jervis Bay*, the enemy began to look for the fleeing ships, but was too late. Most of them had scattered to safety. The enemy had been robbed by the armed merchant cruiser of what must have appeared to him an easy and magnificent prize. Only four ships failed to reach port, though for a time Germany boasted to the world of the annihilation of the whole convoy.

EXPLOITS OF TANKERS

Several of the ships in the convoy had desperate adventures; at least one of them is worthy of record. The *San Demetrio*, an oil tanker, was set ablaze by the raider's gun fire, and the crew abandoned ship. But coming across the ship again the next day, the men, who were in one of the tanker's lifeboats, boarded her, although she was white-hot amidships. They fought the fire for eleven hours, determined to save the ship if it could be done. When some sort of order had been produced again and the engines had been set going once more, it was discovered that the compass, which had been shot from the binnacle, showed the Pole star dead astern, while they were sailing east. So they were forced to disregard its vagaries and steer by the stars, and "by guess and by God." "They were bound to hit something between Narvik and Gibraltar," remarked a Canadian soldier. In eight days the *San Demetrio* sailed 1,000 miles. Reaching port, she discharged, through her own pipes, 11,000 out of the 11,200 tons of petrol with which she had been loaded. The second officer, who had captained this voyage, was awarded, with other members of the crew, a salvage claim of over £14,000, and all the costs of the case were paid voluntarily by the shipowners. Another tanker, the *San Casimiro*, was

SURVIVOR WHO COULDN'T STOP PADDLING

Let an officer of the corvette which rescued him tell this man's story. "Having been ordered to proceed to pick up survivors of a torpedoed ship in the Atlantic, we came across this man, who was a gunner in the merchant vessel. He had drifted about on a spar for twenty-four hours. When we got him aboard he could not, at first, stop the paddling rotation of his arms." Survivors of sunken ships often drifted on rafts for many days before rescue came

captured by the battle-cruiser *Gneisenau*. Some thirty Germans, armed with revolvers, hand-grenades, and machine guns, boarded the tanker. They kept a heavily armed guard over the unarmed British crew. The Germans were quite friendly, and expressed surprise at the quantity and quality of the food on board the tanker, as they believed England to be starving; their officer spoke English, and scoffed at the idea that he might not be able to take his prize through the British naval patrols. He said: "There are no British men-of-war on the sea and you know it. Who's going to rescue you?"

He appeared really to believe this was so until facts proved otherwise—a British warship held up the *San Casimiro*, and took him and his prize crew prisoners.

In the grim war of the sea, escorts had more than once to be left to face the odds with little or no chance of survival. A liner bringing some 1,000 R.A.F. pilots, observers, and navigators from Canada had for escort a destroyer and a corvette. A submarine was sighted; it fired two torpedoes, which missed. The third was right on the mark. But before it could reach the liner, the destroyer dashed to the rescue. There was a terrific explosion and debris rained down, and by the time the smoke had cleared nothing remained but oil and bits of wreckage. The liner dared not wait to search for survivors from the destroyer. Only seven were picked up by the corvette.

FIVE HOURS FIGHT

There were many duels between merchantmen and submarines. The *Carlton* fought an Italian submarine in the Atlantic with one Hotchkiss gun for nearly five hours. "The submarine popped up not more than twelve yards away," said one of the crew, who was rescued after eighteen days in a lifeboat. "We turned our gun on her, but the bullets bounced off the hull like hailstones." After zigzagging in an effort to make her escape, the *Carlton* was

finally hit and sank in six minutes. Of the men in the lifeboat twelve died. There were only four survivors.

More fortunate was another merchantman sailing astern of a convoy. It was dark and the U-boat was sighted nearby. The merchantman fired her machine gun, and when the U-boat had fired and missed, tried to turn and ram it. Again the U-boat attacked, and this time the defensive gun was manœuvred to fire at almost point-blank range, forcing the submarine to crash dive. Surfacing farther away, the submarine was hit again, and started to sink by the stern. Another shot damaged the bows and the submarine sank.

TALES OF SURVIVORS

Germany's inhumanity at sea, violating all traditions, inevitably brought great suffering to large numbers of voyagers. Many have been the hazardous journeys undertaken in open boats, often in face of storms and severe wintry weather, by survivors of ships sunk by the enemy. Many are the sad tales which the survivors have told to us landsmen of hardship, despair and death. Happily there comes now and then a brighter story of Britain's mighty struggle on the seas. No one will ever forget the thrill which ran through our country at news of the rescue of three hundred British sailors from the *Altmark*. It was such an adventure as Captain Marryat would have delighted in for one of his robust sea novels—a cutting-out expedition in an ice-bound fjord, ships grappled together, an armed boarding-party, the task accomplished, a safe return. It was a great day when the destroyer H.M.S. *Cossack* steamed into Leith, her after part crowded with 299 British sailors whom the Navy had snatched from a miserable captivity.

It came at a time when people were jubilant at the triumph by British sailors over the *Admiral Graf Spee*, then lying a scuttled and burnt hulk at the bottom of

DESTROYER ON ESCORT DUTY

Many destroyers are engaged on escort duty, guarding convoys of merchant ships through Britain's western approaches, to protect them from air, surface, and submarine attack. Here captain and navigator of a destroyer are seen in consultation on the bridge. These ships are fast, and heavily armed—a "Javelin" class destroyer having six 4·7 and several smaller guns

the harbour of Montevideo. It was known that the *Altmark* had served as an auxiliary ship to the *Admiral Graf Spee*, whose captain, after sinking British merchant ships, had detained the bulk of their officers in his own vessel. He turned the seamen over to the *Altmark*, thus using her as a prison-ship. The *Admiral Graf Spee* was alone when she met the cruisers H.M.S. *Exeter*, *Ajax* and *Achilles* in the South Atlantic. The *Altmark* disappeared in the ocean wastes, carrying survivors of no fewer than seven destroyed merchant ships. For almost two months she was lost. Then on February 15, 1940, a British aircraft pilot on reconnaissance sighted her creeping southwards along the Norwegian coast, taking care to shelter within territorial waters.

She had put in at Bergen, where her captain was under obligation by International Law and usage to release his prisoners, and the Norwegian authorities were under obligation to see that they were released. Instead, he kept them concealed, and satisfied the Norwegian officers, who made a very perfunctory inspection of the ship—it cannot be termed an examination. Battened down below hatches, the prisoners set up a hullabaloo, hoping thereby sufficiently to announce themselves. The German reply was to put all the ship's steam winches at work to drown the sound of their shouts.

PRISON SHIP TAKES REFUGE

So the *Altmark* resumed her journey south, fully expecting to reach a German port. She was intercepted by the British destroyer H.M.S. *Intrepid*. Here a Norwegian gunboat intervened, and her commander gave assurance that the *Altmark* traversed Norway's territorial waters by permission, that she had been examined, and that she carried no prisoners. H.M.S. *Intrepid* thereafter had no course but to withdraw; and the *Altmark* took refuge in Josing Fjord.

Satisfied that the Norwegian authorities had failed in their duty as neutrals, the Admiralty the same day gave orders that the ship was to be searched, even if it entailed His Majesty's ships entering territorial waters for the purpose, and that the prisoners were to be rescued.

BOARDING THE "ALTMARK"

Captain (now Rear-Admiral) P. L. Vian, in the destroyer H.M.S. *Cossack*, approached Josing Fjord after dark. At its mouth he was met by two Norwegian gunboats. His offer of joint action by both navies to carry out a search of the *Altmark* being rejected, he carried out his orders and steamed into Josing Fjord. It was packed with ice, across which the searchlights played, opening up glittering points of light against the sombre background of high cliffs. Jammed in the ice at the inner end was the *Altmark*.

As the destroyer was drawing alongside, the prison-ship began to work her engines, broke free from the ice, and attempted to ram H.M.S. *Cossack*. By sharply swinging round and by good seamanship the destroyer got clear, and the *Altmark* herself ran aground by her stern. A boarding party of twenty-four men under an officer, with rifles and bayonets, were assembled on H.M.S. *Cossack*, as the destroyer manœuvred to strike the German head on. Touch being made, the ships were grappled together. Quickly the boarders scrambled up the *Altmark's* side, the officer making for the bridge. In a hand-to-hand fight, the gunner was severely wounded; but the fight was brief.

German seamen, among them some put on board as guard from the *Admiral Graf Spee*, got down to the ice over the ship's stern and made their way ashore, where from a low ledge they fired on the British with rifles. This fire was returned with vigour, and two Germans on their

H.M.S. "COSSACK" COMES HOME WITH RESCUED "ALTMARK" PRISONERS

The German ship "Altmark," which had on board as prisoners 300 British seamen captured from ships sunk by the "Graf Spee," tried to get back to Germany with her captives. She was intercepted by the destroyer "Cossack" and took shelter in Josing Fjord. The "Cossack" followed her in, ran alongside and boarded her. After a hand-to-hand fight with the "Altmark's" crew, the "Cossack" released the imprisoned British seamen, and brought them home in triumph. She is seen entering a Scottish port, with the rescued men packed amidships

way over the ice to join the snipers were hit. The German dead were stated by Berlin to number six. Nearly an hour passed before all the Germans in the ship were rounded up. In the mêlée an enemy sailor fell into the sea. Characteristically, two of H.M.S. *Cossack's* officers at once went overboard into the icy water and saved him from drowning.

The captives on the *Altmark* had been thrown into consternation as the ship grounded, the shock sending a shiver through her every plate. At length hatches over the holds were knocked off, and a voice shouted, "Any Englishmen below?"

"Yes," was the resounding answer. Immediately afterwards there came the now historic words: "The Navy's here!" It was the first those below knew of the rescue. A Londoner among them, John Quigley, said afterwards: "We went hoarse with cheering when we heard that. You should have heard our cheer!"

Fifteen hours later H.M.S. *Cossack* was in Leith. The Royal Navy had shown again, as it had shown many times before in its history, that its arm can reach very far out to protect British seamen.

TYRANT OF THE "ALTMARK"

On the *Admiral Graf Spee* the merchant officers were well treated; that is to Captain Langsdorff's enduring credit. The seamen held in the *Altmark* found the order there quite different. Her skipper was a tyrant, as a survivor from the sunken *Doric Star* rightly put it—a man sharing nothing of the chivalry of the seaman's calling, one who took delight in causing misery to those in his power.

The *Altmark* had no fitting accommodation for prisoners, and a company of 299 must, in any case, have taxed the ship's capacity. The hardships they suffered in the eleven weeks confinement which many among them endured, can be imagined. In one compartment under iron hatches, forty-five men were imprisoned together.

"It was a filthy place, with no fresh air," said Frederick Thomas, of the steamer *Trevanion*. "We were lucky to get some carpets from one of the cargoes the ship carried, otherwise we should have had to sleep on bare boards. The conditions were terrible, and the Germans took delight in making us as miserable as they could with their heartless treatment."

TEA LEAVES FOR TOBACCO

And that was not the worst. Even an empty oil tank, which had been used for storing oil, was made to do service, a disgraceful place in which to confine living men. Other crowded prisons were shell-rooms and store-rooms, into which the captives were locked. The Germans would not let them see anything.

"We were confined for a fortnight without once being allowed on deck," was the testimony of William Curtis, of the *Doric Star*. "There was very little food. We ate black bread and were given tea. For a long time we got no cold water. Sometimes we got washing water." The prisoners became so desperate for tobacco that they smoked tea leaves rolled in paper.

They tried to send out an SOS. A message was placed in a tin, which was made watertight—a friendly German carpenter providing solder. A miniature flag was attached, and tin and flag were dropped overboard with slop pails. To the men's discomfiture, the attempt was observed. Those involved were imprisoned in the ship's hold for three days, and the carpenter got three weeks confinement.

All that ingenuity could suggest was done by the prisoners to attract the attention of the Norwegians. But these officers were deaf and blind to a remarkable degree. There was yet a chance, if noise failed, for the prisoners had managed to bore a hole through a hatchway, so that they might spy what was going on upon deck. They shouted and blew whistles to enforce notice by the uproar, and the second mate of the steamer *Ashlea* pushed a home-made Union Jack on a stick through the hole. This, however, a German guard quickly appropriated, and whether it was seen by the inspecting officers remains unknown.

In the last days before relief, conditions were so bad that a few of the prisoners tried to stage a mutiny. The idea was that

found to do it. The ship was 600 miles from land, in a tempestuous sea, at night —conditions which gave small chance to passengers, adult or child, to survive an attack. Without warning, an assassin U-boat fired a torpedo into her side. Most of the children, whose ages ranged from five to fifteen, were in their cots or bunks. The explosion killed some of them out-

RESCUED ONE BY ONE

From the rocky cliff men throw a line to survivors of a sunken tanker, whose lifeboat bobs perilously in the surf. One by one all the men in the lifeboat were hauled to safety

if the three hundred of them once got above deck they could seize control of the ship; but no opportunity came for a breakaway.

The world which had been thrilled by the story of the rescue from the *Altmark* was shaken with horror at the barbarous deed which sent the children's evacuee ship *City of Benares* to the bottom of the Atlantic. It seemed incredible that any German submarine captain could be

right. Escorts shepherding their charges to the alleyways found the boys' quarters a mass of wreckage and broken glass. A boy lay stretched dead across the floor.

The U-boat was never seen. The darkness, the cutting wind and the cold, hailstorms and drenching rain added to the perils of those compelled to take to open boats. Others from the ship clung to rafts in a tumbling sea, enduring exposure to which, in the night, many succumbed. Boats were swamped and their occupants drowned. The *City of Benares*, a big Ellerman liner, was struck two hours before midnight, and quickly began to settle down. Possibly fifteen to twenty minutes—some said less—were available to get the boats out before she sank. Altogether 421 passengers and crew were carried by the *City of Benares*. She

Rehearsals on the voyage for just such a contingency proved their worth. Excellent order prevailed. Passengers mustered in the lounge until the evacuee children were on deck and passing into the boats, then they took their stations. Boat after boat was got off with no loss of time, but the heavy list of the big liner added to the sailors' difficulties in lowering them as the

MID-ATLANTIC RESCUE

The "Kafiristan" was torpedoed and sunk by a German submarine. One of her lifeboats was swamped in launching, and six men were lost. Others managed to right the lifeboat, which is seen nearing the American ship which rescued over thirty of the "Kafiristan's" crew

had sailed from a West of England port during the second week of September, 1940. On board were a party of ninety-two children, who were being sent to Canada; seven only were reported saved. A group of five children came from one London family, whose home had been wrecked by a bomb. In charge of the children were nine women escorts, six of whom lost their lives. Adult passengers included Czech, Dutch and Hungarian refugees, among whom upwards of one hundred were missing after the rescue.

minutes sped by, and all could not leave the ship. A survivor thought there were some ten boats on the water when the ship was engulfed.

It was nearing dusk next day when a British warship came to the rescue of the widely scattered flotilla of boats and rafts.

Loss of life was, at first, given out as 306 persons, three-fourths of all whom the ship had carried; of the ninety-two evacuee children, nearly all were missing. All hope had gone of other survivors, and certainly no one was prepared for the surprising

SAVED AFTER ELEVEN DAYS ADRIFT

After eleven days drifting in the ship's lifeboats, all the crew of a small Allied merchant vessel, sunk in the South Atlantic, were rescued. Their ship was shelled and machine-gunned for half an hour by an Axis submarine in an obvious attempt to conserve torpedoes

denouement. Eight days after the *City of Benares* had gone down, news was flashed across the waters that another of her boats had been found, containing forty-six of the ship's passengers and crew, including six boys from among the evacuee children. All were well, although much exhausted.

RESCUED BY AIR PATROL

This was a joint air and sea rescue. Just before going off patrol a Sunderland flying-boat of the Australian Air Force, on convoy escort, had noticed the floating boat below. As his petrol was running low, the captain signalled the R.A.F. aircraft relieving him to carry out the rescue, giving the exact position by Aldis lamp. Her captain found the boat, which had hoisted a sail and was crowded with people, all sitting or lying down except the man at the tiller. He came down low, circled round, noticed that the castaways seemed pretty exhausted, then made a signal that he would fetch help. Before leaving, he dropped by parachute all the food the aircraft had on board, tying the bag to a lifejacket to keep it afloat. In time a warship approached, following the returning aircraft, which, after observing the rescuing vessel alongside the lifeboat, made off to join the convoy.

Rescue came just in time, for the boat had no water left, and food was practically gone. The rescuing warship picked up six survivors from rafts. All in the boat suffered severely from cold, but rowing night and day helped the stronger of the men.

By the recovery of this last boat-load of sea-tossed survivors, after they had been mourned as lost, the death roll of what, perhaps, was the Germans' most inhuman act of barbarity on the oceans was brought down to 260, and the loss among the children to seventy-nine dead.

Narratives have accumulated in this war of almost incredibly long voyages in open boats, bearing testimony to the seamen's immovable faith that while there is life there is hope—testimony also to their dauntless determination not to give in.

One boat made a journey of no less than 2,500 miles. Two men survived out of seven who had originally set out in her. A planter upon the island of Eleuthera, in the Bahamas, noticed two figures staggering upon the beach. They were sailors from the British ship *Anglo-Saxon*, which had disappeared when on a homeward voyage, and had long been given up for lost. She had been sunk by a raider.

The survivors knew nothing of the fate of other boats. They had themselves been adrift for seventy days. The boat was provisioned, but food gave out and they kept themselves alive by eating flying fish and seaweed. Rain occasionally fell, and was caught and stored in tins, but on eight days of the long voyage they had been without drinking water. Both men were young, one but nineteen. They had been tanned almost black by the sun. Although they were in the last stage of exhaustion when found, they recovered in hospital in Nassau, to which they were flown.

ADRIFT FOR 500 MILES

Twenty-nine survivors of a British freighter sailed an open boat to safety for nearly 500 miles upon the North Atlantic, in intensely cold weather. Their ship, outward bound on her maiden voyage, was torpedoed in the middle of the night to the west of Iceland. The crew, numbering sixty, got away in two boats, but they almost immediately lost sight of one another. The boat in charge of Mr. John Cameron, the chief officer, turned back to rescue four men who were dangling from ropes down the ship's side. A few minutes later the vessel sank.

All was uneventful till a strong wind blew up from the east, and a sea anchor was rigged. For five days no real progress could be made, and only unceasing baling kept the boat afloat. Then the wind changed. So matters went along for

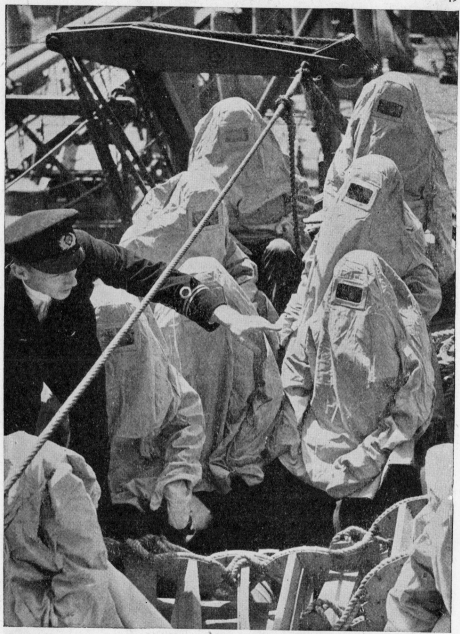

MASKED MEN OF THE TANKERS

Crews of British tankers are being supplied with special protective suits of asbestos clothing to lessen danger from blazing fuel. These hoods and gauntlets are flame-proof. All in one piece, they can be slipped on in an instant. Tanker lifeboats are to be equipped with asbestos blankets. In their hooded suits these men are on their way to lifeboat drill. New regulations on equipment of lifeboats and rafts have much improved safety measures for seamen

BRITISH SHIPS MADE IN SECTIONS

Pre-fabricated standard merchant ships are being launched from British shipyards. They are almost entirely made at inland factories, the various parts then being taken to the shipyards for assembly on the slipways. Top, a pre-fabricated ship on the stocks, showing main frame. Below, a pre-fabricated ship in being. This method greatly speeds up ship production

twelve days, by which time some of the men were fully exhausted. Their only food was biscuits, pemmican, and chocolate.

Luckily it rained on and off, so there was no actual shortage of fresh water, though the cold drenching added to the voyagers' miseries. One man died when they were almost in sight of land. On the fourteenth day, when ten miles from the coast, they were sighted by a British plane, which guided an Icelandic trawler to their rescue.

The castaways were placed in hospital suffering from frostbite. Mr. Cameron was the only man in the boat who knew anything about navigation, and to being kept so busy throughout the terrible voyage he attributed the fact that he was not as badly affected as were the others, who recovered, and were soon at sea again.

A vessel of the New Zealand Shipping Company made a run down the Mediterranean, just after Italy had entered the war, which well deserves a place among epic voyages. This ship had the reputation of being " a perfect beast " to handle and manœuvre—even with a rudder.

GUNS OUT OF ACTION

She was pushed along 400 miles without a rudder by her captain's and the engineers' seamanship and resourcefulness, dodging attack on the way. It began when she reached Suez, and Admiral Sir Andrew Cunningham, Commander-in-Chief in the Mediterranean, asked her captain if he would accept the burdensome honour of taking his ship to Malta, loaded with much-needed supplies for the island. A couple of high-angle guns were placed on board and off she set, in company with

SURVIVORS COME ABOARD

Safe on board the rescue ship, one of the survivors from a merchant vessel sunk in the Atlantic takes a long drink of water from a tea kettle. Another is climbing up the rope ladder. They were members of a crew of twenty-seven, who were all rescued. Great hardships were suffered by merchant seamen. Two men from another ship endured seventy days adrift before reaching land

ONE OF THE SHIP'S LIFEBOATS IS SAFE

Three corvettes were sent to help a merchant ship which had been torpedoed. All they found was this upturned boat. The men clinging to it were the only survivors. Among them can be seen the Chief Engineer, with his broken leg sticking out. Coastal Command aircraft have helped in many rescues of survivors, and flying-boats have sometimes carried them to safety

two other ships, on her perilous voyage. The risks were great and the onslaught duly came. Italian airmen, flying high, dropped bombs, which fell into the sea. A single plane, more daring, came lower to find better fortune. Its first bomb hit the wireless cabin and killed the operator. A second bomb struck the ship's aft gun-mounting, put out of action the two high-angle guns, and smashed the steering-gear. Thereafter she was defenceless. The airman, returning, had the luck with his last bomb to score a miss right alongside the main injector. Water came into the ship, and had almost reached the furnaces, by the time the engineers were able to stop the leak with timber.

Malta was 400 miles away. More raiders were to be expected, as certainly as the rise of the next tide. They came, and the little company of three ships went through a gruelling time. Fortunately, the New Zealander was a twin-screw ship. Night came, and she carried on, steering by her engines. When the Italians arrived at day-break to renew the attack, they found British forces ready for them on the sea and in the air. Five Axis bombers were shot down, and the others dispersed; they were given no chance of approaching near the ships. Rudderless as she was, and bearing her scars, the New Zealander reached Malta and delivered the needed supplies, as did her companions. The master deservedly received a decoration.

WHOLE CREW RESCUED BY AIR

The entire crew of a merchant ship torpedoed in the South Atlantic made what must have been a unique passage. The vessel (name not disclosed) sank rapidly, leaving thirty-six British seamen, mostly Scotsmen, and twenty Chinese adrift. By good fortune they were sighted by a big Sunderland flying-boat, which came down to the water to make a rescue. The pilot's first thought was that he could take twelve men who were wounded.

and no more. He was asked to take them all. "Very well, we'll risk it," he said; "everybody in." By tight packing as they sat in rows along the floor of the flying-boat's cabin the whole company was eventually accommodated.

The plane had to taxi five miles upon the sea before it became airborne, and after a 200-miles flight to shore all were brought to safety. This incident, which would have been regarded as impossible when the war on shipping opened, well illustrates the debt of gratitude which merchant seamen, in their dauntless fight against the new piracy, owe, not only to the officers and men of the Royal Navy, but to the officers and men of the air.

An R.A.F. Squadron-Leader, forced to bale out, paddled his rubber dinghy for 60 miles—57 hours—before being rescued.

IN THE FRONT LINE

Let it never be forgotten that the British merchant sailor is always in the front line in wartime, and that the front line of war at sea was always active—never still. Day in and day out, he faced the menace of bombs, torpedoes, shells and incendiaries, of machine guns and mines; he was beset from above the water, on the water, and beneath the water. And still there remained the old hazards of the sea: hurricanes, fogs, rocks, and storms. The winter of 1941-42 was especially severe; in the North Atlantic there was "a flaming gale" for months, with often a 75-mile-per-hour wind and nothing much less than 35 miles per hour, and waves anything up to 65 feet high. Cold and frostbite, starvation, madness or death from exposure, and an end with the sharks were often the lot of the shipwrecked sailor.

The odds against the merchant seamen were tremendous. They were unequalled in the history of the sea. But no ship left port undermanned, and few ships, ready for sea, were ever seriously delayed for lack of a full crew.

INDEX

(PAGE NUMBERS IN ITALICS REFER TO ILLUSTRATIONS)

A NEW HISTORY OF
IRELAND

A NEW HISTORY OF
IRELAND

CHRISTINE KINEALY

How many Times feminism has been quoted

||||
↑
pag.3
|
guessing
you did
Not get
Past page
3 ☺

Believe it or not women form
Part of Irish history so of
course they are going to be
Mentioned... plus she is Right

SUTTON PUBLISHING

First published in 2004 by
Sutton Publishing Limited · Phoenix Mill
Thrupp · Stroud · Gloucestershire · GL5 2BU

British Library Cataloguing in Publication Data
A catalogue record for this book is available from the British Library.

ISBN 0-7509-2819-0

Typeset in Photina MT 10.5/15 pt
Typesetting and origination by
Sutton Publishing Limited.
Printed and bound in England by
J.H. Haynes & Co. Ltd, Sparkford.

CONTENTS

ACKNOWLEDGEMENTS

The writing of this book has benefited from the work of many scholars working in the field of Irish history. I am also indebted to the following people who have read and commented on various sections of the book. They are Seán Egan, Peter Berresford Ellis, Robert Langford, Honora Ormesher, Francine Sagar, David Sexton and, last but not least, John Walton. The probing questions of colleagues, students and friends have also helped to focus my thoughts, and I would like to thank Scott Brewster, Ivan Cooper, Debra Ferris, George Harrison, Reesa Jenkins, John Joughin, Joie Karnes, Michael Parker, Carol Russell, Marcelline Jenny, William Rogers and Jack Worrall. Finally, I would like to thank my children, Siobhán and Ciarán, for their encouragement and laughter, and to them this book is dedicated.

Legend:

□ Monastery linked to St Patrick and Armagh

■ Monastery linked to St Colum Cille and Iona

◉ Monastery

(Indicates approximate boundaries of provinces)

Iona

Labels on map:

Tory ■   Rathlin ◉
Fahan   Coleraine □   Armoy □
Derry ■   Camus
Raphoe ■   Connor □   Antrim □
Bodoney □   Bangor
Ardstraw ◉   Movilla
Donaghmore □   Dromore ◉   Nendrum
Devenish ◉   Tynan □   Saul □
Clogher □   Armagh □   Downpatrick
Inishmurray ◉   Drumcliff ■
Killevy ◉
Killala □   Achonry ◉   Fenagh ◉   Donaghmoyne □
Louth □   Linnis □
Kilmore □   Granard □
Achagower □   Elphin □   Monasterboice
Mayo ◉   Baslick □   Fore ◉   Kells ■   Slane ■
Inishbofin ◉   Roscommon ◉   Ardagh ◉   Ardbraccan ◉   Holmpatrick
Cong ◉   Tuam ◉   Inchcleraun ◉   Trim ◉   Dunshaughlin □
Annaghdown ◉   Clonard ◉   Finglas ◉   Swords ■
Roscam ◉   Durrow ■   Clondalkin □   Glasnevin
Clonmacnoise ◉   Tallaght ◉
Clonfert ◉   Killashee □
Inís Mór   Kilmacduagh ◉   Lorrha ◉   Seir Kieran ◉   Kildare ◉
Birr ◉   Kilcullen ◉   Glendalough ◉
Kilfenora ◉   Terryglass ◉   Roscrea ◉   Moone ■
Inishcaltra   Sletty □
Killaloe ◉   Killeshin ◉   Aghade □
Leighlin ◉
Inis Cathaig ◉   Mungret ◉   Derrynaflan ◉   Ferns ◉
Cashel ◉   St Mullins ◉
Ardfert ◉   Emly ◉   Ardfinnan ◉   Begerin
Taghmon ◉
Lismore ◉
Inisfallen ◉   Ardmore ◉
Sceilg Mhicil   Cork ◉   Cloyne ◉
Ross Carbery ◉

PROVINCES

Ulaid (Ulster)
Airgialla (Oriel)
Uí Néill
Connacht
Munster
Laigin (Leinster)

Ireland, *c.* AD 650

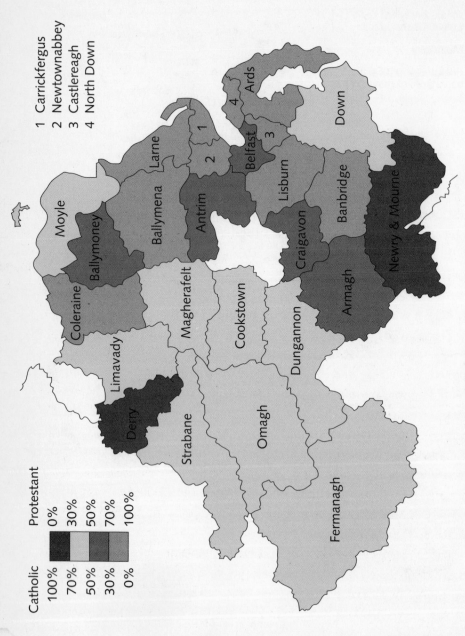

Religious composition of Northern Ireland at the time of Partition

Catholic

- 100%
- 70%
- 50%
- 30%
- 0%

Protestant

- 0%
- 30%
- 50%
- 70%
- 100%

1 Carrickfergus
2 Newtownabbey
3 Castlereagh
4 North Down

Moyle

Ballymoney

Coleraine

Limavady

Derry

Strabane

Larne

Ballymena

Antrim

Magherafelt

Cookstown

Omagh

Fermanagh

Belfast

Lisburn

Dungannon

Craigavon

Armagh

Ards

Down

Banbridge

Newry & Mourne

INTRODUCTION

Irish history, to a large extent, has been influenced by waves of conquest and settlement – from the Celts in the sixth century BC to Eastern European refugees at the beginning of the twenty-first century. Ironically, perhaps, the greatest icon of Irishness, St Patrick, was born in Britain in the fifth century and he demonstrated the close linkages between Britain and Ireland even at this stage. One of the themes of this book is that Irish history cannot be understood without reference to British history, just as British history is diminished without reference to developments in Ireland.

Significantly, different epochs or movements in Irish history have been characterised by the wave of settlers that shaped them: the early Christian period, the Viking and pre-Viking periods, the Norman, the Old English, the New English, the plantation of Ulster, the Protestant ascendancy and the Anglo-Irish period. All had roots in Ireland's relationship with 'England' in its various manifestations, as part of the Angevin Empire, Britain, the United Kingdom, the British Empire and the Commonwealth. At the same time, each phase was firmly grounded in the Irish experience and Ireland's capacity to absorb, assimilate and enrich other cultures and ideologies. Irish identity, in turn, was shaped and enhanced both by its opposition to, and its acceptance of, each of these influences.

Ireland is a small island situated on the periphery of Europe, lying on the margins of the continental land mass, yet despite its size and isolation, it played a central role in shaping the progress of its European neighbours, from the time of the early Christians through to the European Union. In turn, the history of Ireland has also been shaped by wider European developments, notably the spread of Christianity, the Norman expansion, the Reformation, and the growth of ideologies such as liberalism, nationalism, republicanism, socialism and feminism. Each of these advances has brought Ireland closer to Europe, while

Europe has been enriched by Ireland's contribution to its development. Since the eighteenth century also, other parts of the world, most obviously North America, have impacted on developments in Ireland, and vice versa.

The peripatetic Irish monks in the sixth to ninth centuries took their scholarship to all parts of Europe, possibly even getting as far as North America. The spirit of adventure remained powerful, as people left Ireland to be settlers, explorers, soldiers and mercenaries. Other groups of emigrants went in less happy circumstances, as political refugees or economic emigrants – the impact of the Great Famine, in particular, provided a powerful image of emigration as enforced exile. The movement of Irish people did not just change the new societies in which they settled, but also impacted on the country they had left. Irish nationalism (itself an amalgam of American, French and Italian political movements) was to become a model for other colonised peoples. Paradoxically, being part of the British Empire provided increased opportunities for Irish people in the nineteenth century as imperial administrators, military enforcers, or simply settlers. For some nationalists, an unresolved paradox was how could Ireland be both colonial and imperial concurrently?

From the fifth century also, Irish history was dominated by the attempts of the Christian Churches to influence events in Ireland – framed by the emergence of Patrician Christianity in the fifth century – followed by attempts to impose the authority of Rome, the Reformation in the sixteenth century and the constraints associated with the penal legislation, all of which was followed by regroupment and a reassertion of church dominion in the nineteenth century. At the end of the twentieth century, secularisation and the implosion of the Catholic Church as a result of numerous scandals proved to be more challenging to the Church's authority than the subjugation of earlier centuries by a Protestant state. The impact of the Protestant Churches on Ireland was also powerful. From the sixteenth century the Anglican Church was the state church despite being the religion of a minority. Its wealth and political influence made up for its lack of numbers. Its supremacy was challenged in the nineteenth century and increased as the Protestant minority in Ireland formed a united front to resist the new challenge of a nationalist movement that identified strongly with Catholicism. This political alignment along religious lines was not inevitable. Supporters of non-sectarian politics were present in all churches. Irish Protestants in the late eighteenth century proved their patriotic and republican credentials in the struggle for Irish independence. The 1798 Uprising and the Young Ireland movement in 1848 were led by Protestants, many from Ulster, who consistently argued than the Protestant ascendancy should not be replaced with a Catholic ascendancy. At the beginning of the twentieth century, some members of the Orange Order argued for a fresh accommodation with nationalists under the common banner of being Irish, while many of the leaders of the 1960s civil rights movement were Protestant. This book also seeks to give a voice to the diversity of the Protestant contribution to Ireland's development.

Within a relatively small overview such as this, it is impossible to give adequate voice to all groups and contributors, both inside and outside Ireland, who have shaped Ireland's history. Within such broad strokes, however, it is easy to overlook lesser movements and changes in Irish history. Generally, historians have focused on certain key groups and places – thus giving primacy to Christianity over secularism, Catholics over Protestants (especially the smaller denominations), conflict over cooperation, the rich over the poor, Dublin over Belfast, men over women, nationalism over unionism, the victor over the vanquished, and British repression over British radicalism. Much recent history has focused on the twin polarities of nationalism and unionism, but this disguises the diversity of Irish society and range of political opinions – particularly the role of women, atheists, radicals, communists and pacifists. This new history places developments in Irish history in a broader and more nuanced context by looking at the experience of groups that are traditionally underrepresented. As far as possible an attempt has been made to synthesise the multiplicity of experience. A particular theme of the book is the participation of women from all backgrounds in Ireland's development, and how – from St Brigid to Betsey Gray to Bernadette Devlin to Mary Robinson – they had to fight against the patriarchy of the various churches, political organisations and social mores to overcome the inferior position assigned to them by men.

When covering such a wide sweep of history, the sources vary in quality and quantity: for the early period there are few primary sources; for the later period, there are many more, despite the destruction of the Public Record Office at the beginning of the Civil War in June 1922. Since 1990 also, the growth in Irish scholarship and academic publishing has greatly increased the quantity and quality of secondary sources that are available. Moreover, historical debate has been re-energised by challenges to the 'revisionist' orthodoxy, which had dominated Irish history since the 1930s but in its crudest form had become narrowly anti-nationalist.

The starting point for this new history is not just the emergence of St Patrick but also the appearance of written documents. Early Ireland was an oral society. The fact that few written records have survived, however, means that aspects of Ireland's early history remain unknown and there is much scope for conjecture. The changes in the Irish language that took place between the fourth and seventh centuries make it difficult to fully grasp the complexities and subtleties of the earlier period. Propaganda is also evident in the early sources, a prime example being the writings of Giraldus Cambrensis, who was the chronicler of the Anglo-Norman invasion. Writing from the perspective of the victor, he provided a negative picture of Irish society and the Irish people. His twelfth-century writings influenced subsequent generations of English and Anglo-Irish writers.

The Annals are a major source for chronicling the history of Gaelic Ireland, although their main value is in identifying trends rather than in providing detailed accounts. Both Gaelic Annals and Anglo-Irish Annals have survived, although they were not contemporary with the period described. Rather, they were mostly written when paganism had been discredited and the kingship was in decline. The majority of Annals were compiled in the sixteenth and seventeenth centuries and were themselves based on earlier ones. There were exceptions: the writing of the Annals of Inisfallen extended into the thirteenth century, by which time they had become a contemporary record. A team of people generally compiled them over a number of years.

But there are other reminders of Ireland's past, notably physical ones – ranging from the remnants of early Christian Ireland, such as the Gallarus Oratory in County Kerry and the monks' round towers of the tenth century, to the magnificence of eighteenth-century Dublin architecture and, more recently, the constabulary barracks, workhouses and elementary schoolhouses that each became a feature of the nineteenth-century landscape and, in varying degrees, of British control. During the latter part of the nineteenth century also, a network of Catholic churches was built in Ireland, while the small Anglican churches that had become a symbol of Protestant ascendancy struggled to survive as both their income and their congregations shrank. All, however, in their own way, were physical manifestations of Ireland's interaction with the outside world, for better or worse.

The Anglicisation that accompanied the colonial process was never absolute, especially in regard to the Irish language. The introduction of

National Schools after 1831, where everything was taught in English, contributed to the decline. Around the same time, many Irish place names were Anglicised, largely as a result of the Ordnance Survey of Ireland after 1824. One of these consequences of Anglicisation is that there is little standardised spelling, with the English and Irish form of names and places often being used interchangeably. Increasingly, however, the Irish language became an important part of the political and linguistic identity of Ireland. In this book, where appropriate, both forms have been provided, although generally the most common usage of names has been adopted.

Inevitably, the political geography of Ireland also changed after the fifth century. At the beginning of the period Tara was the seat of the high king of Ireland. As the system of high kingship declined, so too did the significance of Tara. For much of the Celtic period the capital of Ulster was Navan Fort near Armagh, while after the tenth century Armagh was the centre of the Christian Church in Ireland, despite challenges from Cashel and Dublin. The prominence of Dublin as a political centre came about after the thirteenth century; until then Kilkenny was an important political and ecclesiastical centre. The rise of Belfast only started in the sixteenth century. Economic and demographic factors made Belfast a nineteenth-century phenomenon, and as the century progressed, it took its place as the centre of Protestant Ireland. Dublin's golden age, in contrast, had been the eighteenth century, after which it went into a slow economic decline, until the birth of the Celtic Tiger at the end of the twentieth century made Dublin one of the wealthiest, most cosmopolitan and most visited capitals in Europe.

From the eighteenth century, Ireland was part of Britain's imperial project. The loss of the American colonies had been a psychological blow to Britain's ambition and created a determination that Ireland should not follow a similar path. The desire of the majority of Irish people for independence was denied even when demonstrated by constitutional means, as occurred during the 1918 general election. The period after 1969 in Northern Ireland is euphemistically referred to as 'The Troubles' but in reality it was a war that was more prolonged and lethal than either the Anglo-Irish or the Civil War. The conflict dominated the politics of Northern Ireland, Britain and the Republic for many years. Moreover, the international media took the images of carnage throughout the world, condemning the inter-community violence but also denouncing the role of the British government. However, it was not until the 1990s that Britain declared it had no strategic interest in Northern

Ireland, although ironically at this stage it played a more active role in the affairs of Northern Ireland than ever before. The Peace Process, though not perfect, has been remarkable for bringing nationalists and unionists from across the political spectrum into talks with representatives of the British and Irish governments. It represented a significant move by the British government from imposing a military solution to finding a political accommodation. The process of disentanglement has been complicated, violent and piecemeal. Consequently, the Peace Process has been battered, and at times its survival has appeared doubtful. By the end of 2003 the Process had reached another deadlock, yet it remains a beacon of hope, not only for the future of Northern Ireland, but for the future of all Irish and British people.

ONE

THE COMING OF CHRISTIANITY
c. Fifth to Eighth Centuries

Before the arrival of Patrick and Christianity in the fifth century, Ireland had a vibrant culture and civilisation. Waves of settlers, most notably the Celts and Goidels, had contributed to the island's rich oral and artistic traditions. The emergence of Christianity coincided with a golden age of Irish scholarship, which was spread throughout Europe largely by the missionary activities of Irish monks.

This chapter examines the beginnings of Christianity in Ireland, in particular its role in shaping Irish culture and religious practices, and its contribution to the spread of learning within Europe. At the same time, the response of Irish kings to the spread of Christianity is considered.

Early Christian Society

An appropriate starting point for understanding modern Irish history is the fifth century, not merely because it coincides with the life of St Patrick, but also because it marks the appearance of written documents. Moreover, in varying degrees since the fifth century, Christianity has shaped Irish society. Although the coming of Christianity to Ireland was sometimes attributed to the endeavours of Patrick, Irish Christianity predated him. According to one chronicle, Pope Celestine ordained Palladius the first bishop in Ireland in 431. Patrick's contribution, however, was to consolidate and extend Christianity's hold.

When Patrick was taken into slavery in Ireland it was a Celtic country, with a population of about one million, but possibly less. It was criss-crossed with a network of roads, a disproportionate number of which led to Tara, the seat of the Irish high king. The poor usually lived in small huts, often made of clay. The homes of the rich were erected on raised mounds and were usually built of wood or stone, with straw roofs. Kings and other powerful members of society lived in protected dwellings, in ring-forts or on lake dwellings known as crannogs. Agriculture was the main occupation of the people, both livestock and tillage, including wheat, oats, barley and flax. The importance of livestock as an indicator of status and wealth was evident from the fact that a person's rank was measured in terms of the number of cows that he or she owned. Entertainment was varied, ranging from storytelling, singing and playing instruments to chariot racing, horse racing and hurling. Some external observers, however, described the favourite pastimes of the Irish as quarrelling and war.

Ireland in the fifth century possessed a vibrant culture and civilisation. The country's development had been shaped by waves of settlers, most notably the Celts (or *Goídil*), who had contributed to the island's rich oral and artistic traditions. According to some narratives, the Celts had come to Ireland in four main waves, that is, the Nemedians, the *Fir Bolg*, the *Tuatha Dé Danann*, and the *Goídil* or Milesians. They first arrived in Ireland from central Europe in the sixth century BC and the last colonisation occurred about 150 BC. At this stage the Celts already controlled much of central and western Europe and Ireland marked the concluding phase of their westward expansion. The *Goídil* were the final wave of Celtic invaders to reach Ireland. They spoke a variety of Celtic known as Q-Celt (earlier settlers had spoken P-Celt). The *Goídil* also settled in the Isle of Man and Scotland. The exact origins of the word *Goídil* are uncertain; it is either derived from the Welsh word *Gwyddel*, meaning Irishman, or the Irish *Gaedhilg*, meaning 'Gaelic'. The *Goídil* were also referred to as Milesians after their leader, Mil Espaine. According to legend, Mil was fleeing from the Roman invasion of his territory in the Iberian peninsula. His successors became the dominant ruling family in Ireland, establishing two main settlements at Tara and at Cashel.

By the fifth century, when Christianity appeared in Ireland, the European Celts had been dispersed and pushed to the western fringes of their empire. The scattered Celtic groups, though, shared a common language, religious beliefs and a similar social organisation. In Ireland the descendants of the *Goídil* were the dominant group. Increasingly, the Irish people described their ethnicity as 'Gael' and this designation increased following the arrival of the Norsemen. An impression was thereby given of the unity and longevity of the Irish race. Just as significantly, the language of the Goidels, known as Celt, had become the common language of Ireland. Ireland, therefore, remained a stronghold of Celtic culture, its influence being only slowly replaced by the coming of Christianity. Despite being displaced by Christianity in Ireland, the

Celts retained an important cultural influence. Their legacy was particularly evident in art and jewellery (such as torques and collars) and in the legends and heroic tales – all of which shared customs and traditions that linked Irish Celts with Celts elsewhere. Unfortunately, it was not until the seventh century that written records were made of the vibrant literature or laws of Ireland, which until that date had been preserved only in oral traditions and passed on by storytellers and poets.

Within Celtic society a high value was placed on scholarship, even though written records were not used. The respect for learning and learned men (and women) meant that kings were not absolute; Druids, poets (*fili*) and Brehons (see p. 16) all had special status. They were regarded as the possessors and protectors of the collective wisdom of the people, which was a gift to be given to each succeeding generation. Their wisdom was preserved and passed on in special Druidic schools. The scholars also played a role in guiding the kings, especially on issues to do with law, genealogy, succession and spiritual matters. A Druid, a poet or a Brehon often adjudicated on judgments made by a king. Usually, a Druid would sit on the right hand of the king and only after he had spoken could the king speak. In matters of law the Brehons would arbitrate and make a judgment based on a complex system known as the Brehon Laws. They would also teach the law to pupils and thus ensure it was passed on to the next generation. If a Brehon issued a wrong or careless judgment, there was a belief that he or she would be punished by nature, nature being both the giver and final arbitrator of all legal matters. Some of the laws were recorded as poems or chants, which made their oral transmission easier. After 550, however, some Irish law texts were committed to writing.

Life at this time was precarious. If internecine warfare or belligerent incursions did not prove to be lethal, then famine, generally caused by bad weather or the plague, frequently could be. Poor food harvests were commonplace in this period, which resulted in food shortages, sickness and mortality. A serious famine lasted for three years between 698 and 700, and was followed by a period of disease. Pestilence was also commonplace. There was a plague in 549, but it was overshadowed by the great plague of 664–6: also known as the 'Yellow Plague', it probably resulted from a virulent form of jaundice, and it had wiped out a good deal of Europe before it reached Ireland. It has been estimated that up to a third of the population perished at this time. Because so many rulers died, it changed the political face of the country. The death toll included Blathmac and Diarmait, the joint high kings of Tara, who both died of plague. Large-scale mortality also resulted from a smallpox epidemic in 742–3. In 773 a widespread drought resulted in famine. As proved to be the case so often, disease followed the famine, and in 774 there was a dysentery outbreak; it returned in 777 and 778. More disasters followed: in 778–9 hunger resulted from cattle disease; in 779 there was famine and smallpox; and in 783 and 786 an influenza epidemic appeared in Ireland. The demographic consequences of plague and famine were serious, as the recovery in population growth was often slow. A consequence of this period of catastrophes was that the population remained fairly static. Some commentators attributed the disasters to overpopulation, while others believed the deaths were caused by the hand of God. In such perilous conditions it is not surprising that the pagan Irish, in common with most societies, placed a great emphasis on pleasing the gods of the harvest and fertility. And, as Christianity spread, the taking on tour of relics, which were believed to have healing powers, became popular. Often the relics were the remains of the founders of a monastery, and this became a lucrative source of income for monasteries.

Celtic Society

When Patrick arrived in Ireland, the country was divided into eight main kingdoms: the Midlands of Leinster, ruled by the Leinster *Goídil*, with their royal seat at Tara; Connacht, ruled by the Tara *Goídil*; South Leinster, ruled by the Laginians, renowned for their independence; the north-west triple kingdom of *Tír Conaill*, *Tír Enda* and *Tír Eóghain*, associated with Niall of the Nine Hostages; *Airgialla* in central Ulster, which had been ruled by the *Fir Bolg*; Munster, ruled by the Munster *Goídil*, whose royal seat was at Cashel; *Dál nAraidi* in east Ulster, ruled by the Cruthin; and finally, the small kingdom of *Dál Ríanta* on the northern coast, also ruled by the *Fir Bolg*. These kingdoms were all subdivided into smaller territories known as *tuatha*, each ruled over by a king or chief. They governed with the help of an assembly known as an *aonach*, which was open to freemen within the community. Joint assemblies were also held between the provincial kingdoms.

Like all early Indo-European societies, early Celtic society was highly stratified and based on a number of political and social hierarchies. Each group had different functions and rights. Kings were at the top and slaves at the bottom of the social structure. Below the level of kings there were distinct hierarchies, although each group contained multiple subdivisions. The highest levels comprised nobles and freemen, which included both landowners and craftsmen. Scholars, who included Druids, bards, Brehons and poets, were highly ranked in society. The 'non-free' classes, on the other hand, which included slaves, labourers and workmen, had neither status nor political power. Although there was some social mobility, it could take generations to move upwards. Inevitably, downward movement was far easier.

Society was organised around a number of small kingdoms, or *tuatha*, and they continued to be the basic political unit until around 600. A *tuath* was hard to define in terms of simply territory, but for people within a *tuath* the common bond was that the same king governed them and they saw themselves as being distinct from other groups. Within the *tuath* the basic social unit was the kin group, which was usually defined by having a grandfather (or older forebear) in common. Descent often gave status and sometimes genealogies were fabricated in order to prove a prestigious lineage. Kinship, like kingship, imposed certain expectations and responsibilities. Kinsmen were liable for each other's offences and therefore liable to pay compensation if the original offender failed to do so. Two responsibilities that cut across all social divisions were the concepts of honour and loyalty. The concept of honour was central in Celtic society. Breaches of honour had to be compensated in full 'body-price', that is, according to the rank, and therefore value, of the offender. If honour was offended, there was an 'honour-price' to be paid. Like many other aspects of society, the system was complex and hierarchical, with kings receiving the highest honour-price. From the seventh century the concept of *enech*, literally 'face' but in reality honour, was recognised by Irish law. Compensation was known as *eneclann*, that is, 'face-cleansing'. If the injured party was dead, compensation would be paid to his or her kinspeople, with the closest relatives receiving the highest amount. Children aged under fourteen had no legal responsibility.

Hostage taking was a means of allowing people to be used as sureties or human pledges to ensure the fulfilment of a contract. Following the inauguration of a new king, or the acquisition of land by one, high-ranking hostages would be given to guarantee loyalty and submission. They were often related to the people proffering submission, including daughters and even wives. Fostering was a commonplace way of rearing and educating children. It was also used to cement alliances between various groups.

Fostering usually involved boys aged from seven to seventeen (when boys were believed to have reached maturity) and girls between seven and fourteen (when girls could marry). There were two main forms: *altramm serce*, that is, fostering for affection for which there was no fee, and fostering for a fee. In the latter cases, the fosterage fee, *iarraith*, provided revenue for the foster parents. As with so much in Celtic society, the fee reflected the wealth and status of the father of the child. The fosterage fee for girls was higher than for boys. The way in which the child was raised and educated also reflected the social status of the child's family. Fostering created filial obligations as strong as natural ones and they were lifelong. The foster child, for example, was expected to look after his or her adoptive parents in old age. It was therefore a further way of ensuring loyalty and cementing social responsibility.

Gender divisions in Celtic society were most evident among the poorest classes, where women had little overt power. Educated women, however, could enter any profession, and they were respected for their scholarship. Prominent female judges included Bríg Bríugaid and Áine ingine Iugairu. In the tenth century Ulluach was for a time the chief bard of Ireland. It was even acceptable for Irish women to lead their clan's people into war. This right was abolished at the Synod of Birr in 697, which forbade women to be military commanders. The Synod also passed the 'Law of the Innocents', protecting all non-combatants in a war. Under the Brehon Laws, wealthy women had more rights than was generally the case in European societies. They had a say in whom they wanted to marry, could divorce, could own property, and if they were badly treated they could sue for damages. After a divorce, a woman would return to her family, and both she and her former partner were free to remarry. She was also allowed to take her original dowry with her. The inheritance laws for men and women were the same. A woman could inherit property from her father and dispose of it as she saw fit. If she had no sons, her female children could inherit her property. Upper-class women who were of marriageable age were valued for their role in making dynastic alliances. A woman had to be of equal rank to her husband, and her main function was to supply heirs. Kings and nobles could be polygamous, and kings usually had more than one wife in order to ensure sons and heirs. Upon marriage, control of a woman's possessions passed to her husband for the length of the marriage; if left unmarried, she remained subject to her father, or, after his death, to her nearest and eldest kinsman. Thus widows were subject to their sons, and wives to their husbands. But women could inherit land where there was no male heir, and continue to hold it independently of their husbands. But even in such cases, when the woman died, property would revert to men. More commonly, women could not pass on land upon death, as it reverted to her kin group. The early Christian Church disapproved of both polygamy and divorce, although it had provided opportunities for women to be educated or to pursue a vocation. The Reformation, however, undermined the position of women and ended many of the rights provided under the Gaelic legal system.

Kings and Kingship

The social structure was intricate. While a king (*rí*) was at the top of the structure and was the ruler of his own kingdom, the status, authority and influence of kings differed. There was a hierarchy of kings: at the lowest level was the *rí tuaithe* (king of one *tuath*); *rí tuatha*, king of several *tuatha*; and *rí ruirech* or *rí cóicid*, king of a province. A sub-king was known as a *uirrí*. A king who only governed a single *tuath* would give allegiance to an over-king – who was usually king of a province. Subordination was often guaranteed by giving hostages to the over-king and, in return, the supplier could receive 'posts of honour'. The most powerful king was known as the high king and, in theory, he had kingship over the whole of the island. The high king was also referred to in some later texts as the king of Tara. Although little is known about the hill of Tara in County Meath, its ancient and important origins are clear from its Neolithic passage tomb, hill forts and stone pillar, which was traditionally believed to have been used in inauguration ceremonies. Some pre-Christian Celts believed that Tara contained the entrance to the 'otherworld'. The first Goidelic high king of Tara was Eochu, whose son achieved notoriety as Niall of the Nine Hostages, largely because of his successful raids on Britain. Niall was killed on one of these forays, but he in turn was the eponymous ancestor of the Uí Néill family, who rose to prominence in the fifth century, extending their kingdom into parts of Ulster. By the end of the fifth century, there were only five main kingdoms in Ireland and the Uí Néill over-king described himself as king of Tara.

Succession to kingship was not by primogeniture. A king was elected from within a family group and his successor was usually chosen during his lifetime. Those descended from a previous king were eligible. The designated successor was known as the *tánaiste*. The new king would ensure support by taking hostages from his opponents. The bonds of blood remained important

– for military and social alliances. None the less, there was social movement, and battles and alliances between kings, together with internal challenges for power, meant that the leaders changed. There were also frequent disputes over the kingship of Tara. This system may have contributed to instability in the late Celtic period. Throughout the late fifth and sixth centuries there were intense battles for the kingship, although the paucity of surviving records means there is a lot of conjecture about the origins and outcomes of various battles. In the second half of the sixth century the most powerful kingdom was Munster, which was ultimately ruled from Cashel. The Uí Néill, however, regrouped, and the following century was dominated by their rise, which included taking over the kingship of Tara and overthrowing the Ulaid, the dynastic group that controlled much of Ulster. It is possible that they were the first high kings who truly had control over the whole of the country by the eighth century. The success of the Uí Néill was representative of a change on the political scene in Ireland, as dynastic government replaced local tribal rule.

Being a king conferred privileges but it could not provide protection against a violent death, with disputes often ending in the losing king being slain. Ireland was a warrior nation, and life at the top levels of Celtic society was undoubtedly precarious – especially for kings and their sons, who were frequently involved in local, internecine, warfare. Fighting for rights of kingship succession was particularly common in some kingdoms. By the sixth and seventh centuries, bloodshed appeared integral to claiming succession among some rulers, with the Uí Néill particularly immersed in violence, in contrast to the more peaceful kingdom of Cashel. Once the kingship had been gained, more fighting was necessary to hold onto it. Internal quarrels within a *tuath* could be as deadly as external ones.

Irish kings had ambitions beyond Ireland, and raids on Britain were frequent. When the Romans withdrew from Britannia around 420, some Irish kings took advantage of the power vacuum and mounted vicious raids on the unprotected Britons. Niall of the Nine Hostages was one of the most successful of the Irish raiders, his hostages being part of the bounty from his raids. Around 500, the Irish king Fergus Mór attacked and conquered Argyll in Scotland, some early historians wrongly attributing his victory as marking the origins of the Gaels in Scotland. Báetán Mac Cairíll, king of the *Dál Fiatach* (*c.* 572–81), made his small northern kingdom the most powerful in Ireland. He also had external ambitions and colonised the Isle of Man in 577, and shortly afterwards forced Aedan mac Gabrann (*c.* 574–608), the Scottish

king of the *Dál Riata*, to submit to him. The attempts at colonisation were
two-way, with Scottish kings also having dynastic aspirations in Ireland.
Following Báetán's death Aedan reversed his actions, invading both the Isle of
Man and the north of Ireland. This resulted in the creation of the joint
Scottish–Irish kingdom and brought together the Scottish *Dál Riata* with the
original *Dál Riata* group in Ulster. The kingdom was subsequently ruled by the
Irish *Dál Riata* until the defeat of Aedan's grandson, Domnall Brecc – who
appeared to lose every battle he ever fought – in 642. He was then slain by
Owen of Dumbarton, the victor.

Irish kings and their nobility were great promoters of art and culture. Royal
courts were centres of sophistication and scholarship. Apart from the poets (*fili*)
and bards, lawyers, theologians, philosophers, medical experts, astronomers and
musicians would gather at the courts. Many religious monuments were
commissioned by kings, including the shrine of St Lachtin's Arm, which was
erected under the patronage of Cormac III. The kings also endowed
ecclesiastical establishments and it was their patronage that enabled the
illuminated manuscripts, the Cross of Cong and the Ardagh Chalice, among
other treasures, to be created. Much of the great artwork associated with early
Christian Ireland was possible only because of the support of Irish kings.

The relationship between each king and his followers was complex, with
variations in different parts of the country and from reign to reign. Overall, kings
were expected to rule with honour and strength, and this in turn gave them the
legitimacy to govern. Fasting – if necessary to death – was the only way to take a
grievance against a king. Gradually, fasting was replaced by an ability to sue a
substitute so that the king suffered no loss of face. Kings could demand the
payment of a cattle tribute, and if it was not paid they could go into battle to
levy it. Because kings were so important in pagan society it was vital to convert
them to Christianity as an example to other people. Kings showed surprisingly
little resistance to this change, but appeared to welcome many aspects of it.
Within the new hierarchy also, members of the Church were accorded a high
status, with bishops being put on the same elevated level as poets. A number of
kings ensured their eminence was recognised in the Christian structure by
declaring themselves to be bishop–kings. Changes were inevitable, though. Kings
were regarded as sacred in pagan Ireland and their inauguration involved pagan
rites and rituals, which included a fertility ceremony. During the ceremony the
king would be symbolically wedded to his land. The ritual could take a variety of
forms, sometimes including a mock mating with a goddess, usually either Medb

or Eithne, the goddesses of fertility. In some cases, the king was mated with a white horse, which was then slaughtered and eaten. Again, this symbolised the linking of the king, the land and his people.

As with many overt pagan rituals, the conversion of kings and other nobles to Christianity meant that this tradition was dying out by the sixth century. Also, rather than all pagan rituals being reviled, as far as possible they were Christianised and absorbed by the new Church. For a number of years, therefore, the pagan and the Christian systems coexisted peacefully. As the Church grew stronger, however, it became confident enough to challenge some pagan traditions that it regarded as unacceptable, including the pagan rituals that accompanied the inauguration of a king. Moreover, the Church attempted to control the telling of Ireland's pre-Christian past. Christian historians either excluded references to pagan practices or rewrote a sanitised history of the past, including turning the pagan deities into humans with Christian virtues. Historians who wrote the later Annals, that is, the chronicles of Ireland from the Gaelic period to the sixteenth century, adopted a similar approach. They also showed their desire to distance themselves from Ireland's pagan past. A common feature of the early histories was that Patrick was given a major role in the conversion of Ireland to Christianity. In the case of the high king of Tara, for example, Patrick allegedly confronted the pagan king, Laoghaire, and his Druid priests at Tara, and his actions resulted in the abandonment of the fertility rites. Whether this took place or not, from the sixth century the high kings discarded these rituals and adopted practices endorsed by the Christian Church.

Laws and Law Makers

Although kings were powerful, they were not absolute. Generally, they were not judges; nor could they enact laws. Instead, there was a complex legal system in existence, which was enforced by learned men and, to a lesser extent, women, known as Brehons. The Brehon legal system had parallels with the equally sophisticated Hindu law system. A distinctive feature of the Brehon Laws was that physical chastisement and capital punishment were kept to a minimum, but rather the focus was on compensation for the victim and the victim's family, and rehabilitation for the wrongdoer. For the Christian Church the challenge was how this arrangement could be controlled and shaped to fit into the new order.

The Brehon system was more than just legal apparatus: it permeated all aspects of Irish society – including fasting, seizing cattle, the position of women, and so on. It also clearly defined relationships, not only within the immediate family, but also in the extended family and over five generations. The laws governing inheritance did not recognise primogeniture; instead, land was shared between sons, women not being able to inherit land. The Brehon Laws were unique to Ireland and were thought to predate the birth of Christ. Although they were associated with Ireland, they had certain features in common with the Celtic laws elsewhere. Many of the Brehon Laws were unwritten but preserved by verbal contract. Information about the Laws, therefore, is sparse and derived from a variety of sources, including the *Senchus Már*, the first Irish legal corpus, which was probably written in the seventh century. These books provided a set of guidance laws for all layers of society. They are also important in providing a tangible link between the laws of pagan Ireland and new Christian laws that are associated with Patrick.

Under the Brehon system legal responsibility largely lay with the individual to pursue a claim against the accused. He or she would hire a legal advocate, or Brehon, and both sides had to agree in advance that they would abide by the decision of the legal advocate. The law was complicated, and because it was not written down, it had to be committed to memory. An expert in law was known as an *ollamh*. If reparation was agreed, the offender had to pay the victim compensation (an 'honour-price') which was proportionate to his or her means. Homicide required an additional payment. The payment of fines was a matter of honour, and if the wrongdoer was unable to pay, his or her kin group would do so. If no payment was made, goods could be distrained from the offender or his family. If payment was still not forthcoming, the offender would be shunned by his kin and lose his place in society.

As with many aspects of life, the coming of Christianity to Ireland changed the practice of law, although some customs were slow to disappear. Patrick and his successors recognised the value of utilising the Brehon Laws, and so endowed the clergy with legal authority. The early Church kept aspects of law that did not clash with God's law or, increasingly, their canon law, and in the short term turned a blind eye to less palatable aspects such as concubinage, polygamy and divorce. Bishops who drew up laws in the fifth and sixth centuries had said that members of the Church could not go before secular courts or use Brehons. The Brehons gradually converted, which was facilitated by the fact that their relationship with the Church had remained friendly. The idea of physical punishment also crept into the Brehon Laws, largely because of the spread of the Christian Penitentials, which were associated with the Roman Church. The Penitentials spread to Ireland, possibly from Wales, after the sixth century, and they provided a register of sins and the fixed penances required for absolution. In Ireland the way in which Penitentials developed borrowed some concepts from the Brehon Laws, notably that each offence had a price and was to be classified according to the nature of the deed and the status of the offender. Many aspects of the Brehon Laws survived up to the twelfth century, with some remnants continuing until the seventeenth century when English law was enforced throughout the country. None the less, the spread of Christianity, especially of Roman orthodoxy, had changed the Brehon Laws. The introduction of the Penitentials in particular had provided an alternative law system, bringing Ireland more in line with the feudal system in other parts of Europe.

Christianity and Patrick

The demise of the Roman Empire left a power vacuum throughout many parts of Europe, which the Christian Church was partly able to fill because it possessed a large organisation, it was international and throughout Europe there was a general desire to convert to cross-border faiths. Because the Roman Empire had not spread to Ireland, the development of the Church's influence was different from elsewhere in Europe. Although there were Christians in Ireland before Patrick, the success of the Christian Church became associated with the achievements of this one man.

Despite Patrick's importance, little is known of him and information comes predominantly from his own writings, notably his *Confession*, which was written as a defence of his calling, and only gave scant details of his life. Patrick's birth and death dates are unknown, as is his exact birthplace, although it was in Roman Britain. At sixteen he was captured by raiders and spent six years in captivity in Ireland, at an unknown location. He escaped to Britain but in a vision was told to go back to Ireland. Patrick returned as a missionary, and baptised thousands of people and ordained clerics. Most of his work was in the northern half of Ireland, north of the line from Galway to Wexford. Initially, pagans, especially Druid priests and pagan kings, resisted conversion – but they were gradually won over to Christianity and, unusually, the resistance produced no martyrs. The dates of Patrick's mission are also unknown, but it probably began in the second or third quarter of the fifth century and lasted for thirty years. The discrepancy in dates led to a possibility that there were, in fact, two Patricks who conflated into one, possibly a combination of Palladius and a later, unknown, bishop. Such suggestions, however, were clearly unpalatable to the Church in Ireland, which attributed its origins and success to the sacred figure of Patrick.

By the seventh century a cult of sainthood had emerged in Ireland, and Patrick was at the forefront. He was depicted in a heroic way, as the person who had defeated his pagan opponents. This cult was largely associated with Armagh, which had much to gain by association with the father of the Irish Church. It was no coincidence that two Armagh monks, Muirchú and Tírechán, wrote hagiographical accounts of the life of Patrick. In the ninth century the cult of Patrick was further promoted and extended with the use of remains and relics, including his bell and crosier. The cult of Patrick not only survived the Norman period but was also actively encouraged during it. Like the pagan kings before them, Anglo-Norman knights appreciated the value of having an organised and disciplined Church within Ireland. In the twelfth century, possibly for the first time, there were references to St Patrick's Purgatory at Lough Derg in County Donegal. At this location, Patrick had purportedly fasted in order to expel demons. Not only did the Church in Ireland adopt this legend, but it was also accepted by Christians elsewhere. Consequently, Lough Derg became a major place of pilgrimage for those who sought penitence. Its existence confirmed the centrality of Ireland's position in the medieval Church. Despite being destroyed by Cromwell's soldiers in the seventeenth century, Lough Derg continued to be regarded as a place of pilgrimage and was an important factor in promoting the popularity of Patrick. Whatever the truth about Patrick, within a relatively short period Christianity had encroached on all aspects of life, its success being helped by its willingness to absorb or adapt aspects of paganism.

The coming of the Church also resulted in an administrative and social revolution in Irish society, although it proved to be a peaceful one. One of Patrick's contributions was to extend the episcopal church government used in Britain and Gaul to Ireland: a system that was based on bishops having jurisdiction over their diocese and the laws of the synod. It took a long time before a national reform was accepted by all the territories. The synod for national reform was held at Ráith Bressail (Rathbreasail) in 1111, and undertook a diocesan reorganisation of the Church. It decided that thirteen dioceses in the north would be subject to Armagh and twelve in the south subject to Cashel, with Armagh as the seat of the primacy. As far as possible, the new dioceses coincided with areas of over-kingships.

Patrick also introduced monastic life into Ireland and the unique feature of the Irish Church, which was different from the rest of western Europe, was that the most important churches were ruled by a monastic hierarchy, with abbots, rather than bishops, having ultimate control. Because there were no towns or villages in Ireland, monastic settlements quickly became an important feature of Irish economic and cultural life and their influence was spread, with monastic houses being founded outside Ireland. From the mid-sixth century there was a massive expansion in monastic foundations in Ireland. Their spread was facilitated by the fact that it was easy to found a church or monastery, with only two monks needed for the establishment of the latter. Once established, their survival was helped by the practice of burying the founder's body in the chief church. Monasteries were autonomous and abbots had a lot of individual power. They also became increasingly self-sufficient, with some monks being involved in agriculture and other manual work. Yet in the larger settlements, most of the labour was done by tenants who lived on the church lands. This interaction brought the Church into closer contact with the people.

Monasteries were also centres of learning, with monks able to read and write. Even wealthy lay people would send their children to monasteries in order for them to receive a good education. The skills of Irish monks in producing illuminated manuscripts based on the gospels and written in Latin also added to their reputation. Although the themes of the illuminated manuscripts were Christian, the artwork was largely Celtic, with religious artists adopting the curves and coils of pagan artists. This fusion of old Celtic art and new Christian values was exemplified in the Book of Kells, the most famous, though not the first, illuminated manuscript. Although it is strongly associated with Irish monasticism, it is possible that the manuscript was begun in Iona and completed in County Meath. The date of production is also unknown, although it probably dates from the late eighth century. The influence of Irish art was also evident in religious work elsewhere, such as in the Book of Durrow and the Lindisfarne Gospel. Some Irish monks were also skilled in other forms of artwork, notably metalwork. Gold, silver and precious stones were commonly used in their work to glorify Christ and his saints. Examples of their craftsmanship include the Ardagh Chalice and the Tara Brooch. The latter, which dates from the eighth century, was crafted from gold, silver, copper and amber. Although it was made in the early Christian period, it became a symbol of Celtic art and culture. Little is known, though, about the early history of the brooch because it was not found until the mid-nineteenth century and fed into the Celtic/Gaelic revival.

Christianity quickly made inroads into all levels of Irish society, and the relationship between the new Church and the rest of society was strong. Abbots usually belonged to the kin-group that gave the land, which contributed to peaceful coexistence. In the early Church, loyalty to God and king and kin-group had to be balanced. However, with the spread of monasteries, the social standing of the Church was in the ascendant. By the end of the sixth century a bishop of a *tuath* had equal rank to a king of a *tuath*, and the status of the lower clerics also rose. Overall, the Church had created an alternative social structure that was challenging the supremacy of the existing one. By the seventh century monasteries had become associated with wealth, learning and power. Some of the large monasteries performed the function of early universities, while others became renowned for the ascetic values they promoted. The location of monasteries varied: some were situated near roads and were accessible and prominent, while others were built in inaccessible and isolated places, such as the Aran Islands and Sceilg Mhicíl (Skellig Michael), both off the west coast. One of the strengths of the Irish system was the diversity within its monastic life.

The early Roman Church did not expect its clerics to be celibate and they could marry. An exception was small groups of aesthetes who chose to devote their lives totally to God. There were some attempts to impose celibacy: the Council of Nice in 325 condemned clerical marriages but did not ban them. Pope Leo IX, however, who was pope from 1049 to 1054, attempted to enforce celibacy on all clergy, as it was part of his broader mission to cleanse the Church of the twin evils of 'simony [selling pardons] and clerical incontinence [lack of sexual control]'. An even more stringent policy was adopted in 1189 by Pope Urban II, who decreed that the wives of priests could be seized and sold as slaves. The attitude of the Irish Church was more liberal and again indicated its autonomy from Rome on some issues. Irish religious houses could be mixed (*conhospitae*) and clergy, and even bishops, could marry. Although Ireland was gradually brought more in line with Rome, as late as the fourteenth century some priests had taken a wife.

In the Irish Christian Church the role of women and female religious establishments was important. The most successful female houses, which had their origins in the fifth century, included St Brigid's home at Kildare and St Moninne's house near Newry. Later female establishments included St Ita's at Killeady in County Limerick, and St Safann's in County Meath. Brigid founded a monastic house in Kildare, and was its first abbess. The Book of Kildare, which disappeared in the sixteenth century, was regarded as the most beautiful of all illuminated manuscripts. An unusual feature of Brigid's foundation was that it was effectively two monasteries, one for men and one for women. They shared the same church and observed the same regulations, and were governed jointly by an abbess and a bishop–abbot. However, the early egalitarian approach to women was of short duration in church history. In general, the status of women declined with the spread of Christianity, and they lost many of the privileges that they had enjoyed in Celtic society.

The earliest life of Brigid was written fifty years after her death by Cogitosus ua hÁeda of Kildare, suggesting her importance in the Church. As with Patrick, early accounts of her life became intertwined with myth and folklore. Although it is known she was born in Ireland, probably in north Leinster, her birth and death dates remain uncertain, but she was probably born towards the end of the sixth century. Like Patrick, she was supposed to come from humble origins – her mother Broiseach was a bondservant. Other accounts say her parents were nobles, and some suggest that her father was a *Dubhtach*, or Druid, and that Brigid herself was a *ban-druí*, or female Druid, before she converted. Some accounts suggest that Brigid had studied under Mel, the bishop of Armagh, and this may have been where she first came into contact with Patrick. According to *The Book of Armagh*, which was a major source for the early history of the Church, Patrick baptised Brigid's parents into Christianity. Patrick and Brigid subsequently became good friends. When the life of Brigid was compiled in the seventh century, legend had overtaken reality. Brigid was praised for her lack of materialism, her virtue, her hospitality and her intelligence – all of which she used in the cause of God. By the seventh century, the church in Kildare, which included a shrine to Brigid, was a major one within Ireland. Such was the attraction of the stories associated with Brigid that she vied with Patrick for popularity. Devotion to Brigid spread beyond Ireland, and she was possibly even more venerated than Patrick at this stage. The elevation of holy people into saints was largely done in response to popular demand, and canonisation was the privilege of local bishops. Apart from living a holy life, those raised to sainthood were expected to have performed miracles and to have suffered for their faith. For the local churches, association with a saint gave a number of benefits, especially if it became a place of pilgrimage. The new custom of taking relics on tour helped to promote Irish saints overseas. Irish scholarship also found an outlet in writing embellished lives of the saints. Rome, however, was becoming increasingly uneasy with this aspect of local independence, and in the twelfth century responsibility for canonisation was transferred exclusively to the Pope.

Although Armagh made some attempts to create a more centralised Irish Church, with Armagh at the centre, a feature of the early Church was its lack of centralisation, reflecting the political structure of Ireland itself. The lack of a central state structure made Ireland vulnerable to outside attacks. It was not until the twelfth century that the Irish Church finally became centralised following the Synod of Rathbreasail, which also recognised the primacy of Armagh. The rise of Armagh was concurrent with the rise of the Uí Néill, and both parties saw advantage in providing mutual support. Armagh's association with Patrick, however, was central to its success. Internal discipline in the Irish Church was helped by the compilation of Irish Canon Law after 710. In 734 the Law of Patrick took all clerics under the protection of Armagh. By the eighth century, therefore, Armagh was challenging places such as Kildare, Iona and Clonmacnoise in claiming to be the ecclesiastical authority in Ireland. Moreover, Armagh claimed to be answerable only to the Papal See, and that other Irish churches were thus accountable to it. By the eighth century even churches that had no affiliation to a monastery pledged allegiance to Armagh. Although Dublin challenged Armagh's predominance in the eleventh century, this was ended by the Pope's recognition of the primacy of Armagh. Yet, regardless of the desire for papal recognition, a feature of the early Irish Church, which continued for many centuries, was that it remained largely independent from Rome. At times there did seem to be a willingness by the Irish Church, especially in Armagh, to adopt Roman ways. After 1640, for example, an Irish deputation was sent to Rome to discuss the way in which Rome had changed its method of computing Easter. Again, Roman policies were not embraced by all Irish clerics. Columbanus argued with Pope Gregory XIII about Rome's adoption of the new calendar. Overall, significant differences remained between the Roman and the Irish approach, which proved a source of frustration to successive popes, especially as the Irish Church had so many admirers in Europe.

Although Patrick claimed to have little education and he wrote an unrefined form of Latin, one of his legacies was the foundation of a scholarly and sophisticated Church that was admired throughout Europe. Within a century of Patrick, missionaries such as Columbanus were fluent in Latin. Irish scribes were also important, and they were particularly admired for the way in which they illuminated their writings. Irish monasticism did not remain confined to Ireland, but Irish missionaries travelled over Europe and possibly even reached America. The Irish monks were influential in founding important monasteries, including those at Iona, Auxerre, Bobbio, Cologne, Salzburg and Würzburg. The monastery at Whitby was founded by Hilda, grand-niece of Edwin of Northumbria. St Aiden made her abbess, and possibly even ordained her as a bishop. Whitby was a mixed community. Even after the Synod of Whitby, Hilda refused to adopt the Roman teachings but continued with her Celtic traditions. Some of the early missionaries viewed their travels as a form of penitence, with overseas missions regarded as exile. A number of monasteries even used being sent on an overseas mission as punishment for a transgression. A valuable source for appreciating the influence of the Irish Church was the scholar–monk Bede from County Durham, who wrote about Irish missionaries on the continent. Although the primary aim of Irish missionaries was to evangelise, they also built up libraries and thus established centres of learning overseas. The fact that Irish monks had their own distinctive style of teaching, and did not follow Rome in many of their practices, also made them stand out. Furthermore, unlike their European counterparts, Irish monks had a heavy reliance on corporal punishment, penitence and aestheticism. The more punitive aspects of monastic life were gradually abandoned, possibly as a consequence of European influences.

Ireland's reputation as a centre of learning and devotion ensured that missionaries throughout Europe knew and emulated its practices. Even at this stage, parts of Britain were still pagan and were regarded as a challenge by Irish monks. In turn British missionaries visited Ireland in the sixth and seventh centuries. By the seventh century also, students from Britain were travelling to Ireland for learning. Scottish and Welsh missionaries were particularly important in establishing monasteries in Ireland. The Welsh missionaries Cadoc and Gildas were associated with the establishment of Clonard monastery. Under the tutelage of Finnian, Clonard produced a remarkable new generation of missionaries, sometimes referred to as 'the twelve apostles of Ireland'. These men each went on to found their own monasteries, including Clonfert monastery by Brendan; Aghaboe monastery by Cainneach; Clonmacnoise monastery by Ciarán; Durrow, Derry and Iona monasteries by Colum Cille; Glasnevin monastery by Mobhi; and Devenish monastery by Molaisse. Learning and the spread of ideas were reciprocal. Irish monks received Latin books from overseas and increasingly Irish monks took their books to the continent. New monasteries invariably included a library.

In addition to the spread of Christianity, other significant changes were taking place in Irish society. The Irish language underwent a number of radical changes between the fourth and seventh centuries, as a consequence of which 'Archaic' (or 'Primitive') Irish was replaced with what became referred to as Old Irish. Early Irish is mostly associated with a form of writing known as 'ogham', which was based on slashes of different length. Its most frequent use was in memorial stones, probably those used by Druid priests. The arrival of Christianity, which made extensive use of Latin, also contributed to the transition from Archaic to new (or 'Old') Irish. Although the Church, especially the monasteries, was associated with learning, a district secular education survived which educated successive groups in law, genealogy, and a wide range of artistic and literary activities. These learned men were the carriers of a secular culture which kept the view of a heroic Celtic past alive. Their knowledge and traditions were not based on the written word but on memory. After Patrick, though, a written tradition emerged and, rather than continue to be distinct, written and oral histories came together and proved to be mutually enriching. One consequence was that oral traditions were written down. An unusual but exciting aspect of the new writings was that they utilised both the Latin and the Irish language, borrowing ideas and techniques from each other's conventions. Learning was also spread by laymen who chose to obtain their education in the monasteries. This, in turn, probably helped spread the knowledge of Latin. By the eighth century, therefore, the gap between the Latin and the Irish worlds had narrowed, as had the gap between laymen and clerics, church and secular symbols, heroic tales and history.

Conclusion

The seventh and eighth centuries are sometimes called the Irish golden age, or even the Irish Enlightenment. Irish society was quite prosperous, while, largely because of the activities of the monks, Ireland was admired in many parts of Europe for its learning and culture. The fact that Ireland's cultural blossoming coincided with a period of stagnation of art and learning in the rest of Europe made the Irish contribution stand out. Ireland became a cultural magnet: by the middle of the seventh century, Durrow monastery, in the midlands of the country, was attended by students from eighteen other European countries. Much of the success of the early Irish Church was attributed to the strong foundations provided by Patrick. His supremacy – which grew in the centuries after his death – overshadowed the contribution of other saints and holy people. By the ninth century, when the Vikings arrived, Irish society was structured, stratified and settled, based on a complex system of reciprocal obligations and duties. Christianity was not only firmly established in Ireland but its success meant that Irish colonies had been established overseas.

Regardless of all the changes that had taken place since the fifth century, by the end of the eighth century Ireland was comparatively stable, and both secular and ecclesiastical traditions had learnt to coexist. Conflict between the rulers continued, although the supremacy of the Uí Néill had contributed to a decline in internecine conflict. The new Church had shown itself to be tenacious and adaptable, responding to both internal and external challenges. The monastic system, however, was in slow decline, and this decline was expedited after 795 when Viking invaders started destroying religious shrines in Scotland. An early warning of the impact of these raids was provided in the religious settlement founded by St Colum Cille in Iona. The Vikings were interested in taking slaves and treasures, and they found both in the monastic settlements, killing monks who got in their way. After their initial raid on Iona in 795, they returned every few years, and in 806 the abbot decided to return to Ireland, taking the remaining valuables. This included the Book of Kells, which was of little interest to the raiders, who were illiterate and pagan. However, the fact that it remained unfinished may be due to the disruption the raids caused. The Vikings then moved westwards and their incursions into Ireland marked the beginning of a new phase of invasion that threatened not only the Gaelic way of life but also the survival of the Christian Church.

TWO

VIKING RAIDS AND THEIR AFTERMATH
c. Eighth to Eleventh Centuries

The Vikings came to Ireland as raiders, but within a few generations they had become peaceful farmers. None the less, their arrival – and the destruction that ensued – contributed to a period of economic and cultural decline. The destruction of many monasteries and the departure of many monks affected all aspects of Irish life.

This chapter focuses on the impact of the arrival of the Vikings in Ireland and the changing balance of power between the settlers, the Irish kings and the Christian Church. Literary evidence is limited but archaeological remains and artefacts, some in Scandinavia, provide insights into the Viking period in Ireland. Irish sources also reveal that by the eleventh century, the integration of natives and Vikings had created a new group in Ireland known as the Hiberno-Norse or Norse-Irish.

The Coming of the Vikings

The Viking period in Ireland is not clearly delineated, although Viking interest in the country started in the late eighth century and continued until the tenth century. The Vikings, or Norsemen, were Scandinavian and came predominantly from Sweden, Denmark and Norway. In Ireland they were referred to as 'Ostmen', that is, 'men of the east'. Their development of the longboat made it possible for them to sail long distances in a relatively short time. When the Vikings first arrived in Ireland, they were still fairly new to raiding, having started a systematic programme of attacks only in 793, when they plundered monasteries in Lindisfarne off the east coast of England. It was only a matter of time before they crossed the Irish Sea. The first Viking raids on Ireland took place about 795, and for the next thirty years they averaged about one a year. After this, the periodic ransacking of Irish treasures had been replaced by permanent occupation. By this stage, the

Norsemen had also started to plunder parts of France, Iceland, Greenland, Russia and Scotland, reaching as far as the coasts of Constantinople, North Africa and North America.

Monasteries were important targets for the first wave of Viking marauders, not only as a source of precious treasures, but also to supply them with slaves and other provisions. The early Viking raids, therefore, were made on the wealthy monastic settlements, and it was the monks who provided the earliest written descriptions of the new raiders. Inevitably, their narratives were not flattering. The attackers were pagans with little respect for Christian icons or sites. The early raids were brutal, with the pillaging and taking of slaves being followed by burning of the site. The monks and scholars were either killed or captured and sold into slavery. In 845 the primate of Armagh was captured and imprisoned by the Vikings. Because the arrival of the Norsemen coincided with the decline of the monasteries, it was also easy to blame them for undermining scholarly learning, especially in the Latin language. They were mostly illiterate and therefore regarded by their victims as philistines. The early attacks were on Irish monastic settlements such as Rathlin Island, Inishmurray, Inishbofin and Sceilg Mhicíl, all of which had little protection. In order to safeguard some of the monastic valuables, the Irish monks deliberately removed them, initially from the islands onto the mainland and then from Ireland to the continent. Some, however, were lost at sea. The customary image of the Vikings, therefore, was of an unskilled, belligerent and boorish people. In popular memory, the Vikings were simply remembered as ruthless plunderers. In contrast, Scandinavian sagas written in the twelfth and thirteenth centuries glorified the Viking adventurers as great warriors with superhuman strength. Reality and mythology became linked in characters such as Ivar the Boneless, who plundered Dublin in the 860s. In literary accounts, he became a heroic figure with extraordinary powers, probably based on the less glamorous character of the Viking warrior Ingwaer.

In reality the Vikings were a diverse people who were proficient in a range of areas. In addition to being renowned as shipbuilders, seamen and looters, they were skilled horsemen, and able to extend their raids inland. They were also farmers, and their desire to establish communities overseas was possibly motivated by population growth in their own lands. Some of the land in Scandinavia was of poor quality, and farming was hampered by long, cold winters. Also, because they practised a system of primogeniture, there was an incentive for younger sons to seek a livelihood elsewhere. Like Celtic society,

Norse society was sophisticated, possessing high levels of technical, mathematical and artistic skills. Norsemen were particularly proficient in metalwork, which was used not only for making jewellery but also for military equipment, such as metal or leather helmets and the iron axes, double-edged swords and spears that made them such fierce warriors. Some of their leaders' swords were elaborately decorated. Their mathematical expertise was reflected not only in their navigational ability, but also in their interest in weights and measures – signified in their mercantile interests. Their skills, as carpenters, technicians, mathematicians and navigators, were apparent in their impressive boats and ability to traverse the unpredictable seas of Europe. Viking ships were not only beautifully crafted vessels, which demonstrated their technical ability, but they were also elaborately decorated, with mastheads usually carved in animal form. Furthermore, although they initially acted as pirates, in their wake new trading and shipping routes were established, linking the towns, markets and waterways of Europe.

The early phase of the Viking attacks was largely unchallenged, the Vikings having both superior weaponry and the advantage of surprise. The monasteries were undefended, the wooden buildings surrounded only by earthen enclosures. The Irish kings were slow to respond to the arrival of the Norsemen. The southern Uí Néill attempted to stop the Norsemen, but they themselves were routed. The Irish kings, however, did not mount a sustained resistance to this onslaught. The fact that Ireland was divided into so many kingdoms made a united front difficult, especially as the two most powerful dynasties, the Uí Néill of Tara and the Eóganachta kings of Cashel, were bitter rivals and sporadically at war. The resumption of internal conflicts between Irish kings coincided with the external Viking assault. The conflict between Irish kings was often violent, and in the ninth century it resulted in more churches being destroyed by the Irish than by the Vikings.

For a few years after 850 the frequency of attacks diminished as the attention of the Vikings seemed to have turned from Ireland to Britain and the Isle of Man. But the respite for the Irish people was short-lived. At the end of the eighth century Viking raids on Ireland became both more numerous and more intrepid. Increasingly also, their desire for treasure, and their tactic of looting and destruction, was replaced by their wish to find fertile land for communities. Their early raids had been on isolated monastic settlements, but by the ninth century the nature of the raids changed, as single ships were replaced with fleets of vessels containing between fifty to one hundred ships.

This made large-scale raids now possible, and rather than the attacks being forays quickly carried out, they became more sustained, with the objective of establishing long-term bases overseas. In addition to monasteries and churches, farms and communities were also plundered. This new pattern of attack, combined with both the numerical strength and superior weaponry of the Norsemen, made them appear unstoppable. By the time the Irish kings had regrouped to mount a counter-attack, the Vikings had started to establish permanent bases in the east of the country. To protect themselves against the native Irish, they usually fortified their settlements. In the second half of the ninth century the Vikings were undertaking incursions into the interior of the country, both on horseback and along the waterways. None the less, the Viking attacks resulted in changes in Irish building practices. The ring-forts and crannogs, which had been the preferred form of dwelling before the Vikings, were replaced by souterrains. These were man-made tunnels that had been used in the early Christian period as places of refuge or for hiding valuables. Their use became more widespread in areas under threat of Viking attack. Round towers were also constructed from the beginning of the tenth century on monastic sites. Although they were bell towers, their primary role was defensive. They were usually at least five storeys high and each floor provided a separate unit of defence, accessible only by ladder. Although monasteries could still be destroyed, the towers provided an early warning system of attacks and some protection for the monks and their possessions.

The first Viking settlements were temporary camps, or *longphorts*, where raiding parties could spend the winter. They were usually situated beside a river, which provided both shelter and good access to the interior of the country. Two of the early longphorts were at Dublin, or *Dubhlinn* (meaning black pool), near the mouth of the River Liffey, and Annagassan in Louth. Smaller camps were located at Dunrally in Laois and Athlunkard in Clare. While the inland bases were quickly abandoned, some of the coastal bases became permanent settlements. The Dublin longphort, which allowed both good internal access and excellent contact with other Viking areas, rose in prominence after 841. The Vikings established a permanent base there that grew into the centre of their system of administration and trade. Dublin was well situated to allow the Vikings in Ireland to maintain communication with Viking settlements elsewhere. It quickly became one of the major Viking settlements in Europe, gaining importance as a centre for selling slaves to Britain. Within Dublin, streets, craft shops and businesses were opened and a *thingmote* or assembly place established, in addition to the creation of designated burial areas. Its security from native attack was maintained by the building of a rampart or wall to surround it. All of these measures suggested the Vikings had long-term plans to stay. Other Viking towns included Waterford, Youghal and Cork, although they could not rival the success of Dublin. The economic system within the Viking towns became so superior to that of the other parts of the country that Irish merchants wanted to trade with these areas. Overall, though, the success of the Vikings in their early period of settlement meant that there was a marked divide between the economies in the Viking and non-Viking areas.

The Viking settlers also brought their own traditions to Ireland. Although the monks regarded them as barbaric, some of them could read and write, and they had their own alphabet, called the *futhark*, based on an elaborate system of marks known as runes. As in Ireland, the oral tradition of storytelling was very important. Both the Vikings and the Irish placed a high value on storytelling and in both societies poets were elevated to privileged positions. Viking poets or *skalds*, like their Irish counterparts, were hired by the rich to recount heroic tales of the past. Death also was taken seriously. Viking burials could be elaborate, with some men buried with their swords or tools, and women with their jewellery or household items. They were usually laid with their head facing east. Eminent warriors were interred in their ships, which were then set on fire. Although the early Viking settlers were pagans, they believed in the other world and Odin, the god of death, was the most powerful of all their deities. The other important Viking gods were Thor, the god of thunder; Njord, the god of travel and trade; Freya, the goddess of fertility; and Freyr, the god of the harvest and of health and wealth. Many of their gods had parallels in Celtic traditions: Lug, for example, was the pagan god of the harvest and his feast day was absorbed into the Christian calendar. Viking mythology included stories of the Valkyrie, who were women warriors, but in reality the Viking warriors and traders were men, although as they settled in Ireland, some women joined them. Clearly, there were significant gender differences between roles assigned to Norse men and women, although the latter had a high level of independence. Apart from looking after the homes, women were spinners and weavers, and were usually responsible for medical treatments. They looked after the farms while the men were away either fighting or trading. A significant difference between Norse women and those elsewhere was that the former had considerable legal rights that did not disappear when they married. A married woman retained control of any wealth or money she brought into the marriage. She could also initiate a divorce based on unreasonable behaviour, and the process was simple.

Viking Settlements

The importance of Dublin as a Viking centre was confirmed when Olaf the White (d. *c.* 871), a Viking chieftain, took control of the town in 853, and ruled for almost twenty years. He was followed by Ivar the Boneless (d. 873). As a result, Dublin became a separate kingdom within Ireland. From this point until the arrival of the Normans, Dublin was ruled by a succession of Norse kings, with the exception of a brief period when it was recaptured by the Irish between 902 and 917. Many of the Norse kings were active not only in Irish affairs but also in England and Scotland, Dublin providing a good base for attacks on the west coast of Britain. In 870 Olaf the White and Ivar the Boneless together captured Dumbarton Rock, which was the fortress of the kings of Strathclyde, and thus a significant victory for the Norsemen. Through the activities of the Norse kings also, Dublin was politically linked with other kingdoms in England, Scotland and elsewhere. The activities of early rulers of Ireland were kept alive by Scandinavian sagas of the heroic Viking age, which glorified the role of these men as warriors and conquerors. The fact that the Dublin kings also ruled elsewhere provided a political link with other Viking areas. Between 1091 and 1094 Dublin was governed by the Isle of Man ruler, Godred. Godred II, who was also king of the Isle of Man (r. 1152–87), tried to extend his control to Dublin. His kingship of Dublin was achieved only following a vicious conflict with his brother. The final years of his rule coincided with the arrival of the Normans in Ireland, in 1169. Their appearance changed the balance of power within Ireland but Godred II attempted to ensure his survival in the new political set-up by marrying his daughter Affreca to the ambitious Norman knight John de Courcy, who became Lord of Ulster.

The integration of Norsemen into Irish life was helped by a period of peace and consolidation in the closing years of the ninth century, but after about 914 the Vikings renewed their attacks on Ireland. One of their first actions was to recapture Waterford from the Irish. In 917 the Vikings recaptured Dublin, which had been controlled by the Irish since 902. Sitric (or Sihtric) Caech, a grandson of Ivar the Boneless, was king of Dublin until his death in 927. From 921 he was also king of York. Sitric accepted Christianity in 926, although his conversion was short-lived and appeared to be motivated by political reasons. At his death he was succeeded by his brother Gothfrith (d. 934), who ruled Dublin only, having lost York to an English king. Gothfrith was succeeded by his son Olaf Gothfrithsson (d. *c.* 941), who attempted to win back the kingdom of York, and briefly ruled it from 939 to 941. Gothfrithsson was followed by Olaf Sihtricsson (d. *c.* 981), who ruled Dublin until 980. He converted to Christianity in 944, and at the end of his reign he became a monk on Iona. Sihtricsson also ruled York intermittently but ultimately was unable to hold onto it, being expelled from York by a fellow Viking, Eric Bloodaxe (d. 954). Bloodaxe, whose name was derived from his violent career, was the last Viking king of York. What these reigns demonstrated was that the Viking kings of Dublin continued to have aspirations to govern in England, rather than expand their interests over Ireland.

The Viking invasions after 914 were also accompanied by the founding of a number of new towns, including Wexford (Weisfjord) in 921, and the following year a Norse town was founded at Limerick, near the mouth of the River Shannon. These new conquests provided bases for incursions into Munster. They met little resistance. Ultimately, though, the Norsemen in Ireland preferred to remain as urban dwellers and coastal traders rather than as farmers. Also, by the middle of the tenth century the Vikings were using many of their resources to control their recently established kingdom in England, known as the Danelaw. A separate kingdom of Normandy had also been established in France. One of the consequences was a division within the Viking territories, with Dublin splitting from the English Viking kingdom in 952. From that point Dublin was ruled as a separate kingdom with its own dynasty of Viking kings.

Although the Vikings established a new system of government in the areas under their control, life in the rest of the country continued largely untouched, and so the two systems existed side by side. The response of the Irish kings to the Viking invasions was partial and incomplete. The overall lack of political unity meant that resistance did not happen on a sustained basis. Moreover, rather than unite against a common enemy, the Irish kings continued to fight among themselves as they had before the arrival of the Norsemen. Many of the conflicts between the Irish kings were either about the high kingship or gaining control of the kingship of Cashel.

Irish Kings

The eighth and ninth centuries were marked by the rise of the northern Uí Néill dynasty, although its members were divided amongst themselves. The Cenél nEóghain branch of the Uí Néill dynasty controlled central Ulster, but after 750 it successfully gained jurisdiction of the eastern part of Ulster, which was governed by the Uliad. The Uí Néill dynasty in the west of Ulster, which was ruled by the Cenél Conaill, resented the growing power of the Cenél nEóghain branch. It was the expansion of the Connacht kings into Breifne, rather than the threat posed by the Vikings, that united the two branches of the Uí Néill at the end of the ninth century. It was a short-lived truce, disintegrating after 940. What it did achieve, however, was an increase in the power and prestige of the Uí Néill kings, and it confirmed them as supreme rulers in the north of the country. Yet, despite their strength, the rulers of Connacht or Munster did not accept them as high kings.

In 908 Flann Sinna, the king of Tara, defeated the king–bishop of Cashel, Cormac mac Cuilennain. Cormac and many of his leading supporters were killed, and Cashel never recovered from this defeat. The new wave of Viking activity after 914, however, galvanised some of the Irish kings into resistance, led by the king of the Uí Néill, Niall Glundub, who, since the demise of Cashel, had become the most powerful king in Ireland. He tried to unite the people of Ulster and Leinster to attack the Norsemen in 917. He was unsuccessful, but two years later marshalled a further assault on the Vikings, this time in Dublin. The Irish were again defeated and Uí Néill was killed.

It took a few more decades before a new powerful group emerged in Munster under the leadership of the Dál Cais of east Clare. In 964 their leader, Mathgamain, secured Cashel from the Eóghanachta and then defeated the Norse in Limerick. These victories not only gave him considerable prestige, but also increased his wealth significantly. His victory was a blow for the Vikings. The Limerick Vikings killed Mathgamain in 976, but his brother Brian Boruma (generally known as Boru) not only took over his possessions, but also sought to extend them. His aspirations were helped by the fact that the Norsemen were starting to demonstrate vulnerability; they had even been defeated in their stronghold of Dublin in 980 by Máel Sechnaill, at the battle of Tara. Following this victory Máel Sechnaill was declared the king of Tara. In the following year he took control of the whole of Dublin and demanded a tribute be paid to him. These victories marked a turning point in the political balance between the Irish and the Vikings, although the Irish remained divided between Máel Sechnaill, who represented the northern Uí Néill dynasty, and Brian Boru, who represented the southern dynasty of Dál Cais. Brian Boru was the victor, defeating both his Irish opponents and the Norsemen in 999. Three years later Máel Sechnaill acknowledged Brian Boru as the high king at Tara, although Brian personally preferred the appellation of 'emperor of the Irish'. This agreement gave him effective control over Munster, Leinster and Dublin. In return, Máel Sechnaill retained the kingship of Connacht and Ulster. Effectively, these two kings had divided Ireland between them, with little consideration given to the Viking claims.

Inevitably, the lords of Leinster and the king of Dublin felt particularly aggrieved at this settlement, and during the remaining years of Boru's kingship, opposition was mounted by a coalition of Irish and Norsemen. Brian Boru responded by taking his army into Dublin and burning down its main fortress in 999. Following this, the Norse king, Sitric Silkenbeard, submitted to Boru's kingship. Brian also sought to woo and control the Irish Church, visiting Armagh in 1005 and leaving a gift of 20 ounces of gold. He also undertook two tours of Ireland, in 1005 and 1006, which confirmed and consolidated his position as the supreme ruler of Ireland.

The challenges to Brain Boru's kingship continued, showing that the various allegiances to him had been based on military expediency rather than genuine loyalty. In 1013 Máel Morda, the king of Leinster, and the king of Dublin again allied against Brian Boru. This revolt had sporadic support in the rest of the country, which divided Boru's forces. His main assault was against Dublin: his army laid siege to the town in the final months of 1013, but was forced to retreat as the weather deteriorated. His retreat allowed the Vikings to regroup and seek help from their Viking allies overseas. Brian Boru's followers returned in spring 1014 and the two armies met at Clontarf, on the border of Dublin. The battle was violent, with thousands of losses on both sides. Boru's army was the victor, but he was killed in the battle. In the wake of their defeat, the Vikings retreated, many leaving Ireland. What the war also showed was that militarily the balance of power between the Norsemen and the Irish had changed, largely because the latter had adopted many of the Viking military tactics and weapons. The victory of an Irish king over an invader – even if the invading group had been in the country for over 200 years – was a symbolic victory for the Irish people, although in military terms it was not as significant. The domination of the Vikings had been in decline for a number of decades. Moreover, as so frequently proved to be the case, the Norsemen had adopted many Irish ways, a process that had been facilitated by their gradual acceptance of Christianity. The battle of Clontarf was as much a power struggle between Irish kings as it was with the Viking invaders. Following Clontarf, Dublin was again under Irish control, although Viking kings were allowed to continue to rule it. Dublin flourished throughout the eleventh century under a combined Norse–Irish influence. Inevitably, the process of becoming Irish, sometimes referred to as 'Hibernicisation', increased even more rapidly. By the end of the century Dublin had overtaken Tara as the capital of Ireland, not only as the centre of economic activity, but also as the heart of political power. For Irish kings, controlling Dublin was an important step in gaining the high kingship of the island.

By the end of the tenth century, changes were taking place within Scandinavia that ended Viking supremacy and the unity that had existed there. At the beginning of the Viking period, there had been numerous kings in Scandinavia, but this gradually reduced to the three kingdoms of Denmark, Sweden and Norway. Christianity had also made inroads into the area, with the king of Denmark, Harald Bluetooth, converting in the 960s. Christianity spread, with Norway becoming Christianised in the early eleventh century and Sweden converting at the end of the eleventh century. As had been the case in Ireland, though, for a while Christianity coexisted with and accommodated the old pagan gods.

Viking ambitions had not ended. In 1066 Harald Hardraada, the king of Norway (r. 1047–66), made a bid to become king of England. He was unsuccessful, being killed by Harold II at the battle of Stamford Bridge in 1066. Harold was himself killed by William the Conqueror at the battle of Hastings, in the same year. Although William became the first Norman king of England, he was himself descended from the Vikings who had settled in France. They had named the territory Normandy, and it was from this area that the Norman invaders of England originated. By the time of the invasion, their Norse ancestry had been subsumed under a Norman French identity.

Despite the generally negative image of the Viking period, some advances had been made. Before the arrival of the Vikings, Ireland possessed a sophisticated and uniform language, and, apart from the monks, scholarly activities were promoted by artists, poets, Brehons, genealogists and historians. Many of these people survived not only the arrival of Christianity but also the coming of the Vikings. Notwithstanding the early ransacking of the monasteries, many of them did survive, although their role as centres of scholarship and hubs of economic activity diminished. The decline of the monasteries as centres of learning, however, gave rise to secular educational establishments. At the same time, many monasteries survived as religious centres which were primarily concerned with spiritual matters. Some accounts, however, referred to a leniency in the morals of the religious orders. The decline of Latin following the ninth century strengthened the use of Irish as the language of the educated.

Poets were traditionally highly regarded and well paid within Celtic society. Hereditary succession ensured that each generation would have its own access to these professional artists. The coming of Christianity, however, initially caused a division between poets who celebrated the Church and those whose compositions were devoted to eulogising the kings and other powerful members of society. By the tenth century, Irish poets had evolved into a bardic class. This period was also associated with the emergence of *dindshenchas* poetry. One of the greatest Irish poets of this period was Cináed Ua hArtacáin, who died in 975. Pilgrimages to the continent continued to be important. Together, the church scholars and the poets became responsible for learning and literacy in Ireland. They reached a compromise about Irish historical traditions, with poets helping to preserve Celtic customs through their writings. The monks, on the other hand, depicted much of the Celtic history as pagan legends, while glorifying the Christian age. These two scholarly traditions continued to coexist until the sixteenth century.

Despite the decline of the monasteries, Irish monks continued to make some impressive contributions to European Christianity. St Catroe of Armagh founded a monastery at Metz in the 970s, and Irish monks were given control of the monastery of St Martin's in Cologne. Irishmen were also prominent in promoting the revival of learning on the continent and continued to produce illuminated manuscripts. Stone sculptures, especially figure carvings and high crosses carved with biblical scenes, developed during the Viking period. The Irish high crosses, which included Flynn's Cross at Clonmacnoise (*c.* 909) and Muiredach's Cross at Monasterboice in Louth (*c.* 924), were at the time probably the most sophisticated stone monuments erected within Europe. Changes also took place in architectural practices, with stone churches taking the place of the earlier wooden buildings. Coins were also in circulation in some of the Viking areas. There were some setbacks. The deadly plague that killed so many on the continent in 1094 arrived in Ireland in 1095, and proved to be devastating.

By the late eleventh century the Viking period in Ireland and elsewhere had ended. By this stage, the Irish Vikings were very different from the marauders who had first appeared in the country almost 300 years earlier. Their main settlements remained along the coast in Dublin, Wexford, Waterford, Cork and Limerick. One of the consequences was to give the east coast political and economic domination within the affairs of Ireland. As permanent settlers, the Vikings had influenced Irish arts, culture, language, trade and warfare. The Viking towns also rivalled the monasteries as centres of economic importance. In turn the Vikings had embraced some of the ways of the Irish: many were Christian and their art showed a Celtic influence. One of the greatest legacies of the Norsemen was the development of Viking towns, notably Dublin, which opened up Ireland to external trade and firmly integrated her within the European marketplace. Norse words had become absorbed into the Irish language, particularly in place names such as Leixlip and Wexford.

Post-Viking Ireland

Following the death of Brian Boru, Máel Sechnaill II, who had preceded Boru as high king, resumed this position until his death in 1022. Between 1022 and 1072, there was no high king in Ireland. The battle of Clontarf and the death of Brian Boru demonstrated the deep-rooted antagonisms and rivalries between the Irish kings. It also ended the emergence of a strong, central monarchy in Ireland. Brian Boru was almost sixty when he became high king and he ruled for only twelve years, yet he proved to be high king in more than just name. Moreover, his jurisdiction was not merely of the Irish areas, but included the Norse towns. Boru's combination of skills as a military strategist, able administrator and astute politician was unusual and hard to follow. The battle of Clontarf, despite being a defeat for the high king, also marked an end to Viking aspirations of extending their control in Ireland. The timing was made noteworthy by the fact that as Viking power was diminishing in Ireland, in England it was reaching a new peak. In 1016 Cnut (Canute) became a Viking king of the English, until his death in 1035. In Ireland, the battle of Clontarf confirmed that the Viking control of Ireland had peaked.

Royal enmity in Ireland did not lessen following Brian Boru's death in 1014, and the eleventh century was dominated by internecine conflicts and warfare between the rulers of Ireland. At this stage Ireland was divided into over 100 kingdoms, with the most important ones seeking the ultimate prize of the high kingship. Consequently, the eleventh century was marked by shifting alliances and alignments. No king or high king attained the unity and stability that had been achieved under Brian Boru. This phase of conflict was only ended by the arrival of the Normans, who themselves came at the invitation of warring Irish kings.

However, the fighting and conflict between the Irish kings disguised the achievements made following Brian Boru's death. The rapid changes in leadership and in allegiance, and the violent disposal of opposition, were not unique to Ireland but a feature of medieval life in Europe. Furthermore, despite the backdrop of constant warfare, Ireland experienced a cultural renaissance in the tenth century that extended into the early Norman period. The revival was more conspicuous because it followed a long period of relative stagnation during the Viking episode. It was also a period of far-reaching church reform, a fact that was deliberately misrepresented by Ireland's Norman neighbours in the twelfth century.

One of the outcomes of the cultural revival in the eleventh century was that the use of the Irish language was strengthened, with learning in Latin being augmented with teaching in the Irish language, even in the monasteries. This change was supported by Latin texts translated into Irish. As a consequence, Ireland was the first modern European country to develop a native literature. It was also the first country to have its own stadardised written grammar. Although some of the writings praised the role of Irish saints, endowing them with such qualities as to verge on hagiography, Irish literature also extended beyond merely religious topics. A new development was the writing – in Irish – of Irish sagas, which suggested a heroic past, exalted Ireland's pagan antecedents and suggested that some of the Gaelic kings were superhuman. The first manuscript to be written completely in Irish was *Lebor na hUidre*, that is, 'The Book of the Dun Cow', which was written in Clonmacnoise around 1100. Much of the book was devoted to what was called 'The Ulster Cycle', which provided epic accounts of Ireland's past. 'The Book of the Dun Cow' also included a version of *Táin Bó Cuailnge*, that is, 'The Cattle Raid of Cooley', which retold the story of Queen Medb of Connacht's invasion of Ulster in pursuit of a brown bull. The Ulster hero Cú Chulainn halted her, and eventually the Ulster bull destroyed the bull of Connacht. This narrative was based on a seventh-century oral story, but it was not written down until the eleventh century. Despite its literary origins,

Táin Bó Cuailnge could also be read as a metaphor for the political and territorial disputes between Irish kings.

A number of histories were also written which promoted the idea of glorious antecedents. The most renowned of these texts was *Lebor Gabála*, which was more popularly rendered as 'The Book of Invasions'. It provided an epic view of Irish history, which glorified the origins of Ireland, particularly the contribution of the Gaels. It also provided a description of the role of kings in Irish development. Overall, *Lebor Gabála* was influential in providing a heroic view of Ireland's past. Some of the subsequent histories provided a more dubious view of Ireland's past. Part of this process was the creation of invented genealogies. More recent events were also glorified. A text written in the twelfth century, *Cogadh Gáedhel re Gallaibh*, that is, 'The War of the Irish with the Foreigners', provided an early written testimony of the unique position occupied by Brian Boru.

Historical events were preserved in the Annals, which provided written accounts of significant aspects of Ireland's past. They were a particularly rich source for the Gaelic period, which had few written records. The Annals of Inisfallen are the earliest example of this type of written history. They were begun in 1092 and completed in the fourteenth century, with a greater number being between the fourteenth and sixteenth centuries. Monks wrote the earliest Annals, which meant that the arrival of Christianity was treated favourably, while some aspects of pagan practice were sanitised. Few of the earliest Annals survived, but some of them were incorporated into later Annals.

A number of church reforms also took place. For a while it appeared that the Irish Church might move closer to papal rule. In 1028 Sitric Silkenbeard, the Viking king of Dublin, and Flannacan, the king of Brega, undertook a pilgrimage to Rome. Following his return, Sitric founded Christ Church Cathedral and appointed Dunan as the first bishop of Dublin. Dunan remained in this position until his death in 1074. These developments demonstrated how entrenched Christianity had become among the Viking community. Following Dunan's death, however, there was a movement by some Irish kings to bring about more ecclesiastical reforms. The need for reform received support from outside Ireland, including from St Anselm, the archbishop of Canterbury, who contacted the king of Cashel urging change. The authorities in Rome disliked the autonomy of the Irish Church, which had been apparent since the time of Patrick.

One outcome was the First Synod of Cashel in 1101. Cashel was an important religious site, although since the fourth century it had been associated with the royal family of Eóganacht. The king of Cashel was usually designated king–bishop, indicating the close relationship between the Church and the rulers. Brian Boru had made himself king of Cashel in 978, and this title passed to his descendants, the Uí Briain. The synod came about largely because of pressure from European church reformers who desired to return church control more clearly to religious bodies. There was also some concern about some lapses in the moral teachings of the Irish Church. Ironically, however, the synod was organised by Muirchertach Ua Briain, the king of Munster. One of the most important outcomes was that Muirchertach agreed to give the site of Cashel for the exclusive use of the Church. From this point, Cashel was associated with ecclesiastical developments rather than royal matters. A number of decrees were also agreed to by the synod, many concerning the involvement of the laity in church affairs. The Church's attitudes to the marriage of clerics were also brought in line with European practices. A unique feature of the Irish Church was that the organisation of the church was monastic rather than diocesan. This structure meant that priests played little role in church affairs. Furthermore, many of the important positions within the Church were hereditary, and they were sometimes held by laymen. The programme of church reform, therefore, continued, and in 1111 the Synod of Ráith Bressail, near Cashel, was convened. It was presided over by Cellach, the primate of Armagh and the high king. One of its main aims was to reorganise the diocesan structure in Ireland. The outcome was that the monastic organisation was replaced with twenty-four sees. Within only ten years, therefore, significant changes had taken place in the organisation of the Irish Church. Many of the churches and reforms, however, despite being driven by an external agenda, were adapted to suit Irish conditions, and this implementation was sometimes piecemeal and faced strong local opposition. Overall though, the Irish Church remained a strong, national organisation.

The desire for reform and to bring the Irish Church closer to Rome found a champion in St Malachy, the bishop of Down and Connor after 1124, and archbishop of Armagh. His goal of church reform found a powerful supporter in Cormac Mac Carthaig, the king of Desmond, although some of the other kings were less enthusiastic. Some were reluctant to support the separation of Church and royal authority, fearing a diminution of their power. When

Malachy became archbishop of Armagh in 1129, he was opposed by the local chieftains of Clann Sinaich, who had controlled clerical positions at Armagh for almost 200 years. This family had traditionally supplied Armagh with abbots, whose lifestyle had been closer to that of laymen, especially in regard to marriage. The marriage of abbots had been forbidden by the Synod of Cashel, and Malachy was determined to enforce this decree. Because the Clann Sinaich refused to cooperate with Malachy he resigned the see in 1137. Malachy desired to move the Irish Church closer to Rome, and in 1139 he undertook a visit to Pope Innocent II. He also wanted papal recognition for the archbishoprics of Armagh and Cashel. The request was refused because Pope Innocent did not believe that Malachy carried the backing of the Irish Church. Instead, the Pope instructed Malachy to convene a church council in Ireland and get total support for the archbishopric.

A more successful outcome of Malachy's journey was that he formed close connections with the Cistercian monastery at Clairvaux, and in 1142, under Malachy's patronage, the first Irish Cistercian monastery was founded at Mellifont. He subsequently brought an Augustinian order to Ireland, based at St Mary's abbey in Louth. A more successful Augustinian house was established at the abbey of St Thomas the Martyr in 1177. Once in Ireland, these and other houses established strong roots, surviving the upheaval following the arrival of the Normans. In 1148 Malachy again travelled to Europe to ask the Pope once more for recognition for Armagh and Cashel. He died en route, probably in the arms of St Bernard, his friend and biographer. Malachy was canonised by Pope Clement III in 1190. Malachy's reforms had helped to reinforce the separation of the functions of the laity and the Church. Moreover, his interaction with the Pope and introduction of new religious houses brought European observances and practices into the Irish Church. Not everyone in Ireland, however, approved of these changes. Some of his attempted reforms came to fruition only after his death. At the Synod of Kells in 1152 Ireland was divided into thirty-six sees with four archbishops, that is, in Armagh, Cashel, Dublin and Tuam. These changes provided Ireland with an administrative structure more in keeping with the demands of the various popes. These reforms make it hard to understand the *Laudabiliter*, a papal letter issued by Pope Adrian IV in 1155, authorising a conquest of Ireland by Henry II to enable a reform of the Church. Its main motivation appears to have been political rather than ecclesiastical, the Pope disliking the autonomy of the Irish Church.

Church architecture also benefited from both the general artistic revival and the reforms within the Church. Much building took place in Cashel following the synod, adopting a Romanesque style that was embellished with sumptuous and numerous carvings, including human masks. This style of building was copied, and it influenced subsequent church building in Ireland, vying with the Gothic style preferred by some religious orders. Cormac's Chapel, named after Cormac Mac Carthaig, king of Munster, was begun in 1127 and was consecrated amid much pomp in 1134. Stone-roofed churches also became common. All these elaborate buildings suggest that the Irish Church was successful, prosperous and flourishing. Moreover, it is unlikely that such ambitious projects could not have taken place without the approval and support of rich patrons, mostly kings. Regardless of the conflicts, therefore, Irish society was stable enough to be capable of innovation and artistic greatness.

In the twelfth century also there was a revival in the building of high crosses. Although a number had been erected in the ninth century, mostly on monastic sites, the process had mostly died out by the tenth century. In the twelfth century, though, there was a revival of this art form, and the crosses were even more decorated than previously. The intricate decorations that adorned the crosses were also used to decorate other church icons, including crosiers, chalices and carrying crosses, such as the Cross of Cong. Some of the designs showed a Viking influence, thus bringing together Norse and Gaelic art in religious icons. Religious links with Europe also continued through the activities of Irish monks and pilgrims. Aaron of Cologne, an Irish-born monk, was consecrated bishop of Cracow in 1049. Irish pilgrims were granted the use of St Peter's church at Regensburg in 1075. Again, one of the consequences of this link was to expose Irish missionaries to church reforms taking place in the rest of Europe. Inevitably, they saw the potential for such reforms within Ireland.

Ireland's cultural blossoming did not go unnoticed overseas. In 1155 Henry II of England discussed a possible invasion of Ireland at the Council of Winchester, although he decided not to proceed with the proposal. However, Henry was not the only person with an interest in Ireland. The Pope, Adrian IV, was anxious to ensure that the restructured Irish Church looked to Rome for leadership. When Henry approached Adrian with his vague proposal for an invasion, he found a willing advocate. Moreover, by depicting the Irish as 'a rude and ignorant people', who needed to be brought more closely under the control of the Roman Church, Henry was constructing a justification that would satisfy both parties, regardless of the fact it had no basis in truth. The outcome was the *Laudabiliter* of 1155, which approved of an invasion of Ireland by Henry at any time that it should be convenient. For Henry, who was busy fighting wars of the eastern flank of his Angevin Empire, the timing was not good, and no action was taken. It was not until 1169 that a local conflict between the Irish kings Diarmait MacMurchada (Dermot MacMurrough) and Ruaidrí Ua Conchobair (Rory O'Connor) provided an opportunity for both Henry and Adrian to involve themselves in the affairs of Ireland. Their intervention had more far-reaching effects than either had anticipated.

THREE

THE NORMAN INVASION
c. 1169–1490

The arrival of Norman knights in Ireland in 1169 (quickly followed by Henry II) marked the beginning of the long political entanglement between Ireland and England.

This chapter examines the coming of the Normans to Ireland and the early attempts to extend English control throughout the country. The Norman influence, however, was increasingly undermined by the willingness of Norman settlers to associate with and integrate into Irish culture and society. None the less, during the Norman period, a number of patterns were established that defined relations between natives and settlers for hundreds of years. Much of our knowledge of the early Norman period is derived from the writings of Gerald of Wales (Giraldus Cambrensis), although his first visit to Ireland took place in only 1183 when the first phase of the invasion was over. Inevitably, his account was culturally located and partisan, extolling the Normans at the expense of the Irish.

The Early Norman Period

The coming of the Anglo-Normans in 1169 marked a new departure in Irish political development. From that point, Irish history was intertwined with that of its nearest neighbour. The Anglo-Normans had come at the invitation of an Irish king and they stayed because Ireland offered many opportunities for ambitious knights and kings.

Their involvement was precipitated by a conflict between Irish kings, Dermot MacMurrough (Diarmait MacMurchada), the king of Leinster (d. 1171) – remembered in Ireland as *Diarmait na nGall*, Dermot of the Foreigners – and Rory O'Connor (Ruaidrí Ua Conchobair), king of Connacht and high king of Ireland (d. 1198). Dermot had ruled Leinster since 1132, but it was the events of the last few years of his life that ensured his notoriety. Dermot was banished from his kingdom in 1166, following a battle against Rory O'Connor. Dermot sought external help from Henry II (r. 1154–89), who appeared disinterested at this time. Henry, however, was an ambitious and belligerent ruler, and the early years of his reign had been marked by territorial expansion and consequently war. In the mid-1160s, Henry was too busy defending and extending his recently acquired Angevin Empire, which at times included England, Anjou, Normandy and Aquitaine, with outposts in Scotland and Wales, to get involved in a dispute between Irish kings. Yet, within a year of becoming king of England, Henry had shown an interest in Irish affairs and a desire to extend his empire westwards. In 1155 Adrian IV, the first and only English pope (from 1154 to 1159), had issued the *Bull Laudabiliter*, a papal decree which authorised the conquest of Ireland by Henry II. Adrian's primary objective was to reform and reorganise the Irish Church and bring it into line with Rome. Although the authenticity of the decree was subsequently challenged, there is no doubt that both Adrian and Henry had designs on Ireland, even if for different reasons.

While Henry did not want to get personally involved in the Irish conflict, he gave permission for Dermot to recruit Norman mercenaries to win back his kingdom. Dermot recruited a number of Anglo-Norman knights in south Wales, who were out of favour with Henry. They were led by Richard de Clare, the 2nd Earl of Pembroke (*c.* 1130–76), a soldier whose nickname was Strongbow. Strongbow had supported Stephen, a rival of Henry, in his unsuccessful bid for the English throne. When Henry II ascended to the throne, Strongbow had to forfeit his titles. Strongbow therefore saw the expedition to Ireland as a way of gaining favour with the king and winning back his titles. In return for his support, Dermot promised Strongbow lands, the hand of Aoífe, his daughter, and the right to the succession of the kingship in Leinster.

A Norman army led by Robert FitzStephen landed in Ireland in 1169 and successfully assaulted the Viking town of Wexford. The advance army included a number of Cambro-Norman families, such as the Fitzhenrys and the Fitzgeralds, and some Flemish-Norman families, including the Prendergasts, the Roches and the Synotts. The Wexford Norsemen were no match for the well-armed foot soldiers, archers and horsemen who were fighting on behalf of Dermot. As a result of this victory, Dermot was able to regain control of his kingdom. When news of his victory spread, O'Connor marched south and met Dermot at Ferns in Wexford. MacMurrough agreed to recognise O'Connor as high king and the status quo appeared to be in place. But this was far from being the case. Strongbow arrived in Ireland in 1170 with more soldiers and captured the town of Waterford. His victory was commemorated with his marriage to Aoífe a few days after the battle was over.

The marriage of Aoífe and Strongbow cemented the political relationship between natives and newcomers. The union was indicative of the role of upper-class women – as useful commodities that could be bartered in dynastic marriages and as child bearers. For the Normans, it was also a way of creating family ties with the natives that soldered political alliances. Following the wedding the Normans moved northwards to Dublin, with a view to deposing the Viking king. Although O'Connor and the Vikings formed an alliance, they were unable to defeat the superior weaponry of the Normans. The taking of Dublin marked a significant victory for the Normans, who had achieved within a few months what the Vikings had taken years to accomplish. Moreover, the position of the Normans was considerably strengthened when Dermot MacMurrough died in 1171 with no male heir and was succeeded by his son-in-law, Strongbow.

Strongbow's accession to the kingdom of Leinster made both the English king and the Irish kings nervous. Henry II feared, as so many subsequent English kings were to fear, that his knight would establish an independent Irish kingdom, which might eventually threaten England's interests. Within a few months of Dermot's death, therefore, Henry took personal control of the situation by travelling to Ireland accompanied by a small but well-equipped army. He stayed in Ireland from October 1171 to April 1172, travelling along the east coast and receiving pledges of loyalty from the Irish leaders, the Viking lords, and the Norman knights. Rory O'Connor, the high king, initially refused to submit to Henry. Henry viewed Strongbow as a potential threat not only in terms of creating an independent kingdom in Ireland, but also because Ireland could provide a base for attempting to win back his lands in Wales. Before travelling to Ireland, therefore, Henry placed troops on Strongbow's property and warned him that his lands would be confiscated unless he recognised him as overlord of Ireland. Strongbow agreed and was allowed to continue as the king of Leinster, although his position was now with the consent of the English king. His title as Earl of Strigoil, based on his castle at Chepstow, was also recognised, although not his title of the Earl of Pembroke. But, to counterbalance Strongbow's power in Ireland, the areas of Meath and Waterford that adjoined the kingdom of Leinster were declared to be Crown property. Dublin was also granted a charter, and the kingdom of Meath was given to Hugh de Lacy.

Henry's follow-up action could be seen as a way of controlling his maverick knights rather than a sudden interest in Irish affairs. Nevertheless, whether intentionally or otherwise, he consolidated English military involvement in Ireland and extended English influence into other areas. Henry was a foreign king yet he quickly rivalled the power of the Irish kings. In recognition of the Pope's support, Henry established a second Synod of Cashel in 1172, which was intended to extend the Pope's authority in Ireland. The first synod had been held in 1111 and had initiated a period of reform in the Irish Church. The second synod, however, achieved little, largely because Henry disagreed with the papal representative. Overall, although church reform as outlined in the *Laudabiliter* was used as the justification for the conquest, Henry put little effort into reforming the Irish Church. Adrian's successor, Alexander III, also realised the benefit of allying with Henry in order to bring about reforms in Ireland. In 1172 he wrote to the remaining kings of Ireland and asked them to give fealty to Henry. The coming of the Normans effectively created two distinct Churches within Ireland. The Irish Church within the Norman area was European in style and more responsive to papal authority. Beyond this area, the old Irish Church remained isolated and more autonomous than it had been prior to 1169.

Henry's attention was diverted from Ireland when in April 1173 his sons mounted a rebellion against him in Normandy. To assist in quelling the uprising Henry took knights from Ireland, including Strongbow. Henry's departure was hasty, and although he had secured his position in a half-conquered Ireland, his power ultimately depended on the interest and loyalty of his Norman knights. However, they were never given sufficient resources to complete the process of conquest. While the Normans were occupied elsewhere, there was an attempt by the native Irish to regain their land.

Given his ongoing troubles in France, Henry was anxious that Ireland should not prove to be a drain on his military resources. He wanted a peaceful settlement in Ireland that would allow him to focus on his problems elsewhere. Henry particularly wanted submission from Rory O'Connor, who was both the high king of Ireland and the man who had initially expelled Dermot. O'Connor, however, wanted to prevent further Norman expansion and maintain his own power base. The consequence was the Treaty of Windsor in 1175, which provided clear evidence of Henry's superior position in Ireland. The treaty, however, symbolically consolidated the relationship between the English king and Irish kings by recognising Rory O'Connor as high king of the unconquered parts of the country. In return, O'Connor acknowledged Henry as his overlord and agreed to donate to him one-tenth of the cattle tribute from areas not under Norman control. The treaty also confirmed Henry as lord of the cities of Dublin, Wexford and Waterford and of Meath and Leinster. The peaceful coexistence of the two systems was short-lived, with neither side fulfilling their promises: O'Connor did not possess sufficient power to act as Henry's agent, while the Norman knights and Henry himself unilaterally seized more Irish land. O'Connor found himself in the position of being trusted by neither the Normans nor the Irish, and in 1183 he abdicated in favour of his son, Conchobar, although he regretted this action and tried unsuccessfully to win back his title. When he died in 1198, Rory O'Connor had the dubious distinction of being the last high king who could claim to have hegemony over the whole of Ireland. The disappearance of this ancient title paved the way for ambitious Norman knights to extend further their position in Ireland. Henry's position in Ireland was strengthened following Strongbow's death in 1176, when the kingdom of Leinster was assigned to Henry. Henry also demonstrated his long-term dynastic ambitions in Ireland when he made his ten-year-old son John the 'Lord of Ireland' in 1177. In less than ten years Henry, without having personally fought on Irish soil, had embedded his influence in Ireland in such a way that it would prove difficult to challenge or remove.

Strongbow, whose actions had such a dramatic impact on Irish development, in fact only had a brief involvement with Ireland. His position as king of Leinster was short-lived. He only survived Dermot by five years, dying in 1176. He was buried in Christ Church Cathedral in Dublin, which he had helped to renovate. During his life Strongbow had repeatedly demonstrated his loyalty to Henry, although this trust was never reciprocated. Following his death, although Aoífe and two children survived him, Henry took most of Strongbow's lands into the protection of the Crown. Aoífe was allowed to hold onto some of Strongbow's Welsh property, including Chepstow, and she also acquired the title *Comtissa de Hibernia*. The only son of Strongbow and Aoífe died in 1185, and their daughter Isabel became their sole heir. Isabel married William Marshal (*c.* 1147–1219), an English soldier. As a reward for supporting Richard I, in 1189 the king gave Marshal the hand of Isabel, together with some of Strongbow's lands in Normandy, England, Wales and Ireland. Marshal also won back more of the lands that had been taken from Strongbow by Henry, including the title of the Earl of Pembroke. Marshal's political importance was evident from the fact that he was regent of England, governing on behalf of the boy-king Henry III from 1216 until his death in 1219. Before his appointment as regent, Marshal also spent considerable time in Ireland, a decision that was influenced by the loss of Norman lands in France. He showed interest in estate management and promoted the expansion of the towns of New Ross and Kilkenny. Marshal and Isabel had ten children, and consequently Dermot MacMurrough's great-grandchildren regained his lands in Leinster, although not his title of king. As a result of Marshal's acquisitions and political acumen, his successors became the most powerful family in England and Ireland. They also carried on a process, which had been started by Strongbow, linking the fortunes of English, Welsh and Irish nobility by blood ties, scattered possessions and shared enemies.

Despite the Treaty of Windsor, the Norman expansion continued. Henry started a process in Ireland of disregarding promises that were made to Irish kings. One of his early actions was to flout the Windsor Treaty by taking land for the Crown, including the cities of Cork and Limerick, and giving away large tracts of land to Norman knights. Moreover, Normans were permitted to expand westwards into Connacht, despite the fact that the kings of Connacht, the O'Connors, had been loyal to Henry. The Normans involved in the conquest of Connacht included the de Burgos, the de Lacys and the Fitzgeralds. Walled towns sprang up in many parts of Connacht as a result of this expansion, but despite building walled towns, castles and garrisons, the Normans in Connacht remained more vulnerable to attack than those in the east. However, by the middle of the thirteenth century, three-quarters of Ireland was under the control of the Normans. What the expansion demonstrated was that the word of the English king meant little, as Ireland was callously divided up between uncontrolled and ruthless Normans.

One of the most fearless and ambitious of Norman knights was John de Courcy. He came to Ireland in only 1177, as part of a second wave of Norman knights. He extended the Norman Conquest northwards. Within a few weeks of his arrival he had captured Downpatrick, which was an important hill fort and religious site. In 1171 he killed the king of Dál nAraidi and thus became the lord of Ulaid (Ulster). He did this without receiving the prior permission of Henry II. De Courcy consolidated his position by dividing up much of his territory among his loyal knights and encouraging them to build a series of castles. De Courcy's building of the magnificent stone Carrickfergus Castle after 1180 was an indication of his strength and supremacy, even among other Norman knights. He ruled this

territory for twenty-seven years, during which time he
towns in Downpatrick, Newry, Carlingford, Carrickfergu
also promoted the fame of Patrick, and linked the sain
with Downpatrick. The Norman towns, castles, fortif
abbeys and monasteries all provided visible evidence of tl
in Ulster. Within a generation, the new settlers had changed the political and
physical landscape of the country.

De Courcy demonstrated his longer-term dynastic ambitions by marrying
Affreca, the daughter of the king of the Isle of Man. This marriage linked him
with the Gaelic–Norse nobles rather than his fellow Normans. They had no
children. Affreca, who was a devout Christian, built a monastery at Greyabbey
dedicated to St Mary. Although de Courcy had angered – and worried – Henry
II by his actions in Ulster, in 1185 Henry appointed him as justiciar of Ireland.
Justiciar was the designation of the chief governor of Ireland from the twelfth
to the fourteenth centuries. He combined administrative, military and judicial
duties. The king appointed the justiciar and had the right to intervene in any
of his judgments. The position was usually given to settler lords and was a way
of increasing royal control in Ireland.

De Courcy's success, however, created powerful enemies among other
Norman knights. These tensions intensified after de Courcy minted his own
coins, a prerogative reserved for the king, with Patrick's name on one side
and his on the other. When John succeeded to the throne one of his first
actions was to dismiss de Courcy and command Hugh de Lacy to capture
him. De Lacy had arrived in Ireland in only 1195. He was ambitious, and
King John (r. 1199–1216) decided to use him to destroy de Courcy's power.
De Courcy was attacked in Downpatrick by de Lacy in 1203, but he retreated
to Carrickfergus where he was finally defeated. De Courcy refused to submit
to John, and his lands were forfeited by the Crown and given to Hugh de Lacy.
Many of his knights transferred their loyalty to de Lacy and so were allowed
to hold onto their lands. Hugh de Lacy was given the title of the Earl of Ulster
by King John, a title that had never been granted to de Courcy. The latter
made an attempt to win back his lands, landing with Norse soldiers supplied
by the king of Man in 1205. He was again defeated and expelled from Ulster,
for a second time by de Lacy. King John eventually fell out with de Lacy. The
land that de Lacy had taken from de Courcy was in turn taken from him and
his knights. King John also took over de Lacy's earldom in 1210. De Lacy left
Ireland but returned in 1223, aggressively taking over property in Meath. In

the earldom of Ulster was returned to him, and his lands were extended return for his participation in the conquest of Connacht. De Lacy died without heirs in 1242, and his lands reverted to the Crown. Ulster was ruled directly by the Crown until it was granted to the de Burgh family in 1263. The Normans clearly saw Ireland as being worth fighting over, even if their opponents were fellow Normans.

Colonisation and Settlement

Norman involvement in Ireland fluctuated according to the personal interest of individual kings. Richard I (r. 1189–99), who succeeded his father, Henry II, had little interest in the affairs of Ireland, much of his reign being devoted to fighting in the Crusades for control of the Middle East. His personal involvement in the Crusades meant that for long periods he was an absentee monarch, while the wars were a drain on both manpower and financial resources. Yet even in his lifetime, Richard was admired throughout Europe for his bravery, winning him the nickname *Coeur de Lion*, the Lionheart. When he returned from the East to England in 1194, he was confronted by troubles in his French possessions, and so left for Normandy, never to return to England. Ireland received little attention from Richard. His brother John, who was governor of Ireland, was left in charge of the Anglo-Norman area; despite his personal unpopularity and attempt at rebellion against his brother, these were relatively peaceful years for Ireland. When Richard died, despite his frequent absences from England, the Angevin Empire was intact, a situation that was rapidly reversed by his successor, John.

The success of the Norman occupation was not just due to their military and diplomatic skills. Their military victories were followed up by other measures that consolidated their hold on society. Overall, there was little displacement of the Irish people, and for ordinary people everyday life hardly changed. Those who suffered most from the Norman arrival were the Gaelic chiefs, who lost their lands, power and status. Yet, just as marriage had been used to consolidate the deal between Dermot and Strongbow, other alliances were made by noble Irish families to help safeguard their position with the settlers. In 1180 de Courcy had consolidated his position by marrying Affreca, the daughter of Godred, the former king of Dublin and the king of Man. In the same year de Lacy married the daughter of the high king, Rory O'Connor. Some years later, William de Burgo married the daughter of Donal

O'Brien, king of Thomond. This marriage demonstrated that leading Gaelic families were not regarded as the social inferiors of the Normans.

Economic integration was also important, and the early Norman period brought economic growth and prosperity to parts of the Irish economy. Moreover, the Normans did not want to expel the natives from the land, but to encourage them to use their agricultural skills. Within his Irish dominions, Henry allowed free trading rights, and this was extended to Ireland in 1175. The Normans also introduced the feudal system to the areas under their control, in which the most important Norman knights and barons granted land to lesser knights in return for mutual protection. The growing of grain was encouraged and estate management introduced into farming. The building of a new infrastructure of roads and bridges helped internal trade, and also facilitated the export of goods to Wales and England, notably of wool, cattle hides, cheese, wheat and other provisions. One of the greatest Norman legacies was possibly the creation of a network of towns, which usually possessed shops, artisans, traders and a church. By the second half of the thirteenth century, trade guilds had been established in the main towns. Regular markets and fairs were held, which increased economic links with the surrounding areas. Few Irish people, though, chose to live in the towns.

The coming of the Normans changed religious practices in Ireland, even if not in the way Adrian had envisioned. Many religious orders came to Ireland from various parts of Europe in the wake of the Normans, although they remained in the areas under Norman control. However, as the Normans expanded throughout Ireland, so too did the influence of the religious orders. The Normans supported a programme of renovating or building churches. Some of them were magnificent edifices, and the cathedrals of the medieval period, just like the castles, provided a reminder to the Irish of the power and ambition of the settlers. These buildings also suggested that the settlers had God on their side.

The Normans made many administrative reforms that proved to be of long duration. Several of these were initiated during the reign of King John, the youngest son of Henry II and Eleanor of Aquitaine. Within England, John's reign was not particularly successful. Unlike his predecessors he was not an accomplished or brave military leader. He had inherited from his brother Richard the Angevin Empire, and by the end of his reign had managed to lose most of it, with the exception of Ireland. The losses of Normandy and Anjou in 1204 were a particular blow to English pride, and John's signing of the Magna Carta in 1215 was a way of punishing him by English barons. Nor was John particularly liked in Ireland. His father had given him the lordship of Ireland in 1177. It seemed that at this time Henry was also contemplating making John the king of Ireland and had gained papal blessing for this. The delay was because Henry became caught up in Normandy politics. In 1185, however, Henry sent John to Dublin to take over the lordship of Ireland directly. In Dublin, John managed the almost impossible task of uniting both the Norman colonists and the Irish kings in their dislike of him. When de Lacy, who had opposed John's involvement in Irish affairs, was assassinated in 1186, plans for John to reside in Ireland were abandoned.

A primary motivation for King John's administrative reforms was to replenish the Crown's depleted finances. None the less, during his reign Dublin Castle was built, which proved to be the focus of English government in Ireland. John also established an exchequer in Dublin, controlled by a treasurer whose main function was to ensure the payment of royal revenues. Before the Normans, only limited use was made of coins, but the growing trading links, both in Ireland and externally, increased the need for currency. In 1207 a system of coinage was introduced which carried a symbol of the harp. In 1210 John visited Ireland for the second time, and during this visit he gained control of the Anglo-Norman knights. His supremacy was short-lived, though, as his position was undermined in England. As a consequence, the Anglo-Norman knights were able to regain their position within Ireland, as exemplified by the rise of William Marshal, the son-in-law of Aoífe and Strongbow.

In the thirteenth century a legal system was also established, based on a system of sheriffs and the use of juries. The county system was also extended into parts of Ireland, including Kerry and Connacht. A structure of government was created with the summoning of a parliament in Dublin in 1297, giving representation to each county and the liberties, which were areas under the jurisdiction of Norman lords rather than the Crown. Yet the Normans could not have maintained a presence in Ireland without the use or threat of force. However, the fighting between Gael and Gall was intermittent, and mostly located in the interface areas. Numerous fortifications and garrisons linked the Norman areas. Initially the fortresses were built of wood, surrounded by a moat. But as the Gaels realised the advantage of setting fire to them, the replacement fortifications were built of stone. Numerous castles were erected, for a combination of economic and military reasons – they were also a powerful visible reminder of the Norman presence. The Normans also had superior military technology, making extensive use of lances, longbows, iron helmets, and chain-mail armour. Moreover, the Norman soldiers were well practised in fighting wars against foreign enemies. Although the Irish were acknowledged as brave soldiers, their military tactics were primitive. They generally wore no armour and used swords and spears; consequently they were massively disadvantaged in any conflict, even if they had more men. The inequality between the armies lessened over time as the Irish adapted to the skill and technology of their opposition. The Irish fighters were also at an advantage using guerrilla tactics in the rocky and boggy terrain of land that lay beyond Leinster.

By the middle of the thirteenth century, the Norman influence stretched over three-quarters of Ireland. To safeguard their interests, they built fortresses and castles throughout the country. At this stage, the Norman expansion was slowing down and had lost its early impetus and energy. There were a number of reasons for this. As the first generation of Norman settlers died, some had left no heirs, and the land passed to absentee owners who took little interest in Ireland. In contrast, those who remained and established families assimilated and began to adopt Irish customs, and they were sometimes referred to as the Norman Irish. In general, the Norman influence was in decline in Europe, while in England the various kings showed a lack of interest in Ireland as local problems pressed for their attention. Continuous wars against Wales, Scotland and France proved to be a large drain on resources.

Again the Irish, especially some of the displaced leaders, took advantage of this lethargy. An early setback to Norman expansion had come in 1220 when the O'Neills had driven the Norman army out of south Ulster. The Normans were expanding westwards, however, into north Kerry, but an Irish force led by the MacCarthys in 1261 decisively defeated the FitzThomas family. This battle ended further expansion in that area. In the north-west of the country also, Áedh O'Connor defeated a Norman force led by Ralph d'Ufford and supported by Walter de Burgo. The Irish victories were partly due to their adoption of some of the military skills of the Normans but also because the Gaelic lords employed gallowglasses, that is, Scottish mercenaries who wore armour and were hardened warriors, in their fight against the Normans. Among the Irish kings and lords there was a recognition that their best chance of stopping further Norman expansion was by banding together. In 1258, various Irish leaders agreed that Brian O'Neill of Cenél Eógain should be king of Ireland. Although his kingship was short and achieved little, it was a significant step in cooperation. A new departure came when the Irish leaders invited King Haakon of Norway to be their leader. Again, this action achieved nothing but arose out of a belief that if the Irish were to regain their independence, they would require help from Europe.

The attempts to expel the Normans were unsuccessful, and by 1300 the Normans still controlled much of the country. Within just over 100 years Ireland had been transformed, and the conquest had become colonisation. Yet the invasion was unsystematic, so the Norman influence remained partial and uneven. They never fully conquered Ireland, lacking the will and the resources to do so. English kings, from Henry II onwards, were sufficiently ambitious to want to control Ireland, but did not have enough interest or resources to pursue a full conquest. Consequently, some aspects of Irish life continued as before, especially for the poor and, at the other end of the social spectrum, for the kings, who continued to fight and challenge each other. Although some Gaels became Anglicised and some Normans became Hibernicised, they were still separate. Ireland therefore remained divided – a divide that was geographically demarcated and reflected in language, culture, religion and politics. Yet, after 1169 Irish and English politics were inextricably linked. External threats occurred sporadically. A challenge to the high kingship came in 1316 when Edward Bruce, brother of the Scottish king, Robert, was inaugurated as king of Ireland. This resulted in two years of internecine warfare. The Scots rather than the Normans had triggered the end of the ancient Irish institution of high kingship, and by doing so, had inadvertently cleared the way for ambitious English monarchs to claim Ireland as theirs.

The government of Ireland was carried out through a combination of attempts at assimilation and separation. There were various attempts to anglicise Ireland. In 1331, for example, ordinances were passed outlining the authority of the Irish government, which included a provision that there should be one law for the Irish and another for the Anglo-Irish. Nevertheless, this proved hard to do. The original Norman invaders had spoken French and English, but as they settled they underwent a process of Gaelicisation, adopting the language, customs and religion of their new home. Use of the English language therefore was mostly confined to the Pale. After 1446, the term 'Pale' was used to denote the area under Dublin control. It was coterminous with counties Louth, Meath, Dublin and Kildare. It was not until Edward VI's plantations in the 1550s that the English made inroads into other parts of Ireland. The Gaelicisation of the Normans worried the authorities, who responded by passing legislation designed to keep natives and settlers separate. The Irish intelligentsia and Irish culture were the particular targets of much of the legislation.

The Statute of Kilkenny in 1366 was the culmination of a series of enactments to keep the English settlers separate. Anti-Irish legislation had commenced in 1297 when Englishmen were forbidden from wearing their hair in the 'Irish way'. The Kilkenny Statute provided a comprehensive attempt to prohibit the use of the Irish laws, customs and language. The Statute stipulated that the settlers should all speak English, although the document was written in Norman French, the formal language of the settlers. Additional laws were passed which demonstrated that Irish people received less protection in law. Educated Irish particularly were treated with suspicion. In the early years of the fifteenth century, various proclamations were passed expelling Irish students from England. In 1435, further legislation was introduced that forbade Irish poets and musicians from being in areas controlled by the English. The ideological division between the two areas was further formalised following the creation of the Pale. After 1494 a ditch was built around the Pale, which provided a physical separation and visible reminder of the distinction between the settler English and the native Irish. The success of these measures to control Irish culture was limited, with Gaelic traditions flourishing rather than disappearing in the late fourteenth and fifteenth centuries. Consequently, in 1537, when Henry VIII was on the English throne, a further attempt was made to prohibit wearing Gaelic hairstyles or clothes. By and large, the various attempts to extend English ways to Ireland had not succeeded.

Although Ireland lay on the edge of Europe, many of the movements that swept the continent also reached its shores. In the 1340s a bubonic plague known as the Black Death swept Europe. It probably arrived in Ireland in 1348 or 1349, when the population had already been weakened by a series of poor harvests in the early decades of the fourteenth century, which had resulted in famine. The cumulative impact of famine and plague on an already vulnerable population was serious and resulted in demographic stagnation and decline. The plague was also endemic, with further outbreaks in 1362, 1373, 1382 and 1391. The very frequency of the attacks helped the population to build up a collective immunity, which made the impact of the reappearance of plague in the fifteenth century less lethal. The exact number of dead was not known but estimated to be between one-third and one-half of the population. Its impact was more serious in towns and ports rather than the countryside. The Black Death, appearing on the heels of the subsistence crises, also contributed to a prolonged agricultural depression. It was not until the early fifteenth century that the Irish population recovered and began to grow and return to its pre-1300 levels. Unlike many other European countries, however, the hysterical response to alleged cases of witchcraft or sorcery did not take place in Ireland in the fifteenth, sixteenth and seventeenth centuries. There were exceptions, such as the much publicised case of Alice Kyteler of Kilkenny (died *c.* 1324), who was accused of sorcery by the bishop of Ossary in the fourteenth century. While she escaped to England, her associate Petronella of Meath was burnt to death.

By the fourteenth century there was resentment of England's presence in Ireland, and this was used by some people to justify their support of the Bruces, who were fighting against Edward II, king of England and lord of Ireland. The role of the English kings in Ireland had changed since the time of Henry II. When Henry's son John had visited Ireland in 1185, he used the title 'Lord of Ireland', and this title remained intact until Henry VIII. In 1361 Edward III sent his second son, Lionel, to Ireland, and in order to sweeten the deal he appointed him lieutenant of Ireland. Following Lionel's death in 1381 the Irish lieutenancy did not pass to his son, but the governance of Ireland was given intermittently to royal relatives or friends of the king. A hereditary title, however, was created in 1385 when Richard II made Robert de Vere (his alleged lover) Marquess of Dublin and a year later Duke of Ireland. Robert's governance was unremarkable, and his later years were spent in exile for being a traitor.

Since the time of Henry II the involvement of English kings in Ireland may have been sporadic, but it was also clearly valued – as a location for younger sons or troublesome knights, or as a reward for trusted friends. When there was a direct involvement of English kings in Irish affairs it was generally arrogant and their appearance on Irish soil usually had more to do with self-interest than good government. And, until the time of William of Orange in the 1690s, English kings usually came at the head of an army. Consequently, the relationship between England and Ireland was defined by war. When Richard II led an expedition to Ireland in 1394, he was the first English king to have been in Ireland since 1210, when John had visited. Since de Vere had vacated the governance of Ireland a number of Irish princes and kings, notably Art MacMurrough, king of Leinster, had reasserted their authority. Richard dealt with this by bringing over 7,000 soldiers to Ireland and forcing a resubmission by the Irish leaders. The submission was short-lived, and unrest in Ireland included the murder of the lieutenant, Roger Mortimer, in 1398. This unrest forced a return to Ireland by Richard II in 1399, with the intention of reasserting his authority over the Irish princes.

Richard's expedition ended in failure: not only did he not succeed in achieving a settlement, but even more fatally his absence provided an opportunity for his overthrow by Bolingbroke, son of John of Gaunt. Bolingbroke, who was crowned Henry IV (1399–1413), had Richard murdered in 1400. Although Bolingbroke inherited the title of the lord of Ireland in addition to king of England, the former was in name only. Ireland remained disorderly throughout his reign, largely because Bolingbroke was absorbed by war with France and internal fighting between the Lancastrians and Yorkists. He also had financial problems, and parliament frequently complained of the cost of the royal household. Consequently, the English king had neither time nor resources to devote to Ireland. His lack of money meant he was unable to respond effectively to uprisings in either Wales or Ireland. Yet, even with little intervention, Ireland continued to be interested in English affairs. This concern was particularly apparent during the Wars of the Roses (1455–85) between the rival Yorkist and Lancastrian (Tudor) families. During this period many Irish earls supported the Yorkist cause against the Tudors. At the same time, without English intervention, there was a realignment of power within Ireland, with Gaelic chiefs reclaiming some of the lands that had been controlled by English colonists, and increased attacks on the Pale. The colonists' appeals for help from both the English king and the Pope were largely unanswered. Yet this constant fighting placed a heavy burden on the entire population of Ireland, especially as the armies were supported by a system of coign (or coyne) and livery, that is, a system of maintaining the armies of both the Gaelic chiefs and Anglo-Irish lords by tenants. Initially, coign and livery had been a Gaelic practice, but Thomas Fitzgerald, the 8th Earl of Desmond, had introduced it to the Pale. Because this system of billeting was so unpopular, there had been an attempt by the Irish parliament to limit its use in 1297. The Irish earls were not united, however, and there was competition between the three most important families, that is, the Butlers of Ormond, and the Fitzgeralds of Desmond and of Kildare.

In 1449 the attention of the English king turned to Ireland by way of sending Richard, the Duke of York, to claim submission from both the Gaelic chiefs and the Palesmen. His success was largely due to his attractive personality and personal popularity. But while in Ireland he only strengthened the links between Ireland and the Yorkist cause. His success was short-lived and in 1459 he was charged with treason by the English parliament. He fled to Ireland, where he was welcomed for the second time and there was an attempt to make him chief governor of the colony. The significance of this episode was that it demonstrated a political cleavage: with Ireland generally supporting the Duke of York, and England remaining loyal to Henry VI. However, York's attempt to take the English throne was unsuccessful and ended with his death in 1460. Yorkist ambitions were realised, however, when the son of the dead Duke of York took the throne in 1461 as Edward IV. Perhaps because of his father's influence, Edward took an interest in Irish affairs and in 1463 he appointed the Earl of Desmond the chief governor of Ireland. The appointment was also a reward for Desmond's part in defeating a Lancastrian uprising in Pilltown in 1462. Although there were reservations about Desmond's Gaelicisation, he was well connected with both the English and the Gaelic chiefs. Like many of the Anglo-Irish nobles, Desmond would have spoken English, French, Latin and Gaelic. Desmond eased trade restrictions between the English towns and the Gaelic people – they were economically interdependent anyway. The English king also asked Desmond not to continue with the unpopular system of coign and livery, because it was an oppressive burden on the people.

Regardless of the apparent integration of native and settler, it was still not safe to travel outside the Pale, and English towns were walled. The nobility on both sides of the Pale lived mostly in tower houses, where the social and economic functions combined with a defensive function. However, this period of cooperation with the Irish earls ended tragically, when Desmond and the two Fitzgeralds were accused of treason and Desmond was executed at Drogheda in 1468. Inevitably, this action soured Irish relations with the English king, which were not eased by Desmond's replacement, John Tiptoft, the Earl of Worcester, whose brutality towards his enemies had earned him the nickname 'the butcher'. Worcester was equally unpopular with the English and the Gaels, and following an uprising by both groups he was withdrawn. He was executed shortly afterwards.

Desmond's death facilitated the rise of the earls of Kildare. Garret Mór Fitzgerald was a particular threat to English rule, especially as he allied with the Gaelic chiefs, including the O'Neills, through the strategic marriage of his daughters. He also supported the Yorkists. When the Lancastrian Henry VII came to the English throne, there were Yorkist plots in Ireland that again demonstrated the independence of political outlook within the country. This was particularly apparent in 1487 when Lambert Simnel, the main Yorkist rival, was crowned Edward VI of England in Dublin. Although he took the title the Earl of Warwick and claimed to be the son of the Duke of Clarence, there were many doubts about his parentage. None the less, his supporters then invaded England, although they were defeated within days and Warwick was taken prisoner. He was not executed but forced to work as a scullion in the royal household. In 1491 a new Yorkist pretender emerged, Perkin Warbeck, who took the title of Richard IV. Although he also was of low birth and his claims to be the brother of Edward were improbable, he did pose a threat to Henry VII, largely because he had support from Ireland, France and Scotland. When Warbeck was unable to land in England in 1495 he returned to Ireland and, supported by the Earl of Desmond, led a rebellion. Edward Poynings defeated them. Warbeck escaped and two years later returned to Ireland hoping, in vain, to mount another rebellion. This time he was captured and eventually executed by Henry in 1499.

What this period of turmoil, executions, alignments and realignment demonstrated was that regardless of infighting within Ireland, without the investment of massive resources, Ireland could not be properly governed by England, and even Anglo-Irish lords such as Desmond could not be fully trusted by the English monarch. In fact, governors who had good relationships with the Gaelic chiefs probably posed more of a threat, as they stood more chance of establishing independent rule in Ireland. The various uprisings had made it clear to Henry that Ireland, uncontrolled, was a danger, not least because it could provide a base for aspiring Yorkist claimants to the throne. His response was to send Edward Poynings to Ireland, a man who combined ruthless soldiering with efficient administration and loyalty to Henry; his mission was to bring all Ireland under English control. At the end of 1494 he introduced legislation that took his name. Furthermore, to protect England's interests, the Pale was to be physically separated from the rest of the country by a double ditch that was six feet high. The most important English castles were to be guarded by men who were born in England. Poynings' Law also confirmed the main provisions of the Statute of Kilkenny, with the exception of the section that had outlawed the use of the Irish language by the English and Anglo-Irish. This omission was a recognition that the use of the Irish language had not diminished but had become more widespread after 1366. Perhaps the most important aspect of Poynings' Law was in respect of the role of the Irish parliament. The parliament in Ireland could only meet if royal permission had been granted, and no measures could be enacted without the approval of the king and council in England. One of the purposes of these provisions was to ensure that a governor in Ireland could not oppose or challenge the authority of the king. As the previous years had shown, with Irish support for Lambert Simnel and Warbeck, this was a real possibility. Overall, however, Poynings' Law defined the internal government of Ireland and the political relationship between England and Ireland until 1800.

Continuity was provided for by the reappointment of the 8th Earl of Kildare – Garret Mór Fitzgerald or 'the Great Earl' – as governor of Ireland in 1496. Despite being suspected by Poynings of still having Yorkist sympathies, and having widespread support among the Gaelic chiefs, Fitzgerald remained loyal to the English king and stayed in position until his death in 1513. In total, he was governor for over thirty years and served no fewer than five kings. Although there were conflicts within Ireland under Fitzgerald's long governorship, Ireland remained relatively peaceful and stable. Moreover, the conflicts that did occur were not simply between native Gael and English settler but cut across these traditional divisions. This regrouping was evident at the battle of Knockdoe in 1504, when Fitzgerald defeated Burke of Clanricard. What made this battle unusual was that both leaders were supported by Gaelic and Anglo-Irish leaders, making it the largest battle between Irishmen.

Fitzgerald's particular skill was that he balanced the diverse and sometimes opposing demands of the Gaelic Irish, the Anglo-Irish and the English kings under whom he served. During his final period of governorship (1496–1513) the Pale remained protected, both against Gaelic incursions and, from the English perspective, as a base of support for the Lancastrian Henry VII. This period of relative stability was also due to the reforms introduced by Poynings, which made both the Pale and the authority of the English king more secure. However, regardless of the clear segregation that was supposed to exist between the residents of the Pale and those outside it, which had been codified by legislation, the separation was never complete. Moreover, Gaelic society and Gaelic culture had not only proved resistant to change, but had undergone a revival. Perhaps even more worrying for the Crown authorities was that, within the Pale also, there were clear signs of Hibernicisation.

FOUR

REPRESSION, CONFISCATION AND CONQUEST
c. 1490–1603

The introduction of Poynings' Law in 1494 marked a new phase in the endeavour to control Ireland politically and culturally. This objective was made more difficult by the willingness of successive waves of settlers to assimilate and Hibernicise.

This chapter outlines the attempts of the Gaelic chiefs to resist the process of Anglicisation pursued by Tudor monarchs. The rebellions culminated in the defeat of Hugh O'Neill and the Flight of the Earls in 1607, which marked the end of Gaelic society. It also examines how the Reformation added to existing political divisions, while creating an enduring religious divide both within Ireland and between Ireland and England. Fresh divisions had also emerged, largely based on religion, which created new alliances between Anglo-Irish Catholics and Gaelic Catholics.

The Reformation

It is widely assumed that neither Reformation nor Renaissance reached Ireland. Both, however, were to influence, directly and indirectly, the development of Irish society. In the late fifteenth century, when the Reformation was sweeping Europe, Ireland was too poor and culturally remote to participate in the artistic and architectural changes evident elsewhere. Moreover, the native Irish intellectuals had either been subsumed beneath the elite settler class or were in exile. Nor was Ireland to benefit from the intellectual changes such as humanism, which advocated civilisation through education, whereas the preferred approach by Tudor kings was to use force. The philosophical challenge proffered by the Renaissance went largely unanswered in Ireland, despite the contribution of individual Irishmen such as Richard Stanihurst and, later, Francis Hutcheson, who was remembered as the 'Father of the Scottish Enlightenment'. Colonisation –

either political or religious – preoccupied Irish minds. However, scholarly debate was kept alive by some religious orders, but the Reformation of the sixteenth century jeopardised the very existence of the Irish Church.

Initially Ireland appeared sheltered from the Reformation sweeping Europe after 1517, by devotion, geography and the fact that Henry VIII (r. 1509–47) provided a bulwark against such apparent heresy. His writing in 1521 of the anti-Reformation text *Assertio Septem Sacramentorum* gained for him the title 'Defender of the Faith'. By the time the Reformation appeared in Ireland, its original theological purpose had been exploited by kings and governors who viewed it in terms of strengthening their power bases and disciplining recalcitrant subjects. Henry VIII was no different.

In the early sixteenth century there were two main groups within Ireland, the Gaelic Irish and the English or Anglo-Irish within the Pale. Internal fighting and political instability among Gaelic chiefs meant that they had little unity. The most troublesome of the Gaelic families were the O'Neills and O'Donnells in Ulster, the MacCarthys and O'Briens in Munster, the Kavanaghs and O'Connors in Leinster and the O'Connors and O'Kellys in Connacht. In addition, the loyalty of many Anglo-Irish lords was doubted by Henry and subsequent Tudor monarchs, who believed that these nobles had become too Hibernicised to be fully trusted. The untrustworthy nobles included the Fitzgeralds of Desmond, the Roches and Barrys in Munster, the Butlers in Leinster and the Burkes in Connacht. Moreover, what all these groups had in common was their religion; Catholicism and the move to Protestantism by Henry had little support within Ireland. Henry's actions not only created fresh discord between England and Ireland, but it also brought native and settler together. One response was for the Crown to bring new settlers in, who were loyal to the English Crown and the new Protestant Church. Nevertheless, the Tudor period is associated with an extension of power in Ireland, with the English lordship being extended from the area known as the Pale to the whole of Ireland. The Tudor 'conquest', however, initially appeared as incomplete as earlier attempts to control Ireland. In reality it was piecemeal, achieved over a number of disparate reigns, and only ultimately accomplished by force. The wars within Ireland culminated with the ending of the Nine Years War in 1603, which also marked the death of Elizabeth and the end of the Tudor line.

One of the consequences of the Tudor conquest was the arrival of a fresh wave of Crown officials, soldiers, planters and new settlers. Those who were descended from the early Anglo-Norman settlers still regarded themselves as English, even though many had become Hibernicised and their families had been in Ireland for generations. To distinguish them from new settlers, the existing groups were referred to as the 'Old English', 'Anglo-Hiberni', 'English Irish' or 'Anglo-Irish'. By the early seventeenth century the term 'Old English' (or *sean Ghaill*) was being widely used to describe the descendants of the Normans, while 'New English' (or *nua Ghaill*) described the Elizabethan and Jacobean settlers. These terms also reflected new divisions within the Pale that were based on religion, as many of the new settlers were Protestant, initially for pragmatic but increasingly for pious reasons. These divisions were reinforced by the fact that from Henry VIII onwards, royal and political patronage was centred on the New English and, unlike in earlier groups of colonists, there was little social interaction or even marriage between the old and the new settlers.

Henry VIII, remembered for his wives and corpulence, changed the relationship between Ireland and England in a number of significant ways. Yet, during the early years of his reign, despite his desire to control Ireland, he achieved little. When Henry VIII ascended to the English throne in 1509 he inherited a relatively peaceful situation in Ireland. This stability was largely due to the administrative reforms of Poynings in 1494 and the skilful and, by Irish standards, lengthy governorship of Gerald Fitzgerald, the 8th Earl of Kildare. Kildare was head of the Geraldine family, which included the powerful earls of Desmond and Kildare. He acceded to his title in 1477, following which he was also referred to as 'the Great Earl', thus acknowledging his powerful position in Ireland. His acquisition of power marked a period of Geraldine supremacy in Ireland. Henry VIII's father, Henry VII, had been anxious to exploit the fact that Kildare was virtually ruler of Ireland. In 1480 he was made lord deputy, which gave official recognition to his unofficial status. Even his support for the impostor Lambert Simnel in 1487 did not lead to his dismissal, although he was briefly imprisoned for his alleged support of Perkin Warbeck in 1494. Amazingly, he survived and was reappointed lord deputy in 1496. Henry VII clearly regarded Kildare as a valuable asset despite his occasional transgressions. Insurance was provided, however, by the fact that Kildare's son, Garret Óge, was kept as a hostage in England from 1497 to 1503. When Henry VIII became king, he recognised the value of allowing some continuity in the government of Ireland. Kildare remained loyal in return, but was killed by an adversary in Ireland in 1513. His son, Garret Óge, succeeded him as lord deputy.

Following Kildare's death, Henry decided to pursue a more interventionist approach to Irish affairs, and in 1519 the Earl of Surrey replaced Garret Óge as governor. This action was an indication that Henry wanted to rely less on Anglo-Irish lords and more on English officials, who were answerable directly to him. Surrey, an Englishman, soon proved to be out of his depth in Ireland, and he was recalled in 1522. Henry had tasked him with bringing all of the country into submission, and after two years Surrey was reporting that this would be impossible without massive military deployment. Surrey estimated 6,000 additional men would be required to bring Ireland under control, and that the building of fortresses throughout the country and a wholesale policy of colonisation outside the Pale would be required to maintain this position. Although a complete conquest appeared impossible, Henry continued with his policy of centralisation and attempted to undermine Irish earls, who were a potential threat to Tudor rule. While Henry would have preferred an Englishman as chief governor of Ireland, what Surrey's brief involvement demonstrated was that the Irish earls would not relinquish power easily. Garret Óge, in particular, made it clear that English rule in Ireland depended on his support. Under his leadership, the fortunes of the Geraldine family declined. Moreover, Henry never really trusted him, and he was imprisoned for treason on a number of occasions. He died in the Tower of London in 1534.

Henry, who was at this stage still regarded as the defender of the (Catholic) Church, also wanted Surrey to Anglicise the Irish Church. Again, Surrey reported to his king that this would not be easy. Although the Irish Church was Catholic, it had little in common with Rome or its sister church in England. Also, it reflected the general divisions within Irish society: it showed little internal unity but was split between the Gaelic Irish and the English settlers. The head of the Irish Church did not live in Armagh, which was geographically outside the Pale, but was generally based at Termonfeckin in Louth. Henry identified with the inhabitants of the Pale in both language and culture. Many of the bishops outside the Pale were of Gaelic origin, and some lived secular lives. More seriously, they invested little in church property, allowing church buildings to decay. What the Church did have in common throughout Ireland was its casual or idiosyncratic adherence to church teachings. Religious teaching and practice within Ireland were largely kept alive through the work of the friars and other orders of brothers. Not surprisingly, when Henry determined to marry Anne Boleyn in 1533 and consequently broke with the Church in Rome, religious orders in England and Ireland made clear their opposition to his action. Henry's response was, in 1534, to declare himself the supreme head of the Church of England. Where England led, the Irish parliament followed, and the Act of Supremacy passed by the Dublin parliament in 1536 proclaimed Henry as supreme head of the Church of Ireland. These titles allowed him to introduce his individual version of Protestantism to England and Ireland that included a rejection of purgatory, ending the cult of images and the continued observation of celibacy by the Catholic clergy. He also sponsored a new official translation of the Bible in 1539. The Act of Supremacy also meant that the Church of Ireland was now the state church in Ireland and it was answerable to royal control. In reality, Henry's control was limited to the Anglo-Irish areas within the Pale, and even there, Catholic practices coexisted with the new Protestant doctrines for a number of years. The muddled situation was left to Henry's successors to sort out, as in the short term his rejection of Rome had given him what he desired. Moreover, in 1537 he had belatedly fathered a son by his third wife, Jane Seymour, and so it appeared that both the royal succession and the Protestant Reformation were safe.

Henry's decision to suppress the monasteries, nunneries and friaries was inevitable in the light of his new beliefs. In Ireland the process of suppression began in 1539 and was completed quickly and with relative ease. The dissolution only affected areas within the Pale, but the majority of Irish monasteries lay in Gaelic areas and, in the short term anyway, they remained untouched by these changes. Moreover, dissolution took place at a time when the monasteries' importance was already in decline, not only ecclesiastically, but also in terms of their role in providing education and social welfare. Dissolution was carried out under the control of the Irish earls, including Anthony St Leger, Sir William Brabazon and Lord Leonard Grey, and they, rather than the Crown, were probably the main financial beneficiaries. The monks who had lost their livelihoods and their homes were given pensions according to their rank. Although they were allowed to work, they were also expected to remain celibate. In England, the dissolution action provided large revenues for the Crown, although these were quickly absorbed by Henry's wars. In Ireland the dissolution of monasteries and the sale of their land brought a number of new adventurers, attracted by prospects of easy profits. Much of the revenue remained within the Pale and added to the economic prosperity of its inhabitants.

Henry's marriage to Anne Boleyn and his break with Rome initially meant that he had less time to pursue his military ambitions in Ireland. His unconcern was short-lived. In 1534 Lord Offaly, also known as Silken Thomas, the son of Garret Óge, led a rebellion against Henry. Thomas was acting governor while his father was in England and his actions appear to have had his father's approval, with Garret Óge having denounced Tudor policies in Ireland and ceremoniously resigned his position. The rebellion was triggered by a false rumour that Garret Óge had been executed. In fact, he died in the Tower of London shortly after the rebellion had begun. More significant, however, was the fact that the new governor of Ireland was to be an Englishman, Sir William Skeffington. Thomas's motives were not totally clear, although one of his demands was that he should be granted governorship of Ireland for life. It is also possible that he disliked the centralisation of Henry's policies and feared that the Kildare family was losing influence as a consequence. Religion, on the other hand, appeared to have little to do with Thomas's rebellion, although he conveniently declared it to be a Catholic crusade and sought support from fellow Catholics in Europe, including the Pope and Emperor Charles V. Yet its timing was ominous for Henry, who was having problems winning support for his adoption of the Reformation in England. He knew he had to act decisively regardless of expense. Henry sent Skeffington to Ireland at the head of an army. Thomas, with little support either from within Ireland or elsewhere, surrendered in August 1537 and was executed in London later that year, together with five of his uncles. The Kildare lands were also confiscated. This effectively ended the Kildare challenge. For Henry, the removal of the Kildares paved the way for the administrative reforms that he had desired for some years. Direct rule by an English governor was introduced, although, as Surrey had warned, this could only be done with the support of an English garrison.

The conquest of Ireland was part of Henry's desire for imperial expansion. A more pressing reason was strategic. This was particularly necessary in the wake of his break with Rome and England's move to Protestantism. In a Europe that was now divided by religion, England was vulnerable to attack by her large Catholic neighbours and traditional enemies, France and Spain. Ireland's devotion to Catholicism made it more threatening than ever before. However, Henry's desire to extend the Reformation to Ireland was made harder by the ongoing desire for independence from England, which appeared to be gathering momentum rather than lessening. A number of Gaelic chiefs formed an alliance in the 1530s, known as the Geraldine League. Conn O'Neill, the 1st Earl of Tyrone, and Manus O'Donnell, a Gaelic scholar and lord of Tyrconnell, led it. Such a coalition, which brought together Gaelic and Anglo-Irish lords, was unprecedented. The League rejected the rule and supremacy of the English Crown and instead offered the kingship of Ireland to James V of Scotland. They invaded the northern part of the Pale with an army of Gaelic supporters and redshanks, that is, skilled mercenaries from the Highlands and Islands of Scotland. Fearing a possible Scottish invasion, Henry responded with military force, and the Geraldine League was decisively beaten at the battle of Bellahoe in 1539 by Lord Deputy Grey. In 1541 Henry created the kingdom of Ireland and began to call himself 'King of Ireland'. Until this point, English kings had been referred to as lords of Ireland. Henry's initial motivation for this change was religious rather than political. Many people associated the right of English kings to be in Ireland to have derived from the 1155 *Laudabiliter* issued by Pope Adrian IV. Henry was anxious that none of his power should be seen as coming from Rome. His decision to change his title was announced by the Irish parliament in 1541 and the English parliament in 1542. ✄

Henry's military victories were a massive drain on Crown resources, and he raised money through the introduction of a policy of 'surrender and regrant' (or submit and regrant). This policy was intended to get Gaelic and Gaelicised Anglo-Irish lords to accept English rule. It exploited the fact that Gaelic lords had no security of tenure, and so the holding of their lands was in the gift of the Crown. This scheme allowed Irish chieftains to hold onto their lands if they formally accepted English rule. However, the submission meant that they were subject to a number of conditions, which included limitations on their ability to trade with other territories. It also hoped to introduce primogeniture to the Gaelic areas. The process involved three formal assurances that were legally binding: firstly, the lord recognised the king as his sovereign and relinquished his lands, while simultaneously applying for a grant and a peerage; secondly, he renounced his Gaelic title, promised to assist in the extension of the English colony, and gave money and military service to the Crown in return for the grant of land and noble titles; and thirdly, he had to ensure the loyalty of his kinsmen and vassals to the king. One of the aims was to make Gaelic lords less autonomous and more dependent on the Crown. If Gaelic lords proved reluctant to participate, as many did, bribes were unofficially used. However, the implementation of submit and regrant was made easier in the wake of the social dislocation that followed the suppression of the monasteries. One of the successes of the scheme was judged to be Conn O'Neill's reluctant acceptance of the title Earl of Tyrone in 1542. O'Neill had hoped to earn the title of Royal Earl of Ulster, but this was refused. In effect, therefore, he suffered a diminution in status, having lost his royal O'Neill title. Although his new title gave him more power than his Gaelic rivals, it also soured relations with them.

By the end of his long reign, Henry had extended the power of the Crown from its stronghold in the south of England to the peripheral (from a London perspective) areas. Whether or not it constituted a Tudor revolution in government, Ireland, Wales and the north of England were brought under the control of Westminster. Henry's rejection of Rome had made a real conquest of Ireland not merely expedient, but a requirement for the survival of the Tudor monarchy. His tactics were unorthodox. He abandoned the traditional English policy of keeping the Gaelic and the Anglo-Irish separate. Instead, he was willing to wage an aggressive war that some Anglo-Irish found unpalatable. And, rather than rely on Anglo-Irish support, his tactics forced a direct dependence on the Crown, via the parliaments in Dublin and London. Although a political conquest appeared to have been achieved, the fact that it was not accompanied by a religious conversion made it a conquest in name only. In England, Scotland and Wales, Church and State adopted the Reformation and the people followed. In Ireland, the people rejected the new religion of Church and State but clung to Catholicism. Consequently, the gap between governed and governors became wider than before, and a new source of conflict, based on religious division, ensured that the gulf between natives and settlers would intensify. Moreover, regardless of having neither popular support nor majority participation, the Church of Ireland remained the established state church until 1869.

Henry was succeeded by his ten-year-old son, Edward VI (r. 1547–53). From his birth Edward had been surrounded by converts to Protestantism and during his brief reign he sought to establish its hold in his kingdoms of England and Ireland. The refusal of his half-sister Mary to convert appalled him, but his premature death meant he did not have time to remove the right of succession from her. Edward introduced a number of enduring reforms to Protestantism, notably a reformed liturgy and new church structures. In 1549 the English Book of Common Prayer, which had been introduced into England a few months earlier, was ordered to be used in Ireland. A second Book of

Common Prayer was introduced in 1552. Edward also permitted a plunder of the resources still held by the Catholic Church. In Ireland there was resistance to his measures, especially the introduction of Protestant bishops and prayer books to the country. Edward's answer was to plant settlers from overseas in specially established colonies in counties Laois and Offaly.

One solution to the ongoing problem of Irish resistance was to create a colony of English settlers. The deliberate plantation of settlers was regarded as a way not only of extending English rule, but also of providing model communities as examples to the barbaric Irish. It was also a way of extending Protestantism beyond the Pale and into the Irish countryside. Moreover, the plantations provided a useful – and possibly economically advantageous – outlet for younger sons and aspiring professionals. However, to facilitate this process, the Gaelic families were banished. In the 1550s, small groups of settlers were planted in counties Laois and Offaly. Laois was renamed Queen's County to honour Queen Mary and its main town, Portlaoise, was renamed Maryborough. Other colonies were established in Munster and Ulster. One problem, though, was that the colonies needed to be protected, as Irish natives, some of whom were clearly hostile having been displaced from their lands, surrounded the English settlers. A further attempt was made to seize the land and distribute it among English families. Although Edward's plan failed, it sowed the seeds for a more comprehensive plantation after 1609.

The move to Protestantism was halted briefly during the reign of Mary I (r. 1553–8). She also attempted to reverse some of the measures introduced by her father and brother, notably by restoring traditional forms of worship and obedience to the Pope. Ironically, Mary argued with the papal legate and so her attempts to restore Catholicism in England had no support from Rome. Her methods, moreover, were brutal, restoring the old heresy laws in 1555, and burning over 300 'heretics'. Mary's marriage to Philip of Spain brought England into a war with France, during which Calais was lost. She died childless, and so the Catholic revival was short-lived. What it also showed was that since the time of Henry, Protestantism had become entrenched in England and even Mary's cruelty and determination did not undermine its hold. In Ireland the opposite was true. An unlooked-for outcome of the Reformation was that in 1555 the Pope, Paul IV, recognised Ireland as a kingdom. It was remarkable because so many preceding popes had despaired of the autonomy of the Catholic Church in Ireland; now its independence was regarded in Rome as a strength.

Henry's daughter Elizabeth (r. 1558–1603) wanted to build on her father's achievements in Ireland. His legacy was mixed, though. More administrative and political unity had been achieved, but religion was creating a new set of divisions that appeared more intransigent than previous ones. Elizabeth quickly moved to restore Protestantism in her two kingdoms, through the Act of Supremacy and Act of Uniformity of 1560. In these, she built on the reforms initiated by her half-brother, Edward, by requiring all Irish clergy to use the second English Book of Common Prayer. Unlike her brother, she was willing to punish those who were recalcitrant. Clergy who refused to use the prayer book could be imprisoned for life, while laity who did not attend church services could be fined. Even though enforcing such legislation was virtually impossible, it demonstrated that religious attendance and practice were no longer matters of choice.

Elizabeth quickly realised that Tudor rule in Ireland could be maintained only through a combination of wholesale plantation, administrative reforms and local government, all underpinned by the threat of military force. By the end of the sixteenth century, the military played a large role in the control of Ireland, with an army of 16,000 based in the country. For Elizabeth, a committed Protestant, an immediate challenge was to restore the Protestant Church, and to continue the work begun by her father and stepbrother. Having early on restored royal supremacy and enforced the use of the English prayer book, she was excommunicated by the Pope in 1570.

Tudor Women

The Protestant Reformation undermined the position of women in the later sixteenth century. Yet in Ireland, upper-class women remained caught between the protection that had been provided by the Brehon Laws and the patriarchy of the Reformation, evident in both the Protestant and the Catholic Churches. Also, despite the gender differences existing in most aspects of life, being female was not an obstacle to being a sovereign, to owning land or being involved in politics or rebellion.

Grace O'Malley (Gráinne Ní Mháille) combined being a pirate, a warrior and, in her spare time, an Irish chieftain. Grace, or as her name was rendered by contemporaries in England, 'Granuail', was probably born in County Mayo around 1530, making her roughly the same age as Elizabeth. She came from a family of seafarers, and her father was Owen O'Malley, a sea captain who was also the chieftain of Umhall Uachtarach. Unlike Elizabeth, Grace married twice and had four children, and had a number of lovers. Her first husband was Donal O'Flaherty, the *tánaiste* (next in line) of the O'Flaherty chief. He owned land and a number of castles, which meant that Granuaile could have led a life of relative ease. To compensate for trade restrictions imposed by England, Grace allegedly took to raiding other territories and piracy. She was ruthless, daring and successful, which particularly annoyed the merchants of Galway, who asked for assistance to capture her. Although she was captured and imprisoned in 1577 during a raid on the lands of the Earl of Desmond, she escaped within two years and returned to piracy. The arrest of one of her sons prompted her to travel to England, where she was allegedly granted an audience with Queen Elizabeth in 1593. She returned with a pardon for her son and a pension for herself. Both Elizabeth and Grace died in 1603. Reality and popular traditions have become intertwined in the lives of both women. Grace represented the continuation of an independent tradition in Ireland that survived years of English centralisation and the straitjacket of the Protestant Reformation. She died in the year that Hugh O'Neill and Hugh O'Donnell were finally defeated, and their rout ended hopes for Irish independence.

Other women were caught up in the sixteenth-century rebellions. Gerald Fitzgerald, the 14th Earl of Desmond, led the Desmond rebellions. Following his defeat at the battle of Affane in 1595, he was imprisoned for six years in the Tower of London. His wife, Eleanor, managed the Desmond estates during this period and intervened personally on her husband's behalf with Elizabeth. During the second Desmond rebellion she vainly attempted to negotiate a pardon for her husband. His assassination left her in poverty, although her second marriage made her wealthy again.

Despite the achievements of Elizabeth and other Tudor women, the position of English women declined in the sixteenth century. Irish women fared little better. Upper-class females, who had been the main beneficiaries of the Brehon Laws and Gaelic system, were the most affected. Although the Catholic Church had disapproved of certain women's rights, especially in regard to marriage and divorce, they had never exerted absolute authority in these matters. The Reformation marked the final demise of women's property rights and the freedom to divorce. The ability of women to obtain an education was also ended with the dissolution of abbeys and convents. The nuns and abbesses who lost their livelihoods, as was the case with the monks, were given pensions.

Elizabethan Rebellions

Elizabeth's foreign policy was largely founded on her determination not to lose any territory, the loss of Calais having proved to be an enduring blot on the reign of her predecessor, Mary. Within Ireland, however, there were periodic attempts to break away from England, most notably in 1561, 1568–73, 1579–1583 and – the most protracted rebellion – between 1594 and 1603. The first occurred only three years after Elizabeth acceded to the throne, and was led by Shane O'Neill. Other rebellions followed. At the same time, Elizabeth was intermittently fighting wars overseas, mostly in the defence of fellow Protestants. One of her most threatening overseas wars was against Spain, leading to the defeat of the Spanish Armada in 1588. In the 1590s her attention was again turned to Ireland, where the Gaelic chiefs were mounting a large-scale rebellion. The final uprising was the most serious because Elizabeth was old and clearly coming to the end of her life, and she did not want her reign to end on the inglorious loss of Ireland. Moreover, the rebellion was led by Hugh O'Neill, an Irish chieftain whose Anglicisation had made him appear tame and loyal.

However, not only did Elizabeth have to contend with opposition from outside the Pale; she also faced entrenched opposition from Catholics within the Pale. The new division between the Old and the New English had become more marked, as the new arrivals began to displace their predecessors. The taking of their authority was accompanied by a propaganda war against the Old English, which depicted them as being more disloyal and untrustworthy than the Irish themselves. A worrying departure for England was when nobles from the Pale joined forced with Gaelic nobles. The response of Elizabeth and her ministers was increasingly brutal, and this expedited the ascendancy of the New English control of the Pale. Initially, though, fighting between various Irish noblemen helped Elizabeth's position in Ireland, as the rebellions were as much motivated by the expansion policies of some lords as by their dislike of Tudor centralisation.

In 1560 Elizabeth convened her first Irish parliament, which restored royal supremacy. It also provided for the restoration of the Church of Ireland. The following year Shane O'Neill initiated a rebellion that lasted, with intermittent breaks, until 1567. O'Neill, a young leader in Ulster, was the legitimate son of Conn O'Neill, the 1st Earl of Tyrone. Upon his father's death in 1559, he was by-passed as successor in favour of his illegitimate brother, Matthew. The state was enabled to intervene in this way as a result of the Tudor policy of submission and regrant. Shane O'Neill killed Matthew in 1558 and demanded his title. Apart from his legitimate entitlement, O'Neill claimed the right to take over his father's title on the grounds that the clan members had chosen him. He was proclaimed a traitor, but a costly military intervention, led by the Earl of Sussex, failed to defeat O'Neill. In 1562 O'Neill submitted to Elizabeth, and in return she accepted his claim to the O'Neillship. The truce was short-lived, as O'Neill still wanted to extend his territories in Ulster. He was defeated at Farsetmore in 1567, and the defeat was compounded by the loss of many of his men by drowning. O'Neill was killed a few weeks later by his former allies, the Macdonnells, probably for head money from the English. Posthumously, his lands were taken from him and the O'Neill title was banned. The English authorities hoped that the ensuing political vacuum would facilitate their expansionist plans in Ulster, in particular a private scheme known as the Enterprise of Ulster. But Shane O'Neill's death left a legacy of confusion among the Gaelic lords, combined with a distrust of the English. Also, despite the ruthless military responses of various governors in Ireland, rebellions against English rule continued.

A sustained rebellion led by the Fitzgerald family of Desmond took place from 1568 to 1583, with a break from 1573 to 1579. It was led by Gerald Fitzgerald, the 14th Earl of Desmond, and his deputy, James Fitzmaurice Fitzgerald. It was largely a revolt against the Tudor policy of centralisation and the financial demands it placed on local lords. The Anglo-Irish nobles, however, were no more united than the Gaelic lords and Desmond was also involved in a conflict with 'Black' Tom Butler, the 10th Earl of Ormond. Ormond was sympathetic to the reform of the Church and to English policies in Ireland. He regarded Desmond as a threat to both. Ormond's conflict with Desmond in 1565 led to the latter being imprisoned in the Tower of London for six years. Upon release, he organised an uprising against English rule. Sir John Perrot, the president of Munster, ruthlessly suppressed the first Desmond rebellion, which began in 1568 and ended in 1573. Within a space of two years, he executed almost 1,000 rebels. Fitzmaurice Fitzgerald surrendered in 1573, but only after he heard that the Earl of Desmond had been released from the Tower of London. Both men then went into exile, seeking assistance from other Catholic powers for a further uprising. Unknown to him, an English adventurer, Thomas Stucley, who was reputedly an illegitimate son of Henry VIII, appealed to the Pope, Gregory XIII, for assistance to help win independence for Ireland. Gregory responded by giving him 1,000 troops. Stucley immediately offered them to the king of Portugal in his invasion of Morocco. Nevertheless, a second rebellion began in 1579. It was supported by the remnants of the papal force. Again, it was ruthlessly suppressed, the English troops destroying the homes and crops of the poor. The ensuing famine contributed to the overall death toll. As the war came to a close, Black Tom Butler was put in charge of Munster. Through a mixture of cruelty and conciliation he brought the rebellion to a close. The revolt finally ended in the killing of the Earl of Desmond in 1583, probably by his own followers, in return for head money.

Elizabeth's victory was consolidated by a large-scale plantation in Munster that utilised the lands of the nobles involved in the Desmond rebellions. Approximately 300,000 acres of land were granted to thirty-five 'undertakers' in lots of up to 12,000 each. The undertakers were a mixture of English soldiers, administrators, courtiers and gentry, and a condition of the grant was that they were to remove the Irish tenants and bring in new ones from England. The Munster plantation did bring in extra revenue for the Crown, but the land survey on which the plantation was based was inaccurate, and the Irish tenants were never fully displaced. The Nine Years War also provided an opportunity for both former tenants and landowners to reclaim their land, if only temporarily.

The suppression of the Desmond rebellions and the plantation of his supporters' lands did not bring the cycle of upheaval to an end. The continuation of rebellions demonstrated that the Tudor hold on Ireland was tenuous and probably opposed by the majority of the population, although often for different reasons. The Baltinglass Rebellion, which began in 1580, was led by the Catholic Viscount Baltinglass. He joined forces with Feagh O'Byrne, whom he had formally regarded as his enemy. O'Byrne was a leader of the O'Byrne in County Wicklow, and he had been a serious impediment to the expansionist plans of the Crown. The lord deputy in Ireland responded quickly and emphatically, executing some innocent Palesmen in the process. O'Byrne's wife and son-in-law were also hanged. The property of the insurgents was taken from them and given to those loyal to the Crown. Some of the original leaders, including Baltinglass, fled to the continent. O'Byrne stayed and briefly allied with Hugh O'Neill until he was killed in 1597. He was decapitated and his head displayed first in Dublin and then in England.

Hugh O'Neill, the 3rd Earl of Tyrone, led the most serious rebellion. His father, Matthew O'Neill, had been killed as a result of the conflict with his brother, Shane O'Neill, in 1558. According to some histories, the eight-year-old Hugh was then brought to the Pale to safeguard him against his father's enemies. Early accounts of his life, however, claim that O'Neill was brought up in England and there was made a ward of Elizabeth. When he returned to his own lands in 1568, there was a hope in the English court that Hugh would be a useful tool in helping to contain the other Irish chieftains, in particular Turlough O'Neill, a powerful lord in west Ulster. Turlough, through a number of skilful alliances, had gained control of much of Ulster, and was beginning to make incursions into the Pale. The fact that Hugh O'Neill's return also coincided with a rebellion by Desmond suggested that he could be a useful asset to England. He was therefore given substantial lands in Ulster and allowed to attend the Irish parliament in 1585 as an earl.

The position of Ulster, and its resistance to English control, continued to worry the English authorities. Various attempts had been made to extend English control northwards but they had met with little success. One of the most concerted attempts was the Enterprise of Ulster, which lasted from 1571 to 1575. The guiding principle was that the colonisation was to be left to individual enterprise. Although a number of private expeditions took place, they achieved nothing, although both money and men were lost in the attempts. Sir John Perrot, who was lord deputy from 1584 to 1588, made an aggressive attempt to extend shiring, and English law and rule, to the north of the country. His partition of Cavan was a first step in this process, although it was achieved only by ruthless suppression of his opponents. The naked desire of some Englishmen to extend the Pale into Ulster inevitably alarmed the local lords and contributed to general political instability. Moreover, Hugh O'Neill, since his return home, appeared torn between loyalty to his fellow Irishmen and fulfilling the expectations of England. While he continued to proclaim his loyalty to the English Crown, he was simultaneously negotiating with Spain for support. Although he intermittently appealed to the Pope for help, the latter's dislike of Spain meant he refused to intervene. O'Neill was also gradually extending his power in Ulster. The proposed marriage of his daughter to Red Hugh O'Donnell, son of the Lord of Tyrconnell, alarmed the English authorities. The lord deputy, Sir John Perrot, responded by imprisoning Hugh O'Donnell in Dublin Castle in 1587. O'Neill helped him to escape and together they defeated O'Neill's enemy, Turlough, in 1592. Hugh

O'Donnell acceded to the lordship of Tyrconnell in the same year. On a personal level, O'Neill also alienated the English marshal of Ireland, Sir Henry Bagenal, by eloping with his sister and making her his third wife.

From 1593 he was recognised as 'the Great O'Neill' by the main Gaelic chiefs. The growing power of O'Neill lessened his dependence on English goodwill. At this stage, however, he probably believed that England had designs on the land held by the lords in Ulster. This was confirmed by the partition of Monaghan in 1593, which effectively provided the trigger for O'Neill's rebellion. The Ulster lords were afraid that this would create a precedent for more English incursions into the north, which had been carried on intermittently since 1570. The resultant alliance of Gaelic lords in Ulster, however, went beyond being merely defensive to attempting to build an alliance based loosely on nationality and religion. The lords came together in a confederacy, which was secret and oath-bound.

O'Neill's actions resulted in a realignment of alliances, with the Crown now propping up Turlough as a buttress against him. When Turlough died in 1595, Hugh inherited the ancient kingship of O'Neill, and he started to appoint lords in other parts of Ireland. In the early months of the rebellion, however, O'Neill continued to claim to support England, although this may have been because he did not want to initiate all-out warfare until he had heard from Spain. In 1595, however, Hugh O'Neill destroyed an English fort in Armagh, which made his allegiance very clear. The English responded by proclaiming him a traitor. In 1596 he made a request to the Dublin parliament for Roman Catholics to have freedom of worship. He also asked Irish landowners to join a military alliance in defence of Catholicism. O'Neill's language and demands also began to refer to gaining the independence of Ireland, thus intertwining Catholicism with national demands.

The Irish confederates fought the war using a mixture of English traditional military methods and their usual Irish guerrilla tactics. They were supplied with some firearms from Scotland and some by Old English sympathisers, but they did not have sufficient weapons to take control of the towns in the east. O'Neill was also actively opposed by a number of Anglo-Irish lords, notably Black Tom Butler, the 10th Earl of Ormond, who had proved such a ruthless enemy of the Desmond rebellions. O'Neill's campaign had some initial successes, which took the English army by surprise, with victories at the Ford of the Biscuits in 1594 and Clontribet in 1595. At this point the English were willing to compromise and offered O'Neill complete control of Ulster, but O'Neill refused – possibly because he no longer trusted the English or because he had received word concerning Spanish support.

His greatest victory was the battle of Yellow Ford near Armagh in 1598. During the battle the English marshal, Sir Henry Bagenal, who was O'Neill's brother-in-law and fiercest adversary, was killed. As a result of his triumph O'Neill was able to extend his authority into Munster. O'Donnell was also having successes in the west of the country following his capture of Sligo Castle. This victory allowed him to extend his control into Connacht, reaching down as far as Thomond. It was not until 1600 that he faced any serious challenge to his advancement. Overall, it meant that the confederate army had reached into each of the four provinces in Ireland, making the war appear truly national. At this stage O'Neill controlled more of Ireland that did the English. From this position of strength, in 1599 O'Neill issued a political manifesto that appealed to the Old English not only as co-religionists but also as compatriots. The proclamation contained twenty-two articles, covering both religious and national demands. Essentially, it provided for an independent Catholic Ireland, which would be run jointly by the Old English and the Gaelic lords. The Crown refused, but the implications of the document were a terrifying prospect to a monarch who saw her mission as being to complete, not abort, the conquest of Ireland. More troops were sent to Ireland and their strategy was to undermine the economy, particularly the food supplies of the north. The proclamation also alarmed many of the Old English, and O'Neill suffered a setback when they refused to support him. Now, however, he had been promised support from Spain, and Spanish troops finally landed in Kinsale in west Cork in September 1601. They were joined by O'Neill and Hugh O'Donnell, but their initial successes against the Crown forces were quickly reversed. O'Neill and his supporters were defeated and the Spaniards withdrew, having achieved little. O'Donnell died in Spain in 1602.

Although the war dragged on, Kinsale was a decisive defeat for O'Neill, and he and his supporters were forced to sue for peace. O'Neill went into hiding, and it was not until 1603 that he surrendered unconditionally at Mellifont. The Treaty of Mellifont in March 1603 officially brought the Nine Years War to a close. When he surrendered, however, he had not been told that Elizabeth was already dead. The treaty ended O'Neill's rule as a chieftain, although he held onto his kingship title. He also received a pardon for his actions and was given new patents for his lands. Although the Crown treated O'Neill's supporters generously, they had lost their independence and they believed that their future was not secure. Ironically, perhaps, O'Neill was one of the peers who signed a proclamation in Dublin accepting James VI of Scotland as James I of England. Financially, the victory had been expensive for England: at £2 million, it had cost more than any previous Irish war. However, as Elizabeth realised, the stakes had been high, and defeat would have done irrevocable damage to the Crown and the Church. Instead, by their victory, for the first time ever England had complete control of Ireland. O'Neill's overthrow, in effect, defeated the Gaelic aspiration of ending English rule in Ireland.

O'Neill's ambitions did not die in 1603, and he continued to negotiate with Spain for military support. The Flight of the Earls in 1607 was a final, desperate attempt to win support on the continent, although it may also have been motivated by a fear that his plans had been uncovered. O'Neill was accompanied by Rory O'Donnell, Earl of Tyrconnell, and Cuconnachy Maguire, the Lord of Fermanagh. Their flight ended ignominiously. Whatever their reasons, it was a turning point in Irish history, as, following the flight, O'Neill, O'Donnell and Maguire were declared traitors, and their lands were confiscated. Their intention of reaching Spain was spoilt by bad weather and they were forced to land in France, where, rather than being welcomed, they were an embarrassment to the French king. O'Neill settled in Rome, where, like O'Donnell and Maguire, he was supported by a papal pension until his death, in 1616. His defeat and the aftermath was a major blow for the aspirations of Gaelic Ireland. It was particularly devastating for the northern Gaelic clans that had lost their leaders. The departure of the earls, however, created new opportunities for the English Crown, and Elizabeth's successor, James VI of Scotland, a Stuart, was the main beneficiary of the Tudor conquest.

FIVE

MAKING IRELAND PROTESTANT
c. 1603–1685

The seventeenth century witnessed a rapid decline in Gaelic culture and the concurrent rise of a Protestant elite, who asserted their dominant position within the country at the expense of both Irish Catholics and Old English Catholics. Yet, increasingly, political and religious changes within Ireland were being shaped by external influences.

This chapter examines how, as early as the 1640s, Ireland had become a sideshow for royal conflicts within England. James I of England, who never visited Ireland, Oliver Cromwell, who spent only nine months in the country, and William of Orange, who spent two months, were all to change Ireland significantly.

The Plantation

During Elizabeth's reign, Scotland and England had moved closer together. The treaty of Edinburgh in 1560, which was an alliance between Scotland and England, ended Scotland's long-term relationship with France. Elizabeth's choice of James VI of Scotland as her heir, despite some initial prevarication, was acceptable to many English people, largely because of his Protestantism. The spread of the Reformation to Scotland had provided a strong link with England, although the Scottish people showed an early preference for Presbyterianism over the Episcopalian form of Protestantism.

Elizabeth's failure to marry and produce an heir resulted in a new development in the royal succession. James VI (r. Scotland 1566–1625), son of the executed Mary, Queen of Scots, had acceded to the Scottish throne at the age of thirteen months. During the later years of Elizabeth's reign, the expectation was that James would inherit the English throne. When he did so in 1603, he became James I of England (r. 1603–25). James became the first ruler of the three kingdoms of England, Scotland and Ireland, but each of these countries continued to have their own parliaments, in London, Edinburgh and Dublin respectively.

James believed that he was king by divine right and disliked the Presbyterian view that he was not the ruler but merely a member of the Church and a subject of Jesus. This approach largely reflected the fact that while the Reformed Church in England had been led by the Crown, in Scotland local preachers such as John Knox had directed it. When James became king he made it clear that he was not going to promote Presbyterianism within England. Throughout his reign, regardless of his actions in Ireland, he was tolerant toward Roman Catholicism and supported some schemes for the reunion of the Western Christian Church.

In October 1604 James I declared himself to be king of 'Great Britain', and he announced his determination to unite England and Scotland through his wise governance. New coins were minted and flags were designed to celebrate the union. James, however, was the monarch of three kingdoms, although promoting what he referred to as a 'perfect union' between Scotland and England was one of his primary aims. Consequently, Ireland was left more in the custody of government ministers than had been the case for many years. The Irish parliament played little part in the government of Ireland. James did not convene his Irish parliament until 1613, by which time the landscape of Ireland had been changed by the plantation of Ulster. The Dublin parliament met for the last time in 1615 and from then on played no part in James's government of Ireland.

The ending of the Nine Years War in 1603 and the Flight of the Earls four years later paved the way for the Crown and Dublin authorities to impose long-desired reforms on Ulster. The north of the country had always proved most resistant to English control, despite the early victories of John de Courcy in the 1170s. Until the end of the sixteenth century, Ulster had been a stronghold of Gaelic, Catholic Ireland. The ending of the war allowed English law, English authority and English armies to be extended northwards. The departure of the Gaelic lords made this process even easier. The plantation was a way of ensuring that the deposed Gaelic world could not return. This aim was consolidated by legislation that served to undermine Gaelic culture. A proclamation of 1605, initiated by Arthur Chichester, the lord deputy, declared that all persons in Ireland were no longer subjects of their lords or chiefs, but were subjects of the king. In 1606 the Irish system of gavelkind, which had permitted partible inheritance in Gaelic areas, was declared to be illegal. Until this date, Irish lands, except what belonged to the *tánist*, were periodically divided among the clan, including illegitimate children. The English state regarded this system as unstable, preferring its own system of primogeniture. Two years later the office of the tanistry was declared illegal. Under Gaelic law, the *tánist* was the designated successor of a king or chief. This ruling was a further blow to the Gaelic traditions of inheritance, especially political succession. The English monarch now held lands that had traditionally been held by Irish kings or chiefs. Overall, the effect of these changes was to bring the Irish legal system more in line with the English one, and to expedite the demise of the Brehon Laws. The Scottish planters added to the existing cultural mix of Irish, Norse, Old English and New English. Apart from division between Catholics and Protestants, many Anglicans did not like the Presbyterian practices of the Scottish settlers.

An experiment in plantation had taken place under Edward VI, in Laois and Offaly. Larger-scale ones were carried out under Elizabeth in Munster. In addition to the plantations initiated by the Crown, some private ones also took place. Although none of the schemes was totally successful, in the short term they provided a way of rewarding people loyal to England and bringing in additional revenues for the Crown. The plantations were viewed as a way of embedding English civilisation and the Protestant religion in Gaelic areas, but this proved hard to achieve. However, as the Nine Years War demonstrated, the natives who had been displaced were awaiting an opportunity to regain their lands. None the less, during the Tudor period the advantages of placing loyal Protestant settlers in Ireland as a bulwark against both foreign and native enemies had proved appealing. Moreover, the frequent wars in Ireland had proved to be a significant cost to the Crown, but plantation meant that Irish land could be used to reward English soldiers with no cost to England. Additionally, the new landowners, or undertakers, gave revenue to England. Clearly, there were financial benefits from such settlements.

Although the Crown adopted a policy of conciliation at the end of the Nine Years War, O'Neill's defeat provided an opportunity to recolonise land that had been claimed back by the original Irish owners, especially in Munster, where the plantation had been overturned in 1598. A major beneficiary of the defeat of the Gaelic lords in Munster was Richard Boyle, 1st Earl of Cork. He personified the ideal both of a successful 'undertaker' and of the rising fortunes of the New English. He was an ambitious younger son from England who made his fortune in Ireland, demonstrating the potential of the country.

Primarily, though, Richard Boyle's achievements were for the benefit of Richard Boyle. Moreover, he cheated, forged and lied in order to obtain social and economic advancement. His determination resulted in his appointment as 'escheater', that is, the main official in charge of Crown lands. Although this office had been in the doldrums for decades, he exploited it to purchase land at reduced prices for his own use. He bought Sir Walter Ralegh's Munster estate, which Ralegh had acquired in the original plantation, for a discounted rate. He acquired a massive estate in County Cork, and within a few years was the richest man in Ireland. Thomas Wentworth, the lord deputy after 1632, only temporally halted Boyle's economic and social ascent. Wentworth wanted to make an example to other New English landowners of the consequences of defrauding the Crown. Boyle paid a fine of £15,000 (his annual income was £20,000), but he and his new dynasty survived. Wentworth's actions, however, had alienated many of the New English in Ireland.

Boyle's unscrupulous tactics did not disguise the potential rewards that plantation could offer. The success of his Cork estates attracted a number of New English settlers, notably to the towns of Kinsale and Youghal. The Munster plantation had a population of approximately 3,000 in 1590, 14,000 in 1610 and 22,000 in 1640. Some of the new settlers made fortunes from the export of timber, wool and cattle. Their control of the local economy through the ownership of land and the control of maritime trade further weakened the standing of the local Irish. It also meant that a small group of English Protestants had become successfully planted in Munster.

The Ulster plantation was conceived on a much larger scale and with much more advanced preparation than previous settlements. One of the purposes of the plantation was to reward those who had provided military service, but within a few years its terms had been broadened and more land was taken than had been originally envisaged. Initially it had been intended to use regrants in order to allow some of the native Irish to hold onto their lands, but this plan was reversed. The scale of the plantation was immense. Lands in parts of counties Armagh, Cavan, Coleraine (later Derry), Donegal, Fermanagh and Tyrone were confiscated and then made available for low rents in packages ranging from 1,000 to 2,000 acres.

The principles of the Ulster plantation were codified in a document drawn up in 1609. Although the first settlers arrived as early as 1610, working out the final details of the plantation took a number of years. There were three main categories of planters: undertakers, servitors and native Irish. The governing conditions of the settlement were that as far as possible the land should be sublet to Protestant tenants, that defences should be built for their protection and that the settlers should not mix with the natives. The best quality land was granted to either English or Scottish undertakers in lots of up to 2,000 acres. They had primary responsibility for the defence of the settlements. A further group of planters, known as servitors, who were generally employees of the Crown in Ireland, were also granted land. They could have a limited number of Irish tenants, but if they brought in English or Scottish tenants their rents would be lower. The third group of planters was native Irish, but they had to pay higher rents that the other grantees and they were restricted in the farming methods that they could use. To ensure that the plantation did not result in confusion and litigation as the Munster plantation had done, the plantation was delayed until a comprehensive map of the area was produced. The area was then divided into twenty-eight precincts, or baronies, sixteen of which were divided equally between English and Scottish undertakers; the remaining twelve were for the joint use of servitors and natives.

The Inishowen peninsula, which had not been part of the original settlement, was also included, even though its Gaelic lord, Sir Cahir O'Doherty, had been loyal to the Crown and had been part of the jury that had found O'Neill guilty of treason in 1607. But his disagreements with the newly arrived English governor of Derry, Sir George Paulet, led to his burning Derry and killing Paulet. This small revolt resulted in O'Doherty being killed by Crown forces in 1608 and his lands confiscated and granted to Sir Arthur Chichester, the ruthless lord deputy from 1605 to 1615. Chichester, who oversaw many of the plantation arrangements, benefited immensely from them. Like Boyle, he came from minor English gentry and was a professional soldier, but his actions in Ireland brought him vast wealth and status, and created a new dynasty, the Donegall family. During the latter period of the Nine Years War, Chichester was governor of Carrickfergus and his callous tactics extended to the civilian population as a consequence of his wholesale destruction of property. In 1603 he was granted lands in Belfast, including the castle, and in 1613 he was made Lord Belfast. The granting of the Inishowen Peninsula in Donegal, together with the addition of lands in Antrim and Down, made him one of the most powerful of the new landlords in Ulster.

Because Derry was regarded as strategically and financially important, it was given special treatment. James I was personally involved in persuading the wealthy merchants of London to put capital into developing and fortifying the county. In 1610 an agreement was reached between the Crown and the merchants of the City of London, with the latter being made collectively responsible for an area west of the Bann, although it was subject to the same conditions as other planted areas. In honour of its new owners, in 1613 Derry City was incorporated as the City of Londonderry, and County Coleraine was extended and renamed County Londonderry. The building of walls around the city of Derry began in 1614. The Irish Society acted on behalf of the London merchants in Ireland. Although the Society retained control of the towns and fisheries, it transferred responsibility for the remainder of the county to individual companies. The initial interest shown by the London merchants in the renamed county of Londonderry was not sustained on the level anticipated by the state. The Society proved to be inefficient about bringing British workers into the City, but continued to rely on Irish inhabitants. By 1630 there were fewer than 2,000 British settlers in the county. In 1635 the City of London and the Irish Society were found guilty of mismanagement in Londonderry, fined £70,000 and forced to forfeit some of their territory, although Cromwell reversed this latter penalty in 1662.

Applications for land were collated in London and Edinburgh. The English undertakers were granted the best quality land, while the Scottish settlers received less advantageous land. In total these two groups accounted for 36 per cent of the land provided. The London companies, through the Irish Society, received 10 per cent; servitors, state officials, army commanders and the Anglo-English in Cavan received 12 per cent; the Church of Ireland, 16 per cent; the newly established Trinity College, 3 per cent, with a further 3 per cent between garrisons and other establishments. Only 20 per cent of planted land was reserved for the native Irish who had supported the Crown during the Nine Years War. However, they were only allowed small portions of land and the strict conditions governing the grants meant that they were forbidden to purchase further land. In some instances the grants were only for the duration of their lifetime. Promises were broken by the government, with the claims of the minor Gaelic lords being ignored. The displaced Irish were to move to land held by a servitor or by the Church. This was to be completed by 1610, but the tardiness in the arrival of the undertakers meant that this was not possible. When they did arrive, they displayed a cavalier attitude to the rules governing the plantations, renting their lands to Irish tenants who could afford the high rents rather than waiting for immigrants from Scotland or England. Overall, the native Irish had much to be discontented about, as even those who had not supported O'Neill's rebellions were in a weaker economic position than they had been. Even if Irish tenants had remained loyal to the Crown, the incoming settlers received preferential terms to those of the native occupiers.

Apart from the displaced tenants, a further problem for the plantation was the existence of semi-professional soldiers, known as idlemen, who had lost their livelihood when the Gaelic lords had been defeated. The lord deputy, Chichester, attempted to reduce the threat by sending 6,000 of them to Sweden, where they were employed as mercenaries. Those who remained in Ireland whom he perceived to be a threat, he simply executed. Some of the Irish soldiers became outlaws, or woodkern, there being no place for them in the new arrangement. In 1615 the hanging of hundreds of woodkern followed an unsuccessful uprising by the O'Neills and the O'Cahans. The draconian approach adopted by Chichester helped to ensure the survival of the plantation, despite an unsteady start.

The new settlers were a diverse group, bound only by their Protestantism. Unlike previous planters who had come almost exclusively from England and had been Anglican, the new ones included a large portion of Lowland Scots and were Presbyterian. Apart from the religious distinctions, there were other differences between natives and settlers. Many of the incomers were involved in arable farming, rather than the pastoral farming that had been preferred by the outgoing Irish tenants. They built timber houses or stone cottages, schools, chapels, marketplaces, all of which were collected together in organised settlements. The Protestant settlements were not only distinctive within Ulster; they were also unique within Ireland. They were made more noticeable by the fact that they remained separate enclaves within Ulster, although not as segregated as the Crown had hoped. Some of the land, usually the poorest quality land, was rented out to Catholic tenants, who remained angry at their recent expulsion. Within a few years of the plantation taking place some of the planters were being penalised because they had not fulfilled the conditions upon which they received cheap land.

Irish Catholics of all levels had been the main losers from the changes. For the Catholic Old English, King James's plantation had some disquieting aspects. It had been implemented without consulting the Irish parliament, and demonstrated that the king did not need the support of parliament in order to rule Ireland. By increasing the number of Protestants landowners, the plantation also increased the number of Protestant members of the Irish parliament. Overall, the Ulster plantation changed the balance of power between Catholics and Protestants in Ireland more extensively than any previous event. The actions of Lord Lieutenant Chichester further weakened Catholicism throughout Ireland. He revived a crusade, begun under Elizabeth I, to get people to attend Church of Ireland services. In 1605 he sent letters, or mandates, to sixteen prominent Dublin Catholics, telling them to attend Protestant services. They were fined and imprisoned for refusing to do so. Chichester extended the mandates to other parts of the country. He also banished Catholic priests from the planted areas, and in 1608 he had the Book of Common Prayer translated into Irish. In 1612 Conor O'Devany, the Catholic bishop of Down and Connor, was executed on the spurious charge that he had aided Hugh O'Neill. This act demonstrated that the Catholic Church had been weakened by the defeat of the Gaelic lords. Chichester's draconian actions may have been counterproductive in some ways, as the resolve of Catholics (or recusants) in their support for the Counter-Reformation was strengthened. Since the 1590s Catholicism had been regrouping in Ireland, and by establishing Irish colleges for the training of priests overseas, it retained a vibrant priesthood. The resurgence of the Catholic Church in Ireland was even more remarkable as it took place within a hostile Protestant state. But this hostility pushed the Catholic Church either underground or into the privacy of people's homes. None the less, the Catholic Church survived, and in the process rid itself of the corruption that had become a feature of the Church in the late Middle Ages.

Just as the plantation undermined Catholicism, Presbyterianism was strengthened. In fact, one of the most enduring legacies of the plantation was the spread of Presbyterianism to Ireland. This change was particularly ironic, as it meant that James, a Scottish king who disliked the Presbyterian Church, was responsible for extending it to Ireland. Whereas earlier plantations had brought English Episcopalian settlers to Ireland, this plantation brought Scottish Presbyterian settlers to the country, adding to existing political tensions. Before the plantation, the Reformed Church had made virtually no inroads into Ulster. The Scottish undertakers, however, had been encouraged to bring their tenants to Ulster. The Crown felt that if Scottish men inhabited the coasts they would promote trade. Scottish tenants, in turn, were attracted by the prospect of cheap land and the protection of the Crown. Some brought their own preachers, who were effectively missionaries in Ireland. A number of the Scottish Presbyterian ministers were tempted to move to Ireland because they disliked the restoration of Episcopacy in Scotland in 1610. Ulster, which had remained immune from the Reformation, the Counter-Reformation and other church reforms, was a fertile ground for their missionary endeavours. By 1630 a religious revival was taking place that attracted hundreds of believers. However, the type of Protestantism practised by the Lowland Scots was very different from the Episcopalian variety preferred by the English settlers. The English parliament and both James I and his successor Charles I disliked the former. Within a short period of the plantation being established, therefore, they were regretting the fact that they had supported the Scottish settlers. The dislike was mutual.

Both the Crown and private plantations had been established only through the displacement of a large number of native Irish. The new settlers knew that they needed to defend themselves with weapons and fortified towns. The early plantations in Laois, Offaly and Munster had been frequently attacked, and the Munster one had been toppled in 1598. Despite the disappearance or decline of many Gaelic lordships after 1603, there was a fear for a number of years that a charismatic leader such as Hugh O'Neill might return. Furthermore, a large number of displaced and landless Irish people remained angry at their dispossession. An early example of their hostility took place in Ulster in 1615, led by the O'Neill and O'Cahan families. The rising was easily defeated and gave an excuse for even more land to be confiscated.

In general, the government was dissatisfied with the slow progress made in the plantations, and the high levels of corruption and inefficiency that had accompanied them. In 1622 Lionel Cranfield was sent to investigate. The Cranfield Commission criticised the London companies for not having fulfilled their obligations. Irish tenants had not been removed as systemically as they should have been, and the fortifications were not as rigorous as was considered necessary. Overall, the Cranfield Commission changed little and the plantation never fulfilled its initial promise. Moreover, the ongoing failure to fortify the settlements left the planters open to attack. One change was that, in recognition of the fact that some native Irish remained on the planted land, new patents were issued in 1628, but their rents were massively increased. The new rent levels proved to be a successful lever for forcing the Irish from the most fertile lands. Significantly, their departure consolidated the hold of Scottish and English tenants on the best quality properties.

Despite James's disappointment with the progress of the Ulster caretakers, more plantations were endorsed. In 1621 the Crown authorised plantations in Leitrim, King's Country, Queen's Country and Westmeath, and in 1635 preparations were begun by the lord deputy for the plantation of Connacht.

Apart from the Crown plantations, a number of private plantations were initiated, encouraged by the relatively peaceful conditions and powerlessness of the Gaelic lords. The Ulster plantation encouraged further movement of people from England and Scotland to Ireland. Informal plantations took place in counties Antrim and Down, where the Enterprise of Ulster scheme had failed to take hold in the turbulent conditions of the previous century. There were smaller private plantations in Queen's County, Leitrim, Longford, King's County and Wexford. English settlers even felt safe enough to settle in western districts such as Thomond. These settlements were made possible by a Crown and a government flexing its muscles and maximising the powers regarding land acquisition created by various Tudor monarchs, especially their ability to grant and regrant land. By 1640 there were 15,000 English and Scottish settlers in Ulster, about 7,000 fewer than in Munster. The fact that many of the new landlords were absentee and did not develop their new properties suggested that avarice was an important factor in England's relationship with Ireland in the seventeenth century. A further aspect of the relationship was that Ireland had little political voice within the relationship. The Stuart monarchs showed no interest in the Dublin parliament, except when it needed it to raise money or troops. James I convened only one Irish parliament, which sat for two years from 1613 to 1615, and the Dublin parliament did not meet again until 1634. What this attitude demonstrated was that even Irish Protestants were politically marginalised within the three kingdoms.

Regardless of the fact that settlers exploited the land and the resources of the country, particularly forestry and fishing, the early decades of the seventeenth century coincided with the growth of the economy. The settlers brought capital and new skills to Ireland. The introduction of new breeds of cattle boosted pastoral farming. Many towns and ports prospered, helped by a growing export sector. The number of fairs and markets also grew, especially in the hinterlands of Ulster, facilitated by a network of roads. A judicial system based on assize circuits, which dealt with civil and criminal cases, was imposed in parts of Ireland that had proved resistant to English law. But three distinct societies existed separately in Ulster: the Scottish, the English and the Irish. For the planters, Protestantism provided protection and opportunities for advancement. The establishment of sixteen new corporate towns that were Protestant-controlled mirrored the changing religious balance in the Dublin parliament. In contrast, the Irish were the poorest group, surviving on marginal lands often at a subsistence level. The plantation and the ministers who implemented it had shown little sensitivity to the Irish, who felt aggrieved at losing their lands. An opportunity to recover their property came in 1641.

Charles and Ireland

Although the Ulster plantation had been achieved with relative ease, it had created within the whole of Ireland new divisions, resentments and factions that emerged mostly after James I's death in 1625. Religion was at the heart of much of the conflict. The Nine Years War had been a loss for Gaelic Ireland, yet Catholicism remained strong among the Gaelic Irish and the Anglo-Irish. Moreover, the Old English, who continued to be major landowners in Ireland, remained faithful both to Catholicism and to the Crown. This loyalty was not reciprocated, as from the late sixteenth century there was an assumption within government that all Catholics were disloyal. The Old English had traditionally played an important role within the Irish parliament, but even this was being eroded. None the less, when the Irish parliament attempted to introduce anti-Catholic legislation in 1613, the Old English flexed their collective muscles to stop them. After this action, the parliamentary power of the Old English was clearly in decline.

Although James never visited Ireland, his policies had a dramatic impact on the political development of the country. Regardless of his devotion to Protestantism, he based many of his policies on appeasing all factions. With the exception of the plantation, his foreign policy was conciliatory, based on a desire to mollifiy rather than fight his Catholic neighbours. This policy was manifested in the arranged marriage of his son and heir, Charles, to a French princess, Henrietta Maria, who was Catholic. His marriage did not please his Protestant subjects who had become suspicious of Catholicism. In Ireland, though, the Old English were hopeful that when Charles became king he might be more sympathetic to them. This hope was short-lived: where James had sought to conciliate, Charles (r. 1625–49), despite his personal charm, was willing to offend. And, while James's reign had been marked by consensus, Charles's was defined by conflict and confrontation. Charles wanted to rule his three kingdoms without the intervention of parliament. In Ireland he did not convene a parliament until 1634, and it sat for only a year. He recalled the parliamentarians only when his monarchy was in crisis in 1640. While the Irish parliament had too little power to demand better treatment, his handling

of the English parliament was to lead to his eventual dethronement. In 1629
Charles dissolved the English parliament and ruled without it until 1640.
These eleven years of personal rule, which were referred to as the 'Thorough',
left Charles vulnerable to faction fighting within England. His isolation was
exacerbated by his policies in Ireland and Scotland, which left him with few
allies. Despite his Scottish ancestry, he showed little interest in the country.
Charles visited Scotland for his coronation only in 1633, and he showed
himself to be insensitive to Scottish customs and traditions. Just as he had
overridden the English parliament and ignored the Irish parliament, he showed
himself to be equally dismissive of the Scottish parliament in Edinburgh and
the Presbyterian Kirk (Church) authorities. For example, he did not inform
either of them of his decision to impose the English Prayer Book on Scotland
in 1637. His arrogance in this matter was indirectly to result in war in each of
his kingdoms and his own execution.

Initially, some Catholics in Ireland regarded Charles's accession with
optimism. Since the late fifteenth century the Old English had been defending
their political and economic power in Ireland. Although they still owned a
large portion of land, their political position had been weakened, as they were
increasingly marginalised within the Irish parliament. The balance of power
had also changed as the plantation increased the number of Protestants in
the Dublin parliament. The Old English feared that the government might
attempt to deprive them of their land. An opportunity to safeguard their
position was provided when Charles I came to the throne in 1625 and
immediately went to war with Spain; war with France quickly followed. He
needed money to finance his military expeditions. The English parliament was
reluctant to give it but the Old English in Ireland were willing, in return for
security of ownership. The 'Graces' was the name given to concessions and
guarantees made to the Old English by Charles. Although the English Privy
Council agreed to the Graces in 1628, they were never fully ratified. When
the wars ended Charles abandoned his promises. Although he made peace
with Spain and France in 1630, the wars had left him with large debts.

In an attempt to sort out various factions and make them less troublesome
to the Crown, Charles sent a new lord deputy, Viscount Wentworth, to Ireland
in 1632. Wentworth's mission was to reform the administrative and legal
structures of the country, and make them more efficient and financially
lucrative. His main objective was to recover income and lands for the Crown
and the Reformed Church. His tactics were ruthless and his treatment of the

old Anglo-Irish classes alarmed the gentry in England. Within the Irish parliament he played off Catholic against Protestant, and Old English against New English, or if this failed, he by-passed the parliament altogether. One of the main targets of his reforms was the Old English, whom he kept vulnerable by not giving sanction to the Graces. In place of the traditional political elites, Wentworth appointed his own officials who were loyal to the Church and the king. Wentworth also forced reforms on the Church of Ireland, causing it to move towards high-church principles. More aggressively, he exploited the existence of some ancient royal titles to plant land in Connacht. The colonisation marked a new political development, in that no distinction was to be made between the Irish and the Old English. A further purpose was to divert the revenues of Catholic landlords to the Crown, which not only weakened their position but left less revenue for the maintenance of the Catholic Church. Wentworth also offended Presbyterians in Ireland. He was responsible for introducing the Black Oath in 1639, by which Scottish settlers in Ireland rejected the Presbyterian covenant. This act was seen as a way of ensuring their loyalty to England at a time when Scotland had just declared war. When Wentworth returned to England in 1639 he had united the disparate sections of Irish society in their dislike of him. He was still valued by Charles, who appointed him his chief adviser, created him an earl and promoted him to lord lieutenant. He was put in charge of preparing an Irish army to invade Scotland.

Although Charles had angered the Irish Catholics and the English parliament, his treatment of Scotland was to lead to his demise. Charles's problems with Scotland had been triggered by his treatment of the Presbyterian Church. When Charles imposed the English Prayer Book on Scotland, the Presbyterians responded by drawing up the Scottish National Covenant in 1638, and then embarking on two years of warfare against Charles, known as the 'Bishops' Wars'. When the Scottish Covenanters defeated the English army on two occasions, Charles was forced to recall the English parliament and to appease the Irish parliament. At this point, both parliaments made clear their dislike of Charles and his loyal ministers. The English parliament was dismissed within weeks of convening, although within a few months Charles was forced to recall what became known as the Long Parliament. He was also forced to agree to the execution of his closest supporter Thomas Wentworth, who had managed to alienate the Irish parliament from Charles's rule. Charles immediately regretted this action, especially when in 1641 conflict in his Irish kingdom demonstrated the post-plantation fragility of Irish politics. The war had left Charles with many enemies. In 1643 his English and Scottish opponents signed a Solemn League and Covenant, as a way of protecting their religious and political rights. For the Scottish signatories this essentially meant the promotion of Presbyterianism, which they regarded as the word of God.

Charles's problems in England and Scotland forced him to appear more conciliatory in Ireland, especially towards the Old English. None the less, the issue of the Graces dragged on without resolution until 1641, when Charles again promised to ratify them, motivated by the fact that he needed the support of the Irish parliament as he had fallen out with the English one. The question of the Graces was also revived by the Old English, who now added to their demand the ending of the colonisation of Connacht, fearing this would undermine their economic domination in this province. They also wanted the Irish parliament to regain some of the autonomy that had been eroded under Wentworth's administration. At the same time, the Old English did not want Charles's personal authority to be too weakened, as Charles, like his father, was tolerant of Catholic worship. In contrast, both the English and Scottish parliaments were aggressively Protestant and were not satisfied with just removing economic and political power from Catholics. Ironically, though, the two Stuart monarchs had done much to undermine Catholicism in Ireland.

During the reigns of both James I and Charles I, not only was the land taken from Catholics but they were also to be segregated from the new Protestant settlers. Inevitably the links between Catholic Ireland and the Catholic monarchs and various popes strengthened. The Counter-Reformation, which sought to regain the souls lost to Protestantism, was also anxious that Protestantism should not make any further inroads into its congregation. The Catholic Church in Ireland received support from Rome. The Church, therefore, despite the onslaught of Protestantism, became doctrinally and organisationally stronger in the seventeenth century and moved closer to Roman orthodoxy. Continental Europe, rather than Britain, became the natural ally of the native Irish.

The 1641 Rising and the Confederate War

The unrelenting erosion of Catholic power in Ireland, especially within the parliament, resulted in a rising in 1641. Those who supported it were a diverse group that included the Old English, displaced Irish, disgruntled Gaelic chiefs and, to a lesser extent, disillusioned New English. They united under the leadership of Sir Phelim O'Neill, the member of parliament for Dungannon; Rory O'More, whose ancestors were a mixture of Gaelic lords and Catholic Palesmen, supported him. Its Catholic leaders believed that their rebellion had some chance of success while Charles was preoccupied with his troublesome British Parliamentarians, yet some also claimed that they were defending the king. To prove this, Phelim O'Neill insisted that each of his followers take an oath of loyalty to Charles. Mostly, though, they viewed their actions as a defence of Catholicism. The rising was to occur in a number of locations, but the Dublin conspiracy was betrayed the day before it was due to begin on 23 October 1641. Following the detection of the Dublin plot, the focus moved to Ulster, where the grievances of the Old English fused with the dissatisfaction of the displaced Irish. The early success of the local Ulster risings encouraged other areas to participate. However, the leaders on both sides were unable to prevent some of the most violent aspects of the uprisings, especially the sectarian killings. Approximately 4,000 of the Protestant settlers were killed, and their murders were followed by vicious reprisals against the Irish living within the planted areas.

The early success of O'Neill and his followers meant that they quickly controlled most of Ulster. They then proceeded southwards and captured Dundalk on 31 October, and a month later defeated the Parliamentarian troops. At the beginning of December, they were joined by some members of the Old English who had lost faith in Charles's commitment to agree to the Graces. This alliance changed the nature of the conflict, as the newly constituted 'Catholic Army' prepared to embark on renewed warfare. The movement spread, and by 1642 had extended into many parts of Ireland. The Old English were personally loyal to Charles but were suspicious that the English parliament wanted to extend Protestantism into all parts of Ireland. In 1642 the English government sent a large number of reinforcements to Ireland and, for the first time, victory appeared to be passing to the English government. By April that year the insurgents had been pushed back into Ulster. A number of them were willing to negotiate a peace, but the English government, sensing that they now had the initiative, refused. They wanted to use defeat of the uprising as an opportunity to finally crush all opposition in Ireland. Even before the uprising had been finally defeated, they borrowed large amounts of money to finance a new wave of land confiscations.

The rising in Ireland led Charles into a fresh confrontation with the English parliament, as they disagreed over who would control the army to be sent to Ireland. This altercation was to evolve into the English Civil War when Charles again withdrew from parliament and raised his standard in Nottingham. Ireland became a side issue, with neither Charles nor parliament willing to give in to the insurgents. Despite the conflicts in Ireland and England, parliament passed the Act for Adventurers in 1642. The other purpose of this legislation was to pay for the rising in the previous year. Investors, who were referred to as Adventurers, were to subscribe money which would be repaid as land when Ireland was reconquered. The intransigence of the English parliament and its declared intention to take land from the Irish Catholics meant that the insurgents had nothing to lose. Consequently, the rising entered a new phase as it changed into a full-scale confrontation. This was made possible as more Old English joined the insurgents and a reconstituted Catholic Army began to organise and prepare for a more extensive war. The resultant Confederate War in Ireland paralleled some of the conflicts taking place in England and Scotland and on the continent, all having in common a desire to either limit or control the power of the monarch.

Charles's main commander in Ireland was James Butler, 12th Earl of Ormond, who was lord lieutenant from 1643 to 1647, and from 1649 to 1650. His ancestors were Anglo-Norman and he was associated with the Old English, but he had been brought up in England as a Protestant. After 1642 Ormond supported the Royalists and fought against the Catholic Confederation on behalf of Charles. He was involved in making a series of short-lived truces with the Confederates. Ormond hoped that if he could resolve the conflict in Ireland, he and his troops would be able to assist Charles's campaign in England. Following Charles's eventual defeat and execution, Ormond allied himself with the various Catholic factions in Ireland.

The conflict with Charles resulted in the establishment of two parliaments in England, while in Ireland an alternative form of government was set up, although it did not refer to itself as a parliament. In June 1642 the Irish Catholics established a confederation, taking an oath proclaiming their rights as Catholic subjects of Charles. A provisional executive was established, following which a representative assembly met in Kilkenny in October 1642. It comprised clergy and lay people, lords, landowners and merchants, Irish and Old English. This assembly, sometimes referred to as the Confederation of

Kilkenny, governed the Catholic-controlled parts of the country. It was anxious to display its continuing loyalty to Charles, summed up in its motto, 'For God, King and Fatherland, Ireland united'. Despite this, the assembly undertook many of the duties of an independent parliament, controlling the army, collecting taxes, minting money and negotiating with foreign powers. Although the Confederate Catholics had hoped to get substantial financial help from the continent, it proved to be disappointing. Since 1618 many European powers had been involved in the Thirty Years War, and this prolonged conflict had proved to be a massive drain on their resources. Some overseas private help was forthcoming, especially in protecting the trade of Catholic Ireland. The Confederates were helped by the return of Irish exiles from the continent, including a number of professional soldiers, such as Colonel Owen Roe O'Neill, a nephew of Hugh O'Neill. The Pope sent a nuncio, Archbishop Giovanni Rinuccini, to Ireland in 1645. He provided the Confederate Army with financial resources, but one of his objectives was to get Charles I to agree to restore Catholicism in Ireland.

Despite displays of unity among the Confederate Catholics, the disparate origins and aims remained. The Old English, who had much to lose from defeat, were anxious for the war to be brought to a speedy conclusion. The Irish, on the other hand, augmented by the return of combative exiles and hardened by decades of enforced humiliation, felt they had little to lose. They wanted a return of their confiscated lands, and safeguards for the Catholic Church in Ireland. A third group, centred on the papal nuncio, Rinuccini, wanted a full restoration of Catholicism, in keeping with the new ideas of the Counter-Reformation Church. These conflicting aims, together with Charles's own problems, made it difficult to reach any accommodation. Moreover, there was personal animosity between two of the Confederate leaders, Phelim O'Neill and Thomas Preston. Their disagreements meant that some campaigns were aborted or abandoned. This discord also meant that while the Confederate Army had a number of significant victories it never consolidated its position, with some of the moderates continuing to have faith in making a lasting peace with Charles. Despite the disagreements among the Confederates, the attempts to end the conflict also proved fruitless. The cessation of hostilities in 1643 had been short-lived, and the various treaties between the Confederates and Charles in 1645 and 1646 were also of brief duration. One of the problems was that Rinuccini opposed any agreement that fell short of giving full promises of restoration to the Catholic Church.

The divisions within the Confederate camp came to a head when O'Neill left the confederacy because he opposed the truce that had been made between Murrough O'Brien, 1st Earl of Inchiquin, and the Confederates. Inchiquin, who had converted to Protestantism as a young man, was governor of Munster. He supported the parliamentary side, although they never fully trusted him, and after 1647 he rejoined the Royalist side. He later reconverted to Catholicism. When the supreme council of the Confederates agreed to the Inchiquin truce in 1647, Rinuccini excommunicated the whole of the council. His action demonstrated that the divisions among the Confederates made a lasting truce difficult.

Scotland was also involved in the conflict in a limited capacity, maintaining an army in Ulster to support the Presbyterian settlements. In 1642 the Scottish army led by Robert Munro landed at Carrickfergus; it had an early victory and was able to take control of Newry. It was convincingly defeated by Phelim O'Neill at Benburb in 1646, the Confederate Army having been replenished with money supplied by the Pope. Under Cromwell, the hold of Presbyterianism deepened even further. The army was accompanied by its religious ministers, and within a few weeks of landing a ministry was established in Ulster. One of the unexpected consequences of the 1641 rising, therefore, was the strengthening of the Presbyterian Church.

Although the Irish rising and subsequent war were largely triggered by a widespread mistrust of the English parliament, ultimately they weakened further the authority of Charles I. The war in Ireland also reflected some of the political divisions in England. In 1642 Charles finally split with the English parliament and set up his own Royalist parliament in Oxford. The resultant Civil War forced realignment in British politics, with the English parliament moving closer to the Scots, and Charles reluctantly negotiating with the Irish Confederates through his Irish commander, the Earl of Ormond. This resulted in a ceasefire in September 1643, but the Confederates gained little advantage from it. Overall, Charles was too absorbed by his problems in England to take control of Irish developments. His main concern was for the conflict in Ireland to be quickly resolved so that he could focus his resources on England. Similarly, the English parliament sent a token army to Ireland, but its priority was the defeat of the king in England. As a result, the war in Ireland dragged on with little prospect of resolution. By 1644, the Civil War in England had reached a stalemate. The Royalist defeats increased, however, following the creation of the New Model Army under Sir Thomas Fairfax, with Lieutenant-General Oliver

Cromwell as his cavalry commander. In 1645 the Civil War ended, and in the following year Charles surrendered to the Scots, belatedly abandoning his previous opposition to their Presbyterian Church. The Scots handed Charles over to the English parliament, but he escaped in 1647. In 1648 a second phase of the Civil War commenced but Cromwell decisively defeated the Scots at Preston in August 1648. Charles was handed over to the English parliament and in January 1649 he was executed. Two weeks before his execution the Irish Confederates had agreed to a further treaty with Charles's commander, known as the second Ormond Peace. At this stage the funds of the Confederate Army were exhausted, and the Irish population had been debilitated by a period of famine and disease. The taxes imposed by the Confederate parliament had also placed a heavy burden on the Catholic population.

With Charles dead, the English parliament under Cromwell began to concentrate on the situation in Ireland in a way that it had not done since 1640. Charles's death also meant that the Irish Catholics now had no buffer between themselves and the Protestant English parliament. Furthermore, the political climate in England had changed as a result of the Civil War, and a dogmatic form of Puritanism had replaced Charles's liberalism. The new Puritan state disliked Catholicism and found it easy to attribute the events since 1641 to Catholic disloyalty and deviousness. At the same time, the violence that had taken place during the 1641 rising was exaggerated and blamed on Catholic sectarianism. When Cromwell arrived in Ireland in August 1649, therefore, there were many scores to settle. The Confederate War dragged on for four more years, and Catholicism appeared to be even more under threat than it had been prior to 1641.

Cromwell

Despite spending less than one year in Ireland, from August 1649 to May 1650, Oliver Cromwell was to have a far-reaching impact on the subsequent development of the country. He was born in 1599 into a minor gentry family in England, but as a result of patronage became an MP in 1628. In the 1630s he converted to the Puritan faith and his providentialism both guided and justified the remainder of his life. When the Civil War commenced he supported the Parliamentary side, though he was critical of the high command. Not only did he regard them as militarily inept; he disliked their alliance with the Scottish Presbyterians and their tolerance of the radical

Leveller group within the Parliamentary army. The Levellers were a radical, libertarian group who wanted the abolition of the monarchy and its replacement by a republican government. They also supported religious toleration. Their ideas had quickly spread in the New Model Army, though Cromwell disliked relying on their support. Cromwell's success at the battle of Naseby in 1645 against the Royalist forces was a major factor in Charles's surrender and catapulted Cromwell into a prominent position. A failure to reach an agreement with Charles and his escape resulted in the beginning of the Second Civil War in 1648. This experience convinced Cromwell that no satisfactory agreement could ever be reached with Charles. Cromwell was a powerful figure in the new English parliament, expelling the Presbyterian party from it, overseeing Charles's trial and execution, and executing or expelling the Leveller group from within the army. His attention next turned to Ireland, where a coalition of Catholics and Royalists had regrouped under the Earl of Ormond.

Cromwell arrived in Ireland on 15 August 1649 in his capacity as commander-in-chief. He was supported by an army of 20,000, together with a large artillery and naval backing. He had the support of leading Protestants within Ireland, and they were a major factor in his success. Cromwell came to Ireland as God's emissary and as a liberator – from royalty, from Catholicism and from Irishness in general. His religious zeal was matched only by his English patriotism. Within a month of arriving in Ireland he had captured Drogheda. His swift defeat of the Irish alliance there forced its leader, Ormond, into exile with Charles I's son and heir, Charles II – upon the Stuart restoration, however, Ormond was reinstated as lord lieutenant. Cromwell moved southwards to Wexford, where he was equally successful. He showed no mercy to the garrisons that refused to surrender. More shockingly, Cromwell's ruthless treatment of the inhabitants of towns demonstrated his determination to have a speedy resolution of the Irish problem, while providing graphic evidence of his mercilessness. In Wexford 2,000 inhabitants were randomly killed in the marketplace, even though the garrison had surrendered and was negotiating with the New Model Army. Although Cromwell was not personally responsible for the massacre, he defended his army's conduct. Moreover, he regarded the Irish as barbaric and deserving of such treatment, referring to the massacre of Protestants during the rising of 1641 as evidence of the brutality of Irish Catholics. Revenge, therefore, informed his actions. The early brutality of the New Model Army may have served as a warning to other Irish towns, many of which surrendered and agreed to terms. A number of Protestant Royalists also deserted the Confederates. In May 1650 Cromwell's army was ambushed as it entered Clonmel: with losses of 2,500 men, it was the heaviest defeat sustained by the New Model Army.

Cromwell left Ireland in May 1650 to deal with a new Royalist threat in Scotland. By that time, he controlled the east of Ireland and his forces had demonstrated that they were dominant within Ireland. Protestant support helped to subdue the provinces of Ulster, Munster and Connacht. Although Cromwell had suffered some minor setbacks, it was clear that he viewed his Irish campaign as a triumph. His tactics had been brutal, but they had succeeded. Moreover, Cromwell's victories in Ireland, followed by his defeat of Scottish Presbyterians, allowed him to return to England as a victor. They also made him the most powerful man within the English parliament, as not only had he defeated the English Royalists, he had also brought the recalcitrant peoples of Ireland and Scotland under English influence again. He did not, however, fully control parliament, and his relationship with it was increasingly tense. In 1653 he dissolved what was referred to as 'the Rump Parliament', although he was not sure what to put in its place, having become disillusioned with both royal and parliamentary government. What his action demonstrated was that he was just as willing as the Stuart monarchs to discard parliament when it suited him. He convened a new type of legislature, known as the 'Barebones Parliament', to which Ireland and Scotland sent six and five members respectively. This act was a precursor of the parliament created by the Act of Union of 1800. In 1653 Cromwell was declared lord protector, which gave him ultimate legislative and executive power. The first protectorate parliament met in September 1654 and included thirty Irish representatives. Although Cromwell promoted Puritanism in England, he proved to be more tolerant of Protestants, Jews and even Roman Catholics than some of his contemporaries. Puritanism, however, was not popular with the public. Ironically also, although he refused the title of king, he and his family lived in increasing splendour until his death in 1658.

Even after he had left Ireland, Cromwell's draconian methods continued and were underpinned by the settlement that followed the war. Despite being opposed to hereditary monarchy, Cromwell made his own younger son Henry governor of Ireland between 1655 and 1659, in a variety of influential roles. Like his father, Henry did not favour the new Protestant denominations such as the Quakers and Baptists, and he increasingly allied with the Ulster Presbyterians, who represented a more conservative brand of Protestantism. He also continued the Cromwellian policy of dealing ruthlessly with opposition by Royalists or Catholics, by imprisonment, transportation and execution. However, those who had taken up arms in the preceding wars were allowed to emigrate, and 30,000 did so. A general pardon was also issued. Once the wars were over, Cromwell's main interest in Ireland lay in controlling the wealth of the country. The war had cost approximately £3½ million, and the Act for Adventurers introduced in 1642 had raised just over £300,000. Consequently, there was wholesale confiscation of land. This was codified in the Act for the Settlement of Land in 1652. Catholics who had taken part in the rebellion lost their estates and their property rights. Catholics who had not been involved in the rebellion were also punished. Although they were allowed to retain a small portion of land, it was to be a different piece of land. Ireland was split into two parts. Six counties situated in Connacht and Clare, which included some of the poorest land in Ireland, were the location to which innocent Catholics were to be transplanted. Catholic land in the other twenty-six counties was used to reward soldiers who had fought for the Parliamentarians, and generally to raise capital for the government.

As a consequence of these changes, landownership in Ireland was dramatically transformed. Unlike with the Ulster plantation, though, the new landlords did not bring new tenants to their land. Catholic landlords who had struggled to protect their position despite the various onslaughts of Tudor and Stuart monarchs were extinguished by a Puritan commoner. In 1641 Catholics had owned 59 per cent of land in Ireland; by 1688 this had fallen to 22 per cent, and it continued to fall, dropping to 14 per cent in 1703. Distinctions between the Old England and the Gaelic Irish were subsumed beneath the generic classification of being Catholic, and to be Catholic had come to mean to be dangerous and disloyal. The demise of Catholic landownership resulted in the creation of a new Protestant landowning elite in Ireland, which extended the work done by the Ulster plantation to other parts of Ireland. The vast majority of the population, however, were Catholic, landless and Gaelic speakers. Language, class and religion divided the two groups. The new elite had achieved an ascendancy and domination that early settlers in Ireland had not. Their position had been achieved only through violence and a systematic removal of the native population from the land.

SIX

THE WAR OF TWO KINGS
c. 1685–1780

The eighteenth century saw the consolidation of power for the Protestant minority, helped by the introduction of the Penal Laws. Consequently, it marked the high point of Protestant ascendancy. Yet, by the end of the century, a Catholic middle class was emerging, while radical Protestants were being inspired by events in America and France.

This chapter charts the period from when the Protestant elite took control of Ireland. Conflicts within Europe, however, were to embroil the country in a fresh wave of warfare.

Restoration and Consolidation

The war in Ireland between James II and William of Orange had little to do with Ireland but was triggered by a constitutional crisis in England. Not for the first time, Ireland provided a backdrop to English politics. William's acceptance of the throne, however, moved the succession crisis in England to centre stage in European politics, and the wars in Ireland provided a battlefield for wider conflicts between Louis XIV of France and his enemies.

Until the political crisis of 1688, the Irish parliament had had little influence on either the government of its own country or on politics within Britain. While the conflicts between the monarch and the English parliament in the 1640s had changed the constitutional development of England, Scotland and Wales, in Ireland little recognition had been given to the existence of an Irish political nation, either Catholic or Protestant. The Dublin parliament was a sideshow to English politics, called into being to raise monies only when necessity required it. Until the beginning of the 'Glorious Revolution', seventeenth-century monarchs felt the need to do so only on four occasions. Consequently, the Irish parliament played no significant role in Crown politics throughout this period.

When Charles I was executed in 1649, his son Charles was proclaimed king in Edinburgh and in Dublin. This assertion meant little, as Charles II spent the succeeding years of the protectorate in exile on the continent. Cromwell's death in 1658 did not bring an immediate return of monarchy, and it took a further two years before the English parliament voted for a restoration. Charles II was proclaimed king in London in 1660, though his reign was formally backdated to 1649, and the Irish government was no less speedy in paying tribute to him as king. Charles's accession marked the end of the English Commonwealth, but one of its legacies was that the king had to concede some of his prerogative powers to parliament, and the days of 'personal' or absolute rule were officially past. The balance of power between parliament and the sovereign had changed as a result of the English Revolution. Charles II had been recalled to England at the invitation of the English parliament and the invitation had been accompanied by a number of conditions, one of which was that that the Cromwellian land settlement should not be overturned. Charles was severely affected by his years of exile and had no intention of returning to them. His reign until his death in 1685 was characterised by his making promises to all sides while trying not to offend opposing groups.

Within Europe, religion continued to be the basis for making alliances and going to war. Although England was a Protestant state, or more precisely an Anglican one, the restored monarchy was not unsympathetic to Catholics. The parliaments in England, Scotland and Ireland were all controlled by Protestants and the English parliament in particular was antagonistic to non-Anglicans, who were described as Dissenters. These groups included Quakers and Independents. Catholics, however, who were a minority within England and Scotland but a majority within Ireland, were particularly disliked and feared, especially as they shared their religion with England's traditional enemies, Spain and France. Religion was an area where Charles II had to balance his own liberal opinions with the overt Protestantism of the state. In Ireland, where many Catholics had remained loyal to the monarchy, this proved to be difficult. Generally in his foreign policy he tried to maintain the semblance of a balance between Protestant Holland, Catholic Spain and Catholic France. For the most part Charles's sympathies were with Louis XIV, whom he believed to be his only likely supporter if ever he were to fall out with parliament. The falling out eventually occurred over the so-called 'Popish Plot', in which anti-Catholic feeling reached a zenith, and Charles dispensed illegally with the calling of parliament for the latter years of his reign. For almost twenty-five years, though, his reign had brought peace to the three kingdoms, and the ferments of his father's reign appeared to have been calmed.

The Restoration was generally welcomed in Ireland. One of Charles's first acts was to reconvene the Dublin parliament, and it sat from 1661 to 1666, making it the longest-running Irish parliament in the seventeenth century. During its relatively short life, the Irish parliament voted Charles a large hereditary income. Thereafter, Charles felt he had no need of its presence, and no further parliament met until the succession crisis after 1688. The real political power in Ireland lay with the Dublin executive, and Charles reappointed the Earl of Ormond as lord lieutenant and awarded him a dukedom. Ormond had served under his father and gone into exile with Charles II when Cromwell had seized Drogheda. Following his appointment, Ormond, a committed Protestant, restored the episcopacy in Ireland. A thornier problem was land. He knew that the maintenance of the land settlement would disappoint Irish Catholics but a reversal was impossible. Ormond attempted to ameliorate some of the most offensive aspects of the Cromwellian settlement by providing for 'Innocents' to receive some of their land back from the new settlers. The latter were reluctant to give up their land and, after much deliberation and confusion, a small amount was returned to approximately 500 Catholics. The new arrangement left everybody dissatisfied. A number of Catholics who were excluded from the settlement literally took to the hills and became outlaws, or, as they were referred to, 'tories'. The Cromwellian settlers were the main targets of their attacks. Some of the tory outlaws, such as James and Patrick Brennan, achieved notoriety for their banditry. Overall, the displaced Irish felt a grievance against the king. They believed that they had lost their lands because they had fought to defend the monarchy, yet the restored monarchy had done little to compensate them. Moreover, those who had rebelled and ultimately executed Charles I had been rewarded. From this point Catholic loyalty to a Protestant monarch became more measured.

The Restoration had coincided with a period of economic growth in the three kingdoms, although England had been the main beneficiary. A number of restrictions were imposed on Irish trade that in the long term were to be damaging. The export of Irish cattle was banned, and Irish wool could be exported only to England. The butter trade flourished, however, and an illicit trade developed in smuggling Irish wool from England to the continent. The ports of Cork, Dublin and Limerick were beneficiaries of the increased volume of trade in dairy produce. The period of peace also encouraged population growth, and by the end of Charles's reign the population had probably reached 2 million. But the distribution of wealth was unequal between Catholics and Protestants. Approximately 75 per cent of the Irish population was Catholic, but Protestants owned the majority of land and dominated trade, commerce, the professions and government positions. None the less, a Catholic gentry class and professional class had survived the Cromwellian onslaught, and they consolidated their position during the Restoration period.

The treatment of the Catholic Church was a further source of disaffection. The Restoration parliament in England quickly demonstrated its ongoing allegiance to the Anglican Church. Episcopacy was restored, and legislation was also passed favouring Anglicans, including the Corporation Act of 1661 and the Act of Uniformity of 1662. The Test Act of 1673 required all office-holders to take Anglican communion. Charles's brother James, who was lord high admiral and in the process of converting to Catholicism, felt compelled to resign. Little sensitivity was shown to the main denominations in Scotland or Ireland. The parliament ordered the burning of the Solemn League and Covenant of 1643 that was regarded by Scottish Presbyterians as an affirmation of their faith. They refused to repeal the Penal Laws against Catholics. Charles, who was a religious liberal, disliked these measures, but his proposal for a Declaration of Indulgence was ignored by parliament. However, because religious dissent had become associated with rebellion, he was also keen not to put his position in jeopardy.

Ormond wanted to seek an accommodation with the Irish Catholics over the issue of religion. In return for religious toleration, he expected Catholics to acknowledge the supremacy of the state even over the authority of the Pope. The Catholic Church could not agree to this, and so Church and State in Ireland maintained an uncomfortable coexistence that only occasionally gave in to anti-Catholic hysteria. When it did, however, the consequences could be as serious, as the imprisonment of Archbishop Peter Talbot and the execution of Archbishop Oliver Plunkett demonstrated. For the most part, however, the lord lieutenants of the Restoration period tolerated Catholic institutions and practices, and it was only the extremities of the Popish Plot and other anti-Catholic alarms which led to occasional clampdowns. These periods of repression could have serious consequences for figures such as Oliver Plunkett, however, who was executed in 1681 for his part in the Popish Plot.

Because Charles II had no legitimate heirs, succession passed to his brother James. James's conversion to Catholicism led to suggestions that he should be excluded from the succession. The Popish Plot, an alleged conspiracy to assassinate the king, brought this issue to a head, with Charles's opposition in parliament seeking to force on him an exclusion bill which would keep James from the succession. However, James's wife and only surviving son had died in 1671, making his elder daughter, Mary, heir presumptive. Both Mary and her sister, Anne, had remained Protestant, and so in the long term the Protestant succession appeared secure. But two years after the death of James's first wife, Louis XIV of France had helped him to find a new wife, Mary of Modena, who was a Catholic. At first James and Mary had no children, which meant the inheritance would still pass to his daughter Mary. The Crown's closeness to Louis XIV, who was not only a Catholic but also king of the most powerful nation in Europe, was disliked in England, and led to suspicions about both Charles's and James's real intentions. The English parliament mistrusted Louis and wanted England to ally with the Netherlands, a Protestant country. Charles II had sealed an alliance with the Dutch through the marriage of his niece Mary to William of Orange, but suspicions as to how deep this alliance really ran continued throughout the Restoration period. Indeed, under Charles, England twice went to war with the Netherlands, the second time in 1672 being an act of open aggression in concert with France. In 1685 James acceded to the throne as James VII of Scotland and James II of England (r. 1685–8). The duke of Monmouth, Charles II's illegitimate son, immediately challenged James's succession to the throne. On 11 June he issued a proclamation asserting his right to the throne. He had about 4,000 supporters, who included a large number of Protestant dissenters. The Royalists defeated the insurgents, and Monmouth was executed in July 1685.

James's Catholicism meant that his three parliaments, the state church and many of his subjects regarded him with mistrust. The belief that Catholics were subversive had been confirmed in the previous century through episodes such as the Spanish Armada, the Gunpowder Plot and the 1641 rising in Ireland. The last event in particular had been the subject of much inflammatory writing, which depicted Irish Catholics as cruel and brutish haters of all Protestants. Such interpretations found a sympathetic audience in England and Scotland. Anti-Catholic feeling was also stirred up by the agitator Titus Oates, son of a chaplain in the New Model Army. Oates blamed everything from rebellion in Ireland to the Great Fire of London in 1666 on Jesuits. He was also involved in fabricating the so-called 'Popish Plot' against Charles II in 1678, an alleged Catholic conspiracy to put James on the throne. These accusations led to the arrest of many prominent Catholics in England, a number of whom were executed. More significantly, Oates's accusations created a climate of fear against Catholics, which also extended to other dissenting groups, including Presbyterians. In 1684 Oates referred to James as a traitor, and this led to his imprisonment. Although he was released in 1688, he no longer had political influence. Oates's actions demonstrated that because of the fear of papism even hysterical accusations could gain credibility. The general dislike of Catholics was also mirrored in legislation. In 1678 parliament passed the Test Act, which forbade any Catholic from holding an influential position, including MP, magistrate, judge or army officer. James disliked the Test Act, and when he became king he asked for it to be repealed, but parliament refused.

Regardless of the climate of anti-Catholic feeling, when he became king, James did not disguise his desire to revive Catholicism. He appointed Catholics to high positions and used his royal prerogative to invalidate the impact of the Test Act. In 1685, within a year of acceding to the throne, James closed parliament, and he gave no indication that he would be recalling it in the near future. In 1687 he issued a Declaration of Indulgence, which suspended all laws against Catholics and Dissenters. He did this without consulting parliament. There was also alarm among some Protestants that James had doubled the size of the army, even though England was not at war. However, James's actions were tempered by his realisation that the established Church had become an integral part of the British monarchy and this arrangement could not be overturned. He was similarly cautious in regard to the land settlement. Lord Clarendon, his Protestant lord lieutenant in Ireland, assured Irish Protestants that no change would be made to the land settlements. Nevertheless, where Charles II had been conciliatory or charming, James was more often confrontational.

Catholics in Ireland were optimistic that the new king would be sympathetic to their situation. Yet James's policies in Ireland were ambivalent. He put his Catholic friend Richard Talbot in charge of the army, even though the army was almost exclusively Protestant. Talbot immediately appointed Catholic officers and encouraged more Catholics to join; within a little over a year, the majority of the army were Catholic. Although this appointment was clearly contentious, James disregarded the alarm expressed by Irish Protestants. Yet, while he encouraged the recruitment of Catholics into the Irish army, he showed no inclination to overturn the Cromwellian land settlement, which had proved so punitive to Irish Catholics. Protestants felt reassured by the appointment of the Protestant Lord Clarendon as lord lieutenant. Concern was increased in 1687 when Lord Clarendon was recalled from Ireland, and Richard Talbot, now the Earl of Tyrconnell, replaced him as viceroy. Talbot immediately appointed Catholics to key positions in central and local government. Even more worrying for Irish Protestants, he persuaded James to agree to quash the Act of Settlement of 1662, which was the basis of the Cromwellian land agreement, and the Act of Explanation of 1665, which had sorted out some of the problems associated with the original settlement. James's apparent willingness to overturn the land settlements increased the hostility of Irish Protestants to the king and his deputy, Talbot. Approximately 2,400 Protestant landowners fled from Ireland, while in Ulster a number of the planters started to arm themselves.

Because James had no sons, succession would pass to his Protestant daughter Mary, who in 1677 had married William of Orange. However, fifteen years after James's second marriage, in the spring of 1688, it was announced that Mary of Modena was pregnant. If the child was a boy, he would have prior claim to the throne over Mary. James issued a second Declaration of Indulgence that he insisted was to be read out in every Protestant church. When seven bishops refused on the grounds that James did not have the power to override parliament, he had them arrested. Although they were tried for sedition, the jury found them not guilty. Overall, James's actions lost him much support and demonstrated that he had misjudged the mood of the country.

Opposition to the king erupted when, on 10 June 1688, a son was born to Mary and James, and instantly rumours circulated that the birth was bogus, the baby probably being the child of a miller. A few weeks later a number of political leaders sent a secret letter to William of Orange, James's son-in-law, inviting him to come with an army and give support to a rising. In fact, they had been involved in negotiations with William since 1685, but the birth of a son changed everything. Apart from being Mary's husband, William was a significant figure within European politics. He was born in 1650, a grandson

of Charles I of England. The United Provinces of the Netherlands had chosen
him as their leader, or *stadholder*, in 1672. That year William had successfully
resisted Louis XIV when he attempted to invade the United Provinces. William
was undoubtedly interested in acquiring the English throne, but was waiting
for an appropriate opportunity. This moment appeared when France became
engaged in fighting in the Palatinate. William immediately sailed to England,
landing there on 5 November with 20,000 soldiers. James made William's
mission easier by fleeing to France. For James, the rejection must have been
particularly hurtful, because both his subjects and his family had betrayed
him. William promptly convened a parliament, which demonstrated its
gratitude by proclaiming William and Mary to be joint monarchs. While
James had lost the throne of England and Scotland, he was still king of
Ireland, and so Ireland, which had played no part in the English
constitutional crisis, was to move to the political centre stage.

The War of Two Kings

Although James II had ruled three kingdoms, he was predominantly
answerable to the English parliament. It was one of the most powerful in
Europe, as the principle of absolute monarchy had ceased to exist in England.
In contrast, the Irish parliament not only had little autonomy but was also
rarely given a chance to participate in the political process. Before the
constitutional crisis with James, the Irish parliament had been convened only
four times in the seventeenth century: from 1613 to 1615, 1634 to 1635,
1640 to 1641 and 1661 to 1666. The constitutional crisis in England
changed this situation.

The Williamite War indirectly involved many other European nations. In
Ireland, though, it was referred to as *Cogadh a Dá Rí*, or the War of Two
Kings. Each side took the name of the leader whom they supported. Following
William's entry to England, James had fled to France. His flight was
convenient for William, who did not have the problem of imprisoning James,
not only the rightful monarch but also his father-in-law. France at this stage
was the most powerful single state in Europe and was overwhelmingly
Catholic. Louis XIV also had a long-standing enmity with William and
wanted to weaken the power of the Netherlands. Louis encouraged James to
fight to regain his throne and promised him the support of French troops.
The larger problem was where the conflict should take place, as James had

little support in England and Scotland. Ireland, however, which contained a Catholic majority that had been dispossessed and disenfranchised by successive English governments, was a perfect base to launch the campaign. Moreover, Talbot (now Earl of Tyrconnell) remained in Ireland at the head of a predominantly Catholic army.

When James was deposed he lost the throne of England and Scotland but he legally continued to be king of Ireland. More practically, he retained control of Ireland through his lord lieutenant, Tyrconnell. James also sought to use the Irish parliament, which had not sat since 1666, to regain his throne. When the Irish Catholic gentry had lost their land, they had lost much of their remaining political power, as parliamentary representation was based on land ownership. Seventeenth-century parliaments, therefore, were dominated by Protestants. James had shown little interest in the Irish parliament until he was deposed. In 1689 elections were held for an Irish parliament, which met in May. It was predominantly Catholic, with only six Protestant members. Although James had convened the parliament, the Irish members demonstrated that they would not be content with a resumption of the status quo. They immediately passed legislation to give Ireland some measure of independence, removing the control of the English parliament and English laws in the country. The parliament's major demand was that the land confiscated by Cromwell should be returned, and that the Catholic Church should be given parity with the Anglican Church. If these changes took place they would support the right of an English king to rule them, although they still wanted their own parliament. James knew that by agreeing to these proposals, ultimately he was weakening his own position if he regained the throne, and undermining his position with potential non-Catholic supporters in England. Yet, without the support of Ireland his chances of becoming king again were slim, and so he reluctantly agreed. James probably underestimated the frustration of Irish Catholics. Without his approval they passed an Act of Attainder that declared as traitors the Protestants who had left Ireland upon Tyrconnell's appointment, and confiscated their land. This action inflamed Protestants and ultimately damaged James's cause.

The Protestants in Ireland were not a united group. The largest number of Protestants was clustered in Ulster; they were predominantly Scottish Presbyterian in origin. The nature of the plantation meant they comprised all social classes. In the other three provinces, Protestants were predominantly Anglicans and included a high proportion of landlords or wealthy merchants.

Ireland also counted a number of Protestant dissenter groups, including – in addition to the Presbyterians – Quakers, Baptists and Independents, all of whom refused to accept the teachings of the Episcopal Church. The Anglican Church, despite being the Church of the minority, was also the state church. Law did not recognise the Presbyterian Church. Although the two main Protestant Churches did not like each other, they were united in their dislike and distrust of the Catholic Church and its members. Traditionally, Protestants in Ireland had felt themselves protected by the English throne against the threat posed by Irish Catholics. James's actions changed the relationship of Irish Protestants with the monarch, and united the Church of Ireland with the Presbyterians.

James's military strategy to regain his throne began in March 1689 when he sailed from France to Ireland, landing at Kinsale. Shortly afterwards he was joined by 3,000 French troops, with a promise of more. They met with Talbot's Irish army. James's military command also included some Irish leaders: Patrick Sarsfield and Neil O'Neill. Sarsfield's ancestry was a mixture of Irish and Old English, which gave him a wide basis of support among Catholics. He had fought for France between 1675 and 1677, and his fearlessness and personal charisma meant that he had quickly risen to prominence in James's army. The Jacobite army, that is, troops that supported James, was led by Richard Hamilton. Initially it was successful, defeating a Protestant force in Dromore, County Down, in March. Triumphant with their victory, the Jacobite forces chose to attack the more strategically significant Protestant strongholds of Enniskillen and Derry. Almost immediately, the Jacobites embarked on the siege of Derry. However, there were some Protestant insurrections against James and in defence of William. The Protestants of south Ulster and Connacht formed a joint force that had headquarters at Enniskillen and Derry.

The city council in Derry decided initially to remain loyal to James, but in March 1689 they changed their allegiance to William. On 7 December 1688 thirteen apprentice boys had closed the gates of Derry against Catholic troops. The circulation of a letter, probably forged, that referred to the impending massacre of the city's Protestant population, had ignited their anger. This letter, rather than support for William, was the immediate trigger for their intervention. The closing of the city gates, however, came to symbolise their resistance to James. Despite the closing of the gates, the garrison of Protestant troops, under the command of Robert Lundy, was still loyal to James. This changed in March

1689 when Lundy accepted a new commission from William. At this stage, James's troops controlled the surrounding countryside, and he appeared confident that the city would fall. In April, James appeared in person to reclaim Derry City, but he was met with hostility and cries of 'No Surrender'. Lundy's willingness to surrender isolated him, and he fled the city shortly afterwards and thus became established in Protestant folklore as a traitor.

Lundy had argued that the walls of Derry were weak, the city was overpopulated and food supplies were limited. Yet James's troops were not well equipped to undertake a siege of a walled city such as Derry, and after a few unsuccessful attempts to assault the walls and gates, they decided to starve the population into surrender. They placed a boom on the estuary of the River Foyle, which made the city inaccessible by water. As a result of the conflict, Protestants from the surrounding countryside had sought refuge in the city. The population increased from its usual 2,000 inhabitants to almost 30,000, in addition to 7,000 troops. Food supplies were quickly exhausted and people started to die of hunger and, more commonly, disease. Relief came at the end of July when two ships carrying food broke through the boom. At this stage the food supplies were virtually exhausted. The siege had lasted for 105 days, and the defiance of the city was a significant victory for Protestant propaganda both at the time and subsequently.

During the summer of 1689 the war continued in a number of other locations. Williamite supporters in Enniskillen, Newtownbutler and Roscommon attacked the Jacobite troops, and on each occasion they were defeated. The Williamite troops captured Sligo town, but they were driven out in October by Patrick Sarsfield. Until this defeat, the Enniskillen troops had been regarded as invincible. In August 1689 William's commander, Marshal Frederick Schomberg, landed at Carrickfergus accompanied by 14,500 men, including English forces. Schomberg, a Protestant mercenary from Germany and a veteran of the Thirty Years War, was a personal favourite with William. Throughout the winter Schomberg's troops consolidated William's hold on Ulster. Although they reached as far as Dundalk, Schomberg decided not to fight James but to retreat to the safety of Antrim for the winter, during which half of his troops died of fever and dysentery. Schomberg's failure to extend the Williamite authority to Dundalk, and from there on to Dublin, lost him William's respect and trust.

Despite suffering a setback at the siege of Derry, James still presented a threat that William could not ignore. In June 1690 William reluctantly travelled to Ireland to take personal control of the fighting. His army, which was predominantly European, was approximately 37,000 in strength and was diverse in terms of its religious composition and nationality mix, Ulster Protestant troops fighting alongside soldiers and mercenaries from all over the continent, including Catholics from the Netherlands. Less than half of his men were English. He was also supported by troops from Brandenburg and Denmark, and French Huguenots, who had joined an alliance against Louis XIV. In spite of the association of James's campaign with Catholicism, William's challenge had papal support, the Pope disliking Louis's high-handed treatment of the Catholic Church in France. Apart from their numerical supremacy, William's troops were mostly well trained and well equipped.

James's army comprised approximately 6,000 French, German and Walloon troops and 19,000 Irish soldiers. His Irish troops had little military training, largely because Catholics had not been allowed to join the Irish army prior to 1685. Despite receiving some firearms from Louis, they were not very well equipped because the Irish treasury had reduced funds. The Jacobites had only twelve field guns, while William's army possessed thirty-six field guns and twelve siege guns. Significantly, James had little faith in his Irish troops, and in March 1690 had agreed with Louis to exchange five regiments of Irish troops for French ones. The Irish troops were to form the nucleus of the Irish Brigade in France. James's generals were also weakened by personality clashes that James did little to overcome. Tyrconnell disliked the French generals Lauzun and, later, Saint-Ruth, and all of them appeared jealous of Patrick Sarsfield, who, after the death of Neil O'Neill, became the most inspirational of the Irish leaders.

William's aim was to move from Ulster and take control of Dublin. The Jacobite troops, in turn, attempted to cut him off. The two armies met in an area north-west of Dublin where James hoped to stop William's progress southwards and where he believed that the River Boyne would provide a natural barrier. The main forces of the smaller Jacobite and Williamite armies respectively camped on the south and north side of the river, near to Oldcastle. Schomberg, however, led a large force up river, where he engaged with a small Jacobite force led by the romantic Gaelic leader Sir Neil O'Neill. By going to their support, James allowed William to cross at Oldcastle and defeat the remnants of the Jacobite army. Although Tyrconnell mounted a counter-attack, the advantage was with William's troops. The Jacobite army, now encircled, retreated without having fully engaged in battle with the enemy. The lack of sustained fighting meant that there were relatively few casualties: the Jacobite army lost 1,000 men, while the Williamite army only lost 500. The Williamite losses included Marshal Schomberg. Within a few days the Williamite troops had occupied Dublin – James was on his way to France and William was making plans to return to England. Despite the defeat at the Boyne and James's hasty departure, the Jacobite troops continued to fight, giving James more loyalty and support than he had earned or deserved in Ireland.

William's victory was celebrated not only in England and the Netherlands, but also throughout Europe by opponents of Louis XIV. In the Netherlands, where Catholics had complete religious freedom, they also celebrated William's victory. The Pope and the Catholic monarchs of Spain and Austria were also pleased, viewing the battle as a defeat for France. The Catholic rejoicing at William's victory was not mirrored in Ireland, where the battle was regarded as a victory for Protestantism. The battle of the Boyne had been, in every respect, an international conflict which had little to do with Ireland. None the less, it became the most commemorated battle in Irish history, and its outcome permeated and shaped subsequent generations of Irish Protestant memory.

In military terms, however, the battle of the Boyne was neither significant nor decisive. Most of the combat took place on one day, 1 July, later incorrectly celebrated on 12 July, partly because of the calendar reform in 1752 and also either a mathematical miscalculation or subsequent confusion with the date of the battle of Aughrim. The battle resulted in relatively few casualties and, more importantly, it did not end the war. Yet its symbolism was important. The battle of the Boyne was unique in that the two rival kings had been present on the battlefield. James's premature departure made him an object of derision on both sides. Propaganda by both sides exaggerated the battle's importance and perpetuated divides. In particular, it became depicted as a war for religious supremacy rather than a struggle between a British king and his parliament. Consequently, it shaped the development of a particular Protestant tradition in Ireland that was rooted in the need to fight to defend Protestantism. However, it was in the character and role of William of Orange that fabrication and embellishment were most marked. It was not until the 1790s that the battle received a central place in Protestant memory. Until that date commemorations of William had been centred either on his birth date (4 November) or the day that he arrived in England, 5 November, which coincided with the anniversary of the discovery of the Gunpowder Plot.

The battle of the Boyne gave William control of Dublin and eastern Ireland although the Jacobites remained dominant in Connacht and Munster. However, the war continued for another year, although without the personal leadership of either James or William. The hub of the fighting moved to the west of the country, where many of the Jacobite forces had gathered at Limerick. The leading commanders disagreed about what they should do next: Tyrconnell and the French commander, Lauzun, wanted to agree to terms with William, but the other Irish leaders, led by Sarsfield, wanted to continue to fight. The Williamite army, still under the command of William, reached Limerick on 8 August 1690, expecting that it would be relatively easy to capture. Sarsfield, however, mounted a counter-attack and delayed William's attack. When it did take place, the first siege was successfully resisted by the inhabitants and Irish soldiers. At this stage William decided to leave Ireland, as he was anxious to return to his European wars. He had been in the country for only ten weeks but had inflicted a psychological blow to both Jacobite aspirations and the prestige of Louis XIV. William was not only anxious to return to England, he also wanted to visit the Netherlands and direct his long-running conflict with Louis. William never returned to Ireland.

Following William's departure, his Dutch general, Ginkel, was put in command in Ireland. He was directed to finish the war as quickly as possible as William wanted his Dutch troops to support his European wars. William was not the only person to leave Ireland. Both Lauzun and Tyrconnell also left, taking the French troops with them. Their departure symbolised the ending of foreign support for the Jacobite cause, and Sarsfield was left with only a small army of Irish troops. The following May, James and Louis sent further French supplies and a French general, the Marquess of Saint-Ruth, to Ireland, but no further French troops were involved in the war. In the summer of 1691 Ginkel led the Williamite army westwards, crossing the Shannon at Athlone. A number of fierce conflicts took place, which forced the Jacobites to retire to Aughrim in County Galway, where a major encounter occurred on 12 July 1691. The Jacobite losses were massive, with about 7,000 fatalities, including Saint-Ruth, who was decapitated by a cannon ball. Sarsfield survived, and he and the remaining Jacobites returned to Limerick. Ginkel consolidated the victory at Aughrim by continuing on to Galway, where the city surrendered on 21 July.

The defeat at Aughrim meant that the Jacobites controlled only Limerick. Ginkel reached the city on 14 August and started a second siege. English warships bombarded the city from the sea and cut off its external links. Both sides wanted a rapid end to the conflict: Sarsfield knew that the remnants of the Irish army had no chance of victory, while Ginkel was anxious to return William's troops to the continent. They agreed to a ceasefire, and on 3 October signed a treaty. A few days later a French fleet arrived on the Shannon River, bringing food and military supplies to the city, but it was too late as the war was over. The treaty was negotiated and agreed to within only a few days. The negotiations were carried out between Ginkel, representing William, and Sarsfield, the leading Jacobite negotiator. The terms were relatively generous. Ginkel agreed that the Jacobite soldiers who had surrendered could return home, or join either William's or Louis's continental armies. Approximately 14,000 joined the French army and 1,000 joined William's army, while 2,000 returned to their homes. Those who left the country did so quickly, on a mixture of French and Dutch ships. Sarsfield went into exile again; he was killed in 1693 fighting on behalf of France. The Irish soldiers who went into exile in France were referred to as the 'Wild Geese'. They augmented Irish troops who were already part of Louis's army and had formed Irish brigades. Together they now formed twelve Irish regiments. Louis gave them the same conditions as French soldiers and granted them French citizenship. By the late eighteenth century the term Wild Geese denoted those who left Ireland to serve in a foreign army.

The Limerick Treaty guaranteed Roman Catholics the same rights of worship as they had enjoyed during the reign of Charles II. Both Ginkel and Sarsfield appeared to believe that Catholics would thus have parity with Protestants. Landowners in areas controlled by Jacobites were allowed to hold onto their lands if they took an oath of allegiance to William. In February 1692 William countersigned the treaty. Essentially the document was drawn up by a Dutch general and agreed to by a Dutch king. Irish Protestants, who were to benefit from William's victory, played no part in the negotiations. Many of them, in fact, were alarmed by the leniency of the treaty towards Catholics, even though they had been comprehensively defeated. They were also disturbed by the fact that much of the Jacobite army remained intact, even if it had relocated to France. They felt that the threat posed by James and by Irish Catholics had not been removed. Irish Protestants, therefore, demanded protection that was not guaranteed by the treaty. In 1691 the Irish parliament made it illegal for Irish men to be recruited by foreign powers. Regardless of this legislation, France and Spain continued to recruit Irish soldiers.

Because many of the articles of the treaty were couched in vague terms they were open to multiple interpretations. Almost immediately one of the main provisions of the treaty in regard to religious tolerance was broken, as in 1691 an act was passed that prohibited Catholics from sitting in parliament. This measure was an inauspicious start for Jacobites remaining in Ireland who had agreed to recognise William as king. The Irish who had fought for James were punished by their land being confiscated and becoming the property of the Crown. The land of Jacobites who chose to go to France was also confiscated. In total approximately 1 million acres of Irish land were confiscated.

As had become the general practice, the confiscated land was given to people who had fought for the victor, in this case William. Although his army was international, William favoured his Dutch followers over other nationalities, and they received particularly generous remuneration. His commander Ginkel was rewarded with a large estate and the title of the Earl of Athlone, while the largest amount of land was given to his two Dutch advisers, Arnold van Keppel and William Bentinck. The favouritism shown to Dutch supporters annoyed the English parliament, which, as had usually been the case, expected English soldiers to be the main beneficiaries. In 1700 it passed the Resumption Act, which William reluctantly agreed to. It stipulated that only seven of the grants made by William could be sustained and that the remainder of the confiscated land had to be sold. Irish Catholics were not permitted to purchase any of this property. Some of the smaller Jacobite landlords who had lost their lands and did not go into exile became 'rapparees', or outlaws. Angry at losing their lands and at the fate of James, they initially directed their resentment at the new Williamite landlords. With the passage of time, however, they blended in with other bandits and outlaws, surviving by plunder.

The war in Ireland had confirmed William as joint sovereign of Britain and Ireland. In England the war consolidated the process begun by the 'Glorious Revolution' in 1688 whereby the parliament asserted its right to authority over the British sovereign. The Irish parliament also benefited, after a century during which it had been only intermittently allowed to play a part in the government of Ireland. Following his defeat, James remained in France, his military standing and prestige having been damaged by his defeats in Ireland.

James's troops, especially the Irish ones, had been more loyal than he deserved. They were pawns in his larger game of regaining the British throne. James's defeat was also a blow for France. Even when the fighting ended in Ireland, England and France remained at war. Louis continued to plot against William, although he was motivated as much by his desire to control the continent as his support for James. In 1692 he planned an invasion of England. The invasion force consisted of 14,000 men, about half of whom were Irish. Patrick Sarsfield led them. The invasion was aborted following the defeat of the French fleet by a combination of the English and Dutch forces. Consequently the Irish Brigade did not get a chance to fight on British or Irish soil again, but had to join the other French regiments on the continent. In the longer term, though, the presence of the Irish Brigade meant that James and his successors were a threat to the security of the throne and the safety of the land settlements in Ireland. France continued to be a centre of Jacobite intrigue, providing a base for a Jacobite rebellion in 1745. In the same year Irish soldiers also fought in the battle of Fontenoy between France and England. It was not until the middle of the eighteenth century that the Jacobite threat seemed to be over, following the defeat of the Jacobites at Culloden in 1746, and France finally ended its support for a Stuart restoration. Although recruitment to the Irish Brigade shrank following this double defeat, it was not finally abandoned until the outbreak of the French Revolution in 1789.

The Penal Age

In the wake of William's victory a body of legislation known as the Penal Laws was passed. The passage of these laws was perhaps surprising because within the Netherlands Catholics enjoyed the same rights as Protestants, and William showed no desire to penalise Irish Catholics. However, after 1691 William regarded Ireland as a small and unimportant part of his large kingdom and he devoted little attention to it. His main concern was that Ireland should be secured against further uprisings and this, in effect, had come to mean that power should lie in the hands of the minority Protestant gentry. Apart from land, the Protestant gentry also again controlled the Irish parliament. The Penal Laws, however, were designed to weaken irrevocably what little economic and political power the Catholic gentry had left. Culturally they were also weakened, as the Irish language and Irish poetry and literature were reviled and marginalised. English, and to a far lesser extent, Scots Gaelic or Dutch were the languages of the new master class. Irish increasingly became the language of the poor native Irish. Above all, Protestantism, or rather Anglicanism, was supreme. What made the Penal Laws different from religious restrictions elsewhere was the fact that in Ireland the persecuted formed the majority of the population. The laws were justified on the grounds that a hostile Catholic population surrounded the Protestant minority. Moreover, Britain was still involved in a European war against France, and the Irish Catholics had shown that France was their ally of choice.

The Penal Laws covered a wide range of social, economic and political areas. Although they were sometimes referred to as anti-Popery legislation, in fact they favoured only members of the Anglican Church, with Catholics and dissenting Protestants being treated as second-class subjects. Some of the legislation was specifically directed against Catholicism. It was not only Catholics in Ireland who were feared but also those who lived in Britain, and so the legislation generally applied to England, Ireland, Scotland and Wales. Many of the Penal Laws were passed by the English parliament, but the Irish parliament did not object as it viewed the legislation as a way of propping up the Irish Protestant parliament. Their enforcement, however, was sporadic. In 1697 an act was passed that banished Catholic bishops and clergy from the country. Parish priests were allowed to stay, though they had to register with the authorities and recognise William as their king. About 1,000 priests accepted these terms and remained in Ireland. Because no new priests could be ordained in Ireland, it was expected that the clergy would cease to exist. A small number of bishops did stay in Ireland secretly and they remained in contact with Rome. France also provided a base for the training of new priests. Because church building was not allowed and the Church had little income, mass and other sacraments were sometimes performed in the open air. A further source of irritation was that Catholics had to pay tithes (taxes) for the upkeep of the minority Anglican Church. This requirement was later extended to include all Protestant dissenters.

While much of the legislation was concerned with undermining the power of the gentry and middle classes, the penal legislation affected all classes of Catholics, and even if it was not always strictly enforced, it was a source of grievance to all members of the Church. Ironically, the legislation may have increased the influence of the Catholic Church over the people, as priests became their natural leaders. At the same time, the legislation had increased the divide between Protestant landlords and Catholic tenants. The opening of schools was also banned by the penal legislation, giving rise to the 'hedge schools'. This legislation was mainly directed at the Catholic gentry and professional class. Trinity College in Dublin, which was the only university in the city, did not allow Catholics to take degrees. Although Catholics could not train as lawyers, they were allowed to be doctors, merchants and traders. The educational restrictions made it difficult, however, for the children of middle-class Catholics to advance. Becoming Protestant ended these restrictions.

Some of the penal legislation had serious long-term consequences by undermining the economic position of Catholics. Land was the key to power, and so it was subject to special consideration. Traditionally, if a landowner died, the land passed to his eldest son. One of the laws stipulated that all land had to be divided equally among all of his sons. If one son converted to Protestantism, he would become the sole inheritor. One of the most serious penal acts was the 'act to prevent the further growth of Popery', which ended the right of Catholics either to inherit or to purchase property. Catholics were also forbidden to purchase land that had belonged to Protestants. The impact of this legislation combined with the Williamite confiscation was swift and comprehensive. At the start of the Williamite War, Catholic gentry owned approximately 22 per cent of land; by 1703 this had dropped to 14 per cent.

It was not only landownership that was affected. The loss of economic power was accompanied by loss of political influence, as after 1691 Catholics could not be members of parliament, county sheriffs or magistrates. Catholics also lost the right to vote in parliamentary elections. They were also denied access to the professions; they were forbidden from becoming army or naval officers. Other restrictions were intended to be demeaning and to undermine the social status of Catholics, such as prohibiting them from carrying a pistol or sword, or riding an expensive horse. Overall, the Penal Laws appeared to Catholics, whether or not they had fought for James and whether or not they had remained in Ireland, to be a betrayal of the Treaty of Limerick. Although there was some laxness in their enforcement especially in the west of the country, the laws confirmed Catholics as second-class subjects within both Ireland and Britain. The harshness of the laws persuaded some Catholics to convert to Protestantism. Inevitably, the laws had a dramatic impact on Catholic landownership, which had fallen substantially in the previous century anyway; within two generations it had fallen to 5 per cent.

William's victory was the death knell for the old Gaelic Catholic world, while the new Penal Laws marginalised the political, social and economic position of the Irish Catholic gentry. Land continued to be the basis of power, being necessary to qualify for both public and political office. During the seventeenth century both land and political powers were taken from Catholics in a number of ways. At the beginning of the sixteenth century, most of the land in Ireland had been in the hands of Catholics; by the end of the century, Catholic landownership had largely been confined to the west of the River Shannon. This process had been achieved through a mixture of policies, war, confiscation and plantations. The Penal Laws were another blow to the aspirations of the leaders of Gaelic and Catholic Ireland. The plantation and Penal Laws together completed what centuries of conquest, anti-Gaelic legislation and occasional conciliation had failed to do.

While much of the penal legislation was directed against Catholics, some of it was intended to penalise dissenting Protestants, particularly Presbyterians. This behaviour was particularly disappointing for Presbyterians in Ulster, who had been one of the first groups to pledge their support to William. Although Scottish Presbyterians had been encouraged to settle in Ireland during the plantation, they did not have equal rights with English settlers. Presbyterian ministers were not recognised in law, which meant that the marriage ceremonies they performed had no legal status. During the Williamite War, restrictions against the Presbyterian Church had been ignored, and many Presbyterians expected this to remain the case after the war was over. The Church of Ireland hierarchy, however, did not so much view the defeat of William as a victory for Protestantism as for the Anglican Church. With the threat posed by Catholicism apparently ended, the Presbyterian Church appeared to be in a position to gain more authority within Ireland, being well organised and financially secure. The various wars and confiscations under Cromwell and William had increased Scottish immigration to Ireland. In Scotland, the Presbyterian Church had benefited from the defeat of James. In return for the Scottish parliament accepting William as the king of Britain, the Presbyterian Church had been made the state church in Scotland. The elevation of the Scottish Church alarmed Irish Anglicans as their supremacy was based on political support rather than numerical strength.

William's success was largely due to his support from all Protestants, and in 1689 the English parliament passed a law granting religious toleration to all dissenters. No similar law was introduced in Ireland. Moreover, additional restrictions were placed on Irish Presbyterians. In 1704 the Irish parliament passed an act that banned Presbyterians from being members of town councils and from being members of parliament. Effectively, this meant Anglicans controlled both local and central government. Concurrently with these restrictions, the Presbyterians did benefit from changes imposed by a grateful William, who had been in favour or religious toleration, but this was opposed by a newly empowered Irish parliament. William revived the *regium donum*, a state grant for the payment of Presbyterian ministers that had been introduced by Charles II but abolished by James II. The payment was short-lived, as in 1716, in response to hysteria among the Anglican Church hierarchy, it was again abolished. In 1719, under George I, Irish Presbyterians were granted freedom of worship, although they were still excluded from holding some offices in local and central government. Unlike Catholics, though, they could carry arms, practise their religion openly and vote in elections. Despite the disabilities, they remained loyal to the Protestant monarch. Overall the treatment of Presbyterians in Ireland contributed to large-scale emigration from the north of Ireland in the second half of the eighteenth century. Many of the settlers went to the North American colonies, where they remained within the British Empire yet encountered religious toleration. By the 1770s an estimated 12,000 Presbyterians were leaving Ireland each year. By this stage, Presbyterianism had established deep roots in Ireland. What the Penal Laws had demonstrated was that Catholics and Presbyterians were both disliked and feared by the Anglican Church.

Parliament and People

The seventeenth century had been characterised by intermittent conflict between the king and the English and Scottish parliaments. The Civil War and the Glorious Revolution had changed the balance of power between king and parliament, with the latter gaining ascendancy. When William and Mary were offered the throne in 1688, the English parliament, supported by the Scottish one, had outlined the terms of settlement, which included the succession and also a bill of rights. The bill outlined a number of civil liberties and renounced the power of a monarch to suspend or dispense with laws. It stipulated that the British monarch might neither be nor marry a Catholic. The monarch was forbidden from keeping an army in peacetime except with the permission of parliament. William's relationship with his

English parliament was just as fraught as that of his predecessor had been, parliament disagreeing with him on his interventions in the Irish land settlements, the size of the civil list, financial support for his army, triennial elections in England, and a political union with Scotland. William, in turn, tried to maintain a balance between the two major forces within English politics, the Whigs and the Tories, while not becoming the pawn of either.

Apart from the land settlements, William showed little interest in Ireland following the battle of the Boyne. The Irish parliament, however, which had returned to its Protestant profile, hoped to benefit from having William as joint monarch. The Irish parliament had played a minor role within both the Irish and the Crown's seventeenth-century government, being convened only four times between the ascent of James I in 1603 and the hereditary crisis of 1688. On each of these occasions the main motivation for calling a parliament had been financial. William, despite his victory over James, needed the Irish parliament in order to obtain funds to implement the Treaty of Limerick. Because he required their financial support, he was unwilling to alienate the parliamentarians by insisting on more religious toleration in Ireland. The Irish parliament, which at the end of the fifteenth century had lost its political autonomy, viewed the various crises in England as a way to regain some of its powers. The 1689 parliament, which was almost completely Catholic, asserted the exclusive right of the Irish parliament to legislate for Ireland. Even James balked at this. The problem was that an independent Irish parliament would threaten both the English and Protestant interest in Ireland, and this was unacceptable to Protestants in Ireland and England. Although the Anglican gentry were beneficiaries of the Williamite War because of the enhanced role given to the Irish parliament after a century of being disregarded, the rights won by the English parliament after 1688 were not extended to Irish parliamentarians. The Penal Laws provided a mechanism for denying Irish Catholics (and Presbyterians) political rights, but even an exclusively Anglican Irish parliament was to remain subordinate to Westminster.

In spite of the wide range of restrictions, not only did Catholicism survive, but by the second half of the eighteenth century a Catholic middle class was emerging. A Catholic party also appeared, led by Charles O'Conor of Belanagare, who argued that being a Catholic did not mean being a disloyal subject. The Seven Years War from 1756 to 1763 provided an opportunity for some middle-class Irish Catholics to demonstrate their loyalty. They promised that not only would they not ally with the Crown's foreign (and

Catholic) enemies, but that they were willing to fight on behalf of the king. The Irish parliament, alarmed by an increase in agrarian outrages by Catholic secret societies, did not support the claims of Catholic loyalty. Instead, in 1766 the Tumultuous Risings Act was passed, which was the first of many coercion acts introduced into Ireland. Father Nicholas Sheehy, who had allegedly incited a group known as the Whiteboys, was hanged, drawn and quartered. Despite the repression, agrarian secret societies continued to flourish, and as relationships between Catholic tenant and Protestant landlord deteriorated, such organisations became the defenders of the peasantry. What these decades showed was that there were significant differences between the aspirations of the poor rural Irish Catholics and those of the urban upper- and middle-class Catholics.

In 1699 the English parliament passed the Wool Act, which prevented the export of wool and woollen cloth from Ireland. The Irish parliament and Protestant landowners objected to this act, as the trade had been extremely lucrative for Irish merchants. It also demonstrated that Irish interests were to be subordinate to English ones. Some Irish MPs, led by William Molyneux, challenged the right of the English parliament to make laws for Ireland. The basis of his argument was not that only Irish people had a right to legislate for Ireland, but rather that as many wealthy Protestants regarded themselves as Englishmen living in Ireland, they should have the same rights as Englishmen living in England. While much of the penal legislation had been welcomed by the Irish parliament, the passage of the Wool Act in 1699 created a division between the English and Irish legislatures. Although the Irish parliament resented its lack of power, ultimately it relied on England for protection, from both Catholics and Jacobites. One solution to the division between the parliaments was to have a political union. In 1703 the Irish House of Commons proposed that England and Ireland should have a single parliament. The English parliament rejected this proposal but instead in 1719 passed legislation reaffirming the right of the English parliament to legislate for Ireland and the English High Court to overrule any judgments made by Irish courts. The English parliament's rejection of the proposed union with Ireland indicated that Ireland was not regarded as politically equal. In 1707, however, a union between the English and Scottish parliaments took place, which, despite a shaky start, marked an important step in the creation of a British identity that shared a common monarchy, religion and parliament.

James II died in exile in France in 1701. William died in the following year after falling off his horse. Mary had died in 1694 and, because she and William had no heirs, the succession moved to her sister, Anne (r. 1702–14), also a daughter of James II. Although Mary had been joint sovereign with her husband, she had chosen to leave all executive authority in his hands. Anne's ascent to the throne in 1702 was unexpected, and she inherited from her brother-in-law both a faction-ridden parliament and an expensive war with France. Her major legacy was the parliamentary union with Scotland, which created the beginning of a unitary British state with a single parliament in Westminster. Although the Scottish union had raised hopes that a similar scheme might be extended to Ireland, this was not the case. However, fear of Irish Catholics was a more powerful concern for the Irish Protestant ascendancy than a desire for political parity with Britain. Anne died without any surviving children and parliament approved of a Hanoverian prince, the Duke of Hanover, to succeed her. He ascended to the British throne in 1714 as George I (r. 1714–27). For Protestants, George's nationality, and the fact that he mostly ruled from Hanover and did not bother to learn English, was of less interest to them than his Protestantism, which they believed would safeguard their position. He left the government of England in the hands of a group of capable administrators, including Sir Robert Walpole, who was mockingly referred to as 'Prime Minister', a label that endured.

Irish Protestants were satisfied with the British succession. None the less, the issue of who had the right to legislate for Ireland and the restrictions that had been imposed on Irish trade continued to irritate them. In 1720, following a dispute over the jurisdiction of England to legislate for Ireland, the British parliament passed the Declaratory Act 'for the better securing the dependency of the kingdom of Ireland on the crown of Britain'. This act confirmed what was already in existence, yet it became a long-running source of grievance to the Irish parliament. The dissatisfaction of middle-class Protestants found an outlet in the satirical pen of Jonathan Swift, who blamed the poverty of the mass of the Irish people on the restrictions imposed on Irish trade. His message that England was the cause of Irish poverty had a wider public appeal that even he had expected. Swift, who was ambivalent about his own nationality – seeing himself as an Englishman in Ireland – had inadvertently also sown the seeds of Protestant nationalism. The fourth of the *Drapier's Letters* significantly was addressed 'To the whole people of Ireland', an inclusive view that was unusual. By satirising the political relationship between England and Ireland and by appealing to the Irish nation, Swift had given the question of national rights priority over the more usual preoccupation with either Catholic or Protestant rights.

The Jacobite struggle continued even after the death of James II. James's son, James Edward, whose birth in 1688 had triggered the Williamite War, continued the struggle to gain the kingdoms of Britain and Ireland. Although he referred to himself as James III, his enemies mockingly labelled him the 'Old Pretender'. Within Britain, Scotland was the stronghold of Jacobite support and it became the base for some attempted coups in the early part of the eighteenth century. The most sustained threat came in 1745 when James III's son, Charles Edward, or the 'Young Pretender', landed in Scotland, where he was joined by an army of mainly Catholic Highlanders, and together they marched on England. They reached Derby before deciding, possibly prematurely, to retreat to Scotland. When Charles Edward landed in Scotland he was accompanied by some of the Wild Geese. The Jacobite uprising also had support in Ireland, including that of some disaffected Protestant gentry. The wider Catholic population, however, played no part in supporting the uprising, as the intervening fifty years since they had first supported the Jacobite cause had left them leaderless, disarmed and demoralised. The latest defeat of a Jacobite possibly added to their disaffection, but in reality had little impact on their everyday lives. Charles Edward's army was convincingly defeated at the battle of Culloden in 1746. It was a crushing blow to Stuart and Catholic hopes of regaining the British monarchy. In 1766 James III, the Old Pretender, died. His death symbolised the end of Stuart aspirations. The Papacy, which had supported William's wars in Ireland, had reverted to its support of Catholic ambitions after the war was over. Following the death of James III, the Pope ceased to support the claims of the Stuart family.

Poverty and Progress

The outcome of the various changes in landownership was to replace a Catholic landowning elite with a Protestant landowning elite. For tenants and agricultural labourers, the impact was less dramatic. The upheavals in parliamentary government also had little impact on the lives of the majority of people. For some of the more enterprising, emigration was an option. The majority, however, stayed in Ireland. The eighteenth century was marked by a growing dependence of the poorer classes on potatoes, a wonder vegetable that had been introduced by Sir Walter Ralegh from America in the late sixteenth century. The vulnerability of the Irish poor had been publicised by Jonathan Swift in his attacks on trade restrictions in a number of widely read pamphlets, such as the *Drapier's Letters* (1724) and the ironic *Modest Proposal* (1729), in which he suggested the Irish poor could eat their own children if they were hungry. The destitution of Irish peasants had less to do with the religion of the landlords than with decades of war, confiscation and unfavourable trading conditions. The growth in population in the eighteenth century also placed pressure on the land, but potatoes provided a means of feeding large numbers of people on small plots of poor-quality land. For the poorer classes, the payment of a tithe to the Anglican Church was both a financial and a psychological burden. The poverty of the country was made more noticeable by the fact that Ireland was socially polarised, with a small middle class of either farmers or professionals.

The majority of Irish people continued to speak Irish, although it had come to be regarded as the language of poverty rather than of a culturally rich civilisation. The Gaelic lords who had given shelter and patronage to itinerant poets had disappeared, and poets were now men of the people, having lost their privileged status. Their songs, stories and poems, however, provided an outlet for political and social grievances. They also kept alive the memory of a heroic, if tragic, past in which Irish identity was both Gaelic and Catholic. But for poor Irish people, with their leaders gone, who could bring such glories back to Ireland? Ironically, perhaps, they did not allude to a return of the old system of Gaelic kingship; instead the aspirations of many Irish Catholics centred on the return of a Stuart monarch. Their faith in the Stuart dynasty was probably imprudent; the Stuart kings had no affinity with Ireland and had shown little interest in the country until the crisis of 1688. Moreover, in the war that ensued, James II used Ireland and brought bloodshed and ruin to his supporters.

Despite widespread poverty, the Irish economy did expand in some sectors. The economic development was not evenly spread but concentrated mostly in Dublin. Since 1600 the population of the city had grown rapidly, largely mirroring its commercial expansion. Within Ireland the city was pre-eminent, containing the only university in the country, the courts of law, the national parliament and the lord lieutenant's viceregal court. Increasingly, the wealthy Irish gentry spent their winters in Dublin, thus promoting the emergence of a leisure industry, notably a lively theatre culture. In the eighteenth century the city underwent an architectural renaissance manifested in the erection of a number of civic buildings, including a new parliament at College Green, an extension of Trinity College, the opening of the Rotunda 'Lying-in' Hospital and the construction of a new Custom House, the Four Courts, the Carlisle Bridge and the Royal Exchange. Much of the rebuilding of Dublin was associated with the architect James Gandon, who was awarded a gold medal for architecture by the newly founded Royal Academy. After 1700 linen production expanded in the north and west of the country, and in 1711 a Linen Board was established to regulate the fast-expanding industry. By the end of the century the lucrative linen business had become concentrated in the north-east of the country, with Belfast being a major beneficiary. The emergence of Belfast as a cultural centre was reflected in the launch of newspapers such as the *News-Letter* in 1737 and the opening of the Linen Hall Library, which was founded by the Belfast Reading Society in 1788. The eighteenth century also witnessed some notable literary and cultural achievements. Although the Gaelic poets lost their privileged position in society, a cluster of Anglo-Irish writers who were Protestant and whose allegiance was to England filled the cultural vacuum. They included Edmund Burke, R.B. Sheridan, Bishop George Berkeley and Oliver Goldsmith. They appealed to an educated middle-class audience in both Ireland and Britain.

In the winter of 1739 to 1740 a great frost descended on Ireland that was remarkable for its longevity and intensity. Throughout Europe the winter was particularly cold, though many European countries were more used to harsh weather than was Ireland. Major lakes and rivers in Ireland, such as Lough Neagh, the Liffey, the Boyne and the Foyle, were frozen, not only killing fish but also limiting access to and from the country. Food and fuel quickly became scarce, and famine and fever followed. Public and private interventions were small and inadequate. Despite the extreme weather conditions, the British parliament showed little interest in intervening. Britain was involved in fighting a war with France and was preoccupied with the possibility of another Jacobite insurrection. Financing social welfare was a low priority, and few suitable administrative structures existed even if such action had been seriously considered. The consequences of the famine were significant. Out of a population of almost 2½ million, as many as 20 per cent died as a result of the catastrophe. Consequently, Ireland had possibly the highest proportionate mortality rate in Europe in the wake of the frost. Among Irish-speakers 1740 was referred to as *bliain an áir*, that is, 'the year of the slaughter'. Centuries of war and conquest had not destroyed the poor population of Ireland as effectively as one freezing winter had.

The Irish population grew rapidly after 1740, although the poorer classes were increasingly dependent on a single crop, the potato. Despite ongoing tensions between the Catholic Gaelic population and the increasingly powerful Protestant landowning elite, there were no major political or religious upheavals. This allowed the hold of Protestant Britain in Ireland to be consolidated, and, significantly, Englishmen were appointed to the main offices of state. The emergence of Protestant opposition to British rule that had been evident at the beginning of the eighteenth century, sometimes referred to as 'colonial nationalism', re-emerged during the American War of Independence. However, the new Irish patriots wanted only the right to government themselves, and not full independence. Their actions were to contribute to a train of events that culminated in a violent uprising in 1798, which changed the course of both Irish and British history.

SEVEN

REBELLION TO REPEAL
c. 1780–1845

The uprising in 1798 marked the start of the republican physical-force tradition in Ireland. It also marked an attempt to take religion out of Irish politics and replace it with citizenship. The British government responded to the uprising brutally (30,000 Irish people were killed – far more than died during the Reign of Terror in France).

This chapter examines the consequences of the rising, in particular the creation of the United Kingdom. After 1800, however, the demands for political independence did not disappear but re-emerged in the form of the repeal movement. Concurrently, militant Protestantism was reorganising, centred on the newly established Orange Order.

Protestant Patriots

While the Jacobite threat and the growth in Catholic secret societies had alarmed the British and Irish governments, the most serious challenge to the eighteenth-century status quo came from an unexpected quarter. A war in a distant British colony was to have dramatic long-term consequences for Ireland, Britain and the rest of Europe. A new factor had also entered British politics, since defence of the empire, which was still growing, became a major consideration.

Britain's empire included thirteen colonies on the eastern seaboard of North America. The intervention of the British parliament in American affairs had been minimal until 1760. America, however, was expected to support Britain during the Seven Years War. The colonies, which were self-governing and highly politicised, objected to the increasing political and fiscal intervention by Britain following the end of the war in 1763. The American War of Independence was triggered by the various taxes imposed by Britain in the 1770s, in particular on stamps and tea. The leaders included Samuel

Adams, Benjamin Franklin and Thomas Jefferson. A number of Irish-born immigrants were prominent supporters of the revolution, including John Dunlop, who had been born in County Tyrone, Charles Thompson of County Derry and Aedanus Burke, born in County Galway.

On 4 July 1776 Jefferson published the Declaration of Independence. The British monarch, George III, was personally blamed for many of the colonies' grievances. Other European countries used Britain's colonial problems as an opportunity to declare war against Britain: France in 1778, Spain in 1779 and the Netherlands in 1780. All of these factors imposed a heavy financial demand that led the British parliament to call for an end to the war. In 1783 Britain agreed to a ceasefire, retaining her colonies of Canada and the West Indies but conceding the loss of the thirteen colonies which were recognised as the United States of America. The loss of the colonies was a major psychological blow to Britain's imperial project.

The American War of Independence popularised a new vocabulary among European radicals, as ideologies such as republicanism, liberalism and nationalism entered the political discourse. These ideologies were given a more immediate relevance by the revolution in France in 1789. In Ireland, however, the parallels between the Irish and the American situations had been clear to many immediately: they shared the same imperial masters and, though both America and Ireland had parliaments or representative assemblies, ultimately power lay at Westminster. Many Irishmen sympathised with the demands of the American colonists. Nor was it just Catholics who felt empathy. The ties between the colonists and the Ulster Presbyterians were strong after decades of emigration to colonial America, and some of the emigrants played a direct role in revolution and drawing up the Declaration of Independence in 1776.

Even before the American Revolution some British politicians had favoured giving political rights to Catholics, primarily as a way of counterbalancing the power of obstructive Irish Protestants. The same Irish Protestants, however, had resisted any dilution of their supremacy. Fighting wars with the colonists and the French changed the situation, as the British government could argue that national security required that a traditionally hostile Catholic population be conciliated. Moreover, the British army needed new recruits and it was not practical to prohibit Catholics from enlisting. The British government initiated a new approach with the passage in 1778 of the first Relief Act, which would allow Catholics to take leases for 999 years and to inherit land in the same way as Protestants. British politicians had underestimated the acrimonious opposition that the bill engendered in the Irish Parliament. The bill was passed because the British parliament coerced Irish MPs into accepting it. One of the arguments used by the opponents of the bill was that once concessions to Catholics had been granted, they would be endless. Middle-class Catholics did regard this act as a beginning, and with each subsequent Relief Act their position strengthened while, conversely, that of the Protestant ascendancy diminished.

The concessions made to Catholics disguised the fact that by the end of the eighteenth century Britain had become an overtly and aggressively Protestant nation – a shared religion having contributed to the emergence of a common British identity. For some Protestants, the lifting of the penal legislation against Catholics was not only misguided but also dangerous. The Gordon Riots in 1780 were prompted by the introduction of the Catholic Relief Act in 1778, which allowed Catholics to join the army. A militant MP, Lord George Gordon, who founded the Protestant Association in 1780, led the opposition. He was against ending religious discrimination towards Catholics in either Britain or Ireland. Gordon also argued that allowing Irish Catholics into the British army was particularly dangerous, as they had already demonstrated their empathy with France and Spain. Approximately 55,000 'No Popery' protesters marched to the Houses of Parliament in London, led by Gordon. The resultant rioting lasted for four days, with as many as 300 fatalities. Roman Catholic churches and homes were destroyed or burned. Twenty-one of the organisers were hanged, though Gordon was acquitted. What the riots demonstrated was that, for some extreme Protestants, being a Catholic was synonymous with being a traitor.

The American Revolution had many repercussions within Europe. France was sympathetic to the American revolutionaries and declared war on Britain in 1778. War with France was not unusual, and it resulted in renewed fears that Ireland might be invaded and used as a back entrance into Britain. The British government, however, anxious to break the sympathetic ties that existed between Irish Catholics and France, responded with conciliatory rather than coercive tactics. Also, while the American revolutionaries had popular support in Ireland, Britain wanted the support of the Irish parliament to help finance the war with France.

In 1778 Britain received a spontaneous expression of support as the threat of invasion by France resulted in Irish Protestants (both Anglicans and

Presbyterians) forming a volunteer militia force in Ireland. The Volunteers replaced the regular army that had been removed to fight in the American colonies. Catholics were excluded from the movement because they were still prohibited from carrying arms. By 1782 an estimated 60,000 Irish middle-class Protestants had enrolled in the militia. They were led by members of the Protestant gentry and aristocracy, including Henry Flood, the Earl of Charlemont, the Duke of Leinster and Henry Grattan. Ireland was not invaded, and the movement transformed into a political lobby group. One of their main grievances concerned the trade restrictions imposed by the British parliament, and after 1779 their campaign centred on the demand for free trade.

The restrictions imposed on Irish exports were a long-standing grievance in the Irish parliament. Unlike Scotland, Ireland was not allowed to trade freely with other British colonies, and some Irish commodities, such as wool, could be exported only to England. Anger mounted after 1776 when an embargo was imposed on food exports as a way of preserving supplies for the army fighting in America. The fact that this measure coincided with a general economic downturn moved the issue of free trade to the top of the political agenda. The Westminster parliament, anxious to appease the Irish government, in 1778 supported the right of Ireland to have free trade with other British colonies. British manufacturers who wanted to retain a monopoly on Irish exports successfully opposed the legislation, however. Their intervention led to a boycott of British goods in Ireland and a number of public demonstrations orchestrated by the Volunteers. They frequently gathered at the statue of William III in Dublin, because William was viewed as a guardian of parliamentary rights, rather than simply as a defender of Protestantism. The language of the protesters was increasingly militant, with the demand for free trade merging with more general appeals for parliamentary reform and more rights for Catholics. The Irish parliament demonstrated its support for free trade by voting taxes for only six rather than the usual twelve months. At the end of 1779 the British government announced that export restrictions would be lifted from glass and wool, and Ireland would be allowed to trade freely with other British colonies.

The success of the Volunteers in acquiring more trading rights encouraged them to extend their agitation. A long-standing grievance was the fact that while English subjects were protected by habeas corpus, which prohibited imprisonment without trial, no comparable legal protection existed in Ireland. In the new climate of patriotism, similar rights were demanded for Irish people, and an act of 1782 extended the rights guaranteed by habeas corpus to Ireland. After 1780 the Volunteers became more overtly political, and this resulted in the meeting of the Dungannon Convention in February 1782. These Protestant patriots demanded the granting of legislative independence for Ireland. They argued that the British parliament's authority over the Irish parliament was both illegal and unconstitutional. The following year a Volunteer National Convention in Dublin developed further their plans for parliamentary reform. The more radical members also added limited voting rights for Catholics to their demands, and more protectionism for Irish trade. The Irish House of Commons, disliking the autonomy displayed by the Volunteers, rejected their suggestions.

War with the American colonies had made Britain vulnerable. The Volunteers combined moral-force tactics – holding large public displays and parades – with belligerent rhetoric. Just as worryingly, the Volunteers had a quasi-military aspect: they were organised into military corps, they were uniformed and they were armed. Visually, therefore, they also presented a challenge to the British government. Of most consequence perhaps was the language of the movement, which suggested that Irish Protestants were acquiring an Irish identity. The Dungannon Convention responded to the Catholic Relief Bill by asserting that 'as men and as Irishmen, as Christians and as Protestants, we rejoice in the relaxation of the penal laws'. Significantly, these Irish Protestants viewed themselves as Irishmen, rather than as Englishmen in Ireland. They also argued that having legislative independence would not diminish their loyalty to Britain. In April 1782 the British government acceded to the demand for legislative independence. The new parliament was named after its first leader, Henry Grattan. In real terms, Grattan's parliament did not have total autonomy. The British parliament still had ultimate control over taxation, and the power to go to war or make truces. Moreover, Britain continued to govern Ireland indirectly though the lord lieutenant in Dublin Castle. Within Ireland also, political power remained in the hands of a small Protestant elite whose supremacy was based on the ownership of land. None the less, the fact that the lifting of trade restrictions and Grattan's parliament coincided with an economic revival meant that parliamentary independence became associated with prosperity.

The early triumphs of the Volunteers encouraged some members to broaden their campaign. The Volunteers were essentially a middle-class movement, but some members wanted it to have a more popular base, including Catholics. James Napper Tandy was one of the advocates of including artisans and the working classes in the movement and radicalising its demands. The inclusion of lower-class Catholics and Protestants alarmed some of its wealthier Protestant leaders, who had no desire to lead a mass popular movement in Ireland. Some Protestant gentry were also unhappy with the inclusion of Catholic demands in their campaign. Although they were willing to grant some concessions, ultimately they desired the maintenance of the Protestant ascendancy. The British government had also become alarmed that an organisation they had created for defence had transformed itself into a powerful political machine. The threat of British intervention allowed conservative leaders, such as the Earl of Charlemont, to regain control of the movement and discourage its radicalism.

In 1788 George III was declared insane and parliament decided that a regent, the Prince of Wales, should rule Britain and Ireland. The Irish parliament, led by Henry Grattan, objected to having a regent foisted on it without consultation. The dispute ended only when George apparently recovered his sanity a few months later. The conflict demonstrated that despite the apparent political stability of Grattan's parliament, aspects of the relationship between Britain and Ireland remained fraught. Yet it was the crisis of the French king rather than the British monarchy that was to shape the political future of Ireland. In the short term the French Revolution generated a new spirit of radicalism in Ireland, which included a brief revival of the Volunteer movement and the formation of a radical nationalist group, the United Irishmen (see p. 138). For a while it appeared that the United Irishmen and the Volunteers might work together for a radical parliamentary reform. A series of repressive measures by the British government undermined any real involvement by the Volunteer movement, while some of its more radical members moved closer to the United Irishmen.

The Catholic gentry and middle classes, who had been the main losers from the land confiscations and Penal Laws, found they had a small but influential number of champions among Protestants in both the Irish and British parliaments in the second half of the eighteenth century. The traditional divide within Protestantism between Anglicans and dissenters was replaced by allegiances based more on political outlook – that is, radical, liberal, conservative or militant Protestantism. This realignment was to have significant consequences for Catholics and Protestants alike.

Rebellion

The outbreak of the French Revolution in July 1789 had dramatic repercussions throughout Europe. Initially the overthrow of the French monarch and the establishment of a National Assembly were welcomed in many parts of Europe. The increasing radicalism of the revolutionaries, which culminated in the execution of Louis XVI and Marie Antoinette in 1793, lost the revolutionaries much support. Nevertheless, a revolutionary fervour had been unleashed and the ideas of nationhood, citizenship, republicanism, the rights of man and even the rights of women had become part of the political vocabulary. In Ireland the revolution resulted in expressions of support, with the *Marseillaise*, which had become the anthem of the revolution, sung on the streets of Belfast and Dublin. Liberals in Belfast were particularly overjoyed at the news of the French Revolution, with the *Belfast News-Letter* describing it as 'the greatest event in human annals'. Their enthusiasm lasted for a number of years, with the anniversary of the fall of the Bastille continuing to be celebrated throughout Ireland.

Although the Catholics' cause was advanced during the period associated with Protestant patriotism, they made even more progress during the early years of the French Revolution. For the British government the revolution made it necessary to conciliate Catholics as a way of containing the revolutionary fervour. This need increased in 1792 when relations between Britain and France deteriorated, culminating in war being declared in February 1793. The Irish Catholic hierarchy was also antagonistic towards the French revolutionaries because of their treatment of the Church. However, the Catholic Committee took advantage of the government's vulnerability to demand full civil rights. The Committee had been formed in 1760 to provide a structured outlet for Catholic demands. It met only intermittently, but after 1791, inspired by events in France, it developed a more militant stance. In December 1792 some delegates from the Committee, accompanied by their Anglican secretary, Wolfe Tone, personally petitioned the king in London. During this period a spate of legislation was passed: from 1792 Catholics were allowed to practise as solicitors and to intermarry with Protestants. Hobart's Catholic Relief Act, passed in 1793, extended the vote in parliamentary and municipal elections to Catholics, though they were subject to the same property qualifications as Protestants. Catholics were also permitted to bear arms. Yet, while Catholics were now eligible for most civil and military posts, they were excluded from the highest offices, including that of lord lieutenant, lord deputy, chancellor of the Exchequer, provost of Trinity College and commander-in-chief of the forces. The impact of the relief acts was immediate. In October 1793 St Patrick's College was opened in Carlow, which was the first Catholic tertiary college in Ireland. In 1795 an act was passed for the establishment of a Catholic seminary at Maynooth.

All of these measures raised the hopes of middle-class Catholics, who felt that equality required full emancipation, that is, the ability of Catholics to sit in parliament. The appointment of Lord Fitzwilliam as lord lieutenant at the end of 1794 suggested that emancipation was imminent. The British government under the premiership of William Pitt appeared unwilling to make any further concessions. Fitzwilliam, however, encouraged Irish Catholics to believe that more measures would be passed, and he supported a new relief bill by the Irish parliamentarian Henry Grattan. Fitzwilliam's indiscretions alienated his colleagues in Dublin Castle and in the British government. He was recalled within a few months and replaced by the ultra-conservative Earl Camden. Fitzwilliam's departure was mourned both by Irish Catholics and liberals, some of whom viewed it as a failure of constitutional agitation. His demise facilitated the spread of more militant nationalism, which was led by the United Irishmen. They in turn attempted to radicalise other political organisations.

The French Revolution contributed to the emergence of a new form of Irish nationalism, although this philosophy also borrowed from the doctrines of the American Revolution and the English Glorious Revolution, combined with Irish patriotism. The new nationalism was distinct from earlier political movements, however, because it aimed to unite all creeds in Ireland under the common banner of being Irish. The most successful new political organisation in Ireland was the Society of the United Irishmen. It was formed in Belfast in October 1791 and in Dublin a few weeks later. Smaller sister organisations were formed in other parts of Ireland. The leaders, Samuel Neilson and Theobald Wolfe Tone, were Protestant, and many of the founding members were also middle-class Protestants. In Belfast members were predominantly Presbyterian, while in Dublin about 50 per cent of the membership was Anglican. In January 1792 the Society launched its own radical newspaper, the *Northern Star*, edited by Samuel Neilson. Its circulation rose rapidly to 4,000 copies, making it the most popular newspaper in Ireland. Initially, the United Irishmen wanted the total removal of England from Irish parliamentary affairs. The programme of the Society became more radical, with some members supporting universal male suffrage and the establishment of an Irish republic. Although the Society was also committed to complete Catholic emancipation, this demand made some Protestants uneasy. While Wolfe Tone was personally dismissive of what he referred to as 'papal tyranny', for him and the other leaders religious equality was a central part of the organisation's philosophy. Wolfe Tone had long been an advocate of complete religious equality, being the author of *An Argument on Behalf of the Catholics of Ireland*. Although he was Protestant, the Catholic Committee had appointed him their paid secretary.

Concurrently with more liberal legislation being passed on behalf of Catholics, repressive measures were introduced to curb some of the radical organisations that were active in Ireland. The existence of the Volunteers, the United Irishmen and the Catholic Committee in the towns, and the Catholic Defender groups in the countryside, was regarded as a threat to a British government on the verge of war with France; this was particularly the case as the moderate leadership and reformist approach of groups such as the Volunteers and Catholic Committee had been replaced by a more confrontational approach. The Defenders were Catholic secret societies that had originally been formed as protection against Protestant groups in the north of Ireland. They had gradually spread into other parts of the country, where they also defended the economic interests of poor Catholics.

The holding of a convention by the Catholic Committee in 1792, therefore, was regarded as subversive and dangerous because it effectively challenged the authority of both the Irish and the British parliaments. The fear that these organisations were in touch with the revolutionary government in France was confirmed when an agent, Reverend William Jackson, was arrested in Dublin in 1794. Jackson, a Church of Ireland clergyman, was gauging the support in Ireland for a French invasion. His arrest and trial for treason resulted in the pursuit of Wolfe Tone and his departure for America.

In 1793 both the Gunpowder Act and the Convention Act were introduced. The latter prohibited large assemblies and thus effectively curtailed the gatherings of the main political groups. The following year the Society of the United Irishmen was suppressed. The effect of this legislation was to drive these movements under ground and transform them into secret, oath-bound societies.

Even more draconian measures were passed in 1796, when a French invasion was attempted. The Insurrection Act made taking illegal oaths punishable by the death penalty and permitted stringent curfews to be imposed on districts regarded as 'disturbed'. Magistrates were also given extensive powers to search for arms. In 1796 habeas corpus was suspended, which allowed imprisonment without trial. It was not re-established until 1806. Another long-term measure was the establishment of a yeomanry. By 1797, only a year after its formation, 30,000 men had joined this part-time militia. Although Catholics could enlist, the recruits were primarily Protestant. Many of the northern ones were also members of the recently established and exclusively Protestant Orange Order, and this led to accusations of sectarianism. Although the yeomanry had been established to deal with the revolutionary threat between 1796 and 1798, the state continued to depend on it for defence. After 1798, however, the yeomanry became increasingly Protestant in composition and more overtly partisan in performing its duties. In addition to these overt measures to repress radicalism, covert measures were also used. In particular, the government employed a network of spies and informers to infiltrate the secret societies.

These counter-revolutionary measures appeared immediately justified. Wolfe Tone had travelled from America to France, arriving in Paris at the beginning of 1796. There he appealed to the revolutionary government, which was now controlled by the Directory, to invade Ireland and assist in a rebellion. Apart from any desire to support Irish nationalism, the war with England made an invasion militarily attractive for France. Wolfe Tone also convinced the French leaders that they would be welcomed in Ireland. In December 1796 a French fleet carrying over 14,000 men, commanded by General Lazare Hoche and accompanied by Wolfe Tone, sailed to Bantry Bay in County Cork. A violent storm prevented them from landing, but they judged the Irish support to have been greatly exaggerated. For the United Irishmen, however, the French participation, minimal as it was, boosted morale among their supporters. Significantly, the internal organisation of the Society was modelled on the experience of France, with local directories being established. The Hoche expedition alarmed Britain, as it proved that the French navy could break through the blockade and that the Irish radicals had external allies. It also alarmed the Irish government, as it suggested that the latter had lost control of the country. The attempted invasion was followed by a brutal attempt to suppress the United Irishmen, under the direction of a British officer, General Gerard Lake. Lake used a scorched-earth policy, with liberal use of torture, to break the United Irish organisation in Ulster. He also arrested some of the local leaders, including Henry Joy McCracken. The success of Lake's methods led to his appointment as commander-in-chief in March 1798, when he extended his tactics to the Dublin area, which was another stronghold of the movement. Yet, regardless of his brutality, the United Irishmen continued to win support, and by the beginning of 1798 had almost 300,000 members. Some of its more militant leaders, including Lord Edward Fitzgerald, a younger son of the duke of Leinster, argued for a widespread rebellion. Just as worrying for the authorities was the fact that the United Irishmen had established stronger links with the Defenders, which were Catholic agrarian secret societies. The rapid growth of the organisation changed its character in some ways, as many of the new members had a more radical, populist agenda than some of its leaders. Consequently the demands for a republican government were augmented by the demand for radical social change. More ominously, as the movement spread, elements of sectarianism appeared.

For the United Irishmen the main predicament concerned the timing of an uprising: if they delayed too long or waited for another French intercession there was a danger that their leaders would have all been arrested. Acting on information provided by an informer, Thomas Reynolds, in March 1798 the Leinster Directory was arrested in Dublin. One of the leaders, Fitzgerald, escaped, but was captured and mortally wounded two months later. His death deprived the movement of one of its best military strategists and charismatic leaders. The government's intervention sparked a series of uprisings. In May uprisings took place in Counties Dublin, Kildare and Meath, spreading out to the adjoining areas. The fact that the rebels had little success in Dublin, which was strongly guarded, was a strategic blow, but risings in Wexford and Waterford were more successful, encouraging the rebels to move westwards. The insurgents in Wexford also briefly took over the running of the main towns, modelling their government on the Committee of Public Safety in France. They were defeated when they attempted to take over New Ross. Consequently, they retreated and regrouped, together with their wounded and local townspeople, at Vinegar Hill near Enniscorthy. They were decisively defeated at Vinegar Hill by a government force led by Lake and which included some Irish Catholic militia. Although many of the insurgents escaped, this defeat marked the end of the Wexford campaign. The rising in Wexford was tainted by accusations of sectarian violence. The killing of as many as 200 Protestant prisoners in Scullabogue led to subsequent accusations of sectarianism, although the deaths may have been the result of indiscriminate violence or desperation. The leaders of the Wexford insurrection were diverse. Father Murphy, the curate of Boolavogue, had been opposed to the United Irishmen, only joining the uprising in response to the violence of the government forces, while Beauchamp Bagenal Harvey was a local Protestant landowner. Harvey and Murphy were both executed in 1798. The leadership of the Ulster rebellion attracted many Presbyterians, both as rank-and-file followers and as leaders. Approximately twenty Presbyterian clergymen were involved in the rising, and four of them were executed.

Uprisings also took place throughout eastern Ulster in 1798, even though the movement had been considerably weakened by Lake's campaign in the previous year. None the less, Henry Joy McCracken and his followers were initially successful in County Antrim, but they were defeated on 7 June when attempting to capture Antrim Town. An amnesty was offered to all except the leaders and they, including McCracken, were hanged. Within a few days of the defeat in Antrim a larger insurrection had taken place in County Down, led by Henry Munro. It was defeated at Ballynahinch and Munro was also executed. These defeats marked the end of the challenge in the north-east. One of the remarkable features of the northern uprising was the involvement of women – Mary Anne McCracken, a younger sister of Henry Joy, shared his radical politics. Betsey Gray, a working-class Presbyterian woman, played a significant role. She fought alongside her brother and her lover at Ballynahinch and was brutally killed.

The defeat of the insurgents in the east meant that the west became the centre of republican aspirations. It was not until the arrival of a French force, led by General Jean Joseph Humbert, that its contribution became significant. By this stage Napoleon was effectively in charge of the Directory in France and although he desired to inflict a blow on England, he was engaged in fighting in Egypt. While he agreed to provide support, overall the French fleet was smaller and later than had been promised, and under the command of a relatively inexperienced general. Humbert and just over 1,000 French soldiers landed at Killala Bay in County Mayo on 22 August 1798. The local support was uncoordinated and ill prepared for their arrival. Nevertheless, the combined forces defeated the government troops at Castlebar. Acting on incorrect information, Humbert advanced into the country but was defeated at Ballinamuck in County Longford by a fortified government force. Lord Cornwallis, the lord lieutenant, commanded the government troops. The French and Irish forces surrendered, but while the former were imprisoned, about

2,000 Irishmen were slaughtered. Meanwhile, a further French force had sailed to Ireland, which included Wolfe Tone who was serving as a French officer. A British squadron at Lough Swilly met it and most of the French ships, including the one carrying Wolfe Tone, were captured. Wolfe Tone was court-martialled but, before he could be executed, he committed suicide. Although he played no direct part in the actual uprising, he became indelibly associated with it and, posthumously, was regarded as the architect of Irish republican nationalism. In the short term, the rebellion convinced the British government that while the insurrection had been defeated militarily, a longer-term solution was required to quell the nationalist spirit that had been awakened.

Regardless of the defeat, the insurrection was not over, as local pockets of resistance survived. Michael Dwyer and Joseph Holt mounted successful guerrilla warfare in the Wicklow Mountains. James Napper Tandy, who accompanied French troops with additional supplies for Humbert, briefly landed in Ireland in September but departed on hearing news of the defeat of the main French force. He was arrested in Hamburg and returned to Ireland, where he was sentenced to death. The treaty of Amiens, which ended the Revolutionary Wars with France, was concluded in March 1802. War resumed in 1803 but Napoleon used the cessation of warfare to intervene on Tandy's behalf and secured his release. In 1802 he was deported to France.

Overall, despite early successes, the 1798 uprising suffered from having little central coordination, which meant that it developed as a series of local, isolated confrontations. Throughout 1797 the British authorities had been preparing for conflict and the ruthless activities of Lake had weakened the United Irishmen. Significantly, the insurgents had not put at risk the strategic towns of either Belfast or Dublin. The response of the government forces was ferocious, General Lake having commanded his subordinates not to take any prisoners. There were also instances of insurgents who were surrendering being slaughtered, as occurred at the Curragh in Kildare on 29 May 1798. Inevitably, mortality rates were high. As many as 30,000 Irish people were killed, out of a population of approximately 5 million. Many of them were non-combatants. The impact of the mortality was localised: County Wexford, for example, lost approximately 25 per cent of its population during the conflict. The government repression also continued after 1798, with 1,500 people being flogged, executed or transported. Overall, therefore, the uprising was the most brutal conflict on Irish – or British – soil since the seventeenth century. Even by contemporary standards, this figure represented massive losses – approximately 11,000 were killed during the Reign of Terror in France in 1793 (out of a population of about 24 million) and there were only eleven fatalities at the Peterloo 'Massacre' in Manchester in 1819, when the yeomanry fired on unarmed protesters. Yet British public opinion appeared unmoved in 1798, indicating that Ireland had become an adversary. Two years later, however, an Act of Union was passed that forged an even closer political association between Ireland and Britain.

Although many of the leaders of the 1798 insurrection were executed, a number of the younger ones escaped, mostly to France. The guerrilla warfare also continued. A number of the veterans of 1798, including Robert Emmet, Thomas Russell and Myles Byrne, returned to Ireland to plan a further uprising in 1803. Emmet, a Protestant radical, had been expelled from Trinity College in 1798 for his political views. He believed that an uprising could only succeed if the insurgents seized the capital, Dublin. This, he assumed, would lead to spontaneous uprisings in the remainder of the country. Russell, however, tried unsuccessfully to rally support in Ulster. An insurrection led by Emmet took place in Dublin on 23 July 1803. The resumption of war between Britain and France in the summer of 1803 led Emmet to hope that he might receive some French aid. Napoleon, however, was concentrating his efforts on an invasion of England. The uprising was defeated within a few hours, although there were losses on both sides. Emmet was captured, tried for treason, and hanged on 25 September. He was aged twenty-five. His trial oration captured the popular imagination of both his contemporaries and subsequent generations – 'When my country takes her place among the nations of the earth, then and only then may my epitaph be written.'

Twenty other insurgents were hanged. Thomas Russell, who had attempted to rescue Emmet, was also captured and hanged in Downpatrick. Michael Dwyer, who had led the guerrilla war in the Wicklow Mountains since 1798, surrendered at the end of 1803 and was transported to Australia. Michael Dwyer's niece, Anne Devlin, was Emmet's housemaid. When Emmet was in hiding, she demonstrated her loyalty to Irish nationalism by taking secret messages from Emmet to his friends in Dublin. Devlin, who was the same age as Emmet, was arrested, tortured and imprisoned for two years, yet she refused to give any information to the authorities. She died in poverty in Dublin in 1851.

In one sense the 1803 uprising led by Robert Emmet had more in common with the events of 1798 than with post-Union Ireland. The fact that Emmet was young, idealistic and publicly executed helped to create a hero who, more than any of the leaders of 1798, captured and kept alive a spirit of romantic nationalism that transcended any short-term political failures. The manner of his death and his speech from the dock were a source of inspiration for nationalists in Ireland and America throughout the nineteenth century. In the short term, though, Emmet's death marked the end of a period of nationalist activity that had commenced with the formation of the United Irishmen in 1791. And, despite subsequent accusations of sectarianism, it marked a zenith of inclusive politics in Ireland that accommodated republican nationalism and Protestant patriotism. While sectarianism had accounted for a relatively small number of the deaths, the few instances where it did occur shaped Anglican and Presbyterian perceptions of the 1798 uprising. The popular memory of the rising also remained strong in America. The emigration of Thomas Emmet, a United Irishman and brother of Robert, to the United States, where he named his son Robert, kept alive the memory of 1798 and the republican nationalist tradition. Robert Emmet grew up to be a supporter of repeal of the Act of Union, and in 1848, fired by events in France and the rhetoric of the Young Irelanders, he helped to establish the Irish Republican Union in New York.

The 1798 uprising and the resultant Act of Union led to a reconfiguration in Irish and British politics – radical Presbyterians were replaced by those who felt their future was better protected if they were part of a Protestant, rather than an Irish, alliance. Conservative Catholicism also increased, and part of its strength lay in remaining distinct from the other Churches – through education and devotional orthodoxy rather than radical nationalism.

A United Kingdom?

The 1798 rebellion convinced the British prime minister, William Pitt, that the political relationship between Britain and Ireland needed to change. Ignoring the patriotic and nationalist fervour that had been evident in Ireland since the 1770s, he advocated a closer political union with Britain. The Irish parliament, however, had different ideas. Led by Henry Grattan, it rejected unification while stressing Ireland's distinctive and separate identity. In 1799 the British government's proposal for a union was rejected by a majority of five. A mixture of bribery, threats and promises was used to ensure that the next vote was successful. The Act of Union was passed by the British parliament in July and by the Irish parliament in August 1800.

On 1 January 1801 the political union between Great Britain and Ireland commenced. The Act of Union brought to an end the Irish parliament, which had existed in Dublin since 1297, replacing it with direct rule from London. It also marked the final stage in the creation of a unitary British state, political unions having taken place with Wales in 1536 and Scotland in 1707. By the end of the eighteenth century these three countries had forged a common identity, based on a shared monarch, a shared economy and a common religion. Ireland did not fit easily into this established configuration, especially as a sea also physically separated it. The Union also brought more economic integration between Britain and Ireland. In 1817 the two exchequers were united and the fiscal systems were gradually aligned. Some differences continued: when income tax was reintroduced to Britain in 1842 it was not extended to Ireland.

The Union created a new political entity, that is, the United Kingdom of Great Britain and Ireland. Its birth was celebrated with a new flag, the Union flag. Its passage was controversial and attracted mixed support: it was welcomed by the Catholic Church, which hoped it would benefit Irish Catholics, and opposed by the Orange Order, who feared that it would benefit Catholics. Pitt had raised Catholic hopes that emancipation would be granted in return for the acquiescence of liberal Protestant MPs. These expectations were short-lived. King George III refused to agree, and so emancipation was abandoned. His untimely intervention was an inauspicious start for the new political relationship. Little sensitivity was shown to the majority Catholic population, with the Act of Union confirming the Anglican Church as the state church. Yet Ireland could not be ignored, politically, economically or demographically. In 1801 England accounted for 54 per cent of the United Kingdom population, Ireland for 33 per cent, Scotland 10 per cent, and Wales for 3 per cent. Consequently, until the devastation caused by the potato blight after 1845, Ireland supplied one-third of the population of the United Kingdom. After the Great Famine, Ireland supplied less than 20 per cent of the United Kingdom population, and its share was falling.

The addition of Irish MPs also changed the composition of the Westminster parliament, but again England remained the dominant partner. After 1801 Ireland sent 100 MPs to sit in the British parliament, where they joined 489 English MPs, 45 from Scotland and 24 from Wales. Following the Reform Act of 1832 the number of Irish MPs was increased to 105, but proportionally Ireland remained under-represented within the British parliament. However, regardless of the Union, an unrepresentative Protestant landed elite continued to govern Ireland. Furthermore, Irish Protestants were transformed from a religious minority within Ireland to being part of the dominant religious group of the United Kingdom. The granting of Catholic emancipation in 1829 was a setback to their supremacy. The Act of Union also changed British politics in unforeseen ways. The prime minister, William Pitt, was an early casualty, resigning in 1801 when King George III refused to accede to Catholic emancipation. Neither prime ministers nor monarchs spent much time in Ireland, although after 1800 it shaped political developments in Britain. King George IV, who briefly visited Ireland in 1821, was the first monarch since William of Orange to do so, and his motivation was similarly selfish, needing to compensate for his unpopularity in England. Queen Victoria, lover of Scotland, visited Ireland only three times during her long reign. Overall, while a legislative union existed on paper, in reality Ireland remained separate from the rest of the United Kingdom by virtue of her religion, geography, culture and customs. The years that followed the Union did little to assuage the fears of either Irish Catholics or Irish Protestants.

Complete integration, however, was never achieved or sought, as Ireland continued to be regarded as a colony. The fact that Ireland was not an equal political partner in the relationship was suggested by the survival of the Dublin Castle administration. Dublin Castle was the medium by which England had traditionally governed Ireland, through the offices of a lord lieutenant, a chief secretary and under-secretary. After 1801 the Dublin Castle executive continued to look after many aspects of Irish government, including the important areas of law and order. Its role also increased, and during the nineteenth century the Castle administration became more interventionist than previously. Inevitably, Dublin Castle became a symbol of the British presence in Ireland. The office continued to exist until 1921.

In the first half of the nineteenth century the intervention of Dublin Castle was most apparent in matters relating to education, poverty and rural crime, the last usually referred to as 'outrages'. The development of an education system in Ireland was chequered, especially for Catholics and Protestant dissenters. From the sixteenth century education was used to promote Protestantism and English culture. The plantation of Ulster had included the establishment of a number of royal schools, which received an endowment from James I. The Penal Law in 1695 banned Catholics from going overseas for education and from running schools within Ireland. These restrictions gave rise to a clandestine system of education, known as hedge schools. Although they were predominantly associated with Catholics, they were also used by Presbyterians in the north of the country. The Catholic Relief Acts of 1782 and 1793 removed the restrictions on education, although no funding was made available for state schooling. Some members of the Catholic Church quickly took advantage of the new climate. In 1802 Edmund Rice opened a school for poor Catholic boys. The system spread and in 1820 the Pope recognised the role of Rice's Christian Brothers in providing Catholic education in Ireland. State funding, however, remained limited to Anglican schools, most notably through the Kildare Place Society, which included bible reading as part of its curriculum. Although as early as 1812 there were calls for money to be available for mixed, or multi-denominational, education, early attempts ended in accusations of proselytism.

In 1831 Ireland became the first country in the United Kingdom to receive statutory state funding for education. A Board of Education was established that was to receive an annual grant of £30,000 to meet building and teaching costs. More significantly, the Board represented the three main denominations in Ireland and the new national schools could receive funding only if they adopted a similarly multi-denominational approach. To avoid controversy in the classroom the Irish language and Irish history were not to be taught, although British poetry was. Also, all teaching was done through English, which contributed to the decline of the Irish language among the poor. The new school system divided the Anglican Church, as some of its conservative members opposed mixed education and formed their own Church Education Society in 1839. Some Catholics, including the Christian Brothers, also opposed the new system, as they did not want their religious curriculum to be diluted. Nationalists increasingly viewed the national schools as a way of promoting English culture and language.

After the Union, Irish poverty and economic underdevelopment were a major concern for the British government. Unlike the rest of the United Kingdom, Ireland had no state system of poor relief. In 1833 a government commission was appointed under Richard Whately to undertake a survey of Irish poverty. After three years' detailed inquiry, the commission reported that 2 million Irish people each year required short-term welfare assistance. They did not recommend that the new English Poor Law system, based on workhouses, should be extended to Ireland, but suggested that state-funded assisted emigration and public works should be used to alleviate the poverty.

Their suggestions were out of keeping with the prevailing orthodoxies concerning poverty, and the report was ignored. Instead, an English Poor Law commissioner, George Nicholls, was sent to Ireland with the primary objective of suggesting how a Poor Law, based on the English model, could be extended to Ireland. Following a six-week tour of Ireland, Nicholls recommended the extension of the English system of poor relief to Ireland, although he paid little attention to the different economic and social structures of the two countries. Consequently, in 1838 a Poor Law was introduced into Ireland. It divided the country into 130 unions, each with its own workhouse. Unions were also areas of taxation, with each workhouse being financed from local poor rates. In total, the Irish workhouses could accommodate 100,000 inmates, to be designated 'paupers'. Yet, while the Irish Poor Law was closely modelled on the English one, there were significant differences. In Ireland relief could be given only inside the workhouse, unlike in England, Scotland and Wales, where outdoor relief was also permitted. Also, the situation in Ireland was unusual in that there was no legal right to relief, which meant that if a workhouse became full, there was no legal requirement to provide alternative relief. These differences demonstrated that the Irish poor were to be treated more harshly than the poor in other parts of the United Kingdom. This attitude was partly based on a belief that Irish people were lazy and would take advantage of any state system of welfare provision. During the early years of the Poor Law, however, few Irish people made use of the workhouses. The failure of the potato crop after 1845 increased demand for workhouse accommodation, and by the end of 1846 many institutions were full.

While a number of governments recognised the need for land reform, little was done because of the entrenched position of vested interests. This was most apparent in the wake of the comprehensive Devon Commission. The Commission was appointed in 1843 by the prime minister, Sir Robert Peel, to inquire into relations between landlords and tenants. Peel wanted to modernise the Irish economy, and he regarded land improvements as a prerequisite. Following two years' detailed investigation, the Commission reported. Although its recommendations were generally moderate, Irish landlords disliked them. Their opposition was evident in 1845 when Peel introduced a bill to give compensation to outgoing tenants who had made improvements to their land. The opposition to this modest measure was so vehement that it was withdrawn. The onset of a subsistence crisis not only meant that there was no immediate opportunity to present further legislation;

the devastation caused by the famine wiped out a high proportion of the rural poor. Approximately 25 per cent of landownership also changed. Regardless of these alterations, relations between landlords and tenants remained a source of discord.

Despite sporadic attempts to conciliate Catholic opinion, most notably between 1835 and 1840 when Thomas Drummond was under-secretary, Dublin Castle was regarded as a symbol of Protestantism and of oppression. After 1801 Ireland was governed by a series of repressive measures and Coercion Acts, even after the threat posed by the United Irishmen had disappeared. In the decades following the Union, Ireland had a professional standing army, usually of 25,000 troops. In periods of unrest this was increased, and during the political unrest of 1847 to 1848 it grew to 100,000. Law enforcement was also a concern of the Dublin Castle authorities, and in 1814 Robert Peel, a member of the executive, introduced the Peace Preservation Force into Ireland. The establishment of this early police force, known as 'Peelers', was in response to widespread agrarian unrest. The Peace Preservation Force was appointed by the government and was controlled by it. It could be quickly dispatched to any area that was regarded as disturbed. Within a few years of its establishment there was a need for a national police force in Ireland, and so in 1822 a permanent national constabulary was introduced. From the outset, it was organised and run along military lines. In 1836 these forces were amalgamated into the Irish Constabulary, which after 1867 became the Royal Irish Constabulary. The Irish Constabulary was also controlled by Dublin Castle. By 1840 there were approximately 8,500 constables in Ireland, and their presence was made more visible by the erection of 1,400 police barracks throughout the country. All of this meant Ireland had a police force before any other part of the United Kingdom, and throughout the nineteenth century Ireland remained more policed that any part of Britain. From the outset also, the Irish constabulary were armed, unlike police in other parts of the United Kingdom.

Although after 1832 Dublin Castle adopted a more liberal attitude towards Catholics, especially middle-class ones, coercion was still a major tool in the government of Ireland. This was apparent from the introduction of the draconian Suppression of Disturbances Act in January 1833. It allowed the lord lieutenant to impose a curfew on a 'disturbed district', and for detention without trial for up to three months. Moreover, the trial would be by military courts rather than by magistrate's court. This legislation was the most repressive passed since the Union. Its passage was largely in response to the activities of agrarian secret societies in Ireland. However, it alarmed radicals in both Ireland and Britain, especially as a Whig government had passed it. In the 1840s some British politicians were expressing alarm at the state of Ireland. Earl Grey, speaking in the House of Lords in 1846, described the British presence as being due to the 'military occupation of Ireland, but that in no other sense could it be said to be governed'. His statement suggested that forty years after the Union had taken place, Ireland continued to be ruled by force.

A Protestant Nation

In the eighteenth century the Protestant ascendancy really referred to Anglicans, but from the end of the century Presbyterianism emerged as a powerful force in both religion and politics. Presbyterianism changed, however, from being an inclusive, progressive and radical influence on Irish politics to a conservative and militant force that increasingly defined itself by its opposition to Catholicism and nationalism. Other radical Protestant voices persisted; they were overshadowed by a mounting polarisation between Catholics and Protestants.

The collapse of the 1798 uprising contributed to a new form of religious segregation, as the rising was increasingly depicted as having been a priest-led, anti-Protestant movement with sectarian motives. Although a number of militant Protestants initially opposed the Union, fearing that it would undermine their ascendancy, they quickly became reconciled to it as a defence against Catholicism. Economic arguments were also added to religious justifications in the nineteenth century. The peaceful conditions of the eighteenth century had benefited Ulster in particular and the domestic system of linen production had flourished. Ulster, and northern Protestants in particular, benefited from Belfast's economic expansion, which followed the Union. Their rising aspirations were demonstrated by the opening in 1814 of the Belfast Academical Institution, a college for Presbyterians, where the majority of the Synod of Ulster's ministers were trained. Belfast's success was also evident from the establishment of a number of civic and educational institutions, such as the Belfast Natural History and Philosophical Society in 1821. The local economy benefited from the development of wet spinning techniques in the 1820s, which ensured that Ulster led the way in Irish industrialisation in the nineteenth century. Moreover, the success of the local linen industry meant that it remained the most important Irish manufacturing industry in the country. Economic arguments were thus added to political ones for remaining within the United Kingdom and part of the British Empire.

In addition to the emergence of republican nationalism in the 1790s, the decade also gave rise to a new form of militant Protestantism that appealed to all classes of Protestants. The Orange Order was founded in County Armagh in 1795 following a sectarian confrontation known as 'the Battle of the Diamond', during which over thirty Catholics were killed. From the outset the Orange Order was a conservative, sectarian body that was exclusively Protestant and avowedly anti-Catholic. It was predominantly Anglican, with Presbyterians being excluded until 1834. From the beginning, the Order was dedicated to sustaining 'the glorious and immortal' memory of William of Orange, and his victory at the battle of the Boyne was chosen as the key commemoration within the Orange calendar. Before his veneration by the Orange Order, William had been widely admired as a liberal monarch, but Orangemen appropriated him and recast him as the conservative defender of Protestant values and the protector of British civil liberties. Yet William was an unlikely icon, either of Protestantism or Britishness. He was Dutch, he was personally tolerant of all religions, and his campaign in Ireland had the blessing of the Pope. Also, unlike the heroic and dashing representation on horseback, William was short, pockmarked and hunch-backed. He left Ireland following his victory at the Boyne and never returned to the country.

The Orange Order appealed to those Protestants who disliked the radical and non-sectarian politics of the United Irishmen. On 12 July 1796 parades took place in various locations throughout Armagh. Their marching in formation and carrying weapons suggested the militarist nature of the Orange Society, as the Order was originally known. The day ended violently with the burning of 7,000 Catholics' homes and their forcible removal from the area. Posters were displayed warning 'Go to hell or Connaught. If you do not, we are all haters of the papists and we will destroy you'. Both the local magistrates and officials in Dublin Castle refused to intervene in the conflict, viewing the Orangemen as a useful counter-revolutionary force against the United Irishmen. The Orange Order quickly spread throughout Ulster, and 330 local lodges had been founded by 1798. In the same year the Grand Orange Lodge was established in Dublin. By this stage, the Protestant gentry had taken control of the movement, realising its value in counteracting the republican agitation. The British government also realised its potential as a counter-revolutionary movement, issuing Orangemen with weapons and ammunition during the 1798 uprising. The political insecurity of the late 1790s meant that the Protestant gentry viewed the Orange Order as a valuable mechanism for defending British interests in Ireland, especially against the nationalist challenge.

The Orange Order opposed the Act of Union, and some of its members campaigned to preserve the 'Protestant Constitution'. Within a few years, however, they had changed from their anti-Union position, seeing a Protestant United Kingdom as their best defence against Catholic advancements. When the threat of a republican uprising had disappeared, the attitude of successive British governments to Orangemen became increasingly ambivalent. The association of the 12 July parades with sectarian violence also resulted in an attempt to proscribe the Orange Order and other political associations in 1824. Some local lodges ignored the legislation, and continued to meet and commemorate the Boyne anniversary. Protestants of all classes regarded the granting of Catholic emancipation in 1829, which permitted Catholics to become members of the British parliament, as a threat to their political supremacy. Anglicans and Presbyterians, directed by the gentry, formed a Protestant alliance to resist the legislation. The opposition to Emancipation united Irish Protestants, the common bond being not only religious identity, but also political objectives. Following emancipation, the parades became even more violent and the government responded by passing more stringent legislation in 1832, banning political processions. Again, militant Orangemen ignored the legislation. In 1835 a government inquiry into the activities of the Orange Order was critical. It reported that Orangemen had successfully infiltrated the army, police force and judiciary in Ireland and Britain. The Duke of Cumberland, the brother of the British king, was grand master of the Orange Lodge in Britain. The inquiry also found that the routes followed on 12 July were deliberately chosen to go through Catholic areas. Despite the adverse publicity, the Orange Society survived, and in 1845 Prime Minister Sir Robert Peel lifted the ban on political marching. The timing was injudicious, as it coincided with the revival of radical nationalism in Ireland. The membership of the Orange Order increased and the Boyne marches were larger than before. In the fifty years since the founding of the Orange Order, conservative Anglicans and Presbyterians had moved closer together, but the distance between Protestants and Catholics had grown.

In addition to the political hostility, a new dimension had been added to the religious cocktail, as proselytism commenced in Ireland. Traditionally, even though Anglicans may not have liked Catholicism, in general they did not want to convert Catholics. Instead, they preferred to remain as a small and privileged elite. This situation changed at the beginning of the nineteenth century largely as a result of the spread of Protestant evangelism. In the two decades following the Act of Union, almost twenty missionary stations were established in Ireland. Although Anglicans managed many of the stations, Baptist, Methodist and Presbyterian organisations were also involved. They usually established schools, where education was free but mostly focused on reading the Protestant Bible. Because the majority of poor Catholics were Irish-speakers, the missionaries were generally bilingual, and the Bible was translated into Irish. A more concerted attempt to convert Catholics to Protestantism, referred to as 'the Second Reformation', was made in the 1820s. The west of the country was particularly targeted, and large missions were established in County Kerry and on Achill Island. A political incentive was added to the religious motivation, as despite the defeat in 1798 Catholics had regrouped and emerged as a significant force in the 1820s. Yet despite the vigour of the Catholic emancipation movement and the growth of the Catholic middle classes, the Catholic Church remained relatively poor and could not compete with the missionaries. Although the missions had only limited success, their activities contributed to a growing cleavage between Catholics and Protestants. Overall, for Protestants, political disillusionment was a feature of the 1830s and 1840s, and it combined with a move towards more theological conservatism, to convert Catholics to Protestantism. This tension was intensified after 1845 when the hunger of the Catholic poor was used as an opportunity to convert them.

The political conservatism of Presbyterians after 1798 was matched by more devotional orthodoxy. Although some Presbyterians continued to be political liberals, from the 1820s a new brand of fundamentalist Presbyterianism also emerged, personified by the conservative yet flamboyant minister Henry Cooke. Cooke had come to prominence in 1821 when he had opposed the appointment of a liberal professor at the Belfast Academical Institution. His actions had been a victory for theological orthodoxy and academic conformism. Cooke was conservative in matters both religious and political. He opposed tenant rights, mixed marriages, concessions to Catholics and the repeal movement. Towards the end of his life he vigorously opposed the disestablishment of the Anglican Church.

The Presbyterian Church was strengthened in 1840 when the Synod of Ulster and the Secession Synod, which had divided in the 1650s, reunited. They formed the General Assembly of the Presbyterian Church. The restructured Church viewed both education and missionary work as particularly important. Their proselytising activities, however, increased the divide with the Catholic Church. Hugh Hanna, a Presbyterian minister who combined evangelical religious observance with membership of the Orange Order, inflamed these antagonisms. His open-air preaching resulted in a number of anti-Catholic riots in Belfast. He was also involved with the religious revival in 1859, which resulted in a large number of conversions to Presbyterianism. The revival was accompanied by visions, stigmata, prophecies and general hysteria. Moderate members of the Church disliked the sectarianism and anti-Catholicism of the Presbyterian evangelicals. None the less, all this demonstrated that the inclusive politics of the United Irishmen had been subsumed beneath religious antagonisms.

A Catholic Country

The Roman Catholic Church had supported the Union, but in the short term it was not a beneficiary of it. The Act of Union confirmed British and Anglican control of Ireland, manifested by the continuation of the Dublin Castle administration, the affirmation of the Anglican Church as the state church, and the denial of Catholic emancipation. The Protestant ascendancy had been confirmed by the Union. Concessions to Catholics in the early decades of the nineteenth century were slow and piecemeal, largely because of opposition from vested interests, including the British House of Lords, but there was also an increasing alliance of conservative and evangelical Protestants. Anti-Catholic feeling remained entrenched in Britain and in parts of Ireland, and proposals to conciliate and appease Catholics caused a Protestant backlash. The opposition also created an alliance of Presbyterians and Anglicans, and, in a reversal of the spirit of the 1790s, the Presbyterians became aggressive partners in the relationship and fierce defenders of what they (misguidedly) believed to be their traditional rights.

The first serious challenge to the Protestant ascendancy came in 1829 with the granting of Catholic emancipation. Ironically two men who were Tories and defenders of Protestantism championed it through parliament. The Duke of Wellington, although born in Ireland, had little interest in the country, and

Peel, who had served as chief secretary between 1812 and 1817, had an abiding – if precarious – relationship with Ireland. This victory was followed by smaller, but none the less significant, triumphs: the abolition of tithes, reform of the corporations (allowing Daniel O'Connell to become mayor of Dublin in 1841), the appointment of Catholics to the judiciary, and an increased grant to Maynooth College, a seminary for training Catholic priests. In 1869 disestablishment, that is, the separation of Church and State, was to be a significant step in undermining the privileged position of the Anglican Church. Within this general picture of advancement for Catholics, the Ecclesiastical Titles Act of 1851, which forbade Catholic clerics to use ecclesiastical titles, can be regarded as an aberration within an overall picture of progress.

The Catholic Emancipation Act was the end of a process that had begun in 1778. From 1812 the British House of Commons had been sympathetic to the granting of emancipation, but vested interests, especially in the House of Commons and by successive monarchs, had blocked it. The formation of the Catholic Association in 1823 made the issue impossible for the government to ignore. The Association, under the skilful direction of Daniel O'Connell, was transformed from a pressure group into a mass movement. The introduction of a fee, known as Catholic Rent, provided the organisation with an income, while priests, who were ex-officio members, effectively ran the local organisations. Other requests were added to the demand for emancipation, including the abolition of the tithes (a tax paid for the upkeep of the Anglican Church) and a less partisan judiciary system. In 1826 a new tactic was added to the one of holding mass meetings, as the Catholic Association became involved in election campaigns. The situation reached a climax in 1828 when Daniel O'Connell stood as a candidate in a by-election in County Clare. His opponent was Vesey Fitzgerald, a Protestant liberal who supported emancipation. O'Connell defeated him with a massive majority, but as a Catholic he was unable to take his parliamentary seat. The result demonstrated to British politicians that middle-class Catholics were a powerful political force that could not be ignored. Wellington and Peel were given the job of persuading the British parliament to agree to Catholic emancipation. Neither man was personally sympathetic, but they justified it on the grounds that it was necessary to avert civil war. Consequently, on 13 April 1829, Catholic emancipation was granted.

A by-product of the act was that Catholics throughout Britain benefited from the legislation, gaining access to the right to vote and to sit in parliament. Irish Catholics, however, suffered some penalties as a result of having obtained emancipation. The ability to vote was greatly restricted, with the franchise being raised from 40 shillings to £10, a five-fold increase. The price was also high in terms of Protestant alienation. The Catholic Association had made little inroads into Ulster, even though emancipation had the support of liberal Protestants and shapers of public opinion, including the *Northern Whig*. In 1828 a Belfast journalist and loyal supporter of O'Connell, Jack Lawless, attempted to rectify the situation by encouraging O'Connell to visit Ulster. Orangemen and their supporters, however, described it as an 'invasion of Ulster'. They were encouraged by the inflammatory rhetoric of the Reverend Horner, who urged all Protestants to resist, using violence if necessary. Lawless achieved little, but his actions had united and provoked Ulster Protestants. The struggle for emancipation widened religious divisions in Ireland. Its passing created a paradox: Protestants, who claimed to be the most loyal of all the people in Ireland, were simultaneously the most politically disaffected. But when challenged, they were willing to use violence to defend their position.

For Irish Catholics, emancipation was the most significant concession made to them since the passage of the Act of Union. It represented a lingering grievance, as emancipation had been expected to follow the Union. Its granting in 1829 was symbolic of the changing power relationships within Ireland and between Ireland and Britain. The agitation, skilfully led and exploited by Daniel O'Connell, marked a high point in his career and a low point in the turbulent career of Robert Peel. Catholic satisfaction was juxtaposed with Protestant anger, with the legislation contributing to the ever-widening gulf between the groups. A further consequence was that the Orange Order (a predominantly Anglican movement) more visibly portrayed itself as the voice of Protestant Ireland, reaching out to Presbyterians and other non-Catholics. Under the broad Protestant umbrella, therefore, divisions were also hardening, as the cleavage widened between liberals and conservatives or evangelicals. Loyalty to Britain was clearly conditional.

Emancipation was won at the cost of a large-scale disenfranchisement, a move that was supported by the socially conservative O'Connell. Certain petty restrictions remained on the statute books, which, even if they were not enforced, demonstrated that tolerance was not total. For example, Catholic churches could not have a spire; priests were not to wear clerical attire; Jesuits could not enter the country; nuns were required to register with the government. None the less it was a significant political and moral victory for the Catholic Church in Ireland, and one that benefited Catholics in all parts of the United Kingdom. The granting of emancipation confirmed O'Connell as the supreme leader of the Irish people. In 1835 he entered into the Lichfield House Compact with the Whig government, which was an informal agreement that he would support the Whigs in return for reforms. This alliance was indicative that O'Connell had within a few years been recognised as a major force in British politics also. But within Ireland, O'Connell made little effort to reassure Protestants that his vision for Ireland included them. By not including them, he allowed more conservative forces to exploit their fears and use emancipation as a tool of division between Catholics and Protestants.

Following emancipation, other legislation benefited Catholics, some of which resulted from the Lichfield House Compact, while some arose from the more liberal atmosphere of the 1830s. The new measures included the introduction of non-denominational elementary education in 1831, the reform of the corporations, the removal of tithes, an increased grant to Maynooth and, in 1845, the establishment of non-denominational universities in Galway, Cork and Belfast. Less tangible but no less important was Dublin Castle's policy of appointing Catholics to important positions. In 1847 Lord Clarendon even invited members of the Catholic Church hierarchy to dine with him, which was condemned in the British press. In 1869 the Anglican Church in Ireland was disestablished, an action that was not repeated in either Wales or Scotland, although it was also a minority Church in those countries. Each measure was challenged and reviled by conservative Protestants.

Although Daniel O'Connell's name is inextricably linked with the repeal movement, in the 1830s, when he forged an alliance with the Whig Party, he demonstrated that he was willing to work with British political parties to achieve reforms in Ireland. In 1840 O'Connell founded the National Association of Ireland for Repeal, which a year later changed its name to the Loyal National Repeal Association. The early years of the newly constituted repeal movement were auspicious, with O'Connell becoming the first nationalist lord mayor of Dublin in 1841. The fact that repeal was being discussed openly by Dublin Corporation, traditionally a Protestant stronghold, was a moral victory for Catholics. For conservative Protestants it was another blow against Protestant supremacy in Dublin. The year 1843 was supposed to be the climax to the repeal agitation, O'Connell hoping that the same tactics and rhetoric that had won Catholic emancipation would again force Peel into retreat. The high-water mark came at Tara – symbolically the seat of the high kings of Ireland. O'Connell held a massive repeal meeting on 15 August 1843 at this symbolic site, reputedly attended by over 1 million people. Tara was a warning to the government, which responded by forbidding the next mass meeting at Clontarf, another symbolic location as it was associated with the hero Brian Boru. The meeting was banned, and O'Connell complied. Following this he lost political credibility, some face saved only by his imprisonment. For the repeal movement Clontarf was a massive blow and the following five years were an anticlimax, with the initiative passing to the Young Ireland group (see below). O'Connell's lack of authority was not helped by advancing years and ill health. He allowed power to pass increasingly to his son John, who was ill equipped to lead such a movement and, compared to the dazzling array of talent of the emergent Young Irelanders, appeared even more uncharismatic.

The political advancement of women was not of particular concern to O'Connell or the repeal party. The French Revolution had prompted some women to seek equality with men, notably Mary Wollstonecraft in England and Olympe de Gouges in France. In Ireland some of the radical female writing was overshadowed by demands for political independence from Britain. Radical women, in a pattern that continued into the twentieth century, allowed their demand for gender equality to take second place to national aspirations. An exception was Anna Wheeler, who, together with William Thompson, wrote *An Appeal of One Half of the Human Race, Women, against the Pretensions of the Other Half, Men, to Retain them in Political and thence in Civil and Domestic Slavery*. Wheeler was born in Ireland, probably in 1775, and was the daughter of a Church of Ireland bishop. Her husband was an alcoholic whom she left after twelve years of marriage. As a result of her radical political views, she met Robert Owen, the British utopian socialist, and she wrote articles in his journal under the pseudonym 'Vlasta'. In London she also met William Thompson, an Irish socialist. Thompson was opposed to capitalism and he supported trade unionism. He was also a vegetarian and an atheist, and he disliked O'Connell's association of Irish nationalism with the Catholic Church. Also, unlike many other radical men, he believed that the rights of women were an integral part of political equality. The *Appeal of One Half of the Human Race* was reprinted in France and the United States. Thompson's writings also had an influence on the socialist writings of Karl Marx and James Connolly.

Socialism and feminism had little support in Ireland in the early nineteenth century. An Irish association that attracted mass support, however, was the temperance movement. Temperance societies had been established in Ireland as early as 1829, largely as a result of the efforts of Presbyterian and other nonconformist ministers. Temperance became a mass movement thanks to the work of Father Theobald Mathew, a Capuchin, who founded his own movement in 1838. Within four years, 3 million Irish people had sworn an abstinence pledge. Although some Protestants took the pledge, its main supporters were rural Catholics. Daniel O'Connell took the pledge in 1840 and his repeal movement borrowed some of the tactics of the temperance movement. Father Mathew, however, received little support or recognition from the Catholic Church hierarchy, who disliked his millenarian methods, playing on fears about the end of the world, and his willingness to work alongside Protestants.

Although the early decades of the nineteenth century had been distinguished by increasing religious tensions between the main Protestant and Catholic Churches, there were some attempts to keep alive the spirit of the United Irishmen. In 1846 Young Ireland, a group of romantic intellectuals, was forced out of the repeal movement, ostensibly over a disagreement on the use of physical force. In reality, the Young Irelanders had become disillusioned with O'Connell's acquiescence with successive governments. They also disagreed on a number of religious questions, the Young Irelanders, many of whom were themselves Protestant, arguing for an inclusive non-sectarian approach to politics. Following Daniel O'Connell's death in 1847, the Young Irelanders provided a radical and dynamic alternative to John O'Connell's inertia. After 1846, however, political developments were overshadowed by a massive famine that was to change radically the course of Irish history.

EIGHT

FAMINE TO HOME RULE
c. 1845–1900

The Great Famine (or An Gorta Mór) was a watershed in modern Irish history. It also was a clear symbol that the Act of Union had failed. In the decades that followed, however, the divisions between those who supported the Union and those who did not became more polarised.

This chapter examines the consequences of the famine both in Ireland and elsewhere. It also assesses the emergence of a successful home rule movement in the late nineteenth century that gave rise to a new, more militant form of unionism. The middle ground contracted and the diversity within each tradition appeared to evaporate.

Famine

By 1845 Irish Catholics were in a stronger position than they had been for 200 years. While a large portion of the Catholic peasantry was poor and depended on a single crop, potatoes, for survival, the lifting of the Penal Laws in the late eighteenth century had allowed an economically strong Catholic middle class to emerge. Political agitation and mobilisation had won them Catholic emancipation in 1829. The symbolism of this victory was lost on neither the British government nor on radical movements within Europe. But the rising middle class alarmed Protestants. Their minority status made them vulnerable and meant that they did not have a peasantry to mobilise if necessary. The emergence of republican nationalism in the 1790s had also unleashed a more extreme form of Protestant militancy. The granting of Catholic emancipation signalled a defeat for conservative Protestantism that united Anglicans and Presbyterians in a collaboration against Catholics. During the 1840s, however, two events indicated that the religious divides could still be bridged. The emergence of Young Ireland as a political force reawakened the inclusive, non-sectarian approach of the United Irishmen.

The onset of the Great Famine after 1845 demonstrated that economic vulnerability was not confined to poor Catholics.

In the early nineteenth century many British politicians and economists regarded Irish agriculture as backward and underdeveloped. Irish landlords and Irish peasants alike were blamed for the refusal of Irish agriculture to modernise. Landlords were criticised for their failure to invest in their properties, for allowing the constant subdivision of land and for their high levels of absenteeism. Potatoes, which were the subsistence crop of approximately half of the Irish peasantry, were also blamed for Ireland's lack of economic progress. Dependence on potatoes had increased after 1750 when the population had grown rapidly. Potato cultivation allowed poor-quality marginal land to be utilised, while providing a plentiful and nutritious food for the Irish poor. The subdivision of land for potato growth allowed landlords to maintain their income, while releasing better-quality land for growing corn and raising cattle. After 1780 exports of corn, cattle and dairy produce to Britain increased substantially. The ending of the Napoleonic Wars in 1815 and the consequent economic dislocation throughout Europe reduced demand for Irish corn. Nevertheless, by 1845 annual food exports to Britain included approximately 250,000 cattle, 90 million eggs and enough grain to feed 2 million people. This high level of exports earned Ireland the title of 'bread basket of Britain'. Consequently, within Ireland a successful export trade existed alongside a large subsistence economy. Despite the high dependence of the poor on potatoes, potato cultivation accounted for only 20 per cent of total agricultural production. Various government inquiries in the 1830s had revealed that the decline of the domestic linen industry had increased dependence on this single crop, especially in the north of the country.

In 1845 an unknown blight destroyed approximately 50 per cent of the potato crop in Ireland. Prime Minister Peel set in train a number of measures to deal with the anticipated shortages in the following spring. His polices included the import of Indian corn from the United States, which not only increased food supplies in Ireland but also helped to stabilise food prices. Peel also saw the subsistence crisis as a chance to repeal the Corn Laws, which ended protection on corn imports into the United Kingdom. This legislation changed the basis of Ireland's agricultural economy from grain to pasture. The repeal of the Corn Laws angered members of the Tory Party, who split into two factions, the Protectionists and the Peelites. The disagreement ended

Peel's premiership and brought the Whigs into government, with Lord John Russell as prime minister.

In the first year of blight there was no excess mortality as a consequence of the shortages. In the summer of 1846, however, when the British parliament was dominated by the Corn Law crisis, the blight reappeared in Ireland. Its impact was more extensive than in the previous year, with almost the total crop being destroyed. The new government, therefore, faced a far more extensive crisis than Peel had confronted. Also, whereas Peel had a large government majority, Lord John Russell was at the head of a minority administration, and his electoral support came from a mixture of landed gentry and the merchant classes. While Peel had a gap of a number of months to put his relief measures in place, the 1846 potato failure had an immediate impact on the poor. The relief measures introduced in 1846 were more parsimonious than in the previous year and were unsuited to providing emergency relief. In the second year of shortages, public works were made the main form of relief, although conditions governing their management were harsh. Employment was for twelve hours a day and entailed demanding, physical labour generally building 'roads that led nowhere and walls that surrounded nothing'. Wages were paid at piece-rates, although a ceiling was placed on the amount that could be earned. The system was tied up in so many levels of bureaucracy as a way of avoiding abuse that the schemes took an average of six weeks to establish. Russell also decided not to resume Peel's policy of importing Indian corn into the country but to leave imports to the merchants. Despite calls from all parts of Ireland to restrict food exports, vast amounts of foodstuffs continued to leave the country, and although corn exports were reduced, the export of cattle, dairy produce and alcohol increased after 1846. In the winter of 1846 sharp increases in evictions, emigration, disease and death were testimony that the government's relief policies had not worked.

The public works were not only ineffective as a mechanism for saving lives; they were also expensive. At the beginning of 1847, in an admission of failure, the government changed its relief polices. The public works were replaced by a network of soup kitchens where the poor could obtain free rations of soup and bread. Although the size of rations was small, for the first time the Irish poor were getting direct relief in the form of food, and during the summer of 1847 the rate of excess mortality declined. By July 1847 over 3 million people were receiving daily rations of food from the soup kitchens.

At the beginning of 1847, duties were lifted from imported corn and the Navigation Laws, which decreed that all imports to the United Kingdom had to be carried on British-registered ships, were suspended. These measures were temporary and to end at the harvest, but because the destitution continued to be widespread, they were extended. All of these changes demonstrated that the relief measures, introduced only a few months earlier and leaving the Irish poor at the mercy of market forces, had not worked. Private relief was offered by a variety of organisations, with donations being sent from all over the world. The fact that a small minority of Anglican and Presbyterian organisations used the hunger of the people as an opportunity to proselytise meant that private relief was regarded with distrust.

The 1847 potato harvest showed little evidence of blight but the lack of seed potatoes and the demands of employment on the public works meant that the crop sown had been small. The relative freedom from blight permitted the government to announce that the famine was over. At the same time, the government's relief measures again changed. The soup kitchens were closed and the Poor Law system was made responsible for both permanent and temporary relief. The workhouses built after 1838 had capacity for 110,000 paupers. To cope with their extended role in relief provision, additional workhouses were built and, subject to stringent conditions, outdoor relief was permitted. For the government the main advantage of this change was that it made the landlords responsible for relief in their own localities, both through management of the workhouses and by payment of poor rates to finance the consolidated relief system. Included in the 1847 Poor Law legislation was the Quarter Acre Clause, the creation of an Irish landlord Sir William Gregory. The clause decreed that no person who occupied more than a quarter of an acre of land was eligible to receive relief. This harsh legislation forced small tenants to choose between obtaining relief and holding onto their land.

The famine clearly was not over, and in 1848 over 1 million people continued to be dependent on the minimal relief provided by the amended Poor Law. In 1848 the potato blight returned to Ireland and was as virulent as in 1846. The blight reappeared in 1849, although its impact was almost confined to the west of the country. The sharp increase in evictions exacerbated the problems of the poor. Between 1849 (when recording started) and 1854, over a quarter of a million people were legally evicted from their homes. Large numbers were also illegally ejected or gave up their properties voluntarily in order to be eligible for Poor Law relief. For landlords the incentive to evict smallholders was that poor rates were heavier on land that was subdivided. As a consequence, after 1847 homelessness joined hunger as a cause of social dislocation, disease and death.

Emigration provided an outlet for those who had the resources and energy to leave the country. Before 1845 emigration from Ireland had been high, but after 1846 the volume and character of the emigration changed. Famine emigration started at the end of 1846 and was carried out in a mood of desperation. Emigrants were willing to risk dangerous winter crossings in order to escape from Ireland, and also chanced travelling in ships that were ill suited to carry passengers. Despite many well-publicised instances of ships capsizing and calls for government regulation, the government was reluctant to intervene, preferring to leave emigration to market forces. Most of the emigrants chose the United States, usually travelling via Liverpool and Canada in order to get the cheapest fares. Most of the emigration was self-financed, with landlords only paying for 5 per cent of the total. Emigration in the later years of the famine was financed by remittances sent back by the original emigrants. This system of chain migration continued into the twentieth century and reinforced ties between Ireland and the new countries of settlement. The outflow of people from Ireland did not end when the blight disappeared, and the early 1850s witnessed an increase in the volume of emigration. Many regarded themselves as economic refugees rather than voluntary emigrants. Protestant landlords and the British government were often the target of the emigrants' anger, and this was translated into nationalist feeling.

Good harvests returned to Ireland after 1851 although the fall in population, changes in landownership, the response of landlords to the British government, and the attempts at proselytising left enduring and painful legacies. Within the space of six years, Ireland's population fell by 25 per cent, making the Irish famine one of the most lethal in modern history. Apart from the short-term impact on population, the famine precipitated a longer-term demographic shock. In 1841 Ireland had one of the fastest-growing populations in Europe, but after the famine, uniquely within Europe, the Irish population diminished. While the population of the rest of the United Kingdom increased during the course of the nineteenth century, the Irish population continued to fall. By 1900 the Irish population had fallen to just over 4 million, which was half of its pre-famine level. The tragedy of the famine occurred in the jurisdiction of the richest empire in the world and at the heart of the United Kingdom. It was a clear indication that the Act of Union had failed.

Revolutionary Nationalism

The divisions within the repeal movement became more apparent after 1843, the year in which Daniel O'Connell claimed the Act of Union would be repealed. His retreat at Clontarf not only damaged him personally, but weakened the entire repeal movement. Following this, the political initiative passed increasingly to a group of radical intellectuals known as Young Ireland. Its leadership was diverse, including Catholics and Protestants, radicals and moderates, landlords and lawyers, while women were also significant among the supporters. The leaders included Thomas Davis, William Smith O'Brien, John Mitchel, Thomas Francis Meagher and Charles Gavan Duffy. The founding of the *Nation* newspaper in 1842 helped the spread of their influence. One of its founders, Thomas Davis, was both a Protestant nationalist and a poet. As a student at Trinity College he implored the college authorities to teach Irish history. He had joined the repeal movement in 1839, but together with a group of other intellectuals became frustrated by O'Connell's lack of tenacity. His premature death at the age of thirty-one deprived Young Ireland of one of its most gifted and original thinkers. His influence persisted long after his death and endured in his popular ballad, 'A Nation Once Again'.

One of O'Connell's achievements was to argue for an Irish press that was cheap and liberal. The success of the Catholic Association and the repeal movement was helped by their connections with a number of sympathetic newspapers, including the *Freeman's Journal*, the *Cork Examiner*, *The Pilot* and, briefly, the *Belfast Vindicator*. The *Nation*, however, wanted to go beyond the reporting of news and political analysis. It aimed to promote cultural nationalism as an antidote to earlier writers and historians who had ignored or been dismissive of Ireland's culture, traditions and history. Initially the *Nation* had a print run of 12,000 copies, but when it was suppressed in 1848, it had a readership of 250,000, making it one of the most widely read papers in Ireland. It also provided a chance for women to participate in the national awakening and cultural revival of Ireland, although the women used pseudonyms. One of the most remarkable female poets was Jane Elgee, who wrote as 'Speranza'. In 1847 she published 'The Famine Year', which was a searing indictment of the British government. She also helped to edit the *Nation* following the arrest of Duffy in 1848. In 1851 she married the Dublin surgeon William Wilde and they had two sons, William and Oscar, who was to become the famous playwright and poet, achieving success (and meeting disaster) in England rather than Ireland.

In 1846 the divisions within the repeal movement reached a climax, and in January 1847 Young Ireland formed the Irish Confederation. It drew most of its support from the towns, and its local organisation was based on a network of confederate clubs. The clubs were in regular contact with each other, those in Dublin, Liverpool and Manchester keeping in touch using carrier pigeons. However, the leadership of the Confederation also suffered from internal divisions over the question of the role of landlords and the rights of property. These differences resulted in the radical John Mitchel leaving the Confederation at the beginning of 1848, which deprived the organisation of one of its most popular and well-known leaders at a crucial time. O'Connell's death in Italy in May 1847 further contributed to the decline of the Old Ireland movement, after an initial flurry of sympathy.

The French revolution in February 1848 created a wave of revolutionary fervour throughout Europe. It was particularly admired because the French monarchy had been overthrown with little bloodshed (the violence came later, in the June Days). The revolution was warmly greeted by nationalists in Ireland, where bonfires were lit and meetings were convened to send messages of congratulation to the French provisional government. The French revolution also raised hopes among moderate nationalists that repeal could be achieved in a similarly bloodless revolution. However, even moderates, angered by the indifference of the British government to the suffering caused by the famine, supported some sort of revolutionary insurrection. The famine complicated the timing, with many radicals arguing that no uprising should take place until the poor had secured the harvest, probably in August.

William Smith O'Brien, a Protestant landlord and MP in Westminster, was one of the leaders of Young Ireland. He believed that external assistance was necessary for the uprising to succeed. In March 1848 he recommended 'the formation of an Irish brigade in America, composed of Irish emigrants, who might, hereafter, serve as the basis of an Irish army'. He also hoped that France would intervene to help the uprising. In April 1848 a delegation of Young Irelanders visited Paris to meet with the provisional government.

Before they arrived, the British ambassador, Lord Normanby, pressured the French government not to support Ireland. The British government regarded the lukewarm French response to the Irishmen as a propaganda coup, and the Irish lord lieutenant printed copies of the French reply and displayed them throughout Ireland. French intervention in Irish affairs, therefore, was neutralised in 1848. However, many Irish emigrants in America – Catholic and Protestant alike – had publicly declared their support for repeal of the Union. Moreover, their views had been infused with American republican ideals, which meant that American support was closer to the views of radical Young Irelanders than those of the repeal party. Both the Young and Old Irelanders also had substantial support in Britain. The Irish Confederation had forged close relations with the British Chartists and this alliance bothered the British government more than the French or American connection. The ignominious conclusion to the presentation of the third Chartist petition on 10 April was not only an anticlimax for the Chartists but a significant victory for the British government propaganda against radicalism. Although the Confederate leaders were not being able to rely on support from either French or British radicals, the deteriorating situation in Ireland in the summer of 1848 hardened their attitudes. In particular William Smith O'Brien was disillusioned with the government's policies during the famine, believing that while these policies had not caused the tragedy, they had added to the suffering of the people.

The nervousness of the British government was manifested in a series of draconian measures introduced in the spring of 1848. The Crown and Government Security Act introduced in April created a new offence of treason–felony. The definition of treason included 'open and advised speaking' in such a way as would encourage rebellion. The Aliens Removal Act was introduced in response to rumours concerning foreigners – especially Frenchmen – coming into the country. This act permitted the removal of any foreigner from the United Kingdom if their conduct could be regarded as 'injurious to the peace of the realm'. In Ireland and Britain plain-clothes policemen attended public meetings of the repealers, while informers reported on the private meetings of Confederate and repeal clubs. What was particularly worrying for the authorities was the fact that the structure and number of Confederate clubs made it difficult to place informers inside them, which meant that information was scant. The Orange Order, which had been growing since 1845, also offered to act as a counter-insurgency force as it had done during the 1798 insurrection. Although the lord lieutenant publicly declined the offer of support, privately he had decided to use the Order as a reserve force if necessary.

Following the introduction of the Treason–Felony Act, Mitchel, O'Brien and Meagher were arrested. O'Brien and Meagher were acquitted, but Mitchel's conviction by a handpicked and predominantly Protestant jury signalled a new determination by the British government. Mitchel's dubious conviction, and his rushed transportation to Bermuda, united moderate and radical nationalist opinions in Ireland, and was condemned by radicals in Britain and the United States. There was talk of rescuing him from his prison ship, and funds were established to give to his young family. The Confederation claimed that Ireland was on the verge of an uprising but urged the people to wait until harvest, after which they avowed that 'armed resistance to the oppressors will become a sacred obligation'. This declaration was printed in newspapers in Ireland, Britain and America. As the summer progressed, the prospects for harvest appeared poor, with potato blight reappearing in Ireland.

At the beginning of July 1848 the British government arrested a number of Confederate leaders, including John Martin of the *Felon*, Charles Gavan Duffy of the *Nation*, and Messrs Williams and Doheny of the *Tribune*. On 12 July a warrant was issued to Thomas Meagher for having made a seditious speech in Limerick. On 20 July the Irish lord lieutenant 'proclaimed' the City and County of Dublin and Counties Cork, Waterford and Drogheda, which meant that any person who carried or had in their possession any weapon (guns, swords, pikes) could be imprisoned for two years' hard labour. Also, any house or premises could be searched between sunrise and sunset. An even more draconian measure was passed on 25 July when the prime minister, Lord John Russell, suspended the Habeas Corpus Act in Ireland, giving the authorities the power to apprehend and arrest any person suspected of 'treasonable designs'. The suspension of the act was a trigger for action, as the leaders knew that if they did not act immediately they would be imprisoned. William Smith O'Brien, who was a reluctant rebel, was persuaded to lead a rebellion immediately. Because Dublin was so well guarded it was decided to locate the uprising in the south-west of the country, near Kilkenny. But the insurgents had been taken unawares and they lacked both weapons and a strategy. O'Brien, who was a man of principle, told his small band of followers that they were not to steal or to damage property. Just as importantly, the Catholic Church hierarchy – alarmed by recent events in France – issued a declaration disapproving of any involvement in an uprising.

On 28 July a small uprising led by William Smith O'Brien took place in Ballingarry in County Tipperary. It was easily defeated with few casualties, only two of the insurgents being killed. Charles Gavan Duffy believed that the uprising had taken place three months too late, allowing the government rather than the rebels to seize the initiative. Although the events in Ballingarry marked an end to Confederate hopes in Ireland, the British and Irish authorities remained alert, as they had received intelligence from an informer in New York about the imminent arrival of 5,000 members of a specially recruited Irish Brigade. The Brigade never appeared, but it suggested that as early as 1848 an Irish-American nationalism had been awakened. Following the defeat at Ballingarry, some of the leaders of the Irish Confederates escaped either to the United States or to France. Others, including O'Brien and Meagher, were captured, found guilty of high treason and sentenced to death. In 1849 their sentences were commuted, and six Confederates were transported to Van Diemen's Land (Tasmania) for life. John Mitchel was taken from Bermuda to join them there. Mitchel and Meagher escaped to the United States in 1852, while O'Brien remained until he received a conditional pardon in 1854, which became a full pardon in 1856. Some of the junior members of the Confederate movement, including James Stephens and Michael Doheny, founded the Fenian movement in 1858.

Although the 1848 insurrection was easily defeated, in the longer term it helped to shape the development of Irish nationalism. Moreover, the events that had led to the uprising were significant in keeping alive a vision of non-sectarian republicanism. They also showed unity between British and Irish radicals was possible and could be fruitful – and, despite the non-arrival of the Irish Brigade, constituted a major step in the development and emergence of Irish-American nationalism. The Young Irelanders had also promoted cultural nationalism in Ireland and their legacy influenced subsequent nationalists and laid the foundation for a revival in Gaelic culture.

Although most of the leaders were in prison or in exile in 1849, a small group of Young Irelanders attempted to revive Young Ireland clubs. Because much of the repressive legislation remained in place, the revived movement was under ground. The main force behind the Young Ireland revival was James Fintan Lalor, whose radical writings, especially on the question of an agrarian revolt, had greatly influenced John Mitchel. Lalor, whose health was bad, died in 1849. Lalor also influenced the emergence of socialist nationalism at the beginning of the twentieth century, most evidently in the writings of James Connolly. The conspirators were willing to use physical-force tactics, plotting the abduction of Queen Victoria during her visit to Dublin in August 1849. The constabulary knew of the plan and arrested some of the leaders before the queen arrived in the city. Their most ambitious scheme was an attack on the police barracks in Cappoquin in Waterford in September 1849. The police knew an uprising was likely, although the timing took them by surprise. The insurgents were easily defeated, although one policeman, James Owens, was killed. This made Owens the first member of the constabulary to be killed in a nationalist uprising. Despite his murder, the leaders of the uprising were transported rather than executed.

The defeat of Young Ireland marked the end to a long period of nationalist activity in Ireland that had begun with Daniel O'Connell in 1840. Ten years later, O'Connell was dead, most of the Young Ireland leadership had been transported or were in exile, the repeal movement was in disarray and physical force had been discredited. The British government had shown its willingness to use draconian measures in order to defeat an uprising and so preserve not only the unity of the United Kingdom but also the sanctity of the British Empire.

The Fenians

The Great Famine, the collapse of the repeal movement and the failure of the 1848 rising meant that the 1840s were a watershed in the social, economic and political development of Ireland. After 1850 the Irish population was greatly reduced, while the poor were dispirited, demoralised and exhausted. Not surprisingly, Irishmen living outside Ireland largely inspired much of the initiative, energy and resources for the next wave of nationalist activity. For Irish Americans in particular, anger at having been forced to leave their country of birth combined with the prejudice and alienation they experienced in the United States. This was associated with the rise of the Know-Nothing Party, which mounted campaigns against foreign immigrants.

The Irish Republican Brotherhood (IRB), or Fenians, was founded in Dublin and New York in 1858. The founders included James Stephens, John O'Mahony, Charles Kickham and Thomas Clarke Luby, most of whom had been involved in the 1848 uprisings. An early recruit was Jeremiah O'Donovan Rossa, founder of the radical Phoenix Society. Although the Fenians borrowed much from the ideology of Young Ireland, especially Thomas Davis's views of nationality, they believed that physical force was the only way to gain an independent Ireland. Their single aim, therefore, was to win independence through an armed uprising. Fenianism also differed from earlier nationalist movements in that most of its support came from the towns and its members were artisans or workingmen. Landlords, the British government and the Catholic Church disliked this secret organisation and its radical aims equally. Although many of the Fenians were Catholic, like the Young Irelanders they argued against replacing the Protestant ascendancy with Catholic ascendancy, but wanted a separation of Church and State. Unlike Young Ireland, the Fenians had little success in winning the support of Protestants. More worrying for the future of Irish nationalism, the Fenians alarmed conservatives and unionists, who distanced themselves from nationalist politics. What also made the Fenians different was that they had large-scale support overseas, particularly in the United States and Britain. Although the repeal movement and Young Ireland had also drawn support in these places, the scale and organisational structure of the overseas Fenians made them much more threatening. Mass emigration had exported Irish nationalism overseas, and the experience of the famine was the latest grievance against British rule. Many of the leaders of Young Ireland distanced themselves from the Fenians, although they used the death of Terence McManus in 1861 as a publicity stunt, bringing his body from exile in San Francisco, via New York, to be buried in Dublin. John Mitchel was also persuaded to leave his exile in the United States to be the Fenian treasurer in Paris. Mitchel, however, found James Stephens arrogant, indecisive and difficult to work with.

The outbreak of the American Civil War in 1861 delayed the Fenian uprising but many Irish Americans used it to gain military experience – something that had been lacking in earlier uprisings. The ending of the American Civil War in 1865 released thousands of trained Irishmen to take up revolutionary activities. The British government responded by arresting many Fenians, including Luby, O'Donovan Rossa and Stephens. Without their leadership, the hope of a successful rising had passed. Stephens was sprung from jail and he assumed command of the American movement. A small rising finally took place in February and a large one in March 1867. As had been the case before, the rising was a series of uncoordinated activities that took place in Ireland, Britain and the United States. As had happened before, the British government had infiltrated the Fenians and was aware of the movements of many of the leaders. By the time the uprising took place most of the leadership was in prison. They also lacked sufficient arms or money to make the uprising effective. The Catholic Church, now firmly under the influence of the conservative cardinal Paul Cullen, was vehement in denouncing the Fenians and, in some cases, consigning them to hell. Although the Fenians were defeated in 1867, their vision lived on and individual members of the IRB kept the hope of a revolutionary uprising alive.

Although the uprising had failed, it had some longer-term consequences. The barrister Isaac Butt, a conservative, former Orangeman and adversary of Daniel O'Connell, defended some of the Fenians. In 1848 he had defended O'Brien and Meagher and started to sympathise with nationalist politics. His defence of the Fenians completed this process and led him to found the Home Government Association in 1870. This transformed into the home rule movement. The long jail sentences and the appalling treatment of the Fenian prisoners resulted in the formation of the Amnesty Association in 1879 to look after the welfare of prisoners. Isaac Butt was president. The Fenian uprising also had a profound impact on a British politician, William Gladstone. He had previously shown little interest in Ireland, but the uprising changed this. Gladstone not only moved Irish issues to the top of his political agenda; he became a champion of Irish home rule. His involvement was to change the course of both British and Irish politics. The Irish Constabulary was given the title Royal Irish Constabulary for its role in repressing the Fenian threat.

The activities of the British Fenians were also to have long-term implications. A number of uprisings were to take place in England in 1867, including an attack on Chester Castle to get arms. Again, the authorities had advance warning and arrested many of the ringleaders. When two of the leading Fenians, Thomas Kelly and Timothy Deasy, were being taken to the jail in Manchester, the police van was attacked and the prisoners released. During the commotion an unarmed policeman was killed. The government responded immediately with blanket arrests, and five men were convicted of murder, three of whom, William O'Meara Allen, Michael Larkin and William O'Brien, were hanged. The hastiness of their trial led to suspicion that the wrong men had been convicted. The hanging created a wave of public sympathy for the three men, who were designated the 'Manchester Martyrs'.

The popular response to the hangings, together with Gladstone's commitment to Irish politics, contributed to a new phase in nationalist politics.

Land, Landlords and Land War

The land question was central to many political developments in the nineteenth century. By then, being an Irish landlord meant more than just the possession of land but represented an outlook and a way of life. Ownership of land conveyed social status, economic power, political participation and a cultural mindset. Landlords were the elite descendants of the Gaels, Normans, Old English, New English, Scottish and various other settler groups in Ireland, and by the nineteenth century they had melded into a new ascendancy group generically known as the Anglo-Irish. Their power was derived from land, and land was largely a Protestant commodity. Irish landlords, especially absentee landlords, were widely regarded as unenterprising and indolent by successive British governments. Yet the generally accepted negative view of Irish landlords overlooked the fact that they were a diverse group and included among their number good managers, innovative agriculturalists, benevolent landlords, women and Catholic proprietors. A number of landlords were insolvent, or nearly so, as a result of lack of investment, long leases and over-dependency on middlemen or land agents. The famine years, when rents were unpaid and taxes were high, proved too much for some landlords. Sale of estates was complicated, and falling property prices after 1846 were a further disincentive to sell. Russell's government, however, viewed the financial problems of landlords as an opportunity to clear Ireland of unenterprising proprietors and pave the way for more cash-rich landlords from Britain. To facilitate the sale of land, special legislation was introduced in 1848, known as the Encumbered Estates Act. To expedite its impact a more rigid act was passed in the following year, which created a special court with compulsory powers to force the sale of property. Land did change hands, although the government's hope that it would be purchased by British capitalists was not realised. Middle-class Catholics bought some land, but buoyant Anglo-Irish landlords purchased the majority of estates. The ascendancy class, therefore, survived the famine largely intact.

Regardless of the changes in landownership, overall there was a high level of stability and continuity before and after 1846. Despite the economic shock of the 1840s, landownership remained in the hands of a small group that was both economically and politically powerful. There were approximately 20 million acres of land in Ireland, and by 1881 it was owned by fewer than 20,000 people: only 750 men owned half of the land, while the ten largest landowners owned 1 million acres. With few exceptions, the largest landowners were Anglican, Anglo-Irish and unionist. Before the famine, most Irish landlords had followed the British political divide of Whig (Liberal) or Tory (Conservative), but by the 1880s these allegiances had been replaced by those of nationalist and unionist. While in Britain, Irish landlords were viewed as an impediment to economic progress, in Ireland they were increasingly regarded as defenders of colonial rule and a barrier to political independence.

Tenant farmers farmed most of the land. Although the average size of farms after the famine was between 15 and 30 acres, the farmers were a diverse group, ranging from those who occupied large farms to those who existed near to subsistence level. For the poor who survived the famine, life changed little. They remained politically and economically weak: the poorest tenants continued to have a high dependence on potatoes, and their economic survival was made possible by remittances from America or by seasonal work in Britain. Their economic vulnerability was apparent during bad harvest years, such as 1860 and 1879. Without external cash injections, it is unlikely that their properties would have been economically viable. Living standards did rise in the second half of the nineteenth century, but this took place against a backdrop of a rapidly declining population and large-scale emigration. The depopulation of Ireland represented the largest movement of people in the nineteenth century in proportion to the size of the population. One of the remarkable changes in agriculture was the move to pasture farming. The repeal of the Corn Laws and the clearance of small tenants from estates facilitated the change to large grazing farms whereby the production of beef and butter overtook corn in importance. By 1881 twice as much land was used for pasture as was used for growing crops. A further incentive for change to pasture was that profits increased as prices rose after 1850, while the price of corn generally remained the same.

The reform of the landholding system had been a central demand of some of the more radical Young Irelanders in the 1840s, although the majority supported the more moderate aim of introducing the Ulster Custom to the whole of the country. The Ulster Custom had been introduced in the seventeenth century to give limited protection to plantation settlers, generally compensating them for improvements made to the land. However, this system had no legal validity and was confined to areas in the north-east of the country. In the 1850s the tenant right movement emerged as a political force in Ireland, uniting both Catholic and Protestant tenants in the demand for reform. William McKnight, the Presbyterian editor of the *Banner of Ulster*, and Charles Gavan Duffy, the Catholic editor of the *Nation*, formed the Tenant League movement in Dublin in 1850. Its demands were referred to as the 'three Fs', that is, the right to freedom of sale, fixity of tenure and fair rents. The League did not support violence but promoted constitutional means to further its demands. This was helped by the extension of the franchise in 1850, which allowed occupiers of land valued at over £12 to vote. To some extent the movement filled the political vacuum left by the demise of the Young Ireland and repeal movements. The Tenant League was short-lived, disbanding in 1858. Although it achieved little, it sowed many seeds and provided a political programme for the more successful Land League.

The economic and religious differences between landlords and tenants were exacerbated by the fact that tenants had few rights, with little protection in law. Many of them were tenants at will, which meant that they could be easily evicted and were vulnerable to unexpected rent increases. An exception was the minority of tenants protected by the Ulster Custom. Following the famine the number of evictions fell, but they were clustered during periods of poor harvest, such as 1859–61 and 1879–80. The fact that they took place when the poor were suffering anyway made them appear particularly heartless. Some of the evictions were widely publicised, such as the Derryveagh evictions in County Donegal in 1861, where the evictions were precipitated by the murder of a land steward. The murder of landlords and stewards, although not common, received widespread publicity. These assassinations shocked public opinion in Britain, being regarded as proof of the lawlessness of the Irish. The evictions, however, attracted adverse publicity in sections of the British press, suggesting that a new challenge to the landlord ascendancy was emerging outside Ireland. A recent but influential convert to the need for land reform was William Gladstone. In 1870 his Landlord and Tenant Act gave legal validity to tenant right where it existed and extended it to other parts of the country. This legislation made it difficult to evict tenants for reasons other than non-payment of rent, and allowed outgoing tenants to receive compensation for improvements.

Evictions increased after 1879 following a series of bad harvests. In 1880 alone, over 2,000 families were evicted. The evictions prompted an immediate increase in rural crimes or 'outrages'. In that year there were over 2,500 recorded outrages throughout Ireland. A young Irishman, Michael Davitt, harnessed this anger to a powerful political machine. His own family had been evicted from County Mayo during the famine, and he spent his childhood in Lancashire working in a factory until he lost his right arm in machinery in 1857, when he was aged eleven. In 1865 Davitt joined the Fenian movement in England and was imprisoned for fifteen years for gunrunning. He was released early and, despite being on a ticket of leave, he resumed his political activities. The subsistence crisis in 1879 prompted Davitt to establish a Land League. His intention was to lead a nationwide campaign for the establishment of the three Fs. Peasant proprietorship was the ultimate aim of the League, together with the eradication of the landlord system. The position of the League was strengthened when Charles Stewart Parnell, a leading home rule politician, accepted its presidency. A further strength of the League was that it united diverse social groups; also, farmers were usually in the vanguard of the movement rather than landless labourers, who had less to gain. There were some divisions. A minority of supporters wanted more radical social and political demands to be included in their programme. Some large farmers, though, were opposed to a total social revolution, wanting landlords' estates to be broken up, rather than a complete redistribution of land. Moreover, the League was not able to establish strong roots among the Protestants of Ulster. The foundation of the Land League initiated the Land War. It was based on mutual support and civil resistance. A particularly successful tactic was the system of boycotting, named after the Irish land agent Captain Boycott. Boycott, who was agent on Lord Erne's estates in County Mayo, responded to the refusal of local labourers to work on the property by bringing Orangemen from the north to replace them. The new workers had to be protected by 1,000 troops. Overall, the League's use of isolation or boycott, sometimes underpinned by a threat of violence, proved to be successful.

The 1881 Land Act gave legal recognition to the three Fs, and established a Land Commission to decide on fair rents and make loans to tenants of up to 75 per cent of the purchase price. The act created divisions within the League, as some supporters felt that it had not gone far enough in weakening the landlord system, while others felt that there was no need for the Land War to continue. The protests resulted in the imprisoning of Parnell and other leaders, who issued a 'no rent' manifesto from jail. The authorities responded by outlawing the League. One of the most talented young barristers who adjudicated on behalf of the tenants was Edward Carson. He was subsequently linked with unionism and the Conservative Party, yet in his early career he was sympathetic to measures introduced by the Liberal Party, even being asked to stand as a Land League candidate in Waterford. Within a few years, however, he was representing the government against the tenants (see p. 188).

Michael Davitt responded to the imprisonment of Parnell and the outlawing of the Land League in an imaginative and unprecedented way by asking Parnell's sister Anna to take over the management of the Land War. In 1881, therefore, Anna founded the Ladies' Land League. Even before Davitt's invitation, the two Parnell sisters, Anna and Fanny, had recognised the value of organising women not simply as appendages to men but as an independent political force. In 1880 Fanny had founded the New York Ladies' Land League and attempted, unsuccessfully, to extend the women's organisation to Ireland. Fanny was also a talented writer, and her powerful poem 'Hold the Harvest', written in response to the food shortages in Ireland, had resonance with Speranza's poetry written during the famine. The Ladies' Land League, under Anna's leadership, not only filled the leadership vacuum but also extended the activities of the outlawed League. She proved indefatigable in organising tenants to resist evictions and providing accommodation for those who were evicted. Her support of small tenants and desire for a social revolution alarmed the more conservative male members of the Land League and larger tenants, who were proving to be the main beneficiaries of the activities. Anna, in turn, grew to dislike the social conservatism of the new farming class. The Ladies' Land League was remarkable because, for the first time, it gave Irish women a recognised role in nationalist politics. The involvement was short-lived, however. When Parnell was released from prison in May 1882, he dismantled both the Land League and the Ladies' Land League. Five months later, the Irish National League was founded to carry on some of the work of the Land League, though Parnell was not involved.

Despite the short existence of the Land League and its contentious demise, the passing of the 1881 Land Act was a milestone for Irish tenants. As landlords feared, it also marked the beginning rather than the ending of the process of land reform. Further legislation followed. In 1885 the Purchase of Land Act allowed tenants to receive loans covering the full purchase price of the property, while the Purchase of Land Act of 1891 introduced bonds to facilitate land sale. More importantly, in the long term it established the Congested Districts Board, which had powers to purchase and redistribute land and to relocate tenants where necessary. The Board was also responsible for improving the infrastructure of the west of Ireland and for bringing new farming techniques and technologies to the country. The various land acts did not bring an end to rural poverty. Although Parnell had little involvement in agricultural affairs after 1881, one of his supporters, William O'Brien, initiated a 'Plan of Campaign' in 1886. In cases where a landlord refused a rent reduction, the tenants would deposit the rent in an estate fund, and this could be used to support evicted tenants. The spread of the campaign through the south and west of the country alarmed landlords and the government alike, and both resisted it. For nationalists, though, it was a drain on resources and was called to an end in 1890.

Successive Conservative governments also showed their commitment to land reforms as part of their plan to 'kill Home Rule with kindness'. This strategy of 'constructive Unionism' was associated with the period between 1895 and 1905, and its success was partly due to the absence of effective nationalist opposition. The Land Act of 1903 (also known as the Wyndham Land Act) finalised the transfer of land from landlords, by providing funds for estates to be sold if three-quarters of the tenants wanted to buy. They did, especially as the terms were favourable, with the annual repayments often being lower than their existing rents. This act resulted in the transfer of 11 million acres of land. Birrell's Land Act of 1909 modified Wyndham's Act by making the purchase terms less favourable to the tenants. Following this, the number of purchases decreased.

By the outbreak of war in 1914, two-thirds of former Irish tenants now owned their own properties. When the Congested Districts Board was finally dissolved in 1923, it had purchased over 1,000 estates. The various land acts constituted a social revolution in Ireland, which was even more remarkable as it pre-dated a political revolution. Although poor tenants benefited from fair rents, the main beneficiaries were larger tenants. Even more significantly, the various land acts led to the rapid demise of Irish landlordism. The extinction of the landlord class was accompanied by the disappearance of a way of life which was embodied in the disappearance of the 'Big House'. For the landlords who did survive, years of revolutionary warfare and the creation of the Free State provided the death knell of the Protestant ascendancy.

Political Union and Division

Following the defeat of the 1867 Fenian uprisings, the nationalist struggle again returned to constitutional methods. Since 1832 there had been 105 Irish MPs in parliament. Although they followed the divisions of the British political parties, a high portion of them were briefly united by O'Connell in support of repeal. It was not until the emergence of the home rule movement in the 1870s that Irish MPs again demonstrated a similar unity of purpose. Isaac Butt, who proved to be a brilliant but flawed leader, founded the home rule movement. The takeover by Charles Parnell and Joseph Biggar transformed the movement from being an irritant in Westminster politics to a powerful political machine. In 1879 over sixty MPs supported the Home Rule Party; by 1885, this had increased to eighty-six. More success followed when Parnell decided to work with other political groups, even though their goals and methods appeared incompatible. In 1879 Parnell, Davitt and the Fenian leader, John Devoy, made a compact, known as the 'New Departure', which accepted a link between nationalism and the land question. Although this link was regarded as original, John Mitchel and Fintan Lalor had argued for a similar alliance in the 1840s. The New Departure also recognised that there were substantial differences in some areas: while the Fenians refused to work with any British government, Parnell viewed the Parliamentary Party as crucial to success. In the short term, though, the alliance proved beneficial to all nationalists, especially as it coincided with the onset of the Land War. Within the alliance also, Parnell appeared supreme, as by 1880 he was both president of the Land League and chairman of the Irish Parliamentary Party.

Charles Parnell had been born into a Protestant landowning family in County Wicklow. He had grown up surrounded by remarkable women. His Irish-American mother, Delia Parnell, had been a critic of American slavery and had supported women's rights. He also had two remarkable sisters, Anna and Fanny, who each made a significant contribution to nationalist politics. Because they both spent much time in the United States, they helped to extend the influence of the Land League, especially among Irish-American Fenians. An early significant success was the 1881 Land Act, yet it left Parnell in a dilemma regarding the continuation of the Land War. His decision to call off the agrarian struggle angered his more radical supporters, including his sisters. Following this, he concentrated on making his parliamentary supporters effective at Westminster and in this aim he was very successful, particularly following his alliance with William Gladstone.

Gladstone's long career in the British parliament began in 1832. Although he had served under Peel's Tory government in the 1840s, he subsequently joined the Whig–Liberal Party. Gladstone had shown little interest in Irish affairs until the Fenian uprisings of 1867. Although he decried their violent intent, they convinced him that Ireland was the most important issue in British politics and that the country needed to be 'pacified'. As Liberal prime minister from 1868 to 1874 he was responsible for the 1870 Land Act and the disestablishment of the Anglican Church in 1869. The disestablishment was of particular significance as Gladstone was a devout Anglican, and the queen, the Conservative Party and the Anglican Church itself opposed this measure. While it pleased both Catholics and Presbyterians in Ireland, militant Protestants, notably the Orange Order, used it to arouse anti-Catholic feeling. Gladstone also attempted to appease Catholic demands for higher education with his University Bill of 1873, although it was the Conservative leader Disraeli who brought this scheme to fruition.

Gladstone's Land Act of 1881 demonstrated that he was willing to weaken Irish landlords in order to pacify Ireland. Moreover, the Kilmainham Treaty of 1882, which marked the official end of the Land War, initiated an alliance between Parnell and Gladstone. A few weeks later the alliance was threatened by the murder in the Phoenix Park in Dublin of the chief secretary and under-secretary. A secret assassination club, the Invincibles, carried out the murders. Although a new Coercion Act was passed, Gladstone did not allow the murders to interfere with his programme. The Invincibles were caught, and five of them were hanged in the following year.

After 1882 Irish and British politics entered a new phase as the political priority of Gladstone and Parnell became home rule for Ireland. This marked a genuine new departure in the Irish struggle, which traditionally had the support of only a handful of radicals within the British parliament. The emergence of Gladstone – in his reinvented post-1867 manifestation – gave Ireland a committed champion of home rule, moreover one who held the most important position within the House of Commons. His conversion to home rule in 1885 not only split the Liberal Party, but it resulted in the emergence of a more militant and united form of unionism.

The general election of 1885 was remarkable not only because home rule was an issue, but also because the franchise extensions in 1867 and 1884 meant that it was the most democratic election ever held. Women, however, no matter how rich or educated, had no right to vote. Parnell made a passionate appeal to support home rule, saying 'No man has the right to set a boundary to the onward march of a Nation. No man has the right to say: Thus far shalt thou go, and no further.' The outcome of the election was a victory for Liberals in Britain and Parnell in Ireland. Gladstone, aged seventy-six, again became prime minister and announced that his political priority was home rule for Ireland. Gladstone's support for home rule was not only based on his desire of justice for Ireland but was also premised on the fact that it would strengthen rather than undermine the United Kingdom. Yet he did not take account of the substantial number of Irish Protestants who wanted to remain fully integrated into the United Kingdom. Gladstone's 1886 Home Rule Bill envisaged an Irish parliament in which power was devolved from the Westminster parliament. The home rule parliament would have responsibility for domestic issues, while the imperial parliament would decide on issues concerning security, taxation and foreign relations. Irish politicians would also continue to sit at Westminster, thus retaining a voice in imperial affairs but also – to the chagrin of its opponents – a say in British affairs. Gladstone, however, was unable to get the whole of the Liberal Party to support home rule. Joseph Chamberlain led a revolt by some Liberals to vote against it with the Conservatives. The bill was defeated in the House of Commons by a majority of thirty. It was also a personal defeat for Gladstone. None the less, it was the first time that a general election in the United Kingdom had been fought on a home rule issue. Some British radicals also believed that the government was treating Irish nationalism less sympathetically than nationalism elsewhere. These double standards were pointed out by the British MP Charles Bradlaugh in the House of Commons on 23 March 1887, when he posed the question, 'Was it so very wicked to talk about the nationality of Ireland? . . . But it did not lie in the mouth of an English government to denounce the doctrine of nationality after the encouragement that England had given to the nationalities of Poland and Italy, Greece and Bulgaria.'

For Parnell, regardless of the home rule defeat, merely having it brought before a British parliament was a personal victory. Parnell's success, however, worried some conservative opinion in Britain, and in 1887 *The Times* published a series of letters under the heading 'Parnell and Crime' which claimed that Parnell was linked with violent groups. These accusations united nationalist opinion in support of Parnell, and a commission in 1890 proved that the letters had been forged. Parnell's triumph was short-lived. In December 1889 he was cited as co-respondent in a divorce case brought by Captain O'Shea, a former ally and friend. Parnell, who had had a long-term and widely known relationship with Katherine O'Shea, married her in June 1891. But it was too late, and too many powerful factions, including former colleagues, had chosen to condemn him. British nonconformists, who had been committed supporters of home rule, declared him unfit to lead his party. The Catholic Church hierarchy, whom Parnell had made little attempt to woo, denounced him. Unionists and Conservatives were also delighted at the fall of such an effective nationalist leader. Gladstone reluctantly asked that Parnell temporarily retire from politics. His refusal to do so split the Home Rule Party more than the original scandal. He tried, unsuccessfully, to regain his leadership, but died in October 1891. He was aged only forty-six and his achievements in a short life had been remarkable.

Despite his defeat and loss of a political ally, Gladstone's commitment to home rule continued. In 1893 he introduced a second Home Rule Bill, which passed in the House of Commons but was overwhelmingly defeated in the House of Lords. At this stage Gladstone was aged eighty-four. He resigned the following year, bringing to an end his extraordinary political career. Between them Gladstone and Parnell had not only brought significant benefits to Ireland but had laid the foundations for a new phase of nationalism that was organised, confident and determined. Their common failure, however, was in ignoring the views and aspirations of Irish Protestants, despite the fact that they themselves were Protestant. Both men had underestimated the strength of feeling and consequent opposition of Irish and British Protestants. Because they failed to woo or convince them, a schism had emerged in Ireland that proved more difficult to heal than earlier political divisions. The voice of liberal Protestantism shrank and was drowned out by conservative elements.

Unionism

Although unionism had existed in the first half of the nineteenth century, it lacked a coherent structure or political organisation, but was loosely based on an allegiance to Protestantism, the Crown and the Act of Union. The Great Famine, however, was a damning demonstration of the failure of the Union and resulted not only in mass Catholic excess mortality, but also the deaths of thousands of poor Protestants, yet in its aftermath allegiance to Britain increased among Protestants of all classes. The creation of a unionist political machine was largely in response to the actions of nationalists rather than the activities of Protestants. Despite the crisis of the famine, throughout the nineteenth century middle-class Catholics were becoming more economically and politically successful. Concurrent with this was the rise of a strong, centralised, authoritarian Catholic Church. Catholic emancipation had alarmed many Protestants, and disestablishment had finally ended the special privileges and protections given to the Anglican Church. The revolutionary activities of the Fenians had alarmed even liberal Protestants, and many expressed their concern by joining the Orange Order. The home rule crisis after 1885, however, involving support for this policy from the British Liberal Party, was the final straw.

Unionist opposition to home rule was based on a variety of reasons, but most usually religious and political affinities with Britain. In the second half of the nineteenth century, economic reasons were added to the list. Although the province of Ulster accounted for only 26 per cent of the land mass of Ireland, most of Ireland's industries were concentrated in the eastern part of the province. By 1911, 50 per cent of all industrial jobs in Ireland were located in Ulster, while one in five was in Belfast. This concentration was largely due to the success of a number of industries, including linen production, shipbuilding and rope making, which contributed to the spectacular economic growth of the town of Belfast. In the second half of the century, as the population of the country declined dramatically, Belfast experienced the fastest growth in the United Kingdom. Demographic expansion was matched by a growth in civic pride and this was rewarded when Belfast was granted city status in 1888. The beautiful architectural façade disguised the fact that the poor of Belfast, especially but not only the Catholic poor, lived in abject poverty. For much of the second half of the nineteenth century, Belfast had the highest rate of infant mortality in the United Kingdom. Unlike Dublin, Belfast was a predominantly Protestant city, and inevitably it became the focal point for unionist agitation and for Protestant patriotism. In the aftermath of the famine, the percentage of Catholics increased in the town, although sectarian employment practices ensured that they were confined to the lowest-paid jobs. Since the eighteenth century much of Belfast had been segregated into Catholic and Protestant areas, and these areas became polarised into nationalist and unionist enclaves. Serious – and deadly – rioting occurred in Belfast in 1857, 1864, 1872, 1886 and 1893, the latter years being connected with home rule agitation. By this stage, it was the most policed area in the United Kingdom. Overall more people were killed in the sectarian riots in the north of Ireland in the second half of the nineteenth century than in nationalist risings during the course of the whole century.

A powerful argument used in Britain in the nineteenth century was that Irish independence would be the first step in the dismemberment of the empire. As support for imperialism cut across all classes, this was a particularly powerful argument. Being part of the empire also created a paradox for Irish people. While independence – either total or limited – was a preferred option for many people, yet they were also active participants in the empire, as soldiers, administrators and settlers. Overall, the ties of religion, monarch, commerce, union and empire meant that by the end of the nineteenth century a new form of Protestantism had emerged that saw itself as British – if only as a defence against Catholicism and nationalism.

In 1885 a Unionist Party machine had been established in Dublin and Belfast and by the time of the home rule vote in the following year, the Parliamentary Unionist Party was in place. Concurrent with parliamentary activity, militant loyalism was also evident on the streets in the north of Ireland, as rioting accompanied each victory for the Home Rule Party. Within Britain the new Unionist Party had some powerful support, including most members of the British Conservative Party. The most provocative was Lord Randolph Churchill. He was the leader of a minority group within the Conservative Party, but most of his colleagues regarded him as a maverick whose frequent threats to resign were part of his histrionic behaviour. During the course of the year, however, Churchill had made a brief but memorable visit to the north of Ireland, to rally support for the unionists. His slogans 'Ulster will fight; Ulster will be right' and 'the Orange card was the one to play' were not only powerful rallying calls for unionists; they were also indicative that the militancy was underpinned by a threat of violence. Churchill, who had been an advocate of popular Tory democracy, also played to the fears of many British people by warning that home rule would be the first step in the break-up of the empire. Although Churchill's popularity was in the ascendant in Ireland, he resigned as chancellor of the Exchequer in Salisbury's cabinet in December 1886, which removed him from the centre of British politics. However, while

Churchill judged the determination of the unionists perfectly, most British politicians, especially Gladstone, underestimated them.

As with the supporters of home rule, the new Unionist Party was helped by the extension of the franchise in 1884 but, as they were aware, it benefited Catholics more than Protestants. The Unionist Party, though, was buoyed by the involvement of the Orange Order, which provided a mass base of popular support. From the viewpoint of Catholics, however, the Orange Order, especially its 12 July marches, had become associated with violence. The killing of five innocent people in the Catholic village of Dolly's Brae in 1849 – through which the Order had never previously marched – had caused public outrage in both Britain and Ireland. As a consequence, the government was forced to take action against the Order, sacking Lord Roden, a local Orange leader and member of the House of Lords, from the magistracy. More significantly, in 1850 political parades had been banned, although hard-line Orangemen continued to march, generally unhindered by the constabulary or judiciary. The ban on marching did not end sectarian attacks. In 1857 there were anti-Catholic riots in Belfast, which were incited by an inflammatory anti-Catholic sermon by an Anglican minister, the Reverend Thomas Drew. Following a series of defiant marches led by William Johnston, a minor landlord, militant Orangeman and son-in-law of Reverend Drew, Gladstone decided to make marching legal again. The Party Processions Act was repealed in 1872. The implication of Gladstone's intervention (supported by the British parliament) was that defiance and civil disorder were successful tools for Orangemen. The marches resumed and so did the annual displays of violence. Following the formation of the Unionist Party, however, 12 July became an occasion for unionist politicians to make defiant speeches against home rule. The appearance of bowler hats, smart outfits and other regalia at the end of the nineteenth century disguised a potentially violent political force.

Despite the increasing militancy and overt anti-Catholicism of some Protestant groups, liberal and nationalist Protestants had not disappeared. In 1903 an Independent Orange Order was formed that called for a return to the basic principles of Protestantism. Its Protestant fundamentalism was combined with a radical approach to politics. In 1905 the Order issued the *Magheramorne Manifesto*, which suggested that members should return to the site of the battle of the Boyne and 'hold out the right hand of fellowship to those who, whilst worshipping at other shrines, are yet our countrymen – bone of our bone and flesh of our flesh'. The manifesto continued by suggesting that Irish Protestants needed to re-evaluate their attitude to Catholics. The impact of this radical political manifesto was to win praise from the nationalist press, which regarded it as representing support for home rule, but opprobrium from many Orangemen. Some members from the Independent Orange Order returned to the mainstream movement, and some of the leaders distanced themselves from the document. More deserted in the following year when, in order to defeat the Liberals in the general election, the Unionist Party called for unity. Following this, support for the Independent Orange Order declined rapidly.

The Unionist Party was initially a nationwide party, representing interests ranging from Anglican landowners to Presbyterian factory workers. Although Anglican landowners were disproportionately powerful within Ireland, the successive Land Acts eroded both their economic power and their political influence. As a consequence the influence of landlords within the movement declined. Increasingly the party looked for support from its mass base, mostly the northern industrial workers, whom their opponents dismissed as 'Protestant plebeians'. The supremacy of northern unionism was confirmed by the formation of the Ulster Unionist Council in 1905, which linked unionist associations with Orange lodges throughout Ulster. Its foundation was an attempt by middle-class militants to regain control of the party. Its main support was from Belfast's industrial workers. By focusing only on issues to do with the north, a new, more limited version of unionism was emerging, which marked an important step in the demand for a separate Ulster. The formation of the Council not only heralded a move away from national unionism; it also marked the end of liberal unionism. It quickly established itself in the vanguard of unionist politics and directed the campaign against home rule during the crisis of 1912 to 1914.

Unionism was also helped by the emergence of a number of dynamic leaders, in particular James Craig and Edward Carson. Carson was born in Dublin in 1854 and joined the Irish bar in 1877. Initially he was a Liberal Unionist but gradually shifted allegiance to the Conservative Party. Carson was a brilliant lawyer who had helped to defend tenants following the 1881 Land Act. His political conversion was also reflected in his legal work. The government responded to the nationalists' Plan of Campaign after 1886 with the traditional tactic of coercion. The Crimes Act of 1887 was designed to counteract the new campaign as part of the Land War. The first prosecution under this legislation at Mitchelstown District Court ended in a riot, with the deaths of three protesters. The Crown prosecutor was Edward Carson, and in this capacity he came directly into contact with leading nationalists. His strong defence on behalf of the government gained him prominence and promotion. In 1889 he became the youngest QC in the United Kingdom, and three years later he was promoted as the solicitor-general for Ireland. At the same time he launched his political career, and successfully stood as Liberal Unionist candidate for Trinity College. His parliamentary status increased following his robust attack on the 1893 second Home Rule Bill. His legal career also continued to attract attention, especially his defence of the Marquess of Queensberry against Oscar Wilde in 1895. Wilde had been Carson's contemporary at Trinity College. In 1900 Carson became solicitor-general for England, and in the same year led the prosecution for treason against Arthur Lynch, the MP for Galway and commander of the Irish Brigade who had fought against the British during the Boer War. Carson was also knighted that year.

Even though the Conservative and Unionist Parties were defeated in the 1906 general election, Carson remained a major force in British and Irish politics. By accepting the leadership of the Irish Unionist Parliamentary Party in 1910, Carson demonstrated a renewed commitment to unionist politics. His timing was appropriate, as after 1912 Ireland was plunged into the third home rule crisis.

NINE

REBELLION AND PARTITION
c. 1900–1921

The first decade of the twentieth century was marked by a rise of political and cultural organisations that challenged traditional political structures. Unlike earlier movements, these were distinguished by their mass participation and the contribution made by women. After 1912, however, both Irish and British politics were dominated – and changed – by the home rule issue.

This chapter examines the turbulent period in Irish politics that encompassed a nationalist uprising, unionist threats of civil war and a period of vicious war with Britain. The partition of Ireland in 1920 marked an attempt by the British government to provide a compromise solution to the two conflicting ideologies of nationalism and unionism, but for some nationalists it was a disappointing outcome to their years of struggle. Partition, however, did not solve the problems of Ireland, but created new divisions, while exacerbating existing religious tensions. It also created a new form of confrontation as a civil war began in Ireland.

New Nationalism

The demise of Parnell left a large vacuum in nationalist politics. His downfall not only split the movement into Parnellites and anti-Parnellites, but allowed nationalism again to retreat into its various factions. Ironically, this meant that the second Home Rule Bill was largely the result of the determination of a British politician, Gladstone. This bill was the highlight of home rule achievements in the decade following Parnell's death. It was not until 1900 that the Nationalist Party, which included the Irish Parliamentary Party, achieved some unity, when John Redmond was elected its leader. He had been a devoted supporter of Parnell and led the minority that had supported the leader after 1890. Redmond benefited from the reform of county government in 1898, which was handed over from grand juries – which had been landlord-dominated – to popularly elected county and district councils. This change allowed nationalists to gain valuable experience in local politics. Although Redmond led the Nationalist Party until 1918, he did not have the unifying skills of his predecessor. He also inherited a party that was largely trapped in the vision of home rule created in 1886, that is, an Irish parliament with limited powers, which remained part of the United Kingdom, and in which British institutions and the English language remained predominant.

However, a different kind of nationalism also arose that claimed to be non-political but based on Irish culture. Although the cultural resurgence at the end of the nineteenth century had some similarities with the cultural nationalism of Young Ireland, the new Anglo-Irish and Gaelic revivals were not attached to political organisations. Yet, ultimately, the cultural revival helped to shape Irish nationalism because, unlike nationalism elsewhere, in Ireland it was not founded on either language or an identifiable culture. A poet, William Butler Yeats, led the Anglo-Irish literary revival. He was the centre of an array of talent that included Lady Gregory (whose husband had introduced the punitive Gregory Clause in 1847, forbidding many tenants from receiving relief), Æ (the pen-name of George Russell), James Joyce and J.M. Synge. They sought out Celtic legends, some of which had been retained only in oral tradition, and rewrote them, adding their own combinations of poetry, mysticism and romanticism. Recent history, with all its disappointment and failures, was ignored in favour of a heroic past which seemed to point to a glorious future. This aspiration was personified in Yeats's dramatic creation of *Cathleen Ni Houlihan*, a poor old woman who became queen. The Anglo-Irish literary revival was dominated by Protestant middle-class males, who wrote in English and idealised both the Irish peasantry and the nationalist struggle. Its appeal was largely confined to other intellectuals. Within Catholic Ireland, also, there was some suspicion that some of these writers were too 'Anglo' and not sufficiently Irish. However, James Joyce, a Catholic and the most linguistically innovative of the writers, left Ireland in protest at the bigotry of the Catholic Church. Overall, these writers made a remarkable contribution not only to Irish literature, but also to international culture.

A more consciously Irish revival, centred on the Gaelic League, had a much wider appeal, especially among the lower middle classes. The League was an Irish-language organisation founded by Eoin MacNeill in 1893. Its first president, Douglas Hyde, the son of a Church of Ireland clergyman, had learnt to speak Irish from servants in his family home. His concern that the

Irish language was disappearing had been the subject of his lecture in 1892 to the National Literary Society, 'The Necessity for De-Anglicizing the Irish People'. The main objective of the Gaelic League was to revive Irish as a living language. Hyde and others believed that if Ireland could prove that it had a distinct language, then its claim to be a separate nation would be irresistible. The League held classes and competitions, and in 1909 it succeeded in having Irish made a compulsory subject for entrance to the National University of Ireland. It also suggested that de-Anglicisation entailed not playing English games, dressing in the English way or adopting other symbols of Englishness. In this way, it provided an inverted form of some of the Kilkenny Statutes of the fourteenth century. The establishment of the Gaelic Athletic Association (GAA) by Michael Cusack in 1884, which rejected the playing, or even watching, of any English sports, helped this programme of de-Anglicisation. At the same time it promoted games such as hurling, which was regarded as peculiarly Irish and associated with the myths of Cú Chulainn. In 1885 Gaelic football was provided with its own set of rules, and two years later the first all-Ireland championship was held. Female members of the Gaelic League devised their own version of hurling, camogie, which was first played publicly in 1904. From the outset the GAA was linked with the Fenian movement (IRB) and it was openly nationalist in its politics. The Gaelic League, however, claimed to be non-political, and initially Protestants and unionists joined it. It also attracted some influential members, such as Horace Plunkett, an Anglo-Irish landlord, who founded the Irish cooperative movement. As the League became involved in various campaigns, to promote Irish at all levels, to celebrate St Patrick's Day and to close pubs on the same, it assumed the characteristics of a political organisation. The increasing politicisation of the movement, and its infiltration by the IRB, led to Hyde's resignation in 1915. The fact that many of its members supported or participated in the 1916 rising also suggested that it was political. In 1919 the British government declared it to be an illegal organisation.

The Gaelic revival was a major development in the emergence of a new type of nationalism. Yet, while many aspects of it were distinctly Irish, it was also part of a Europe-wide movement that resulted in large-scale participation in political organisations, the growth of spectator sport and a desire to rediscover a glorious past before modernisation had wiped out all vestiges of it. In Ireland, however, this was carried out within the parameters of desiring national independence. Unfortunately, though, the Gaelic revival contributed to existing political divisions as it was increasingly associated with Catholics, and even liberal Protestants came to feel excluded. The Gaelic revival had, unintentionally, excluded many Protestants from the new view of Irishness, which had its roots in an imagined heroic past which was exclusively Catholic. Protestants appeared to have little role either in Ireland's heroic past or its glorious future. The authority and narrowness of the Irish Catholic Church had become apparent in the closing years of the nineteenth century. Its role in the downfall of Parnell was indicative of a more restrictive moral climate. This new respectability was also apparent in other aspects of Irish life, including Irish theatres. When Yeats's play *The Countess Cathleen* appeared in 1899, the police were required to restore order, objections being that it offended Catholic morality by its portrayal of Ireland. *Ne Temere*, a papal decree passed in 1907 that laid down that children of mixed marriage, that is between a Catholic and a Protestant, must be brought up as Catholics, inflamed existing religious divisions. Yet, while the decree might have been offensive to non-Catholics in general, it provided a propaganda gift for conservative Protestants by providing evidence of papal intolerance and giving proof to the adage 'Home Rule is Rome Rule'.

Apart from the Gaelic revival, other ideologies, such as socialism, syndicalism and feminism, gave Irish politics a new dynamism and focus. Although these ideologies were influential in other countries, in Ireland they operated through the prism of nationalism. The main problem was how such conflicting aims and aspirations could coexist. Overall, however, these extra-parliamentary organisations not only revitalised Irish nationalism, but also extended the view of independence beyond the narrow parameters set by Parnell and Redmond. In 1905 Arthur Griffith and Bulmer Hobson founded a new political organisation, *Sinn Féin* ('ourselves alone'). It evolved out of the articles Griffith had written in the *United Irishman* since 1899. The premise of his philosophy was that the Act of Union was illegal and that the Irish Parliamentary Party, by sitting in Westminster, was perpetuating this falsehood. As the name of the new party suggested, the solution was to withdraw from the imperial parliament and participate in a self-governing council in Ireland. Moreover, the country should strive for economic self-sufficiency and thus break the financial connection with Britain. Yet Griffith was a separatist rather than a republican. He accepted, largely to broaden Sinn Féin's appeal, that the link with the British Crown should continue, but that Ireland should be an equal partner under the dual monarchy. He also believed that this form of independence could be achieved through passive resistance, and he did not support violence. Although Sinn Féin drew a wide spectrum of support, including frustrated nationalists, feminists and pacifists, it was not numerically strong. It also had limited political success. Despite having opposing views on the use of violence, Sinn Féin worked closely with the IRB, which was being revitalised by the return of Tom Clarke from exile and the involvement of Seán Mac Diarmada. Tom Clarke was a veteran republican who had been sentenced to penal servitude for life for organising a bombing campaign in Britain. Following his release in 1898 he had emigrated to the United States, but he returned to Ireland in 1907 and, together with Seán Mac Diarmada, was instrumental in reviving the IRB. Mac Diarmada, who was a leading figure in Sinn Féin, also helped to publish the IRB paper, *Irish Freedom*. Sinn Féin's influence increased during the First World War when it opposed recruitment. Although it was involved in the 1916 rising, it did not play the prominent role that was later assumed. Nevertheless, Sinn Féin was the major force behind Irish nationalism after the rising.

Although the British Independent Labour Party had attempted to organise in Ireland in the 1890s, early Irish socialism made few inroads. James Connolly, who was invited to Dublin in 1896 to establish the Irish Socialist Republican Party, encountered similar resistance. Connolly had been born in Edinburgh to poor Irish immigrant parents, and as a teenager he had joined the British army. His humble background made him a new phenomenon in Irish politics. Disillusioned with his lack of success, though, in 1903 he moved to the United States, where he became involved with the International Workers of the World. At this stage it appeared that Belfast rather than Dublin would be the centre of Irish socialism, largely because of the skills and organising ability of William Walker, whose early career had been as a joiner at Harland and Wolff, the shipbuilding company. While there, Walker became involved with the British Labour Party and the trade union movement. In 1905 he was only narrowly defeated in a by-election in North Belfast where he had stood as a Labour Party candidate. Walker personified some of the complexities of Irish politics at the beginning of the twentieth century. He was a Protestant, a socialist and a unionist. Connolly, in contrast, was an atheist, a socialist, a nationalist and a fervent supporter of women's rights.

In 1910 Connolly was invited back to Ireland to run the newly founded Socialist Party of Ireland. He was also appointed the Belfast organiser of the Irish Transport and General Workers' Union, founded by the Liverpool-born

James Larkin in 1909, and in 1912 he persuaded the Irish Trade Union Congress to establish a Labour Party. He and Connolly worked closely together to promote socialism in Ireland. Connolly had a number of early successes in Belfast, including unionising the women linen-workers. However, he viewed Walker as an impediment to the development of Irish socialism and nationalism, and while the home rule crisis was raging, the two men debated their respective ideological positions in print. Although Connolly was an internationalist, he attempted to give socialism an Irish heritage, arguing that Gaelic society was based on a primitive form of communism, founded on a common ownership of resources. His radical position on the home rule question, whereby he refused to accept the exclusion of Ulster, lost him the support of some moderate nationalists.

Opposition to trade union activity, culminating in the Dublin lockout of 1913, offered a reminder of how much Irish industrialists disliked the new labour politics. Yet the lockout also demonstrated that many Irish workers were surviving on the economic margins. At that time, Dublin had the highest death rate of any European city. This was due to a combination of inadequate nutrition, low wages and unsanitary living conditions, with 21,000 families living in one-room tenements. The lockout was precipitated when a group of employers attempted to compel their workers to leave the Irish Transport and General Workers' Union. If they refused to do so, they would be dismissed. The Union responded by calling out other workers, and so within a few weeks 22,000 workers were either on strike or locked out. It was a bitter and prolonged dispute, with the leaders, including James Connolly and Jim Larkin, being imprisoned, and the workers being intimidated and starved into submission. The police killed two during a riot. Some women's organisations established soup kitchens, but they could not meet the demand of a population that, even before the dispute, was malnourished and unhealthy. In January 1914 the strikers returned to work, on whatever terms they could get. Larkin, disillusioned and exhausted by the lockout, emigrated to the United States, where he helped to found the American Communist Party. For Connolly, though, the lockout was a grim insight into the vulnerability of the workers when pitched against the combined forces of the state and the determination of the employers. During the strike he had established the Irish Citizen Army, the first socialist militia in Ireland. When the strike was over it continued to meet and grow and, despite only having about 350 members, it played an active role in the 1916 rising.

The Home Rule Crisis

The disparate political and cultural movements functioning in Ireland in the early twentieth century, although they had different tactics and objectives, had frequently supported each other. They were brought together by the crisis precipitated by the third Home Rule Bill in 1912. Yet while the possibility of home rule united various groups, it led to increased polarisation between nationalists and unionists.

Since the deaths of Parnell and Gladstone little progress had been made on the home rule issue. The home rule movement was split. Following Gladstone's retirement from politics, the Conservative Party, which had allied with the Unionists, was in power. Home rule was also in the doldrums. In contrast, extra-parliamentary nationalist activities had been energised by the Gaelic revival and increasing involvement of women in politics. The IRB, in particular, which had been languishing since the end of the Land War, was revitalised after 1910, largely because of the involvement of the veteran Tom Clarke, but also as a result of the fresh approach and vision offered by Sinn Féin. The IRB attracted a new generation of supporters who combined their love of Ireland with a passion for Gaelic culture. They included Patrick Pearse, Thomas MacDonagh, Joseph and Mary Plunkett and Eamonn Ceannt. In 1910 the IRB had founded *Irish Freedom* to promote its activities. A major propaganda coup, however, was achieved in 1915 at the burial of Jeremiah O'Donovan Rossa, one the first members of the Fenian Brotherhood. Pearse started the oration in Irish, which was not only a tribute to the work of the Gaelic League, but demonstrated that the Irish language was being integrated into Irish nationalism.

Politics within Britain were also changing. In 1910 the Liberal government that had been elected four years earlier was returned to office, but needed the support of the Nationalist Party to have a majority. Home rule therefore seemed a real possibility. Moreover, in 1911 the power of the House of Lords to veto legislation was curbed, limiting it to delaying bills for two years. Despite the rise of other nationalist groups, the majority of Irish people still saw home rule, achieved though constitutional means, as their objective. The prospect of a successful Home Rule Bill in 1912 drew support from different groups, and in the same year Patrick Pearse spoke in support of the legislation. That year also the House of Commons passed the bill, although the House of Lords exercised its right to delay it for two years. The Home Rule

Bill, like the earlier ones, gave no recognition to the aspirations of Irish unionists. The latter by this stage had adopted an increasingly militant approach to the issue, and the two-year delay meant that they had time to organise resistance to the bill. For unionists the twin enemies were now the nationalists and the British government. Increasingly, the vision of unionist separatism was limited to Ulster.

In the previous year, when the Home Rule Bill was being discussed, Edward Carson, MP for Dublin University and leader of the Unionist Party, told a mass rally in Dublin they should prepare to take over the government of Ulster if the bill was passed. Apart from religious and political considerations, the economic argument remained powerful. Ulster was the richest and most industrialised province in Ireland, yet in an all-Ireland parliament the community would always remain in a minority. Following the passage of the bill, Carson put into place a massive programme of civil resistance and disobedience, which had the support of the majority of the Conservative Party. The activities culminated in a 'day of declaration' or 'Ulster Day' on 28 September 1912, which marked the end of a week of demonstrations and protests throughout Ulster. Protestant communities in the north of Ireland treated Ulster Day as a public holiday: the streets were decorated with Union flags, bunting and Orange arches. The religious dimension of their struggle was also prominent, with the distribution of free bibles and the holding of religious services. The climax of the day was the signing of 'Ulster's Solemn League and Covenant', which was a shrewd means of uniting unionist leaders and people in one common oath. It was also named after the agreement made in 1643 between the Scottish and English adversaries of Charles I, which had helped to precipitate the English Civil War. The Covenant stated that a home rule parliament 'would be disastrous to the material well-being of Ulster as well as the whole of Ireland, subversive of our civil and religious freedom, destructive of our citizenship and perilous to the unity of the Empire . . . And in the event of such a Parliament being forced on us, we solemnly and mutually pledge ourselves to refuse to recognize its authority.' Supporters of unionism in Britain also signed a separate document. Folk tradition related that some people signed in their own blood. At this stage, the Council envisaged that only the nine counties of Ulster would be excluded from the home rule parliament. An estimated 218,000 men signed the Covenant, and a parallel declaration was signed by an even higher number of women. The role of women in the unionist movement had been increasing in the previous few years. In 1911 a Women's Ulster Unionist Council had been formed which within twelve months had recruited over 40,000 members. The women were active in canvassing support for the Covenant, especially among their own gender.

In September 1913 a provisional government was set up in Ulster to take control if home rule became law. The threats of armed resistance were made more real by the formation of a paramilitary force in January 1913. Local Protestant groups had been organising and drilling since 1910, although they lacked weapons. Frederick Hugh Crawford, a militant unionist leader, had been secretly importing arms into the north since the second Home Rule Bill. In 1910, as the new bill loomed, he organised a secret subcommittee within the Ulster Unionist Council with the particular aim of importing arms. Crawford's role increased after 1913. The formation of the Ulster Volunteer Force (UVF) provided the Unionist Party with its own militia. Almost 100,000 men joined the UVF, including retired officers from the British army. Crawford took control of organising the illegal importation of arms for the Ulster Volunteers: 25,000 rifles and 3 million rounds of ammunition were secretly imported to Larne, Donaghadee and Bangor, all ports near to Belfast. This act of defiance was a propaganda coup for the unionists and a warning to the nationalists. For the government a worrying aspect of this new militancy was that prominent officers in the British army made it clear that they would be reluctant to fight against the unionists. When Asquith ordered the army in Ireland to be ready to march on Ulster in March 1914, sixty British cavalry officers in the Curragh Camp in County Kildare resigned their commissions, on the grounds that they would not fight the unionists.

The British government appeared unsure how to cope with the mounting crisis and so did very little. Carson, regardless of the illegality of the actions of the unionists, defied the government to stop them. They were also assured of the support of the Conservative Party, now led by Andrew Bonar Law, son of an Ulster Presbyterian minister. Bonar Law told a pro-unionist rally in England in June 1912 that there was 'no length of resistance to which Ulster can go in which I would not be prepared to support them'. The prime minister, Herbert Asquith, supported by Redmond, decided that taking action against the unionists would increase their support in Ireland and Britain. They therefore did nothing. Diplomacy had failed and the British government lacked the tenacity to stand up to the unionists, who by 1914 were not only armed, but had the support of leading members of the British army. Asquith continued to believe in constitutional tactics and secretly met with Carson and Bonar Law, promising a fresh amendment. Although home rule was due to become law in the summer of 1914, last-minute attempts were made to change it. On 23 June the House of Lords decreed that the nine Ulster counties should be allowed to exclude themselves from the home rule parliament for six years. At the end of the period, parliament could reconsider the issue. Within the Lords, this bill was amended to allow the permanent exclusion of Ulster. Overall, Asquith had created a constitutional mess. Home rule was due to become law, but now Asquith had publicly accepted that some degree of exclusion should be allowed. By doing so, he had strengthened the hands of the unionists, although Protestants living outside Ulster were alarmed that they would be even more isolated in the new set-up. Ironically, it was a southern unionist, Carson, who was the architect of the separation.

Asquith had further meetings with Carson and Redmond, but his main concern was the extent of the territory to be excluded, given that much of the west of Ulster was predominantly Catholic. With war looming in Europe, everybody wanted a quick solution, including the king. At Asquith's suggestion, a conference was held in Buckingham Palace from 21 to 24 July 1914; John Redmond and John Dillon represented the nationalists, while Andrew Bonar Law, Edward Carson, James Craig and Lord Lansdowne represented the unionists. There was disagreement not about the integrity of maintaining the Home Rule Bill (and Ireland) intact, but about whether County Tyrone, which had a 55 per cent Catholic majority, and County Fermanagh, with a 56 per cent Catholic majority, should be included or excluded from a home rule parliament. No agreement was reached, although Carson offered a compromise: he would not demand all of Ulster to be excluded but would settle for the counties of Antrim, Armagh, Londonderry, Down, Fermanagh and Tyrone, and the cities of Belfast and Derry. The conference broke up without achieving anything, although Carson had a clearer idea of the geography of unionist demands. Redmond lost the support of some nationalists, however, for agreeing to the exclusion of part of Ireland. Overall, the politicians had reached an impasse, although a civil war was still a possibility. For the British government, therefore, the start of the First World War in August 1914 offered a drastic solution. The previous two years had shown that civil disobedience, when used by unionists, was successful. In contrast, decades of constitutional home rule agitation by the nationalists had proved futile.

The increasing belligerence of the unionists alarmed nationalists. Some militant members of the Gaelic League called on nationalists to arm themselves in order to defend home rule. The Irish National Volunteers were founded in Dublin in November 1913, although the strongest support initially came from Catholics in the north, which looked to the Volunteers to counteract the UVF. John Redmond was concerned that the Volunteers would become a tool of the IRB, but the deteriorating situation encouraged him to negotiate with them. In June 1914 Redmond gave his official approval to the organisation and in return was allowed 50 per cent control of the organising committee. Following this recruitment increased sharply, reaching 160,000.

The Irish Volunteers lacked weapons and, like the UVF, they looked to Germany to supply them. Erskine Childers and Darrell Figgis travelled to Germany in May 1914 to purchase rifles and ammunition. Childers, who was born in London, had been a clerk in the British House of Commons. In 1903 he published a novel, *The Riddle of the Sands*, which was a fictional account of German attempts to invade England. After 1910 he devoted himself to political activities. The Dublin-born Figgis started his career as a tea-broker in London and Calcutta, but gave this up in 1910 and became a writer and political activist. The first consignment of arms was landed safely in County Wicklow, but, in an attempt to rival the publicity that the Larne gunrunning had attracted, a larger consignment was landed at Howth in County Dublin. Childers sailed into Howth on his own private yacht, the *Asgard*, which was full of weapons. However, unlike in Larne, in Howth the authorities decided to intervene, and troops were sent to prevent the landing. They only captured a small amount of weapons but, as they returned to the barracks in Dublin, they opened fire on a crowd of hecklers. Three civilians were killed and thirty-eight were wounded.

The outbreak of the First World War created a dilemma for the Volunteers, forcing them to decide whether or not to support the British government. The British government, however, had no problem in abandoning home rule. Although it received royal assent on 18 September, its operation was indefinitely suspended. None the less, Redmond's attitude was clear: support for the war would ensure that support for home rule was sustained. He also argued that rather than being an imperial war, it was a war to defend the rights of small nations. The vast majority of Irish Volunteers followed Redmond and formed the National Volunteers. This left a much reduced group of approximately 10,000 Volunteers, led by Eoin MacNeill, who opposed the latest imperial war. Moreover, they despaired that a British government would ever grant home rule without a further struggle. Redmond's policy also split nationalist groups in the United States, most of whom condemned the war. The American group *Clan na Gael* urged the United States government to maintain its neutrality, while the Ancient Order of Hibernians openly supported Germany. For Britain, which hoped that the United States would enter the war as its ally, this development was also worrying.

1916

The decision to engage in a further uprising was a reaction to the duplicity, intimidation and disappointments of the two years that had followed the passage of the third Home Rule Bill in 1912. Upon Britain declaring war on Germany, leading members of the IRB and the Irish Volunteers decided to prepare for an insurrection. James Connolly, who viewed the conflict as an imperialist, capitalist war, agreed that the Citizen Army would support an uprising. The British political situation was also unpromising for Irish nationalists. In 1915 a coalition government was formed under David Lloyd George, leader of the Liberal Party. It included Bonar Law and Carson. The latter had also been appointed attorney-general. Clearly, despite Carson's repeated defiance and unconstitutional actions, he continued to be one of the dominant figures in British politics.

In May 1915 the Supreme Council of the IRB established a Military Council. Leading members of the Irish Volunteers, including Patrick Pearse, Joseph Mary Plunkett, Thomas MacDonagh and Eamon Ceannt, were involved, although Eoin MacNeill, the supreme commander of the Irish Volunteers, was initially unaware of their activities. He was involved in the rising only in its later stages. The original plan was that a nationwide uprising would take place at Easter 1916. On the eve of the uprising, things went wrong. John Devoy, a veteran Fenian in the United States, had been in touch with the German government to arrange for supplies of arms for the insurgents. A retired British diplomat, Sir Roger Casement, had travelled to Germany to finalise the deal. For Germany, supplying arms meant that it created a diversion for British troops at a critical point in the war. The Allies appeared exhausted, Gallipoli had just been evacuated and France, Russia and Britain had all suffered defeats. On 20 April 1916 a consignment of German rifles and machine guns, including 25,000 captured Russian rifles, was carried on board the *Aud* to Ireland. As had been so frequently the case, British intelligence had been intercepting messages to and from activists in New York, and the full details of the *Aud*'s movements were known. When the *Aud*'s captain arrived at Tralee Bay and realised that they were trapped, he scuttled the ship.

Casement, who had travelled from Germany to Ireland, feared that the rising would be hampered by insufficient weaponry, and he asked his co-conspirators to postpone the rising. Shortly after landing at Banna Strand in County Kerry on 21 April (Good Friday) he was arrested. His trial received a lot of publicity and some appeals for clemency. He had been born in Ireland and joined the British Colonial Service in 1892. His humanitarian work, especially in exposing the brutal treatment of plantation workers in the Belgian Congo and Peru, and won him international admiration. But his nationalist views had been intensifying, and when he retired in 1913 he dedicated himself to the cause of Irish independence. During his trial, a worldwide campaign was organised to save his life, but the government, releasing extracts of his diaries revealing his homosexual activities, undermined this. This information, whether true or false, damaged him both in the eyes of Irish Catholics and British public opinion. Casement was hanged in August 1916, after converting to Catholicism. In 1965 his remains were returned to Ireland, where he was belatedly given a state funeral.

Apart from the shortage of arms, the planned rising was further undermined by confusion about the timing. The leaders of the insurrection, in an attempt to avoid betrayal, were wary about releasing details, and so it was not until 19 April that the date was made known to the Volunteers. This allowed little time for preparation. The rising was opposed by some of their supporters, notably the leader of the Volunteers, Eoin MacNeill, who published a countermanding order cancelling the involvement of the Volunteers in the rising of Sunday 23 April. The other leaders, however, had already decided that they would rise in Dublin, even if they lacked sufficient arms. They knew that they had little chance of success. Even before a shot was fired, the leaders regarded the rising as a heroic gesture, and one that would probably end in their death. But the rising was less about realism than about idealism and symbolism.

The rising began on 24 April 1916, which was Easter Monday. Patrick Pearse of the Irish Volunteers and James Connolly of the Irish Citizen Army led it. Various places in Dublin and other parts of the country were occupied, but the focal point was the occupation of the General Post Office in Dublin. A proclamation was read on the GPO steps in the name of the Irish provisional government, and the tricolour flag was flown. The proclamation recognised the rights of both men and women in the new republic, which was the first time that a revolutionary declaration had done so. Initially only 800 Volunteers supported the call to arms, although the number doubled during the course of the fighting. Their numbers included fifty 'Hibernian Rifles' from the United States. *Cumann na mBan* (see p. 208), which had been formed as an auxiliary to the Irish Volunteers, also took part, although the women's role was predominantly as nurses, cooks and dispatch-runners. This work could be dangerous and one of its members, Margaretta Keogh, was killed. Countess Markievicz (see p. 208), a leading political activist who was a commandant in the Irish Citizen Army, was based at the College of Surgeons in Stephen's Green. While most of the fighting was concentrated in Dublin, supporting uprisings took place in Galway, Wexford and County Dublin. In Cork the Volunteers, led by Thomas MacCurtain and Terence MacSwiney, were engaged in a stand-off with the military for one week. Symbolically, however, Dublin represented a particular blow against the British forces because neither in 1798 nor in 1848 had the insurgents felt strong enough to attack it.

Initially the British were unprepared. Easter Monday was a holiday and only 400 of the troops were on duty. But reinforcements were quickly brought in from the rest of the country and from England. Within two days, therefore, the troops outnumbered the insurgents by twenty to one. Apart from military opposition, the insurgents also faced opposition from Dublin civilians. This hostility increased as Dublin burned, food became scarce and rumours proliferated that the wives of Irish soldiers fighting against Germany would not be paid. On Saturday, after five days of fighting, Pearse and Connolly officially surrendered. The centre of Dublin had been devastated. The greatest number of casualties had been among Dublin civilians, with 230 fatalities; 64 of the insurgents were killed and 132 troops. The dead included the pacifist Francis Sheehy-Skeffington, shot while trying to prevent looting. Regardless of the defeat and the fact that Dublin was still in flames, Pearse believed that the action had redeemed Ireland's honour. The citizens of Dublin did not appear to agree, since they booed the republican prisoners as they were marched through the streets to their captivity. But as the numbers of civilians killed by

British troops and the damage caused by them became evident, feelings changed. The continuation of martial law and the wholesale policy of arresting sympathisers alienated the Dublin civilians. The decision to execute the leaders and the manner of executing them caused a further change in public opinion in favour of the nationalists. Fifteen leaders were executed between 3 and 12 May. Three months later Sir Roger Casement was hanged in London. Although Countess Markievicz was court-martialled and sentenced to death, her execution was cancelled because of her gender. The rising had failed as the leaders knew it would, but it inspired a new and even more militant wave of national struggle, and in this way it succeeded.

British public opinion, however, was outraged that a rebellion had been perpetuated while Britain was fighting a war. Unionists were able to exploit this anger. Sir Edward Carson, who was working at the heart of the British government, was particularly well placed to do so. Sympathy for unionism was made easier by the participation of Ulster Protestants in fighting on behalf of Britain, especially in one of the most shocking actions of the whole war, the battle of the Somme. Members of the Ulster Volunteer Force had been allowed to form their own unit, the 36th (Ulster) Division, and they were present at the opening of the battle of the Somme on 1 July 1916. In commemoration of the battle of the Boyne, a number of the Ulster Division wore orange lilies or orange sashes, and as they went into battle shouted 'No Surrender' or 'Dolly's Brae'. In the first two days of action, 5,500 of the Ulster Division had been killed or wounded. In many parts of Ulster, 12 July 1916 was treated as a day of mourning, with even the annual parade being called off. Not only had the losses been great, but also unionists juxtaposed their loyalty and sacrifice for king and country with the treachery of the nationalists. The appalling losses endured at the Somme became embedded in unionist memory and commemorative tradition. In the short term, though, the actions of both nationalists and unionists in the spring and summer of 1916 appeared to be another nail in the coffin of home rule. In June 1916, the Ulster Unionist Council voted in favour of a partition of Ireland. The granting of home rule appeared even more elusive in 1916 than it had in 1914.

However, it was not only Protestants who made sacrifices on behalf of Britain during the war; Catholics also answered Lord Kitchener's call to arms. Kitchener, who had been the embodiment of the British struggle, was in fact born in County Kerry in Ireland. Although the Kitchener poster was displayed in Ireland to help recruitment, it said 'Your first duty is to take your part in ending the war . . . Join an Irish regiment today'. References to fighting for king and country were tactfully omitted. By 1915, 90,000 men from all parts of Ireland had enlisted. This represented only 4 per cent of the total recruitment within the United Kingdom. After 1916 Irish enlistment dropped to less than 2 per cent of the whole. In total, more Irish Catholics than Protestants fought in the war, with recruitment rates being highest in Ulster. Very few Irish women took part in the war, accounting for less than one-thousandth of total British female recruitment. Connolly and other socialist leaders attributed the high recruitment in Dublin to unemployment and pauperism rather than loyalty, which he categorised as the 'enlist or starve' policy. In total, almost 30,000 Irish recruits died during the war.

Women Activists

Irish nationalism received much of its energy from the involvement of women. It was not that they had not involved themselves before, but they now did so in large numbers and in their own right, rather than as sisters or wives. Overwhelmingly, these women were middle class, educated and generally Protestant. Also, unlike male political activists, the women were breaking social and gender roles, and not all men welcomed their participation. The patriarchal Catholic Church hierarchy also disliked the activities. The women brought fresh perspectives to the nationalist struggle, their nationalist politics having been enriched by their involvement with the suffragette movements and other social issues. This vitality was reflected particularly in the radical politics of women such as Hanna Sheehy-Skeffington, Maud Gonne and Countess Markievicz. Also, through their involvement with the poor and children, nationalist politics were often brought onto the streets of Ireland, rather than being left in meeting rooms. Irish women were involved in various ideological battles, but most of them believed in the primacy of nationalism over any other struggle. Nevertheless, Margaret Cousins, Hanna Sheehy-Skeffington and Charlotte Despard each made a major contribution to the winning of votes for women in 1918. Not all the women were nationalists. Louie Bennett, for example, the secretary of the Irishwomen's International League for Peace and Freedom, was a pacifist, and was uncomfortable with the nationalist agenda that underpinned many women's activities. The fact that the 1916 proclamation assigned equal rights to men and women was a testament to the achievements of Irish women in a relatively short period. The question of women having the vote was initially a low priority for many male nationalists. In the late nineteenth century, though, a women's movement was establishing roots throughout Europe. Within the United Kingdom the franchise had been extended in 1832, 1867 and 1884, but to men only; women, like convicts and the insane, were excluded. Two early Irish supporters of Irish suffrage were Anna and Thomas Haslam, who had married in 1854. They were Quakers who viewed women's suffrage as a question of social justice. In 1876 they founded the Women's Suffrage Association, which later became the Irish Women's Suffrage and Local Government Association. Although the Haslams did not support physical-force tactics, they worked alongside militant nationalist and suffragette groups. Their work laid the foundations for the later phase of the suffrage struggle.

In England the demand for women's votes had begun in the nineteenth century but had become a powerful force only following the founding of the Women's Social and Political Union (WSPU) in 1903 by the Pankhurst family. From the outset it was committed to physical force rather than the constitutional methods used by its predecessors. The WSPU inspired two radical Irishwomen, Hanna Sheehy-Skeffington and Margaret Cousins, to establish their own Irish organisation, the Irish Women's Franchise League (IWFL) in 1908. The women came from different backgrounds: Hanna from a middle-class Catholic, nationalist family, while Margaret had working-class unionist, Protestant origins. Both she and her Protestant husband became ardent nationalists and feminists.

While the new organisation was inspired by the English suffragettes, and worked with them, Sheehy-Skeffington and Cousins realised the contexts were very different. They believed that, in Ireland, women's freedom was indivisible from national freedom. The IWFL was a women-only body, although men, including the husbands of the two founders, provided support. The trade unionist leaders Jim Larkin and James Connolly were also champions of their activities. Although individual members of the Nationalist Party supported votes for women, Redmond did not, fearing it would undermine the main struggle. Sinn Féin included votes for women in its programme and, unusually for an organisation founded by men, it had a female vice-president, Jennie Wyse-Power. The members of the IWFL were drawn from a wide range of social and economic groups. However, some of the more radical women's organisations did not join because they were opposed to the League's tactics of attempting to achieve the vote by simply pressurising the British parliament, preferring to use direct action instead. For these reasons, Markievicz, a prominent figure in a number of political organisations, did not join, although she spoke at many of the League's rallies. Despite having different strategies, the IWFL worked successfully with various socialist and nationalist groups in 1910 to get school meals extended to Ireland. Christabel Pankhurst spoke in Dublin in 1910 to a meeting of over 3,000 people. Margaret Cousins also took part in a suffragette protest in London, during which she threw missiles – including potatoes – at various ministers' windows. She was imprisoned for one month in Holloway prison.

The IWFL hoped that the third Home Rule Bill in 1910 would include votes for women. In 1910 a Conciliation Bill was introduced into parliament, which would have given votes to women throughout the United Kingdom. The Irish Party voted against it, afraid that it might weaken the government on the eve of the Home Rule Bill. Their action outraged suffragettes in Ireland and Britain, but when Irish suffragettes protested at home rule meetings, they were roughly treated. However, a mass suffrage rally was held in Dublin in June 1912 and it called on the government to include women's votes in the Home Rule Bill. Two weeks later a number of suffragettes broke the windows of government offices in Dublin, refused to pay their fines and so were imprisoned. Two English suffragettes visiting Dublin in July attacked a coach carrying Prime Minister Asquith and Redmond. This attack angered public opinion, and suspected suffragettes were beaten. The English women were sentenced to five years' penal servitude and went on hunger strike, demanding to be treated as political prisoners. A number of Irish suffragettes, also in prison, including Sheehy-Skeffington, joined them in sympathy. This was the first time that a hunger strike was used in Ireland as a political weapon. However, the distance between the Nationalist Party and the suffragettes was growing. The former voted against the Women's Suffrage Bill at the end of 1912, and, even more controversially, in 1913 they supported the so-called 'Cat and Mouse' Act, by which hunger strikers could be released on licence and then rearrested. Consequently, the IWFL was fighting not just against the British government, but also against its Irish representatives. The period of intense activity was brought to an end by the outbreak of the First World War, during which League worked closely with other groups. In response to the possibility that conscription would be extended to Ireland in

1918, various women's groups organised a day of action and a petition stating that women would not take the jobs of conscripted men. While the war was still raging, votes for women were granted. In February 1918 the Representation of the People Act was passed, which gave votes to men over twenty-one and women over thirty, providing they met the property qualifications. It applied to the whole of the United Kingdom. In November a further act allowed women to stand for parliament. Yet, although women had obtained the vote, the national question remained unresolved.

Two of the most charismatic and flamboyant of the female nationalists were Maud Gonne and Countess Markievicz. Gonne was born in England in 1865, although she was educated in Dublin and Paris. John O'Leary, a Fenian activist, introduced her to Irish nationalist politics and she was sent to Donegal to help organise resistance against the evictions. In 1889 she met William Butler Yeats. Although she refused to marry him, she involved him in nationalist politics. Maud Gonne's beauty was an inspiration for Yeats's poetry, his unrequited love untarnished by the reality of an actual relationship. But Maud's passion was for politics, not Yeats, and she repeatedly turned down his marriage proposals. In 1887 she moved to France to be with her French lover, Lucien Millevoye, and together they had two children. From Paris, Gonne published a newspaper, *L'Irlande Libre*. It achieved notoriety for including an impassioned poem by Gonne objecting to the visit of Queen Victoria to Ireland in 1900 to raise troops for the Boer War. The poem referred to Victoria as 'the Famine Queen', an appellation that proved to be enduring.

When Gonne returned to Ireland she founded *Inghinidhe na hÉireann* ('Daughters of Erin') in 1900. Again it grew out of the protest at Victoria's visit. Many other female activists were involved, including Countess Markievicz and Louise Gavan Duffy. Although the organisation was overtly nationalist, it was involved in a range of social issues, including feeding the poor children of Dublin during the 1913 lockout. The organisation was critical of the wealth and authoritarianism of the Catholic Church, which meant that it had some powerful enemies. It also supported women's suffrage although it believed that independence should be the priority and women's rights would follow. Gonne married John MacBride in Paris in 1903. MacBride was an ardent republican who had fought for the Boers in the Irish Brigade. Following the birth of their son, she divorced MacBride. She also converted to Catholicism. During the First World War she worked with the Red Cross in France. She did not return to Ireland until 1917. She took no part in the Easter Rising, but her former husband, John MacBride, was executed for his role in it.

Constance Markievicz, like many other Irish nationalist leaders, was born into a privileged Protestant world. Yet she died in poverty in 1927. Constance and her equally radical sister, Eva, were descended from the Gore-Booths of County Sligo, a family that had a reputation for being liberal landlords. Constance's surname resulted from her brief marriage to a Polish count. Like other women of her period she supported women's rights, believing that once Ireland had gained its independence, equality for women would be automatically granted. She therefore regarded winning independence as the priority. Despite her background, Markievicz was concerned with the problems of the poor, and in 1913 worked alongside James Connolly to provide soup kitchens for the strikers. In 1916 she fought in the rising as a commandant, and only her gender saved her from being executed. Although she was imprisoned, upon release she resumed her activities.

Markievicz was a leading figure in both *Inghinidhe na hÉireann* and *Cumann na mBan* ('the League of Women'). After 1914 *Inghinidhe na hÉireann* went into decline, although the vacuum was partly filled by *Cumann na mBan*. Its origins lay in the decision by the male Irish Volunteers to exclude women: 100 excluded women decided to form their own organisation in April 1914. It was strengthened when it was joined by Markievicz, who was then president of *Inghinidhe na hÉireann*. The women combined first aid with fund-raising and drilling. The fact that it was an auxiliary to the men's organisation angered some fellow radicals, who refused to become involved. Hanna and Francis Sheehy-Skeffington, who were feminists, nationalists and pacifists, viewed the setting up of *Cumann na mBan* as a regressive step that kept women in a subordinate position. Although Francis took no part in the Easter Rising, he was shot by an insane British officer. Hanna continued to work for the nationalist cause. She and Nora Connolly (James's daughter) toured the United States in order to raise money for the republicans and sympathy for their cause. With so many men in prison, the involvement of these women was a crucial factor in the reorganisation of Sinn Féin. The Anglo-Irish Treaty of 1921 was a bitter disappointment to many female activists, with all the women members of the Irish parliament voting against it. Hanna, who outlived many of her comrades, was later saddened by the treatment of women in the new Free State, especially the domestic role assigned to them by the 1937 constitution.

Civil War and Partition

In the wake of the 1916 rising the British government, under the premiership of David Lloyd George, decided some settlement had to be made for Ireland. Britain was anxious to conciliate public opinion in the United States, as the government still hoped for American support in the war. Although Lloyd George initiated a series of negotiations, the nationalist representative, Redmond, no longer represented the aspirations of revolutionary Ireland. Nor was Redmond any match for the political astuteness of Carson. In the final stages of the war, therefore, while a new revolutionary movement was being formed in Ireland, in London a policy of partition was taking shape. The prime minister even suggested that they should not wait until the end of the war to pass a Home Rule Bill, from which the six Ulster counties of Antrim, Armagh, Down, Derry, Fermanagh and Tyrone were excluded. While Redmond accepted the partition, he refused to agree to Carson's demand that it be permanent. Undaunted, in May 1917 Lloyd George established an Irish Convention, which was to represent all interests in Ireland. As a gesture of goodwill, he had released hundreds of internees who had been arrested in the wake of the rising and imprisoned without trial. He also released those who had been tried. Their release, however, reinforced the revolutionary movement in Ireland, Redmond's activities in London almost being irrelevant. When he died in 1918, though still leader of the Parliamentary Party, he had lost authority over nationalist politics. The Irish Volunteers were also being revived, though Sinn Féin had manoeuvred itself into being the political wing of the movement. That the pendulum had swung from home rule politics to revolutionary nationalism was made clear by the results of two by-elections, in Roscommon in February and Longford in May. The home rule candidates were unable to defeat those of Sinn Féin. Moreover, Sinn Féin made its disparagement of Westminster politics clear by reaffirming its commitment not to take its seats in parliament. None the less, the Irish Convention met in July 1917, chaired by Sir Horace Plunkett. Sinn Féin refused to take part, and the unionists refused to budge from their intransigent position. The Convention had no chance of success. Although southern unionists were present, they also felt that their demands were being ignored. The majority of those present were home rulers, and they did get the Convention to support a home rule parliament for all of Ireland. By this stage, it had become irrelevant and the Convention's recommendations were ignored.

In contrast to the lethargy of the home rule supporters, Sinn Féin had energised and revitalised the nationalist movement, helped largely by the unstinting efforts of radical women, including Countess Markievicz and Hanna Sheehy-Skeffington. In October 1917 Sinn Féin held a national conference (*ard feis*) in Dublin and appointed a new president, Eamon de Valera. A hero of 1916, de Valera escaped execution because of his American birth – he and Markievicz were the only two commandants who survived the insurrection. In 1917 de Valera won the election in East Clare with a massive majority. In November he was elected president of the Irish Volunteers, which gave him ultimate control of both wings of the revolutionary movement. He was a shrewd politician who relished his supreme position within the revolutionary movement. The Volunteers appointed Michael Collins as director of organisation. Collins was only twenty-six at the time of the rising and had played a subordinate role in it. Nevertheless, he had been interned and had become a leader when in prison. The experience of 1916 led him to believe that only guerrilla warfare would defeat the government forces.

Although they had an organisation in place, the leaders of Sinn Féin were not sure of their next step. Anti-government feeling remained high, as large-scale arrests and house searches were continuing. The government's control was slipping away and the vacuum was immediately filled by Sinn Féin who, through its success in local elections, took over the running of county councils, poor law boards and other forms of local government. The government's handling of the conscription issue broke the deadlock. Conscription had been introduced to Britain in 1916 but not extended to Ireland. In 1918 the British government was considering extending conscription to Ireland as part of its final push to defeat Germany. Sinn Féin's vociferous opposition to conscription won it much support and this was translated into votes in the general election in December 1918, when Sinn Féin won 73 out of the 105 parliamentary seats in Ireland. The unionists won 26 and the Parliamentary Party only 6 seats. The election marked the demise of the Nationalist Party, which since 1912 had been increasingly out of step with the mood of Ireland. Moreover, the most persuasive and charismatic of the Irish nationalists had channelled their energies into extra-parliamentary activities. Unlike Parnell, Redmond did not have the foresight or the personality to harness these forces to the benefit of the Parliamentary Party. This election was the first, and last, time that Irish people (women over thirty also had the vote) voted in a British general election. The

Representation of the People Act in 1918 had enfranchised all adult males, and this mass electorate worked to the benefit of Sinn Féin. Apart from voting, women had also been allowed to stand as MPs, and Countess Markievicz was the first woman to be elected to the British parliament. With her fellow Sinn Féin MPs she refused to take an oath of allegiance to the monarch or to take her seat in Westminster. Consequently, Lady Astor later became the first woman to sit in the British House of Commons. Sinn Féin believed that the election results gave legitimacy to its demands and demonstrated that, in the two years since the rising, popular opinion had shifted in favour of an Irish republic.

The electoral victory convinced Sinn Féin that it was the optimum time to seize the initiative. They refused to sit at Westminster but constituted themselves into an Irish parliament (*Dáil Éireann*). It included no members of the Unionist or Nationalist Party. Members of the Dáil were referred to as *teachtaí dála*, or TDs. They were pledged to an Irish republic and they hoped to achieve this by ignoring all things British, including Westminster. The Dáil met for the first time on 21 January 1919. Eamon de Valera was elected president and Arthur Griffith (the founder of Sinn Féin) was his deputy. Countess Markievicz was appointed minister for Labour, and Michael Collins was put in charge of the military campaign to resist British intervention. Despite having no legal or constitutional status, at the first meeting of the Dáil three items were sanctioned. The Dáil ratified the 1916 Proclamation of a Republic, it asked for the world to recognise that republic and it issued a Democratic Programme, which outlined the social aspirations of Sinn Féin. Although the Dáil had asked for world recognition, its main target was the American president, Woodrow Wilson. He, however, despite being an enthusiastic supporter of the League of Nations and of self-determination, was less than wholehearted in his support for the Irish Republic. The British government proscribed the Dáil, which disrupted some of its work although the Irish parliament did have some impact, notably in the area of local government.

The activities of the Dáil were carried on against a backdrop of war. The Anglo-Irish War, or War of Independence, opened with the killing of two policemen in Soloheadbeg in County Tipperary on 21 January 1919. The Irish Volunteers, who were increasingly referred to as the Irish Republican Army (IRA), mounted a guerrilla war directed by Collins. Its tactics included ambushes, assassinations and raids on police barracks. These proved to be both ruthless and efficient, and, in response, the British government formed two new forces – the Black and Tans (which described the colour of their uniform) and the Auxiliaries – to supplement the regular troops. The new forces proved to be just as brutal in their tactics as the IRA, responding with summary shootings and the indiscriminate burning of buildings. So-called 'flying columns' of IRA men were created to mount quick attacks and escapes. Repressive legislation was passed, including the Restoration of Order Act in August 1920, which extended the provisions of the Defence of the Realm Act, replacing coroner's juries with military courts and extending the power of courts martial. The draconian response of the government achieved little, except to win more support for the IRA, and led to even more violence. Many of the Royal Irish Constabulary casualties of the violence were Catholic. Terence MacSwiney, the Sinn Féin lord mayor of Cork, was imprisoned for possessing a code belonging to the RIC. He went on hunger strike in Brixton prison and died on 25 October 1920, on the seventy-fourth day. His sister, Mary, who was also a political activist, continued to agitate on his behalf. One of the most violent episodes occurred on 21 November 1920, or 'Bloody Sunday'. The IRA shot dead fourteen secret service agents. The Black and Tans responded by indiscriminately firing on the spectators at a Gaelic football match in Croke Park. Twelve people were killed. One week after Bloody Sunday, fifteen Auxiliaries were killed in an ambush in Kilmichael in County Cork. A few weeks later, much of Cork was burnt to the ground by the Black and Tans.

The violence during the Anglo-Irish War was mostly confined to Leinster and Munster. The conflict resulted in an increase in sectarian violence in the north. This reached a climax in the summer of 1920, when Catholics were expelled from the shipyards and other factories in Belfast. Riots in August resulted in thirty deaths and a curfew being imposed on the city. The Irish Volunteers were greatly weakened when they attempted to take over the Custom House in Dublin but were outnumbered by Crown forces. This action depleted their already small supply of weapons. British and American public opinion was shocked by the indiscriminate violence, and in July, Britain negotiated a truce. At this stage the IRA's weapons were exhausted. They had controlled only small areas of the country, which had also stretched their resources and meant that they offered local pockets of resistance rather than a national campaign. During the course of the war, almost 2,000 of the Crown soldiers had been killed, while 752 IRA men had lost their lives, with 866 wounded.

While the conflict was becoming ever more violent, a constitutional solution was being prepared in London. On 23 December 1920 the coalition government led by Lloyd George passed the Government of Ireland Act. It was largely the work of Walter Long, a Conservative who sympathised with unionism. The electoral success of the Conservative Party in the 1918 general election meant that the Liberals were in a minority, and so their party had little influence on the crucial question regarding the exclusion of the six counties of Ulster. Long's original proposal was that Ireland should have two parliaments, both subordinate to Westminster, one in Belfast to look after the nine Ulster counties and the other in Dublin. A Council of Ireland was also to be created, consisting of twenty members from Ulster and twenty from the south of Ireland, which was to work towards an all-Ireland parliament. Unionist opposition, however, rendered the Council ineffective. A few weeks after the Government of Ireland Act was passed, Carson resigned as leader of the Ulster Unionists, and James Craig was elected by the Unionist Council in his place. Craig feared that the proposed Protestant government in Belfast would be weakened by the inclusion of Counties Cavan, Donegal and Monaghan, and began to lobby for a six-county partition, to ensure a safe Protestant majority. This proposal was agreed to, and so the Government of Ireland Act included the six-county alternative. The remaining twenty-six counties were to be constituted as 'Southern Ireland'. Despite the backdrop of conflict, in May 1921 general elections were held to the parliaments of Southern Ireland and Northern Ireland. In the former, 124 Sinn Féin and 4 independent candidates were returned unopposed, while in the Northern Ireland elections, 40 unionists, 6 nationalists and 4 independents were returned. On 7 June 1921 the Northern Ireland House of Commons met and appointed James Craig the prime minister. On 22 June, King George V officially opened the Northern Ireland parliament, even though it was using the City Hall as a temporary meeting place until a custom-built parliament could be erected at Stormont in Belfast. King George used it as an occasion to plea for reconciliation, saying 'I appeal to all Irishmen to pause, to stretch out the hand of forbearance and conciliation, and to join in making for the land which they love a new era of peace, contentment and goodwill.' In the south, the Sinn Féin candidates met in the Mansion House in Dublin and convened as the second Dáil on 16 August. It was short-lived, lasting for less than a year, but it brief duration was overshadowed by the events that followed the treaty negotiations after July 1921.

In December 1921, following months of intense negotiation, a treaty was signed between British and Irish representatives. The early discussions had been carried out between de Valera, the president of the Dáil, the British prime minister, Lloyd George, and Craig, the new unionist leader. In June, de Valera had travelled to London to meet with the other two leaders. Although their talks dragged on for five months, in reality the parameters had been set from the outset, the British government stipulating that all of Ireland was to remain within the British Empire and that Northern Ireland was not to be coerced into a union. If these terms were agreed to, Ireland would be granted self-government; but the government was not willing to negotiate on these terms. Initially de Valera rejected these conditions, although he continued to negotiate. The Sinn Féin leadership was divided on the issue of whether or not to compromise: Arthur Griffith believed that conciliation was necessary, while Austin Stack and Cathal Brugha opposed it. De Valera favoured the more uncompromising approach, yet he chose not to take part in the later negotiations. Instead, he sent Arthur Griffith, Michael Collins and Robert Barton in his place. They were invested with plenipotentiary powers, though de Valera appeared reluctant to relinquish control and told them not to sign anything until it had been approved in Dublin. De Valera also hoped that, by prolonging the negotiations, they might eventually win recognition for a republic. In London, however, both Collins and Griffith had realised that Britain was unyielding regarding its two conditions. Collins also knew that a resumption of war by the IRA was unrealistic and would end in quick defeat. Furthermore, outnumbered by astute and experienced British politicians, they allowed themselves to get bogged down in the symbolism of the oath to the king rather than the reality of partition. Lloyd George, who was anxious to get a quick resolution, exploited their concerns, even using the threat of a renewed conflict with Britain. He also urged them to agree swiftly without first consulting Dublin.

The Anglo-Irish Treaty was signed at 2.30 a.m. on 6 December 1921. Essentially the document was the one that had been put on the table by the British government in July. It provided that twenty-six counties, to be designated the 'Irish Free State', were to become a self-governing dominion within the British Empire, with similar status to that of Canada. Members of the Irish parliament had to take an oath of allegiance to the British Crown, and Britain was to be allowed to maintain naval bases in Irish ports. The negotiators had hoped to win the status of republic for Ireland, but this had proved elusive. Instead, they had, in their words, won 'the freedom to achieve freedom'. More pessimistically, disappointed that they had not achieved more after so many years of struggle, Collins – prophesying his imminent assassination – lamented, 'I have signed my own death warrant.'

The partition of Ireland was the first step in the dismemberment of the British Empire. Since the Act of Union came into effect in 1801, religious and political divisions within Ireland had become more polarised into the camps of nationalists and unionists. As the century progressed, there appeared to be diminishing room for compromise. A British prime minister imposed a solution of sorts in 1920, which created two new states, each with its own parliament. Ironically, Irish unionists, who had argued so defiantly for a continuation of the Union, achieved self-government before any other part of the United Kingdom. The advantage for the British government was that the problems caused by nationalism and unionism had been removed from Westminster to Dublin and Belfast. Yet the political difficulties of Ireland were not solved by the partition; rather a new set of problems had been created. Ireland had achieved limited independence, but fresh divisions had arisen that almost immediately plunged the country into civil war.

TEN

TWO STATES
c. 1921–1969

The partition of Ireland created fresh divisions and new problems within Ireland. After 1921 the two states increasingly grew apart in a number of spheres, making the political partition a reality. Both states were born in violence and their creation was followed by a prolonged period of anarchy, lawlessness and civil war. The two respective states responded with repression – both utilising and extending the tactics devised by the British government in the previous decades.

This chapter examines the consequences of the partition of Ireland and the divisions within and between the two newly created Irish states. In Northern Ireland, these divisions found an outlet in the civil rights movement in the 1960s – inspired by events in the United States – which had an impact on the whole of Ireland and Britain.

Civil War

Many Irish people were disappointed with the terms of the Anglo-Irish Treaty, though, like Michael Collins and Arthur Griffith, they viewed it as a means to an end rather than the end itself. When the negotiators returned to Ireland they tried to persuade the Irish people that it was the best outcome that could have been achieved. The British threat of renewing the war had forced them to reach a decision, as had the promise of a Boundary Commission, which they believed would result in the transfer of large portions of land to the Free State. They were hopeful that by reducing the size of Northern Ireland its separate status would become unsustainable.

De Valera's opposition to the treaty was unequivocal. He argued that the delegates, regardless of their plenipotentiary status, had no right to sign the treaty. He also stated, disingenuously, that 'The sad part of it is that a grand treaty could at this moment be made.' De Valera had the support of other Sinn Féin leaders, including all of the female members of the Dáil. They were offended by the continuation of the oath of allegiance attesting their loyalty to the monarch, the fact that they had dominion status rather than full independence, and the creation of a governor-general who was the representative of the British government in the Free State. The role of the governor-general was to maintain a link with the imperial parliament. It was his responsibility to summon and dismiss the Dáil, although the Dáil could choose its own dates to assemble. After 1927 the office disappeared but, for nationalists, this arrangement had been an uncomfortable reminder of their subordinate position within the empire. These issues, rather than the partition, dominated much of the debate in the Dáil.

The debate on the treaty in the Dáil lasted from 14 December 1921 to 7 January 1922, with each member being called on to contribute. The deliberations were long and acrimonious, with Griffith and Collins pitted against de Valera, Cathal Brugha and Austin Stack. On 7 January 1922 the treaty was ratified by sixty-four votes to fifty-seven. De Valera resigned his presidency, and he and other opponents of the treaty withdrew from the Dáil. Griffith was elected as de Valera's replacement. Although members of Sinn Féin were disappointed with the treaty, initially it had much support in the country, with many people welcoming the prospect of peace. De Valera's sustained opposition did undermine the early support, but a majority of people remained loyal to Collins and Griffith. The anti-treaty group, however, argued that morally the Irish people had no right to reject the Republic.

The Anglo-Irish Treaty had also provided for seventeen MPs elected under the Government of Ireland Act to meet in January, ratify the treaty and select a provisional government. Collins was the chairman of the provisional government until his assassination later in the year. Until September there was a system of dual government in Ireland, with the Dáil and provisional government functioning concurrently, although the British government only recognised the latter. Republicans who were pro-treaty dominated the provisional government. In accordance with the treaty, one of their first duties was to draft a new constitution and organise elections for a constituent assembly. The arrangements were in place by the beginning of summer. Simultaneously, the process of withdrawal by the British was underway. On 16 January 1922 Viscount Fitzalan of Derwent, the last British viceroy, formally handed over power to Collins, together with Dublin Castle. The castle had been built by King John in 1204 and it had become an emblem of British authority and, increasingly, British repressiveness, especially after 1801. The

Black and Tans and RIC were disbanded and given government pensions. British troops began to withdraw, marking a symbolic end to British rule. Their barracks and equipment were handed over to the IRA, which was regarded as the official army of the provisional government. The IRA, however, was increasingly splitting into pro- and anti-treaty factions. Dubliners celebrated on the streets and quaysides as the British troops left. The celebrations were short-lived, as a civil war thrust the country into a new phase of conflict.

While Collins was absorbed with setting up the new state apparatus, de Valera undertook a propaganda campaign against the treaty. He was supported by leading members of the IRA, who in March officially left to form a separate organisation. Both pro- and anti-treaty groups claimed to be the real IRA, but the latter were widely referred to as the Irregulars. They included some of the most experienced troops of the IRA, although they had few weapons. The pro-treaty IRA, however, although they were fewer in numbers, had superior weapons supplied by the British government. The anti-treaty IRA, supported by the IRA in Northern Ireland, felt that their best chance of success was if they could provoke a renewal of conflict with Britain.

On 16 June a general election was held. It was bitterly contested. Out of the 128 parliamentary seats available, the pro-treaty group won 58, while de Valera's followers won 36 seats. The others seats were won by Labour (17) and various independents (also 17 including 4 unionists), all of whom accepted the treaty. Overall, therefore, the election appeared to be an endorsement of the treaty. The election marked the end of the second Dáil, which had sat from August 1921 to June 1922 and paved the way for the third Dáil in less than four years. De Valera still refused to accept that the popular support for the treaty had given it any legitimacy. The Irregulars appeared determined to provoke Collins and the British government into warfare, and on 27 June they kidnapped the governor-general, forcing Collins or Britain to take some action against them.

Although the Free State had appeared to be on the brink of a civil war for months, its actual commencement was precipitated by the intervention of the British government. The occasion was the assassination of Sir Henry Wilson, a former soldier and Unionist MP who was associated with the Belfast pogrom (see p. 227), in London on 22 June 1922 by two anti-treaty IRA members, probably acting autonomously. Following his death, the British government issued an ultimatum to Collins, forcing him to take action against the IRA. The assassination, together with the kidnapping of the governor-general, forced Collins to issue an ultimatum to the Irregulars, which was rejected. On 28 June 1922 Collins, now the commander-in-chief of the Free State Army, ordered his troops to attack the Four Courts building in Dublin, using artillery borrowed from the few British forces remaining in Ireland. This building was the headquarters of the Irish judiciary, but had been occupied by the Irregulars since April. The Irregulars surrendered two days later but before they vacated the building, it caught fire, destroying the Public Record Office and its collection of historical records.

The attack on the Four Courts was the trigger for the war to start. Because the Irregulars were dispersed and lacked central coordination, they suffered some initial defeats, especially in Dublin. They reverted to the tactics that many of them had learned while fighting under Collins during the War of Independence, that is, those of guerrilla warfare. These tactics proved to be more successful against the government forces. The provisional government responded with repressive measures, including the Public Safety Act of 1923 that permitted internment and made possessing arms punishable by death. These measures undermined the Irregulars, who could no longer count on the sympathy of the Irish population as they had when they were fighting Britain. By December they were effectively defeated. They kept fighting, though, until the death of their chief of staff, Liam Lynch, in April 1923. His death marked the end of the Civil War, with his successor, Frank Aiken, calling for a unilateral ceasefire. Three weeks later, Aiken asked the Irregulars to 'dump' their arms and wait until a new opportunity presented itself for the struggle to resume. In total 927 people had been killed, which included 77 people executed by the provisional government. In the final six months of the Civil War, the Irish government had executed twice as many people as were executed by the British during the turbulent years between 1916 and 1921. The atrocities did not stop even when the war was officially over. The Free State government continued to execute anti-treaty prisoners, who had had no proper trial, until the end of 1922. By the beginning of 1923 approximately 12,000 anti-treaty soldiers were still in captivity, the new state lacking both the resources and the expertise to deal with them. Britain stepped into the breach, offering the island of St Helena (where Napoleon had spent his final days) for the republican prisoners. The Irish provisional government in Dublin responded with enthusiasm. However, the replacement of Lloyd George's Liberal coalition government with a Conservative one meant the project never came to fruition as it did not have the support of the new administration.

While the war was being fought, De Valera had established an alternative government, of which he was president. He claimed that it had the legitimate authority of a republic. But he failed to convince the public, the majority of whom simply wanted the conflict to end. The Catholic Church also condemned the actions of de Valera and the Irregulars, asking the country to support the Free State government. Before a ceasefire was finally declared, de Valera announced that he was willing to discuss terms with the government, but the latter was not willing to make any concessions. When the Irregulars finally surrendered, de Valera blamed the supporters of the treaty for destroying the Republic.

The pro-treaty dead included Michael Collins, who had been killed at an ambush in Beal na mBlath in County Cork in August 1922. His premature death at the age of thirty-two deprived the new Free State of a gifted soldier and statesman who had the leadership qualities to heal many of the rifts that had emerged in Ireland. Many other men who had given their lives selflessly for the republican cause also died during the Civil War. They included Erskine Childers, who was executed by the provisional government in 1922, and Rory O'Connor, a hero of 1916 who was executed on the order of Kevin O'Higgins, at whose wedding he had been best man. The Irish Civil War, like all civil wars, made allies out of long-standing enemies. Tragically, the war had pitted brother against brother and former comrade against comrade. Men who had fought so strenuously to end British rule now lost their lives at the hands of their fellow Irishmen. The divisions and recriminations lasted long beyond the ending of the war itself. An independent Irish state, which had been the object of desire for so many years and had resulted in so much death and suffering, was in place, but its creation was tainted by the loss of many who had brought it into existence.

During the Civil War the Free State had lost its leadership. Arthur Griffith had died on 12 August 1922 and ten days later Collins had been killed. Together, these two men had been the architects of the Free State and had delivered a political settlement that exceeded many people's expectations. But they had not been able to bring peace to Ireland. De Valera, however, who had ignored the wishes of both the Dáil and the electorate, survived, and in the following decades he proved to be the main beneficiary of the conflict. The British government had remained largely detached from the problems of Ireland after 1920, except when they directly conflicted with its own interests. Yet successive British governments had proved to be weak and vacillating in the face of unionist opposition. The decades that followed partition were defined by a similar lack of intervention. For many British politicians the Government of Ireland Act marked a major step in disengagement from what they viewed as 'the Irish problem'. Lloyd George, faced with the imminent collapse of the Liberal Party, wanted Ireland to sort out its own problems.

In December 1922 the existence of two separate states was copper-fastened by the coming into force of a constitution in the Free State, while the Northern Ireland parliament, under Article XII of the treaty, formally asked to be excluded from the jurisdiction of the Free State. Both states believed that they had made sacrifices in order to arrive at this stage, but many lives had been lost or ruined during the process. After 1923, despite sporadic outbreaks of localised violence, the two governments concentrated on building their states, but the way in which they developed was divergent, making the border, which had been offered as a temporary solution by Lloyd George, an enduring political reality.

A Free State?

Following the deaths of Griffith and Collins, the Free State government passed to W.T. Cosgrave, with Kevin O'Higgins as minister for home affairs. Together they were responsible for rebuilding a country devastated by years of conflict and turmoil. A constitution, which was the work of the provisional government, had been approved by the Dáil in October 1922, and it came into effect on 6 December. The document did not appease republican sentiment as, at the insistence of the British, it included clauses relating to the oath of allegiance and the governor-general. The constitution did provide for a system of government that was distinct from the British model in a number of ways. It declared that government and its authority were derived from the people. The Irish legislature (or *Oireachtas*) comprised the monarch, who was represented by the governor-general, and two chambers, the lower chamber (or Dáil) and the Senate, or upper house. While executive authority was vested in the monarch, his or her power was nominal, with power lying with an executive council governed by a president nominated by the Dáil. Voting was by proportional representation, and provision was made for referendums to be held. The Senate consisted of sixty elected members. Because the election process was not fully operative, Cosgrave nominated half of the members of the first Senate. He gave Southern unionists special representation. The popular election of the Senate was abolished in 1928 when it was elected by the legislature. In 1936 de Valera abolished the Senate, which had refused to support a bill ending the oath of allegiance. Referendums were also abolished. Overall only half of the Free State constitution remained intact before the 1937 constitution of Ireland supplanted it.

The turmoil of the early years left its imprint on the subsequent development of the new state. In February 1922 a police force, *Gárda Síochána*, was established as an unarmed police force to replace the Royal Irish Constabulary. It had responsibility for the twenty-six counties outside Dublin city, but the high level of civil unrest meant it could not cope and it was restructured within a year by Eoin O'Duffy. At the time of the ceasefire there were approximately 12,000 republican prisoners in the overflowing jails and prison camps of Ireland. Many were kept in appalling conditions and treated brutally. The public campaign to get them released was led by Maud Gonne. In 1923 a number of prisoners went on hunger strike in Mountjoy Prison in Dublin; 425 men, including 10 members of the Dáil, volunteered to go on strike. The support spread into other prisons, although not all inmates adhered to it. By November, there were about 200 men and women on hunger strike. On 20 November, Commandant Denis Barry died in Newbridge camp, and on 22 November, Captain Andrew Sullivan died in Mountjoy. The next day the prisoners agreed to call off the strike. Following this, 300 women republican prisoners were released, but the men were offered a discharge only if they signed a document accepting the Free State. More were gradually released, including de Valera in July 1924. Although the prisons had generally been emptied, the state continued to rely on draconian measures, mostly directed aimed at the IRA. Public Safety Acts were passed in 1923 and 1924 permitting internment. They were only temporary measures, but more permanent legislation, the Public Safety (Emergency Powers) Act, was passed in 1926. It meant that internment was now part of the state apparatus, although it was to be implemented only following the declaration of a state of emergency. In July 1927 Kevin O'Higgins, the minister for justice and external affairs, was assassinated in Dublin while on his way to mass. He had joined Sinn Féin while a student and played an active role in the War of Independence, but his support for the treaty and his ruthless treatment of those who opposed it resulted in his assassination by a former comrade. His murder resulted in the introduction of a more stringent Public Safety Act in

1927. This provided for the establishment of special criminal courts that had no juries, the imprisonment of members of proscribed organisations and the banning of additional organisations. De Valera was its most vociferous opponent, and when he came to power in 1932 he suspended it. Within a short time, however, de Valera's administration was depending on a wholesale policy of subjugation to maintain its power. The early decades of the state were defined by a level of institutionalised repression that exceeded the policies of the British government in the nineteenth century.

The Anglo-Irish Treaty had divided Sinn Féin, and this separation was confirmed by the Civil War. Yet while the pro-treaty side had lost its two leaders, Griffith and Collins, those against the treaty continued to be led by de Valera. Despite their defeat they still aspired to a republic. The fact that Ireland had only been granted dominion status was a disappointment even to supporters of the treaty. In the succeeding decade, however, Irish Free State politicians, working with their counterparts from Canada, were instrumental in transforming the British Commonwealth (which had replaced the term 'British Empire' after 1914) into an association of independent states. These changes were enacted in the Statute of Westminster in 1931, which gave the dominions constitutional independence and recognised them as being equal partners within the Commonwealth and not subordinate in any way to Britain. They did, however, share a common allegiance to the Crown, although all members of the Commonwealth had to be consulted in matters relating to the royal succession. A number of British Conservatives, notably Winston Churchill, were unhappy that the Free State should achieve independent status, viewing it as a threat to the Anglo-Irish Treaty. They were in a minority, and the Free State was included in the statute. Although de Valera was dismissive of the Westminster statute, when he came to power the following year, he used its provisions to change Ireland's constitution.

Boundary Commission

During the negotiations in London, Griffith and Collins had been led to believe that large tracts of Catholic Ulster, including Counties Tyrone and Fermanagh (which had Catholic majorities), together with Derry City and Newry, would be transferred later to the Free State by a Boundary Commission. The final version of the treaty, however, added the proviso that the aspirations of the local population had to be compatible with the broader economic and geographical considerations. For opponents of partition, the promise of a Boundary Commission meant that the borders of the Northern state would be redrawn in accordance with the wishes of the local population. The idea of such a commission had first been mooted in 1912, but the Government of Ireland Act adopted the existing boundaries of the six counties. The Anglo-Irish Treaty provided for such a commission, consisting of a chairman appointed by the British government and a representative from both the Irish Free State and Northern Ireland. The Civil War, dislocation following the First World War and political upheaval in Britain, leading to the downfall of Lloyd George's coalition, delayed its implementation.

The Northern Ireland government refused to participate in the Boundary Commission, arguing that it had not agreed to its establishment. In reality, the fact that the Commission could recommend border changes was a source of concern for unionists. When the Civil War ended, the Free State government tried to expedite the convening of the Commission by establishing the North-East Boundary Bureau, partly to assuage the anger of Catholics near the border areas. They were optimistic that if the Commission transferred the land where there was a Catholic majority to the South, Northern Ireland would become too small to survive as a separate state. In 1923 the Free State appointed Eoin MacNeill as its Boundary Commission representative. MacNeill, a poet and revolutionary, was minister of education in the Dáil. Sir James Craig, the prime minister of Northern Ireland, and his ministers were still refusing to participate. The British government, now headed by Ramsay MacDonald, brought in legislation allowing it rather than the Northern Ireland government to appoint the second commissioner. The man appointed was J.R. Fisher, a staunch unionist. The British government appointed the chairman, Richard Feetham, a judge in the Union of South Africa. The Commission's remit, defined by Article XII of the treaty, was to 'determine in accordance with the wishes of the inhabitants, so far as may be compatible with economic and geographic conditions, the boundaries between Northern Ireland and the rest of Ireland'.

By the time that the Boundary Commission finally sat in 1924, the state of Northern Ireland had become established. A reluctance to alter the existing situation, therefore, influenced the chairman into wanting to maintain the status quo. The vague language of the document, especially over the question of who was to be consulted and in what manner, was a deterrent to initiating any changes. Also, while many Catholics had made submissions to the Commission, asking that they be transferred to the Free State, the distribution of the Catholic population further complicated the situation. In County Tyrone, for example, although there was a majority Catholic population, they were located in the interior of the country. Conservative and unionist opinion in both Britain and Northern Ireland was opposed to any reduction in the boundaries of Northern Ireland, which would be likely to lead to renewed conflict. The outcome of the Commission was that it refused to transfer any of the land or to implement any apparatus to consult any of the border population on the situation. Instead, the Commission recommended that 'Northern Ireland shall continue to exist as a province of the United Kingdom, in accordance with the provisions of the Government of Ireland Act, 1920'. Although the Commission had been given the power to revise the boundaries, an overriding consideration was that it was dealing with 'two ascertained territorial entities [and] must start from the existing boundaries of those entities; that is, it must start its examination of the whole question on the basis of the division marked by the existing boundary, and must treat that boundary as holding good where no sufficient reason . . . is shown for altering it'.

MacNeill resigned from the Commission before the report was published. Its conclusions were leaked to the press at the end of 1925 (probably by Fisher), stating that the proposed changes were minor and favoured Northern Ireland. Irish nationalists were outraged, but they lacked the resources to challenge it. The Commission was abandoned and replaced by a tripartite conference between the three prime ministers. They agreed not to change the borders at all. Craig was delighted with the outcome; Stanley Baldwin, British prime minister, was relieved; but the Irish premier, William Cosgrave, had only disappointing news to deliver. Many who had supported the treaty had viewed the Boundary Commission as a way of making the partition more palatable, but this was not to be. Catholics, who accounted for one-third of the population of Northern Ireland, felt they were trapped in a hostile state in which sectarianism had increased since the partition. The Boundary Commission's report was not made available (it was only published in 1969). The border remained in place, although both states were given some financial compensation. Nevertheless, it was an inauspicious start for the two newly created states, as Catholics on both sides of the border felt let down. This betrayal was evocative of what had occurred at the time of the Act of Union, when the promises made during the negotiations had not been kept, and constitutional methods had been discredited.

The Six Counties

While the Civil War was confined to the Free State, the Northern Ireland state faced a situation just as violent and divisive. Although a new state of Northern Ireland had been created, its future and longevity were still controversial. Protestants were in the majority overall, accounting for 66 per cent of the Northern Ireland population, but in Counties Fermanagh and Tyrone there was a majority of Catholics. Catholics throughout Northern Ireland were unhappy with the situation, but many believed that the partition would be short-lived. In the short term they refused to cooperate with the unionist government, confirming in the eyes of Protestants that all Catholics were enemies of the new state. The actions of militant Protestants, especially those employed in the constabulary, inflamed rather than assuaged the existing rifts between Catholics and Protestants, who increasingly conformed to the categories of nationalists or unionists, with shrinking common ground.

Not only were nationalists on both sides of the border opposed to the partition, but also unionists who resided in the Free State felt isolated, some choosing to relocate to the North. The 70,000 Protestants who lived in the three excluded Ulster counties of Cavan, Donegal and Monaghan felt particularly aggrieved, as many of them wanted to be part of Northern Ireland. For Protestants in Northern Ireland, the greatest threat to the future of the new state was the Catholics who lived within its borders. In the first elections held in Northern Ireland in May 1920 the nationalist candidates declared that they would not take their seats in the parliament. Following the disappointing outcome of the Boundary Commission in 1925, they did take their seats but refused to act as an official opposition. Their dilemma was how they could participate in a state that their declared objective was to overthrow. The Anglo-Irish Treaty in December 1921 had applied to all of Ireland, but the Northern Ireland government was allowed to opt out, which it did immediately. While the North did not undergo the horrors of civil war, lawlessness and anarchy were commonplace. Sectarian attacks had intensified during the Anglo-Irish War. In July 1920 Catholic employees in some of the shipyards had been attacked. This was followed by days of looting and burning Catholics out of their homes. Some of the worst conflict took place in Lisburn, near Belfast. The shooting of District Inspector Swanzy in August 1920 was followed by attacks on the homes and offices of Catholics, resulting in the evacuation of the Catholic population from the town.

The political problems of the Northern Ireland state were compounded by a downturn in the local economy. In June 1921, 40 per cent of the local population was unemployed. Unemployment increased the tensions between Catholics and Protestants, especially as the former were summarily dismissed from their jobs. The violence, in turn, inflicted substantial damage on the economy. Throughout Northern Ireland, over £3 million worth of property was destroyed, mostly Catholic businesses. The human cost was also high. Violence was most intense in Belfast where, in the two years following July 1920, 453 people were murdered, 257 of whom were Catholics. In the same period 8,750 Catholics were driven from their employment and 23,000 from their homes, leading to the appellation 'pogrom'. When over 1,000 Catholic refugees arrived in Glasgow, the British government became alarmed. They responded by pressurising the two Irish governments into reaching an agreement. The resultant Craig–Collins Pact in 1922 promised that the boycott on Northern goods would be ended by the Free State, that the Catholics driven out of the shipyards would be re-employed, and that negotiations would take place relating to the border. A further meeting between Craig and Collins and a second pact reiterated the earlier promises, and added an assurance that IRA activity in Northern Ireland would be stopped and a mixed Catholic and Protestant police force would be established. In reality, the pacts made little difference to the violence in Northern Ireland.

Because the combined forces of the army and the regular armed police could not cope with the situation, James Craig persuaded the British government to create a special Ulster constabulary, to be composed of part-time volunteers who were well disposed towards the new government. They were to be paid for by the British government. In such a politically fraught atmosphere it was inevitable that only Protestants would join the 'B-Specials'. The B-Specials did not have to meet the usual entrance requirements for the Constabulary, although they were allowed to carry arms. They were also poorly disciplined, and many were overtly anti-Catholic. On 5 April 1922 the Royal Ulster Constabulary was formed, based on its predecessor the Royal Irish Constabulary. Within a few months, there were 50,000 full- and part-time police in Northern Ireland. Faced with such an overwhelmingly hostile police force, many Catholics turned to the IRA for protection. Others simply relocated to the Free State.

The increase in the Crown forces was accompanied by more repressive legislation, similar to the Coercion Acts passed in the nineteenth century by the British government. The legislation of the Northern Ireland government, however, exceeded that of its predecessor in terms of ruthlessness. The Special Powers Act, passed in April 1922, gave the RUC comprehensive powers to arrest and detain suspects for an indefinite period without trial, while special courts could sentence detainees to penal servitude or death. Houses could be searched without a warrant, and people involved with explosives, firearms or blackmail could be punished by flogging, a provision that remained in place until 1968. The minister for home affairs was given the power to proscribe political organisations and ban or re-route marches. This legislation was primarily targeted at Catholics. While the act had been passed in response to the anarchy that followed partition, the Northern Ireland government decided to renew it annually, and made it permanent in 1933. The new Northern Ireland government had been born in violence and even when the violence had diminished, it continued to govern by draconian legislation that exceeded the most repressive measures passed by the British government.

The IRA responded with a wholesale campaign of destruction, burning down Protestant businesses and the 'Big Houses' which for decades had been a symbol of Protestant ascendancy. Protestants murdered Catholics in reprisal and expelled Catholics from their homes. In May 1922 the assassination of W.J. Twaddell, a unionist MP for Belfast, resulted in the imposition of internment, with 200 Catholic prisoners being kept on an old ship in the Larne Lough. In the month of Twaddell's death, forty-four Catholics and twenty-two Protestants were killed in Belfast alone. A raid by the Donegal IRA to Fermanagh alarmed even the British government and the British colonial secretary, Winston Churchill, ordered several hundred troops, artillery and military cars to the small villages of Belleek and Pettigo. The villages were shelled with howitzers, resulting in the deaths of three members of the IRA and one special constable. Collins, who was head of the Free State government, did not intervene, even though British troops based themselves in County Donegal. He was still hoping to prevent a civil war in the country and did not want to offend the British when the survival of the Free State appeared so fragile. In May, Collins met Craig in London and promised to curb the hostile actions of the IRA against the Northern state, in return for a promise that the unionist government would do more to protect the Catholic minority. In the wake of this meeting, sectarian violence in the North diminished, and within twelve months some level of stability had been achieved. In contrast, the South was plunged into a divisive and violent civil war, which pitted Catholic against Catholic.

While the main concern of the unionist government in its early years of existence was the violence that following partition, a system of administration was concurrently put in place that shaped the future development of the State. Partisan employment practices further alienated the Catholic population and kept many of them unemployed or in the lowest income groups. Although one-third of the RUC was supposed to be Catholic, the proportions never rose above one-sixth, and no attempts were made to correct this imbalance. Government employees were overwhelmingly Protestant, from high-ranking civil servants to gardeners. Richard Dawson Bates, the minister for home affairs, refused to use the telephones when he found that a Catholic telephonist had been hired. The discrimination against Catholics was most blatant in the political arena. One of the first things the government did was to change the local government electoral boundaries in order to prevent certain parliamentary and council seats from falling to the nationalists. This was in response to the fact that in a number of Catholic areas, Nationalist Party–Sinn Féin coalitions controlled the local councils, who had pledged allegiance to the Dáil. The hostility of many Catholics to the new state was used to justify these measures, and so sectarianism became embedded in many of the government policies and structures.

In 1921 the Northern Ireland parliament passed a bill dissolving recalcitrant (by which they meant nationalist) local authorities. Within a year, twenty-one local authorities had been disbanded and replaced by government-appointed commissioners. Michael Collins objected to the British government, arguing that the real purpose of the measures was to disenfranchise Catholics, which would be particularly damaging on the eve of the sitting of the Boundary Commission. Winston Churchill, fearing an outbreak of further hostilities, agreed to withhold royal assent. The unionists, however, threatened to resign. Not for the first time, the British government backed down, being unwilling to alienate the unionists even if it meant estranging Catholics in Northern Ireland. An act for the rearrangement of local government boundaries was finally passed in April 1922. The following year proportional representation was abolished in local government elections. There had been a period of consultation; Sinn Féin and nationalist councillors had refused to participate, although their involvement probably would have made little difference. The blatant redrawing of electoral boundaries in favour of unionists, or gerrymandering, had an immediate impact on local government results. Even in areas where Catholics constituted a majority of the population, they lost their control of local government. In the 1924 local elections, nationalists won control of only two of the eighty councils. These changes had consolidated unionist control over local government and they then turned their attention to national politics.

In the general election in 1925, the vote for unionists was slightly reduced, with the Labour Party winning three seats. The fact that each of the Labour MPs was Protestant and that they had criticised the Unionist Party convinced Craig of the need to end proportional representation. It was abolished in 1929, shortly before the general election. Electoral boundaries were also redrawn to reduce the number of seats held by nationalists and the Labour Party. The changes contributed to more polarised political divisions between Catholics and Protestants, by disempowering the moderates on both sides who wanted a more just system of government. Westminster, establishing a pattern of behaviour that characterised the next forty years, did not intervene to protect the rights of minorities within the Northern Ireland electorate. In November 1932 the Prince of Wales opened the new parliament buildings at Stormont in east Belfast. A statue of Sir Edward Carson was prominently located near to the entrance. For unionist politicians the opening was treated as a day of celebration, but nationalist MPs took no part, seeing the building as a symbol of a new form of Protestant ascendancy.

The de Valera Era

During the 1916 Rising, the Anglo-Irish War and the Civil War, many nationalist leaders had been lost. Eamon de Valera (1882–1975) survived all of these conflicts and, despite playing such a subversive role in the Civil War, was not executed. He dominated Irish politics for almost fifty years, during which time Ireland changed from being part of the United Kingdom, to winning partial independence as a free state and dominion, to unilaterally claiming status as a republic. He played an important role in each of these transformations. De Valera was born in New York but raised in Limerick. In 1908 he joined the Gaelic League and became a strong supporter of the Irish language. During the 1916 Rising he was commander at Boland's Mill in Dublin. Although he was sentenced to death, he was reprieved, probably because of his American birth. He thus became the senior male survivor of the rising. By virtue of this circumstance alone, he was in an ideal position to present himself as rebel leader in the popular imagination. In 1917, when he was released from prison, he was elected MP for County Clare and also became the president of Sinn Féin. Following his escape from Lincoln Jail in 1919, which was a massive propaganda coup for Sinn Féin, he was elected president of the first Dáil. In 1919 he went to America and raised over $5 million for the republican cause, but he failed to get official recognition for the republic. De Valera chose not to lead the delegation to negotiate a treaty to end the Anglo-Irish War, sending Collins in his place. He then refused to accept the treaty and resigned as president of the Dáil. His actions helped to trigger the Irish Civil War. At the end of the war, he was arrested and spent a year in jail. In 1926 de Valera left Sinn Féin and formed a new political party, *Fianna Fáil* ('Soldiers of Ireland'). Its constitution included its desire 'to secure the unity and independence of Ireland as a republic' and 'to restore the Irish language as the spoken language of the people'. In 1927 de Valera was re-elected to the Dáil. Although he and his supporters signed the book containing the oath of allegiance, they did so in silence. The election of Fianna Fáil as the majority party in 1932 marked the beginning of a period of Irish politics dominated by de Valera, as he led the Free State parliament for sixteen years. It also marked a more conservative phase in Irish history that culminated in the writing of the 1937 constitution. De Valera personally benefited from the new constitution, later serving two consecutive terms as president, from 1959 to 1973.

After 1932 de Valera sought to dismantle the treaty and other vestiges of the connection with Britain. One of his first actions in government was to remove the oath of allegiance, although the Senate opposed him in his attempt to do so. Nevertheless the oath was officially removed in 1933. In 1936 de Valera abolished the Senate. He also used the disarray caused by the British abdication crisis to rush the External Relations Act through the Dáil. It abolished all of the functions of the monarch in the internal affairs of Ireland but endorsed them in the State's external affairs. One of de Valera's most enduring legacies to Ireland was the 1937 constitution. Although it was written by a small group of civil servants, it was done under de Valera's close supervision. The new constitution retained the administrative structures of that of 1922, including the *Oireachtas* and the legal framework. There were significant differences. Controversially, Article 2 referred to the national territory as 'the whole island of Ireland'. Although the succeeding articles referred to the twenty-six counties as the State's area of jurisdiction, for unionists the second article amounted to a declaration of intent by the Free State government. The constitution provided for the creation of a head of state or president. A president was to be elected by the people every seven years. He or she also had some discretionary powers over the *Oireachtas* and was commander-in-chief of the armed forces. Some opponents felt that the president had too much power for the head of a democracy. Douglas Hyde, a Protestant, was inaugurated as first president of Éire in 1938.

The Senate, which de Valera had abolished in 1936, was reintroduced, although its composition was restructured. Of the sixty seats in the upper house, designated groups elected forty-nine members, including the unionists; the other eleven were nominated by the *taoiseach* (prime minister). The position of *taoiseach* was provided for in the constitution to replace the existing president of the Executive Council, which had been the title of the prime minister in the Free State. It also provided for the Free State to be officially referred to by the Irish name, Éire. The most controversial – and conservative – articles in the constitution were those referring to social and personal matters, including the role of women, which suggested that they belonged exclusively in the domestic sphere. Article 41 stated that 'the State recognises that by her life within the home, woman gives to the State a support without which the common good cannot be achieved'. Article 44 referred to the Catholic Church as holding a 'special position' in the State, which not only excluded Protestants but reinforced the accusations of unionists that the Free State was a Catholic state for a Catholic people.

When de Valera came to power, he also promoted a policy of economic self-sufficiency (autarchy), which he hoped would protect Irish industries. Before partition Sinn Féin had adopted a policy of protection and economic self-sufficiency. This policy was abandoned by the Free State government under William Cosgrave, largely for practical reasons. In the period immediately following independence, Britain and the Irish Free State continued to share a unified currency. The Free State was predominantly agricultural, with over 50 per cent of employment being on the land, compared with 25 per cent in Northern Ireland. The State therefore had a high dependence on external trade, particularly with Britain and the rest of the Commonwealth. In 1926, 65 per cent of all imports to the Free State were from Britain, and 83 per cent of all exports were to Britain. Cosgrave's cautious economic policies appeared successful and, in the decade following partition, unemployment was lower in the Free State than in Northern Ireland. When de Valera became president he wanted to end not only the political link with Britain, but also the cultural and economic ties. He therefore pursued a policy of economic autonomy, based on Sinn Féin's original policy of self-sufficiency. On coming to power, he also refused to continue the repayments of land annuities to the British Treasury, that is, the repayment of loans from the various land acts at the turn of the century. The British government retaliated by imposing high duties on a number of agricultural imports from Ireland and introducing a system of quotas. De Valera responded with placing tariffs on British goods. This trade dispute, which was referred to as the Economic War, lasted from 1932 to 1938. It coincided with an international trade depression, with a number of other countries introducing similar protection for their goods. The impact of the Economic War was to promote some native industries, although agriculture suffered. Some areas of trade continued – throughout the 1930s, non-food imports from Britain increased. In reality, the Economic War was more significant in promoting political rather than economic separation. It was also a propaganda coup for de Valera at an important stage in his political career. The war did benefit Northern agriculture, which had continued to receive British government subsidies and had preferential access to British markets.

De Valera's electoral success raised the hopes of republicans both in the Free State and in the North. Some of his early actions included releasing political prisoners, dissolving military tribunals, and suspending special powers and detention. These actions appeared to confirm that a new phase of republicanism would begin. De Valera exploited his popularity and the disarray of the opposition Cumman na nGaedheal (literally 'Party of the Irish'), calling an election in 1933 in which he gained 5 seats, giving his party 77 out of the 153 seats in the Dáil. The number of seats won was deeply symbolic, as it equalled the number of republicans executed in 1922–3. A new element had entered Irish politics with the formation in 1932 of the Army Comrades' Association, or 'Blueshirts'. Some of its members were as much alarmed by de Valera's electoral victory as they were attracted by the ideology of fascism. After 1933 the Blueshirts adopted the appearance and method of European fascist groups and (now calling themselves the National Guard) joined with Cumman na nGaedheal to form Fine Gael ('People of Ireland'), with Eoin O'Duffy as their leader. In 1936 O'Duffy and some of his followers travelled to Spain to fight on the side of General Franco. They had the support of many members of the Catholic Church hierarchy.

The IRA and the Blueshirts were implacable enemies, and there were numerous violent clashes between the two groups. Initially the State arrested more Blueshirts, but by 1935 large numbers of the IRA had been imprisoned. The IRA had also been weakened by internal splits and by the vehement opposition of the Catholic Church. In the Lenten Pastoral of March 1935, the Church had forbidden its followers to belong to the IRA. Despite de Valera's republican credentials, as his hold on power became more secure, he turned his back on former comrades. Although, when in opposition, de Valera had described Cosgrave's Public Safety Act as 'the most abominable piece of legislation this House was ever asked to pass', in government he showed himself to be as willing as his political predecessors to use repressive measures against political dissenters and republicans. In 1934 he introduced legislation similar to the Public Safety Act, although he justified it by pointing to Blueshirt activity. In 1936 the IRA were banned and their imprisoned members were no longer allowed political status. Despite being outlawed in their own country, in 1939 the IRA started its 'English campaign', placing explosives in seven different English towns. The Northern Ireland government responded to this renewal of hostilities by introducing internment; de Valera's solution was the introduction of the Offences Against the State Act, which provided for the establishment of military tribunals and internment without trial. Although there was an attempt to show that internment was unconstitutional within the Free State, an amending act reintroduced it in 1940. The act remained in place and was used by successive governments against the IRA. The demand for political status led to the death by hunger strike of two IRA men in 1940, followed by a third death in 1946. This situation had parallels with the actions of the British government in Northern Ireland thirty years later. Overall, the legislation against the IRA demonstrated that many in the republican movement had moved to constitutional government, even if that government could only be maintained by a system of institutionalised repression on both sides of the border.

A Conservative State

The period between 1932 and 1973, which was dominated by de Valera, was a conservative phase in Irish development. In his traditional St Patrick's Day speech in 1943, in a declaration which was to become one of his most quoted speeches, de Valera praised the benefits of a 'frugal' lifestyle, describing Ireland as a country 'whose countryside would be bright with cosy homesteads, whose fields and villages would be joyous with the sounds of industry, with the romping of sturdy children, the contests of athletic youth and the laughter of comely maidens'. De Valera's view of women appeared particularly traditionalist when compared with the promising origins of the republican movement. The 1916 proclamation had made an explicit reference to women, being addressed to 'Irishmen and Irishwomen', thereby becoming one of the first revolutionary declarations to place women at the heart of the revolutionary demands. Constitutionally also, the political rights of women had been enhanced as a consequence of the 1918 Representation of the People Act.

Following the defeat of the 1916 Rising, with many men in prison, it was female activists who ensured that the sympathy that followed the execution of the leaders was maintained. They also travelled throughout Britain, Ireland and the United States in order to raise funds for the republican cause. In 1918 Maud Gonne, Hanna Sheehy-Skeffington, Kathleen Clarke, Countess Markievicz and a number of other republican women were arrested for their involvement in the anti-conscription campaign. They were interned in Holloway prison in London. The active role of women such as Countess Markievicz, Kathleen Clarke, Kate O'Callaghan and Margaret Pearse in the first and second Dáil ensured that women's rights were acknowledged. In 1922 women in the Free State were given full equality of citizenship, six years before British women, although a source of grievance was the fact that they remained excluded from jury service. The period that followed partition did little to demonstrate that women were seen as equal to men. On the contrary, in the Free State the status of women deteriorated in many ways and women activists were marginalised, silenced and even imprisoned.

Leading republican women, including Maud Gonne and Countess Markievicz, opposed the Anglo-Irish Treaty. Because of their support for the anti-treaty forces, they were imprisoned in 1923 without charge. The women had been jailed before, but this time they were imprisoned not by the British but by the Irish Free State government. Gonne and ninety-one other women went on hunger strike, and most were released after twenty days. Undaunted, some women continued with their political activities although they had been driven from mainstream politics. For the remainder of her life, Gonne worked on behalf of republican prisoners and their families, which was unpopular in the authoritarian atmosphere of post-partition Ireland, both sides of the border. Markievicz joined the Fianna Fáil Party, which was founded in 1926.

She died the following year in a public ward in a Dublin hospital. Yet she, more that any other individual, appeared to be an embodiment of the spirit of *Cathleen ni Houlihan*, Yeats's female representation of Ireland.

Irish activist women quickly became disillusioned with the Free State government, particularly its social conservatism and association with Catholicism. Their feminism and radicalism were at odds with the traditionalism of the new State. Some of the women, including Rosamund Jacob, warned that the outcome of women being squeezed out of the political arena would be anti-women legislation. She was right. The role of women further declined in the 1930s, especially during de Valera's administration. In 1935 there was an attempt to limit the ability of women to work outside the home, and their domestic role was confirmed in the 1937 constitution. Although women protested, they not only faced opposition from traditionalist politicians but also the authoritarianism of the Catholic Church. The identification of many people with the Catholic Church, however, had been evident during the Eucharistic Congress in 1932, which was part of a series of international congresses to support devotion to the Blessed Sacrament. The climax of the congress was a public mass in Phoenix Park in Dublin, which was attended by over a million people – approximately one in five of the population. The congress demonstrated how closely an Irish identity had been combining with a Catholic one.

The conservatism of the Free State politicians towards women extended into other areas of life. Successive governments, backed by an increasingly conservative and arrogant Catholic Church, tried to protect Ireland from cultural influences that were regarded as foreign or risqué. External cultural influences were particularly threatening because of the revolution in international communications and the growth of mass media. Cars, cinema, radio and telephones linked rural and urban Ireland, and more slowly, Ireland and the rest of the world. The establishment in 1927 of the Electricity Supply Board, which was the first Irish state enterprise, helped the spread of technology. Many houses in rural Ireland, however, remained without electricity or running water. The extension of the national grid after 1947 amounted to a social revolution in Ireland. A rural electrification programme brought the outside world into rural homes via television.

But for a new state, anxious to establish its own identity following centuries of subjugation, the intrusion of the outside world was not totally welcome. Censorship was one of the tools employed by successive governments. In the nineteenth century, censorship had been used by the British government as a way of controlling political sedition and, increasingly, to ban obscenity. During the First World War and Anglo-Irish War, further measures had been introduced to control anti-British propaganda. The new Free State made use of censorship not only for political reasons but also in a wide range of social and cultural areas. Much of it was introduced as a result of the lobbying of the Catholic Church. In 1923 film censorship was introduced by the new State. The job of the newly appointed censor was to protect Irish people from 'indecent, obscene or blasphemous material' or anything that threatened 'public morality'. In 1926 a Committee on Evil Literature was established. The Irish Censorship Board, which was founded in 1929, had even broader powers: it could ban any literature that was regarded as indecent, encouraged crime, or promoted contraception or abortion. The broad remit of the act resulted in hundreds of bannings, which peaked in 1936 when 171 orders were issued. The books banned included Robert Graves's *I, Claudius* (1936), John Steinbeck's *The Grapes of Wrath* (1940) and Joseph Heller's *Catch 22* (1962). Ironically, James Joyce's *Ulysses* was not banned in Ireland but was banned in the United States and Britain until 1936. Although some opposition was voiced, overall these interventions were accepted by the majority of the Irish population and, with few amendments, continued for decades. At the same time as the introduction of the censorship laws, the Free State government actively encouraged traditional forms of cultural activities such as storytelling, Irish dancing, music and singing. None the less, foreign culture acquired a glamour and excitement with which home-grown culture found it difficult to compete.

The 1930s in Northern Ireland

The 1930s were a time of frustration for nationalists in Northern Ireland. Despite being a large minority within the state, the nationalists found it difficult to be an effective constitutional opposition. In 1928 Joseph Devlin and Cahir Healy, who wanted to bring the disparate nationalist groups together, founded the National League in the North. Joseph Devlin, who was a leading member of the Nationalist Party, came from a working-class Belfast family. He had won the parliamentary seat for West Belfast from the Unionist Party in 1906, and after 1916 he had supported the Nationalist Party in campaigning for a temporary partition. This had lost him the support of radical Catholics, especially as the partition became more established. Devlin hoped that the National League would provide a forum for all shades of nationalists to reunite. Although by 1928 there were ten nationalist and three Labour MPs in the Stormont parliament, the National League was weakened by being opposed by both Sinn Féin and the Catholic Church. It was disbanded following Devlin's death in 1934. The passing of Devlin and the National League left the Northern Catholics bereft of effective leadership, which made them even more vulnerable to the partisan policies of the Unionist Party in the decades following the partition.

The new Northern government, which was overwhelmingly unionist, declared itself to be governing 'an Orange state'. The political outlook was exemplified by the declaration of the first prime minister, Sir James Craig, who stated, 'I have always said that I am an Orangeman first and a politician and a Member of Parliament afterwards . . . All I boast is that we are a Protestant parliament and a Protestant state.' Clearly Protestantism rather than Britishness was the vital part of the identity of the new State. None the less, British symbols were appropriated by the Northern State with the Union flag being used as the symbol of the Unionist Party. Popular attachment to the British monarchy remained strong among Protestants in Northern Ireland, although it was not always reciprocated; Edward VIII, for example, tried to avoid a visit following his coronation in 1936. The allegiance to William of Orange also continued. The first unionist government decided that 12 July should be recognised formally as a public holiday. Although support for the Unionist Party was broadly based, its leaders were drawn from the landed gentry or were wealthy industrialists who had little in common with the mass of their supporters. Despite its apparent unity, the Unionist Party was not monolithic. Although it claimed to speak for Northern Protestants, in reality this meant Presbyterians and Anglicans, rather than smaller denominations such as the Quakers, Baptists and Moravians. In the 1920s Protestant pressure groups, such as the Temperance Reformers, the Labour Party and the 'Unbought Tenants' Association' (who wanted a fairer distribution of housing), were deviating from the unanimity expected from the unionist leaders. These groups attracted considerable support and, by the system of proportional representation, electoral success. In 1925 the Labour Party won three seats in Stormont and the Unbought Tenants' Association candidate was elected in County Antrim, where he defeated a mainstream unionist. The ending of proportional representation in 1929 was as much aimed against dissident Protestants as troublesome Catholics, the former being more likely to take seats from unionist members than the latter.

The ending of proportional representation gave the Unionist Party even firmer control over the Protestant vote, with political allegiances being along nationalist and unionist lines. The Unionist Party was politically unassailable, with 50 per cent of candidates being returned unopposed. Their political dominance resulted in decades of political stability at the level of central government, with a small, wealthy and educated unionist elite controlling Northern Ireland. Moreover, the leadership of the Unionist Party remained remarkably stable, with Craig as prime minister from 1921 until his death in 1940. His successor, J.M. Andrews, resigned after only two years in office, while Sir Basil Brooke (later Viscount Brookeborough) was premier from 1943 to 1963. This high degree of political continuity was in strong contrast with democracies throughout the rest of Europe, including Britain, where the four decades after 1920 witnessed the rise of new political parties on both the right and left. The unionist politicians were exposed to changes taking place in Britain because in addition to its representation in Stormont, Northern Ireland was entitled to send thirteen MPs to Westminster. Again the unionists dominated, holding eleven of the Westminster seats.

The political authority of the Orange Order increased in the Northern state, and, between 1921 and 1968, 138 out of the 149 unionist MPs were members of the Orange Order, as were the prime ministers. Yet sectarian conflicts accompanied the 12 July anniversaries, especially if Protestant supremacy appeared to be challenged. The re-emergence of de Valera as a popular leader in the 1930s worried some Orangemen. His popularity in Northern Ireland had been demonstrated by his election as MP for Down between 1921 and 1929, and for South Down from 1933 to 1937, but he did not take his seat. In 1931 the Orange Order led an attack on Catholics which led to counter-attacks and reprisals. In 1932 the shooting dead of a Catholic publican in Belfast was the first sectarian murder since 1922. The attacks and retaliations increased, culminating in the 12 July parade in 1935, when two civilians were killed. Fearing widespread disorder, the Northern Ireland government had attempted to outlaw the march but, like the British government before, backed down in the face of determined opposition by the Orange Order. Yet the resultant conflict was the most violent since the post-partition period. Despite the presence of troops and constabulary, the rioting continued until the end of August, by which time eight Protestants and five

Catholics had been killed. Over 2,000 Catholics and fewer than ten Protestants had been driven from their homes. The cruelty and regularity of the attacks were even worrying people in Britain, and fifty-nine Westminster MPs called for an official inquiry. The British prime minister refused to accede on the grounds that the matter was totally the responsibility of the Northern Ireland government. The Anglo-Irish Treaty had recognised the need to safeguard the minorities in Northern Ireland, yet since the inception of the State there had had been little evidence that this had occurred. Once again, however, the majority of the British parliament had demonstrated that they were unwilling to intervene to protect the rights of the minority population.

In the 1930s the political turmoil of the new Northern State was overshadowed by the deteriorating state of the local economy. Northern Ireland had remained part of the United Kingdom economy and the British parliament remained responsible for its financial affairs. In the nineteenth and early twentieth centuries the north-east of Ulster had been the most industrialised part of Ireland. Unionists had used their economic superiority as an argument against home rule. The new Northern State had inherited a more developed industrial base than in the Free State, although it had a high dependence on shipbuilding, linen production and engineering. Industry was also localised and concentrated around the greater Belfast area. The creation of Northern Ireland coincided with a sharp decline in staple industries, especially shipbuilding and textiles. Between 1923 and 1930, unemployment reached 19 per cent. This made it one of the poorest areas in the United Kingdom. Its poverty was most obvious in education, housing and health. In each of these fields, poor Catholics were more disadvantaged than Protestants. Catholics also had the highest unemployment rates.

The British parliament was responsible for the Northern Ireland economy but did not provide sufficient money to tackle problems effectively, even if the political will had existed. The international recession that followed the Wall Street crash had a detrimental impact on the Northern Ireland economy. By 1932, 28 per cent of the registered workforce was unemployed, which was comparable to unemployment levels in south Wales. Shipbuilding, which had been a mainstay of Protestant workers, was particularly badly affected: Harland and Wolff's profits fell sharply, while the shipbuilders Workman Clark closed down in 1935. A survey produced in 1938 showed that the death rate in Northern Ireland was 25 per cent higher than in any other part of the United Kingdom. On the eve of the Second World War unemployment still remained at 20 per cent.

The main source of relief for the unemployed was outdoor relief provided via the Poor Law Unions. While the Poor Law had been abolished in the Free State following independence and in Britain in 1929, it was retained in Northern Ireland until 1948. The assistance provided by outdoor relief was minimal, and as the winter of 1932 approached, church leaders warned the politicians that the 78,000 unemployed were on the verge of starvation. Moreover, the unemployed men were required to do task work – usually road-building – to qualify for relief, which added to their general debilitation. Anger at the high unemployment in 1932 had briefly cut across sectarian divisions, and joint meetings and marches were held, organised by the Unemployed Workers' Committee. Their aim was to have unemployment allowances increased. On 3 October they began a strike, and on the same evening 60,000 Catholics and Protestants marched in Belfast singing 'Yes, We Have No Bananas', apparently because this was the only non-sectarian song they had in common. In the days that followed, similarly large demonstrations took place. When protesters refused to obey a police order to stop the protests, the RUC responded violently with baton charges, showing that it was willing to use force against demonstrating Protestants. However, guns were used by the RUC in only the Catholic areas. Violence was particularly bad in the Protestant Sandy Row district and in the Catholic Lower Falls area. The authorities remained intransigent, the Poor Law guardians refused to increase outdoor relief, the government banned all marches, and police reinforcements were drafted into Belfast. Further riots followed, during which two Catholics and one Protestant were killed and dozens of others wounded. The government was alarmed – it was used to confronting the Catholic working classes but was unsettled by being in conflict with people regarded as its natural supporters. The government forced the guardians to increase outdoor relief. It was a victory for the Belfast unemployed, but the unity between Catholic and Protestant poor was short-lived, as both sides retreated into their separate spheres. Furthermore, the unity was restricted to the poorest social groups.

Economic divergence between the economies of the North and South reinforced political divisions. Before 1920 the United Kingdom was a single economic unit, sharing internal and coastal trade, despite the Irish and British economies being structurally different. From the summer of 1920 all Northern goods had been boycotted in the South as a protest against partition. The IRA had enforced this action. In March 1922 Michael Collins, now committed to constitutional tactics, met James Craig in London, and promised to call off the boycott and other hostile actions by the IRA. In the post-partition period, despite the political upheavals, cross-border trade continued. But within twenty years, this situation had changed, largely because of de Valera's policy of protectionism and his 'Economic War' against Britain. A common feature of the two Irish economies was that they both fell behind that of Britain. The Second World War, during which the Free State remained neutral, increased the economic divisions, as the war facilitated a revival in the Northern economy. Moreover, while the war helped to revive the Northern economy, living standards in the Free State were declining and would have dropped further if high levels of emigration had not provided an outlet. An economic division had augmented the political partition between the two states.

War and its Aftermath

The Second World War (1939–45) increased the political and economic void between Northern Ireland and Éire, and Éire and the United Kingdom. At the outbreak of the war, de Valera proclaimed Éire's neutrality during what was referred to as the 'National Emergency'. Éire, however, was the only Commonwealth country to remain neutral. The British government was uncomfortable with this declaration because of the country's strategic importance. Section 7b of the Anglo-Irish Treaty stated that 'The Government of the Irish Free State shall afford to His Majesty's Imperial Force . . . In time of war or strained relations with a Foreign Power such harbour and other facilities as the British Government may require for the purposes of such defence as aforesaid', but in 1938 the ports had been handed back to the Irish government. Britain was now afraid that Éire's neutrality would allow it to be used as a centre of espionage; nevertheless, 43,000 men and women enlisted for the British army, which was a higher number, in absolute terms, than volunteered in Northern Ireland. Dublin was bombed by Germany in May 1941, possibly by mistake. Thirty-four people were killed. De Valera gave covert support to the British government, including passing on weather reports from the west of Ireland and releasing Allied, but not German, airmen who landed in the country. Nevertheless, de Valera's declaration of neutrality was symbolic that Éire viewed herself as totally independent from Britain.

Although conscription was not extended to Northern Ireland, 38,000 people, both Catholic and Protestant, enlisted as volunteers. This number included 7,000 women. The conscription issue divided the Stormont parliament. Many unionists supported conscription on the grounds that it would give them more control over the defence of their state. The British government, however, nervous about provoking nationalist opposition, insisted that the ultimate responsibility for defence lay with the Westminster parliament. The civilian population also underwent many of the same hardships as in Britain, including rationing and air raids. New military bases were built and after 1942 American troops began to arrive. Wartime activities boosted the local economy and attracted workers from Éire, although it was made clear they would not be welcome in the longer term. Yet little effort was put into providing protection for Northern Ireland. In 1940, despite being a major port and centre of wartime production, Belfast had no searchlights or anti-aircraft battery. The city's only protection was seven heavy guns. This lack of protection proved lethal when in April 1941 the city was bombed and over 700 people were killed. A few weeks later, 200 German planes dropped 86,000 incendiary devices on Belfast. Although fewer people were killed than in the first attack, many local industries were destroyed. In the course of the bombings, half of the homes in the city were damaged. During both raids, fire engines from Éire, some from as far away as Dublin, went to the assistance of the people of Belfast.

The neutrality of Éire increased the strategic importance of Northern Ireland. Many important defence bases were situated in the state, and from 1942 until the end of the war 300,000 American troops were stationed there. Airfields were built that were an important base for protecting convoys travelling across the Atlantic. Munitions, aircraft and ships were assembled in Belfast. The American troops required barracks and supplies. These activities all helped to regenerate the economy, and by the end of the war, unemployment had fallen to only 5 per cent. The economic boom continued after the end of the war and new businesses, including DuPont and Courtaulds, set up in Northern Ireland, creating thousands of jobs. As a consequence of this economic revival, the Northern economy far outstripped that of Éire.

The Second World War provided further indications of how far the two states had diverged. The unionists believed that their support for Britain, and their suffering during the bombing raids, had proved yet again their loyalty. Winston Churchill, the British prime minister, said that the contribution of the people of Northern Ireland had created an unbreakable bond between them and Britain. His praise was disingenuous because during the war he had raised the idea of supporting Irish unity in return for regaining control of the ports in Éire. Publicly, the gulf between Britain and Ireland had grown. The war also changed Britain. In 1945 the Labour Party won a massive election victory, which changed the face of British politics. A further consequence of the war was the dismantling of the British Empire.

The Éire government used the postwar dislocation as an opportunity to take a further step in moving Ireland towards autonomy. The government also repealed the External Relations Act in 1948, ending the nominal role of the British monarch in the external affairs of Éire. In the same year a coalition government passed the Republic of Ireland Act. The country was now a republic and its political association with Britain had finally ended. Éire's new republican status made the Unionist Party uncomfortable. The British government, bowing to unionist pressure but also annoyed with Éire's unilateral action, passed the Ireland Act in 1949, which provided that neither Northern Ireland nor any part of it could cease to be part of United Kingdom without the consent of its parliament. The special citizen status and preferential trading terms accorded to Northern Ireland were also maintained. For republicans, a united Ireland appeared as elusive as ever.

Despite the tensions between the governments of the Republic and Northern Ireland, there was some cooperation between the two states. In 1950 they collaborated in a drainage scheme of Lough Erne to enable a hydroelectric generating station to be constructed. In 1951 the Republic took over the running of the Great Northern Railway and in 1952 established the Foyle Fisheries, all of which forced the governments and their civil servants to work together.

Economic growth in the Republic was slow in the postwar period, evidenced by high levels of emigration since the creation of the Free State. It was not until the 1960s that the main political parties began seriously to consider Ireland's economic development. They were partly motivated by the desire to become a member of the European Economic Community. After 1966 the Republic enjoyed a period of economic prosperity and growth, despite slumps in 1974 and 1979. Industry was helped by the foundation of the Industrial Development Agency, which helped to develop new industries, including electronics and electrical goods. Irish agriculture also prospered after the country was admitted to the European Community in 1973. Economic growth had a significant impact on Irish society, most notably in relation to the population, which, after a century of decline since the Great Famine, slowly began to rise in the 1960s.

In the decades following the new constitution, the relations between the government of the Republic and the Catholic Church appeared to be growing stronger. The 'devotional revolution', which had been associated with the second half of the nineteenth century, showed little signs of diminishing, and Catholic church attendance was generally in excess of 90 per cent. Catholic religious orders also remained a dominant force in education and in social welfare provision. Both sectors remained under-resourced, however, and the religious orders had a lot of autonomy from the state. From the 1950s some real advances were also made in health care. This was largely due to the efforts of Noel Browne, a medical doctor and minister for health after 1948. The number of hospital beds was greatly increased, and Browne introduced mass radiography and free treatment for sufferers of tuberculosis, a scourge of the poorer classes. Overall, these improvements made health care more efficient and accessible, though the Republic lagged behind the rapid advances that had followed from the introduction of the National Health Service in the United Kingdom. Browne also drew up a scheme that would give free medical relief to mothers and children under sixteen. The Catholic Church hierarchy opposed this scheme, arguing that the responsibility for these areas lay with the family, not the state. The Irish Medical Association, which saw it as undermining its members' income, also opposed the measure. Browne was discredited and forced to resign. The incident not only showed the sway that the Catholic Church held over politicians; it also showed the power of vested interests to avert measures of social justice. A scheme similar to that proposed by Browne was introduced a year after his resignation.

A more unpalatable incident occurred in the small town of Fethard-on-Sea in County Wexford in 1957, when a Protestant woman, married to a Catholic man, refused to educate her children in Catholic schools, a promise that was generally made at the time of marriage. A local Catholic priest, supported by members of the church hierarchy, implemented a boycott against local Protestants, which was only ended following adverse publicity and the intervention of a papal envoy. The special place accorded to the Catholic Church by the constitution and its intervention in politics gave some justification to the old Protestant adage that 'Home Rule is Rome Rule'. Since 1900 the Protestant population had been declining in the twenty-six counties that formed the Free State, and by the 1950s Protestants accounted for less than 5 per cent of the population, representing a 50 per cent fall. However, economic prosperity and contact with the outside world slowly loosened the hold of the Catholic Church on the people. Although the majority of Catholics continued to attend church on Sunday, the Church's teaching on matters to do with individual morality was being challenged.

The postwar British Labour government put in place a massive programme of social reconstruction, which transformed the United Kingdom into a welfare state. The population in Northern Ireland benefited from this change. Housing, which had suffered from little investment, benefited from the setting up of the Housing Trust in 1945. To bring Northern Ireland in line with rest of United Kingdom, its welfare system was enhanced, and the education system and health and social services were all extended. The Poor Law system, introduced to Ireland in 1838, was finally abolished in 1948. Northern Ireland's new welfare provision reinforced its links with Britain, while strengthening the social disparity between it and the South. Postwar prosperity, better housing and improved educational opportunities in Northern Ireland benefited Protestants more than they benefited Catholics. A significant exception was the reform of the education system in 1947, which meant that by the 1960s a generation of Catholics was emerging that was educated, articulate and committed to social justice. Their challenge to the Northern Ireland state was to have far-reaching consequences.

In the postwar period emigration from Northern Ireland declined, while it remained high in Éire. Women on both sides of the border benefited from the expansion in light industries and the growth in health services. They were also able to take advantage of the increasing educational opportunities open to women. By the 1960s the Northern economy was adjusting to the decline of its staple industries, helped by a move to the production of man-made fibres. Between 1960 and 1973 the Northern Ireland economy was growing faster than any other part of the United Kingdom. Northern Catholics benefited from the coming of the welfare state and the growth of the economy, and for some it made the border less objectionable, and ending discrimination within the Northern Ireland state became the primary objective. For the IRA, however, ending partition continued to be their prime objective. In 1956 they launched a new campaign, 'Operation Harvest', which involved bombing military and police installations in Northern Ireland. The campaign had little popular support. The British government deployed MI5 agents to infiltrate and defeat the movement, and in 1962 the campaign was called off. At this stage, the IRA seemed powerless.

Within Northern Ireland, however, discrimination against Catholics continued. The treatment of Catholics as second-class citizens within the State had begun in the 1920s. Protestants owned most of the industries in Northern Ireland and, encouraged by militant members of the Orange Order, employment practice favoured Protestant workers. The prejudice against Catholics increased in times of recession, as occurred after 1958. Throughout the 1950s also, a number of Orange marches were deliberately re-routed to pass through Catholic areas. Clearly, the parades were being used as a sectarian tool against Catholics. The unequal treatment of Catholics was also apparent in the symbols of the Northern Ireland state. The introduction of the Flags and Emblems (Display) Act in 1954 made it illegal to interfere with the Union flag when it was in a public place, while other flags could be removed from either private or public property. This act resulted in the removal of a number of Irish tricolours, and it inflamed nationalist opinion.

A further grievance was that many Catholics were disqualified from having full voting rights within the Northern Ireland state. Gerrymandering had excluded Catholics from having fair representation within the Stormont parliament, and the local election system was also manipulated. Before 1945 only owners or tenants of dwellings could vote, which excluded lodgers and adult children who lived in their parents' homes. After the war, the franchise was restricted further. Families who lived in overcrowded houses were effectively disenfranchised. Furthermore, businessmen and universities, which were predominantly Protestant, were allocated additional votes. By the 1960s approximately 25,000 adults were disenfranchised, a disproportionate number being poor Catholics. The stranglehold of Protestants in local government appeared unassailable. All of these measures not only perpetuated inequality but also kept alive divisions between Catholics and Protestants, especially those in the low-income groups.

Catholics were discriminated against in council housing allocation which, combined with their low wages, meant that they became ghettoised in some of the poorest districts. By 1961 almost 20 per cent of houses in Northern Ireland had no piped water supply and 23 per cent did not have flushing toilets. In Dungannon, a small town in County Tyrone, between 1945 and 1963 no new council houses were built in the nationalist areas of the town. Although the partisan housing allocation policies of the council were repeated in other parts of Northern Ireland, the Dungannon Catholics took action against it. In 1963 seventeen Catholic families occupied bungalows listed for demolition in Dungannon. The unionist council wanted to evict them but was dissuaded by the news coverage – and sympathy – the occupation was attracting, and so promised to speed up the building of homes for Catholics. This action was coordinated by the Homeless Citizens' League, which had been founded a few months earlier by Patricia McCluskey. The following year her husband, Dr Conn McCluskey, founded the Campaign for Social Justice. He compiled a dossier of evidence to demonstrate the level of discrimination in housing, especially in the area west of the River Bann.

In the early 1960s Northern Ireland was relatively peaceful. It had the lowest crime rate in the United Kingdom and, though the community remained segregated, actual sectarian attacks were rare. This was also a period of progressive unionism, associated with Terence O'Neill, who became the prime minister of Northern Ireland in 1963. Like his predecessors, O'Neill was Protestant and a member of the Orange Order, but unlike many of them, he believed that if Catholics were treated better they could be co-opted into the state. O'Neill also encouraged a rapprochement between the liberal unionist government in the North and the government of the Republic. A symbolic meeting took place between O'Neill and Séan Lemass, the *taoiseach*, in Belfast in 1965. The meeting was described as friendly, although constitutional and political issues were avoided. O'Neill's action divided Protestant opinion. Some progressive Protestants, including members of the Northern Ireland Labour Party, urged him to initiate more egalitarian policies for Catholics. Militant Protestants, represented by Ian Paisley, regarded the talks as a first step in uniting Northern Ireland and the Republic. A number claimed that they were willing to fight rather than acknowledge Catholics as equal citizens. The great majority of Protestant public opinion appeared uninterested, simply wanting to preserve the status quo, preferring not to question the prejudice at its foundation. Change was inevitable, however, as Catholics in Northern Ireland were beginning to organise and challenge the system of institutionalised sectarianism.

In the late 1950s, a period generally associated with moderate unionism, a new leader appeared who embodied the re-emergence of belligerent Protestants. In 1959 Ian Paisley, a young Presbyterian minister, formed Ulster Protestant Action, whose stated purpose was 'to keep Protestants and loyal workers in employment in times of depression in preference to their fellow Catholic workers'. He also rejected the teaching of the Presbyterian Church and formed his own breakaway one, the Free Presbyterian Church. Paisley's rejection of compromise with non-Protestants was evident when he threw a bible at a Methodist minister, Lord Soper, who had preached in favour of conciliation with Catholics. Paisley exploited the fear of some Protestants that a united Ireland would be a Catholic state in which Protestants would be outnumbered. In 1966 he started his own newspaper, *The Protestant Telegraph*, which warned against any association with Catholics or nationalists. It also attacked the policies of liberal unionists such as O'Neill. In the same year he formed the Ulster Defence Committee to resist the reforms proposed by O'Neill. Paisley's actions were more of a threat to the Unionist Party than generations of nationalists had been. Paisley was not only disillusioned with unionist politicians; he was also angered by the General Synod of the Presbyterian Church, which was debating working more closely with Catholics. In April 1966 parades were held throughout Ireland to celebrate the fiftieth anniversary of the Easter Rising. Paisley called for them to be banned in Northern Ireland, but O'Neill refused to comply. Paisley took direct action, leading a march that ended in attacks on Catholics. His more militant supporters, predominantly from the Shankill Road area of Belfast, formed a paramilitary group, the Ulster Volunteer Force (UVF), named as a tribute to the group formed in 1912–14. In June 1966 the UVF shot a number of Catholics whom they mistakenly believed to be IRA leaders. The government invoked the Special Powers Act to proscribe the UVF, and three of its members were sent to prison. For Catholics this intervention was inadequate; for Protestants it was an act of betrayal by fellow Protestants.

In 1967 the Northern Ireland Civil Rights Association (NICRA) was founded in Belfast. It was a non-sectarian association that brought together diverse political groups, including communists, liberal Protestants, students and republicans. Its immediate inspiration was Martin Luther King's civil rights campaign in the United States. Young people, especially students, had taken to the streets in many cities in Europe – in London against nuclear armament, in Paris against the government – and so events in Ireland can also be seen as part of a wider protest movement. NICRA's main objective was universal suffrage and the end of multiple votes, summed up in the Labour Party slogan 'one man, one vote'. It also wanted an end to discrimination, which had become institutionalised in the employment and housing policies of successive governments, and the repeal of various repressive measures introduced by the state that had predominately been used against Catholics. After 1968 the chairperson of the movement was Betty Sinclair, a radical Protestant who had been active in both the Communist Party and the trade union movement since the 1930s. Her involvement with the Civil Rights Association, however, was short, as she resigned from the executive in 1970 after disagreeing with the People's Democracy, a radical group formed by students at Queen's University. Despite the participation of liberal Protestants such as Betty Sinclair and Ivan Cooper, a Protestant civil rights activist, the support for NICRA came overwhelmingly from Catholics.

The tactics of NICRA were peaceful and non-violent, yet when a number of protest marches were organised, the government responded by banning them. Increasingly the marches became opportunities for sectarian violence. The first civil rights march took place in August 1968, when about 2,500 people marched from Coalisland to Dungannon. In October 1968 a march took place in Derry. Its route included the centre of the city, which had long been regarded as a bastion of Protestantism. The Protestant Apprentice Boys planned to march on the same day. Both marches were banned, though the civil rights march went ahead. It ended violently, with the RUC indiscriminately beating up men, women and children. This form of police violence was not new, but the fact that it was shown on television screens throughout the world was. Following this conflict, the support for the Civil Rights Association grew.

A number of splinter groups were formed, including the Derry Housing Action Committee at the beginning of 1968, led by Eamonn McCann. Homeless Catholics were encouraged to squat in houses and to disrupt council meetings. Their actions concerned some of the moderate members of NICRA. After 1968 NICRA moved closer to the People's Democracy, but some of the original founders, including Betty Sinclair and Dr Conn McCluskey, left. People's Democracy organised a march from Belfast to Derry in January 1969. It did not have the support of the leadership of the civil rights movement because it was routed through staunchly Protestant areas. The small march was ambushed by Protestants at Burntollett Bridge in County Derry. Fifty of the eighty marchers were injured. When the marchers arrived in Derry City, rioting ensued, with members of the RUC joining in the attacks on Catholics. The Cameron Report, which was an official investigation on behalf of the British government, stated that 'our investigations have led us to the unhesitating conclusion that on the night of the 4/5 January a number of policemen were guilty of misconduct which involved assault and battery and malicious damage to property in the streets in the mostly Catholic Bogside area'. The report also accused the Protestant attackers of using 'provocative sectarian and political slogans'. Following this attack, the local population started to build their own defences to protect themselves not just from militant Protestants, but also from the RUC. The IRA also helped to defend the local population. This incident at Burntollett inflamed opinion on both sides, and was the precursor to a new period of intense, bitter conflict.

Terence O'Neill's response was contentious as he condemned the march, laying most of the blame for the violence on the marchers. The evidence from the television cameras suggested otherwise, however. Catholic opinion was further outraged when O'Neill proposed recalling the B-Specials. O'Neill attempted to be conciliatory by appointing a commission chaired by Lord Cameron, a Scottish judge, to investigate the conflict. The appointment of a commission angered some of O'Neill's unionist colleagues, including Brian Faulkner, who resigned from the cabinet. Many unionists were calling for O'Neill's resignation, but he responded by calling a general election. The results of the election reflected the factions and divisions within Northern Ireland politics. For the Unionist Party the election was the greatest challenge to its hegemony since its inception, with O'Neill opposed by a group from within his own party and by Paisley's followers. Of the thirty-nine unionist seats, O'Neill won twenty-seven, while ten were won by anti-O'Neill candidates. None of Paisley's Protestant Party were elected. Paisley, however, who had recently been released from prison for organising a counter-demonstration in Armagh, came close to defeating O'Neill in his own constituency. His ostentatious campaign and his ability to win a large number of votes made him appear to be the defender of popular unionism against O'Neill's brand of liberal unionism.

The Nationalist Party also faced challenges, with Paddy Devlin winning a seat for the Labour Party and John Hume, Ivan Cooper and Paddy O'Hanlon taking seats from nationalists and winning as independents. Although the People's Democracy stood in nine constituencies and won over one-quarter of the vote from both Catholics and Protestants, none of its candidates were elected. In a by-election on 17 April 1969 Bernadette Devlin, standing on a socialist and cross-community platform, was elected MP for mid-Ulster. She had the support of a wide range of nationalist groups, including the IRA. At the age of twenty-one she was the youngest woman ever to be elected to the Westminster parliament, and because of her gender she represented a significant break with the patriarchy of Northern Ireland politics. Her emergence into mainstream politics alarmed both unionists and the British government. Just as Daniel O'Connell and his middle class had benefited from the relaxation of various penal laws after the 1780s, Devlin belonged to a generation of working-class Catholics who had benefited from postwar educational opportunities, a generation that included John Hume, Eamonn McCann and Seamus Heaney.

O'Neill's position remained precarious. When, on 22 April, he gave his support to 'one man, one vote' in local elections, there was an immediate backlash, with Major James Chichester-Clark resigning from government. O'Neill then resigned, and was replaced by Chichester-Clark, who beat his main rival, Brian Faulkner, by only one vote. The Northern Ireland government, which had been ruled with such stability and mass support since 1921, was now under threat. O'Neill had lost the support of his own Unionist Party and he had angered both Catholics and Protestants. He had raised expectations among the Catholic community, although he had delivered little. By doing so he had not only divided his own party, but also contributed to the rise of populist unionism on the streets of Northern Ireland.

Throughout 1969 sectarian incidents increased in Northern Ireland. In March and April a number of bombs damaged electricity and water supplies. At the time this was blamed on the IRA, although it was the work of the UVF. Chichester-Clark proved to have no more ability to control the rioting or the militants within unionism than had his predecessor. This was evident during the 'the Battle of the Bogside' in August 1969, a fierce conflict that followed the annual Apprentice Boys' march in Derry. Bernadette Devlin, MP received a six-month prison sentence for her part in it. Coverage of the fighting was transmitted internationally and shocked public opinion. This conflict demonstrated that the new prime minister had lost control of the situation. The violence in Northern Ireland was alarming people in the Irish Republic, and in August 1969 the *taoiseach*, Jack Lynch, stated on television that 'the present situation is the inevitable outcome of the policies pursued for decades by successive Stormont Governments. It is clear that the Irish Government can no longer stand by and see innocent people injured and perhaps worse.' The rise of the civil rights movement forced the British government, after years of indifference, to focus reluctantly on Northern Ireland. The British government, which had for so long ignored Stormont, now regarded it as a liability. However, the international media had turned its full attention on Northern Ireland, and Britain was forced to do the same. On 14 August 1969 the British army was sent to Derry and Belfast to help the police to restore order. Initially the Catholic population welcomed the army, whereas many Protestants resented its intervention. Within a short period, both sides had changed their opinion.

ELEVEN

CHANGING THE QUESTION
c. 1969 to the Twenty-First Century

By the end of the twentieth century the Republic of Ireland and Northern Ireland were following increasingly divergent routes. De Valera's vision of a Catholic, Gaelic and self-sufficient society was fast disappearing. Instead, by the 1990s, the Republic was becoming a secular, Eurocentric, cosmopolitan society, which combined economic success with cultural renaissance. Northern Ireland, in contrast, remained economically weak and politically divided. The restoration of direct rule from Westminster in 1972 demonstrated the fragility of the Northern State. At the same time, developments in Ireland were taking place within the context of a devolved United Kingdom and an increasingly important European Union. Moreover, the violent conflict within Northern Ireland dominated British politics and captured the attention of the international media and, increasingly, of American presidents, culminating in the direct intervention of Bill Clinton.

This chapter examines the recent history of the Irish Republic and Northern Ireland, and their relationships with Britain, Europe and the United States. The future of Northern Ireland – and those of the Republic of Ireland and the United Kingdom – remains unclear, but as Tony Blair observed when introducing the Good Friday agreement, 'The Hand of History is upon us'.

Troops In

The 1960s had been a decade of frustration for Catholics in Northern Ireland because of the political intransigence of hard-line unionists for both economic justice and civil rights. The actions of militant unionists also brought to an end the years of liberal unionism represented by Terence O'Neill. The escalating inter-community conflict resulted in O'Neill's resignation in April 1969. The new prime minister of Northern Ireland,

Chichester-Clark, was a country gentleman by birth, and his style of government tended to be aloof and autocratic, which was little suited to the violent situation that he had inherited. Nor did he attempt to disguise his disdain for Catholics, even when he was trying to be conciliatory. In May 1969 he asserted in a newspaper interview that 'It's frightfully hard to explain to Protestants that if you give Roman Catholics a good job and a good house they will live like Protestants, because they will see neighbours with cars and television sets . . . They will refuse to have 18 children, but if a Roman Catholic is jobless and lives in a most ghastly hovel, he will rear 18 children on National Assistance . . . If you treat Roman Catholics with due consideration and kindness, they will live like Protestants in spite of the authoritarian nature of their church.' Like his predecessor, Chichester-Clark was not willing to stand up to militant unionists, and he allowed the 12 July and Apprentice Boy (12 August) parades to go ahead, despite the likelihood of violence. The latter march was one of the largest ever, and as it passed around the Bogside area in Derry the marchers were attacked with stones. The so-called 'battle of the Bogside' lasted a week and was a watershed in Catholic and Protestant relations. Furthermore, on 14 August, British troops arrived on the streets of Northern Ireland. Their involvement was regarded as a short-term expedient.

Fifty-one years after the state of Northern Ireland had been created by a British politician, the British parliament had been compelled to intervene to salvage a deteriorating situation. In the intervening period it had repeatedly claimed that it did not have the power to intercede in the internal affairs of the six counties. Significantly, the events in Northern Ireland were broadcast throughout the world and international opinion was shocked by the daily violence in part of the United Kingdom. Attempts to resolve the conflict with suggestions such as power-sharing did not work and perhaps demonstrated that Westminster had grown too distant from what had happened in Stormont to fully comprehend how deeply entrenched the divisions had become. Northern Ireland had developed separately and independently of intervention from either Britain or the Republic, whose governments had shown little interest in it until forced to do so by events after 1969. By this time sectarianism had become institutionalised and piecemeal gestures of reform were inadequate – the Catholic population desired more, while hard-line Protestants would concede nothing. Britain had neglected Northern Ireland for decades, and the cost of this abandonment proved to be high. The people whose lives were most disrupted by the conflict, however, were the poor on both sides of the community.

The onset of the conflict coincided with a Labour government in Britain, led by Harold Wilson. Many Labour MPs had been sympathetic to the demands of the civil rights movement which, coupled with the increasing violence and weakness of the unionist government, led them to urge immediate reforms. These demands were outlined in the Downing Street Declaration of 19 August 1969, which stated that every citizen of Northern Ireland was to have the same rights as citizens in the rest of the United Kingdom. The declaration supported the continued existence of the Northern Ireland government but insisted on immediate reforms, especially regarding electoral boundaries, housing allocation and hiring practices in public employment. Although moderate Catholics and Protestants welcomed this intervention, for others these reforms made little difference; they were too late for embittered Catholics and too extensive for militant Protestants. A problem, however, was that the partisan policies had become so embedded in the state structures that they could not be unravelled quickly. More problematically, some of the people in charge of dismantling the system were opposed to anything that would undermine the position of Protestants in Northern Ireland.

To prove that the Labour Party was committed to change, in August 1969 James Callaghan, the British home secretary, travelled to Northern Ireland. His visit included some of the poorest Catholic enclaves in Belfast and the Bogside in Derry, which had been declared a 'no go' area for the police and army. In Derry he was accompanied by John Hume, who had recently been elected to the Northern Ireland parliament. From the bedroom of a small house in 'Free Derry', Callaghan made a speech promising further reforms. He was cheered by the listeners, and his visit, which was filmed by the world's media, appeared successful. Callaghan also visited Protestant areas and he promised them the sanctity of the Northern Ireland state. Privately, Callaghan was more despondent. He estimated that the reforms demanded by the Catholics would take at least ten years to implement, even with Protestant cooperation. And he was pessimistic about the willingness of even moderate Protestants to acquiesce in their dominant position being eroded.

The self-assurance of Protestants, however, was dented by the publication of two official reports in autumn 1969. The publication of the Cameron Report in September provided full and objective evidence of the ways in which Catholics had been discriminated against. Lord Hunt's report on policing in

Northern Ireland was released in October and its recommendations were dramatic. It recommended that the Ulster Special Constabulary should be disbanded; the RUC was to be disarmed, while a new military force, the Ulster Defence Regiment, would replace the B-Specials. A new chief constable was also brought to Belfast from England to head the police force. Protestants responded angrily to the release of the Hunt Report, and there was fighting on the streets of Belfast, with Catholics being burned out of their homes. The police were unable, or unwilling, to stop the rioting, and the army had to be used. During the conflict, two Protestants were killed by the British army. Despite Protestant opposition, some of Hunt's reforms were introduced. In March 1970 the B-Specials were disbanded and reforms were made to the RUC. The Ulster Defence Regiment was also formed to replace the B-Specials, whose role in the civil rights marches had been violent and partisan. The UDR was composed of both part- and full-time members, both male and female, and included former members of the B-Specials. Initially the British government hoped that it would be a cross-community force, but from the outset it was Protestant-dominated and bore similarities to the disgraced B-Specials. Some members of the UDR were also involved – directly or indirectly – in the murder of Catholics. Overall, despite the searing criticisms contained in the Hunt Report, Northern Ireland's policing remained overwhelmingly Protestant.

In the absence of normal policing within Northern Ireland, paramilitary organisations increasingly filled the void. In general the IRA, and its political counterpart, Sinn Féin, had played little active part in either the civil rights movement marches or in the rioting that had followed, leading some detractors to suggest that the initials now stood for 'I ran away'. The failure of its border campaign, Operation Harvest, had weakened its resources, and at the start of the new round of troubles it was ill prepared to play a significant role. Moreover, it was occupied with internal divisions. In November 1969 the republican movement split into two political wings, Sinn Féin and the Workers' Party, and their respective military wings, the Provisional and the Official IRA. The division reflected an ideological split that had been taking place within the IRA for a number of years. The Officials were mostly based in the Republic and wanted to reunite Ireland by peaceful means. Their doctrines had been influenced by Marxist philosophies, largely because of the efforts of Cathal Goulding. The Provisional IRA was predominantly based in Northern Ireland and, led by Seán Mac Stiofáin, believed that the British occupation could be ended only by the use of force. The Provisional IRA became involved in street fighting for the first time in June 1970. It attracted support from nationalists who were angered by the violent response of some Protestants – including the police – to the civil rights protesters, believing that they needed to defend themselves, by equal force if necessary. Members of the Provisional IRA, who endorsed violence and were equally opposed to unionism and the British occupation of Ireland, were well placed to position themselves as defenders of the people. In the early months of 1970 recruitment grew, which alarmed the British government. The government urged the unionist government to ban an Orange march due to take place on 1 April. It refused to do so, and the march was followed by serious fighting, especially in the Catholic Ballymurphy estate in Belfast. The conflict provided a boost to the IRA's recruitment.

The failure of the Labour Party to win the general election in 1970 brought to power the Conservative Party – or more correctly, 'The Conservative and Unionist Party' – led by Edward Heath. The new British home secretary, Reginald Maudling, visited Northern Ireland and when he left, he was reported to have said 'For God's sake bring me a large Scotch. What a bloody awful country.' At this stage, rioting, gun battles and shootings had become commonplace. Moreover, a new area of conflict had emerged between the army and the Catholics, who had at first been welcoming, but increasingly came to see the soldiers as an occupying force. This feeling was consolidated when a violent conflict occurred between the Catholic population of the Falls Road and the army at the beginning of July. It had been triggered by the army searching houses in the area, looking for weapons belonging to the IRA. Many of the houses were wrecked in the process. In total 104 firearms were discovered. When the inhabitants protested, the army used CS gas on the rioters and imposed a curfew on the area. These tactics marked the onset of a more draconian approach by the Crown forces. They became viewed as another tool of state repression rather than as impartial peace-keepers.

The Social Democratic and Labour Party (SDLP) was formed in 1970. Its founders included Gerry Fitt, a Belfast socialist, John Hume, a Derry-born social democrat, and Paddy Devlin, Labour Party MP for the Falls area. Fitt led the party until he was replaced in 1979 by Hume. Its supporters were drawn from members of the Northern Ireland Labour Party, the civil rights movement, the Nationalist Party and various other radical bodies. Although the SDLP supported a long-term goal of Irish unity, in the short term it focused on reforms that would benefit Catholics, all of which was to be achieved through constitutional means. However, the party abstained from the Stormont parliament between 1971 and 1972. It also supported a province-wide rent and rates strike from 1971 to 1974. Its programme appealed to middle-class and moderate Catholics. The SDLP saw itself as part of a broader socialist movement, establishing links with the British Labour Party and socialist groups within the European parliament. Although the SDLP initially won support for its constitutional methods, the deteriorating situation in 1971, especially internment, discredited constitutional politics in Northern Ireland.

The early weeks of 1971 were violent. In February the Provisional IRA shot Gunner Curtis, who was the first soldier to be killed since the troops had been sent to Northern Ireland. Unable to cope with the mounting crisis, Chichester-Clark resigned and was replaced by Brian Faulkner, the son of a wealthy shirt manufacturer who had sat in Stormont since 1949. As minister for home affairs he had been largely responsible for the failure of the IRA's Operation Harvest, using internment against the republicans. Faulkner's policies were based on a mixture of reform and repression. His reforms included the creation of 7,000 jobs and the building of over 14,000 houses. His premiership, however, was dominated by his decision to introduce internment. Both the Free State and Northern Ireland governments had made liberal use of internment after 1921 and again during the Second World War. Internment was reintroduced in August 1971 and was not suspended until December 1975. During this period, 2,060 Catholics and 109 Protestants were interned. On the first day that it was implemented, 9 August, Catholic women banged their dustbin lids on the pavements as both a protest and a warning. On that one day, 342 men (including only 2 Protestants) were taken from their homes, 226 of whom were interned. Most of them were sent to the Long Kesh internment camp, where they were locked in high-security prisons known as 'H-blocks'.

Internment alienated Catholics, who viewed it as another demonstration of their lack of civil rights. It also united them. Not only was internment used far more extensively against the working-class nationalist population than against Protestants; it was sometimes based on inaccurate information. Moreover, after arrest the prisoners were subjected to brutal interrogation methods. Many of the internees saw themselves as prisoners of war and claimed that the British government had contravened Article 14 of the 1948 Geneva Convention. Their treatment was condemned by the European Court of Human Rights and by radical groups in Britain, Canada, Australia, New Zealand and the United States. In November 1971 a government-appointed commission, led by Sir Edmund Compton, reported on the alleged ill-treatment of internees. The report was regarded by Catholics as a sham, especially as his conclusions were contradicted by other independent, but non-official, reports. Internment had another, unexpected, effect, as mixed communities of Catholics and Protestants began to move apart into single-denominational, segregated areas, where they felt safe. Within three weeks of internment being introduced, 1 in every 100 families in Belfast had moved, as a result of fear or intimidation. This mass movement of people was a sign that the middle ground in Northern Ireland politics was disappearing and being replaced by a society separated by mutual fear and animosity.

While violence on the streets increased following internment, a different form of protest was taking place. The rent and rates strike that began spontaneously in 1971 proved to be a powerful form of civil resistance. It was coordinated by the Northern Resistance Movement. Within weeks over 40,000 households had joined in. In some areas local government ground to a halt as its income dried up, and some nationalist councillors withdrew from the councils, forcing central government to take over their functions. The unionist government responded by introducing the punitive Payment for Debt (Emergency Powers) Act, although it made little impact. This campaign of civil resistance demonstrated that the unionists had lost control of the normal functions of government.

In the short term the introduction of internment increased violence. Before its introduction there had been 30 sectarian killings in Northern Ireland: a further 143 people were killed in the following months. Internment shifted support away from constitutional politics and helped to win new recruits for the IRA. In the years after 1969 the IRA also had considerable support in the United States, especially among Irish Americans, notably Senator Ted Kennedy. The Irish Northern Aid Committee (Noraid) allegedly sent arms and financial support to the IRA. By the mid-1970s this supply was slowing down because of a mixture of repugnance at the indiscriminate violence and rigorous pursuit by the FBI and the CIA. The re-emergence of the IRA as a military force not only alarmed the British government; it also worried the Dublin government. This concern increased when, in May 1970, two members of the Dáil, Charles Haughey and Neil Blaney, were dismissed from the Fianna Fáil government for smuggling guns to the IRA. A third minister,

Kevin Boland, resigned in protest at this action. Haughey was subsequently acquitted and Blaney was discharged. Haughey did not return to the front bench until 1975 and subsequently became *taoiseach* at the end of 1979.

In 1971 the government of the Republic banned broadcasts from organisations linked with 'terrorism', which included the IRA and other paramilitary republican groups. The United Kingdom introduced a similar measure in 1988. For the British government, however, winning the propaganda war had been an essential part of the conflict since 1969 and the British media had been deliberately denied information and fed misinformation. For decades, however, the situation in Northern Ireland had been ignored by the British press, and when the civil rights movement exploded into people's consciousness, few understood the background. It was therefore easy to attribute the conflict to the actions of a small number of belligerent IRA terrorists. Concurrent with the military war being fought on the streets of Northern Ireland, a propaganda war was being mounted. The Northern Ireland Office had its own public relations office, which ran advertising campaigns asking the public to inform on terrorists, and produced glossy brochures explaining the legal and penal system in Northern Ireland. By 1976 the British army in Northern Ireland had over forty press officers, and at the same period there were approximately eighteen people working in the RUC press office. Throughout the 1980s there was a general tightening up of information released from these press offices.

For nationalists in working-class areas, who regarded the RUC and, increasingly, the army, as both hostile and partisan, the IRA provided the only buffer and protection. Throughout the 1970s house searches, roadblocks, stop and search tactics, and constant patrolling became commonplace. Again, they were most frequent in the poorest Catholic districts of Northern Ireland. A further source of anger for nationalists was the brutality of the Crown forces against the Catholic population, which received little coverage in the mainstream media of either Britain or Ireland. This approach was particularly evident in the reporting of violence by the police and army, especially when it was officially authorised. In 1970 the use of rubber bullets was permitted, and they were described as a 'soft' or 'minimum force' alternative to the real thing. They were replaced by plastic bullets, which were supposed to be more accurate than the rubber variety. Within twelve years of their introduction they had killed fourteen people, blinded one person and maimed many others. In 1981 alone, almost 30,000 rounds of plastic bullets were fired by the police and army. Those wounded included two press photographers, one of whom had recently published an unflattering image of a British soldier. Many of the victims were children, yet there was little outcry against this form of violence, even when eleven-year-old Stephen McConomy was killed by a plastic bullet in the back of his head in April 1982. In the following month the European Court voted for a ban on plastic bullets. In 1983 the National Council for Civil Liberties launched a campaign against them. Their usage, however, continued. Furthermore, although repeatedly denied by state authorities, accusations of collusion between members of security forces and loyalist paramilitaries were repeatedly upheld by independent observers, including Human Rights Watch at Helsinki. None the less, successive British and Irish governments addressed the problem in terms of inter-communal or religious conflict, and they were reluctant to look at the role of the state authorities in exacerbating or promoting it.

To counterbalance the rise of the IRA, hard-line unionists also began to organise. On the same day that internment was introduced, the Ulster Defence Association (UDA) was formed, which acted as a coordinating body for Protestant paramilitaries. They described themselves as 'loyalists', although their loyalty to either the British or the unionist governments was clearly conditional. Within a short period the UDA had 40,000 members, including breakaway groups such as the Ulster Freedom Fighters, who specialised in attacking republicans. In November 1971 Ian Paisley formed the Democratic Unionist Party (DUP). Paisley, who combined religious fundamentalism with political conservatism, marked a move away from the traditional middle-class domination of unionist politics to a more populist, working-class approach. His entry into mainstream politics came when he won Terence O'Neill's seat following his resignation in April 1969. In the following year Paisley became Westminster MP for North Antrim and a year later he formed the DUP. For his supporters, his fiery rhetoric, anti-Catholicism and populist chauvinism were reassuring, but to Catholics and many external observers he was a symbol of Protestant bigotry. Both the DUP generally and Paisley personally had an ambivalent relationship with Protestant paramilitaries. Although he denied direct involvement, at times he supported and encouraged them. The DUP grew rapidly in the disturbed years of the 1970s. In 1979 it won three Westminster seats, and in the European elections that year it won more votes than any other party in Northern Ireland. In 1981 the DUP had overtaken the Ulster Unionist Party in local elections. Moderate unionists and many members of the British government disliked the extremism that was associated with Paisley's politics.

A more overtly militant Protestant group was the Ulster Vanguard, which was formed at the beginning of 1972 by William Craig. An experienced, but volatile and individualist, politician, Craig had been minister for home affairs in O'Neill's government, but had been dismissed in 1968 for his mishandling of the civil rights agitation. Craig saw Vanguard as a way of uniting some of the most discontented yet volatile members of the unionist community, including Orangemen and paramilitaries – the self-styled loyalists. Like Paisley, he excelled in militant anti-Catholic rhetoric, even talking publicly about the need to 'liquidate the enemy' if the unionist government was unable to control them. He was also sceptical about the longer-term objectives of the British government, and outlined his view of creating an independent Northern Ireland. Vanguard initially possessed its own paramilitary wing, the Vanguard Service Corps. In 1973 Craig appeared to desire a more constitutional path when he founded the Vanguard Unionist Progressive Party. However, he alienated his supporters by suggesting a coalition with the SDLP. Although the VUPP ceased to exist, Vanguard remained as a pressure group. Craig and his deputy, David Trimble, entered the Ulster Unionist Party and in 1995 Trimble became its leader.

Existing paramilitary groups expanded as a result of the hostilities. The Ulster Volunteer Force had been revived in Belfast in 1966 in opposition to O'Neill's reforms. Despite being illegal, by 1972 it had over 1,500 members. In 1974 the UVF was legalised but its continuing association with violence meant that it was again banned in 1975. Until the ceasefire in 1994, the UVF was the foremost loyalist paramilitary group in Northern Ireland, being associated with many of the sectarian killings of Catholics. Within the UVF a particularly sadistic splinter group developed after 1975 called the 'Shankill butchers'. They indiscriminately abducted random Catholics and then carved them up with butcher's knives. As had been intended, the outcome of the crusade was a terrorised Catholic community. One unexpected outcome, however, was that it drove Catholics into seeking protection from the IRA.

Regardless of the appearance of more militant political organisations, a large portion of people in Northern Ireland still desired to find an accommodation between all sides. In April 1970 the Alliance Party of Northern Ireland was formed as a way of promoting centrist, consensual politics. Rather than end the association with Britain, it sought to reconcile people to being part of the United Kingdom. The Alliance Party mostly appealed to the urban middle classes, especially in the east of the province. It also had the support of liberal Protestants, who felt the two main unionist parties no longer reflected their views. While the Alliance Party never achieved more than 10 per cent of the vote, it was a participant in many high-level negotiations.

Although the Civil Rights Association had been overtaken by the emergence of many new political groups, a large number of people still supported its aims. On 30 January 1972 a civil rights march was organised in Derry to protest against internment. The government had banned marches in the previous year, which made the march illegal. The army, however, decided to allow it to go ahead, though it controlled the route, trying to contain it within the Bogside. The soldiers who were put in charge of monitoring the march were the 1st Battalion of the Parachute Regiment, who were not generally involved in operations requiring crowd control. In the late afternoon, some troops began firing on the marchers, although they subsequently claimed that they were firing only in retaliation. Thirteen unarmed civilians were killed and one other person died later. The Catholic community in Northern Ireland was united in its grief. Anger was renewed following the release of the Widgery Report which, while admitting that some of the shooting by the soldiers had been 'reckless', was generally uncritical of their actions. The evidence of 700 eyewitnesses was largely ignored, or, in some cases, their information was distorted. The shootings on what became known as 'Bloody Sunday' caused outrage in many parts of the world. In Britain, however, most of the media coverage condemned the marchers, blaming them for starting the shooting. In the Republic the *taoiseach* announced a day of mourning, and 30,000 people marched in Dublin to the British embassy, which they burnt down. The fear that the conflict might spread south of the border resulted in the government setting up a special criminal court, to consist of three judges without a jury. In the British House of Commons, Bernadette Devlin slapped the face of the British home secretary, Reginald Maudling. The Official IRA responded by bombing the officers' mess of the Parachute Regiment at Aldershot. The dead included women clerks, the Catholic padre and a gardener. Bombs also exploded in Belfast without warning. On 21 July, or 'Bloody Friday', 22 separate explosions went off in Belfast, killing 19 people and injuring 130. The tragic events in Derry marked a new phase of conflict in which the combat was taken to Britain.

After Bloody Sunday the unionist government had lost what little control it had in Northern Ireland, having influence over neither the Catholic community nor the militant unionists. The deteriorating situation was evidenced by the increasing number of fatalities arising from political violence: in 1970, 25 people died; in 1971, 173; and in 1972, 467. A worrying aspect of the violence was the increase in 'tit for tat' killing, especially among paramilitary groups. In March 1972 Faulkner and his ministers were summoned to London, where Heath told them that he was going to transfer control of security to London, appoint a secretary of state for Northern Ireland and end internment. The unionist ministers were annoyed at being dictated to in this way, and, as Heath had probably anticipated, Faulkner and his cabinet resigned. Heath responded by proroguing the Stormont parliament. The Northern Ireland government, which had been formed in the midst of controversy and violence by a British politician, ignored and disregarded for decades, was suspended in response to more bloodshed and carnage in March 1972. The political experiment in Northern Ireland had failed.

Direct Rule

The dissolution of Stormont was followed by a period of direct rule from Westminster. The British parliament, which had ignored Northern Ireland for decades, now moved it to the top of the political agenda. To facilitate the transfer of administrative responsibilities, a Northern Ireland Office was created within the British civil service. Responsibility for Northern Ireland government was transferred from the home secretary to the secretary of state for Northern Ireland. The Westminster parliament was responsible for all Northern Ireland legislation. Twelve Northern Ireland MPs sat in Westminster; this was increased to seventeen in 1983 and to eighteen in 1997. Initially, unionists hoped that the suspension would be brief, but this seemed unlikely when the Stormont parliament was abolished in July 1973. The accompanying Northern Ireland Constitution Act, however, reinforced the sanctity of the Northern Ireland state. The survival of the state was increasingly dependent on repressive legislation introduced by the Westminster parliament. The Special Powers Act, first introduced in 1922 as an emergency measure, was repealed in 1973 but replaced by the Northern Ireland Emergency Provisions Act. In the following year, the Prevention of

Terrorism Act (Temporary Provisions) was passed in response to the bombing of public houses in Guilford, Woolwich and Birmingham, which resulted in twenty-eight dead and hundreds injured, all of whom were predominantly civilians. Most British public opinion, including that of the Irish community, was repulsed and demanded strong measures to deal with the IRA. A small minority continued to agitate for troops to be withdrawn from Northern Ireland. The Prevention of Terrorism Act prevented suspects from any part of Ireland from entering Britain, and allowed British police to hold suspected terrorists for up to seven days without charge.

In December 1973 the British Conservative government attempted to introduce a scheme that would allow Catholics and Protestants to share power. It was based on months of negotiation at Sunningdale in England, with representatives from the British and the Irish governments, and the leaders of the Ulster Unionist, Alliance and SDLP Parties. The involvement of the government of the Irish Republic had been a source of concern to both the British government and many unionists, but they had been relieved when the general election in February 1973 had ousted Fianna Fáil, which was viewed as being sympathetic to a united Ireland. It was replaced by a coalition of Fine Gael and the Labour Party, led by Liam Cosgrave, Garrett Fitzgerald and, from the Labour Party, Conor Cruise O'Brien. Fitzgerald and O'Brien made it clear that their sympathies were not just with the Catholic nationalists, but also with the Northern Protestants. Largely because of the influence of John Hume, supported by the *taoiseach*, Cosgrave, Heath was persuaded to assign an all-Ireland Council of Ireland a more prominent role than had been intended. The significance was that the Sunningdale Agreement moved from simply being concerned with the internal affairs of Northern Ireland to having what was referred to as 'an Irish dimension'. This change, however, which acknowledged the involvement of the Republic in the affairs of Northern Ireland, was abhorrent to many unionists.

The Sunningdale Agreement was announced by the British home secretary, William Whitelaw, in November 1973. A new power-sharing assembly was to be established, supported by the British government. The power-sharing executive comprised in the first instance four SDLP, one Alliance and six Unionist members. The Council of Ireland, run by an indirectly elected assembly, was to look after cross-border issues. Radicals and militants on both sides were sceptical that the Sunningdale Agreement would have any lasting value. Bernadette McAliskey (formerly Devlin) opined that 'It is an attempt to con Nationalists into thinking they have gained a great victory and loyalists into believing they have lost nothing. This agreement is doomed.' A few weeks after its announcement, the Ulster Unionist Council voted to reject the all-Ireland Council, forcing Brian Faulkner to resign as Unionist leader. All militant political groups, who predominantly represented the working classes, had been deliberately excluded from the Sunningdale negotiations. Whitelaw maintained that he and his government would negotiate only with constitutional organisations; but in secret he had also opened talks with the Provisional IRA.

In 1974 elections were held for the new assembly. The results showed that the unionist members had lost some of the backing of their traditional supporters and so a majority of seats were won by anti-Sunningdale unionists. Although Faulkner resigned as party leader, he remained the leader of the executive. The latter was short-lived, being rendered ineffective by the Ulster Workers' Council strike in May 1974 that brought the province to a standstill. The Ulster Workers' Council had been established at the beginning of 1974 specifically to oppose the Sunningdale Agreement. It had links with the Vanguard movement, Paisley's DUP and the Ulster Defence Association, and it also appealed to more moderate unionists. The strike ended only when the Northern Ireland executive resigned. In the midst of the civil disorder in Northern Ireland on 17 May two bombs went off in Dublin and Monaghan, without warning. Twenty-six people, including two babies, were killed in Dublin and seven in Monaghan. Although the IRA was initially blamed, the bombs had been planted by the UVF. The total death toll of thirty-two made it the highest loss of life in a single day during the whole of the conflict. It also brought the war out of Northern Ireland and into the Republic. The Sunningdale Agreement had failed: indeed, it had not survived long enough to be formally ratified. Once again civil disorder and threats of violence by unionists had disrupted constitutional government. By doing so, militant unionists had discredited constitutional methods and made a compromise settlement appear hopeless. After 1974 Faulkner led the newly established Unionist Party of Northern Ireland (UPNI), but it made little impact on a still deteriorating situation. In August 1976 he retired from politics and he was replaced as leader of the UPNI by Anne Letitia Dickson, her appointment marking a break with the general patriarchy of the unionist leadership. Within a few years, the party was defunct.

Direct rule solved none of the problems apparent in Northern Ireland. In particular few measures were taken to eliminate anti-Catholic discrimination.

Despite the creation of new jobs in the early 1970s, Catholic unemployment remained twice as high as that of Protestants, and Catholic emigration was double the Protestant rate. It was not until the 1990s that Protestant emigration began to exceed Catholic emigration. Sectarian violence had continued while the Sunningdale negotiations were taking place. In 1974 there were 216 political killings and 217 in the following year, which included 16 members of the RUC and the Ulster Defence Regiment. By this stage, violence had become endemic in Northern Ireland. The Provisional IRA had also taken its bombing campaign outside Northern Ireland. At the end of 1975 a new republican group was formed, the Irish Republican Socialist Party (IRSP), which was a breakaway from the Official IRA. Some of its members formed a military wing, the Irish National Liberation Army. The Protestant paramilitaries retaliated with an equally violent counteroffensive. Some of the murders were indiscriminate, being perpetrated simply because the victim was Catholic or Protestant, a member of the Crown forces or a politician. These murders included the killing of three Catholic members of the Miami Showband by the UVF, and the deaths of five Protestants in the Bayardo Bar on the Shankill Road, both in 1975. The UDR was implicated in these atrocities. In 1976 the British ambassador to the Irish Republic was killed in Dublin by a landmine placed under his car by the Provisional IRA. His wife responded to her loss by supporting the women's peace movement, formed by Mairead Corrigan and Betty Williams in August 1976.

The women's peace movement, or Peace People, attracted mass support. A rally in Belfast in August 1976 was attended by over 20,000 people. On 5 December a large gathering of Peace People from the North and the Republic took place near Drogheda. Militants on both sides of the political spectrum disliked the movement; Ian Paisley accusing it of being 'priest-inspired', while some nationalists believed that it was government-sponsored. At the end of 1977 Corrigan and Williams received the Nobel Peace Prize in Oslo. Peace, however, was still far away.

In Britain the Labour Party had been returned to power in 1974, and following Harold Wilson's sudden resignation in March 1976, James Callaghan became prime minister. His relationship with the nationalists was very different from what it had been in 1969, showing how rapidly the relationship with the British government had deteriorated. From the outset his administration was weak, and after 1977 depended on support from the Liberal Party to stay in power. Callaghan's conflict with the British trade unions came to a head at the end of 1978, which was referred to as the 'winter of discontent'. The situation in Northern Ireland was temporarily overshadowed by Britain's domestic problems. None the less, the Labour Party oversaw the introduction of more repressive measures by the government. In March 1976 'Special Category' status for political prisoners in the prisons of Northern Ireland was ended. This meant that imprisoned activists no longer had political status, and marked an attempt by the British government to treat political activists as ordinary criminals. In September some of the prisoners protested by wearing only blankets.

In 1977 the number of political deaths decreased, which led Roy Mason, the secretary of state, to declare optimistically that 'We are squeezing the terrorists like rolling up a toothpaste tube.' His confidence was premature, and in 1978 more repressive legislation was introduced. The Emergency Provisions Act (1978) provided for non-jury trials in what became known as 'Diplock courts'. However, a pattern of violence had been established that even the wide-ranging repressive legislation could not end. Moreover, the violence was not confined to the protagonists in the conflict. In January 1978 the European Court of Human Rights cleared Britain of using torture against internees, but found the British government guilty of 'inhuman and degrading treatment of prisoners'.

In May 1979 a Conservative government led by Margaret Thatcher came to power. She knew little about Ireland. In the same year the Provisional IRA became involved in a campaign that was intended to force Britain into ending its occupation of Northern Ireland. In March, Airey Neave, the Conservative Party shadow spokesman on Northern Ireland, had been killed by a bomb under his car, planted by the INLA. Neave had been a close confidant of Thatcher, and his death gave her a personal interest in the conflict in Northern Ireland. In August, on the tenth anniversary of the sending of troops to Northern Ireland, the IRA killed Lord Louis Mountbatten, Prince Charles's uncle, when he was on a sailing holiday off the coast of Sligo in the Irish Republic. The explosion also killed two children who were holidaying with him. Shortly afterwards, nineteen British soldiers were killed by booby-trap bombs in Warren Point in County Down. For the IRA and the INLA, these were a military triumph against the British presence in Ireland. The newspaper of the IRA, *An Phoblacht*, asserted, 'The British Army acknowledge that after ten years of war they cannot defeat us but yet the British Government continue with the oppression of our people and the torture of our comrades in the H-Blocks. Well, for this we will tear out their sentimental imperialist heart.' International opinion was shocked, however, and British public opinion was repulsed by these atrocities. In October 1979 Pope John Paul II visited the Republic of Ireland, but was advised against travelling to the North. During his visit he made an appeal for peace, saying 'I wish to speak to all men and women engaged in violence . . . On my knees, I beg you, to turn away from the paths of violence and return to the ways of peace . . . violence only delays the day of justice.' After 1978 the number of violent deaths in Northern Ireland stabilised at around 100 per year, although it was to rise again during the hunger strikes.

In December 1979 Charles J. Haughey replaced Jack Lynch as *taoiseach*. Some members of Fianna Fáil had disliked Lynch's conciliatory policies towards both the unionist and the British government, and they hoped that Haughey would be more resolute. On gaining office Haughey stated that resolving the Northern Ireland situation would be the main objective of his premiership, although in reality he quickly became absorbed by the Republic's economic problems and the internal divisions in his party. Haughey's alleged sympathy for the IRA worried some unionists, who feared that the Republic might become involved in the affairs of Northern Ireland. However, much of his involvement revolved around meetings with Margaret Thatcher, with little change to the situation on the streets of Northern Ireland. The meetings between the two premiers alarmed some unionists, and in February 1981 Ian Paisley led a 'Protestant army' of 500 men to an isolated mountain side where each man vowed that he was 'ready to fight and die rather than accept an all-Ireland Republic'. Paisley claimed that there were thousands of other men who had made a similar pledge to him.

Despite the increasing polarisation between nationalism and unionism, some British and Irish activists felt that a first step to resolving the problem of Northern Ireland should be a withdrawal of British troops. One of the most outspoken British politicians was the Labour MP Tony Benn, who consistently spoke out against the atrocities being perpetrated in Northern Ireland at a time when most debate focused on the violence caused by the IRA in Britain. He believed that a solution would be possible only through a radical reassessment of the situation. In 1981 he declared:

The present policy is a dead-end. There is no future for Ireland based on the presence of British troops. There has got to be a political solution, and the way in which it has got to be done needs to be discussed. The tragedy is that we haven't had a proper discussion on Ireland. I think it was quite wrong to partition Ireland . . . I should be content if we got a discussion going about how we could get British troops out and a solution in Ireland.

Neither the British not the Irish government, however, was willing to negotiate with, or even listen to, the people who were at the heart of the conflict. Moreover, the British government was promoting a policy of 'Ulsterisation', that is, reducing the role of British troops in favour of local police and, to restrict the negative reporting in the international media, to make Northern Ireland appear a 'normal' rather than a war-torn society. Part of this process was the criminalisation of all political prisoners.

It was republican prisoners who attempted to end the seeming impasse in the political situation. In October 1980 the first hunger strike was started by seven IRA prisoners in the H-blocks to protest against the withdrawal of political status, which meant that they had to wear prison clothes, were denied freedom of association and had to do prison work. On 1 December, three women republican prisoners – Mairéad Farrell, Mary Doyle and Mairéad Nugent – in Armagh prison joined in, followed by a further twenty-three prisoners in the H-blocks. The hunger strike ended on 18 December after fifty-three days, when the British government promised to make certain concessions to the prisoners. The women, more sceptical about the governement's promises, called off their strike on the following day. When it became clear that the promises would not be honoured, it was decided to have a second hunger strike. The decision was made by the IRA and INLA prisoners, led by a young IRA activist, Bobby Sands. Although the prisoners had already participated in blanket and 'dirty' protests, they realised they had achieved nothing. On 7 February the republican prisoners in the H-blocks announced their intention to go on hunger strike; women were not involved this time. It began on 1 March, which was the fifth anniversary of the ending of prisoner political status. Bobby Sands was the first to refuse food. When the MP Frank McGuire died in office, a massive campaign was mounted to get Sands elected in his place. The Northern Ireland Office refused to allow the press access to the hunger strikers, even when Sands became a candidate in the by-election. None the less, Sands was elected MP for Fermanagh–South Tyrone on 9 April, demonstrating the wide spectrum of support for the hunger strikers.

The fact that Sands was now an elected MP to the Westminster parliament did not change the policy of the government, and within a few weeks of being elected, he died. Sands had won 30,000 votes and 100,000 people attended his funeral, yet the British government remained intransigent. The international media that attended his funeral included 23 camera crews, 400 journalists and 300 photographers. Sympathy was largely for the dead man. Yet when Ken Livingstone, the new leader of the Greater London Council, spoke publicly in support of the hunger strikers, he was vilified in much of the British press. Sands's death on 5 May 1981 was shortly followed by that of Francis Hughes. As one man died, another would enter the strike. As more men died, the Catholic Church, the Red Cross and other external agencies attempted to negotiate with the British government. Despite the attention of the world media, Thatcher refused to negotiate or to compromise. The deaths of Raymond McCreesh, Patsy O'Hara, Joe McDonnell, Martin Hurson, Kevin Lynch, Kieran Doherty, Tom McElwee and Micky Devine followed. In total, between 5 May and 20 August 1981, ten hunger strikers had died. The hunger strikes were called off on 3 October 1981. The government had not agreed to the political demands, but pressure from the families, the SDLP and the Catholic Church had mounted to call off the strike. Many of the republican prisoners were not pleased, blaming the Catholic Church hierarchy for their intervention. Within a short period of the strike ending, the demands of the strikers had been granted, although they were not officially recognised as political prisoners. The months of the hunger strike had been accompanied by increasing rioting and violence on the streets: sixty-four people were killed in disturbances between March and October. The intransigence of the British prime minister and the sacrifice of the hunger strikers had shifted some public opinion in favour of the nationalists. More importantly, the hunger strike marked the re-entry of Sinn Féin into electoral politics, their twin strategy summed up by the phrase 'the Armalite and the ballot box'.

Following the ending of the strike, more attempts were made to find a constitutional solution to the problems of Northern Ireland. At the end of 1981 the meetings between Haughey and Thatcher resulted in the setting up of an Anglo-Irish Intergovernmental Council, which was to meet in January 1982. Again Ian Paisley responded angrily, and in November organised a loyalist day of action, which brought much industry to a standstill. In April 1982 Jim Prior, the secretary of state, published a White Paper, *Northern Ireland: A Framework for Devolution*, which promoted a programme of rolling devolution. The ultimate aim was to restore self-rule to Ireland following the election of an assembly by proportional representation. The rights of Catholics were to be protected. In October elections to the new assembly were held. The SDLP refused to take part in these elections, but Sinn Féin gained 10 per cent of the vote. Although Sinn Féin MPs had been democratically elected, in December the British government banned them from visiting Britain.

The intentions of the British government towards the nationalist community remained ambiguous. The 1980s were associated with a 'shoot-to-kill' policy on the part of the army and RUC. In cases where members of the British army were tried for murder they were almost always acquitted, generally on grounds of self-defence. In the period from 1969 to 1993, however, the army was responsible for over 300 of the 357 killings by the police and army combined. The murder by the RUC of six people in County Armagh in 1982 resulted in the Stalker Inquiry in 1984. John Stalker, deputy chief constable of Manchester, was obstructed in numerous ways from carrying out a thorough investigation, and he was removed from the inquiry on a spurious charge three days before he was due to make his report. An inquiry undertaken by a group of international lawyers, however, found the killings to be in violation of the European Convention on Human Rights. They recommended that other tactics should be employed by the British army and RUC. In 1988 a more controversial example of shoot-to-kill occurred in Gibraltar, when three unarmed members of the IRA were shot dead by the British SAS. The murders set in train a chain of events culminating in particularly violent brutality on the streets of Belfast. Despite the condemnation in the European Court of Human Rights, a Conservative Party spokesman, Michael Portillo, opined that the real message of the shootings in Gibraltar was 'Don't mess with Britain'.

The entry of Sinn Féin into electoral politics following the hunger strikes caused realignment in nationalist politics. Support for Sinn Féin, the political wing of the Provisional IRA, was apparent in the general election of June 1983 when it won 42 per cent of the Catholic votes. Clearly the Sinn Féin political machine was in a position to offer a serious challenge to the SDLP. For the British government the clear message was that despite their association with violence, Sinn Féin had popular support. In the election Gerry Adams, a young republican who had been interned in the 1970s, defeated Gerry Fitt, the sitting SDLP MP for West Belfast. None of the Sinn

Féin candidates took their seats at Westminster. In November 1983 Gerry Adams was elected the new president of Sinn Féin.

Despite the entry of Sinn Féin into constitutional politics, the military campaign continued. In July 1982 IRA bombs killed ten soldiers in their barracks in London. In addition to targeting members of the British army and of the RUC and other security forces, the IRA also killed civilians in indiscriminate attacks. The INLA killed seventeen people in a bar in Ballykelly in December 1982. The bombing of Harrod's department store in London a year later was proof that despite years of repressive legislation the IRA remained capable of taking its deadly campaign to the heart of Britain. Despite years of oppression and opprobrium, the IRA also had some public triumphs. They were continuing to receive support in the United States, and in a landmark judgment in November 1982 a United States court set free five men known to have been smuggling arms to the IRA. In September 1983, thirty-eight IRA prisoners escaped from the Maze prison, which was supposed to be a top-security jail.

The success of Sinn Féin at the polls not only alarmed unionists and British politicians; it also worried the main parties in the Republic. The next initiative in breaking the stalemate, the New Ireland Forum, was started by the Fine Gael government in the Republic, which invited 'constitutional' parties from both the North and the South to gather and discuss the Irish situation. The delegates included Garret Fitzgerald, the *taoiseach*; Charles Haughey, the leader of Fianna Fáil; Dick Spring, the *tánaiste* (deputy *taoiseach*); and John Hume of the SDLP. The chairman was Colm Ó hEocha, the president of University College, Galway. No members of the unionist parties or of Sinn Féin were present, the former refusing to stand. Also, the membership of the Forum was weighted in favour of Southern politicians, with Fine Gael having eight members, Fianna Fáil, nine members, Labour, five members and the SDLP, five members. Members of the public were invited to submit their views to the Forum. In May 1984 the Forum's report was released. It had come up with three alternatives for the future of the country: a federal Ireland, a unitary Irish state or joint Irish–British authority in Northern Ireland. Margaret Thatcher and the unionist parties rejected all of these recommendations. Jim Prior, the secretary of state, wanted to resign but was persuaded to stay in place. The Forum had been an attempt to give primacy to constitutional politics but, like many nationalist organisations before it, there had been a failure to take into account unionist viewpoints. Despite appearing to achieve little, the Forum was a significant step in implanting the idea that Northern Ireland was the joint responsibility of the Republic of Ireland and Britain.

The Forum had suggested that Ireland could be united by peaceful means, but in 1984 the violence continued from all parts of the political spectrum. In August the arrest of forty-seven Protestants for membership of the UVF was followed by serious rioting in the Shankill district of Belfast. The conflict in 1984 was overshadowed by the IRA bombing in October of a hotel in Brighton where the entire Conservative cabinet was staying. Five people were killed and some were badly injured. Margaret Thatcher, however, escaped unscathed. The media in Britain was outraged. The bombing proved that the IRA still had the capability of striking at the centre of the British government.

A further attempt to find a constitutional settlement to the problems of Northern Ireland occurred on 15 November 1985 with the signing of the Anglo-Irish Agreement at Hillsborough in County Down by the Dublin and London governments. It was partly motivated by the ongoing high levels of violence and the increasing threat the conflict posed to their own internal security. A further purpose was to draw support away from Sinn Féin. But it also marked recognition by the British government that it could not solve the internal problems of Northern Ireland without recognising an all-Ireland dimension. The agreement provided for the British and Irish governments to consult regularly on issues relating to Northern Ireland. To facilitate this process, a joint secretariat was established near Stormont, comprising British and Irish civil servants. Within Northern Ireland, however, the SDLP was the only major party to support the agreement. The government, yet again, had underestimated the reaction of the unionist population, with the agreement being disliked by both moderate and extreme unionists. Ten days after the agreement was signed, over 100,000 unionists marched on Belfast City Hall. The fifteen Unionist MPs who sat in Westminster resigned their seats, forcing by-elections which would be a forum for demonstrating opposition to the agreement. The outcome of the elections was a resounding anti-agreement vote, although the SDLP candidate Séamus Mallon won a marginal seat in Newry from a Unionist MP. On 3 March 1986 a day of action, or general strike, was held. Although it had widespread support, the unionists were unable to replicate the success which had brought the Sunningdale Agreement down. This was a significant moment for unionists, whose defiant tactics had traditionally been successful. Consequently after 1985 an Irish dimension had been added to what unionists had insisted for decades was an exclusively British responsibility.

In the late 1980s there was a backlash against Sinn Féin when the IRA's bombing campaign intensified, especially following the deaths of eleven people at Enniskillen in November 1988. Antagonism towards the IRA increased after the Warrington bombing, which killed two young boys in 1993. People in Northern Ireland were also war-weary. In 1992 Gerry Adams lost his West Belfast seat to the SDLP. At this stage Adams, representing Sinn Féin, and John Hume, representing the SDLP, entered into negotiations about how to bring about a resolution to the situation. The fact that Hume had conferred with the IRA led to his being criticised by mainstream politicians in Northern Ireland and Britain. Secretly, however, while condemning people who collaborated with 'terrorists', the Conservative government was carrying on discussions with leading members of the IRA. These clandestine meetings laid the foundations for the Peace Process. John Major, whose premiership was undistinguished in many ways, showed a willingness to negotiate with all sides, and by doing so he paved the way for Tony Blair's later high-profile interventions.

The political turmoil in Northern Ireland overshadowed the other significant developments that were taking place in society. Despite the intense period of conflict, the economy had continued to grow until 1973. After 1974, however, it started to decline, partly because of lower levels of investment by the British government. Inevitably, the violence discouraged investment from new companies. Some of the successful industries, such as the man-made fibre industry, also closed down or downsized their workforce. Unemployment increased, especially among the working classes. Yet even as the manufacturing sector shrank, new white-collar jobs were created in the service sector. Young Catholics, who had benefited from the changes in educational provision, were well placed to take advantage of the growth in clerical opportunities. In contrast, the apprenticeships and factory jobs that had been the preserve of working-class Protestants had contracted massively. The impact of these changes was not immediate and by the mid-1980s Protestants were still wealthier than Catholics, but the balance of economic power was changing.

The Republic

While the eyes of the international media and the attention of increasingly nervous British politicians were focused on Northern Ireland, the Republic was also going through a period of change. Politically the years after 1960 were relatively peaceful, and Ireland settled into a system dominated by the two main parties, Fianna Fáil and Fine Gael, with Labour as a third alternative. The political stability was helped by the longevity of Eamon de Valera, who served two consecutive terms as president, from 1959 to 1973. When he retired, he was aged ninety. Throughout his career he had built up a formidable international reputation, and during his presidency his distinguished visitors included Charles de Gaulle of France and John F. Kennedy, president of the United States. However, when de Valera died in 1975, his aim of achieving Irish unity appeared no closer to being achieved.

From the 1960s the Irish Republic benefited from increasing prosperity, although inflation remained at a high level, poverty and poor health were endemic in some parts of the country, and emigration continued. None the less, the 1970s and 1980s were periods of social and economic growth, despite some temporary downturns in the economy. This expansion contrasted sharply with the stagnation associated with the de Valera era. The groundwork for many of these changes had been carried out in the 1960s or earlier. In 1958 T.K. Whitaker, the head of the civil service, had published a groundbreaking document entitled *Economic Development*, which suggested ways in which the economy could grow, and unemployment and emigration reduced. The government had embraced many of these recommendations and at the end of 1958 had published a *Programme for Economic Expansion*. Whether this was attributable to Whitaker or not, in the years after 1958 the economy grew, on average by 4 per cent a year. Thus encouraged, in 1963 Seán Lemass's Fianna Fáil government introduced a *Second Programme for Economic Expansion*, which provided a plan for the period from 1964 to 1970. The government was hopeful that an economic downturn in 1965 would be a temporary setback, but the plan had to be abandoned before it reached its 1970 deadline.

The condition of the Republic's economy in 1965 was overshadowed by a historic meeting between the *taoiseach*, Seán Lemass, and Terence O'Neill, the prime minister of Northern Ireland. This meeting led to an Anglo-Irish Trade Agreement and appeared to augur more beneficial relations between the three states. The agreement provided for a phased dismantling of tariff barriers which had been in place since the 1930s. Its aim was to achieve free trade by 1975. An impetus for the accord was the common desire to join the European Community. In 1973 the Republic of Ireland and the United Kingdom were both admitted to the European Economic Community. Irish politicians hoped that their traditional dependence on the British economy would thereby be reduced. The fact that it required a small loss in neutrality was seen as a small price to pay. Membership of the EEC did bring benefits to the Irish economy, especially the agricultural sector. The Common Agricultural Policy brought subsidies and higher prices to Irish farmers. Because Irish farmers were eligible to receive financial support from the Community, their average income rose. There were also benefits for Irish industry, which now had access to a broad range of European markets. Irish industry was helped by the Industrial Development Agency, which specialised in encouraging companies from overseas to establish bases in Ireland. It was particularly successful in attracting electronics and electrical goods companies. A further consequence was that the Republic became less dependent on trade with Britain. Moreover, the EEC provided financial grants for a range of programmes, many of which helped to develop the infrastructure of the Republic.

Entry to the EEC achieved what de Valera had failed to do in the 1930s: it ended Ireland's dependence on the British economy. The break seemed to be complete when the Republic joined the European Monetary System in 1979 even though Britain refused to do so. A consequence was that Ireland's monetary links with Britain ended after an association of over 150 years. In the 1980s and 1990s, while the United Kingdom continued to have an ambivalent relationship with Europe, the Irish Republic became more closely integrated, giving full support to the Single European Act in 1988, the Maastricht Treaty in 1992 and the Nice Treaty in 2002. The Republic was also among the first group of countries to transfer to the euro currency in 2002.

Ireland's successful participation in the European Community culminated in her providing the president of the European Council in 1979 and again in 1990. During both terms of office, Irish representatives gained considerable standing within Europe. Politicians from the Republic had also been playing a full role in the United Nations Organisation (UNO), which had been formed in 1945 to manage postwar international relations. Ireland entered the UNO in December 1955 but did not make an impact until the external affairs minister, Frank Aiken, became involved in 1957. Aiken's prolonged involvement was made possible by the fact that he was *tánaiste* from 1959 to 1969. By winning the support of other small nations, he placed Ireland in a position that far exceeded its small size. He was a supporter of the nonproliferation of nuclear weapons and welcomed Ireland's role in supplying troops to UN peace-keeping forces. In the 1960s and 1970s Irish troops served in the Congo, Cyprus, Israel and Lebanon. Some of these measures did not make him popular at home, but they won Ireland friends and respect on the international stage. Following the onset of violence in Northern Ireland after 1969, Jack Lynch's government attempted to get the UN Security Council to discuss sending a peace-keeping force to the province. The proposal was vetoed by the British representative. Ironically, while the Irish Republic made an important contribution to the conflicts of many nations, in regard to the Northern Ireland situation it proved to be unimaginative and irresolute.

From the 1960s more investment was placed in education and vocational training, both having suffered from years of underinvestment. An exception had been the founding of the Dublin Institute for Advanced Studies in 1940, which attracted world-renowned scholars. In 1967 the Industrial Training Authority (*An Chomhairle Oiliún*, or AnCo) was established. There was investment in primary and post-primary education, and changes in school curricula. Higher education was also expanding. In 1967 the *Commission on Higher Education, 1960–67* was published, which recommended that the constituent colleges of the National University should become independent; Trinity College, Dublin, was to remain a separate university; and a Commission for Higher Education was to be set up. By 1968 most of the recommendations had been introduced. In the same year Maynooth College, which had been founded as a seminary, was allowed to admit lay students for degree programmes. The changes in higher education laid the foundation for the creation of a highly educated labour force.

The increased prosperity and rising expectations had an impact on many other areas of life. New policies on social housing helped to clear many of Dublin's worst slums. The trade union movement became stronger, and social welfare payments improved. Emigration, however, remained high, although the new wave of emigrants was generally attracted to Britain or the United States by the prospect of higher wages and secure employment. Economic growth within the Republic was reflected in rapid social change. One of the most remarkable changes occurred in the size of the population. One of the long-term legacies of the Great Famine had been the fall in population, which had continued after 1850. By 1961 the population of the twenty-six counties had fallen to only 2,818,000, but from this low point the population slowly started to rise. Much of the increase was concentrated in Dublin. This demographic change provided Ireland with a young population that contributed to Ireland's buoyancy after 1990.

Economic growth was boosted by the expansion of the tourist industry, helped in turn by cheaper air travel. Irish Americans used this as an opportunity to rediscover their roots, although the conflict in the North meant that the destination of tourists was overwhelmingly the Republic. Apart from economic success, a number of social and cultural changes were transforming Irish society. The establishment of *Radio Telefís Éireann* in 1960 not only helped to promote Irish culture, but also brought the outside world directly into Irish homes. This external exposure undermined the traditional authoritarianism of Church and State, which had little control over what people watched on television. The death of de Valera in 1975 ended a link not only with the Republic's political past, but also with a period of social and cultural conservatism.

The various changes in Irish society also had an impact on the role of the Catholic Church in the state. While the 1960s had seen the emergence of more secular societies, in Ireland the position of the Catholic Church remained strong, and its influence permeated many aspects of life. It also remained a powerful force in politics, especially in areas of personal morality. It was not until June 1970 that the Catholic bishops lifted the restrictions on Catholics attending Trinity College in Dublin.

A symbolic change was made in December 1972 when a referendum approved of the removal from the constitution of the article referring to the special position of the Catholic Church. In September 1973 an inter-church meeting was held in County Louth, which was represented by all of the main Irish Churches. It was followed by a series of ecumenical conferences. Overall, however, the Catholic Church remained authoritarian, exclusive and patriarchal, and its influence was helped by the fact that it retained control over many aspects of education and social provision.

It was in the area of private morality that the Catholic Church appeared most entrenched. The more tolerant attitude that was evident in many other European countries in relation to divorce, abortion, contraception, homosexuality and women's rights made little headway in Ireland, either north or south of the border. Irish women, who had been marginalised in Irish politics, were at the forefront of each of these campaigns. Contraception had been banned in the Irish Free State in 1935 by the Criminal Law

Amendment Act. There were some objections on the grounds that the ban would force contraception under ground, while the inability to control family size kept people in poverty. The 1937 constitution, however, had reaffirmed the sanctity of the family within Irish life. In July 1968, in an attempt to reassert the Church's authority, Pope Paul VI issued an encyclical, *Humanae vitae*, which condemned all artificial forms of contraception. In 1974 the Irish Supreme Court upheld the right of people to import contraceptives for their own use, and in 1979 the sale and distribution of contraceptives were liberalised. This was followed by the lifting of all restrictions on the sale of contraceptives, although it took some years before they became widely available.

Divorce was another subject where the Republic was out of line with many other European countries, in contrast with the situation in Northern Ireland, where it was legalised after 1939. Although there had been a limited number of divorces following the creation of the Free State, they had been opposed by Catholic groups. The 1937 constitution placed a ban on all divorces. It was not until 1995, following intense campaigning by women's groups and civil liberty groups, that divorce was made legal. The question of abortion remained more controversial. It had been outlawed in Ireland in 1861 under the Offences Against the Person Act, and as late as the 1990s, abortion was not available in either the Irish Republic or Northern Ireland. The 1967 Abortion Act passed in Britain included a clause saying 'This Act does not apply to Northern Ireland.' The exclusion was largely due to opposition from the Churches. However, within Northern Ireland women were given advice about clinics in Britain. The Northern Ireland assembly in its brief existence also showed that the majority of parties remained opposed to abortion. In the Republic, abortion was illegal, and outside Dublin, advice was scarce, and Irish women who wanted an abortion travelled to Britain surreptitiously. The issue came to a head in the 1980s, largely precipitated by the activities of the 'pro-life' group. In 1983 they persuaded the government to hold a referendum which affirmed the equal right to life of the mother and the foetus. Following an acrimonious referendum campaign, the new clause – called the Pro-Life Amendment – was added to the constitution. The clause effectively conferred equal rights on the foetus, making it difficult for abortion legislation to be introduced. One of the major pro-life organisations, the Society for the Protection of the Unborn Child (SPUC), successfully insisted that the government initiate legal proceedings against Dublin clinics that were offering advice on abortions in Britain. A tragic personal situation that received massive press coverage forced a further change in policy. In 1992 the High Court refused to allow a fourteen-year-old girl who had been raped to travel to England to get an abortion. The decision was overturned by the Supreme Court. A few months later a referendum agreed to an amendment to the constitution allowing women to travel to Britain and to obtain relevant information on abortion. Laws governing homosexuality were also relaxed. In June 1993, in compliance with a ruling from the European Court of Human Rights, the age of consent was set at seventeen, making the legislation more liberal than its equivalent in the United Kingdom. This measure was largely due to the work of Justice Minister Máire Geoghegan Quinn. All of these changes were a sign that the Republic was becoming a more secular society. It also showed that the traditionalism of the Irish Catholic Church was being challenged. However, the greatest threat to the authority of the Catholic Church was the succession of scandals and accusations of child abuse that rocked its foundations in the 1990s.

Women played an important role in bringing about changes in the law and they benefited from the more liberal attitudes to divorce, contraception and abortion. Their social and economic position improved slowly, although Irish women had started from a low base. By the late 1960s the Republic had a lower level of female participation in the workforce than many other European countries, including Northern Ireland. Their wages tended to be lower, and various restrictions were in place forbidding married women from working in certain professions. Again, the Irish women's movement was active in bringing about changes in legislation and in attitude. By the 1990s women were playing a much more prominent role in the public life of Ireland, but they remained under-represented in some areas, especially politics.

Overall the years between 1969 and 1990 had been a period of unprecedented change and progress. The transformation was remarkable because it permeated all aspects of society – economic, social, political, cultural and religious – and it also affected people from all socio-economic groups. During this period, not only did the relationship between the Republic and Britain change, but Ireland took her place as a dynamic force within European politics. However, the paradox of the Northern Ireland conflict remained unresolved, and it cast a long shadow over the affairs of Ireland and Britain.

Peace and Prosperity since 1990

For the Republic the period after 1990 was marked by further prosperity, increasing secularisation and more international recognition. After the mid-1990s the success of the Irish economy, referred to as the 'Celtic Tiger', was remarkable not just by previous Irish standards, but also by international ones. The growth was largely due to the expansion of information technology, high inward investment, a thriving tourist industry and the judicious use of regional development funds from the European Union. In 1993 GDP grew by 4 per cent, and by 1995 it had grown by 7½ per cent per annum. What made its growth stand out from other economies was that the state did not play a central role. Moreover, not only did emigration slow down, but for the first time there was a repatriation of Irish nationals. Economic success in the shape of the Celtic Tiger created new problems. The social structure became more unequal. The growth was uneven, with Dublin benefiting most. The Dublin infrastructure was unable to cope with the demands being made on it. Insufficient affordable housing and social housing were available to meet growing demand for accommodation. Wealth brought an influx of refugees, especially from eastern European countries. Ireland, which for so long had had an outflow of its population, now had to respond to the latest influx of settlers, who came not as conquerors but as economic or political refugees.

A sign of the changing times was the election of Mary Robinson as president in 1990. Not only was she the first female president of Ireland, but as a member of the Labour Party she represented a break from the Fianna Fáil and Fine Gael domination of politics. She transformed the office of president by her energy, her liberal attitudes – including support for abortion rights, homosexual rights and divorce – and her inclusive approach. In 1992 she visited famine-stricken Somalia, where she drew parallels with Ireland during the Great Famine. More controversially, in 1993 she attended a cultural festival in Belfast, despite concerted opposition by church and political leaders in Britain and Ireland. Her shaking the hand of Gerry Adams, the local MP, caused widespread outrage. A feature of her presidency was her concern for Irish people who lived outside Ireland or were of Irish descent. One of the ways in which she 'cherished the Irish Diaspora' was by keeping a light at the window of the president's house as an emblem of remembrance. When Robinson resigned as president, her successor was another woman, Mary McAleese. As president, Mary Robinson had been an excellent ambassador for Ireland, and her contribution to world politics was consolidated when she was appointed UN high commissioner for human rights after 1997. Her outspokenness against the foreign policies of many Western governments, however, lost her support, especially in Washington.

Internationally, the beauty of Ireland and its unique culture were attracting notice. The success of U2 had already brought Irish music to the attention of young people throughout the world, and they were followed by the Cranberries, the Corrs, Boyzone, Enya and Daniel O'Donnell, each of whom appealed to different audiences outside Ireland. The international success of the stage show *Riverdance*, based on a revamped form of Irish dancing, made a traditional Irish pastime appear sexy and cutting-edge. The acclaimed writings of Roddy Doyle, in contrast, provided a reminder of the continuation of the social problems still facing Irish society. The opening of Irish theme pubs, however, not only in Britain but throughout the world, further demonstrated that Irish culture, no matter how contrived or trite, was regarded as being unique, pleasurable and marketable.

Changes in Northern Irish society were overshadowed by the continuation of conflict. Although the political turbulence continued, there was a renewed attempt to find a political solution to the problem both at the level of high politics and in the rise of various cross-community projects within the province. The Peace Process had its origins in the talks that had taken place between John Hume and Gerry Adams in the late 1980s. John Hume believed that the British government no longer had a strategic or political interest in maintaining the link with Northern Ireland. For Hume the challenge was how nationalists and unionists of all descriptions could work together to create a new political situation. The British government reopened negotiations with the Dublin government and held a series of inter-party talks, separated into various components, or 'strands'. The Ulster Unionist Party, the Democratic Unionist Party, the SDLP and the Alliance Party were invited to participate, but Sinn Féin was excluded because of its association with the IRA. During Strand One, each party was to outline its vision for the future of Northern Ireland. The SDLP believed that the future of a new Northern Ireland assembly could only be safeguarded if an external, probably European, party was involved, but it had little support. Strand Two proved to be more contentious as it was concerned with the future relationship between Northern Ireland and the Republic. The unionist parties, however, claimed there was insufficient common ground for agreement, and so effectively ended the talks.

John Major's Conservative government, in an extraordinary move for a party that was still linked with unionism, had opened talks with the Provisional IRA in an attempt to end the violence and move all paramilitary groups towards an acceptance of constitutional methods. Members of the Catholic Church were important contributors to these preliminary confidential talks. The Church, which had for so long been an opponent of republican violence, acted as a conduit for peace. Intense debates had already been taking place within Sinn Féin, which in 1992 produced the document *Towards a Lasting Peace in Ireland*. Sinn Féin believed that peace would be possible only if both the London and Dublin governments were involved, and that one of the main tasks of the British government was to persuade the unionists that the political link between Northern Ireland and Britain was not permanent. Adams was also working with John Hume to produce a common nationalist approach to the situation, and in 1993 they issued a joint statement accepting the existing relationship between Northern Ireland and Britain, but stipulating that any future settlement had to include an Irish dimension.

The unionist community reacted strongly, many being unwilling to allow a representative of Sinn Féin (and, it was suggested, the IRA) to have a say in their political future. The loyalist paramilitaries, who were overtaking the IRA in terms of violence and killings, responded angrily. Their murder of Catholics initiated a further round of 'tit for tat' killings. Consequently, the number of sectarian murders again began to rise. The British government remained undeterred, and in December 1993 issued the Downing Street Declaration, whereby the *taoiseach*, Albert Reynolds, and John Major announced that they had agreed on a set of principles for a settlement. The document admitted to the right of self-determination within Northern Ireland, but only if agreed to by separate referendums in the Republic and in the North. This meant that a majority in Northern Ireland had to agree to any settlement. In essence, therefore, the 1993 declaration reaffirmed the content of the 1949 act requiring the consent of the unionist people to any change. An appeasement was offered to Catholics by the historical declaration that Britain no longer had a 'selfish strategic or economic interest in Northern Ireland'. Both Major and Reynolds hoped the declaration would provide the preconditions for a general ceasefire which they believed was the precursor to a long-term settlement.

For some unionists, their dislike of aspects of the declaration was overtaken by a leaked story to the press that the British government had been involved in top-level secret dialogue with the IRA since 1991. John Major was accused of having done a secret deal with the IRA, but he was able to assure leading unionists that this had not been the case. The way seemed clear for a ceasefire, if the leaders of both the loyalist and republican paramilitaries could persuade their followers to comply. The level of violence suggested that this might be difficult. The Provisional IRA had planted a bomb in a fish shop in the Shankill Road in November, killing innocent shoppers. Retaliation by the loyalist paramilitaries included the murder of eight people by the UDA in a gun attack in the Rising Sun Bar in Greysteel, County Derry. Despite the fact that the activities of the IRA continued to dominate news coverage, more political killings in the early 1990s were perpetrated by loyalist paramilitaries than by republican groups. The UDA in particular had increased its campaign of violence, claiming that its targets were the entire 'pan-nationalist front'. In 1992 they had been responsible for twenty-one of the thirty-nine loyalist murders. In 1993, the UDA killed thirty-one people. The UVF had also been preparing for an 'intensification' of the war, smuggling large supplies of weapons and Semtex to Belfast. The consignment was intercepted by Customs and became the largest arms seizure ever made in Britain.

Some of the paramilitaries were also admitting that the violence had achieved nothing except the perpetuation of more violence. Just as the republican movement was involved in internal debates, a number of loyalists realised that they needed to adapt to the changing situation. Both the UVF and the UDA developed their own political wings, the Progressive Unionist Party and the Ulster Democratic Party respectively. Their formation was an acknowledgement that the military conflict was moving into a new phase. In November 1993 an unidentified spokesman for the UVF appeared on Ulster Television and appealed to all paramilitaries to lay down their weapons, pleading 'Let our people move on together'. The anonymous spokesperson was David Ervine, who subsequently became leader of the Progressive Unionist Party.

On 31 August 1994 the IRA declared a cessation of violence and on 13 October 1994 the Combined Loyalists Military Command also announced a ceasefire. Both sides, however, viewed the ceasefire as a means to achieve their own ends, which still remained separate and irreconcilable, one side seeing it as an end to the relationship with Britain, the other as an affirmation that the relationship would continue. Both sides had in common the fact that the ceasefire was viewed as a means of allowing a peaceful solution to be found, rather than a permanent undertaking. The ceasefire immediately raised the question of the decommissioning of the weapons of the paramilitaries in order to ensure the permanence of the ceasefire. An outside assessor, Senator George Mitchell from the United States, was appointed to report on the likelihood of weapons decommissioning. Talks were delayed until this issue was resolved. The British and Irish governments, still working closely together, published *Frameworks for the Future* in February 1995. The document provided for the creation of a Northern Ireland assembly and the establishment of cross-border institutions to bring more unity and cooperation. Again, this document, especially the latter provision, made many unionists nervous. Their anger and fears were manifested by the protests and violence that accompanied the traditional 12 July commemorations.

While the peace negotiations were taking place, militants in the Orange Order were demonstrating their resistance to the process. In 1994 their frustrations found an outlet at the annual battle of the Boyne march in the small village of Drumcree, near Portadown, in County Armagh, where the local Orange Order insisted on parading down the almost exclusively Catholic Garvaghy Road. The protest attracted support from loyalist paramilitary organisations that opposed both the loyalist ceasefire and the Peace Process. In its early stages the protest at Drumcree appeared to be a microcosm of the wider fears of the Protestant community. These apprehensions were summed up by Joel Patton, a member of Vanguard in the 1970s, who formed the hard-line 'Spirit of Drumcree' group. He explained:

In many ways it's not about 800 Orangemen marching down a road. It's about the survival of a culture, of an identity, of a way of life. It's about our ability to still hold onto parts of the country. The Ulster people have their backs to the wall. They're in retreat. They have been chased from quite a large area of their country and they feel that [Portadown], the citadel of Orangeism, where Orangeism was born 200 years ago, that is the place where they want to take their stand. Drumcree represents that . . .

They believe intensely if it's taken away from them there, then there isn't anywhere in Ulster that will be safe. If they're beaten in Portadown then they believe that they can be beaten anywhere and that's why I don't think they are about to give in.

In its early years the Drumcree protest attracted mass support, with Orangemen coming from all over Ireland and other parts of the world to support it. But apart from skirmishing and street fighting, the Drumcree conflict also resulted in a number of brutal murders, which turned public opinion against it. On 12 July 1998 three young Catholic bothers, Jason Quinn, aged eight, Mark Quinn, aged nine, and Richard Quinn, aged ten, were killed when their home was petrol-bombed. The RUC declared the murders to be sectarian. Many of the Orangemen in Drumcree celebrated. In the following year, Rosemary Nelson, the solicitor for the Garvaghy Road residents, was killed by a bomb planted by the UDA. Before her death she had complained of receiving repeated death threats from the local RUC. The actions of the Orangemen were condemned by all the major Churches, including the Anglican primate of Ireland, Archbishop Robert Eames. The smaller Protestant denominations also denounced the protests at Drumcree, which the protesters claimed were being held in defence of Protestantism.

Despite the violence and atrocities associated with the Drumcree march, successive British governments proved unwilling to confront the Orangemen or to force them to choose an alternative route to march. By employing the same tactics of confrontation and violence that they had used in the previous 200 years, the marches were allowed to continue. For the local Catholic population, this decision suggested that their opinions still did not matter in the Northern Ireland state. In the short term, militant Orangeism seemed to have triumphed again, but ultimately the demonstrations at Drumcree were counterproductive, attracting negative international coverage and reinforcing an image of Orangemen as dour, intransigent and violent. Moderate unionists and Protestants were also appalled at what was being done in their name. By 2003 support for the march had again fallen back to a hard core of followers. It also damaged the Orange Order. Membership of the society had been dropping since 1960, and this process was expedited after Drumcree. A beneficiary of the events in Drumcree was David Trimble, the local MP. In 1995 the Orangemen had been allowed down the Garvaghy Road only if they agreed to march in silence, but when they reached the bottom of the road they celebrated noisily, led by an uncharacteristic partnership of Ian Paisley and David Trimble, literally hand in hand. Trimble successfully used the conflict to boost support for his leadership challenge within the UUP. After he had achieved this, he increasingly distanced himself from the excesses of the Orange Order.

On 24 January 1996 Senator Mitchell published his report on the future of the peace talks. He recommended the gradual disarming of the IRA during the course of the talks. In the interim period, the question of decommissioning had achieved a centrality to the whole of the Peace Process, some people, predominantly unionists, arguing that it should be a condition of involvement in the talks. Mitchell's recommendation disappointed these people, as he believed that decommissioning was unlikely until talks were under way. Therefore, he suggested that talks should begin, which would allow decommissioning to begin. The prime minister, John Major, accepted these recommendations, but he decided to delay the talks until a Northern Ireland assembly had been elected as a way of determining who should take part. Both the prime minister and the unionist parties, however, insisted that evidence of decommissioning was a precondition of any further action.

This stipulation, which had not been part of the original agreement, appeared to republicans to be a betrayal of their trust. They responded by ending the ceasefire in a brutal way. On 9 February 1996 a bomb exploded in London. Two shopkeepers were killed. Moreover, the location of the bomb was at the hub of Britain's financial centre. This bomb marked a renewed campaign of violence by the IRA, which in turn inflamed loyalist anger, as was evident by the violence that accompanied the 12 July march in Drumcree. The renewed violence meant that the future of the Peace Process was uncertain. Moreover, a general election was looming and the Conservative Party appeared to have lost the support and the trust of the British people. In the final years of John Major's period in office his parliamentary majority was so reduced that a handful of Unionist MPs increasingly held the balance of power. Major responded by doing nothing, and the great expectations that he had raised two years earlier rapidly evaporated. None the less, he had acknowledged that isolating the republican movement and denouncing its tactics had not worked, and his actions laid the foundations for genuinely inclusive talks on the future of Northern Ireland.

The election of a Labour government led by Tony Blair in May 1997 appeared to herald a new phase in Anglo-Irish relations. Not only was the Labour Party less ideologically constrained than the Conservative Party, but Blair had a massive parliamentary majority. The Labour Party was also committed to devolved government in Scotland and Wales. Blair, however, declared that Northern Ireland was a political priority. He appointed Dr Mo Mowlam as secretary of state for Northern Ireland, the first woman to hold this position. Her informal style of engagement, her willingness to listen to ordinary people, and her gender were a breath of fresh air in the suffocating and formal atmosphere of Northern Ireland politics. Many unionist politicians appeared uncomfortable with this approach, but many nationalists and members of the Irish and British governments welcomed her passionate involvement. Blair and Mowlam also involved Bill Clinton, the president of the United States, and the *taoiseach*, Bertie Aherne, in reviving the peace talks. In July 1997 the IRA resumed their ceasefire, and by the end of 1997 a new Peace Process was in place.

Blair realised the importance of historical memory to both sides of the community. In 1997 he used the occasion of an international event at Millstreet in County Cork to commemorate the 150th anniversary of the Great Famine to issue a statement that admitted that those 'who governed in London at the time failed their people by standing by while a crop failure turned into a massive human tragedy'. Although the word 'apology' was not used, Blair's statement marked a retrospective admission of national guilt. Many nationalists welcomed this assertion; unionists and the British conservative press hated it. At the beginning of June the *Daily Telegraph* accused Blair of giving succour to 'the self-pitying nature of Irish nationalism [and] the grievance culture which allows nationalist Ireland to place the blame for all the country's ills at the door of the Brits, ultimately justifying terrorism'.

Despite the ongoing hostilities at Drumcree and elsewhere each 12 July, Blair also made attempts to conciliate Orangemen. In a draft copy of a speech outlining his policy in 1998 he stated:

The anti-parade case is better understood outside Northern Ireland than is the case of the loyal institutions: the Orange Order, the Apprentice Boys and the Royal Black Institution. We know that members of these organisations feel that their culture is under attack. But let me assure them that, as far as my government is concerned, this is not the case. In fact, as a result of the valued efforts made by the loyal institutions to reach out to the other community, we are looking at ways to show the wider world the positive contribution to British culture that the Orange Order and other loyal institutions have made, both locally and internationally. They are international organisations, many of whose principles are deserving of attention.

In January 1998 Tony Blair announced that there would be a new Bloody Sunday inquiry, giving official endorsement to the fact that the first one had been flawed. The early months of 1998 were a period of intense negotiations, marked by arguments, disagreements, phone calls from the White House and threats of a renewed military campaign. Despite opposition from both militant unionists and nationalists, on 10 April 1998 the Good Friday Agreement was signed. For the majority of people in Ireland, the agreement was a remarkable step in attempting to find a peaceful solution in Northern Ireland. Its popularity was quickly demonstrated when, in May, a dual referendum was held. Despite vociferous unionist opposition, 71 per cent of those voting in Northern Ireland and 94 per cent in the Irish Republic approved of the agreement. A referendum was also held in the Irish Republic to remove articles two and three, which were concerned with territorial claims over Northern Ireland, from the constitution. A large majority voted in favour of the changes. The purpose of this referendum was to reassure the unionists that the Republic had no covert agenda for the Peace Process. For the British government, the massive majorities augured well for the future of the agreement. The question of IRA disarmament, however, continued to haunt the process.

The Good Friday Agreement provided for the establishment of a Northern Ireland assembly which was open to all parties if they agreed to accept its democratic principles and rejected the use of violence. The rejection of violence was regarded by some as entailing the decommissioning of weapons so that the ceasefire could become permanent. A number of committees were also established to examine traditional sources of contention among the nationalist community, including the issue of the parades and the policing of Northern Ireland. In June 1998 elections were held for the Northern Ireland assembly. International recognition for what had been achieved in the Peace Process was given when John Hume and David Trimble were jointly awarded the Nobel Peace Prize in October 1998.

A remarkable feature of the new Forum was the involvement of women through the formation of a new party, the Women's Coalition. They not only provided an alternative to the mainstream parties, but they drew support from women on both sides of the community, building on the cross-community links created by women's groups in both republican and loyalist areas. Despite being formed only six weeks before the elections for the Forum, they won 1 per cent of the vote. The Women's Coalition argued that any talks should be genuinely inclusive and be open to Sinn Féin. Inevitably, the unionist parties that dominated the Forum were virulent opponents of the women, leading to accusations of misogyny.

Gerry Adams's involvement in the Peace Process had won new electoral support for Sinn Féin. In 1997 Adams retook his parliamentary West Belfast seat, and in the same year Sinn Féin won its first seat in the Dáil since 1957. Sinn Féin had endorsed the Good Friday Agreement, seeing it as a step towards a united Ireland. Just as the signing of the treaty in 1921 had represented a compromise for republicans, so did their signing of the Good Friday Agreement. Moreover, breaking with their tradition of abstention, Sinn Féin candidates also agreed that they would take their seats in the cross-party Northern Ireland assembly. This was the first time that they had sat in the Stormont parliament since its foundation. Not all members of the IRA approved of their entry into the Peace Process, and again the republican movement split, with two new groups, the 'Continuity IRA' and the 'Real IRA', forming breakaway groups. The bombing of Omagh in County Tyrone in 1998 by the Real IRA, which resulted in the deaths of twenty-nine people, was condemned internationally, and there were some calls for the republican representatives to be expelled from the peace talks.

Despite the opposition of hard-line loyalists and republicans, the Peace Process survived, and by 1999 the assembly appeared ready to begin work. But the Ulster Unionist Party demanded disarmament first. The new government, due to operate in July 1999, was brought to a standstill. During this crisis, the unionists made it clear that they mistrusted Mo Mowlam, who was accused of having nationalist sympathies, and they wanted to negotiate directly with Tony Blair. In July 1999 Blair and Bertie Aherne spent a week working out a template for decommissioning. At the same time they set 15 July 1999 as the date for the new assembly to meet and appoint ministers. David Trimble's Unionist Party refused to attend, thus rendering the assembly inoperative. Trimble, who was first minister of the assembly and leader of the largest unionist party, agreed to depart temporarily from his 'no guns, no government' position to allow the government to begin work. However, he threatened to withdraw and shut down the assembly if disarming had not commenced by 31 January 2000. Moreover, both the Ulster Unionist Party and the Democratic Unionist Party opposed Sinn Féin having a role on the executive until the IRA had disarmed. Sinn Féin, however, argued that the IRA had honoured its ceasefire, and that decommissioning had never been part of the original agreement. Moreover, while the focus was exclusively on the arms of the IRA, the Crown forces and the Protestant paramilitaries continued to possess arms, yet there were few public calls for them to decommission.

Blair ordered a review of the Peace Process to be undertaken by George Mitchell. In the interim period the Patten Commission issued its report on the future of policing in Northern Ireland. Mowlam was replaced by Peter Mandelson, a close confidant of Blair. The unionists viewed him as somebody that they could work with. In November 1999 Mitchell reported that all paramilitaries would decommission by May 2000. This assurance resulted in the recovering of the assembly, and on 29 November ministers were appointed. On 2 December the assembly took control of its devolved powers. The fact that decommissioning was not progressing at the rate anticipated led the British government to suspend the executive on 3 February 2000. Direct rule was again imposed.

The impasse was ended by the IRA, which announced in May 2000 that it had put its weapons 'beyond use', supervised by international inspectors. The Northern Ireland assembly reconvened on 30 May. Trimble, however, was losing support within his own party as hard-liners argued that he was being too soft on republicans, and in October there was an unsuccessful attempt to oust him from the leadership. For Trimble, political survival depended on being tougher on Sinn Féin and exploiting the fact that he was viewed in Britain as the acceptable face of unionism. In the early months of 2001 the Peace Process appeared to have stalled again. Although the IRA agreed to meet with the Disarmament Commission, little progress was made. In the period leading up to the 2001 general election, Trimble threatened to resign as first minister unless the IRA disarmed. His policy of brinkmanship was intended to bolster support for him. He was re-elected, although his party lost ground to the DUP. Trimble resigned as first minister, blaming the IRA for this action. In August the commission responsible for disarming announced that the IRA had agreed to place its arsenal of weapons permanently beyond use. The British and Irish governments welcomed this as a breakthrough, but unionist leaders still viewed the action as inadequate. The new secretary of state, John Reid, suspended the power-sharing government as a way of allowing discussion to take place within Northern Ireland and without having to resort to an election. At this stage, much of the enthusiasm that had initially accompanied the Peace Process had dissipated. It seemed likely that

David Trimble would lose his seat in an election; the British government was afraid that the 'middle ground' in unionism was disappearing. The IRA initially withdrew its offer to disarm, but in October announced that the process had begun. The assembly prepared to take over government again, and Trimble was elected first minister, with Mark Durcan (John Hume's successor) as his deputy first minister.

Despite the progress made at the governmental level, sectarian violence, firebombing and punishment beatings continued on the streets of Northern Ireland. Again this was mostly confined to working-class areas, especially the interface between Catholic and Protestant communities. Although the IRA had continued to decommission, the arrest of three IRA men in Bogotá in Colombia provided their critics with an opportunity to cast opprobrium on their intentions, accusing them of still being involved in a military struggle. The fact that some working-class unionist communities were feeling vulnerable and isolated as a result of the Peace Process was brutally demonstrated at the gates of Holy Cross Catholic Primary School in Belfast in September 2001. Catholic schoolchildren and their parents were daily attacked, with petrol bombs, stones, bottles and even guns. These attacks were transmitted throughout the world until they were overshadowed by the tragic events on 11 September in New York. In the same year a census was taken in Northern Ireland that confirmed what many people had suspected. The demographic profile of the six counties had changed radically since 1921, and the Protestant majority had almost disappeared.

In July 2002 the IRA apologised to the families of the 650 civilians its members had killed since the late 1960s. However, the Peace Process still seemed in danger. The following months saw Trimble, as he attempted to preserve his position within his party, threaten to bring the assembly down unless the IRA disbanded. He also asked for Sinn Féin to be excluded. The assembly's closure was then precipitated by an unfounded allegation that an IRA spy was working within the assembly. On 14 October 2002 John Reid suspended the assembly, making this the fourth time that direct rule had been imposed since its foundation in 1999. Negotiations were held at the beginning of 2003, but Blair followed the unionist line of not allowing the assembly to reconvene unless Sinn Féin made an 'unambiguous pledge' to renounce paramilitary methods. The fact that the IRA had honoured its ceasefire and Sinn Féin had received a large electoral mandate to participate in the assembly appeared to count for little. Instead the whole democratic process in Northern Ireland was suspended and the local population effectively disenfranchised. Elections to the assembly were cancelled by the British government. This was explained on the grounds that it wanted total rather than partial decommissioning to take place and street violence to end. Some nationalists, however, suggested that the government was simply attempting to protect David Trimble, whose position as leader of the Unionist Party had become increasingly precarious. The government was also criticised for denying the people in Northern Ireland the democratic right to vote. In October 2003, following further agreement by the IRA to decommission, Tony Blair announced there would be an election in the following November. However, the secrecy surrounding the decommissioning angered some unionists, leading to yet another breakdown in talks.

At the end of 2003, therefore, the Peace Process had reached another impasse. The eyes of the world, however, were no longer on Northern Ireland, the destruction of the Twin Towers and the subsequent 'war on terrorism' dominating political developments throughout the world. None the less, the Peace Process had survived, but not intact. Despite their short time in power, members of the executive showed that they were capable of cross-party cooperation and had some imaginative and constructive policies to offer. But some things had not changed over thirty years: Gerry Adams, David Trimble and Ian Paisley, men who had been involved in the violent events in the 1970s and 1980s, were still the dominant figures in Northern Ireland politics. John Hume had resigned as leader of the SDLP, though he was still involved in the political process. With the departure of Bill and Hillary Clinton from the White House, Northern Ireland had lost a powerful ally as the new administration led by George Bush had little interest in the affairs of Ireland. The majority of people in Northern Ireland had shown a commitment to peace, but they had been let down by a small number of politicians and paramilitaries who were willing to sacrifice democratic rights and a peaceful future for partisan or personal ambition. None the less, the Peace Process was a remarkable development in the history of a society that had been torn apart for so long by internecine conflict. Its progress remains crucial not only to the people of Northern Ireland but also for the political future of Britain and the Irish Republic.

FURTHER READING

General Surveys

One of the most detailed overviews is the nine volumes of the *New History of Ireland* (Oxford, Clarendon, 1976–96). J.C. Beckett's *Making of Modern Ireland, 1603–1923* (London, Faber, 1981) remains one of the most lucid and balanced. Other general surveys include T.W. Moody and F.X. Martin (eds), *The Course of Irish History* (Cork, Mercier, 1994); Roy Foster, *Modern Ireland, 1600–1972* (London, Allen Lane, 1988); Michael Cronin, *A History of Ireland* (Basingstoke, Palgrave, 2001); and James Lydon's excellent *The Making of Ireland: From Ancient Times to the Present* (London, Routledge, 1998). Liz Curtis's *The Cause of Ireland: From the United Irishmen to Partition* (Belfast, Beyond the Pale, 1994) is one of the few general histories that give recognition to the role of women. Flann Campbell's *The Dissenting Voice: Protestant Democracy in Ulster from Plantation to Partition* (Belfast, Blackstaff, 1991) is an excellent introduction to radical Protestantism.

More specialised surveys include Jonathan Bardon's masterful *A History of Ulster* (Belfast, Blackstaff, 1992–2001); Cormac Ó Gráda, *Ireland: A New Economic History 1780–1939* (Oxford, Clarendon, 1995); Nicholas Canny (ed.), *The Origins of Empire* vol. 1 of *The Oxford History of the British Empire*, ed. W.R. Louis (Oxford, Oxford University Press, 1999); Alvin Jackson, *Ireland, 1798–1998: Politics and War* (Oxford, Blackwell, 1999); Christine Kinealy, *A Disunited Kingdom: England, Ireland, Scotland and Wales, 1800–1949* (Cambridge, Cambridge University Press, 1999); and Finlay Holmes, *The Presbyterian Church in Ireland: A Popular History* (Dublin, Columba, 2000).

The writing of women's history has undergone a welcome blossoming in recent years: for example, Margaret Ward, *The Missing Sex: Putting Women into Irish History* (Dublin, Attic, 1991), and Peter Berresford Ellis, *Celtic Women: Women in Celtic Society and Literature* (London, Constable, 1995). Other significant contributions have been made by Mary Condren, *The Serpent and the Goddess: Women, Religion and Power in Celtic Ireland* (San Francisco, Harper & Row, 1989); Mary Cullen and Maria Luddy (eds), *Female Activists: Irish Women and Change, 1900–60* (Dublin, Woodfield, 2001); Dolores Dooley, *Equality in Community: Sexual Equality in the Writings of William Thompson and Anna Doyle Wheeler* (Cork, Cork University Press, 1996); Margaret Ward, *Unmanageable Revolutionaries: Women and Irish Nationalities* (London, Pluto, 1983); Bernadette Whelan, *Clio's Daughters: Essays on Irish Women's History* (Limerick, University of Limerick Press, 1997); Diane Urquhart, *Women in Ulster Politics* (Dublin, Irish Academic, 2000); and Rosemary Cullen Owens, *Louie Bennett* (Cork, Cork Univerisity Press, 2001).

Fifth to Eleventh Centuries

Recommended texts include Laurence Ginnell, *The Brehon Laws: A Legal Handbook* (London, Unwin, 1894); F.J. Byrne, *Irish Kings and High-Kings*, 2nd edn (Dublin, Four Courts, 2001); Liam de Paor, *St Patrick's World* (Dublin, Four Courts, 1993); and Peter Berresford Ellis, *Celtic Inheritance* (London, Muller, 1985). Also worth reading are Dáibhi Ó Cróinín, *Early Medieval Ireland, 400–1200* (London, Longman, 1995); C.E. Meek and M.K. Simms, *The Fragility of Her Sex: Medieval Irishwomen in their European Context* (Dublin, Four Courts, 1996); P. Harbison, *Pilgrimage in Ireland: The Monuments and the People* (London, Barrie & Jenkins, 1991); H. Clarke, M. Ní Mhaonaigh and R. Ó Floinn, *Ireland and Scandinavia in the Early Viking Period* (Dublin, Four Courts, 1998).

Twelfth to Fifteenth Centuries

A classic account is provided in J. Lydon's *The Lordship of Ireland in the Middle Ages* (Dublin, Gill & Macmillan, 1972). Other useful surveys are provided in Marie Therese Flanagan, *Irish Society, Anglo-Norman Settlers, Angevin Kingship: Interpretations in Ireland in the Late Twelfth Century* (Oxford, Clarendon, 1989); Seán Duffy, *Ireland in the Middle Ages* (Basingstoke, Macmillan, 1997); Robert Frame, *English Lordship in Ireland, 1318–1361* (Oxford, Clarendon, 1981); Steve Ellis, *Reform and Revival: English Government in Ireland, 1470–1534* (Woodbridge, Boydell, 1986); Art Cosgrove, *Late Medieval Ireland, 1370–1541*

(Dublin, Helicon, 1981); P. Duffy, D. Edwards and E. Fitzpatrick (eds), *Gaelic Ireland, c.1250–1600* (Dublin, Four Courts, 2001).

Sixteenth and Seventeenth Centuries

A good general introduction is John McGurk, *The Elizabethan Conquest of Ireland* (Manchester, Manchester University Press, 1997), and an excellent account of the Williamite war is provided in W.A. Maguire (ed.), *Kings in Conflict: The Revolutionary War in Ireland and its Aftermath, 1689–1750* (Belfast, Blackstaff, 1990). The following books also provide good insights: W.T. MacCaffrey, *Elizabeth I: War and Politics, 1588–1603* (Princeton and Oxford, Princeton University Press, 1992); Colm Lennon's *Sixteenth-Century Ireland* (Dublin, Gill & Macmillan, 1994) and Brendan Fitzpatrick's *Seventeenth-century Ireland* (Dublin, Gill & Macmillan, 1988); Alan J. Fletcher, *Drama, Performance and Polity in Pre-Cromwellian Ireland* (Cork, Cork University Press, 2000); Pádraig Lenihan, *Confederate Catholics at War 1641–49* (Cork, Cork University Press, 2001); Richard Doherty, *The Williamite War in Ireland, 1689–1691* (Dublin, Four Courts, 1998).

Eighteenth and Nineteenth Centuries

Valuable introductions to the eighteenth century are provided by Thomas Bartlett and D.W. Hayton, *Penal Era and Golden Age Essay in Irish History 1690–1800* (Belfast, Ulster Historical Foundation, 1979); G.Ó Tuathaigh, *Ireland before the Famine* (Dublin, Gill & Macmillan, 1990); and Edith Mary Johnston, *Eighteenth-Century Ireland: The Long Peace* (Dublin, Gill & Macmillan, 1984). There is a vast literature on the nineteenth century including Cormac Ó Gráda, *Ireland: A New Economic History* (Oxford, Clarendon, 1995). Good insights are provided in R.J. Dickson, *Ulster Emigration to Colonial America, 1718–1775* (Belfast, Ulster Historical Foundation, 1988); Thomas Bartlett, *The Fall and Rise of the Irish Nation: The Catholic Question, 1690–1830* (Dublin, Gill & Macmillan, 1992); Marianne Elliott, *Wolfe Tone: Prophet of Irish Independence* (London, Yale University Press, 1989); Christine Kinealy, *The Great Irish Famine: Impact, Ideology and Rebellion* (Basingstoke, Palgrave, 2002); D. George Boyce, *Nineteenth-Century Ireland* (Dublin, Gill & Macmillan, 1990); Paul Bew, *Land and the National Question in Ireland, 1858–1862* (Dublin, Gill & Macmillan, 1978); A.T. Q. Stewart, *The Narrow Ground: Aspects of Ulster, 1609–1969* (Belfast, Blackstaff, 1997).

The Twentieth Century

Excellent introductions are provided by Eamon Phoenix's *Northern Nationalism: Nationalist Politics, Partition and the Catholic Minority in Northern Ireland, 1890–1949* (Belfast, Ulster Historical Foundation, 1994), Dorothy Macardle's *The Irish Republic* (London, Transworld, 1968) and J.J. Lee's *Ireland, 1912–1985: Politics and Society* (Cambridge, Cambridge University Press, 1990). The are many other excellent publications, including *Report of the Irish Boundary Commission 1925* (Shannon, Irish University Press, 1969); A.T.Q. Stewart, *Edward Carson* (Dublin, Gill & Macmillan, 1981); Anne Haverty, *Constance Markievicz* (London, Pandora, 1988); Tom Garvin, *The Evolution of Irish Nationalist Politics* (Dublin, Gill & Macmillan, 1981); Michael Hopkinson, *Green against Green: the Irish Civil War* (Dublin, Gill & Macmillan, 1988); Richard Dunphy, *The Making of Fianna Fáil in Power, 1923–1948* (Oxford, Clarendon, 1995); Ronan Fanning, *Independent Ireland* (Dublin, Helicon, 1983); B. Girvin and G. Roberts (eds), *Ireland and the Second World War* (Dublin, Four Courts, 2000).

The literature on Northern Ireland, especially since the start of the latest round of conflict, is extensive. The Protestant perspective is well represented by Susan McKay's *Northern Protestants: An Unsettled People* (Belfast, Blackstaff, 2000) and Peter Taylor's *Loyalists* (London, Bloomsbury, 1999); Roger Blayney's *Presbyterians and the Irish Language* (Belfast, Ulster Historical Foundation & Ultach Trust, 1996); Norman Porter's *Rethinking Unionism: an alternative vision for Northern Ireland* (Belfast, Blackstaff, 1996); and the polemical *The Faithful Tribe: An Intimate Portrait of the Loyal Institutions* (London, HarperCollins, 1999) by Ruth Dudley Edwards. Good insights are also provided in Tim Pat Coogan, *The Troubles* (London, Arrow, 1996); Chris Ryder and Vincent Kearney in *Drumcree: The Orange Order's Last Stand* (London, Methuen, 2001); Dennis Kennedy, *The Widening Gulf: Northern Attitudes to the Independent Irish State* (Belfast, Blackstaff, 1988); Equality Working Group, *The Directory of Discrimination* (Belfast, 1991); Liz Curtis, *Ireland: The Propaganda War. The British Media and the 'Battle for Hearts and Minds'* (London, Pluto, 1984); David Miller (ed.), *Rethinking Northern Ireland* (London, Longman, 1998); Human Rights Watch, *To Serve Without Favor: Policing, Human Rights and Accountability in Northern Ireland* (New York, 1997); John McGuffin, *Internment* (Tralee, Anvil, 1973); Paul Bew and Gordon Gillespie, *The Northern Ireland Peace Process* (London, Serif, 1996).

INDEX